Lecture Notes in Computer Science 4163

Commenced Publication in 1973
Founding and Former Series Editors:
Gerhard Goos, Juris Hartmanis, and Jan van Leeuwen

Hugues Bersini   Jorge Carneiro (Eds.)

Artificial Immune Systems

5th International Conference, ICARIS 2006
Oeiras, Portugal, September 4-6, 2006
Proceedings

 Springer

Volume Editors

Hugues Bersini
IRIDIA, ULB, CP 194/6
50, av. Franklin Roosevelt, 1050 Bruxelles, Belgium
E-mail: bersini@ulb.ac.be

Jorge Carneiro
Instituto Gulbenkian de Ciencia, Apartado 14
2781-901 Oeiras, Portugal
E-mail: jcarneir@igc.gulbenkian.pt

Library of Congress Control Number: 2006931011

CR Subject Classification (1998): F.1, I.2, F.2, H.2.8, H.3, J.3

LNCS Sublibrary: SL 1 – Theoretical Computer Science and General Issues

ISSN   0302-9743
ISBN-10   3-540-37749-2 Springer Berlin Heidelberg New York
ISBN-13   978-3-540-37749-8 Springer Berlin Heidelberg New York

Springer is a part of Springer Science+Business Media

springer.com

© Springer-Verlag Berlin Heidelberg 2006
Printed in Germany

Typesetting: Camera-ready by author, data conversion by Scientific Publishing Services, Chennai, India
Printed on acid-free paper   SPIN: 11823940   06/3142   5 4 3 2 1 0

Preface

ICARIS 2006 is the fifth instance of a series of conferences dedicated to the comprehension and the exploitation of immunological principles through their translation into computational terms. All scientific disciplines carrying a name that begins with "artificial" (followed by "life," "reality," "intelligence" or "immune system") are similarly suffering from a very ambiguous identity. Their axis of research tries to stabilize an on-going identity somewhere in the crossroad of engineering (building useful artifacts), natural sciences (biology or psychology—improving the comprehension and prediction of natural phenomena) and theoretical computer sciences (developing and mastering the algorithmic world). Accordingly and depending on which of these perspectives receives more support, they attempt at attracting different kinds of scientists and at stimulating different kinds of scientific attitudes. For many years and in the previous ICARIS conferences, it was clearly the "engineering" perspective that was the most represented and prevailed through the publications. Indeed, since the origin of engineering and technology, nature has offered a reserve of inexhaustible inspirations which have stimulated the development of useful artifacts for man. Biology has led to the development of new computer tools, such as genetic algorithms, Boolean and neural networks, robots learning by experience, cellular machines and others that create a new vision of IT for the engineer: parallel, flexible and autonomous. In this type of informatics, complex problems are tackled with the aid of simple mechanisms, but infinitely iterated in time and space. In this type of informatics, the engineer must resign to partly losing control if he wishes to obtain something useful. The computer finds the solutions by brute force trial and error, while the engineer concentrates on observing and indicating the most promising directions for research.

Fifteen years ago, two groups of researchers (one from France at the instigation of Varela and the other from the USA at the instigation of Perelson) simultaneously bet that, like genetics or the brain, the immune system could also unleash a stream of computational developments grounded on its mechanisms. The first group was more inspired by the endogenous network-based regulatory aspects of the system. Like ecosystems or autocatalytic networks, the immune system is composed of a connected set of cellular actors whose concentration varies in time according to the interactions with other members of the network as well as through environmental impacts. This network shows an additional plasticity since it is subject to structural perturbations through the appearance and disappearance of these members. The most logical engineering inspiration lay in the realm of distributed and very adaptive control together with parallel optimization. The resulting controllers should keep a large degree of autonomy, an important emancipation with respect to the designer, a potentiality slowly revealed through their interaction with the world and an identity not predetermined but constantly in the making.

The second group concentrated all its attention on the way the immune system treats and reacts to its exogenous impacts. It insisted in seeing the immune system, first of all, as a pattern recognition or classifier system, able to separate and to distinguish the bad from the good stimuli just on the basis of exogenous criteria and a limited presentation of these stimuli. It successfully stimulated the mainstream of engineering applications influenced by immunology: new methods of "pattern recognition," "clustering" and "classification". This vision of immunology was definitely the most prevalent among immunologists and certainly the easiest to engineer and to render operational. Whether or not this line of development offers interesting advantages as compared to more classical techniques, less grounded in biology, the future will tell. However, some members of this still modest community realized more and more that the time had come to turn back to real immunology in order to assess these current lines of research and to reflect on the possibility of new inspirations coming from novel or so-far neglected immunological facts: network, homeostasis, danger, are words appearing more and more frequently in the recent papers. Only a re-centering on theoretical immunology and a shift from the engineering to the "modelling" perspective could allow this turning point. This is how we saw this year's ICARIS, as the right time to question the engineering avenues taken so far and to examine how well they really fit the way theoretical immunologists globally construe what they study on a daily basis.

To consecrate this re-focusing, the organizers decided to invite four prestigious theoretical immunologists to present and debate their views, first among themselves but equally with the ICARIS community: Melvin Cohn, Irun Cohen, Zvi Grossman, Antonio Coutinho. Additionally, they decided to place more emphasis on the modeling approaches and favored in this conference proceedings papers with a more "biological" than "engineering" flavor. Sixty papers were submitted among which 34 were accepted and included in the proceedings. More than for the previous ICARIS, the first half of the papers are about modeling enterprises and the other half about engineering applications. We would like to thank the members of the Program Committee who did the right job on their fine selection of the papers and Jon Timmis for his very kind and precious collaboration.

June 2006   Hugues Bersini and Jorge Carneiro

Organization

ICARIS 2006 was organized by the IRIDIA laboratory of Universite Libre de Bruxelles and by the Instituto Gulbenkian de Ciencia.

Executive Committee

Conference Chair: Hugues Bersini (IRIDIA - ULB) and Jorge
                                             Carneiro (Instituto Gulbenkian de Ciencia)

Program Chair: Hugues Bersini (IRIDIA - ULB) and Jorge
                                             Carneiro (Instituto Gulbenkian de Ciencia)

Referees

H. Bersini	V. Cutello	P. Ross
J. Carneiro	L. de Castro	S. Stepney
P. Bentley	A. Freitas	A. Tyrrell
J. Timmis	E. Hart	A. Tarakanov
S. Garrett	J. Kim	A. Watkins
U. Aickelin	W. Luo	S. Wierzchon
S. Cayzer	M. Neal	F. von Zuben
C. Coello Coello	G. Nicosia	T. Lenaerts

Table of Contents

Computer Simulation of Classical Immunology

Computer Simulation of Idiotypic Network

ImmunoInformatics Conceptual Papers

Pattern Recognition Type of Application

Optimization Type of Application

Control and Time-Series Type of Application

Danger Theory Inspired Application

Text Mining Application

Did Germinal Centers Evolve Under Differential Effects of Diversity *vs* Affinity?

Jose Faro[1,2], Jaime Combadao[1], and Isabel Gordo[1]

[1] Estudos Avançados de Oeiras, Instituto Gulbenkian de Ciência, Apartado 14,
2781-901 Oeiras, Portugal
jfaro@igc.gulbenkian.pt, combadao@igc.gulbenkian.pt,
igordo@igc.gulbenkian.pt
[2] Universidade de Vigo, Edificio de Ciencias Experimentáis,
Campus As Lagoas-Marcosende, 36310 Vigo, Spain
jfaro@uvigo.es

Abstract. The classical view on the process of mutation and affinity maturation that occurs in GCs assumes that their major role is to generate high affinity levels of serum Abs, as well as a dominant pool of high affinity memory B cells, through a very efficient selection process. Here we present a model that considers different types of structures where a mutation selection process occurs, with the aim at discussing the evolution of Germinal Center reactions. Based on the results of this model, we suggest that in addition to affinity maturation, the diversity generated during the GC reaction may have also been important in the evolution towards the presently observed highly organized structure of GC in higher vertebrates.

1 Introduction

Vertebrates have evolved a complex immune system (IS) that efficiently contributes to protect them from many infectious and toxic agents. To cope with such large variety of agents the IS generates a large diversity of lymphocyte receptors. This occurs through various mechanisms activated during lymphocyte development. The first one consists in the random recombination of relatively few gene segments into a full variable (V) region gene of immunoglobulins(Ig) heavy and light chains, allowing the formation of many different receptors [1]. In higher vertebrates (birds, mammals) the relevance of this mechanism for diversity generation in the primary B-cell repertoire varies with different species, being followed in some of them by other mechanisms like V-region gene conversion or somatic hypermutation (SHM) that act on rearranged V-region genes [2]. This initial repertoire is submitted to selection before B cells reach full maturity, thus getting purged of overt self-reactivity [1].

During an immune response to a protein antigen (Ag) the SHM mechanism is triggered in some of the responding, mature B cells. Most mutations are deleterious (decrease the antibody (Ab) affinity for Ag) or neutral, but a few may increase the affinity [3]. This is followed by an increase of serum affinity starting

H. Bersini and J. Carneiro (Eds.): ICARIS 2006, LNCS 4163, pp. 1–8, 2006.
© Springer-Verlag Berlin Heidelberg 2006

after about the peak of the immune response until it reaches a quasi-plateau several weeks later [4]. This process, termed affinity maturation, implies that a selection process for higher affinity Abs takes place during that time. In higher vertebrates the SMH and selection processes take place at Germinal Centers (GC) [2]. These are short-lived structures, generated within primary follicles of secondary lymphoid tissue by migration of Ag-activated lymphocytes, and characterized by intense proliferation and apoptosis of Ag-specific B cells. In contrast, lower vertebrates do not generate GCs [2] so that SHM during immune responses to protein Ags takes place more or less diffusely in lymphoid tissue. Correspondingly in them the serum affinity during immune responses increases significantly less than in higher vertebrates. This indicates a less efficient selection process, currently attributed to their lack of GCs [2].

A higher rate affinity maturation process requires a more efficient (stronger) selection than a poorer affinity maturation process. On the other hand, the higher the efficiency the more specific the selected Abs will be, but the lower the remaining diversity related to the triggering Ag. However, thinking in evolutionary terms, keeping the diversity in the Ab repertoire seems at least as important as having the ability to selectively expand B cells producing Abs with higher specificity. For instance, while a 'selection structure' (*i.e.*, GCs) has been selected for in higher vertebrates, many lower vertebrates have life spans similar to many higher vertebrates. Also, mutant mice that lack an enzyme essential for the SHM process get strong intestinal inflammation due to massive infiltration of normal anaerobic gut flora [5].

Because the more efficient the selection the less the diversity, and because of the importance of both affinity maturation and diversity, a trade-off between those two goals possibly emerged during the evolution of vertebrates in those species endowed with the physiologic possibility to generate GC-like structures. We hypothesize that such trade-off may have determined the size, life span, organization, etc. of GCs. In order to approach this issue, we have developed a simple stochastic/CA hybrid model that allows us to compare the degree of affinity maturation and diversity generated in different scenarios, intended to represent evolutionary stages of species with increasing GC size. In this model the process of affinity maturation within GCs is formally equivalent to a population genetics model of the evolution of clonal populations under mutation and selection. This allows us to put our findings in context with a number of analytical results from population genetics.

2   The Model

A model of the immune response incorporating SHM and selection, in which lymphoid tissue is represented by a 25×25 square grid with periodic boundary conditions, was implemented in language C. In it B cells are assumed to be distributed evenly in the small squares of the grid and are modeled as a large population with many subpopulations of equal size named demes. More specifically, each single square holds a deme of N_d B cells (thus the whole system contains $N_t = N_d \times 625$ B cells). Individual B cells are defined by strings representing V-regions with 300 nucleotides in size. The processes of SHM/selection take place only in particular demes named MS demes. Cells can migrate from one deme to any of the 8 neighbour demes with probability m_r (see arrows in figure 1).

In each time step (generation) B cells within MS demes mutate in the V region of their Igs with rate U per B cell per generation. The number of mutations occurring per cell is a Poisson random variable with mean U. Once a mutation occurs it can either decrease (with probability p_d) or increase (with probability $1 - p_d$) the affinity of targeted Abs.

Outside of the MS demes, mutation does not occur and all cells have the same probability of survival. In the MS demes the probability of survival for each cell is directly proportional to its fitness W_{ij}, which depends on the affinity of its Igs for the Ag. W_{ij} corresponds to the probability of survival of a B cell with i mutations that decrease the affinity and j mutations that increase affinity. To calculate the fitness of each B cell, we use the multiplicative fitness assumption for the interaction between mutations. With this assumption the fitness of B cells containing i low affinity and j high affinity mutations is calculated as: $W_{ij} = (1 + s_b)^j (1 - s_d)^i$, where s_b is the effect of mutations that lead to an increase in affinity and s_d is the effect of mutations that lead to a decrease in affinity.

To understand how different degrees of 'GC' aggregation/organization could affect the process of affinity maturation and the resulting diversity, five topologies were considered. These topologies are used to model different sizes of 'GC' represented by different areas where SHM and selection could take place. These were meant to model the evolution of GC size along a phylogenetic scale, going from vertebrates species where the SHM and affinity maturation did occur in less structured lymphoid tissue, to current higher vertebrates where these processes take place in finely organized GC structures. We have considered the following topologies (in figure 1 an example of the grid corresponding to topology A3 is shown): *(i)* topology A1 consists of 64 single, unconnected MS demes; *(ii)* topology A2 consists of 16 groups of 2×2 MS demes; *(iii)* topology A3 consists of 7 groups of 3×3 MS demes; *(iv)* topology A4 consists of 4 groups of 4×4 MS demes; and *(v)* topology A5 consists of 1 group of 8×8 MS demes.

Each group of MS demes is placed at random in the grid. The simulations were performed using the following set of parameter values. Each deme is assumed to hold $N_d = 100$ B cells (this number is adjusted every generation, after the migration process has occurred). Within MS demes the mutation parameters are $U = 0.3$ and $p_d = 0.998$, and the selection parameters, s_d and s_b, were varied. The migration rate was set to $m_r = 0.00625$. This Monte-Carlo algorithm was run for different periods of time. In particular, analyses of the time for the mean affinity to approach the expected equilibrium were performed. To relate the time steps in the algorithm with the time scale of present day GCRs, we assume that B cells in the MS demes divide every 8 hours [3]. Thus 60 time steps in the algorithm correspond to about 21 days, which is the average life of GCs

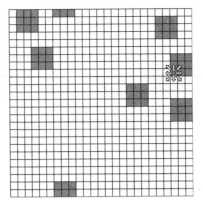

Fig. 1. An example of the 25 × 25 grid with a possible A3 topology. The full squares (MS demes) indicate the places where mutation and selection occur. Arrows indicate the eight possible directions for a migration event.

in primary immune responses. In order to obtain a variance due to stochastic events each simulation was repeated 20 times.

3 Results

3.1 Some Results from Genetics Population Theory

We first summarize some analytical results from population genetics that are relevant to understand the results shown for this model of GC evolution. Let us consider a large population of individuals (*e.g.*, B cells) undergoing mutation at rate U_d per individual per generation. Lets assume that every mutation has a negative effect, decreasing the fitness ($\propto$ affinity) by an amount s_d. Then, after approximately $1/s_d$ generations (each constituting a cycle of mutation and selection), the distribution of bad mutations in the population is Poisson with mean U_d/s_d. This means two things: first, if s_d is small it takes a lot of time to achieve this distribution; second, when it is achieved it can have a very large mean and variance. In the simulations s_d was around 10% the initial fitness so that the equilibrium distribution was reached in a period shorter than the time of a typical GC reaction of a primary immune response. Let $a(t)$ be the mean number of negative mutations at time t after the start of the SHM process, then the distribution at time t is Poisson with mean given by: $a(t) = \left(1 - (1 - s_d)^t\right)U_d/s_d$ [6]. Population genetics theory also shows that, if the population is not very large and/or s_d is small, the equilibrium above is not stable and a continuous accumulation of deleterious mutations can occur [7]. This is likely to happen if the condition $N \times Exp(-U_d/s_d)$ is satisfied, where N is population size.

If positive (affinity increasing) mutations are allowed to occur at rate U_a per cell per generation then for $U_a \ll U_d$ the distribution of negative mutations (decreasing affinity or deleterious) stays close to a Poisson [8].

3.2   Average Affinity Increases with Aggregation Until a Plateau Is Reached

We were interested in how 'affinity' (fitness) levels vary with the level of aggregation, that is, how 'affinity' levels vary with the size of the structure where the GCR occurs. Figure 2 shows the results for different values of the effect of mutations that increase and decrease affinity and for different times of the GCR. When considering short periods for the GCR, the average level of 'affinity' is low, even lower than the germ-line level of 'affinity', which by definition is 1. But as we consider longer periods, we observe that the level of affinity increases as the size of the structures increase. In particular, given sufficient time, above a given size of the structures, the level of affinity reaches a plateau. This qualitative result is independent of the exact values of the selection parameters s_d and s_b.

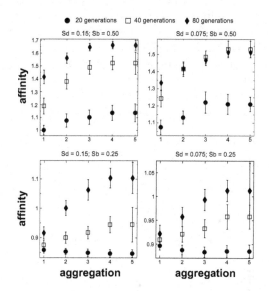

Fig. 2. Level of Ab affinity for increasing levels of aggregation at different times of the GC reaction

The reasons for this behaviour are as follows. When the size of the (GC) structure is small, the number of cells within each structure that are undergoing mutation and selection is small, so the contribution of the stochastic effects to the process is large. This means that, in order for a key mutation to overcome the effects of drift, the increase in affinity of that mutation has to be extremely high. Otherwise, most likely the mutant will be lost by chance. Thus, unless s_b is very strong, for low values of the aggregation the level of affinity is low. When the size of the aggregate is large the stochastic effects are small, and so the probability that the key mutation spreads is higher. From population genetics theory of simple models of mutation and selection we know that the effects of selection are more important than the effects of drift when $s_b > 1/N_e$, where N_e is the effective population size [9]. In our model, since both beneficial and deleterious mutations can occur, the value of N_e depends on the mutation rate and on s_d [8][10].

The above result suggests that there is a critical GC size that leads to a maximal level of affinity. GCs of sizes above this value do not lead to further improvements in affinity. We can also see that organisms in which the process of SHM/selection is spread out in tiny structures may not achieve high levels of affinity maturation. This is compatible with what is observed in lower vertebrates.

3.3   Changes in Average Diversity with Aggregation

Next we have studied how the GC size influences the level of diversity for the whole set of reactions. The diversity of the surviving cells is measured by counting the number of pair-wise differences in the Ig V sequences between two random clones sampled from the GC population.

Figure 3 shows the results for different values of the mutation effects s_d and s_b and for different times of the GC reaction. Obviously, for short reaction times the diversity level is low, but as time increases this level approaches equilibrium. This depends on the values of the parameters governing mutation and selection, as discussed in the previous section.

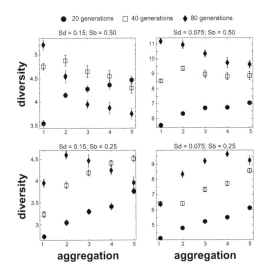

Fig. 3. Level of Ab diversity at different times of the GC reaction for increasing aggregation level

Initially the diversity generated is mainly due to deleterious mutations, but as time proceeds key mutations start to increase in frequency and they out-compete lower affinity clones. This may lead to an actual reduction in diversity. As larger aggregates lead to a higher probability of fixing key mutations the decrease in diversity is more pronounced for the larger aggregates. The wiping out of diversity in clonal populations is a well-established phenomenon in population genetics [11]. From this result we conclude that there is an intermediate value of the GC size for which the level of diversity generated is maximum.

Taken together, the above two results indicate that only GCs of some intermediate size lead to high levels of both affinity and diversity.

4 Discussion

The present preliminary results show that for lower values of aggregation, diversity and affinity maturation act together as a positive selection force for further aggregation increase. However, beyond a certain degree of aggregation there is a trade-off between diversity and affinity maturation. This leads to an optimal size of GCs, for which both high affinity Abs and a highly diverse pool of slightly different ones is produced. An important point that deserves mentioning is that the present results depend quantitatively on the particular definition of the fitness W_{ij}. However, we expect the qualitative behaviour will be much less affected by the fitness definition. On the other hand, the present multiplicative fitness definition of W_{ij} is the most commonly used because of two major reasons: its simplicity and the fact that, as far as we know, to date there is no data relevant to establish a 'fitness landscape' linked to mutations affecting a particular phenotype, and in particular to those affecting the affinity of antibodies.

The classical view of GCs assumes that their major role is to generate high affinity levels of serum Abs, as well as a dominant pool of high affinity memory B cells, through a very efficient selection process [1]. However, in addition to affinity maturation, the diversity generated during the GCR may be also important. Two kind of experimental observations support this view. First, although all vertebrates display similar diversity generation by SHM during immune responses to protein Ags, lower vertebrates have significantly lower efficiency in selecting high affinity Ab mutants than higher vertebrates. However, lower and higher vertebrates have similar life spans. Second, mutant mice with impaired SHM get sick because of strong intestinal inflammation due to massive infiltration of normal anaerobic gut flora [5].

The preliminary results that we have presented here suggest an alternative view of the role of SHM in immune responses. According to it in present day higher vertebrates, the GC reaction not only facilitates the selection of high affinity mutant B cells, but also allows for a rapid generation of (refined) diversity with the potential to recognize changes in the originally immunizing Ag (for instance, virus that mutate with high rate). In other words, the selection process may be only moderately efficient, and in some sense imperfect at leading to the creation of the best (highest affinity) possible memory B cell pool, but may have evolved just so to allow incorporation into the memory pool enough Ig diversity around the specificity of the initial triggered Igs. In this way different individuals can have a good coverage of the different mutational variants of a pathogen generated during its replication. That is, there would be an increased fitness for those individuals able to deal with pathogen variants, while conserving a large enough amount of Abs with increased affinity to the initial pathogen strain. We further speculate that the SHM mechanism could have co-evolved with mutational mechanisms in virus and bacteria focusing in each case in recognition molecules (*e.g.,* Ig V regions in the first case and invasiveness molecules, like influenza hemaglutinin, in the second case), leading after a race similar high mutation rates and similar diversity generation compatible with the physiology of those molecules.

Many related important questions remain to be explored. What determines the SHM rate? Is it optimal? What determines the time of duration of the GCR? Under the view suggested above this time would be related not only to the mutation rate, but also to the diversity generated. For a given mutation rate, the diversity generated and the probability to spoil the physiologyof the Abs will increase with the duration of the GC reaction. Thus, the mutation rate and the duration of the mutational process will be the maximum compatible with preserving the role of the Abs, while the mutational mechanism of microorganisms must be limited also in their rates and the length of the period time in which it is active, being at rest in non-stressing environments.

Acknowledgments

The authors thank Jorge Carneiro and Joana Moreira for constructive comments on this work. This work was supported by Fundação para Ciência e Tecnologia, Portugal (grant to JF, POCTI/36413/1999, SFRH/BPD/8104/2002 to IG and SFRH/BD/5235/2001 to JC). JF is supported by an Isidro Parga Pondal research contract by Xunta de Galicia, Spain.

References

1. Janeway, C., Travers, P., Walport, M., Shlomchik, M.: Immunobiology: the immune system in health and disease. 6th edn. Garland Science, New York (2004)
2. Flajnik, M.F.: Comparative analyses of immunoglobulin genes: surprises and portents. Nat Rev Immunol. **2** (2002) 688–698.
3. MacLennan, I. C.: Germinal centers. Annu. Rev. Immunol. **12** (1994) 117–139.
4. Kelsoe, G.: In situ studies of the germinal center reaction. Adv Immunol. **60** (1995) 267–288.
5. Fagarasan, S., Muramatsu, M., Suzuki, K., Nagaoka, H., Hiai, H. and Honjo, T.: Critical roles of activation-induced cytidine deaminase in the homeostasis of gut flora. Science **298** (2002) 1424–1427.
6. Gordo, I. and Dionisio, F.: Nonequilibrium model for estimating parameters of deleterious mutations. Phys Rev E Stat Nonlin Soft Matter Phys. **71** (2005) 031907.
7. Gordo, I. and Charlesworth, B.: On the speed of Muller's ratchet. Genetics. **156** (2000) 2137–2140.
8. Bachtrog, D. and Gordo, I.: Adaptive evolution of asexual populations under Muller's ratchet. Evolution Int J Org Evolution. **58** (2004) 1403–1413.
9. Kimura, M.: The neutral theory of molecular evolution. Cambridge University Press, Cambridge [Cambridgeshire] New York (1983)
10. Charlesworth, B., Morgan, M. T. and Charlesworth, D.: The effect of deleterious mutations on neutral molecular variation. Genetics. **134** (1993) 1289–1303.
11. Smith, J. M. and Haigh, J.: The hitch-hiking effect of a favourable gene. Genet Res **23** (1974) 23–35.

Modelling the Control of an Immune Response Through Cytokine Signalling

Thiago Guzella[1], Tomaz Mota-Santos[2],
Joaquim Uchôa[3], and Walmir Caminhas[1]

[1] Electrical Engineering Dept., Federal University of Minas Gerais
Belo Horizonte (MG) 31270-010, Brazil
{tguzella, caminhas}@cpdee.ufmg.br
[2] Biochemistry and Immunology Dept., Federal University of Minas Gerais
Belo Horizonte (MG) 31270-010, Brazil
tomaz@icb.ufmg.br
[3] Computer Science Dept., Federal University of Lavras
Lavras (MG) 37200-000, Brazil
joukim@dcc.ufla.br

Abstract. This paper presents the computer aided simulation of a model for the control of an immune response. This model has been developed to investigate the proposed hypothesis that the same cytokine that amplifies an initiated response can eventually lead to its downregulation, if it can act on more than one cell type. The simulation environment is composed of effector cells and regulatory cells; the former, when activated, initiate an immune response, while the latter are responsible for controlling the magnitude of the response. The signalling that coordinates this process is modelled using stimulation and regulation cytokines. Simulation results obtained, in accordance with the motivating idea, are presented and discussed.

1 Introduction

The immune system is a complex aggregate of cells, antibodies and signalling molecules. The Clonal Selection Theory [1] has been, for nearly 5 decades, the dominating base to explain how the immune system discriminates between self and nonself. This discrimination is extremely important, because the system must be able to eliminate nonself components that infiltrate the body, while remaining unresponsive to self. The Clonal Selection Theory argues that the system's tolerance to self is accomplished through a process denominated negative selection, when self-reactive B and T lymphocytes are eliminated during their development.

However, there's increasing evidence that some self-reactive cells eventually escape from the clonal deletion [2]. Therefore, these lymphocytes are present in the periphery, and could give rise to hazardous autoimmune diseases. Various models have been proposed to explain why, most of the times, these cells remain inactive, ignoring self antigens. These models are based on passive or recessive mechanisms, such as low avidities of their receptors for self-antigens and

H. Bersini and J. Carneiro (Eds.): ICARIS 2006, LNCS 4163, pp. 9–22, 2006.

lack of costimulation from antigen presenting cells (APCs). There is, however, a dominant mechanism [3], based on active downregulation of the activation and expansion of self-reactive lymphocytes by certain T cells [4], named regulatory T cells.

In addition, as discussed in [5], there's not much information regarding the mechanisms that terminate immune responses. After a response to an antigen, the immune system is returned to a state of rest, just like before the initiation of the response. This process, called homeostasis, allows the immune system to respond to new antigenic challenges (because the lymphocyte repertoire is closely regulated), and is also conducted by regulatory T cells.

To understand how the control of an initiated immune response is important, it is interesting to notice that, according to [6], the tissue damage that follows the chronic inflamation of tuberculosis is caused not by the bacillus, but by an uncontrolled response to it. In this sense, this work presents a model for the control of an initiated immune response, based on regulatory cells and cytokine secretion and absorption. The model has been motivated by the hypothesis that the same cytokine that improves an initiated response can lead to its termination, if this cytokine acts on more than one cell type with different affinities.

This paper is presented in the following way: first a short description of the cytokines included in the proposed model is presented. Afterwards, regulatory T cells are discussed, focusing on their interesting features for the simulation, followed by a detailed description of the proposed model and its parameters. In the end, results obtained by a simulation are presented and discussed.

2   Cytokines

Cytokines are control proteins secreted by the cells of the immune system, in response to microbes, other antigens or even other cytokines. For greater details regarding cytokines, the reader is invited to read [7] and [8].

Most cytokines are pleiotropic (capable of acting on different cell types), and influence the synthesis and actions of other cytokines. Besides, their secretion is a brief, self-limited event, and they may have local and systemic actions. They usually act close to where they are produced, either on the same cell that secretes them (autocrine action) or on a nearby cell (paracrine action), and initiate their actions by binding to specific receptors located on the membrane of the target cells. The expression of these receptors (and, thus, the responsiveness to cytokines) is controlled by external cell signals (in B and T cells, the stimulation of antigen receptors). In the proposed model, there are two cytokines of interest, described below:

Interferon-γ (IFN-γ) : IFN-γ is the cytokine that allows T lymphocytes and natural killer (NK) cells to activate macrophages to kill phagocytosed pathogens. Besides, IFN-γ improves the ability of antigen presenting cells (APCs) to present antigens, by increasing the expression of MHC and costimulation molecules. Therefore, it can be seen as an stimulation cytokine, that acts in order to increase the magnitude of a response;

Interleukin-10 (IL-10) : IL-10 acts inhibiting the activation of macrophages, being involved in the homeostatic control of innate host immune responses. It prevents the production of IL-12 and TNF by activated macrophages. Because IL-12 is a critical stimulus for IFN-γ secretion and induces innate and cell-mediated immune reactions against intracellular pathogens, IL-10 is responsible for downregulating these reactions. Therefore, it can be thought of as a regulatory cytokine, decreasing the magnitude of an established immune response.

3   Regulatory T Cells

The maintenance of immunologic tolerance by natural CD25$^+$ CD4$^+$ T cells was presented in [9], where autoimmune diseases were induced in normal rodents by removal of a specific subpopulation of CD4$^+$ cells. Recently, it was found that these cells, responsible for the maintenance of self-tolerance, can be identified by the expression of the *Foxp3* marker [10]. These cells are capable of exerting suppression upon stimulation via the T cell receptor (TCR), and their engagement in the control of self-reactive cells is related to the recognition of self-antigens in the normal environment. Besides, once stimulated, the suppression mediated by CD25$^+$ CD4$^+$ regulatory T cells mediate is antigen non-specific. Therefore, they are capable of suppressing the proliferation of T cells specific for the antigen that lead to their activation, but also other T cells specific for other antigens, a mechanism known as *bystander suppression* [11].

In this sense, the defining feature of CD25$^+$ CD4$^+$ T_{reg} cells is the ability to inhibit the proliferation of other T cell populations *in vitro*. This suppression requires the activation of the regulatory cell through its TCR, doesn't involve killing the responder cell and is mediated through a mechanism based on cell contact or mediated by IL-10 and other cytokines [12] [13].

These cells play a crucial role not only in preventing self-reactive T cells that have escaped negative deletion from initiating an immune response against self-antigens. Induced regulatory cells are engaged in the control of a "legitimate" response in the periphery, preventing local or systemic immunopathology (such as septic shock), due to the excessive production of pro-inflamatory cytokines by activated cells [14]. This is an interesting feature, with little exploration available in the literature. An important work in this line is [15], where the role of Toll-like receptors (TLRs) in the process of inflamation is discussed. In addition, these cells are responsible for preventing the complete elimination of the invading microbe, because its persistency, in low levels, is important for the continuous stimulation of long-lived functionally quiescent memory cells [5].

The immune system can be studied in a context of infection, characterized by a response to antigenic pathogens, or in healthy, normal individuals, when the internal activities of the system are dominant. In both cases, regulatory T cells play an important role. In the former, these cells are responsible for the control of both the inflamatory activity and the intensity of the response. In the latter, they prevent autoimmune diseases, given the existence of self-reactive B and T lymphocytes. A recent work presented in [16] discusses two hypotheses in this context: the tuning of activation thresholds of self-reactive T lymphocytes, making them reversibly "anergic", and the control of the proliferation of these cells by specific regulatory T cells.

4   Model Description

As previously discussed, this paper is aimed at modelling the control of an initiated immune response through cytokine signalling, involving effector and regulatory cells. The proposed model is based on microscopic mechanisms, and, due to the lack of numerical data from *in vivo* or *in vitro* experiments, most of the governing equations were arbitrarily selected. However, even if numerical data were available, it is important to emphasize that a complete modelling the immune system is not trivial, given its complexity [17] [18].

Before modelling the actual process of controlling the immune response, some considerations were made about the environment. The tissue where the response would occur is approximated by a rectangular region, whose dimensions are given as parameters to the simulation. Also, the number of iterations and the time step are additional necessary parameters. Cytokines are represented by two-dimensional matrices, equivalent to a discrete representation of the environment. In this sense, there are two cytokine matrices, which separately store the concentrations of the stimulation and regulatory cytokines. Each cell occupies a single square in the grid, and, currently, remains fixed in this position. Besides, the simulations performed so far don't take cell clonning into consideration. Finally, all data presented in this paper is adimensional (i.e.: no physical units for the concentrations or other variables are used), because this has no effects on the simulation outcome. However, if the results are to be compared to real world data, the introduction of physical units in the governing equations is necessary.

The simulation is started after an effector cell is stimulated, after, for example, contact with a specific antigen. It is important to mention that this model doesn't consider antigen dynamics, once the response has been initiated. This cell will secrete an amount of an stimulation cytokine that will be diffused through the environment. The remaining cells (both effector and regulatory) will, then, absorb some of this cytokine, and be activated, secreting, in turn, more cytokines, until a steady state is reached. Effector cells secrete the stimulation cytokine, while regulatory cells secrete the regulatory cytokine; on the other hand, effector cells absorb both stimulation and regulatory cytokines, while regulatory cells absorb only the stimulation cytokine. Based on the discussion presented in [5], the expected response should be an increase of the number of activated effector cells, with little influence from regulatory cells, until the response suppression is initiated, with the activation of regulatory cells and eventual termination of the response. These steps are represented graphically in figure 1.

Each cell stores its position in the tissue and a value representing its activation level. This activation level reflects the immunological status of the cell, and is a real number in the interval $(0, 1)$. The greater the activation level, the

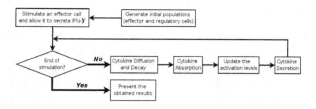

Fig. 1. Steps for the simulation of the proposed model

"more" activated and immunocompetent a given cell can be considered to be, in contrast to a resting condition, represented by an activation level close to zero. The affinity between a cell and a cytokine, a key point of the motivating hypothesis, is modelled by constants used to update the cell activation level, based on the cytokine absorption, that will be described in greater detail. This cytokine affinity is proportional to the increase in the cell activation level, so that cells with a large affinity will be highly stimulated upon absorption of a given stimulation cytokine. This approach to the simulation is very similar to the proposal of [18], where a cellular automaton is used to simulate the dynamics of the immune system during immunization.

Due to the complexity involved, each distinct step in the simulation is presented separately, in the following sub-sections.

4.1   Cytokine Decay and Diffusion in the Environment

Updating the cytokine concentration in the environment is conducted in accordance with the discrete two-dimensional diffusion equation [19], using equations 1 for diffusion and 2 for decay, where $\psi(x, y, t)$ is the cytokine concentration at the point defined by the coordinates (x, y) at the time instant t, k_d is the cytokine diffusion rate, Δt is the simulation time step, ζ is the decay constant, $n(x, y)$ is the number of valid slots surrounding the position defined by points (x, y) (representing the tissue boundary conditions) and h_x and h_y are the environment dimensions. The artificial tissue has been modelled as a compartment isolated from the body, so that there's no cytokine flux coming in or out of the simulation environment. Therefore, all cytokines secreted by the cells in the tissue remain confined to the environment, without taking the decay into consideration.

$$\psi(x, y, t + \Delta t) = \psi(x, y, t) + \frac{k_d \cdot \Delta t}{h_x \cdot h_y} \cdot (\psi(x - 1, y, t) +$$
$$\psi(x + 1, y, t) + \psi(x, y - 1, t) + \psi(x, y + 1, t)) - n(x, y) \cdot \psi(x, y, t))$$
$$1 \leq x \leq h_x, 1 \leq y \leq h_y \qquad (1)$$

$$\psi(x, y, t + \Delta t) = \psi(x, y, t) \cdot (1 - \zeta), 0 \leq \zeta \leq 1 \qquad (2)$$

4.2   Cytokine Absorption

Following the cytokine diffusion and decay in the tissue, each cell in the population proceeds to absorb cytokines located in the position where it is located. According to the model being simulated, effector cells can absorb both IFN-γ and IL-10, while regulatory cells can only absorb IFN-γ. For simplicity, this process has been modelled by a first degree polynomial of the cell activation level, according to equation 3. This equation determines the absorption rate, that is, the relative amount of a given cytokine to be absorbed, where ϕ_{max}^{in} is the maximum cytokine input rate, to be absorbed when the cell is fully activated, ϕ_{min}^{in} is the minimum cytokine input rate, absorbed when the cell has received little or no stimulation and α is the cell activation level. As mentioned, the value given by equation 3 is relative to the total cytokine concentration located in the position where the cell is located. Therefore, to determine the absolute amount of cytokine to be absorbed, the total cytokine concentration is determined, and multiplied by $\phi(\alpha)^{in}$, as shown in equation 4. To illustrate the function used to determine the absorption rate, it is shown in figure 2, for two different values of ϕ_{min}^{in} and ϕ_{max}^{in}.

$$\phi(\alpha)^{in} = \phi_{min}^{in} + (\phi_{max}^{in} - \phi_{min}^{in}) \cdot \alpha \tag{3}$$

$$\Delta\psi(x, y, t, \alpha)^{in} = \phi(\alpha)^{in} \cdot \psi(x, y, t) \tag{4}$$

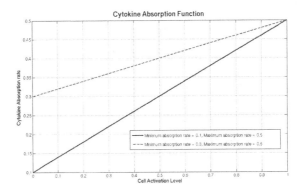

Fig. 2. Plots of the cytokine absorption rate as a function of cell activation for $\psi_{min}^{in} = 0.1, \psi_{max}^{in} = 0.5$ and $\psi_{min}^{in} = 0.3, \psi_{max}^{in} = 0.5$

4.3   Determination of the New Activation Level

After cytokine absorption, the simulation continues to determine the new activation level for each cell, given as a function of the cytokine inputs. As previously discussed, effector cells have $\psi_{stimulation}^{in} \geq 0$ and $\psi_{regulation}^{in} \geq 0$ (because they can absorb both IFN-γ and IL-10), and regulatory cells have $\psi_{stimulation}^{in} \geq 0$ and $\psi_{regulation}^{in} = 0$ (because regulatory cells can absorb only IFN-γ). In the motivating hypothesis, the different affinities for the stimulation and the regulatory cytokine for the effector cells plays an important role in this model. Therefore, the constants involved in this step have great influence on the model, because the cell activation level is used as a measure of the response magnitude. Given the cytokine inputs, the resultant input is then determined, according to 5, where k_r and k_s are positive values, named regulation and stimulation constants, respectively.

$$\chi = k_s \cdot \psi^{in}_{stimulation} - k_r \cdot \psi^{in}_{regulation} \tag{5}$$

Effector Cells. Closer inspection of equation 5 reveals that the resultant input, when negative, implies that cell regulation exert domination over cell stimulation, and the cell activation level should be decreased. On the other hand, a positive resultant input should increase the activation level. To model the activation level update process, the sigmoid function is used. The new cell activation level, given as a function of the resultant input and current activation level, is given by equation 6, where α_0 is the current activation level, χ is the resultant input and σ is the sigmoid function steepness. To illustrate the activation function, it is shown in figure 3, as a function of the resultant input (χ), for two values of α_0 and σ ($\alpha_0 = 0.2, \sigma = 0.1$ and $\alpha_0 = 0.8, \sigma = 0.2$).

$$\alpha(\chi, \alpha_0) = \frac{1}{1 + \frac{1-\alpha_0}{\alpha_0} \cdot exp(-\sigma \cdot \chi)} \tag{6}$$

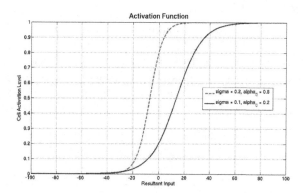

Fig. 3. Plots of the new cell activation level as a function of resultant input for $\alpha_0 = 0.2, \sigma = 0.1$ and $\alpha_0 = 0.8, \sigma = 0.2$

The activation function shown in figure 3 has two interesting characteristics:

– the current activation level (α_0 in equation 6) is related to the horizontal translation of the activation curve. As a matter of fact, the curve is translated so that $\alpha(\chi = 0, \alpha_0) = \alpha_0$; thus, in the absense of input stimuli, the cell activation level will remain constant. In this sense, each cell can be seen as a processing unit with an activation level controlled by a given externally received input

– the steepness (σ in equation 6) is inversely proportional to the transition region between 0 and 1 in figure 3. As an example, consider the first curve ($\alpha_0 = 0.2, \sigma = 0.1$), where a resultant input equals to approximately 5.4 units is needed to increase the activation level by 0.1, while, for the second curve, this value is around 4.1 units. Therefore, the steepness, together with the stimulation and regulation constants, can be seen a parameter representing the affinity for the absorbed cytokines.

Regulatory Cells. Due to the fact that, in this proposal, regulatory cells react only to IFN-γ, the resultant input (χ, according to equation 5) is either positive or zero. Therefore, using equation 6 is not appropriate, because the activation level would never decrease. Thus, update of the activation level for regulatory cells is governed by equation 7.

$$\alpha(\chi) = \frac{2}{1 + exp(-\sigma \cdot \chi)} - 1 \tag{7}$$

According to equation 7, the new activation level for regulatory cells is not dependant on the current activation level (α_0), in contrast to equation 6. In this sense, regulatory cells have no memory of past states (in this case, the activation level), and act based only on the current environment conditions.

4.4 Cytokine Secretion

In this step, each cell secretes an amount of a given cytokine. As previously discussed, effector cells secrete IFN-γ (referred to as a stimulation cytokine), while regulatory cells secrete IL-10 (referred to as a regulatory cytokine). The amount of cytokine to be secreted is directly proportionally to the cell's activation level, and has been modelled according to equation 8, where $\Delta\psi$ is the

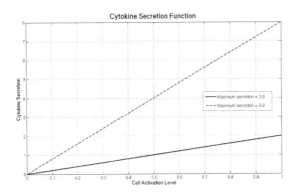

Fig. 4. Plots of the cytokine secretion as a function of cell activation for two sensitivity values

target cytokine secretion amount (which increases the cytokine concentration in the position where the cell is located), ψ_{max}^{out} is the maximum secretion allowed and α is the cell activation level. The secretion function is shown in figure 4, for two maximum secretion values ($\psi_{max}^{out} = 2$ and $\psi_{max}^{out} = 8$).

$$\Delta\psi(\alpha)^{out} = \psi_{max}^{out} \cdot \alpha \tag{8}$$

This equation has been chosen for both simplicity and ease of calculation, so that the simulation of the model is not limited by an excessive computational load. As previously mentioned, no assertion about the validity of this modelling can be performed for now, due to the absence of numerical experimental data.

5   Results and Discussion

In order to verify the response of the designed model, a simple simulation scenario was selected. The artificial tissue is represented by a 3x3 square region, with the cell positioning shown in figure 5, where E and R are used to designate the cell type (effector and regulatory, respectively), and the number located right under the cell type designates the cell number, to be used when analysing the simulation results, with the x and y axis in the horizontal and vertical directions, respectively.

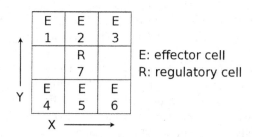

Fig. 5. Artificial tissue where the simulation took place

The cell populations for the simulation are composed of, according to figure 5, 6 effector cells and 1 regulatory cell. Therefore, the initial cell population is composed of 14.3% of regulatory cells, a number close to values verified experimentally [9].

Before starting the simulation, the cell identified by number 2 in figure 5 was stimulated, by setting its activation level to 0.999. This could be caused by the recognition of an antigen, for example. The remaining cells were initialized with an activation level equals to $1 \cdot 10^{-4}$. Afterwards, the simulation was executed for 30 iterations, with a time step of 1 second. The diffusion rates of stimulation and regulatory cytokines were chosen as 1.5 and 2, respectively, while decay rates were chosen as 0.25 and 0.05, respectively. Therefore, regulatory cytokines diffuse more easily and decay less into the environment than stimulation cytokines.

Table 1. Simulation parameters

Parameter	Value	
	Effector cells	Regulatory Cells
Max. cytokine secretion (ψ_{max}^{out})	2	45.5
Min. stimulation cytokine absorption (ϕ_{min}^{in})	0.4	0.05
Max. stimulation cytokine absorption (ϕ_{max}^{in})	0.8	0.5
Min. regulation cytokine absorption (ϕ_{min}^{in})	0.3	-
Max. regulation cytokine absorption (ϕ_{max}^{in})	0.5	-
Stimulation constant (k_s)	10	3
Regulation constant (k_r)	10	-
Activation steepness (σ)	1	2

Additional parameters for both effector and regulatory cells, chosen empirically, are shown in table 1.

As previously discussed, a key feature of the hypothesis motivating the development of the proposed model is the ability of the stimulation cytokine to be absorbed with different affinities by effector and regulatory cells. In order to obtain the expected system dynamic response (increasing the magnitude of the response, followed by its decline), it is analysed the case when the effector cell affinity for the stimulation cytokine is greater than the affinity by regulatory cells. In this situation, the regulatory cell would only be activated once a large amount of stimulation cytokine (secreted by activated effector cells) is present in the environment.

The model parameters shown in table 1 were chosen to reflect this assumption. Special care was taken not to select large diffusion rates, leading to instability when determining the cytokine diffusion. The activation steepness for effector cells is twice as low as for regulatory cells, while the stimulation constant for effector cells is greater than for regulatory cells. Afterwards, the selected parameters were tuned to lead to a desired characteristic, where the response is initiated (by the initially stimulated cell), increased (by the recruitment of surrounding effector cells) and terminated (by suppression of the activated cells). It is important to mention that some combinations of values have lead to oscillations in the response (data not shown), with the activation level of effector and regulatory cells increasing and decreasing, without reaching a steady state. This oscillatory response of the model is undesirable, because there are no reports from a similar behavior in the natural immune system.

The simulation results obtained for the selected parameters are presented in figures 6, 7, 8 and 9. By the end of the simulation, the effector cells identified by numbers 4, 5 and 6, according to figure 5, were not activated, remaining in a resting state during the simulation. Thus, simulation results for these cells are not presented. On the other hand, the effector cells identified by the numbers 1 and 3 in figure 5 were successfully recruited for the immune response initiated by effector cell number 2. Some iterations after the beginning of the simulation, the regulatory cell (number 7) began to be stimulated, acting, at some time, to

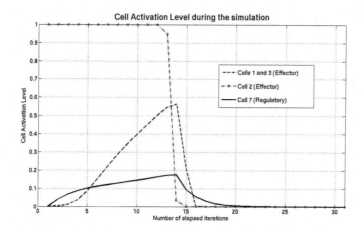

Fig. 6. Cell activation levels during the simulation

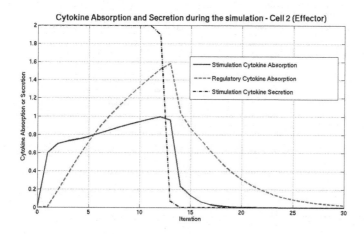

Fig. 7. Cytokine secretion for the initially stimulated effector cell 2

end the initiated response. Figure 6 shows the activation level for effector cells 1, 2 and 3, and regulatory cell 7, during the simulation procedure, while figures 7, 8 and 9 show the cytokine absorption and secretion for these cells.

The results indicate that the model, with the parameters presented in table 1, is able to exhibit the expected response characteristic, with the recruitment of cells and, after some time, termination of the response. Figure 6 shows that cell number 2 (initially stimulated) remains highly active (with an activation level close to 1) for 12 iterations, and quickly decays, reaching a resting condition by iteration 15. In the same figure, it can be seen that effector cells 1 and 3 have reached a peak activation level equals to 0.57 at iteration 14, quickly declining and reaching a low activation level by iteration 16. The regulatory cell (number 7) has reached a peak activation level equals to 0.18 at the same time than effector cells 1 and 3 have. One interesting characteristic of the response shown

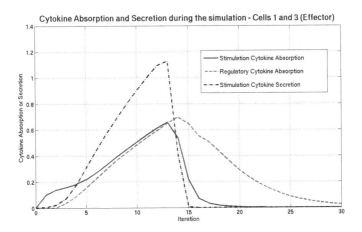

Fig. 8. Cytokine secretion for effector cells 1 and 3

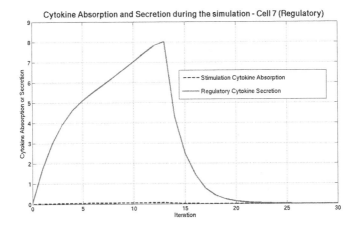

Fig. 9. Regulatory cell cytokine secretion and absorption

in figure 6 is that the initially stimulated effector cell is suppressed before cells 1 and 3, reaching, an activation level of 0.04 at iteration 14, exactly when cells 1 and 3 have reached peak values. This activation delay is due to the time taken by the secreted cytokines to diffuse in the environment and reach nearby cells.

In addition, the cytokine activation and secretion data (figures 7, 8 and 9) reveal interesting information. Cytokine secretion by the regulatory cell reaches a peak value equals to 8, at iteration 13, while cytokine absorption is maintained at low levels, never exceeding 0.2. Therefore, it is possible to conclude that regulatory cells, in this model, need a low absorption rate to terminate the response, resulting in little environment disturbance when not suppressing effector cells. Because the governing equation for cytokine secretion was chosen as directly proportional to the activation level 8, both variables have the same waveforms;

this can be notice when comparing figures 6 to 7, 8 and 9. Inspection of figure 7 reveals that the regulatory cytokine absorption is nearly zero for the first 3 iterations, intersecting the absorption cytokine absorption curve around iteration 6.

6   Conclusion

In this paper, a model for the control of an immune response, based on regulatory cells and cytokines, was presented. Althought based on relatively simple and arbitrary functions, the model simulation has lead to interesting results, with an expected response characteristic obtained. Therefore, this model can be considered as an initial validation to the hypothesis that has lead to its development, that the same cytokine that stimulates the immune system, upon initiation of an immune response, can eventually lead to the downregulation of this response, if the secreted cytokine affects more than one cell type, with different affinities.

However, there are some points that need further investigation, such as a mathematical explanation for the oscillatory response obtained for some model parameters, and the influence of antigen dynamics and persistence in the system. In addition, the model should take cell clonning and movement into consideration, two aspects not considered in the simple simulation presented. In this sense, this paper can be thought of as only an starting point for the simulation of more complicated and accurate scenarios.

Acknowledgements

The authors wish to thank the reviewers for the insightful comments and suggestions. This research was sponsored by UOL (www.uol.com.br), through its UOL Bolsa Pesquisa program, process number 200503301636a. Besides, the authors would like to thank the financial support by PQI/CAPES, CNPq and FAPEMIG.

References

1. Burnet, F.M.: The clonal selection theory of acquired immunity (1959) Cambridge Press.
2. Apostolou, I., Sarukhan, A., Klein, L., von Boehmer, H.: Origin of regulatory T cells with known specificity for antigen. Nature Immunology 3(8) (2002) 756–763
3. Coutinho, A.: The Le Douarin phenomenon: a shift in the paradigm of developmental self-tolerance. Int. J. Dev. Biol. 49 (2005) 131–136
4. Sakaguchi, S.: Naturally arising $CD4^+$ regulatory T cells for immunologic self-tolerance and negative control of immune response. Annu. Rev. Immunol. 22 (2004) 531–62
5. Parijs, L.V., Abbas, A.K.: Homeostasis and self-tolerance in the immune system: Turning lymphocytes off. Science 280 (1998) 243–248
6. Mason, D.: T-cell-mediated control of autoimmunity. Arthritis Research 3(3) (2001) 133–135

7. Janeway, C.A., Travers, P., Walport, M., Shlonmchik, M.: Immunobiology: the immune system in health and disease. 5 edn. Garland Publishing, Inc, New York, USA (2002)

8. Abbas, A.K., Lichtman, A.H., Pober, J.S.: Cellular and Molecular Immunology. 4 edn. W.B. Saunders, Philadelphia, USA (2000)

9. Sakaguchi, S., Sakaguchi, N., Shimizu, J., Yamazaki, S., Sakihama, T., Itoh, M., Kuniyasu, Y., Nomura, T., Toda, M., Takahashi, T.: Immunologic tolerance maintained by $CD25^+CD4^+$ regulatory T cells: their common role in controlling autoimmunity, tumor immunity, and transplantation tolerance. Immunological Reviews **182** (2001) 18–32

10. Hori, S., Nomura, T., Sakaguchi, S.: Control of regulatory T cell development by the transcription factor foxp3. Science **299** (2003) 1057–1061

11. Schwartz, R.H.: Natural regulatory T cells and self-tolerance. Nature Immunology **6**(4) (2005) 327–330

12. Maloy, K.J., Powrie, F.: Regulatory T cells in the control of immune pathology. Nature Immunology **2**(9) (2001) 816–822

13. Levings, M.K., Bacchetta, R., Schulz, U., Roncarolo, M.G.: The role of IL-10 and TGF-β in the differentiation and effector function of t regulatory cells. Int Arch Allergy Immunol **129** (2002) 263–276

14. Sakaguchi, S.: Control of immune responses by naturally arising $CD4^+$ regulatory T cells that express toll-like receptors. J. Exp. Med **197**(4) (2003) 397–401

15. Caramalho, I., Lopes-Carvalho, T., Ostler, D., Zelenay, S., Haury, M., Demengeot, J.: Regulatory T cells selectively express toll-like receptors and are activated by lipopolysaccharide. J. Exp. Med. **197**(4) (2003) 403–411

16. Carneiro, J., Paixao, T., Milutinovic, D., Sousa, J., Leon, K., Gardner, R., Faro, J.: Immunological self-tolerance: Lessons from mathematical modeling. Journal of Computational and Applied Mathematics **184**(1) (2005) 77–100

17. Perelson, A.S.: Modelling viral and immune system dynamics. Nature Reviews in Immunology **2** (2002) 28–36

18. Celada, F., Seiden, P.E.: A computer model of cellular interactions in the immune system. Immunology Today **13**(2) (1992) 56–62

19. Boyce, W.E., DiPrima, R.C.: Elementary Differential Equations and Boundary Value Problems. John Wiley & Sons, Inc. (2000)

Modeling Influenza Viral Dynamics in Tissue

Catherine Beauchemin[1,*], Stephanie Forrest[2], and Frederick T. Koster[3]

[1] Adaptive Computation Lab., University of New Mexico, Albuquerque, NM
cbeau@cs.unm.edu
[2] Dept. of Computer Science, University of New Mexico, Albuquerque, NM
[3] Lovelace Respiratory Research Institute, Albuquerque, NM

Abstract. Predicting the virulence of new Influenza strains is an important problem. The solution to this problem will likely require a combination of in vitro and in silico tools that are used iteratively. We describe the agent-based modeling component of this program and report preliminary results from both the in vitro and in silico experiments.

1 Introduction

Influenza, in humans, is caused by a virus that attacks mainly the upper respiratory tract, the nose, throat and bronchi and rarely also the lungs. According to the World Health Organization (WHO), the annual influenza epidemics affect from 5% to 15% of the population and are thought to result in 3-5 million cases of severe illness and 250,000 to 500,000 deaths every year around the world [1]. The rapid spread of H5N1 avian influenza among wild and domestic fowl and isolated fatal human cases of H5N1 in Eurasia since 1997, has re-awakened interest in the pathogenesis and transmission of influenza A infections [2]. The most feared strain would mimic the 1918 strain which combined high transmissibility with high mortality [3,4]. Virulence of influenza viruses is highly variable, defined by lethality and person-to-person transmission, but the causes of this variability are incompletely understood. The early events of influenza replication in airway tissue, particularly the type and location of early infected cells, likely determine the outcome of the infection. Rate of airway tissue spread is controlled by efficiency of viral entry and exit from cells, variable intracellular interferon activation modulated by the viral NS-1 protein, and by an array of extracellular innate defenses. Although molecular biology has provided a detailed understanding of the replication cycle in immortalized cells, influenza replication in intact tissue among phenotypically diverse epithelial cells of the human respiratory tract remains poorly understood. We are missing a quantitative accounting of kinetics in the human airway and an explanation for how one strain, but not a closely related strain, can initiate person-to-person transmission.

Although the viral structure and composition of influenza are known, and even some dynamical data regarding the viral and antibody titers over the course of the infection [5,6,7], key information such as the shape and magnitude of the viral burst, the length of the viral replication cycle (time between entry of the

---

* Corresponding author.

H. Bersini and J. Carneiro (Eds.): ICARIS 2006, LNCS 4163, pp. 23–36, 2006.
© Springer-Verlag Berlin Heidelberg 2006

first virus and release of the first produced virus), and the proportion of productively infectious virions, is either uncorroborated, unknown, or known with poor precision. This makes modeling influenza from data available in the literature a near impossibility, and it points to the need for generating experimental data aimed directly at the needs of both computational and mathematical models.

This paper describes the computer modeling side of a project that is integrating in vitro experiments with computer modeling to address this problem. We are focusing on the early dynamics of influenza infection in a human airway epithelial cell monolayer using both in vitro and computer models. The in vitro model uses primary human differentiated lung epithelial cells grown in an air-liquid interface (ALI) culture to document the kinetics of influenza spread in tissue. The computer model consists of an agent-based model (ABM) implementation of the in vitro system. Its architecture is modular so that more details can be added whenever data from the in vitro system justifies it. Here, we will describe the implementation of the computer model and report some initial simulation results.

To our knowledge, only four mathematical models for influenza dynamics have ever been proposed. The first and oldest one is from 1976 and consists of a very basic compartmental model for influenza in experimentally infected mice [8]. After a gap of 18 years, Bocharov et al. proposed an exhaustive ordinary differential equation model based on the basic viral infection model but extended to include 12 different cell populations described by 60 parameters [9]. More recently, one of us co-authored a paper presenting another ordinary differential equation model with very slight modifications from the basic viral infection model [10] and a second paper presenting a simple ABM for influenza [11]. All of these models either perform poorly when compared to experimental data or are too simplistic to capture the dynamics of interest in influenza.

2   Agent-Based Modeling

The spatial distribution of agents is an important and often neglected aspect of influenza dynamics. We capture spatial dynamics through the use of an agent-based model (also known as an individual-based) cellular automata style model. Each epithelial cell in the monolayer is represented explicitly, and a computer program encodes the cell's behavior and rules for interacting with other cells and its environment. The cells live on a hexagonal lattice and interact locally with other cells and virions in their neighborhood following a set of predefined rules. Thus, the behavior of the low-level entities is pre-specified, and the simulation is run to observe high-level behaviors (e.g. to determine an epidemic threshold). This style of modeling emphasizes local interactions, and those interactions in turn give rise to the large-scale complex dynamics of interest.

This modeling approach can be more detailed than other approaches. The programs can directly incorporate biological knowledge or hypotheses about low-level components. Data from multiple experiments can be combined into a single simulation, to test for consistency across experiments or to identify gaps in our knowledge. Through its functional specifications of cell behavior, our can potentially bridge the current gap between intracellular descriptions and infection dynamics models. Similar approaches have been used to model a variety of host-pathogen systems ranging from general immune system simulation platforms [12,13,14,15,16] to models of specific diseases including tuberculosis [17,18], Alzheimer's disease [19], cancer [20,21,22,23,24,25], and HIV [26,27].

The spatially explicit agent-based approach is an appropriate method for this project. The ALI is a complex biological system in which many different defenses (e.g. mucus, cytokines) interact and biologically relevant values cannot always be measured directly. In addition, recent high-profile publications have demonstrated that entry of avian and human-adapted influenza viruses into different airway epithelial cells depends on the cell receptor which in turn is dependent on cell type and location in the airway [28,29]. Our modeling approach will facilitate the exploration of spatially heterogeneous populations of cells.

3 Influenza Model

Our current model is extremely simple. We plan to gradually add more detail, ensuring at each step that the additions are justified by our experimental data. Here, we describe the model as it is currently implemented.

We are modeling influenza dynamics on an epithelial cell monolayer in vitro. The monolayer is represented as a two-dimensional hexagonal lattice where each site represents one epithelial cell. The spread of the infection is modeled by including virions. Rather than treat each virion explicitly, the model instead considers the concentration of virions by associating a continuous real-valued variable with each lattice site, which stores the local concentration of virions at that site. These local concentrations are then allowed to change, following a discretized version of the diffusion equation with a production term. The rules governing epithelial cell and virion concentration dynamics are described below.

3.1 Epithelial Cell Dynamics

The epithelial cells can be found in any of the four states shown in Fig. 1, namely healthy, containing, secreting, and dead. For simplicity, we assume that there is no cell division or differentiation over the course of the infection. The parameters responsible for the transition between these states are as follows.

Infection of Epithelial Cells by Virions (k): Each site keeps track of the number of virions local to the site, $V_{m,n}$. But while there are $V_{m,n}$ virions at site (m, n) at a given time step, depending on the length of a time step, not all of these virions necessarily come in contact with the cell, and some may contact it more than once. Alternatively, a particular strain of virions may not be as successful at binding the cell's receptors and being absorbed by the cell. To reflect this reality, we introduce the parameter k which gives the probability per hour per virion

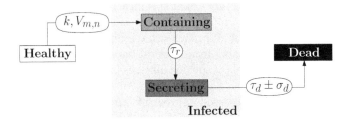

Fig. 1. The agent-based model's four states for epithelial cells, (Healthy, Containing, Secreting, and Dead), and the parameters responsible for controlling the transitions between these states

that a healthy cell will become infected (enter the containing stage). In other words, $k \times V_{m,n}$ gives the probability that the healthy cell located at site (m, n) will become infected over the course of an hour. In order to fit experimental data, we set the rate of infection of cells per virions in our model to $k = 8$ per virion at that site per hour.

Duration of the Viral Replication Cycle (τ_r): This variable represents the time that elapses between entry of the first successful virion and release of the first virion produced by the infected cell. From the experiments, we found this to be about 7 h, and hence we set $\tau_r = 7$ h in the ABM.

Lifespan of Infectious Cells ($\tau_d \pm \sigma_d$): Once infected (containing), a cell typically lives 24 h–36 h (from experimental observations). Given that the replication cycle lasts $\tau_r = 7$ h, this means that once it starts secreting virions, an infectious cell typically lives 17 h–29 h or about 23 ± 6 h. Thus, we set the lifespan of each infected cell individually by picking it randomly from a Gaussian distribution of mean $\tau_d = 23$ h and standard deviation $\sigma_d = 6$ h. In our ABM, cell death is taken to mean the time at which cells cease to produce virions. Note that in vitro, a cell undergoing apoptosis will eventually detach from the monolayer and will be replaced by a differentiating basal cell. For the moment, we neglect these processes and reduce their impact by fitting our ABM to experimental results over no more than the first 25 h after virion deposition.

3.2   Virion Dynamics

As mentioned earlier, virions are not represented explicitly. Instead, we track the concentration of virions stored as a real-valued continuous variable at each site of the lattice. The diffusion of virions is then modeled using a finite difference approximation to the diffusion equation. The continuous diffusion equation of the concentration of virions, V, is described by

$$\frac{\partial V}{\partial t} = D_V \, \nabla^2 V \; , \tag{1}$$

where V is the concentration of virions, ∇^2 is the Laplacian, and D_V is the diffusion coefficient. The simulation is run on a hexagonal grid. The geometry of the grid and the base vectors we chose are illustrated in Fig. 2.

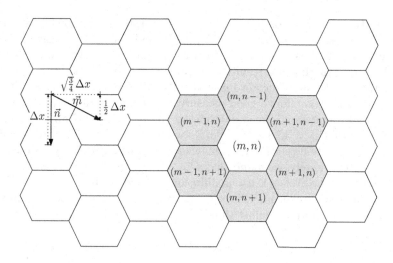

Fig. 2. Geometry of agent-based model's hexagonal grid. The honeycomb neighborhood is identified in gray, and the base vectors m and n are shown and expressed as a function of Δx, the grid spacing which is the mean diameter of an epithelial cell.

We can express (1) as a difference equation in the hexagonal coordinates (m, n) as a function of the 6 honeycomb neighbors as

$$\frac{V_{m,n}^{t+1} - V_{m,n}^{t}}{\Delta t} = \frac{4D_V}{(\Delta x)^2}\left[-V_{m,n}^{t} + \frac{1}{6}\sum_{\text{nei}} V_{\text{nei}}^{t}\right] , \qquad (2)$$

such that $V_{m,n}^{t+1}$ at time $t+1$ as a function of $V_{m,n}^{t}$ and its 6 honeycomb neighbors V_{nei}^{t} at time t is given by

$$V_{m,n}^{t+1} = \left(1 - \frac{4D_V\Delta t}{(\Delta x)^2}\right) V_{m,n}^{t} + \frac{2D_V\Delta t}{3(\Delta x)^2}\sum_{\text{nei}} V_{\text{nei}}^{t} , \qquad (3)$$

where $\sum_{\text{nei}} V_{\text{nei}}^{t}$ is the sum of the virion concentration at all 6 honeycomb neighbors at time t.

Because we want to simulate the infection dynamics in an experimental well, we want the diffusion to obey reflective boundary conditions along the edge of the well. Namely, we want $\frac{\partial V}{\partial j} = 0$ at a boundary where j is the direction perpendicular to the boundary. It can be shown that for such a case, (3) becomes

$$V_{m,n}^{t+1} = \left(1 - N_{\text{nei}}\frac{2D_V\Delta t}{3(\Delta x)^2}\right) V_{m,n}^{t} + \frac{2D_V\Delta t}{3(\Delta x)^2}\sum_{N_{\text{nei}}} V_{N_{\text{nei}}}^{t} , \qquad (4)$$

where N_{nei} is the number of neighbors a cell really has. Note that for $N_{nei} = 6$, (4) reduces to (3).

The virion-related parameters D_V, Δx, Δt in (4), and the release rate of virions, g_V, have been set as follows.

Diffusion Rate of Virions (D_V): The diffusion rate or diffusion coefficient for virions, D_V, measures how fast virions spread: the larger D_V, the faster virions will spread to neighboring sites and then to the entire grid. One way to determine D_V from experimental results is to take a measure of the "patchiness" of the infection, i.e. the tendency of infected cells to be found in batches. The autocorrelation function offers a good measure of patchiness. Hence, we calibrated D_V by visually matching our simulation to the experimental autocorrelation. We started with $D_V = 3.18 \times 10^{-12}$ m^2/s which is the diffusion rate predicted by the Stokes-Einstein relation for influenza virions diffusing in plasma at body temperature. Ultimately, we found that $D_V = 3.18 \times 10^{-15}$ m^2/s, a value 1,000-fold greater than the Stokes-Einstein diffusion, yielded the best agreement to the experimental autocorrelation. This is illustrated in Fig. 3 where the experimental autocorrelation is plotted against simulation results for different values of D_V.

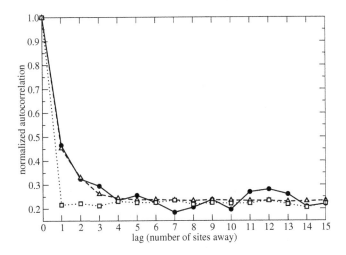

Fig. 3. Autocorrelation at 24 h post-harvest for the experiments (full line, full circles) compared against the autocorrelation produced by the simulation when using a diffusion coefficient of $D_V = 3.18 \times 10^{-12}$ m^2/s (dotted line, empty squares), and $D_V = 3.18 \times 10^{-15}$ m^2/s (dashed line, empty triangles). All parameters are as in Table 1 except for the $D_V = 3.18 \times 10^{-12}$ m^2/s simulation where k was set to 4 per virions per hour to preserve the same fraction of cells infected at 24 h post-harvest. The autocorrelation have been "normalized" to be one for a lag of zero.

Grid Spacing or Diameter of Epithelial Cells (Δx): The diameter of epithelial cells was estimated from "en face" and cross-section pictures of the experimental monolayer. The average epithelial cell diameter was found to be about 11 ± 1 μm. We use $\Delta x = 11$ μm.

Duration of a Time Step (Δt): The stability criterion for the finite difference approximation to the diffusion equation presented in (4) requires that

$$\Delta t \leq \frac{(\Delta x)^2}{4D_V} \; , \tag{5}$$

which is a more stringent requirement for larger values of D_V or smaller values of Δx. We use $\Delta x = 11$ µm which is the diameter of lung epithelial cells, and $D_V = 3.18 \times 10^{-15}$ m$^2 \cdot$s^{-1} such that in order to satisfy the stability criterion, we need $\Delta t \leq 2.6$ h. We found that setting $\Delta t = 2$ min satisfies the stability criterion of the diffusion equation and accurately captures the behaviour of the system.

Virion Release Rate (g_V): As seen above, $\tau_r = 7$ h after becoming infected, an epithelial cell will start secreting virions. In the model, secreting cells release virions at a constant rate until the cell is considered "dead", at which time secretion is instantaneously stopped. This "shape" for the viral burst was chosen arbitrarily as very little is known about the shape, duration, and magnitude of the viral burst. We found that setting the release rate of virions by secreting cells to $g_V = 0.05$ virions per hour per secreting cell in our ABM yields a good fit of the simulation to the experimental data.

3.3   Setting Up the Model

The infection of the epithelial cell monolayer with influenza virions in our in vitro experiments proceeds as follows. An inoculum containing 50,000 competent virions (or 50,000 plaque forming unit or pfu) is deposited evenly on the cell monolayer. The solution is left there for one hour to permit the infection of the cells and at time $t = 0$ h, the inoculum is harvested with a pipette. At that time, not all the virions are removed: some are trapped in the mucus and get left behind.

To avoid having to model the initial experimental manipulations and the uncertainty in the viral removal, we start the ABM simulations at time $t = 2$ h post-harvest. At that time, a fraction of cells have been infected by the inoculum and a few virions have been left behind at harvest-time. To account for this fact, we define two more parameters, V_0 and C_0, which give the number of virions per cell and the fraction of cells in the containing stage at time $t = 2$ h post-harvest, the initialization time of our simulations. In order to determine the number of virions per cell, we also defined N_{cells}, the number of epithelial cells in the experimental well. Parameters N_{cells}, V_0 and C_0 were set as follows.

Number of Epithelial Cells in the Experimental Well. (N_{cells}): We computed N_{cells}, the number of epithelial cells in the experimental well using the measured diameter of the epithelial cells, $\Delta x = 11$ µm, and the known area of the experimental well, $A_{well} = 113$ mm^2. Assuming that the sum of the surface area of all the epithelial cells fully fills the well's area and that the surface area of each cell is roughly circular, such that $A_{cell} = \pi(\Delta x/2)^2$, we can compute the number of epithelial cells in the experimental well

$$N_{cells} = \frac{A_{well}}{\pi \left(\Delta x/2\right)^2} \tag{6}$$

$$= \frac{113 \text{ mm}^2}{\pi \left(11 \text{ μm}/2\right)^2} \tag{7}$$

$$\sim 1,200,000 \text{ cells} . \tag{8}$$

For our ABM, we found that setting the well radius of $R_{well} = 160$ cells, which corresponds to about 93,000 simulated cells, is sufficient to accurately capture the behaviour of a full scale simulation.

Initial Number of Virions per Epithelial Cell (V_0): At time $t = 2$ h post-harvest, the time at which we begin the simulation, 635 ± 273 virions were found on the monolayer. Hence, we can compute the number of virions per epithelial cell present on the monolayer at time $t = 2$ h post-harvest,

$$V_0 = \frac{635 \text{ virions}}{N_{cells}} \tag{9}$$

$$\sim 5.3 \times 10^{-4} \text{ virions/cell} , \tag{10}$$

which corresponds to the number of virions per cell at initialization time.

Fraction of Cells Initially Infected (C_0): The parameter C_0 gives the fraction of cells which are initially set to the containing state. Those are the cells that were infected during incubation with the inoculum. Staining the ALI monolayer with viral antigen at $t = 8$ h post-harvest revealed that approximately 1.8% of the cells contained influenza protein, i.e. were producing virions. Hence, we set $C_0 = 0.018$ in the ABM such that 1.8% of cells are set to the containing stage at initialization time.

4   Preliminary Results

In its current implementation, the ABM has 11 parameters shown in Table 1. A screenshot of the simulation grid is presented in Fig. 4, and Fig. 5 presents the dynamics of the various cell states and viral titer as a function of time against preliminary experimental data. We can see that the ABM provides a reasonable fit to the experimental data.

Table 1. The 11 parameters used in the computer model, with a short description of their role and their default value. In the Source column, C stands for computed, M for measured experimentally, L for taken from the literature, and F for parameters adjusted in order to fit the model to the experiments.

Symbol	Description	Value	Source
	Fixed Parameters		
R_{well}	radius of simulation well in # cells	160 cells	C (Sect. 3.3)
Δt	duration of a time step	2 min/time step	C (Sect. 3.2)
Δx	grid spacing (diameter of epithelial cells)	11 μm	M (Sect. 3.2)
τ_r	duration of the viral replication cycle	7 h	L (Sect. 3.2)
$\tau_d \pm \sigma_d$	infectious cell lifespan (mean $\pm$ SD)	23 ± 6 h	C (Sect. 3.1)
	Adjusted Parameters		
C_0	fraction of cells initially infected	0.018	F (Sect. 3.3)
V_0	initial dose of virions per cell	5.3×10^{-4} virions	F (Sect. 3.3)
k	infection rate of cells by virions	8 /h	F (Sect. 3.1)
g_V	rate of viral production per cell	0.05 /h	F (Sect. 3.2)
D_V	diffusion rate of virions	3.18×10^{-15} m^2/s	F (Sect. 3.2)

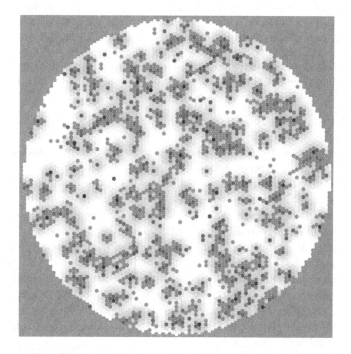

Fig. 4. Screenshot of the simulation taken at 18 h post-harvest for a simulated grid (well) containing 5,815 cells using the parameter values presented in Table 1. The cells are color-coded according to their states as in Fig. 1 with healthy cells in white, containing cells in green, secreting cells in red, and dead cells in black. The magenta overlay represents the concentration of virions at each site with more opaque magenta representing higher concentration of virions.

32

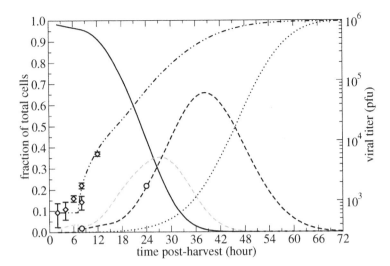

Fig. 5. Simulation results using the parameter set presented in Table 1. The lines represent the fraction of epithelial cells that are healthy (solid black), containing the virus (dashed grey), secreting the virus (dashed black), or dead (dotted black), as well as the number of competent virions (or pfu) on the right y-axis (dash-dot-dot black). The diamonds and the circles represent experimental data for the viral titer and the fraction of cells infected, respectively.

Note added in press: Recent experiments have revealed a highly variable dynamic range of the replication rate, but the basic structure of the model remains intact.

5 Proposed Extensions

As mentioned earlier, the current model is extremely simple, and we plan to gradually increase the level of detail.

One of the first improvements would be the inclusion of different cell types. The epithelial cells that make up the simulation grid are assumed to be a homogeneous population of cells, with no distinction, for example, between ciliated and Clara cells. We plan to add more cell types; each cell type would have the same four states illustrated in Fig. 1, and the transitions between those states would still be dictated by the same processes, but the value of the parameters controlling these processes would differ from one cell type to another and from one virus strain to another. With such a model, we could, for example, explore differences in the spread of the infection on a sample constituted of 90% ciliated cells and 10% Clara cells against the spread on a sample constituted of 50% ciliated cells and 50% Clara cells.

We also plan to break existing parameters into sub-models. Let us illustrate this process with an example. At the moment, we describe viral release using the parameter g_V which describes the constant rate at which virions are released by secreting cells. In the future, this simple model of viral release could be replaced by a much more elaborate intracellular sub-model of viral assembly and release that takes account of factors such as viral strain and cell type to more accurately depict the dynamics. These sub-models could either be agent-based simulations or ordinary differential equations when the spatial distribution of the agents involved is not critical.

We also would like to refine the process of viral absorption, which is currently described by the parameter k. It has recently been shown [28,29] that susceptibility to a particular influenza strain is different depending on the cell type. For example, human influenza virions preferentially bind to sialic acid (SA)-α-2,6-Gal terminated saccharides found on the surface of ciliated epithelial cells of the upper respiratory tract while avian influenza H5N1 prefers (SA)-α-2,3-Gal found on goblet cells in and around the alveoli [28,29]. One easy way to take this type of heterogeneity into consideration would be to define a virion absorption rate rather than an infection rate, and consider different production rates, g_V, for each strain of virus and for each cell type. Eventually, the parameter for the absorption rate of virions, for example, could be broken into a sub-model describing the molecular processes involved in virion absorption which would explain in which way virus strains and cell receptors affect its value.

Eventually, when mechanisms such as viral absorption and release have been modified to take on the form of molecular sub-models, the ABM will be calibrated against a few different known influenza strains. This will provide pointers as to which characteristics of an influenza viral strain drive these mechanisms. Ultimately, we hope to be able to take a newly isolated influenza strain, infect our in vitro system, and then fit our ABM to the experimental results. Doing so would reveal the value of the parameters characterizing this particular strain and hence reveal the lethality and infectivity of that strain.

6   Simulation Platform

The model is implemented on the MASyV (for Multi-Agent System Visualization) simulation platform. MASyV facilitates the visualization of simulations without the user being required to implement a graphical user interface (GUI). The software uses a client-server architecture with the server providing I/O and supervisory services to the client ABM simulation. The MASyV package consists of a GUI server, `masyv`, a non-graphical command-line server for batch runs, `logmasyv`, and a message passing library, `ma_message`, containing functions to be used by the client to communicate with the server. The simulation framework is written in C and was developed on a Linux (Debian) system.

With the MASyV framework, a user can write a simple two-dimensional client program in C, create the desired accompanying images for the agents with a paint program of her/his choice (e.g. GIMP), and connect the model to the GUI using the functions provided in the message passing library. The flexible GUI of MASyV, `masyv`, supports data logging and visualization services, and it supports the recording of simulations to a wide range of video formats, maximizing portability and the ability to share simulation results collaborators. The GUI, `masyv`, is built using GTK+ widgets and functions. For better graphics performance, the display screen widget, which displays the client simulation, uses GtkGLExt's

OpenGL extension which provides an additional application programming interface (API) enabling GTK+ widgets to rapidly render scenes rapidly using OpenGL's graphics acceleration capabilities. Capture of the simulation run to a movie file requires the software Transcode [30] and the desired compression codecs be installed on the user's machine.

For non-graphical batch runs, a command-line interface, `logmasyv`, is also implemented. This option is designed to run multiple simulation runs (e.g. for parameter sweeps on large computer grids). This option requires only that a C compiler be available, and it eliminates the substantial CPU overhead cost incurred by the graphical services. Communication between the server program (either `masyv` or `logmasyv`) and the client simulation is done through a Unix domain socket stream.

MASyV is open source software distributed under the GNU General Public License (GNU GPL) and is freely available for download from SourceForge [31]. It has a fixed web address, it is well maintained and documented, has an on-line tutorial, and comes with a "Hello World" client simulation demonstrating how to implement a new client and how to make use of the message passing library. MASyV also comes with a few example pre-programmed clients such as an ant colony laying and following pheromone trails (`ma_ants`) and a localized viral infection (`ma_immune`) which was used in [11,32]. Our influenza model was derived from `ma_immune` and is now distributed with MASyV under the name `ma_virions`.

7   Conclusion

We have described the implementation of an agent-based simulation built to reproduce the dynamics of the in vitro infection of a lung epithelial cell monolayer with an influenza A virus. At this time, model development is still in its preliminary stage, and many details remain to be elucidated. However, preliminary runs with biologically realistic parameter values have yielded reasonable results when compared with the currently available experimental data.

Recent results from the in vitro experiments revealed that large numbers of virions were being trapped by the mucus. While at 1 h post-harvest viral assays revealed that the experimental well contained about $4,701 \pm 180$ virions, it contains a mere 635 ± 273 virions only 1 h later at 2 h post-harvest and 720 ± 240 virions at 4 h post-harvest. These new results suggest that trapping of the virions by the mucus and the absorption of virions by the epithelial cells upon infection plays a crucial role in controlling the rate of spread of the viral infection. In light of these new results, we plan to direct our future research towards better characterizing the role of the mucus in viral trapping and its effect on viral infectivity.

This recent development is an excellent example of just how much we still need to learn about influenza infection. It also shows that our strategy of combining in vitro and in silico tools will prove a useful tool in this quest.

References

1. World Health Organization: Influenza. Fact Sheet 211, World Health Organization (Revised March 2003) Available online at: http://www.who.int/mediacentre/factsheets/fs211/
2. Webster, R.G., Peiris, M., Chen, H., Guan, Y.: H5N1 outbreaks and enzootic influenza. Emerg. Infect. Dis. **12**(1) (2006) 3–8
3. Tumpey, T.M., Basler, C.F., Aguilar, P.V., Zeng, H., Solórzano, A., Swayne, D.E., Cox, N.J., Katz, J.M., Taubenberger, J.K., Palese, P., García-Sastre, A.: Characterization of the reconstructed 1918 Spanish influenza pandemic virus. Science **310**(5745) (2005) 77–80
4. Tumpey, T.M., García-Sastre, A., Taubenberger, J.K., Palese, P., Swayne, D.E., Pantin-Jackwood, M.J., Schultz-Cherry, S., Solórzano, A., Van Rooijen, N., Katz, J.M., Basler, C.F.: Pathogenicity of influenza viruses with genes from the 1918 pandemic virus: Functional roles of alveolar macrophages and neutrophils in limiting virus replication and mortality in mice. J Virol **79**(23) (2005) 14933–14944
5. Belz, G.T., Wodarz, D., Diaz, G., Nowak, M.A., Doherty, P.C.: Compromized influenza virus-specific CD8$^+$-T-cell memory in CD4$^+$-T-cell-deficient mice. J. Virol. **76**(23) (2002) 12388–12393
6. Fritz, R.S., Hayden, F.G., Calfee, D.P., Cass, L.M.R., Peng, A.W., Alvord, W.G., Strober, W., Straus, S.E.: Nasal cytokine and chemokine response in experimental influenza A virus infection: Results of a placebo-controlled trial of intravenous zanamivir treatment. J. Infect. Dis. **180** (1999) 586–593
7. Kilbourne, E.D.: Influenza. Plenum Medical Book Company, New York (1987)
8. Larson, E., Dominik, J., Rowberg, A., Higbee, G.: Influenza virus population dynamics in the respiratory tract of experimentally infected mice. Infect. Immun. **13**(2) (1976) 438–447
9. Bocharov, G.A., Romanyukha, A.A.: Mathematical model of antiviral immune response III. Influenza A virus infection. J. Theor. Biol. **167**(4) (1994) 323–360
10. Baccam, P., Beauchemin, C., Macken, C.A., Hayden, F.G., Perelson, A.S.: Kinetics of influenza A virus infection in humans. J. Virol. **80**(15) (2006)
11. Beauchemin, C., Samuel, J., Tuszynski, J.: A simple cellular automaton model for influenza A viral infections. J. Theor. Biol. **232**(2) (2005) 223–234 Draft available on arXiv:q-bio.CB/0402012.
12. Celada, F., Seiden, P.E.: A computer model of cellular interactions in the immune system. Immunol. Today **13**(2) (February 1992) 56–62
13. Efroni, S., Harel, D., Cohen, I.R.: Toward rigorous comprehension of biological complexity: Modeling, execution, and visualization of thymic T-cell maturation. Genome Res. **13**(11) (2003) 2485–2497
14. Meier-Schellersheim, M., Mack, G.: SIMMUNE, a tool for simulating and analyzing immune system behavior. arXiv:cs.MA/9903017 (1999)
15. Polys, N.F., Bowman, D.A., North, C., Laubenbacher, R.C., Duca, K.: PathSim visualizer: An Information-Rich Virtual Environment framework for systems biology. In Brutzman, D.P., Chittaro, L., Puk, R., eds.: Proceeding of the Ninth International Conference on 3D Web Technology, Web3D 2004, Monterey, California, USA, 5–8 April 2004, ACM (2004) 7–14
16. Warrender, C.E.: CyCells. Computer Software distributed on SourceForge under the GNU GPL at: http://sourceforge.net/projects/cycells. (2005)
17. Segovia-Juarez, J.L., Ganguli, S., Kirschner, D.: Identifying control mechanisms of granuloma formation during *M. tuberculosis* infection using an agent-based model. J. Theor. Biol. **231**(3) (2004) 357–376

18. Warrender, C., Forrest, S., Koster, F.: Modeling intercellular interactions in early Mycobaterium infection. B. Math. Biol. (in press)

19. Edelstein-Keshet, L., Spiros, A.: Exploring the formation of Alzheimer's disease senile plaques *in silico*. J. Theor. Biol. **216**(3) (2002) 301–326

20. Abbott, R.G., Forrest, S., Pienta, K.J.: Simulating the hallmarks of cancer. Artif. Life **in press** (2006)

21. Gerety, R., Spencer, S.L., Pienta, K.J., Forrest, S.: Modeling somatic evolution in tumorigenesis. PLoS Comput. Biol. **in review** (2006)

22. González-García, I., Solé, R.V., Costa, J.: Metapopulation dynamics and spatial heterogeneity in cancer. PNAS **99**(20) (2002) 13085–13089

23. Maley, C.C., Forrest, S.: Exploring the relationship between neutral and selective mutations in cancer. Artif. Life **6**(4) (2000) 325–345

24. Maley, C.C., Forrest, S.: Modeling the role of neutral and selective mutations in cancer. In Bedau, M.A., McCaskill, J.S., Packard, N.H., Rasmussen, S., eds.: Artificial Life VII: Proceedings of the 7th International Conference on Artificial Life, Cambridge, MA, MIT Press (2000) 395–404

25. Maley, C.C., Reid, B.J., Forrest, S.: Cancer prevention strategies that address the evolutionary dynamics of neoplastic cells: Simulating benign cell boosters and selection for chemosensitivity. Cancer Epidem. Biomar. **13**(8) (2004) 1375–1384

26. Strain, M.C., Richman, D.D., Wong, J.K., Levine, H.: Spatiotemporal dynamics of HIV propagation. J. Theor. Biol. **218**(1) (2002) 85–96

27. Zorzenon dos Santos, R.M., Coutinho, S.: Dynamics of HIV infection: A cellular automata approach. Phys. Rev. Lett. **87**(16) (2001)

28. Shinya, K., Ebina, M., Yamada, S., Ono, M., Kasai, N., Kawaoka, Y.: Influenza virus receptors in the human airway. Nature **440**(7083) (2006) 435–436

29. van Riel, D., Munster, V.J., de Wit, E., Rimmelzwaan, G.F., Fouchier, R.A., Osterhaus, A.D., Kuiken, T.: H5N1 virus attachment to lower respiratory tract. Science **312**(5772) (2006) 399 Originally published in Science Express on 23 March 2006.

30. Östreich, T., Bitterberg, T., et al.: Transcode. Computer software distributed under the GNU GPL at: http://www.transcoding.org. (2001)

31. Beauchemin, C.: MASyV: A Multi-Agent System Visualization package. Computer software distributed on SourceForge under the GNU GPL at: http://masyv.sourceforge.net. (2003)

32. Beauchemin, C.: Probing the effects of the well-mixed assumption on viral infection dynamics. J. Theor. Biol. **in press** (2006) Draft available on arXiv:q-bio.CB/0505043.

Cellular Frustration: A New Conceptual Framework for Understanding Cell-Mediated Immune Responses

F. Vistulo de Abreu[1,2], E.N.M. Nolte-'Hoen[2,3], C.R. Almeida[2], and D.M. Davis[2]

[1] Depto. Física, Universidade de Aveiro, 3810 Aveiro, Portugal
abreu@fis.ua.pt
[2] Division of Cell and Molecular Biology, Imperial College, London, UK
{d.davis, crda}@imperial.ac.uk
[3] Department of Biochemistry and Cell Biology, Utrecht University, The Netherlands
e.n.m.nolte@vet.uu.nl

Abstract. Here we propose that frustration within dynamic interactions between cells can provide the basis for a functional immune system. Cellular frustration arises when cells in the immune system interact through exchanges of potentially conflicting and diverse signals. This results in dynamic changes in the configuration of cells that interact. If a response such as cellular activation, apoptosis or proliferation only takes place when two cells interact for a sufficiently long and characteristic time, then tolerance can be understood as the state in which no cells reach this stage and an immune response can result from a disruption of the frustrated state. Within this framework, high specificity in immune reactions is a result of a generalized kinetic proofreading mechanism that takes place at the intercellular level. An immune reaction could be directed against any cell, but this is still compatible with maintaining perfect specific tolerance against self.

Keywords: self-nonself discrimination, tolerance, homeostasis, cellular frustration, generalized kinetic proofreading.

1 Introduction

Distinguishing self from non-self is understood in many systems at the level of specific molecular processes between individual cells. In contrast, relatively little progress has been made in understanding how the complexity of interactions between populations of many different cells contribute to the functional discrimination between self and non-self. Some theoretical models have attempted to study such complicated interactions at the population level [1-5]. Broadly, present theoretical models of both innate and adaptive immunity assume that effector functions are triggered when a non-self pattern is recognized. In all these models, recognition is not the outcome of an optimization process; rather it is a non-linear (often binary) response to a pattern. This happens when an antibody binds to an antigen (as modeled by affinity shape space models [6,7]), or when a T cell detects agonist peptide-MHC complexes (pMHC) [2,8,9]. High specificity in the recognition process is helped by

H. Bersini and J. Carneiro (Eds.): ICARIS 2006, LNCS 4163, pp. 37–51, 2006.

kinetic proofreading mechanisms [10-12] during the scanning of APC ligands. Although, strong discrimination can be achieved during an intercellular interaction, this is likely insufficient in establishing a reliable and safe discrimination of self and nonself.

Broadly, there are usually two points of view regarding how a binary response to a pattern can result in a functional immune system: Either that this discrimination may be imperfect [2, 8, 9] and hence killing self cells happens at a certain rate, even in the absence of antigen, or that alternatively it is assumed that a certain pattern (which can even be the ubiquity of certain peptides) allows perfect discrimination. Both these approaches raise questions that only future research may clarify. For instance, the notion that some cells are killed 'by mistake' is inefficient and requires a continuous supply of new cells. This in turn requires functional selection of, for example, T cells throughout adult lifetime, perhaps using the adult thymus. It remains uncertain how adult thymus involution can be compatible with this (discussed further in [2]). The notion that patterns can perfectly define self and non-self is not easily reconcilable with evidence that pathogens can often mimic self patterns. In addition it is unclear how immune cells would robustly coordinate their responses and minimize the existence of holes in shape space (that is, regions of non-self peptide sequences not covered by any immune cell) [8, 9, 13], while keeping autoimmunity to a minimum.

Here, motivated by some recent experimental findings in immunology and a recent theoretical work in evolutionary biology, we derive a new conceptual framework to understand how an adaptive immune system could work. Self and nonself emerges as a whole system property: the *self* is defined as the set of cells that can keep short lived intercellular contacts, without ever mounting an immune reaction. Our assumptions require the introduction of a new concept, cellular frustration. Cellular frustration enables accomplishing two apparently incompatible tasks, namely, a highly specific and sensitive reaction against nonself, together with the possibility of maintaining absolute tolerance in the absence of the antigen.

2   What Is Cellular Frustration?

Frustration can be simply understood through the following example: Can one be friends of two mutual enemies? Frustration arises because no stable configuration exists that simultaneously satisfies all the elements interacting in the system. Consequently, the system fluctuates among several possible configurations. Frustration has already been studied in the context of immunology by Bersini and Calenbuhr [14, 15], who showed that a frustrated idiotypic network could display rich dynamics with chaotic behavior, and that frustration in these systems helped maintain tolerance after antigen detection.

In the present work frustration operates in a different way and with a different purpose. The mechanism we propose received inspiration from a work discussing the origin of species [16]. These authors showed that robust reproductive barriers emerge especially when no barriers exist at the level of individual mating rules. This apparently paradoxical result resulted from the existence of a complex (competitive) mating dynamics that strongly enhanced some mating associations over others (i.e., the assortativeness). Hence, mating barriers at the individual level emerged from the mating dynamics within the population.

Establishing an immune system has some parallels with this view of speciation in that tolerance and high specificity in immune responses arise in a system with high degeneracy, i.e. where many cells can interact with each other. The situation is nevertheless more complex in an immune system because tolerance to self requires that interactions between 'healthy' self cells should not be productive in terms of effector functions.

Consider three cells, A, B and C, each with a diverse set of ligands and receptors. For the purpose of simplicity, assume that each cell can only maintain interactions with one cell at a time. Consequently, if two cells are conjugated and a third cell starts an interaction with one of the cells in the conjugate, the conjugated cell has two alternatives: either it engages in this new interaction or it does not favor the new interaction and maintains the former one. This decision process implies that cells perform an integration of the signals they receive and respond after an optimization process. Cellular frustration arises if a chain of interactions, as shown in Fig.1, persists such that interactions are never long-lived.

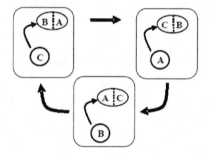

Fig. 1. Cellular frustration among three cells. A system of cells is frustrated if intercellular interactions do not allow long-lived interactions to emerge. This is schematically presented here: Initially, cells A and B are conjugated (configuration in the first square). Then C interacts with cell B, which prevents maintaining the interaction between cells A and B and leads to the second configuration. If then cell A approaches cell C, the conjugate CB is destroyed and a new conjugate AC is formed (third configuration). As in other, physical or social, systems, no stable configuration is reached, and the system fluctuates over several possible states.

Cellular frustration requires several assumptions:

Assumption 1: Cellular Crossreactivity
Cells can interact and potentially react with a large set of other cells.

Assumption 2: Cells are selective
Each cell selects among alternatives and can only maintain interactions with a limited number of cells. (Here, we use the approximation that one cell can only maintain long-lasting interactions with one other cell at a given time).

Assumption 3: Cellular Conflict

Ligands and receptors in different cells of the immune system lead to conflicting interactions (for instance, while one cell promotes interaction with one other cell, this other cell may promote interactions with another different cell, provided it is given the opportunity).

A fourth assumption will also be required in order to render cellular frustration a functionally powerful mechanism that establishes both tolerance and selective reactivity against non-self.

Assumption 4: An effector response takes place only after two cells have been interacting for a characteristic amount of time.

3   Evidence for Cellular Frustration?

Although no experimental proof of the cellular frustration concept exists, here we argue that important experimental results are at least consistent with the possibility. Readers not initially concerned with experimental details may skip this section without any loss in understanding the model proposed.

Assumption 1: Cellular crossreactivity. There is extensive experimental evidence that immune cells display a huge variety in their capacity to interact with other cells. Dendritic cells (DC), for example, can interact with CD4+ or CD8+ T cells, regulatory T cells [17], B cells [18], other DC [19], granulocytes [20], Natural Killer cells [21], or with non-hematopoietic cells, such as splenic stroma cells [22].

There is also wide variety in T cell interactions. CD4$^+$ T (helper) cells can be activated by cells that present antigen in the context of class II Major Histocompatibility Complex (MHC), such as DC, macrophages and B cells. In addition, T cell function can be stimulated by NK cells [23] and mast cells [24]. T cells can also contact many different types of target cells in the effector phase. Cytotoxic T cells for example monitor all the cells of the body. Interestingly, even neuronal cells have been described to influence T cell function [25].

Interactions among T cells themselves play an important role in regulatory activities of the immune system. Regulatory T cells can either target effector T cells directly [26] or modulate the T cell activating capacity of APC [17, 27]. Anergic T cells in their turn can pass on immune responsiveness by down regulation of other T cell responses [28, 29]. Moreover, pMHCs from APC can be acquired by T cells and internalized in such a way that T cells became sensitive to peptide-specific lysis by neighboring T cells [30]. Hence, immune cells are capable of interacting with a wide variety of other cells.

Assumption 2: Immune system cells are selective. During the induction phase of an immune response it is likely that immune cells encounter a variety of stimulatory cells. An important question is whether cells in this case select for interaction with cells that offer the highest stimulus. Regarding the T cell-APC interactions, T cells were observed to have short interactions with different APC, before engaging in a long-term interaction with a particular APC [31, 32]. The sequential encounters of T cells could indicate selection of the APC that offers the strongest stimulus. In favor of this hypothesis, Valitutti's group recently showed that helper T cells are indeed able to scan several adjacent APCs, thereby selecting for the APC loaded with the highest amount of antigen [33].

Assumption 3: Intercellular Signals are Bidirectional and potentially conflicting. Due to the use of one-sided read-out systems in immune cell stimulation studies, interactions between immune cells have often been regarded as unidirectional in terms of information transfer. However, evidence is now accumulating that during immune cell interaction there is an exchange of signals, leading to changes in behavior of all cells involved. Numerous membrane-associated proteins that bind receptors on the opposing cell surface have been shown to possess signal transduction capacity. This process of "reversed signaling" is most obvious in members of the Tumor Necrosis Factor (TNF) family members, like TNF, CD40L, FasL, TRAIL and others [34].

Although the interaction between APC and T cells has long been regarded as a unidirectional process leading to a change in activation status of the T cell, potential activation of signaling pathways within the APC during this interaction has been tested sporadically. For example cross-linking of MHC class II molecules by TCR or antibodies can lead to changes in adhesive capacity [35], apoptosis, or maturation [36]. Also interactions between T cells and mast cells were found to be bidirectional, with mast cells being able to activate T cells, and to release both granule-associated mediators and cytokines as a result of interaction with T cells [24].

Another example of bidirectionality between immune cells is the interaction between NK cells and DC [37]. During NK-DC interactions, activated NK cells can induce DC maturation. Cytokines produced by activated DC, on the other hand, enhance the proliferation, cytokine production and cytotoxicity of NK cells.

Assumption 4: An effector function takes place only if two cells have been interacting for a characteristic amount of time. This assumption has also been receiving increasing experimental support. The signal strength of T cell stimulation by APC can be determined by both the concentration of antigen, the presence of co-stimulation and the duration of the T cell-APC interaction [38]. Prolonged interaction with APC was shown to be important for both effective T cell priming [39] and polarization of the T cell response, e.g. into different helper subsets [40]. Importantly, in vivo studies also show that interaction times of CD4+ and CD8+ T cells with APC are significantly increased in the presence of specific antigen compared to T cell-APC interaction times in the absence of antigen [32]. It therefore seems realistic to assume that in order to establish a productive contact, i.e. a contact that leads to induction of T cell effector function, prolonged interaction between T cells and APC is a necessity. Although for induction of a cytotoxic response by NK cells and CTL interaction times can be much shorter than in the priming phase, a minimal duration of the interaction between effector and target cell is nevertheless necessary in order to elicit effector cell function [41]. There is a significant body of evidence that the assembly of an immunological synapse occurs in stages (reviewed in [42, 43]). Thus, cells must interact for a certain amount of time to elicit at least some types of responses.

Thus, cells require a finite amount of time and only after a characteristic time is an effector function triggered.

4   Cellular Frustration Can Establish the Principles of an Immune System

The purpose of this work is to show that cellular frustration provides an alternative framework that explains self-nonself discrimination not as a two-cell process, but as an emerging principle of the whole system. Cellular frustration is compatible with a somatically generated immunological repertoire; it avoids the existence of holes in shape space, while maintaining perfect specific tolerance.

To understand why this can happen we question whether there can be a system of mutually interacting elements, which can all potentially react but never reach this state because they are frustrated due to interactions with other elements in the system? Here by interaction we mean the process during which two cells sense each others ligands through their receptors and by reaction it is meant an effector function that only takes place if two cells interact for a time longer than a characteristic time T.

As it is known from the study of the stable roommate problem [44], it is possible to define a set of mutually interacting elements that never reach the reaction state described above. To exemplify this, consider a simple system made of 3 cells, A, B and C. Assume that each of these cells promote interactions according to an interaction list (Table 1), in such a way that, if given a chance, they always promote interactions with cells that are on upper positions in their interaction list (IL). Then it is easy to verify that all associations are unstable due to the possibility of contacting with the third cell.

Table 1. Interaction List (IL) for a system of three frustrated cells. In each column the IL of the cell on the top line is defined. According to this list, cell A tries to bind to cell C, if it is unbound: however,if given the opportunity, it would bind to cell B and detach from cell C. This sequence of interactions corresponds to the one described in Fig.1.

A	B	C
B	C	A
C	A	B

Consider a simple algorithm in which at each time-step each cell is given an opportunity to interact with another cell. Thus, in each time-step, a new conjugate can be established and a former one terminated. In the simple case in Table 1, at each time-step the probability that a new interaction is established at the expense of a former interaction, is 1, because there is always one bound cell that interacts but prefers another cell. In this particular system, provided interactions do not lead to instantaneous reactions, the system is frustrated, and thus in a tolerant or homeostatic state.

An interesting situation arises when one adds a new cell into the frustrated system. If one considers that there are no identical cells, then cell D has to appear on the bottom of the ILs of all the other cells, otherwise the system comes out of the tolerant state. Hence, to keep the system in the tolerant state, the fourth cell D has very specific ligands. Yet, the IL of cell D is arbitrary. Hence, tolerance or 'foreignness' is determined by the system itself and the system is very sensitive relatively to the introduction of new cells. In fact, from all the possible ILs for cell D, only $1/27 < 4\%$ keep the system frustrated in this simple system.

Another important point to remark is that if cell D behaved exactly as one of the other cells already present in the system then the system would not stay in the tolerant state. This shows that in this model cells are recognized according to how they function with respect to the whole system. This is a useful property for a protection system, because it implies that clonal proliferation of an infected cell would not be a successful strategy for a pathogen. Rather pathogens need to mutate in order to successfully infect the host. Further, it also shows that a certain level of arbitrariness exists concerning the definition of the ligands and receptors in the system. What is required is that cell A senses cell B with maximal avidity, cell B senses with maximal avidity cell C, and so on. This says nothing about what cell's A receptors are, allowing them to be somatically defined, as required in an adaptive immune system.

Although the previous solution allows the system to remain in the frustrated state, it requires that cell D has low avidity relative to all the other cells in the system. This may not always be achieved in a particular system provided thymic positive selection has selected reactive cells to span uniformly a complete space of sequences. To see this more clearly, imagine that a ligand or a receptor are defined through a sequence of bits and that affinity is proportional to the number of bits in common between the ligand and the receptor (i.e. through a Hamming distance). Then, provided the set of receptors in the system is uniformly distributed, it is not possible to define a ligand that is simultaneously *more* anticorrelated with *all* the receptors in the system. This remark is important, because it shows that thymic selection may have a double function which is not only to select reactive cells, but also to provide a uniform distribution of receptors and ligands. A more detailed analysis of thymic repertoire selection in the light of the present theory will be discussed in a forthcoming paper.

The previous results are restricted to populations with a small number, N, of elements. Can we generalize these results to arbitrary N? For N odd it is easy to establish that there exists a system exhibiting full frustration. Considering that the cell at position j at the interaction list of cell i is $L_i(j)$, then the list verifies the requirement:

$$L_i(j) = L_u(N-j), \text{ where } u = L_i(j). \tag{1}$$

Hence, if cell i has on the top position $(j=1)$ of its IL, cell j, then cell j has on the bottom of its IL cell i. This simple rule forces frustration. For a system with an odd number of elements, it then becomes straightforward to show that such a system never attains a stable configuration, as there is always at least one unbound element that is at the top position of the IL of one in the system. Consequently it is always possible to destabilize at least one pair of bound cells.

The same argument does not apply to systems with N even, in which case the system can converge to a stable configuration. However, due to the complexity of the cellular interactions, for populations with N even the system converges very slowly to the stable solution. In Fig.2 we see that the number of iterations required grows exponentially fast with N. Hence, although for N even the system has a stable configuration, the dynamics of the system is governed by the proximity to a computationally hard problem [45]. Hence, from a biological point of view, the system behaves as in the N odd case. And in fact the duration of cellular contacts behaves as in the N odd case (Fig.2 *(left)*).

Fig.2 *(left)* also shows that interactions' lifetimes decay exponentially. This is not an obvious result, because Almeida and Vistulo de Abreu [16] obtained a power law decay. However, a fundamental difference exists between both models. In the present case interaction lists have a particular order that establishes a global frustration state in the system. On the contrary, in [16] lists were random which allowed a much greater diversity of interactions lifetimes. Hence, in that work, power law (scale free) behavior reflected the absence of a typical lifetime.

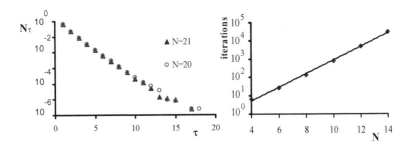

Fig. 2. *Left:* Frequency of interactions that lasted τ iterations in populations with *21* or *20* elements. These histograms were calculated using one population for 10^6 iterations. The first 10^3 where not considered to avoid including transient effects. *Right:* The number of iterations required to reach the stable configuration for a population with N even. There is an exponential growth of the number of iterations N_{it} required: $N_{it} \sim exp(0.8N)$. For a population with $N=20$, around 10^7 iterations would be required.

In order to better understand this result consider a conjugate formed between cells i and r. At each time-step each cell has a probability respectively p and q to find a higher ranked cell to interact with, and to terminate the former i-r conjugate. Hence, the probability that the i-r conjugate terminates is:

$$P=p+q\text{-}pq . \tag{2}$$

The probability that a conjugate lives for exactly τ time-steps is then:

$$P_\tau =(1\text{-}P)^{\tau-1} P. \tag{3}$$

This equation implies that *any* conjugate displays a typical exponential lifetime decay behavior: $P_\tau =(1\text{-}P)^{\tau-1} P \cong P/(1\text{-}P) \, exp(\text{-}P\tau) \sim exp(\text{-}P\tau)$. In the particular case of the IL in (1), equation (2) is simplified because $q=1\text{-}p$, which leads to $P=1-p+p^2$. Hence, in this case P varies between 3/4 and 1, whereas in the most general case of random ILs, P can vary between 0 and 1. This is fundamentally different because it implies that in the former case interactions are short-lived, whereas in the last case there are interactions that never terminate. In order to calculate N_τ, a sum over the possible interactions has to be considered. Assuming for simplicity that all conjugates occur with an equal frequency f_P, then we get:

$$N_\tau = \int_a^b f_P \, (1- P)^{\tau-1} P \, dP \sim \int_a^b (1-P)^{\tau-1} P \, dP . \tag{4}$$

The integral can be integrated by parts. The difference between the two cases is now in the correct choice of the limits of integration a and b. In the frustrated case $a=3/4$

and $b=1$, leads to: $N_\tau \sim \exp(-1.38\tau)$. In the numerical simulations (Fig.3) we obtained exponents close to 1, instead of 1.38. The difference between the two values is due to the crude approximation of f_P used above (see Fig.3 (*right*)). In the random case, we obtain: $N_\tau \sim \tau^{-2}$. Here again the exponent is not the same as the one found in [16] (which was -2.5), again due to the approximations used. Nevertheless with this calculation we were able to understand how two distinctive behaviors can be found and that the power law behavior in N_τ signals the existence of processes with many different lifetimes. Hence, Fig.3 shows that, even if the system could display a continuum of different lifetimes, the frustrated system displays a single well defined lifetime.

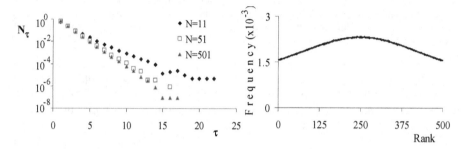

Fig. 3. The distribution function N_τ (calculated as in Fig.2) converges quickly to the asymptotic distribution, when the number of cells in the system varies from $N=11$ to $N=501$ *(Left)*. The distribution for $N=51$ and $N=501$ is almost the same, and given by an exponential $N_\tau \cong A\exp(-\tau)$. This quick convergence shows that the properties of the model do not depend crucially on the number of cells involved. This shows that the model is robust in the sense that generalizations to account for spatial effects should not produce different results (provided the densities are not too low). *(Right)* The distribution of the rank in the IL occupied by a conjugated cell in the other cell's IL. We used a population with $N=501$. This distribution is directly related to f_p (see equation (4)), which is not uniform as assumed in the calculation of the exponents.

The previous analysis is important to discuss the impact of the introduction of a new cell into the system. What happens if the frustration is broken? Does the system break up into a set of long lived interactions (as could happen after introducing a random cell into the $N=3$ system discussed above)?

The recursive (self-similar) structure given by (1) provides a simple answer: for large N, after removing any number of cells from the system, we again obtain a system in which ILs for the remaining cells have the same structure as the initial ILs. Hence, if a new randomly generated cell is introduced in the system it can produce a long lived conjugate and we can view the resulting system as being composed of the conjugate involving the new cell and the remaining fully frustrated system. This guarantees that the system remains stable upon introduction of a pathogen.

It should also be remarked that, contrary to the cases where $N=3$ or $N=4$, recognition of the external pathogen should not require an infinitely long-lived binding. Thus, to define a functional immune system, we invoke *assumption 4*, and determine that a response will occur for interactions whose lifetimes significantly exceed a typical lifetime. For instance, in the example of Fig.2, it could be determined that only if a conjugate lived for 20 units of time, then an effector function would take place.

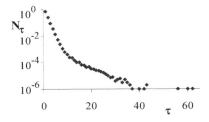 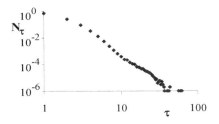

Fig. 4. The distribution N_τ for the frustrated system with N=50 cells and 1 pathogenic cell with a random set of ligands. The distribution function was calculated using the same procedure as in Fig.3. On the left the distribution function is plotted as in Fig.3, showing that a long tail appears corresponding to long-lived interactions. On the right the same distribution is plotted in a double logarithmic scale to highlight the power law behavior emerging for the long-lived interactions.

In order to be more precise, we now consider some numerical examples. Consider a population with N=51 cells from Fig.3 where one cell has been replaced by a pathogenic cell, i.e., a cell that presents a foreign peptide. This population can be simulated constructing the ILs as in (1), for N=51 cells, but where the presence of the pathogenic cell (say cell 1) in the others cell's ILs is moved a random number of positions (up or down). The IL for cell 1 stays the same. In this way we assume that only the ligands of the pathogenic cell change while the receptors of this cell remain the same. It is interesting to remark how the distribution N_τ changes so dramatically with this single cell substitution (see Fig.4). A power law tail now appears which is due to the appearance of long-lived interactions. These long-lived interactions involve the pathogenic cell. In over 100 populations simulated, all the interactions lasting longer than τ=20 iterations steps involved cell 1. This is interesting because it shows that the system is performing self-nonself recognition with high specificity.

In order to understand how sensitive this discrimination is, we next performed the same simulation but where the range of changes in the ILs was restricted: the position of the pathogenic cell in the other cell's ILs was moved only 1 position, up or down. Typical examples are shown in Fig.5, where it can be seen that there are long lasting interactions occurring, although in smaller number than in the previous case.

How the system achieves such high sensitivity and specific self-nonself discrimination can be seen as arising from a *generalized kinetic proofreading mechanism,* and was first discussed in [16]. In the frustrated state interactions have a probability to terminate given by equation (2), with $q=1-p$. If ILs are changed due to a change in the rank of the pathogenic cell, then q increases for some interactions and decreases for others. Hence, certain interactions involving the pathogenic cell can decrease their unbinding probability to P^*, while in a first approximation interactions not involving the pathogenic cell do not change their unbinding probability P, given by (2). Considering the probability that a conjugate remains bound for τ time-steps, we obtain (using (3)):

$$P^*_\tau / P_\tau = [(1-P^*)/(1-P)]^{\tau-1} P^*/P . \tag{5}$$

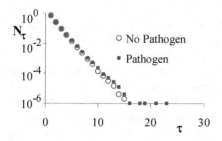 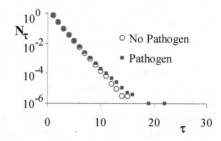

Fig. 5. Distributions N_τ for a system with N=50 cells and 1 pathogenic cell with slightly randomly changed ligands. Each case corresponds to a different pathogenic cell. All cells have ILs given by (1), except that the position occupied by the pathogenic cell in the ILs have randomly been displaced one position up or down. Even with this small difference the system is able to perform self-nonself recognition, because several long lasting interactions emerge involving the pathogenic cell.

Although in principle P and P^* can be similar, as happens in a kinetic proofreading mechanism [2, 11, 12, 46, 47] this ratio can become significant because of the exponent $\tau-1$, that accounts for the several steps required before any effector function takes place. However here, contrary to what happens in conventional kinetic proofreading mechanisms, a pre-defined sequence of interactions does not need to be imposed. Rather, it emerges naturally from the frustrated dynamics. For this reason we call this a generalization of the kinetic proofreading mechanism.

{A}	{B}	{C}
{B}	{C}	{A}
{C}	{A}	{B}
{A}	{B}	{C}

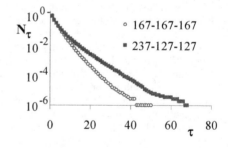

Fig. 6. A system with three distinct cell types or classes (N=501) and an IL constructed using a structure analogous as in (1). *(Left)* Cells belonging to class A, have on the top of their ILs cells from class B (specific cells within that class being randomly ordered), then those from class C (randomly ordered), and at the bottom those from their own class (also randomly ordered). *(Right)* The distribution N_τ is approximately exponential in the absence of pathogens and when the frequencies of each class of cell are adjusted to their equilibrium values ($N_A=N_B=N_C=167$). When one class of cells increases considerably relatively to the others (dark squares; $N_A=237$, $N_B=N_C=127$), long-lasting interactions are formed by cells from classes A and B. This result shows the possibility of homeostatic control of the outgrowing population of cells. In this case, cells from the self were seen as non-self.

Another important issue concerns the nature of the cells involved in the long-lived interactions: *all* long-lived interactions involved a cell that ranked in top positions in the IL of the pathogenic cell. Due to the requirement of frustration, the other cell must have a low avidity for the pathogenic cell before infection, but which has increased the most after infection. In other words, recognition in this system results from changes relative to the remaining population of interacting cells and not on the absolute values of the affinities between ligands and receptors.

Towards modeling the physiological immune system, we next generalized our approach to include different cell types (or classes), such that ILs are structured according to (1), with respect to interactions between cells of different cell types. This means that cells belonging to class A would first have all cells belonging to class B, then those of class C and at last the remaining cells of their own type, on their IL. The way cells of a same type are organized in the appropriate region of the IL, can also be structured, but in the next example they were randomly distributed. This arrangement of ILs allows defining a new system that still preserves a frustrated dynamics, as shown in Fig.6, and where it is again possible to detect pathogens as described above.

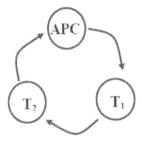

Long-Lived Conjugate	Effector Function
APC-T_1	T_1 cell activation/ T_1 cell proliferation
T_1-T_2	T_2 proliferation/ T_1 cell apoptosis, inhibition or anergy
T_2-APC	T_2 apoptosis, inhibition or anergy

Fig. 7. The mechanism of recognition in lymph nodes may result from a frustrated dynamics involving APCs and T cells of at least two types. *(Left)* Given a chance, T_1 cells conjugated to APCs and detecting a T_2 cell, should promote interactions with T_2 cells and terminate previous interactions with the APC. A similar analysis would apply to the other possible interactions in the system. *(Right)* If long-lived interactions emerge, immune reactions take place that allow a negative feedback loop to stabilize the system. For instance, if a long-lived APC-T_1 cell conjugate emerges (resulting for example from the presentation of a foreign peptide or from the uncontrolled proliferation of self cells), then convenient effector function that leads to negative feedback consists in T_1 cell activation (which will reduce the presentation of this peptide in the future) or/and T_1 cell proliferation (to increase the attack of pathogens).

Interestingly, as cells belonging to the same type can interact and possibly react with each other, the system is able to respond to significant changes in the number of cells in each class. Hence, if one cell type expands considerably relatively to its numbers in the frustrated dynamical equilibrium , it would be possible to detect and react against this growth. This is an interesting homeostatic property of the system useful to fight virus infected cells or tumor growth. Here again we observed that the long-lived interactions were formed involving cells belonging to the cell type that grew and those cells for which these cells have bigger avidity (in the example of Fig.6, long-lived interactions involve cells of type A and B). This happens because there are cells of type A that became highly ranked in the ILs of some cells of type B, in comparison to the stable configuration situation.

This example is the simplest that could describe interactions between T cells and APCs in lymphoid organs. It can describe a scenario where one T cell type could suppress the activation of the other in order to maintain tolerance. It is then possible to establish several types of effector functions that introduce negative feedback and stabilize the system in its homeostatic equilibrium (Fig.7). A similar frustrated dynamics could also take place at sites of inflammation. However in this case the mechanism should be confined, e.g. to environments where the several T cells are present in such a way that frustration is sustained. Otherwise disruptive selection could take place and lead to autoimmune disease. Hence, we propose that the cellular frustration mechanism could take place first in the thymus (during the selection of the system) and then in lymph nodes for the activation of T and B lymphocytes.

5 Conclusions

This work presents a conceptually new approach to the problem of modelling cellular interactions in the adaptive immune system. As in previous models, it assumes that kinetic proofreading mechanisms take place when a cell scans the ligands on another cell [11] to build specific ILs. To establish strong discrimination between self and nonself in our model, we assumed that the cells of the immune system were frustrated. In this system of frustrated interactions, immune responses can be triggered because the introduction of pathogenic cells leads to a disruptive cellular selection. This is achieved with high sensitivity as a result of a generalized kinetic proofreading mechanism, that is, a kinetic proofreading mechanism that takes place at the level of cells. In this framework *all* cells are surveilled and susceptible to immune responses. Consequently, the system is also intrinsically capable of maintaining homeostasis. In our framework, the self is defined as the set of cells that can keep short lived intercellular contacts, without ever mounting an immune reaction. In this manner, discrimination of self and nonself emerges as a property of the whole system.

Acknowledgments. FVA greatly benefited from discussions with Brigitte Askonas. FVA also acknowledges encouragement by Douglas Young. FVA thanks FCT for the grant SFRH/BSAB/531. CRDA thanks FCT for the grant SFRH/BD/10587/2002.

References

1. Casal, A., Sumen, C., Reddy, T.E., Alber, M.S., Lee P.P.: Agent-based modeling of the context dependency in T cell recognition. Journal of Theoretical Biology (2005) **236**(4): 376-391
2. Leon, K., Lage, A., Carneiro, J..: Tolerance and immunity in a mathematical model of T-cell mediated suppression. Journal of Theoretical Biology (2003) **225**(1): 107-126
3. Chan, C., Stark, J., George, A.J.T.: The impact of multiple T cell-APC encounters and the role of anergy. J. Comp. App. Mathematics (2005) **184**(1): 101-120
4. Leon, K., Perez, R., Lage, A., Carneiro, J.: Three-cell interactions in T cell-mediated suppression? A mathematical analysis of its quantitative implications. Journal of Immunology (2001) **166**(9): 5356-5365
5. Leon, K., Perez, R., Lage, A., Carneiro, J.: Modelling T-cell-mediated suppression dependent on interactions in multicellular conjugates. Journal of Theoretical Biology (2000) **207**(2): 231-254

6. Perelson, A. S. and Weisbuch, G.: Immunology for physicists. Reviews of Modern Physics (1997) **69**(4): 1219-1267
7. Varela, F. J. and Coutinho, A.: 2nd Generation Immune Networks. Immunology Today (1991) **12**(5): 159-166
8. Chao, D. L., Davenport M. P., Forrest, S , Perelson, A.S.: A stochastic model of cytotoxic T cell responses. Journal of Theoretical Biology (2004) **228**(2): 227-240
9. Scherer, A., Noest, A., de Boer, R.J.: Activation-threshold tuning in an affinity model for the T-cell repertoire. Proc. Roy. Soc. B (2004) **271**(1539) 609-616
10. Van Den Berg, H. A., Rand, D. A. ,Burroughs N.J.: A reliable and safe T cell repertoire based on low-affinity T cell receptors. Journal of Theoretical Biology (2001) **209**(4) 465-486
11. McKeithan, T. W.: Kinetic Proofreading in T-Cell Receptor Signal-Transduction. Proceedings of the National Academy of Sciences of the United States of America (1995) **92**(11) 5042-5046
12. Chan, C., George, A. J. T. , Stark, J.: T cell sensitivity and specificity - Kinetic proofreading revisited. Discrete and Continuous Dynamical Systems-Series B (2003) **3**(3) 343-360
13. Ji, Z., Dasgupta, D.: Real-valued negative selection algorithm with variable-sized detectors. Genetic and Evolutionary Computation - Gecco 2004, Pt 1, Proceedings. (2004) **3102:** 287-298
14. Bersini, H., Calenbuhr, V.: Frustrated chaos in biological networks. Journal of Theoretical Biology (1997) **188** (2) 187-200
15. Calenbuhr, V., Bersini, H., Stewart, J., Varela, F.J., Natural tolerance in a simple immune network. Journal of Theoretical Biology (1995) **177** (3) 199-213
16. Almeida, C. R., de Abreu, F.V.: Dynamical instabilities lead to sympatric speciation. Evolutionary Ecology Research (2003) **5**(5) 739-757
17. Cederbom, L.,Hall, H. , Ivars F.: CD4(+)CD25(+) regulatory T cells down-regulate co-stimulatory molecules on antigen-presenting cells. European Journal of Immunology (2000) **30**(6) 1538-1543
18. Wykes, M., Pombo, A., Jenkins, C., MacPherson, G.G.,: Dendritic cells interact directly with naive B lymphocytes to transfer antigen and initiate class switching in a primary T-dependent response. Journal of Immunology (1998) **161**(3) 1313-1319
19. Knight, S.C., Iqball, S., Roberts, M.S., Macatonia, S., Bedford, P.A.: Transfer of antigen between dendritic cells in the stimulation of primary T cell proliferation. European Journal of Immunology (1998) **28**(5) 1636-1644
20. van Gisbergen, K.P., Sanchez-Hernandez, M., Geijtenbeek, T.B.H., van Kooyk Y.: Neutrophils mediate immune modulation of dendritic cells through glycosylation-dependent interactions between Mac-1 and DC-SIGN. Journal of Experimental Medicine (2005) **201**(8) 1281-1292
21. Ferlazzo, G.: Natural killer and dendritic cell liaison: recent insights and open questions. Immunology Letters (2005) **101**(1) 12-17
22. Zhang, M., et al.: Splenic stroma drives mature dendritic cells to differentiate into regulatory dendritic cells. Nature Immunology (2004) **5**(11) 1124-1133
23. Hanna, J., et al.: Novel APC-like properties of human NK cells directly regulate T cell activation. Journal of Clinical Investigation (2004) **114**(11) 1612-1623
24. Mekori, Y.A., Metcalfe, D.D.: Mast cell-T cell interactions. Journal of Allergy and Clinical Immunology (1999) **104**(3 Pt 1) 517-523
25. Flugel, A., et al.: Neuronal FasL induces cell death of encephalitogenic T lymphocytes. Brain Pathology (2000) **10**(3) 353-364
26. Thornton, A.M.,E. Shevach, M.: CD4(+)CD25(+) immunoregulatory T cells suppress polyclonal T cell activation in vitro by inhibiting interleukin 2 production. Journal of Experimental Medicine (1998) **188**(2) 287-296

27. Taams, L.S., et al.: Modulation of monocyte/macrophage function by human CD4+CD25+ regulatory T cells. Human Immunology (2005) **66**(3) 222-230
28. Nolte-'t Hoen, E.N., et al.: Uptake of membrane molecules from T cells endows antigen-presenting cells with novel functional properties. European Journal of Immunology (2004) **34**(11) 3115-25
29. Taams, L.S., et al.: Anergic T cells actively suppress T cell responses via the antigen-presenting cell. European Journal of Immunology (1998) **28**(9) 2902-2912
30. Huang, J.F., et al.: TCR-Mediated internalization of peptide-MHC complexes acquired by T cells. Science (1999) **286**(5441) 952-954
31. Gunzer, M., et al.: Antigen presentation in extracellular matrix: interactions of T cells with dendritic cells are dynamic, short lived, and sequential. Immunity (2000) **13**(3) 323-332
32. Mempel, T.R., Henrickson, S.E., U.H. Von Andrian: T-cell priming by dendritic cells in lymph nodes occurs in three distinct phases. Nature (2004) **427**(6970) 154-159
33. Depoil, D., et al.: Immunological synapses are versatile structures enabling selective T cell polarization. Immunity (2005) **22**(2) 185-194
34. Eissner, G., Kolch, W., Scheurich, P.: Ligands working as receptors: reverse signaling by members of the TNF superfamily enhance the plasticity of the immune system. Cytokine Growth Factor Rev (2004) **15** 353-366
35. Lehner, M., et al.: MHC class II antigen signaling induces homotypic and heterotypic cluster formation of human mature monocyte derived dendritic cells in the absence of cell death. Human Immunology (2003) **64**(8) 762-770
36. Lokshin, A.E., et al.: Differential regulation of maturation and apoptosis of human monocyte-derived dendritic cells mediated by MHC class II. International Immunology (2002) **14**(9) 1027-1037
37. Walzer, T., et al.: Natural-killer cells and dendritic cells: l'union fait la force . Blood (2005) **106**(7) 2252-2258
38. Gett, A.V., et al., T cell fitness determined by signal strength. Nature Immunology, (2003) **4**(4) 355-360
39. Iezzi, G., Karjalainen, K., Lanzavecchia, A.: The duration of antigenic stimulation determines the fate of naive and effector T cells. Immunity (1998) **8**(1) 89-95
40. Iezzi, G., et al.: The interplay between the duration of TCR and cytokine signaling determines T cell polarization. European Journal Immunology (1999) **29**(12) 4092-4101
41. Wulfing, C., et al.: Stepwise cytoskeletal polarization as a series of checkpoints in innate but not adaptive cytolytic killing. Proc Natl Acad Sci U S A (2003) **100**(13) 7767-7772
42. Davis, D.M.: Assembly of the immunological synapse for T cells and NK cells, Trends in Immunology (2002) **23** (7): 356-363
43. Davis, D.M., Dustin, M.L.: What is the importance of the immunological synapse?. Trends in Immunology (2004) **25** (6) 323-327
44. Gusfield, D., Irving, R.W.: The stable marriage problem: structure and algorithms, MIT Press, Cambridge, MA, USA(1989)
45. Mertens, S.: Computational complexity for physicists. Computing in Science and Engineering (2002) **4**(3) 31-47
46. Hopfield, J.J.: Kinetic proofreading – new mechanism for reducing errors in biosynthetic processes requiring high specificity Proc Natl Acad Sci U S A (1974) **71**(10) 4135-4139
47. Ninio, J.: Kinetic amplification of enzyme discrimination. Biochimie (1975) **57** (5) 587-595

The Swarming Body: Simulating the Decentralized Defenses of Immunity

Christian Jacob[1,2], Scott Steil[2], and Karel Bergmann[2]

[1] Dept. of Biochemistry & Molecular Biology, Faculty of Medicine
[2] Dept. of Computer Science, Faculty of Science
University of Calgary, Calgary, Alberta, Canada

Abstract. We consider the human body as a well-orchestrated system of interacting swarms. Utilizing swarm intelligence techniques, we present our latest virtual simulation and experimentation environment, *IMMS:VIGO::3D*, to explore key aspects of the human immune system. Immune system cells and related entities (viruses, bacteria, cytokines) are represented as virtual agents inside 3-dimensional, decentralized and compartmentalized environments that represent primary and secondary lymphoid organs as well as vascular and lymphatic vessels. Specific immune system responses emerge as by-products from collective interactions among the involved simulated 'agents' and their environment. We demonstrate simulation results for clonal selection and primary and secondary collective responses after viral infection, as well as the key response patterns encountered during bacterial infection. We see this simulation environment as an essential step towards a hierarchical whole-body simulation of the immune system, both for educational and research purposes.

1 Introduction

Computer-based tools and virtual simulations are changing the way of biological research. Immunology is no exception. Computers become even more capable of running large-scale models of complex biological systems. Recent advancements in grid computing technologies make high-performance computer resources readily accessible to almost everybody [1]. Consequently, even highly sophisticated – and to a large extent still poorly understood – processes such as the inner workings of immune system defense mechanisms can now be tackled by agent-based models in combination with interactive visualization components. These agent models serve as an essential complement to modeling approaches that are traditionally more abstract and purely mathematical [6,7].

Our *Evolutionary & Swarm Design Laboratory* is building and promoting agent-based models, with distributed simulation and visualization capabilities, utilizing swarm intelligence methodologies [2]. The combination of visual and intuitive user interfaces, in combination with the latest technology in visualization (including 3D-immersive environments in CAVES) and distributed high-performance computing, makes our models more accessible to researchers in the

H. Bersini and J. Carneiro (Eds.): ICARIS 2006, LNCS 4163, pp. 52–65, 2006.
© Springer-Verlag Berlin Heidelberg 2006

life sciences community, who usually do not have any programming background or any aspiration nor time to learn how to use a modeling environment. Making simulation tools (almost) seamless to use for researchers and introducing such tools into classrooms in biology and medicine greatly increases the understanding of how useful computer-based simulations can be in order to explore and facilitate answers to research questions and, as a side effect, gain an appreciation of emergent effects resulting from orchestrated interactions of 'bio-agents'.

In this paper we present our latest version of a swarm-based simulation environment, which, we think, fulfills these criteria, and implements an interactive virtual laboratory for the exploration of the interplay of human immune system agents and their resulting overall response patterns. The rest of the paper is organized as follows. In Section 2 we give an overview of related simulation and modeling approaches regarding immune system processes. A biological perspective of the decentralized immune defenses is presented in Section 3. The key design aspects and main results of our *IMMS:VIGO::3D* simulation system are described in Section 4, where we also discuss simulation experiments for clonal selection, primary and secondary responses to viral infection, as well as reactions to bacterial infection. Finally, in Section 5, we conclude the paper with a summary of our work and suggestions for the necessary next steps towards an encompassing immune system simulation environment.

2   Related and Previous Work

The immune system (IS) has been studied from a modeling perspective for a long time. Early, more general approaches looked at the immune system in the context of adaptive and learning systems [3,4], with some connections to early artificial intelligence approaches [5]. Purely mathematical models, mainly based on differential equations, try to capture the overall behaviour patterns and changes of concentrations during immune system responses [6,7,8,9,10]. A more recent algebraic model of B and T cell interactions provides a formal basis to describe binding and mutual recognition, and can serve as a mathematical basis for further computational models, similar to formalisms for artificial neural networks [11].

Agent-based computational approaches, in the form of cellular automata, introduced spacial aspects to immune system simulations [12]. In the context of clonal selection, the influence of different affinities among interacting functional units, which leads to self-organizing properties, was recognized and studied through computational models [13,14]. These models have been expanded into larger and more general simulation environments for various aspects of the human immune system [15,16]. There is also a large number of modeling approaches within specific areas in the context of immune system-related processes, such as for HIV/AIDS [17]. An excellent overview of these modeling strategies can be found in [18].

Most current methods consider immune response processes as emergent phenomena in complex adaptive system [10], where agent-based models play a more and more dominant role [19,20], even in the broader application domain of bio-molecular and chemical interaction models [21]. We see the most promising potential in agent models that incorporate swarm intelligence techniques [2,22], as this results in more accurate and realistic models, in particular when spacial aspects play a key role in defining patterns of interaction, in understanding their emergent properties, and in helping to shed some light on the inner workings of complexity as, for example, displayed by the immune system. Biological systems inherently operate in a 3-dimensional world. Therefore, we have focused our efforts on building swarm-based, 3-D simulations of biological systems which exhibit a high degree of self-organization, triggered by relatively simple interactions of a large number of agents of different types. The immune system is just one example that allows for this bottom-up modeling approach. Other models include the study of chemotaxis within a colony of evolving bacteria [23,24], the simulation of transcription, translation, and specific gene regulatory processes within the lactose operon [25,26], as well as studies of affinity and cooperation among gene regulatory agents for the λ switch in *E. coli* [27].

3   The Decentralized Defenses of Immunity

One aspect that makes the human immune system particularly interesting—but more challenging from a modeling perspective—is its vastly decentralized arrangement. Tissue and organs of the lymphatic system are widely spread throughout the body, which provides good coverage against any infectious agents that might enter the body at almost any location. Even the two key players responsible for specific immunity originate from different locations within the body: T cells come from the thymus, whereas B cells are made in the bone marrow. The lymphocytes then travel through the blood stream to secondary lymphoid organs: the lymph nodes, spleen, and tonsils. Within these organs, B and T cells are rather tightly packed, but can still move around freely, which makes them easier to model as agents interacting in a 3-D simulation space.

Lymph nodes can then be considered the primary locations of interactions among T cells, activated by antigens. T cells, in turn, activate B cells, which evolve into memory B cells and antibody-producing plasma B cells. Both types of activated lymphocytes will subsequently enter the lymphatic system, from where they eventually return to the blood stream. This enables the immune system to spread its activated agents widely through the body. Finally, the lymphocytes return to other lymph nodes, where they can recruit further agents or trigger subsequent responses. Hence, B and T cells as well as other immune system agents (antibodies, cytokines, dendritic cells, antigen presenting cells, etc.) are in a constant flow between different locations in the human body [28].

4   Simulating Decentralized Immune Responses

Our overall goal is to build a whole body simulation of the immune system (Fig. 1). This, of course, does not only require a large amount of computing

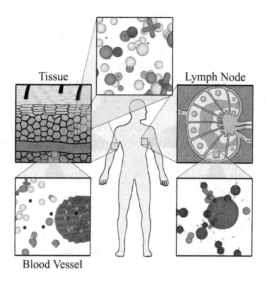

Fig. 1. The decentralized defenses of immunity. Three compartmental modules, that exhibit distinct but interconnected functionalities within the human immune system, are implemented in our *IMMS:VIGO::3D* simulation environment: (1) tissue, (2) blood vessels, and (3) lymph nodes.

resources, but also requires a modular and hierarchical design of the simulation framework. Modelers – i.e., immunologists as well as researchers and students in health sciences – should be able to look at the simulated immune system at different levels of detail. The whole body simulation will not be as fine grained as when looking at the interactions within a lymph node or at the intersection between the lymphatic and vascular system.

In our current implementation we have incorporated three distinct, but interconnected sites within the human body that are related to the immune system:

- **Lymph Nodes:** Within a lymph node section we incorporate adaptive immune system processes during clonal selection, in response to viral antigens entering the lymph node. Different types of B cell strands can be defined. In case of a high degree of matching with an antigen, rapid proliferation is triggered.
- **Tissue:** Within a small section of tissue we model the immune system processes during primary and secondary response reactions among viruses (with their associated antigen components), tissue cells, dendritic cells, helper T and killer T cells, memory and plasma B cells (with their associated antibodies), and macrophages.
- **Blood Vessel-Tissue Interfaces:** At the interface between blood vessels and tissue, we simulate red blood cells moving within a section of a blood vessel, lined with endothelial cells, which can produce selectin and intercellular adhesion molecules (ICAMs). This causes neutrophils to start rolling

along the vessel wall and exit the blood stream into the tissue area. Any bacterium within the tissue is subsequently attacked by a neutrophil. During ingestion of a bacterium by a macrophage, tumor necrosis factor (TNF) is secreted and the bacterium releases lipopolysaccharides (LPS) from its surface. In turn, TNF triggers selectin production in endothelial cells, whereas LPS induces endothelial cells to produce ICAM.

The following sections explain our model in more detail with respect to clonal selection as well as primary and secondary responses within a lymph node area and a tissue region (Section 4.1). The IS processes triggered during a bacterial infection within the interface area between a blood vessel and tissue is described in Section 4.2.

4.1   Simulated Viral Infection

Figure 2 gives an overview of the immune system agents and their interaction patterns in our model. Each agent is represented by a specific, 3-dimensional shape, which are also used in the (optional) visual representation of the agents during a simulation experiment. We demonstrate one experiment to show a typical simulation sequence.

Clonal Selection within a Lymph Node: In this experiment, we first focus our attention on a selected lymph node in order to observe the IS agent reactions after a virus enters the lymph node area (cf. Fig. 1). Initially, 50 B cells as well as 20 helper-T cells of 8 different types (signatures) are present. Figure 3f shows that there is a fairly even initial distribution of the different strands of B and T cells. Around time step $t = 14.6$, dendritic cells enter the lymph node and present a single type of viral antigen (Fig. 3b), which stimulates a nearby helper-T cell and causes a matching B cell (following the Celada-Seiden affinity model [12]) to replicate. Soon after ($t = 57.1$), a significantly larger population of matching B cells proliferates the lymph node area (Fig. 3c), where B cells have already started to emit antibodies. In Fig. 3f the concentration of these fast proliferating B cells is represented by the green plot. At time point $t = 225.0$, memory B cells of the matching strand have become more common. Around $t = 256.4$, the same virus is introduced into the lymph node again. Now it is mainly the memory B cells that trigger the secondary response and replication of plasma B cells which secrete antibodies (compare the increase of the matching B cell concentration (green) towards the last third of the graph in Fig. 3f).

Primary and Secondary Response in Tissue: At the same time, while the simulation of the interactions within the lymph node are running, a concurrent, second simulation models the response processes in a selected tissue area (cf. Fig. 1). Circulation of IS agents is implemented by a communication channel between lymph node and tissue areas. Within the tissue simulation space (Fig. 4a), we start with 10 dendritic cells, 5 killer-T cells, 5 helper-T cells, 5 macrophages, 60 tissue cells and 5 copies of the same virus introduced into the lymph node as

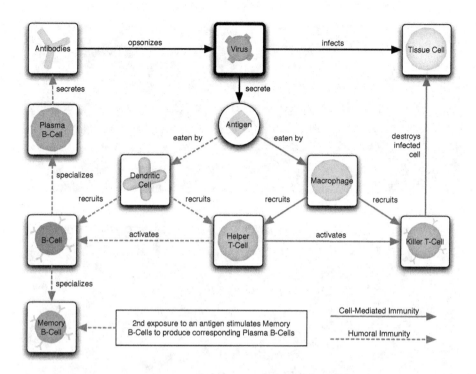

Fig. 2. Interactions of immune system agents triggered by viral infection: A virus is usually identified by its antigens, which alert both dendritic cells and macrophages to ingest the viruses. Both actions lead to recruitment of further IS cells. Dendritic cells recruit B cells, which – in particular when activated by helper-T cells – replicate as memory B cells or proliferate into plasma B cells, which in turn release antibodies to opsonize the virus. On the other hand, macrophages with an engulfed virus stimulate an increase in the proliferation of both helper and killer T cells, which are the key players in cell-mediated immunity and destroy virus-infected tissue cells to prevent any further spreading of the virus.

described above. In Fig. 4b a cell has been infected by the virus and antibodies (from the lymph node) start entering the tissue area. Figure 4c shows a close-up of the important agents: one virus is visible inside an infected cell, another virus has docked onto the surface of a tissue cell and is about to enter it. A third virus has already been opsonized by an attached antibody. Now macrophages will start to engulf opsonized viruses and more macrophages are recruited in large numbers (Fig. 4d). This triggers an analogous spike in the number of killer-T and helper-T cells (also compare Fig. 5). The increase in killer-T cells makes it more likely for these cells to collide with an infected tissue cell and initiate its apoptosis.

After about 120 time steps, the infection has been fought off, with no more viruses or antigens remaining in the system (Fig. 5). The concentrations of T cells and macrophages return to their initial levels. At $t = 150.0$, the same virus

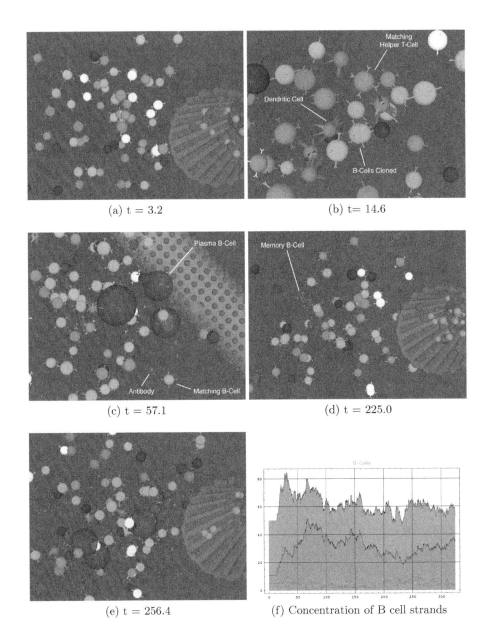

(a) t = 3.2

(b) t= 14.6

(c) t = 57.1

(d) t = 225.0

(e) t = 256.4

(f) Concentration of B cell strands

Fig. 3. Interactions in a **Lymph Node** after a viral infection: (a)-(e) Screen captures (with time point labels) of the graphical simulation interface during clonal selection and primary and secondary response to a virus. The virtual cameras are pointed at a lymph node, in which 8 different strands of B cells are present. (f) The change in concentration of all B cells (brown filled plot) and per strand. The virus that most closely matches one of the B cell strands triggers its increased proliferation (green filled plot). The concentrations of all other strands remain low (line plots at the bottom).

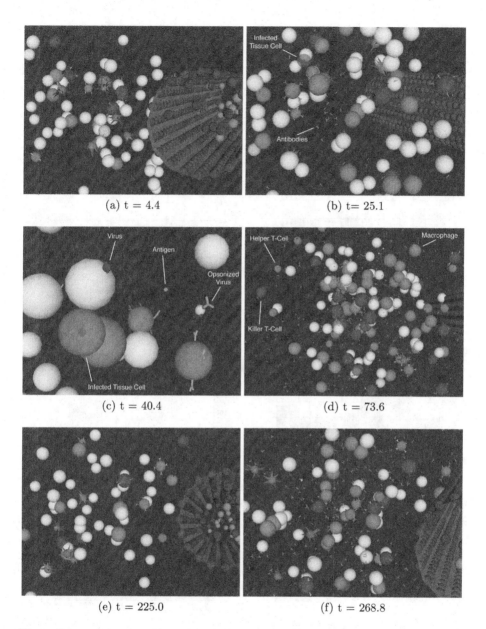

(a) t = 4.4   (b) t= 25.1

(c) t = 40.4   (d) t = 73.6

(e) t = 225.0   (f) t = 268.8

Fig. 4. Interactions in a **Tissue Area** after a viral infection: Screen captures of the graphical simulation interface during clonal selection and primary and secondary response after viral infection. The virtual cameras are pointed at a tissue region close to a blood vessel.

is reinserted into the system. Memory B cells inside the lymph node create an influx of plasma B cells almost immediately. Due to the increased amount of antibodies emitted, the infection is stopped within a much shorter time interval.

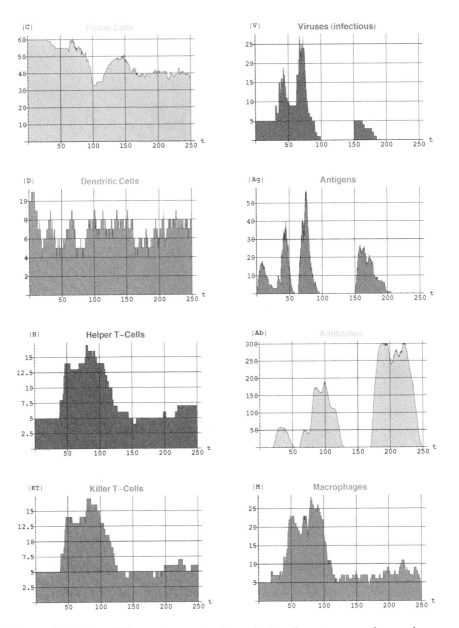

Fig. 5. Evolution of IS agent concentrations during the primary and secondary responses in a tissue area

As a result, the infection is stopped within a much shorter time interval, due to the increased amount of antibodies. Cell-mediated immunity reactions do start faster as well, but are not as intense as during the first response since the infection is eliminated more quickly. Consequently, T cells and macrophage concentrations can remain at a lower level.

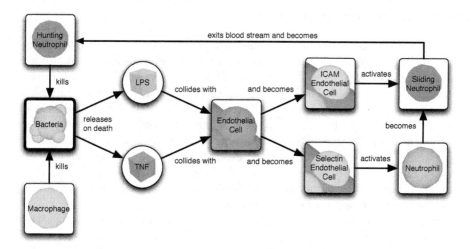

Fig. 6. Bacterial Infection: A summary of the interaction network between bacteria, macrophages, neutrophils, and endothelial cells that line the blood vessel

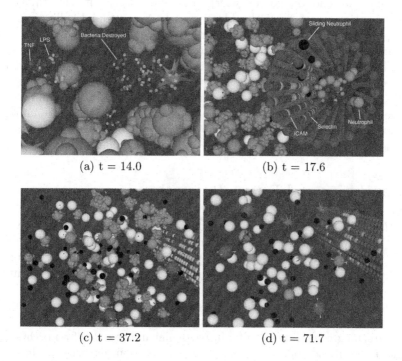

      (a) t = 14.0   (b) t = 17.6

      (c) t = 37.2   (d) t = 71.7

Fig. 7. Fighting Bacterial Infection: (a) macrophages attacking bacteria, (b) endothelial cells, neutrophils and red blood cells inside the blood vessel, (c) neutrophils (blue) on their hunt for bacteria, (d) all bacteria have been eliminated

4.2 Simulated Bacterial Infection

Bacteria within the tissue multiply; their waste products, produced from a large concentration of bacteria, can be damaging to the human body. Therefore it is important that the immune system kills off bacterial invaders before this critical concentration is reached. The following experiment demonstrates immune system response processes during bacterial infection. The key players and their interactions are outlined in Fig. 6. As this involves not only bacteria and macrophages but also neutrophils that enter tissue from the vascular system, the simulation space comprises a segment of a blood vessel (Fig. 7). The tissue-vessel interface area is initialized with tissue cells, B cells, helper-T cells, macrophages, and a number of bacteria acting as infectors. The blood vessel, lined with endothelial cells, contains red blood cells and neutrophils.

Macrophages that engulf bacteria release TNF (tumor necrosis factor) while lipopolysaccharides (LPS), which are major structural components of Gram-negative bacterial cell walls, are released into the tissue area (Fig. 7a). Once endothelial cells get in contact with TNS or LPS, they release selectin or intercellular adhesion molecules (ICAMs), respectively (Fig. 7b). When a neutrophil collides with an endothelial cell which produces selectin, it will start to roll along the interior surface of the blood vessel. A neutrophil rolling along an ICAM-producing endothelial cell will exit the blood stream and head into the tissue area. Once in the tissue area, neutrophils—together with macrophages—act as complementary hunters of bacteria (Fig. 7c). Notice the high number of activated endothelial cells in the blood vessel wall. A bacterium colliding with a neutrophil is engulfed and consumed, while LPS and TNF are again released into the system. Finally, all bacteria have been eliminated and the number of activated endothelial cells is decreased (Fig. 7d). Neutrophils will soon disappear since the system has recovered from the bacterial infection.

5   Conclusion and Future Research

The *IMMS:VIGO::3D* simulation environment is currently used as a teaching tool in biology, medical, and computer science undergraduate and graduate classes. Due to its visual interface and the ability to specify many simulation control parameters through configuration files, it serves both as an educational device as well as an exploration tool for researchers in the life sciences. Students seem to gain a more 'memorable' understanding of different aspects of immune system processes. Although visualizations can also be misleading, they usually help in grasping essential concepts, in particular in the case of an orchestrated system of a multitude of agents. Consequently, from our experience, the visualization component is important for a proper understanding of emergent processes resulting from the interplay of a relatively large number of agents of different types with simple but specific local interaction rules. Gaining a proper understanding and 'intuition' about emergent properties as in the immune system plays a key role in building today's biologically accurate computer simulations.

Of course, our current version does not even come close to the actual numbers of interacting IS agents (e.g., billions of B cells within a small lymph node section). However, according to our experience, key effects within an agent-based interaction system can already be observed with much smaller numbers. Usually, only a 'critical mass' is needed. This is certainly an area that requires further investigation, which we currently focus on. Using evolutionary computation techniques, we also explore the effects of different control parameter settings, as well as how changes in the set of agent interaction rules influence the overall system behaviour. Being able to easily change agent interaction rules and the types of agents makes models of complex adaptive systems useful for large-scale scientific exploration.

Currently, we only have incorporated some of the earlier and basic theories of how immune system processes might work. Now that we have a flexible and powerful simulation infrastructure in place, calibrating and validating our models as well as including more of the recently proposed models is one of our next steps. We are also expanding our simulations to demonstrate (and help students to investigate) why the generation of effective vaccines is difficult and how spontaneous auto-immunity emerges.

Up-to-date details about our latest immune system model and other agent-based simulation examples, which are investigated in our *Evolutionary & Swarm Design Lab* can be found at: http://www.swarm-design.org.

Acknowledgements

Financial support for this research is provided by NSERC, the Natural Sciences and Engineering Research Council of Canada.

We thank Ian Burleigh for creating VIGO::3D, a C++ library for multi-agent simulation and visualization in 3D space [29], on which the *IMMS:VIGO::3D* system is built. VIGO is an open source project available at:
http://sourceforge.net/projects/vigo.

References

1. Przybyla, D., Miller, K., Pegah, M.: A holistic approach to high-performance computing: xgrid experience. In ACM, ed.: Proceedings of the 32nd annual ACM SIGUCCS conference on User services. (2004) 119–124
2. Bonabeau, E., Dorigo, M., Theraulaz, G.: Swarm Intelligence: From Natural to Artificial Systems. Santa Fe Institute Studies in the Sciences of Complexity. Oxford University Press, New York (1999)
3. Farmer, J.D., Packard, N.H.: The immune system, adaptation, and machine learning. Physica D **22** (1986) 187–204
4. Bagley, R.J., Farmer, J.D., Kauffman, S.A., Packard, N.H., Perelson, A.S., Stadnyk, I.M.: Modeling adaptive biological systems. BioSystems **23** (1989) 113–138
5. Rössler, O., Lutz, R.: A decomposable continuous immune network. BioSystems **11** (1979) 281–285

6. Salzberg, S., Searls, D., Kasif, S., eds.: Computational Methods in Molecular Biology. Volume 32 of New Comprehensive Biochemistry. Elsevier, Amsterdam (1998)
7. Bower, J.M., Bolouri, H., eds.: Computational Modeling of Genetic and Biochemical Networks. MIT Press, Cambridge, MA (2001)
8. Hanegraaff, W.: Simulating the immune system. Master's thesis, Department of Computational Science, University of Amsterdam, Amsterdam, The Netherlands (2001)
9. Bezzi, M., Celada, F., Ruffo, S., Seiden, P.E.: The transition between immune and disease states in a cellular automaton model of clonal immune response. Physica A **245** (1997) 145 – 163
10. Tay, J.C., Jhavar, A.: Cafiss: a complex adaptive framework for immune system simulation. In: SAC '05: Proceedings of the 2005 ACM symposium on Applied computing, New York, NY, USA, ACM Press (2005) 158–164
11. Tarakanov, A., Dasgupta, D.: A formal model of an artificial immune system. BioSystems **55** (2000) 151–158
12. Celada, F., Seiden, P.E.: A computer model of cellular interactions in the immune system. Immunology Today **13**(2) (1992) 56–62
13. Celada, F., Seiden, P.E.: Affinity maturation and hypermutation in a simulation of the humoral immune response. European Journal of Immunology **26** (1996) 1350–1358
14. Atamas, S.P.: Self-organization in computer simulated selective systems. BioSystems **39** (1996) 143–151
15. Kleinstein, S.H., Seiden, P.E.: Simulating the immune system. Computing in Science & Engineering (July/August) (2000) 69–77
16. Puzone, R., Kohler, B., Seiden, P., Celada, F.: Immsim, a flexible model for in machina experiments on immune system responses. Future Generation Computer Systems **18**(7) (2002) 961–972
17. Guo, Z., Han, H.K., Tay, J.C.: Sufficiency verification of hiv-1 pathogenesis based on multi-agent simulation. In: GECCO '05: Proceedings of the 2005 conference on Genetic and evolutionary computation, New York, NY, USA, ACM Press (2005) 305–312
18. Guo, Z., Tay, J.C.: A comparative study on modeling strategies for immune system dynamics under hiv-1 infection. In Jacob, C., Pilat, M., Bentley, P., Timmis, J., eds.: Artificial Immune Systems, 4th International Conference, ICARIS 2005. Volume LNCS 3627., Springer (2005) 220–233
19. Johnson, S.: Emergence: The Connected Lives of Ants, Brains, Cities, and Software. Scribner, New York (2001)
20. Wolfram, S.: A New Kind of Science. Wolfram Media, Champaign, IL (2002)
21. Pogson, M., Smallwood, R., Qwarnstrom, E., Holcombe, M.: Formal agent-based modelling of intracellular chemical interactions. BioSystems (2006)
22. Camazine, S., Deneubourg, J.L., Franks, N.R., Sneyd, J., Theraulaz, G., Bonabeau, E.: Self-Organization in Biological Systems. Princeton Studies in Complexity. Princeton University Press, Princeton (2003)
23. Hoar, R., Penner, J., Jacob, C.: Transcription and evolution of a virtual bacteria culture. In: Congress on Evolutionary Computation, Canberra, Australia, IEEE Press (2003)
24. Penner, J., Hoar, R., Jacob, C.: Bacterial chemotaxis in silico. In: ACAL 2003, First Australian Conference on Artificial Life, Canberra, Australia (2003)

25. Burleigh, I., Suen, G., Jacob, C.: Dna in action! a 3d swarm-based model of a gene regulatory system. In: ACAL 2003, First Australian Conference on Artificial Life, Canberra, Australia (2003)
26. Jacob, C., Burleigh, I.: Biomolecular swarms: An agent-based model of the lactose operon. Natural Computing (2004) (in print).
27. Jacob, C., Barbasiewicz, A., Tsui, G.: Swarms and genes: Exploring λ-switch gene regulation through swarm intelligence. In: Congress on Evolutionary Computation, Vancouver, BC, Canada, IEEE Press (2006)
28. Nossal, G.J.: Life, death and the immune system. Scientific American (1993) 53–62
29. Burleigh, I.G.: A journey to the center of the cell. Master's thesis, Department of Computer Science, University of Calgary, Calgary, Canada (2004)

Analysis of a Growth Model for Idiotypic Networks

Emma Hart

School of Computing, Napier University
e.hart@napier.ac.uk

Abstract. This paper presents an analysis of the global physical properties of an idiotypic network, using a growth model with complete dynamics. Detailed studies of the properties of idiotypic networks are valuable as one the one hand they offer a potential explanation for immunological memory, and on the other have been used by engineers in application of AIS to a range of diverse applications. The properties of both homogeneous and heterogeneous networks resulting from the model in an integer-valued shape-space are analysed and compared. In addition, the results are contrasted to those obtained using other generic growth models found in the literature which have been proposed to explain the structure and growth of biological networks, and also make a useful addition to previous published results obtained in alternative shape-spaces. We find a number of both similarities and differences with other growth models that are worthy of further study.

1 Introduction

The study of the structure and growth of biological networks (e.g idiotypic networks or protein-protein interaction networks) has received much attention from various disciplines in the past, for example statistical physics, mathematics and immunology, as it becomes apparent that understanding the architecture and construction process by which these networks are formed plays a crucial role in understanding the dynamics that can then take place on such networks. Studies in all these areas have led to the observation that biological networks are not structured randomly. Frequently, a topology is observed in which there are a few nodes which interact with a large number of other nodes (known as the *hubs*), and many nodes which interact with only a few nodes. The same type of topology is also observed in other real-world networks, such as social and technological networks, for example co-authorship of physics papers or the world-wide-web — such networks are referred to as scale-free, and the networks exhibit a number of interesting properties when compared to random graphs of equivalent size.

A number of growth models have been proposed in an attempt to describe the origins of these real-world networks. Perhaps the most prevalent is due to Barabasi and Albert [1] which proposes a growth model based on preferential attachment of new nodes to existing nodes with high degree, which results in a network with scale-free properties. Whilst this model makes sense in the case of

H. Bersini and J. Carneiro (Eds.): ICARIS 2006, LNCS 4163, pp. 66–80, 2006.
© Springer-Verlag Berlin Heidelberg 2006

technological networks such as the Internet, it has serious flaws from a biological perspective as it implies an mechanism by which a cell or protein decides to attach to another cell based on a knowledge of the other's connectivity. In order to address this, a number of more biologically focussed models have been proposed. For example, [18] put forward the gene-duplication model, in which preferential attachment arises as a result of similarity between genes producing proteins and the initial topology of the network [4]. This model has been shown to explain biological structure in the case of gene-duplication, yet it has yet to be generalised to other biological areas, for example the idiotypic network proposed by Jerne in [12]. In response to this, [13,4] propose a more generalised growth model which can be extended to a number of different biological networks, yet retains the important property that it makes no implicit assumption of preferential attachment based on current node connectivity. Using this model, they show that under certain conditions, networks can be produced that have scale-free properties; however, these conditions are reminiscent of those used in a gene-duplication network in which there is an endogenous production of new nodes. The results do not extend to networks such as the idiotypic immune network in which there is an exogenous production of new cells (in the immune case from the bone-marrow).

Yet, idiotypic networks may play a crucial role in advancing our understanding of the natural immune system. For example, they have been postulated to play a crucial role creating immunological memory [12], in preventing auto-immunity [17], and knowledge of their architecture is critical for describing population dynamics of B-lymphocytes and antibodies [5]. Thus they have received a great deal of attention from the immunological community, e.g [17]. At the other extreme, the properties that are integral to the idiotypic network have also captured the attention of engineers and computer scientists; thus we see them deployed in applications ranging from robotics [19] to data-classification [14]. Attempts to unify understanding and thus progress both disciplines have been made by [3,10], whose work has gradually begun to build a picture of the properties of idiotypic networks. In this paper, we extend a previous analysis concerning the dynamics of emergent idiotypic networks and their resulting properties with an in-depth analysis of the physical properties of the underlying network itself. We attempt to map our observations to those that have been made in theoretical immunology and other studies of biological networks in the hope that the work can impact on both immunological and engineering studies of the immune system. In the next section we review some related work on growth models for idiotypic networks, and then present our model and the experimental results derived from it.

2   Related Work

Interest in modelling idiotypic networks is not new — over a decade ago models were proposed independently for example by [7,16] and the emergent properties of these models analysed. These models raised interesting questions regarding the properties of idiotypic networks, but tended to focus on explaining observed immunological phenomena. Over a decade later, a resurgent interest in networks has come about in which new understanding in the area of statistical physics has led to a greater focus on undertanding the properties of the network itself.

Thus, Brede and Behn in [5,6] focus on analysing the dynamics and architecture of an idiotypic network. Their model incorporates two important principles specific to immune networks; the first is that the dynamics and network evolution should be driven by a continuous influx of new idiotypes from the bone marrow, and that secondly, that idiotypes should die out if they become *under* or *over stimulated*. Their model adopts a bit-string approach: for a bit-string of length d, there are 2^d possible antibodies (representing vertices of a hyper-cube). By defining recognition to occur between vertices which are either perfectly complementary or have only n matching bits ('n-mismatch'), the network can be represented as a graph in which some vertices are connected (e.g a "1-mismatch" rule on a hypercube of dimension 3 has all space and side-diagonals connected). Growth dynamics are simulated by simply selecting at random a set of vertices of the hypercube and occupying them. The neighbourhood of each occupied vertex is then checked, and any vertex having a degree less than t_l or greater than t_u is deleted. The upper bound t_u prevents unlimited growth of the network in the first instance and can lead to instantaneous removal of nodes, whilst the lower bound t_l is responsible for maintaining a memory of perturbations which can last over many iterations. They obtain results which show that their model produces a non-trivial seemingly realistic network topology. Although the model is appealing in it's simplicity it has some drawbacks from a biological perspective in that it makes no reference to the concentration of cells, and instead appeals to cell degree as the deciding factor in determining whether cells survive or not.

On the other hand, Bersini *et al* [4] propose a general model that fits well with the biological perspective and has the added advantage of being generalisable to either exogenous production of nodes (such as the immune network) or endogenous production (as in protein networks) and to both homogeneous and heterogeneous networks. The model again utilises a binary shape-space. Bitstrings are able to bind if the Hamming distance between two strings is greater than some threshold t. The key features of the model are that: each node has a different identity based on it's physical properties which define it's *type* and an associated *concentration* that changes over time; the model is *type-based* rather than *instance-based* as in technological or social networks; nodes connect based on mutual attractiveness (affinity); the nodes that are added to the network depend on the dynamics of the existing network. At each iteration of the model, new instances of types are introduced to the network, and they are added only if they can bind to other instances in the network — links only appear if the types of the two instances had not previously been bound. This essentially forms a biological interpretation of the preferential attachment rules proposed in [1]. Using this model, they obtain results which suggest that scale-free distributions are only obtained using an endogenous production scheme and that exogenous production models as observed in the immune system can lead to in the worst case, an exponential distribution. However, their model is incomplete in the sense that it only contains birth-dynamics, i.e. there is no mechanism by which nodes may disappear due to environmental constraints, and therefore nodes can increase in concentration indefinitely. This is clearly unrealistic from a biological perspective, and likely impacts on the type of networks we can expect to obtain from such a model.

Therefore, in this paper, we present an analysis of an alternative model which in keeping with biologically motivated spirit of [4] is type-based and depends on node concentration, yet includes complete birth and death dynamics as in [5]. We investigate whether the inclusion of a complete dynamics can lead to a scale-free distribution in a network with an exogenous production scheme. The experiments are performed using an integer-value shape-space. Much of the previous work in this area has made use of binary shape-space — this partly has historical roots, dating back to the first ideas in AIS proposed by Farmer [8], but also has some advantages in the richness of matching-rules it facilitates. However, using an integer shape-space only provides an interesting comparison to existing work with binary shape-spaces, but has advantages from the engineering perspective in that it lends itself more readily to the kind of real-world engineering problems we wish to address with AIS technology, and in that the networks can be readily visualised. The next section presents the model used and discusses the differences between it and the general model proposed in [4].

3   Immunological Model

The model used in this paper has previously been presented in [2,10,9] and is shown in outline below.

1. Generate at random a new antibody cell at location (x,y) with radius r and add to the simulation with concentration 10.
2. Calculate the stimulation S_{Ab} of each antibody cell present according to equation 1
3. For each cell present, if $L < S_{Ab} < U$, increase the concentration of the cell by 1, otherwise decrease it by 1, where L and U represent a lower and upper stimulation limit, respectively.
4. Remove any cells whose concentration has reached 0.
5. Repeat

$$S_{Ab} = \sum_{\text{antigens } A} A_c(r - ||A - Ab'||) + \sum_{\text{cells } E} E_c(r - ||E - Ab'||) \qquad (1)$$

In equation 1, Ab' represents the complementary position of an antibody Ab. A_c/E_c represents the *concentration* of the antigen A or antibody E, and r represents the recognition radius of the cell. Although the generic equation given covers the most general case in which a simulation can contain both antibodies and antigens, in all simulations reported in this paper, no antigens are added, therefore only idiotypic interactions between cells are considered.

A key ingredient of any network growth model is defining the allowed interactions between nodes in the network; in graph terminology, we can consider any two nodes which interact to be linked or connected. In popular immunological terminology, two nodes which interact are said to recognise each other. In the model described in this paper, a node defined by integer-coordinates in 2-dimensions can recognise any other nodes which lie in a circular region of radius r centered on a point which is complementary to the node, i.e. at a point $(X - x, Y - y)$, where X and Y are the dimensions of the grid, and (x, y) the coordinates of the cell. In the growth model proposed by Bersini *et al*, a node defined by a binary string recognises another node if the Hamming distance between the two nodes is greater than some threshold T. Thus r and T in the respective models play identical roles in limiting number of potential partners of any given node. If r or T is fixed, then the network is *homogeneous*; a *heterogeneous* network on the other hand can be produced if each node (type) has it's own associated value of r, T (and r, T is drawn from some pre-defined range). This model contains many similarities to that proposed in [4] but differs in the following respects:

- In the model proposed above, at least one node is added to the simulation at each step, regardless of whether of not the node has an affinity with other nodes in the network. In [4,13], only nodes that can connect with another node are added. Nodes are added with concentration 10; if they are not able to make any connections within the following 10 iterations, their concentration will be reduced to 0 and they will be removed from the system. They have therefore a small window of opportunity in order to make the connections necessary to survive.
- When a node is added, all existing nodes in the network are checked to determine whether they lie in the recognition region of the new node; on the other hand, in [4], potential partners are restricted to only those that are selected in a trial of size P, in which nodes are selected with a probability related to their concentration.
- In both models, the concentration of a node is increased by 1 if it receives sufficient stimulation; in the model proposed in this paper, stimulation is calculated via equation 1 and must reach a minimum threshold of *low*. In Bersini's model, connecting to one other partner is sufficient to cause the concentration to increase.
- If the stimulation exceeds a pre-defined value U, then the concentration of the node decreases. This models the suppressive effects observed in real immune-networks. Nodes whose concentration reaches 0 are removed from the network, therefore the network incorporates a death mechanism, unlike that of [4].
- In [4], the simulation is terminated when the number of types added to the network reaches 1000. No limit on the possible number of types is imposed during the simulation described in this paper.

4   Experimental Parameters

All experiments reported are derived from simulations on a grid 100x100, giving a total of 10,000 possible types. This is of the same order of magnitude as those experiments reported in [4] in which types were represented by a binary string of length 13, resulting in 2^{13}=8192 possible types. All experiments used a lower threshold of 1000, the maximum upper threshold is stated in each experiment, and took values $U \in 10,000, 100,000, 200,000$. Connectivity is determined by the radius of a cell r — the minimum radius allowed in heterogeneous experiments is 10 which has been shown in previous work·to be the percolation value, i.e. the minimum radius at which a network is able to spring into existence. The maximum radius is limited to 15 in heterogenous experiments, and is fixed at 15 in homogeneous experiments. Again, this value has been shown in previous work to give interesting network behaviour. $r = 15$ allows a maximum of 708 potential partners; this compares to the maximum number of partners in [4] of 378, obtained by using a threshold of 9. At the lower radius limit of 10, there a 316 potential partners. Due to lack of space, all experiment results obtained cannot be shown here — typical results are presented to illustrate trends, and more detailed results are expected to be presented in a forthcoming publication.

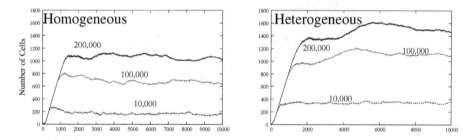

Fig. 1. Number of cells against time plotted for homogeneous and heterogeneous networks for values of $U \in 10K, 100K$ and $200K$. All experiments are run using the same seed value.

5   Experimental Results

In this section, we present results obtained from running simulations of the model over 10,000 iterations. The growth model is clearly dynamic, therefore, the network obtained at iteration 10,000 is merely a snap-shot of the network at some moment in time, and it is unrealistic to assume that all networks will be in the same state at the same moment in time. Therefore, where it makes sense, results presented are averages over a number of runs of the simulation, otherwise, they give a snap-shot of a particular individual run, but can be considered representative of the general trend.

Homogeneous   Heterogeneous

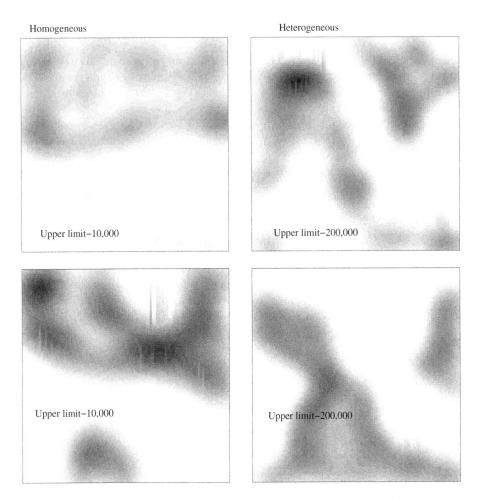

Fig. 2. Cells in the network define tolerated and non-tolerated zones in the space. Blank areas are tolerant to any added cells; the darker the shading, the more reactive the region to added cells.

5.1 Overview of Emergent Network Structure

Figure 1 shows the evolution of two networks using a homogeneous and heterogeneous growth model. In both cases following a rapid growth period, the networks rapidly stabilize to a relatively constant size. For the three values of upper limit U investigated, the heterogeneous growth model tends to produce larger networks. Previous work with homogeneous networks in [10,9] showed that the resultant emergent networks segregate the 2D space into a number of regions which define tolerant and non-tolerant regions of the space (without any need to pre-label cells as a particular type). The results obtained here with a heterogeneous growth model concur exactly with the homogeneous case. In both models, visualisation of the networks in the 2D space shows that cells that are sustained by the network form sharp line-boundaries which separate the space into tolerant and non-tolerant regions. Figure 2 shows new evidence that within these non-tolerant or reactive regions, the tolerance varies quite widely; in figure 2, the darker the shading, the more reactive the spot. Blank (white) regions are those in which any cell is tolerated. Highly intolerant regions are created when the recognition regions of a number of cells overlap, thus providing high stimulation to a cell. It is interesting to observe that the heterogeneous and homogeneous approaches result in markedly different different divisions of the space. Furthermore, increasing the upper-limit is expected to lead to thicker boundaries between zones (see [10]) — however, figure 2 shows that an entirely different pattern of reactivity is observed at the upper limit U is increased from 10, 000 to 200, 000.

5.2   Network Properties

Table 1 compares the physical properties of the networks evolved over 10,000 iterations for various values of U, in both the homogeneous and heterogeneous cases. These results show average values obtained using 100 different seed values (with the same set of seeds used for homogeneous and heterogeneous experiments). Firstly, as previously shown in figure 1, the size of the networks increases as U increases, and as we switch from a homogeneous birth dynamics to a heterogeneous dynamics. The maximum and average degree increase with increasing U, as does the cluster coefficient. A heterogeneous model tends to lead to networks with lower clustering coefficient and lower average degree than a homogeneous model for any given U. All differences are statistically significant.

Table 1. Physical properties of homogeneous/heterogeneous networks obtained after 10,000 iterations from the same seed value

	homo			hetero		
	10,000	100,000	200,000	10,000	100,000	200,000
Number of Nodes	167.8	357.6	786.5	326.9	986.7	1286.2
Max Degree	29.4	58.0	121.2	37.7	117.9	165.6
Average Degree	4.7	7.9	14.3	3.7	8.9	12.5
Clustering Coefficient	0.022	0.023	0.027	0.016	0.016	0.017

Although the maximum degree increases with U, due to cells being able to achieve a higher stimulation from multiple connections before being penalised, figure 3 also clearly shows that the the maximum degree fluctuates up and down; this is just a consequence of the concentration rule; the concentration of the cell with maximum degree with be gradually reduced to zero due the high stimulation it will inevitably receive at which point it is removed from the system. Following this, a eventually a new cell will likely take its place and begin to acquire new connections; the cycle will then repeat.

Homogeneous

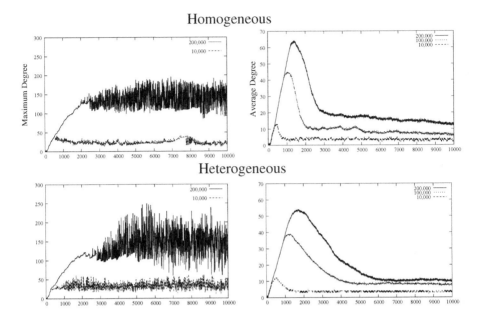

Fig. 3. The graphs show of maximum cell degree vs time and average cell degree vs time for homogeneous and heterogeneous networks for values of $u \in 10K, 100K$ and $200K$. All experiments are run using the same seed value. $U = 100,000$ is omitted from the maximum degree graph for clarity — points are joined by lines in these graphs to indicate the trend.

5.3   Clustering Coefficient

A clear indication that a network deviates from that of a random graph with an equivalent number of vertices and edges can be obtained by examining the clustering coefficient of a network, which is expected to differ by a factor of order n (where n is the number of nodes) [15]. It has been observed experimentally that biological networks have high cluster coefficient. However, table 1 shows that we find the clustering coefficients of the networks obtained with our model to be low in all cases with no obvious trend as either U is increased or the network is evolved with either heterogeneous or homogeneous types. This is not unexpected — due to the complementary affinity function used in the 2D space, a large number of cells are physically unable to form clusters (i.e. if A recognises B, and B recognises C, then C cannot recognise A for the majority of (x, y) coordinates. On the other hand, some clustering does occur; the cluster coefficients are markedly higher than those found by [4] which produced clustering coefficients of the order $< 10^{-5}$.

5.4   Degree Distribution

Figure 3 provides evidence that natural hubs do exist in the network: the left-hand plot shows that very high levels of connectivity are achieved by a few cells in the network in comparison to the average degree of the network cells shown in the right-hand plot of figure 3, which for all experiments stabilises to a low value. One consequence of the growth model which includes death dynamics however is that these hubs are transient, as observed by the spiking nature of the left-hand plot of maximum degree vs iterations. The existence of hubs at all however is contrary to the results found in [4] using an exogenous growth model without death dynamics.

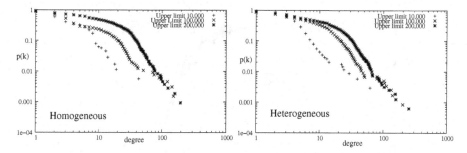

Fig. 4. The graphs show the cumulative degree distribution P(k) for homogeneous and heterogeneous networks for values of $u \in 10K, 100K, and 200K$. Distributions were derived by taking at snapshot of the network at the instant when the maximum degree was observed.

An understanding of the degree distribution in a graph can be obtained by plotting the cumulative distribution function $P(k) = \sum_{k'=k}^{\infty} p_{k'}$, where p_k is the probability that a randomly chosen vertex will have degree k, and therefore P_k the probability that the degree is greater than or equal to k. In a random graph, a binomial distribution of node degrees is observed; in real-world networks, and particularly biological networks, a power-law or scale-free distribution is observed. This shows up as a power-law in the cumulative distribution, with $P_k \approx k^{-(\alpha-1)}$, and is therefore easy to spot experimentally by plotting the cumulative distributions on logarithmic scales. This is given for both homogeneous and heterogeneous networks in figure 4. These appear to show a truncated power-law distribution in the tails of the graphs, particularly as U is increased, though the distributions deviate from this law at small degree (or possibly two separate power-laws contribute). Again, this is contradictory to the results of [4] which show an exponential degree distribution for their exogenous production model.

[4] found that hubs do occur when an endogenous birth-dynamics is used, due to nodes of high concentration preferentially attaching to new nodes, in a model where "the rich get richer". The results we present however suggest that hubs do exist — yet there is no preferential attachment to nodes of high degree (as in the Barabasi *et al*'s model, or to nodes of high concentration as in [4]. Figure 5 plots the relationship between concentration and degree in Bersini model. This shows an inverse correlation between degree and concentration, which is in fact opposite to that presented in [4] using the endogenous production dynamics. Again, the explanation lies partly in equation 1 — nodes with high degree receive a high

stimulation, due to the contribution from each node they are connected to; this drives the concentration down at each iteration as S_{Ab} quickly rises above U, ultimately resulting in the node being removed from the network. (The rise and fall of the graphs of maximum degree vs iterations shown in figure 3 has already been noted).

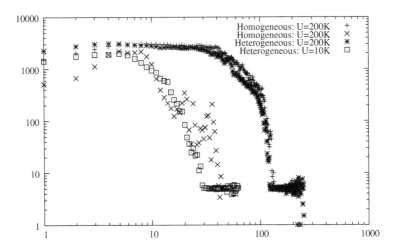

Fig. 5. Correlation between average concentration and degree, averaged over 10,000 iterations of network evolution. Note the log/log scale.

5.5 Topology of Networks

Results presented in previous work e.g [10] provided a visual interpretation of the layout in 2D shape-space of the network of cells that are sustained by the growth model presented here. Further investigation of the topology of the network itself can be obtained by considering the cells of the network as nodes in a graph, with edges connecting pairs of nodes (a, b) if a cell b lies within the complementary region of the cell a. Note that as the recognition function is symmetrical in this case (circular), the links are undirected. Figure 6 shows the topological arrangement of two example networks obtained from the same seed under the homogeneous and heterogeneous production model. Vertices are labelled with the iteration at which the node was "born". Note that the most highly connected nodes were generally "born" within the penultimate few hundred iterations of the simulation. This is inevitable due to the transient nature of the hubs discussed above.

Brede and Behn discuss the requirements of the topological structure of an idiotypic network in [5]. They state that the networks necessarily must realise a trade-off between containing a large number of small components (in order to retain a memory of previously encountered antigen) which requires a *low* connectivity, but at the same time reflect the fact that a large number of antibodies must be able to detect many different types of antigen, therefore resulting in a

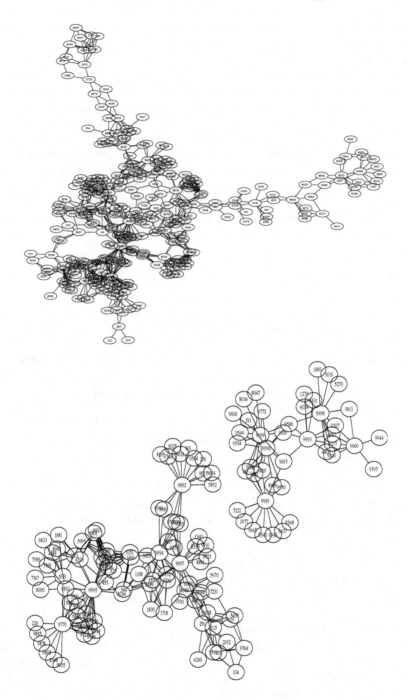

Fig. 6. Topological representation of networks. The upper plot and lower plots respectively shows the heterogeneous and homogeneous networks obtained after 10,000 iterations with an upper concentration limit of 10,000.

high connectivity. Their model suggests that above the percolation transition, the network consists of on a large connected cluster (the central part of the idiotypic network) with a number of weakly connected constituents, and co-exists with a number of small isolated clusters. Figure 6 shows some similarities to this view; in the homogeneous case (lower graph), the network is disconnected and it consists of two isolated clusters. The upper graph showing a heterogeneous network consists of one large cluster which clearly has a highly connected central part weakly connected to a number of smaller clusters. In addition, from a purely visual inspection, the network appears to shows sign of being disassortative, i.e. that nodes with high degree are connected preferentially with nodes with low degree (note several nodes in the lower diagram connected to a large number of nodes which have degree 1). This is a trait which is frequently observed in topological analysis of biological networks (e.g for protein-protein interactions in yeast [11]).

6   Conclusions

An in-depth analysis of a growth model for an idiotypic network and the resultant architecture has been presented, and provides an addition to existing literature in building a picture of how an idiotypic network might emerge and function. Despite the simplicity of the model, we find networks which are in accordance with biology; both homogeneous and heterogenous network models stabilise to a relatively constant size following an initial growth period, and do not either collapse or expand indefinitely. Although the model is simplistic compared to those proposed a decade ago, the topologies of the resultant networks at least contain glimpses of those features we observe from immunological studies — in heterogeneous networks we observe the formation of a large cluster with a number of weakly connected constituents, and the networks show signs of being disassortative. However, more work is needed before definite conclusions can be made in relation to this, particularly in the light of the important role the network topology may play in influencing immunological memory.

Surprisingly, we find some results which contradict the observations made by [4] using an exogenous production model. In particular, our model suggests that hubs can emerge, although they are clearly transient, and that a power-law degree-distribution emerges at least over some range of degrees, even if it is somewhat truncated. The hubs do not arise through a preferential attachment mechanism related to the degree of a node as in the growth model proposed by [1]. However, neither can they be explained through a positive feedback mechanism which rewards nodes with high concentration as in the endogenous production model of [4,13]. It seems likely that the identity of the hubs is in part a lucky accident of the placing of the first few random nodes in the simulation, which sets up the environmental conditions for nodes to exist at certain points in the shape-space where they are able to maintain a balance between becoming over and under stimulated. However, the role that concentration plays needs further investigation, to explain the relationships observed between degree and concentration, and the lack of correlation between degree and clustering coefficient. It is hoped to shed further light on this matter in a publication in the near future.

Acknowledgements

The author is grateful to Hugues Bersini from IRIDIA, and to ARTIST (funded by EPSRC) for providing financial support to enable travel to IRIDIA to discuss aspects of this work.

References

1. L. Barabasi and Albert.R. Emergence of scaling in random networks. *Science*, 286:509–512, 1999.
2. H. Bersini. Self-assertion vs self-recogntion: A tribute to francisco varela. In *Proceedings of ICARIS 2002*, 2002.
3. H. Bersini. Revisiting idiotypic immune networks. In W. Banzhaf and *et al*, editors, *Advances in Artificial Life, 7th European Conference, Proceedings of ECAL 2003*, Lecture Notes in Computer Science, pages 164–174. Springer, 2003.
4. H. Bersini, T. Lenaerts, and Santos.F. Growing biological networks: beyond the gene duplication model. *Journal of Theoretical Biology*, 2006.
5. M. Brede and U. Behn. The architecture of idiotypic networks: Percolation and scaling behaviour. *Physical Review E*, 64(1), 2001.
6. M. Brede and U. Behn. Patterns in randomly evolving networks: Idiotypic networks. *Physical. Review E*, 2003.
7. J. Carneiro, A. Coutinho, and J. Stewart. A model of the immune network with b-t cell cooperation. ii - the simulation of ontogenesis. *Journal of Theoretical Biology*, 182:531–547, 1996.
8. J.D. Farmer, N. Packard, and A. Perelson. The immune system,adaptation and machine learning. *Physica D*, 22:187–204, 1986.
9. E Hart. Not all balls are round: An investigation of alternative recognition-region shapes. In *Artificial Immune Systems, Proceedings of ICARIS 2005*, pages 29–42, 2005.
10. E. Hart and P. Ross. The impact of the shape of antibody recognition regions on the emergence of idiotypic networks. *International Journal of Unconventional Computing*, 2005.
11. H. Jeong, S. Mason, A. Barabsi, and Z. Oltavi. Lethality and centrality in protein networks. *Nature*, 411(41-42), 2001.
12. N.K. Jerne. Towards a network theory of the immune system. *Annals of Immunology (Institute Pasteur)*, 1974.
13. T. Lenaerts, H. Bersini, and F. Santos. How scale-free type-based networks emerge from instance-based dynamics. In *Proceedings of 10th ALife Conference*, 2006.
14. M. Neal. Meta-stable memory in an immune network. In J. Timmis, P. Bentley, and E. Hart, editors, *Artificial Immune Systems: Proceedings of ICARIS 2003*, volume 2787 of *Lecture Notes in Computer Science*, pages 168–180. Springer, 2003.
15. M.E.J Newman. The structure and function of complex networks. *Society for Industrial and Applied Mathematics Review*, 45(2):167–256, 2003.
16. K. Takumi and R. De Boer. Self assertion modeled as a network repertoire of multi-determinant antibodies. *Journal of Theoretical Biology*, 183:55–66, 1996.

17. F. Varela and A. Coutinho. Second generation immune network. *Immunology Today*, 12(5):159–166, 1991.
18. F. Vasquez, A. Flamimi, A. Maritan, and A. Vespignani. Modelling interaction of protein interaction networks. *ComplexUs*, 1:38–44, 2003.
19. Y. Watanabe, A. Ishiguro, Y. Shiraio, and Y. Uchikawa. Emergent construction of a behaviour arbitration mechanism based on the immune system. *Advanced Robotics*, 12(3):227–242, 1998.

Randomly Evolving Idiotypic Networks: Analysis of Building Principles

Holger Schmidtchen and Ulrich Behn

Institute for Theoretical Physics,
University of Leipzig, POB 100 920, 04009 Leipzig, Germany
Ulrich.Behn@itp.uni-leipzig.de
http://www.physik.uni-leipzig.de/~behn/

Abstract. We investigate a minimalistic model of the idiotypic network of B-lymphocytes where idiotypes are represented by bitstrings encoding the nodes of a network. A node is occupied if a lymphocyte clone of the corresponding idiotype exists at the given moment, otherwise it is empty. There is a continuous influx of B-lymphocytes of randomly (by mutation) generated idiotype from the bone marrow. B-lymphocytes are stimulated to proliferate if its receptors (antibodies) are cross-linked by complementary structures. Unstimulated lymphocytes die. Thus, the links of the network connect nodes encoded by complementary bitstrings allowing for a few mismatches.

The random evolution leads to a network of highly organized architecture depending on only few parameters. The nodes can be classified into different groups with clearly distinct properties. We report on the building principles which allow to calculate analytically characteristics as the size and the number of links between the groups previously found by simulations.

1 Introduction

B-Lymphocytes express on their surface receptors, i.e. antibodies which are proteins with highly specific binding sites, which enable them to bind to complementary sites of an antigen, which is thus marked for further processing, e.g., for eating by macrophages. A given B-cell has exactly one specific type (the idiotype) of antibody. When stimulated, i.e. crosslinked by complementary structures, they proliferate and, after a few cell cycles, differentiate into plasma cells and memory cells, the former secreting large amounts of the useful antibodies. Thus, useful clones survive, while others, lacking stimulation, die [1].

B-lymphocytes are capable of mutual interaction if their receptors have complementary specifity. Hence, the entirety of the B-lymphocyte system forms a functional network, with nodes representing the idiotypes and links between complementary idiotypes. This is the central idea behind the concept of idiotypic network presented in 1974 by Jerne [2]. Jerne's idea got an immediate enthusiastic resonance. B-lymphocytes of a given idiotype and their anti-idiotypic counterparts have been experimentally identified. However, the search for deeper

H. Bersini and J. Carneiro (Eds.): ICARIS 2006, LNCS 4163, pp. 81–94, 2006.

network structures was not really successful. Parallel with the rapid success of molecular immunobiology the initial enthusiasm of experimentally working immunologists decayed. Today there is a renewed interest in idiotypic interactions, for example in the context of autoimmune diseases [3,4]. The progress in experimental methods seems to make a new generation of experiments feasible. An excellent review and a thorough discussion of the historical development of immunological paradigms has been given in [5], cf. also [6].

Idiotypic networks stayed always attractive for theoretical biologists interested in the systems behaviour, but they attracted also the interest of theoretical physicists. Also computer scientists are interested in the concepts that living organisms have developed to fight against foreign invaders and develop artificial immune systems.

The estimated size of the potential idiotypic repertoire of men is of truly macroscopic order 10^{12}, the expressed repertoire is of order 10^8 [7,8]. Interactions between B-cells of complementary idiotype are genuinely nonlinear. Thus, modeling idiotypic networks is an inviting playground for statistical physics, nonlinear dynamics, and complex systems. More generally, networks, especially random and randomly growing networks, with applications in a plethora of different, multidisciplinary fields [9,10,11] experience rapidly increasing interest in the community of statistical physicists.

A minimalistic model of the idiotypic network was proposed in [12] where idiotypes are represented by bitstrings which can interact with complementary bitstrings allowing for a few mismatches [13]. In the model, an idiotype population may be present or absent.

For survival it needs stimulation by sufficiently many complementary idiotypes, but becomes extinct if too many complementary idiotypes are present. The dynamics is driven by the influx of new idiotypes generated by mutations in the bone marrow.

The model has a minimal number of parameters, namely the length of the bitchain, the allowed number of mismatches, upper and lower thresholds for stimulation, and the influx of new idiotypes. This allows us to also derive some analytical results. However, unrealistic features, such as the extinction of a clone within one time step, are the price of simplicity.

A first study for one and two allowed mismatches was presented in [12]. For typical parameter settings a random evolution towards a highly nontrivial complex functional architecture of the emerging network was observed. To characterize this architecture the nodes can be classified into different groups with clearly distinct properties. They include densely connected core groups and peripheral groups of isolated nodes, resembling the notion of central and peripheral part of the biological network [14,15].

The potential idiotypic network consisting of all idiotypes an organism is able to generate and the links connecting complementary idiotypes allowing a few mismatches is modeled as in [12] by an undirected base graph $G = (\mathcal{V}, \mathcal{E})$. Each idiotype $v \in \mathcal{V}$ in the network is characterised by a bitstring of length d: $b_d b_{d-1} \cdots b_1$, with $b_i \in \{0, 1\}$ for all $i \in \{1, 2, \ldots, d\}$. For every pair of vertices the degree of complementarity is evaluated: If the Hamming distance d_H between the bitstrings of two vertices $v, w \in \mathcal{V}$ equals the length of the bitstring d, there is a link $l = \{v, w\}$ representing a perfect match, if $d_H(v, w) = d - 1$, we call it a one-mismatch link, etc. Allowing m mismatches, the base graph consisting of all bitstrings of length d and the allowed links is denoted by $G_d^{(m)}$.

The expressed idiotypic network is only a fraction of the potential network, the nodes of the expressed idiotypes and their links are a subgraph of $G_d^{(m)}$.

Driven by the random influx of new idiotypes the network evolves towards a stationary state of nontrivial architecture. Crucial for that is that beside the occupation of previously empty nodes, occupied nodes can become empty if linked with too many or too few nodes of complementary idiotype. To be specific, the rules for (parallel) update are

(i) Choose I unoccupied sites (holes) randomly and set them occupied. They represent the influx of new idiotypes from the bone marrow.

(ii) Count the number of occupied vertices $n(\partial v)$ in the neighborhood of every vertex $v \in G$. If $n(\partial v)$ is outside the window of lower and upper threshold (t_l, t_u), the vertex v will be set empty.

(iii) Iterate.

A similar model was proposed by Stewart and Varela [16], who also apply a window update rule to simulate the internal dynamics and a 0–1 clone population. However, their shape space differs from our model: While we consider a discrete d-dimensional hypercubic shape space, in [16,17] the complementary idiotypes live on different sheets of a 2D continuous shape space.

In the following section we describe the typical course of the random evolution of the network as found in extensive numerical simulations. The evolution tends toward a steady state of highly organized architecture. We describe how this architecture can be characterized classifying nodes into different groups with clearly distinct statistical properties and how these groups are linked together. In Sect. 3 we show that the empirical findings can be explained analytically once the building principles are understood. In the final section concluding remarks and an outlook are given.

2 Random Evolution of the Network

We performed simulations on the basegraph $G_{12}^{(2)}$ for $(t_l, t_u) = (1, 10)$ for different values of I starting with an empty base graph. The base graph contains 4096 nodes each of which has 79 links to other nodes. In the first step only those nodes survive which have at least one occupied neighbor (having more than 10 occupied neighbors is unlikely in the beginning). The surviving nodes represent seeds to which other occupied nodes easily can attach. That leads to a rapid growing towards a giant cluster. Parallel to that many stable holes are created, i.e. nodes with the number of occupied neighbors above the upper threshold.

Going through a state with one giant cluster determines –in a sense– the pattern towards which the system will evolve.

Depending on the influx I we observe with varying probability either a decay of the giant cluster into numerous small identical clusters or the formation of one large cluster accompanied by many isolated occupied nodes.

In any case, the system reaches a stationary state in which the influx of new idiotypes and the loss of old ones stay well-balanced, cf. Fig. 1. The stationary states may have a complex architecture, in which we can classify the nodes into groups with clearly distinct statistical characteristics.

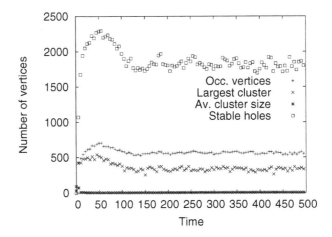

Fig. 1. The time series of the number of occupied vertices $n_T(G)$, the size of the currently largest cluster $|C_T^{\max}|$, the average cluster size $\langle|C|\rangle_{\mathcal{C}_T}$, and the number of stable holes $h_T^*(G)$ on a base graph $G_{12}^{(2)}$ with $t_l = 1$, $t_u = 10$ and $I = 110$

The empty base graph is a highly symmetric object. Due to the random influx the symmetry is broken and the system falls into a network configuration of lower symmetry depending on the individual history. Increasing the influx may lead to transitions between different patterns where the formation of intermediate unstable giant clusters play a role. For a more detailed account of the transient behavior and the transitions see [12].

In the simulations we measured the behavior of the whole system, as well as the time averages of local quantities characterizing every single node. In this way groups of nodes can be distinguished with clearly distinct properties. Figure 2 shows the time average of the number of occupied neighbours of every node as a function of the influx. We find distinct regions in dependence of the influx I. For small and moderate influx a clear group structure is visible. Considering also other characteristics, e.g. the mean life time, we can describe them as static ($I < 90$) and dynamic ($90 \leq I < 260$). For higher influx the clear distinction of groups becomes impossible, we call these patters transient ($260 \leq I$), and random ($350 \ll I$). Static patterns have groups of occupied nodes which have a high mean life time. Many of the other groups are stable holes or sparsely occupied vertices. In dynamic patterns there still are some stable hole groups, however, we do not find any groups of permanently occupied nodes. The mean life time generally is small, and the graph of occupied nodes changes permanently. While in static and dynamic patterns all vertices remain in their groups, for high influx the patterns become transient, i.e. groups dissolve and rearrange themselves. For very high influxes the dynamics is entirely random.

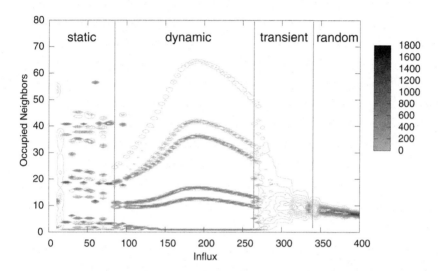

Fig. 2. We measured the time averages of the number of occupied neighbors of each vertex. The graph shows a top view on histograms giving the frequency of vertices with a given average number of occupied neighbors for different values of the main parameter I. Regimes of different temporal behavior are indicated.

3 Building Principles

3.1 Determinant Bits and Pattern Module of the 2-Cluster Patterns

For moderate influx, $I = 10$, one can distinguish, looking at local statistical characteristics, three groups of nodes, cf. Table 1.

We find a group of frequently occupied nodes (S_1) with a mean occupation $\langle n(v) \rangle_{S_1}$ close to 1 and a high mean life time $\langle \tau(v) \rangle_{S_1}$, a group of stable holes (S_3) never being occupied, and a group of potential hubs (S_2) which are rarely

Table 1. Characterization of groups by local quantities for the case $I = 10$

	S_1	S_2	S_3
occupied neighbors $\langle \overline{n(\partial v)} \rangle_{S_i}$	1.16	10.96	53.26
mean life time $\langle \tau(v) \rangle_{S_i}$	4699	3	0
mean occupation $\langle n(v) \rangle_{S_i}$	0.95	0.01	0.00

occupied. However, if occupied, they function as hubs linking together up to t_u 2-clusters. The sizes of the groups are $|S_1| = |S_2|/2 = |S_3|$. For illustration see Fig. 3.

Fig. 3. A typical pattern found for $I = 10$, and similarly for $I = 60$. The occupied vertices form 2-clusters, some of which are interlinked via hubs. The vertices are labeled with the decimal expression of their bitstring. The sum of the indices within a 2-cluster is always 6207 in this 2-cluster configuration. The determinant bit positions are 7 and 12. Figure produced using yEd [18].

Looking at the vertex indices i_v in decimal representation we made a surprising observation: The sum of the two indices in a 2-cluster is constant in the whole graph.

A look at the bitstrings of the nodes of all 2-clusters revealed, that they are identical in exactly two bits, say at position k and l. The remaining $d-2$ bit positions assume all 2^{d-2} possible values. Inside a cluster the two bitstrings are complementary in these positions. Thus, the 2-clusters have a two-mismatch link and we write symbolically

$$\cdots b_k \cdots b_l \cdots \quad \text{connects to} \quad \cdots \overline{b_k} \cdots \overline{b_l} \cdots , \tag{1}$$

where the bar denotes the bit inversion.

The other groups, S_2 and S_3, have similar structural properties. The bitstrings of all stable holes are also equal in the same two bit positions k and l. However, they are inverse to b_k and b_l of the occupied vertices. Potential hubs have exactly one inverse and one equal bit in these positions. As only these two bits play the crucial role of determining the pattern, they shall be called determinant bits. In summary we have

$$
\begin{array}{ll}
\text{occupied vertices } S_1 & \cdots b_k \cdots b_l \cdots \\
\text{potential hubs } S_2 & \begin{array}{l} \cdots \overline{b_k} \cdots b_l \cdots \\ \cdots b_k \cdots \overline{b_l} \cdots \end{array} \\
\text{stable holes } S_3 & \cdots \overline{b_k} \cdots \overline{b_l} \cdots
\end{array}
\tag{2}
$$

These very few principles allow to explain all observations made in the simulations. We can construct a perfect 2-cluster pattern, a configuration in which all nodes of group S_1 are occupied and the others remain empty. It is perfect in the sense that there are no defects but also no hubs. Such a configuration is $2^2 \times \binom{d}{2}$-fold degenerated where the first factor represents the choice of the two determinant bits, and the second factor gives the number of possible positions of these bits in the bitstring of length d.

We further can compute the number of occupied neighbors $n(\partial v)$ of a vertex v of any group. Since all nodes of S_1 are occupied in the perfect pattern, $n(\partial v)$ is given by the number of links between v and the other elements of S_1. A link between two nodes exists if their bitstrings are complementary except for up to two mismatches. If $v \in S_1$, it has two bits in common with all other vertices in S_1, namely b_k and b_l. Thus, all remaining bits must be exactly complementary. There is only *one* vertex $w \in S_1$, $w \neq v$, which obeys the constraints. If $v \in S_2$ or $v \in S_3$, there is one pre-determined mismatch or none, respectively. The remaining mismatches can be distributed among the $d - 2$ non-determinant bits. Thus

$$
n(\partial v) = \sum_{j=0}^{1} \binom{d-2}{j} \quad \forall\, v \in S_2 \quad \text{and} \quad n(\partial v) = 11 \text{ for } d = 12,
\tag{3}
$$

$$
n(\partial v) = \sum_{j=0}^{2} \binom{d-2}{j} \quad \forall\, v \in S_3 \quad \text{and} \quad n(\partial v) = 56 \text{ for } d = 12,
\tag{4}
$$

which is in good agreement with the simulations, cf. Table 1.

This regularity encouraged us to the following concept. Considering the two determinant bits as coordinates of a two-dimensional space, they will define the corners of a two-dimensional hypercube, which is called a pattern module.

The corner with coordinates (b_k, b_l) represents an occupied vertex, the opposite corner $(\overline{b_k}, \overline{b_l})$ is a stable hole, and the neighboring corners of (b_k, b_l) are potential hubs. The module is the building block for the entire regular configuration which can be understood as consisting of 2^{d-2} congruently occupied 'parallel worlds'. Any choice of the two determining bits is of course possible, all corresponding patterns are equivalent, the 2-cluster pattern is $2^2 \times \binom{d}{2}$-fold degenerated. The individual history (the realization of the random influx) selects the determining bits. Thus the degeneracy is lifted, a symmetry breaking has occurred.

Figure 4 illustrates the concept of pattern modules in the smallest possible two-mismatch graph $G_3^{(2)}$.

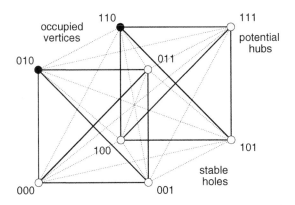

Fig. 4. The complete graph $G_3^{(2)}$ with a 2-cluster configuration. On $G_3^{(2)}$ every vertex is connected to any other. We find two congruently occupied two-dimensional modules (*solid links*), each consisting of one occupied vertex (*black*, · **10**), two potential hubs (*gray*, · **00** and · **11**) and one stable hole (*white*, · **01**). The upper threshold has to be adjusted to $t_u = 1$.

The 2-cluster pattern resembles in a sense the structures found in [16]. There, chains of complementary idiotypes emerge with a fixed distance, which amounts to the preferred occurrence of idiotype–anti-idiotype pairs with a given mismatch. In the ideal case our 2-cluster pattern consists of an ordered array of idiotype–anti-idiotype pairs with the maximal number of mismatches. However, this is only the simplest of a multitude of possible patterns, which occur for larger values of the main control parameter, the influx I. As described in the following, all of these can be explained in a similar way.

3.2   Generalizations and Combinatorics

Many results for 2-clustered patterns on the $G_{12}^{(2)}$ base graph can be generalized to other choices of d and m. For instance, the 2-cluster pattern on 1-mismatch graphs described in [12] can be explained in a similar way. For base graphs $G_d^{(m)}$ we proved: We can construct 2-cluster patterns by means of pattern modules with exactly one occupied corner. The dimension of the pattern module d_M equals the number of allowed mismatches m, the number of qualitatively distinguishable groups is $d_M + 1$, and the size of group S_i is $2^{d-d_M} \binom{d_M}{i-1}$. A 2-cluster pattern can emerge if the lower threshold is $t_l = 1$ and the upper threshold obeys $1 \leq t_u \leq d - d_M$.

In the static pattern regime there exists a dominating 8-cluster pattern, in which the clusters of occupied vertices appear as cubes. Furthermore, 24- and 30-cluster patterns appear, cf. Fig. 5.

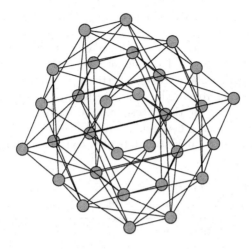

Fig. 5. The regular 30-cluster found for $I = 30$. It has the shape of a 6-dimensional hypercube projected into the plane. Figure produced using yEd [18].

All of these patterns can be explained considering modules with more than two determinant bits. As explained above, the dimension d_M of the module is just the number of determinant bits. Many results for the 2-cluster pattern also hold for the patterns of higher complexity. Given a module dimension d_M the number of groups, and their (relative) sizes can be calculated and arranged as in Pascal's triangle, cf. Table 2.

Table 2. Pattern modules in $G_{12}^{(2)}$

d_M	$\lvert S_i\rvert/2^{d-d_M}$ with $i \in \{1,\ldots,d_M+1\}$							observed patterns in $G_{12}^{(2)}$
0				1				
1			1		1			
2			**1**	2	1			2-cluster
3		**1**	3	3	1			24-cluster
4	1	**4**	6	4	1			8-cluster
5	1	5	10	10	5	1		
6	1	6	**15**	20	15	6	1	30-cluster

The third column shows examples of patterns that are really observed in simulations on $G_{12}^{(2)}$ and that can be explained by means of the pattern modules of the respective dimension. The bold numbers indicate groups which are occupied in these example patterns. For instance, the 2-cluster pattern described above has three groups: one occupied group, a group of potential hubs, which is twice as large, and a group of stable holes.

The possible links between vertices of different groups are –of course– constrained by the mismatch rule.

We find that the bitstrings of a vertex $v_i \in S_i$ always deviates in exactly $i-1$ determinant bits from those of a vertex $v_1 \in S_1$. When calculating the number of links of vertex v_i to vertices $v_j \in S_j$ we have to take into account that the bitstring of v_j also deviate in j–1 determinant bit positions from that of a $v_1 \in S_1$. Among the vertices in S_j there exists a vertex v_j with a minimum number of mismatches with respect to v_i. The non-determinant bits of v_i and v_j can be chosen to be inverse, but for the determinant bits there are constraints. The lowest number of mismatches between v_i and v_j can be achieved if we arrange without loss of generality all deviating bits of v_i to the left and all deviating bits of v_j to the right:

$$
\begin{array}{ll}
v_i: & \underbrace{\overline{b}_{k_1}\,\overline{b}_{k_2}\,\cdots\,\overline{b}_{k_{i-1}}}_{i-1\ \text{bits}}\ \underbrace{b_{k_i}\,\cdots\qquad\cdots}_{m_{ij}^{\min}:=d_M-i-j+2\ \text{bits}}\ \underbrace{\cdots\qquad\cdots\ \overline{b}_{k_{d_M}}}_{} \\[2mm]
v_j: & \overline{b}_{k_1}\,\overline{b}_{k_2}\,\cdots\qquad\cdots\,\cdots\,b_{k_{d_M-j+1}}\ \underbrace{\overline{b}_{k_{d_M-j+2}}\,\cdots\,\overline{b}_{k_{d_M}}}_{j-1\ \text{bits}}
\end{array}
$$

If $m_{ij}^{\min} < 0$, the deviating bits will overlap in the arrangement, and if $m_{ij}^{\min} > 0$, there will be a gap. Considering all allowed arrangements of bits we can thus calculate the number of links of a given vertex $v_i \in S_i$ to vertices in S_j by elementary combinatorics:

$$
\sum_{k=0}^{k'}\sum_{l=0}^{l'}\binom{i-1}{k+\max(0,m_{ij}^{\min})}\binom{d_M-i+1}{k+\max(0,-m_{ij}^{\min})}\binom{d-d_M}{l}, \tag{5}
$$

where $k' = \lfloor (m-|m_{ij}^{\min}|)/2 \rfloor$, and $l' = m - |m_{ij}^{\min}| - 2k$. Details of the calculation are given in [19] and in a forthcoming publication.

3.3 The Six-Group Pattern

A remarkable pattern found empirically in [12] on $G_{12}^{(2)}$ for $I = 90$ is the dynamic pattern consisting of a six-groups, cf. Table 3.

Table 3. Characterization of the six empirical groups. Data from [12].

	$\widetilde{S}_1$	$\widetilde{S}_2$	$\widetilde{S}_3$	$\widetilde{S}_4$	$\widetilde{S}_5$	$\widetilde{S}_6$
group size $|\widetilde{S}_i|$	1124	924	924	134	330	660
life time $\langle\tau(v)\rangle_{\widetilde{S}_i}$	0.0	3.8	5.4	10.0	18.1	35.6

We now denote the empirically found groups by $\widetilde{S}_i$ to distinguish them from the groups S_i defined analyzing the pattern modules. $\widetilde{S}_1$ is the group of stable holes, $\widetilde{S}_2$ and $\widetilde{S}_3$ are central groups, which have connections among each other, as well as to the peripheral group $\widetilde{S}_5$. $\widetilde{S}_2$ additionally has got links to the other peripheral group $\widetilde{S}_6$. The group $\widetilde{S}_4$ is somewhat special, because it is entirely surrounded by stable holes, cf. Fig. 6. Occupied vertices of this group are sustained solely by the random influx. Figure 7 shows a snapshot of the occupied

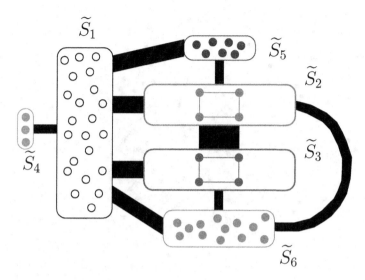

Fig. 6. A visualization of the six-group structure taken from [12]. The size of the boxes corresponds to the group size. The lines show possible links between vertices of the groups and their thickness is a measure of the number of links.

graph at some time step. We clearly see the central and the peripheral part of the idiotypic network.

We were able to explain this sophisticated structure by means of an 11-dimensional pattern module. From this we can derive the correct group sizes and the observed links between the groups. Also the observation, that $\widetilde{S}_1$ and $\widetilde{S}_4$ decay into subgroups [20], can be fully understood. Table 4 gives the mapping $\{S_i\} \rightarrow \{\widetilde{S}_j\}$ and the derived group sizes $|S_i|$. For example, groups S_8, S_9, S_{10}, S_{11}, and S_{12} are the subgroups of the empirical group $\widetilde{S}_1$. Their calculated size adds to 1124, which is *exactly* the statistically measured size of group $\widetilde{S}_1$.

Table 4. The pattern module of the six groups structure

	S_1	S_2	S_3	S_4	S_5	S_6	S_7	S_8	S_9	S_{10}	S_{11}	S_{12}
empirical group	$\widetilde{S}_4$	$\widetilde{S}_4$	$\widetilde{S}_4$	$\widetilde{S}_5$	$\widetilde{S}_6$	$\widetilde{S}_3$	$\widetilde{S}_2$	$\widetilde{S}_1$	$\widetilde{S}_1$	$\widetilde{S}_1$	$\widetilde{S}_1$	$\widetilde{S}_1$
group size	2	22	110	330	660	924	924	660	330	110	22	2

Applying (5) we can also calculate the number of links from a given vertex $v_i \in \widetilde{S}_i$ to vertices in group $\widetilde{S}_j$. The results are given in Table 5. This table is *identical* to the table of measured links in [20]. The non-integer number of links of $v_1 \in \widetilde{S}_1$ is due to the division of $\widetilde{S}_1$ into subgroups. (They are weighted averages.)

In contrast to the static patterns that emerge for low influx I in this structure we also find perfect matches and 1-mismatch links, but they are simply outnumbered by the 2-mismatch links.

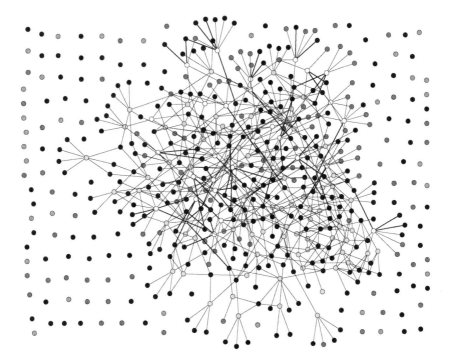

Fig. 7. Snapshot of the occupied graph Γ of a six-group configuration. The five different shades of gray indicate the mean life time of the different groups $\widetilde{S}_i$ from low (*white*) to high (*black*) mean life time, cf. Table 3. Figure produced using yEd [18].

Table 5. The number of links from one given vertex $v_i \in \widetilde{S}_i$ to vertices of $\widetilde{S}_j$

	$\widetilde{S}_1$	$\widetilde{S}_2$	$\widetilde{S}_3$	$\widetilde{S}_4$	$\widetilde{S}_5$	$\widetilde{S}_6$
v_1	0	12.3	16.4	9.4	15	25.8
v_2	15	12	32	0	10	10
v_3	20	32	12	0	0	15
v_4	79	0	0	0	0	0
v_5	51	28	0	0	0	0
v_6	44	14	21	0	0	0

4   Conclusions

We considered a minimalistic model to describe the random evolution of the id-iotypic network which is, given very few model parameters, mainly controlled by the random influx of new idiotypes and the disappearance of not sufficiently stim-ulated idiotypes. Numerical simulations have shown that after a transient period a steady state is achieved. Depending on the influx and on other parameters, the emerging architecture can be very complex. Typically, groups of nodes can be distinguished with clearly distinct statistical properties. These groups are linked together in a characteristic way which leads to the found architecture.

We achieved a detailed analytical understanding of the building principles of these very complex structures emerging during the random evolution. Modules of remarkable regularity serve as building blocks of the complex pattern. We can calculate for instance size and connectivity of the idiotype groups in perfect agreement with the empirical findings based on numerical simulations [12].

For a suitable parameter setting the network consists of a central and a peripheral part, as proposed in [15]. The central part of the immune system is thought to play an essential role, e.g., in the control of autoreactive clones. In this view, the peripheral part provides the response to external antigens and keeps a localized memory. An *ad hoc* architecture similar to the one described here was used in [21] to investigate the role of the idiotypic network in autoimmunity.

The analytical understanding opens the possibility to consider networks of more realistic size and to investigate their scaling behaviour, e.g. exploiting renormalization group techniques [22]. We are optimistic that we can explain and predict many statistical results of the six-group structure for arbitrary parameters d and m, too, if we consider the idiotypes as situated in a mean field created by its surrounding vertices, which in turn act according to the expected behavior of their group.

Future steps will include to check whether a similar understanding can be reached for more realistic models. For example, we think of matching rules allowing bitstrings of different lengths, of links of different weight for varying binding affinities, of several degrees of population for each idiotype and a delay of take-out of understimulated clones.

Furthermore, we are interested in the co-evolution of the network in the presence of self-antigens or an invading foreign antigen in terms of whether the network tolerates them or rejects them, respectively. We also think about modeling the development of the architecture during the life time of an organism.

References

1. Burnett, F.M.: The clonal selection theory of acquired immunity. Vanderbuilt Univ. Press, Nashville, TN (1959)
2. Jerne, N.K.: Towards a network theory of the immune system. Ann. Inst. Pasteur Immunol. **125C** (1974) 373–389
3. Shoenfeld, Y.: The idiotypic network in autoimmunity: Antibodies that bind antibodies that bind antibodies. Nature Medicine **10(1)** (2004) 17–18
4. McGuire, K.L., Holmes, D.S.: Role of complementary proteins in autoimmunity: an old idea re-emerges with new twists. Trends in Immunology **26(7)** (2005) 367–372
5. Carneiro, J.: Towards a comprehensive view of the immune system. PhD thesis, University of Porto (1997)
6. Coutinho, A.: A walk with Francisco Varela from first- to second generation networks: In search of the structure, dynamics and metadynamics of an organism-centered immune system. Biol. Res. **36** (2003) 17–26

7. Perelson, A.S., Weisbuch, G.: Immunology for physicists. Rev. Mod. Phys. **69** (1997) 1219–1267

8. Perelson, A.S., Oster, G.F.: Theoretical studies of clonal selection: Minimal antibody repertoire size and reliability of self-non-self discrimination. J. Theor. Biol. **81** (1979) 645–670

9. Strogatz, S.H.: Exploring complex networks. Nature **410** (2001) 268–276

10. Dorogovtsev, S.N., Mendes, J.F.F.: Evolution of Networks: From Biological Nets to the Internet and WWW. Oxford University Press, Oxford (2003)

11. Barabási, A.L., Albert, R.: Statistical mechanics of complex networks. Rev. Mod. Phys. **74** (2002) 47–97

12. Brede, M., Behn, U.: Patterns in randomly evolving networks: Idiotypic networks. Phys. Rev. E **67** (2003) 031920, 1–18

13. Farmer, J.D., Packard, N.H., Perelson, A.S.: The immune system, adaption, and machine learning. Physica D **22** (1986) 187–204

14. Coutinho, A.: Beyond clonal selection and network. Immunol. Rev. **110** (1989) 63–87

15. Varela, F.J., Coutinho, A.: Second generation immune networks. Immunology Today **5** (1991) 159–166

16. Stewart, J., Varela, F.J.: Morphogenesis in shape space. Elementary meta-dynamics in a model of the immune system. J. Theor. Biol. **153** (1991) 477–498

17. Detours, V., Bersini, H., Stewart, J., Varela, F.J.: Development of an idiotypic network in shape space. J. Theor. Biol. **170** (1994) 401–414

18. yEd - Java^TM Graph Editor, v2.3.1_02, http://www.yWorks.com

19. Schmidtchen, H.: Architecture of randomly evolving networks. Diploma Thesis, Leipzig University, Leipzig (2006)

20. Brede, M.: Random Evolution of Idiotypic Networks: Dynamics and Architecture. PhD Thesis, Leipzig University, Leipzig (2003)

21. Sulzer, B., van Hemmen, J.L., Behn, U.: Central immune system, the self and autoimmunity. Bull. of Math. Biology **56** (1994) 1009–1040

22. Brede, M., Behn, U.: The architecture of idiotypic networks: percolation and scaling behaviour. Phys. Rev. E **64** (2001) 011908, 1–11

The Idiotypic Network
with Binary Patterns Matching

Krzysztof Trojanowski[1] and Marcin Sasin[2]

[1] Institute of Computer Science, Polish Academy of Sciences,
Ordona 21, 01-237 Warsaw, Poland
[2] Warsaw School of Information Technology,
Newelska 6, 01-447 Warsaw, Poland

Abstract. A new specification of an immune network system is proposed. The model works on a set of antibodies from the binary shape-space and it is able to build a stable network and learn new patterns as well. A set of rules based on diversity of the repertoire of patterns which control relations of stimulation and suppression is proposed. The model is described and the results of simple experiments with the implementation of the model without and with presentation of antigens are presented.

1 Introduction

Ability to learn to distinguish and discriminate the self patterns from non-self ones present in the immune systems is explained by the immune network theory proposed by Jerne [6]. The hypothesis assumes that the system is composed of a set of molecules, i.e. antibodies and antigens. There are also rules that control interactions between antibodies and between antibodies and antigens. The interactions turn this set of molecules into a self regulated network which has its own mechanisms responsible for insertion and elimination of molecules. The rules are based on the molecules' traits which assembled all together can be interpreted as points in the multidimensional space where each of dimensions represents a single trait. The result of these interactions is a continuous proces of modification i.e. growth or depreciation of the concentration of molecules in the organism. Depreciation of the concentration of selected antibodies or antigens brings them to elimination from the system. Eliminated molecules can be replaced by new ones and this way the system is able to rebuild itself according to its metadynamics. For the summary of the first models based on this theory which were developed by Farmer et al. and Varela see [3].

In recent years a set of different practical specifications of the models was already proposed. For extended discussion on properties of immune networks based on two types of shape-space: the multidimensional real space and the binary space see the Bersini's publication [2]. Our network manages binary patterns and its activity is controlled by the rules that are easy to implement and of low computational cost. However there is also a set of assumptions which differentiates it from the networks presented by Bersini. In [4] Galeano et al. present

H. Bersini and J. Carneiro (Eds.): ICARIS 2006, LNCS 4163, pp. 95–108, 2006.

a genealogical tree describing dependency relationship between the models. Our approach would be the closest to the *Hunt & Cooke* branch which started from the model proposed in 1996 [5].

In [3] a general–purpose framework of AIS is proposed where the three key layers are distinguished: immune algorithms, affinity measures and representation. The following section describes the first and the last layer of the framework. The proposed idiotypic network model is presented, i.e. the main loop of the process and the rules of affinity and enmity which control the concentration of the molecules are discussed. The formula of evaluation of new concentration levels of the molecules is given. In Section 3 a description of the second layer of the framework including affinity measures can be found. A set of measures is presented as well as a novel transformation operator for binary strings. Section 4 includes results of the first group of experiments where the model was tuned and average life span of antibodies was observed. Section 5 presents the last group of experiments where a set of five antigens was cyclically presented to the system. The paper is concluded with a summary of the current work and plans for further research.

2   The Idiotypic Network Model

The model represents a network which consists of a set of antibodies and rules of relationship between them. In our specification of the model different types of antibodies are represented as objects in a binary shape space. Each of them is equipped with a 32-bit paratope and a 32-bit epitope, and with two numerical attributes: a concentration and a lifetime. It is assumed that each antibody have just one binding site therefore every object represents all the antibodies with the same patterns of the paratope and the epitope. The quantity of a set represented by an object is defined by the concentration attribute. It should not be allowed to exist two or more objects with the same paratope and epitope in the population of objects at the same time [1]. The remaining two components of the object, the two numerical attributes do not participate in binding rules. The second attribute, the object's lifetime allows us to observe robustness of each of the sets of antibodies. When a new object is added to the population its lifetime is set to zero and then it is increased at the end of every iteration of the process as far as the object exists in the population. The concentration of a newly created object is set to an initial value which was equal to 1 in the experiments presented below. During the lifetime of the system the objects stimulate each other to increase or decrease the concentration of the antibodies which they represent.

The proposed specification allows also to introduce antigens into the system. Different types of antigens are represented by objects equipped with epitope and two numerical attributes, i.e. the concentration and the lifetime. The objects representing antigens interact with the objects representing antibodies in

---

[1] It is hardly likely that such a situation will take place because the total number of possible patterns is 2^{64}. Therefore our software application did not have any special procedures for elimination of redundant objects.

the same manner like the antibodies interact with each other and this way the concentration levels of antigens are also able to be modified.

For both types of objects the lifetime attribute values are just gathered during experiments. The values of lifetime do not influence the activity of the system but they are introduced only for easier and more thorough observation of the system behavior.

2.1 The Main Loop of the Process

At the beginning of the experiment an initial number of objects representing different types of antibodies is randomly generated and their attributes are set to initial values. Then the process of life starts. The main loop models the life of the organism. The main task of the loop is to execute the dynamics and metadynamics of the model by updating the levels of concentrations in all the existing objects. During the execution of the main loop some of the objects disappear when their concentration shrinks below the minimum threshold. The deleted objects are replaced by mutated clones of those which concentration is high. The concentration shrinks when the object representing given type of antibodies is suppressed by the other types. When the object is stimulated its concentration grows but it does not grow to infinity. In our experiments the upper limit of concentration level was set to 9999.

2.2 The Antibodies Relationships

There are rules in the system steering the levels of concentrations. They are based on affinity between paratopes and epitopes of different types. It is important to stress that in contrast to other network models the rules depend on the number of other types that a type interact with and they do not depend on the concentration of those types. This is an unusual assumption because in the existing models of the networks the concentration of antibodies plays the significant role in suppression and activation mechanisms. However a rule promoting a growth of diversity in the population of antibodies could stimulate the system to build more stable nets of stimulative relations between the molecules. In such a net a large number or even most of the relations are redundant i.e. lost of one or two types of antibodies does not cause gaps in the chains of relations. Therefore in the presented approach the concentration is responsible just for the lifetime of the particular type of antibodies or antigens.

When the value of the affinity between any two objects is above the specified level the rule is activated and the object's concentration is modified. There are five rules of stimulation and suppression defined. The first two rules describe interactions between types of antibodies while the three latter are used when objects representing types of antigens are introduced into the system. All of them define values which the concentration will be increased or decreased by. In addition they are not disjoint i.e. more than one of them can be satisfied simultaneously for one object. In that case the values from the rules are summarized and the cumulative modification of the concentration is evaluated.

1. For the objects representing type of antibodies there exist two kinds of relation: *to recognize anybody* and *to be recognized by anybody*. In the first case we can say that the object B_1 will recognize the object B_2 if the affinity between B_1 paratope and B_2 epitope is above the specified threshold. In this case B_1 will be activated. In the second case – B_1 will be recognized by B_2 if the affinity between B_1 epitope and B_2 paratope is above specified threshold. In this case B_1 will be suppressed. The thresholds for both relations do not need to be equal.

2. If neither the objects's paratope nor the epitope interact with any other object in the system (i.e. the given type of antibodies neither recognizes nor is recognized by any other type of antibodies) it will be suppressed.

3. If the object representing type of antibodies recognizes any object representing type of antigens i.e. affinity between the antibodies' paratope and the antigens' epitope is above the specified threshold the object representing types of antibodies will be activated and the object representing type of antigens will be suppressed.

4. If the object representing type of antibodies neither is recognized by any other type of antibodies in the system nor recognize any type of antigens the object will be suppressed.

5. The real-world antigens try to proliferate continuously in the infected organism so for each of types of antigens a concentration growth proportional to current level of concentration is evaluated in every iteration.

The five rules presented above require to define the affinity measure and three thresholds. The first threshold at controls the relation of the first type when B_1 recognizes B_2 and causes activation of B_1. The second threshold st controls the relation of the second type when B_1 is recognized by B_2 and causes suppression of B_1. The last threshold t controls the relation between types of antibodies and types of antigens.

2.3   Evaluation of a New Concentration Level

To evaluate new values of concentrations of types of antibodies and types of antigens in the time t of the process the first step is to check current relations between them. For each of the types of antibodies B^i the total number of other types of antibodies which are recognized by B^i (called $A^i_{B2B}(t)$) and the total number of types of antibodies which recognize B^i (called $S^i_{B2B}(t)$) are evaluated using the first rule. Then in case of presence of antigens the third rule is used to evaluate the number of types of antigens which are recognized by B^i (called $A_{B2A}(t)$) and for each of the types of antigens the number of types of antibodies which recognize them $(S_{B2A}(t))$ is evaluated.

In the second step for each of B^i a change of its concentration $c^i(t)$ based on each of the rules of interaction is evaluated. The change of concentration is controlled by two factors: an activation factor η_a where $\eta_a > 1$, and a suppression factor η_s where $\eta_s < 1$. There are four components of concentration change $\Delta c^i_1(t)$, $\Delta c^i_2(t)$, $\Delta c^i_3(t)$ and $\Delta c^i_4(t)$ which come from the former four rules:

$$\Delta c_1^i(t) = \begin{cases} c^i(t)\eta_s(1 - \frac{S_{B2B}(t) - A_{B2B}(t)}{pop\_size}) - c^i(t) & \text{iff } S_{B2B}(t) > A_{B2B}(t) \\ c^i(t)\eta_a(1 - \frac{A_{B2B}(t) - S_{B2B}(t)}{pop\_size}) - c^i(t) & \text{iff } S_{B2B}(t) < A_{B2B}(t) \end{cases} \tag{1}$$

$$\Delta c_2^i(t) = \begin{cases} c^i(t)\eta_s - c^i(t) & \text{iff } (S_{B2B}(t) = 0) \wedge (A_{B2B}(t) = 0) \\ 0 & \text{otherwise} \end{cases} \tag{2}$$

$$\Delta c_3^i(t) = c^i(t)\eta_a^{A_{B2A}(t)} - c^i(t), \tag{3}$$

$$\Delta c_4^i(t) = \begin{cases} c^i(t)\eta_s - c^i(t) & \text{iff } (S_{B2B}(t) = 0) \wedge (A_{B2A}(t) = 0) \\ 0 & \text{otherwise} \end{cases} \tag{4}$$

In case of a model including antigens a new concentration for the objects representing types of antigens has to be evaluated too. Since the change in the concentration level of each type of antigens depends on its natural continuous proliferation in the organism (5th rule) and the number of types of antibodies which recognize the given type of antigens (3rd rule) the new concentration $c^j(t)$ of the object representing j-th type of antigen is evaluated as follows:

$$c^j(t+1) = c^j(t)\eta_{pro}\frac{pop\_size - S_{B2A}}{pop\_size} \tag{5}$$

where η_{pro} is an antigens' proliferation factor where $\eta_{pro} > 1$ (in our experiments η_{pro} was equal η_a).

3   Affinity Measures

The shape space model described above is still not complete because we have not defined a relation for the shapes in the defined space yet. Binary pattern matching problem belongs to classic and a set of different similarity or distance functions was already proposed [1]. It is closely connected with a problem of classification of binary patterns (see e.g. [9] for discussion). In our case it is assumed that the significance of the bits in the patterns is the same for all the bits. So eventually the following set of affinity measures was selected for tests [7]: 1. Russel and Rao, 2. Jaccard and Needham, 3. Kulzinski, 4. Sokal and Michener, 5. Rogers and Tanimoto, 6. Yule. They were compared with a Hamming distance and a r-contiguous bits matching rule.

For the formal description we shall use the following definition of the binary strings: $X, Y \in \{0, 1\}^N$ and the following reference variables:

$$\begin{aligned} a = \sum_{i=1}^{n} \xi_i, \quad \xi_i &= \begin{cases} 1 & X_i = Y_i = 1, \\ 0 & \text{otherwise.} \end{cases} \\ b = \sum_{i=1}^{n} \xi_i, \quad \xi_i &= \begin{cases} 1 & X_i = 1, \ Y_i = 0, \\ 0 & \text{otherwise.} \end{cases} \\ c = \sum_{i=1}^{n} \xi_i, \quad \xi_i &= \begin{cases} 1 & X_i = 0, \ Y_i = 1, \\ 0 & \text{otherwise.} \end{cases} \\ d = \sum_{i=1}^{n} \xi_i, \quad \xi_i &= \begin{cases} 1 & X_i = Y_i = 0, \\ 0 & \text{otherwise.} \end{cases} \end{aligned} \tag{6}$$

Note, that the total: $a + b + c + d$ is a constant value and equals n, i.e. the length of the binary string. Tested affinity measures are as follows:

$$\text{Russel and Rao:} \quad f = \frac{a}{n} \; , \tag{7}$$

$$\text{Sokal and Michener:} \quad f = \frac{a+d}{n} \; , \tag{8}$$

$$\text{Jaccard and Needham:} \quad f = \frac{a}{a+b+c} \; , \tag{9}$$

$$\text{Kulzinski:} \quad f = \frac{a}{b+c+1} \; , \tag{10}$$

$$\text{Rogers and Tanimoto:} \quad f = \frac{a+d}{a+d+2(b+c)} \; , \tag{11}$$

$$\text{Yule:} \quad f = \frac{ad-bc}{ad+bc} \; . \tag{12}$$

A Hamming distance d_H is a well known measure and it could be denoted in terms of a, b, c, d as $d_H = b + c$.

The last of the discussed measures is the r-contiguous bits matching rule. The rule is a classifier rather than a measure because it returns just two values, true and false. True is returned (i.e. the classifier says that two patterns match each other) if there will be a sequence of bits of size r which are identical in both patterns. False is returned otherwise.

Additionally a transformation T operator [8] was applied to the measured bit-strings. Before the evaluation every pair was modified by a T operator working as follows. For every two patterns $A, B \in \{0,1\}^N$:

$$\forall_{i \in \{0,1,...,N\}} A[i] = 0 \Rightarrow (A[i] = 1 \vee B[i] = 1 - B[i]) \tag{13}$$

The operator reduces the search space, e.g. for a set of 65536 pairs of 8-bit binary strings we obtain 256 different transformed pairs. After transformation one of the strings is always turned into a sequence of digits "1", while the other includes information about differences between the input strings. The operator is simple and of low computational cost and it significantly modifies properties of the measure and improves their sensitivity.

The operator should be applied just before matching. Every matched pair of strings is at first turned into a new pair with the T operator and then the measure is applied to the new pair of strings. The returned value is assigned to the original pair of strings, i.e. the pair before transformation. The transformed $X[i]$ never equals zero (one of the resulting strings is always a sequence of digits "1") so the values c and d in (6) are equal zero for all pairs of transformed binary strings.

All the measures except from Yule (12) were applied to the transformed pairs of binary strings too. In case of Yule the transformed pair of bit-strings cannot be evaluated because of division by zero problem (the denominator always equals zero). The definitions of the measures (7) – (11) changed as follow:

$$\text{T1:} \quad f = \frac{a}{a+b} \tag{14}$$

$$\text{T2:} \quad f = \frac{a}{b+1} \tag{15}$$

$$\text{T3:} \quad f = \frac{a}{a+2b} \tag{16}$$

where (14) originates from both (7), (8) and (9), (15) – from (10), and (16) – from (11). The transformed Hamming distance turns to the formula $d_{HT} = b$.

4 Tuning the Network

In the first phase of our research we observed the dynamics of the model i.e. the change of concentration of different types of antibodies. The change is expressed by life spans of the objects since the objects with high concentration live longer (and even *forever*, i.e. as long as the experiment continues) while the ones with decreasing concentration quickly reach the minimum value and are eliminated from the system. This way the life span of the objects tells a lot about the environment where they have to live. Another parameter good for observing the properties of the system is average number of types of antibodies. For better understanding of the graphs it necessary to note, that in contrast to other network models the size of repertoire of types of antibodies was fixed. Therefore new types were recruited only if some other disappeared and made room in the repertoire.

This group of experiments was performed for the system without antigens thus just the first and the second rule of interactions influenced on the concentration levels. Verification of ability of the system to build a stable structure of interactions was the goal of this part of experiments. This group of experiments allowed us also to tune the system. The role of selected measures as well as the two thresholds mentioned above, *at* and *st* which control the sensitivity of the antibodies were compared in these experiments.

4.1 Average Life Span and Average Number of Antibodies

The results of experiments with different values of thresholds *at* and *st* are presented in Figure 1 (average life span of types of antibodies) and 2 (average number of types of antibodies). Each of the figures consist of eight graphs for eight affinity measures and for six of them (7) – (10) and r-contiguous bits rule two versions of measures were tested: without and with transformation T. Thus for each of the six there are two landscapes in the graph except for the Yule affinity measure (12) which can not be applied with transformation T and the Hamming – applied just with transformation T. Every experiment was repeated 20 times therefore every point in the graphs is the mean of the obtained 20 average life spans or average numbers of types of antibodies.

The activation factor η_a was set to 1.11111 and the suppression factor η_s – to 0.9. The thresholds *st* and *at* for Hamming distance and r-contiguous bits rule changed from 1 to 15 with step 1 while for the remaining six measures – from 0.1 to 0.9 with step 0.1. For all the cases minimum level of concentration was set to 0.1 and the maximum – to 9999. The population consisted of 1000 objects representing different types of antibodies and every experiment took 500 iterations. Thus the minimum average number of types of antibodies in the system is 1000 and their maximum average life span is 500.

There are two extreme behaviors observed in the graphs. The first behavior is the case where all the types of antibodies die immediately after introduction into the

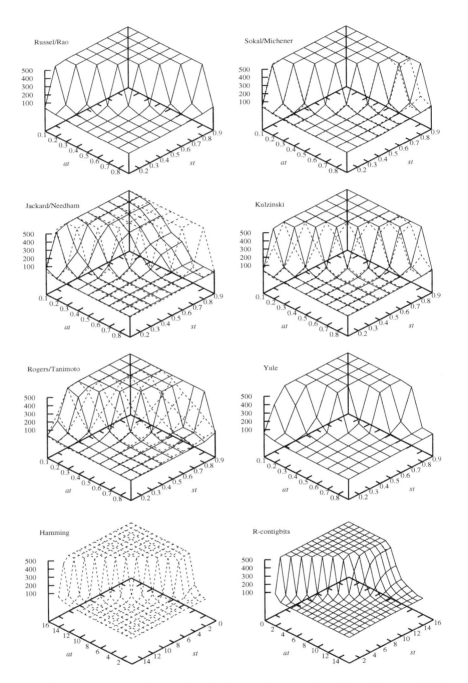

Fig. 1. Average life span of types of antibodies in the system for different types of affinity measures. Solid line – the measure without transformation T, dashed line – the measure with transformation T.

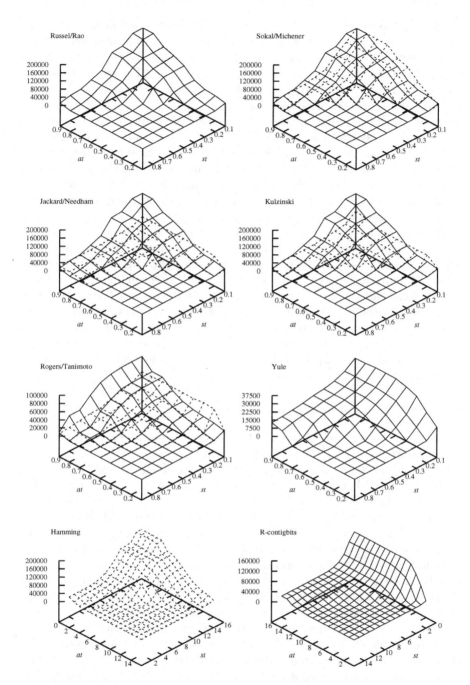

Fig. 2. Average number of types of antibodies in the system for different types of affinity measures. Solid line – the measure without transformation T, dashed line – the measure with transformation T.

system. This is the case when the average life span reaches minimum value and the average number of types of antibodies – maximum. The concentration decreases immediately and the types of antibodies are eliminated from the system. The new ones which replaced the eliminated types live shortly too. The second behavior is the case where all the antibodies live forever and the life span is maximal while the average number of antibodies – minimal. In the first case the suppression pressure is stronger than the activation one. The concentration of all the types of antibodies goes down just after their appearance in the system so the set of antigens is continuously changing. Just the opposite situation is in the second case where the activation pressure is much stronger than the suppression and the concentrations of each of the types of antibodies quickly reach maximum level. So the set of types is constant from the beginning till the end of experiment. None of the two cases represents a system which would be able to learn anything.

The most promising case is the result where the life span as well as the average number of types of antibodies is between the minimum and the maximum value. Unfortunately there are measures that do not satisfy this requirement. Especially when we look at the life span it can be seen that for Russel and Rao (with and without T), Sokal and Michener (with and without T), Rogers and Tanimoto without T, Kulzinski without T, Yule, Hamming and r-contiguous bits matching rule it is very difficult or even impossible to find the values for thresholds at and st giving the requested behavior of the system. The remaining measures allows to be tuned and in those cases it is expected that the system will construct a stable set of dependencies between types of antibodies.

4.2   Histograms of Ages of Antibodies

To confirm our conjectures based on the average life span and average number of types of antibodies we gathered more detailed information about the lifetime of types of antibodies appearing during the experiments. Figures 3 and 4 present sample histograms with mortality of types respecting to their maximum age for three different settings of thresholds at and st.

The histograms in Figures 3 and 4 represent distribution for the lifetime of objects representing types of antibodies in the system. The histograms **3.a** ($at = 0.6$ $st = 0.7$) and **4.a** ($at = 0.2$ $st = 0.3$) obtained for Jaccard and Needham affinity measure without and with transformation T represent the most requested situation. It can be seen that there is a set of objects living for short and even very short time but there are also the types of antibodies which live longer or even for the time of the entire experiment, and so the distribution stretches out to the right. Between these two extremes there are also some types of antibodies which live neither very short nor forever albeit among them there could be also those which were created in the middle of the experiment and which lived till the end of the test. Besides it can be seen that the histogram obtained with transformation T is more regular than the one without T. This observation indicates that the transformation T makes results of Jaccard and Needham affinity measure more predictable.

The histograms **3.b** and **4.b** (both obtained with $at = 0.1$ $st = 0.5$) as well as **3.c** and **4.c** (both obtained with $at = 0.6$ $st = 0.1$) represent the system working with

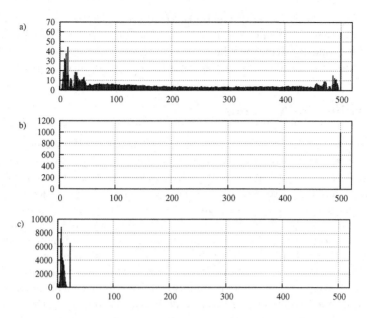

Fig. 3. Histogram of ages of antibodies for Jaccard and Needham without transformation T. X axis – lifetime, Y axis – number of antibodies died at that age.

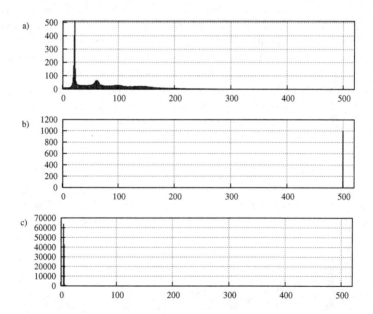

Fig. 4. Histogram of ages of antibodies for Jaccard and Needham with transformation T. X axis – lifetime, Y axis – number of antibodies died at that age.

two extreme parameters setting. The **b** histograms represent the case when the activation pressure is too strong and all the antibodies live forever. The **c** histograms show just the opposite situation where the suppression pressure outweighs and all the types of antibodies die immediately after they are introduced into the system.

5   Learning the Antigens

The last part of our experiments is concerned with testing of the system with antigens. For our tests we selected Jaccard and Needham affinity measure with transformation T and a set of five types of antigens. We searched for such a set of five types where the affinity to each other was the smallest. A new object representing a type of antigens was injected into the system after every 5 iterations of the algorithm. After a copy of the fifth type of antigen the next injected object was a copy of the first one. Figure 5 presents two sample histograms with life spans of the subsequently injected objects. Every bar in the histograms represents a life span of a single object. There are five colors of bars because these are life spans of objects of the five types of patterns. There is a hundred life spans in each of the histograms so each experiment took 500 iterations. The bars are grouped by the number of presentation of the five types of antigens – each of them was presented 20 times. Initial concentration of the added objects was set to 1.

In Figure 5 the histogram shows the case where all the five types of antigens were presented from the beginning of the experiment. It was expected that shortly after the beginning of experiment there would appear multiple copies of objects representing the same types of antigens. However it was also expected that after some time the network would modify its set of types of antibodies and new types that are able to recognize the injected antigens would appear. Eventually the modification of the network would produce the desired effect i.e. the concentration of the objects representing antigens would shrink below the minimal limit and they would be eliminated. The histogram shows that after some time the network of antibodies adapted to the presence of new types of antigens.

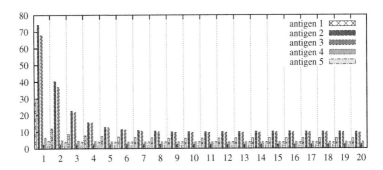

Fig. 5. Histogram of lifetime of objects representing five types of antigens presented cyclically. X axis represents the number of the presentation of a type of antigen and Y axis – the lifetime of the injected object

6   Conclusions

In this paper the new specification of the immune network model is proposed. The specification differs in a set of fundamental assumptions from the others [2]. Among the differences we could mention the following: the network is build of the objects representing types of antibodies and types of antigens instead of just antibodies or antigens, there is a constant size of repertoire of types of antibodies during the experiment, strength of stimulation or suppression depends on the number of different types being above the affinity threshold and does not depend on their concentration, the concentration is responsible only for the lifetime of the type of antibody or antigen, relations of stimulation and suppression between types of antibodies as well as relation between types of antibodies and types of antigens can be controlled by different affinity thresholds. Some of these assumptions are not in accordance with commonly accepted biological point of view.

The experiments show that proposed rules of dynamics and metadynamics of the system based on the binary shape-space build a stable network. Three types of the network behavior can be observed: two of them when the network is not able to establish itself because all the new objects die immediately after introduction into the system or in the opposite case all the objects once added live forever. The third type of behavior is the requested one where some of the antibodies live longer but a recruitment of the new ones is also performed and this way the stable network is build. It was observed that the chances for stable network strongly depends on the type of affinity measure. For some of the measures it was impossible to tune the affinity thresholds successfully. A new transformation T operator was proposed which significantly influenced the properties of the measures and when applied gave a set of three new measures resulting in more regular and predictable behavior of the network. Further work could be focused on testing all the selected efficient measures applied in the network where a set of new patterns is presented.

References

1. V. Batagelj and M. Bren. Comparing resemblance measures. *Journal of Classification*, 12(1):7–90, 1995.
2. H. Bersini. Revisiting idiotypic immune networks. In W. Banzhaf, T. Christaller, P. Dittrich, J. T. Kim, and J. Ziegler, editors, *Advances in Artificial Life, 7th European Conference, ECAL 2003, Dortmund, Germany, September 14-17, 2003, Proceedings*, volume 2801 of *LNCS*, pages 164–174. Springer, 2003.
3. L. N. de Castro and J. Timmis. *Artificial Immune Systems: A New Computational Approach*. Springer-Verlag, London. UK., 2002.
4. J. C. Galeano, A. Veloza-Suan, and F. A. González. A comparative analysis of artificial immune network models. In H.-G. Beyer and U.-M. O'Reilly, editors, *Genetic and Evolutionary Computation Conference, GECCO 2005, Proceedings, Washington DC, USA, June 25-29, 2005*, pages 361–368. ACM, 2005.
5. J. E. Hunt and D. E. Cooke. Learning using an artficial immune system. *Journal of Network and Computer Applications*, 19:189–212, 1996.

6. N. K. Jerne. Towards a network theory of the immune system. *Ann. Immunol. (Inst. Pasteur)*, (125(C)):373–389, 1974.

7. M. Nadler and E. P. Smith. *Pattern Recognition Engineering*. John Wiley and Sons, New York, 1993.

8. K. Trojanowski and M. Grzegorzewski. A look inside the artificial immune algorithm inspired by clonal selection principle. *Artificial Intelligence Studies, Special Issue, M.Kłopotek, J.Tchórzewski (Eds.)*, 2(25), 2005.

9. J. D. Tubbs. A note on binary template matching. *Pattern Recognition*, 22(4):359–365, 1989.

Tolerance vs Intolerance: How Affinity Defines Topology in an Idiotypic Network

Emma Hart[1], Hugues Bersini[2], and Francisco Santos[2]

[1] School of Computing,Napier University
e.hart@napier.ac.uk
[2] IRIDIA, Universite de Bruxelles
{bersini, fsantos}@ulb.ac.be

Abstract. Idiotypic network models of the immune system have long attracted interest in immunology as they offer a potential explanation for the maintenance of immunological memory. They also give a possible justification for the appearance of tolerance for a certain category of cells while maintaining immunization for the others. In this paper, we provide new evidence that the manner in which affinity is defined in an idiotypic network model imposes a definite topology on the connectivity of the potential idiotypic network that can emerge. The resulting topology is responsible for very different qualitative behaviour of the network. We show that using a 2D shape-space model with affinity based on complementary regions, a cluster-free topology results that clearly divides the space into tolerant and non-tolerant zones in which antigen are maintained or rejected respectively. On the other hand, using a 2D shape-space with an affinity function based on cell similarity, a highly clustered topology emerges in which there is no separation of the space into isolated tolerant and non-tolerant zones. Using a binary shape-space, both similar and complementary affinity measures also result in highly clustered networks. In the networks whose topologies exhibit high clustering, the tolerant and intolerant zones are so intertwined that the networks either reject all antigen or tolerate all antigen.

1   Introduction

Part of a Nobel lecture that Niels Jerne gave the 8th December 1984 in France [7] focusing on idiotypic networks was also more specifically concerned with the definition of affinity between two clones. In this lecture, he compared this affinity with the matching problem between pieces of sentence (for example referring to Chomsky's work on universal grammar). He suspected that the way this affinity would be defined might provide the final network of connected clones with very different properties. From very early papers of Varela and Coutinho dedicated to immune idiotypic networks [11,12], the in-depth attention paid to the topology of the connectivity is obvious.

Despite the lack of empirical data relating to the connectivity matrix which made it impossible to make any definitive statement on the analytical nature

H. Bersini and J. Carneiro (Eds.): ICARIS 2006, LNCS 4163, pp. 109–121, 2006.

of the topology, it is evident that Varela did not see the connectivity of this system as simply random like in Erds graph, but rather well structured and playing a key role in the functionality of the system. For instance, he discussed the topology of this connectivity as a possible cause or signature of some auto-immune diseases whose treatment was inspired by this new network perspective. He showed, using again very scant data, that people suffering from auto-immune disease could present a less densely connected network than healthy ones. This default in connectivity could decrease the network effect and thereby provoke homeostatic failure by perturbing the emergent regulatory effect of this network.

It is hard not to see in these studies (together with the critical quest for more experimental data), a pioneering approach to discovering the structure and the functionality of biological networks. Today, this is receiving renewed attention, and advancements in our knowledge and understanding are being made by a new generation of physicists enthusiastic about small-world effects and scale-free topology [1,9]. This paper carries on this quest with new and very unexpected findings.

1.1 Affinity: Complementarity or Similarity ?

The study of the effects of affinity between cells was facilitated by by the notion of shape-space introduced by [8] as a method for representing biological molecules and therefore capturing affinities between them. There have been numerous attempts to exploit this simple idea. The most typical interpretations (by both immunologists and computer scientists) utilise either a real-valued universe or bit-string universe to represent cells. Biologically, it is well established that two cells *recognise* or have an *affinity* with each other if the cells contain complementary shaped regions that can "fit" together — the "lock and key".

In a bit-string universe, it is straightforward to model the notion of a complementary matching. Hence, a number of affinity functions have been proposed which are physiologically plausible based on finding complementary matching regions between two strings [8]. For example, this could take the form of counting complementary bits or identifying contiguous regions of complementary bitwise matches along two strings. A study of the properties of a bit-string shape-space with affinity defined in terms of Hamming distance by Bersini in [3] suggested that this model can give rise to tolerant and intolerant zones in the shape-space, in which some antigens can be tolerated and others rejected, although this work has not since been replicated.

Complementarity can also be defined in a real-valued universe. Bersini [2] proposed a shape-space model implemented in 2D in which affinity was based upon complementary matching between cells by supposing that a cell exerts a domain of affinity in a zone which is situated in region obtained by reflecting the cell through the centre of symmetry of the space. This is consistent with the biological notion of a lock-and-key. [2] showed that this led to model in which regions of tolerance and intolerance emerged naturally from the dynamics of the idiotypic network, without need for pre-defining cells as being of a particular type. This model was later explored in greater depth by Hart in [6,5] which confirmed that these zones exists and further more showed that the shape of the zones, and therefore the subsequent properties of the network could be controlled by altering the shape of the domain of affinity exerted by a cell.

However, in recent years, as the AIS community has focussed it's attention more and more on producing tools to solve engineering problems, it is almost always the case that affinity in a real-valued shape-space has been re-defined in terms of *similarity*. Thus, for example, Timmis [10] introduces an idiotypic network model in which real-valued vectors represent B-Cells (for example, attributes of a data-set). In this discrete immune network, cells are connected simply if the Euclidean distance between two cells is less than some threshold they refer to as the *network affinity threshold*. This approach is now endemic in most practical applications of AIS that utilise vector representations. It seems surprising that such little attention has been paid to whether the use of complementarity of similarity has any effect on the dynamics of network formation and performance – in fact, it is even observed by [4] that "(surprisingly) it is not that important in most cases".

In this paper, we show that contrary to opinion, the definition of affinity imposes a very definite topology on an emerging network, which has subsequent important consequences for the properties that we can expect a network to exhibit. The paper is organised as follows. First, two different network models are introduced, in 2D and in a bit-string universe. We then show how the 2D model with complementary matching gives rise to tolerant and intolerant zones in the shape-space. This is then contrasted to the bit-string shape-space with both complementary and similar matching functions. Finally, we explain the anomalous results we find by analysing a 2D model with a similarity-based affinity function which can be visualised in a straightforward manner.

2   Network Models

In this section, we describe the 2D and binary network models in which we obtain our results.

2D Shape-space model. The following 2D shape-space model was first proposed by Bersini in [2] and subsequently adopted in further work by [6,5] in which the effect of the shape of the cell recognition region was explored. The shape-space is defined on a 2D integer-grid of dimension X, Y. A cell is specified by a position (x, y) on the grid. The potential network therefore consists of a possible $X \times Y$ cells. Cells can be considered as connected nodes on a graph if one cell is *stimulated* by another cell. The manner in which one cell stimulates another depends on the affinity function defined. If affinity is defined as complementary, then a cell A stimulates another B if B lies within a circular region of radius r centered on the point $(X - x, Y - y)$. On the other hand, if affinity is defined between *similar* cells, then A stimulates B if B lies within a circular region of radius r centered on A itself. Using these definitions, the following algorithm can be used to simulate the growth on an idiotypic network in which there are potential interactions between both cells and cells, and cells and antigens:

1. Generate at random a new antibody cell (x,y) and add with concentration 10.
2. (Possibly) add a new antigen with coordinates (x_a, y_a) and concentration 1000.
3. Calculate the stimulation S_{Ab} of each antibody cell
4. If $L < S_{Ab} < U$, increase the concentration of the cell by 1, otherwise decrease it by 1
5. Calculate the stimulation S_{Ag} of each antigen cell
6. If $L < S_{Ag}$, decrease the concentration of the antigen according to $S_{Ag}/(L * 100)$.
7. Remove any cells whose concentration has reached 0.

Stimulation of cells and antigens is calculated according to the equations below. For the complementary model, then Ab' and Ag' represent the complementary position of an antibody Ab or an antigen Ag, given by $(100 - x, 100 - y)$ for a grid of dimension 100x100. For the similarity model, then $Ab' = Ab$ and $Ag' = Ag$. The terms A_c and E_c represent the *concentration* of the antibody A and the antigen E respectively, and r represents the recognition radius of the cell and assumes a circular recognition region surrounding each complementary point.

$$S_{Ab} = \sum_{\text{antigens } A} A_c(r - ||A - Ab'||) + \sum_{\text{cells } E} E_c(r - ||E - Ab'||) \qquad (1)$$

$$S_{Ag} = \sum_{\text{cells } E} E_c(r - ||E - Ag'||) \qquad (2)$$

Binary Model. Except for the definition of clone identity, the binary model closely follows the previous description regarding the 2D-shape space. Instead of a point in a plane, each cell is now identified by a binary bit-string of N bits and the affinity a cell i exerts on another cell j is defined by the following equation

$$Affinity(i, j) = 100.C_i.(HD(i, j) - T)/(N_{bits} - T) \qquad (3)$$

with C_i being the concentration of the cell i, HD the hamming distance between the two bit-strings and T, the affinity threshold, playing an equivalent role of the parameter r in the 2D shape-space model. Like before, the total affinity (field) received by a cell i, S_i, is obtained by summing the affinity for all cells present in the system, given that this affinity can either be positive or null. Note that antibodies can be stimulated by antigens and antibodies, while antigens can only be stimulated by antibodies.

Keeping the system as resembling as possible to the 2D shape-space model, the algorithm is as follows:

1. Generate at random a new antibody cell (bit-string) having an affinity field between L and U, with concentration 75.
2. (Possibly) add a new antigen with concentration 100.
3. Calculate the stimulation S_{Ab} received by each antibody

4. If $L < S_{Ab} < U$, increase the concentration of the antibody by 1, otherwise decrease it by 1
5. Calculate the simulation S_{Ag} received by each antigen according
6. If $L < S_{Ag}$, decrease the concentration by 1.
7. Remove any cells whose concentration has reached 0.

3 Experimental Results

We first consider models with complementary affinity function. In 2D shape-space, in order to be consistent with work reported previously in [6,5] and by [2], experiments are performed on a grid of size 100x100, resulting in 10000 potential cells. The values of the lower limit L and upper limit U are fixed at $L = 100$ and $U = 10,000$. Previous work shows that interesting network behaviour is obtained when $r = 15$, therefore this value is used in these experiments unless otherwise indicated. (Below this value, percolation does not occur therefore a network does not emerge; at high r, the high suppressive effect of cells also does not result in a stable network). Antibody cells are added to the simulation with concentration 10; antigen cells are added with concentration 1000.

In the simulations with bit-strings, we consider strings of length 13, creating a space of 8192 possible cells, a potential repertoire size of similar size as the 2D shape-space. The lower limit L and upper limit U take respectively values 5000 and 10000. T is the affinity threshold (similar to r in the 2D shape-space model) and define the lower limit of complementarity to get stimulation. Regarding the idiotypic network as just a graph, we may say that a cell A is connected with a cell B, if the Hamming Distance between A and B is higher than this threshold T. A high T value imposes a system where an almost perfect complementarity is needed for stimulation, whereas a low T tolerates very poor complementarity for the network to pop up. Each combination of parameters gives rise to different stabilized networks. The size of the stable network will depend primarily on the Threshold level (T) and the size of the window (U and L). For low specificity (low T), the network exhibits a high average degree, which may result in a excess of stimulation depending on the Upper limit of the stimulation window. In this case of over-stimulation, the network is not able to pop up since the majority of nodes can hardly remain under the upper limit. The opposite can also happen. When almost perfect complementarity is needed for stimulation (very high T), the average degree of the network will be so low that nodes cannot be stimulated over the lower stimulation limit. So, for an idiotypic network to pop up, an optimal individual average stimulation value must be found, which depends on a balance between the cells' initial concentration, upper and lower limit of the stimulation window, and the affinity threshold.

As reported in previously, the 2D shape-space model results in the physical space being clearly separated by a line of sustained antibody cells into two distinct regions. In one of these regions, antigens are tolerated; in the other all antigens are suppressed. The position of these zones, and the resultant ability of cells to be maintained by the network, emerges only from the network dynamics.

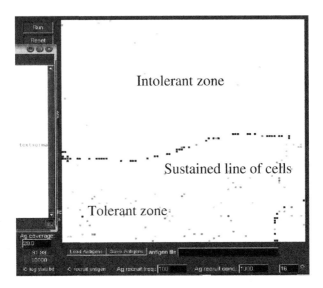

Fig. 1. Snapshot of a network obtained after 10000 iterations of a network in 2D shape-space with a complementary affinity function

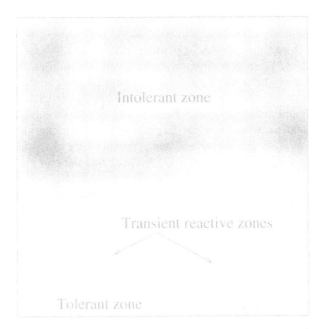

Fig. 2. Field experienced by a cell occupying each potential site of the grid following emergence of the network

There is no need to pre-label cells as being of a particular type, e.g antigen or antibody. Figure 1 illustrates an example of a network obtained using this model after 10,000 iterations. Although the two zones are easily seen, we can obtain

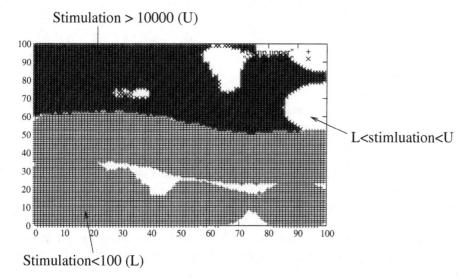

Stimulation > 10000 (U)

L<stimluation<U

Stimulation<100 (L)

Fig. 3. Stimulation observed at potential site of the grid following emergence of the network

more insight into the model by examining the field that would be received by a hypothetical cell occupying each of the potential sites on the grid given the existing network. This field is calculated according to equation 1. Concentration of all cells is assumed to be 1 to make visualisation of the field easier (without loss of generality). The result is illustrated in figure 2, in which darker shading indicates higher field, and vice-versa. The top half of the diagram clearly shows a zone in which all potential sites experience some field; the strength of the field itself varies throughout the zone. In the lower half of the diagram, the majority of sites experience no field at all (antibodies cannot survive in the complementary zone) therefore are tolerant to any cell. Transient reactive regions occur in this region; due to the nature of the algorithm, cells are continuously added to the grid and survive for a minimum of 10 iterations. If these cells occur in the intolerant zone, they temporarily stimulate cells in the lower half — observe however that the shading indicates the reactivity is very low at these sites. The effect the field has on survival of potential cells is illustrated in figure 3 for antibody cells. This figure does account of the concentration of cells at iteration 10000 when calculating stimulation at each site: the upper zone shows sites in which the total stimulation received at a site is greater than 10000 (therefore concentration of a cell at that site decreases). The marked sites in the lower zones represent sites at which the stimulation received at the site is less that 100 which also results in a concentration decrease. Sites at which nothing is marked indicate those places in which the stimulation falls between the lower and upper limits and therefore the concentration of cells at these sites rises. The sites therefore occur along the boundary lines of the zones, and in the transient regions. For antigens, their concentration is decreased if their total stimulation exceeds the lower limit L.

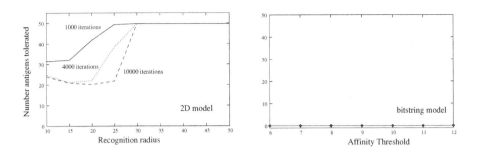

Fig. 4. Comparison of antigen tolerance in 2D and bitstring models

However, as their concentration is decreased according to $stimulation/(100*L)$, if $L = 100$ then in practice, an actual decrease in concentration is only observed when the total stimulation exceeds 10000 (concentration takes integer values only in the model). Therefore, antigens will be rejected from the exactly the same upper zones of the diagram shown in the previous antibody figure where stimulation $> U$.

The shape of the boundary separating the regions, and the resulting ability of the network to reject or tolerate antigen is dependent on the radius of the recognition region used. The left hand side of figure 4 illustrates the number of antigens tolerated by the network when a set of 50 randomly generated antigens are presented to the network at iteration i and evolution continued for a

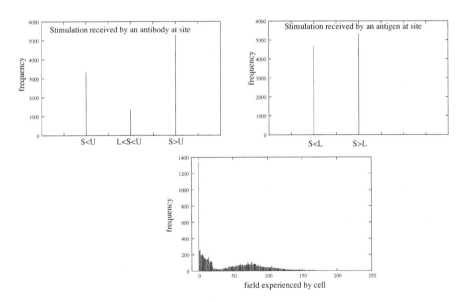

Fig. 5. Field experienced by cells occupying each potential site of the grid following emergence of the network. In the upper diagrams,S=stimulation, L=lower limit (100) and U=upper limit (10000). Field refers to stimulation calculated using constant concentration of 1.

further 2000 iterations. This shows a smooth transition in the number of tolerated antigen as r is increased. At large r, all antigens are tolerated by the network. This is due to the fact that at extreme values of r, the recognition region covers this entire grid; thus every cell stimulates every other cell, resulting in very large value of stimulation which cause any cell added to the network to be suppressed. Antigen cells are tolerated as they are added at higher concentration than antibody cells, therefore outlive any antibody cell that may potentially kill them.

The right hand diagram of figure 4 shows results obtained using a bit-string model using a complementary affinity function. Surprisingly and in contrast with the 2D shape-space, no antigens are tolerated by the network.

4   Why do the Models in Binary and 2D Shape-Space not Concur?

The results in the previous section have shown that surprising results are obtained when comparing a 2D shape-space to a bit-string shape-space. In an attempt to explain this, we examine the distribution of the field received at

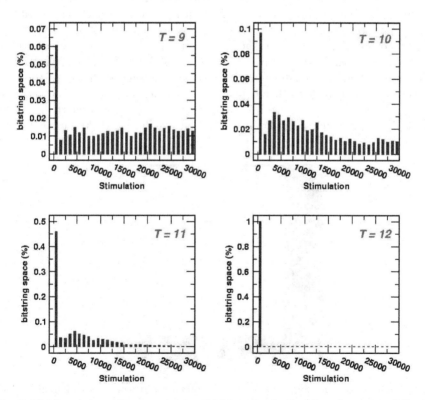

Fig. 6. Field experienced by every potential bit-string in the bit-string space, following emergence of the network, for four different affinity thresholds.

each potential site in both the bit-string and 2D universes. If the space is really separated into tolerant and intolerant zones, then we expect to find a distribution in which a large number of the cells receive little or no field, and the remainder receive high field. Figures 5 and 6 illustrate the result for both shape-spaces. The histograms obtained show very similar distributions — in both cases show a power-law distribution (e.g $y = x^{-a}$) is observed. For the 2D shape-space, as expected, a large number of sites receive no field whatsoever. The remainder receive a spread of field-values, indicating their reactivity. Thus, the different shape-spaces appear to *both* support the notion that tolerant and non-tolerant regions should be observed in the shape space. Yet we have just shown in the previous section that this is not the case! In the next section, we offer an explanation for this effect.

5   Complementarity Is not the Same as Similarity

An explanation for the inability of the networks obtained in bit-string shape space can be gleaned by first considering the behaviour of a network in 2D shape-space with an affinity function based on *similarity*. Consider figure 7 which shows a snapshot of a network obtained after 10000 iterations of a network in which cells a and b stimulate each other if b lies within a recognition region centered on a. Contrast this picture with the snap-shot of the network obtained with a complementary affinity function shown in figure 1. There is now no separation of the physical space into distinct zones; rather we see a "Jackson Pollock" like distribution of cells throughout the shape-space. Figure 8 illustrates the field now received by hypothetical cells placed at each potential site in the network, and those sites at which the total stimulation received is greater than 10,000. The field is now much more homogeneous across the network, caused by the

Fig. 7. Snapshot of a network obtained after 10000 iterations of a network in 2D shape-space with a similarity affinity function

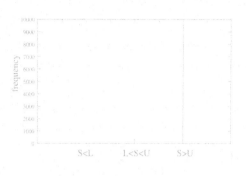

Fig. 8. Examination of field and stimulation received at potential network sites for 2D shape-space with similarity based affinity

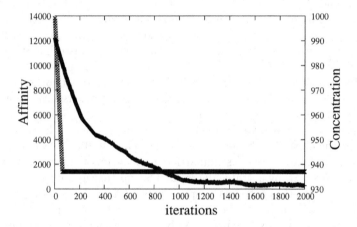

Fig. 9. Stimulation and Concentration of an antigen added to a network evolved using a similarity based affinity function

intertwining of tolerant and intolerant regions which averages out the total field received at any site. Almost every site appears to be potentially reactive. One therefore might expect the network to be intolerant of any antigens at all — simulation and experimentation proves the opposite. In fact, the network is tolerant of *all* antigens presented. Although at first glance surprising, the result is clearly explained: figure 9 plots the stimulation and concentration received by a single antigen randomly added to the network for 2000 iterations. Initially, the stimulation received by the antigen is high and it's concentration therefore decreases. This in turn results in a decrease in the stimulation of the antigen as the antigen now stimulates corresponding antibody cells less – therefore its stimulation (and concentration) continue to decrease. However, when the stimulation of the cell is reduced to below 10000, this is no longer sufficient to cause any further decrease in concentration of the cell (recall that concentration decreases by an amount $stimulation/(100 * L)$). Therefore, at this point, although its stimulation continues to decrease, it's concentration remains constant from this point onwards.

We can now offer an explanation for the observed results based on the clustering observed between cells that arises from the network topology. In a bit-string space, the networks that emerge will necessarily have high cluster coefficient due to the nature of the affinity function, whether it is defined in a complementary or similar manner: if a interacts with b which interacts with c, there is a good chance that a can also interact with c due to the affinity measure which allows such connections via a series of different matching sequences. Consider a trivial example in a 3-bit universe; if the affinity function is such that cells with 2-mismatches can connect, then $a = 000$ can connect to $b = 110$ which connects to $c = 011$ which in turn connects back to $a = 000$. Thus, any antigen will always find itself with two kinds of responding antibodies closely located in the space, one in high and the other in low concentration. At the end, the response of the network to any antigen intrusion just depends on the initial concentration of this antigen and therefore no longer on the position of this antigen. The space has been uniformly filled up with all kinds of antibodies. No clustering of antibodies with similar concentration would be possible. Similarly, using a similarity affinity function in the 2D model, we also obtain highly clustered networks, in which it is possible to form the triangle $a - b - c$, therefore we observe the same effects as just described for th binary network.

In 2D shape-space using a complementary affinity function however, then it is clear that the cluster-coefficient is necessarily close to 0 and no clustering can occur — if a stimulates b and b stimulates c, then c cannot stimulate a. This can easily be seen by drawing a simple diagram. The only exception to this is for cells located very close to the centre of the space, where $(X-x, Y-y)$ is approximately equal to (x, y), and therefore the triangle $a - b - c$ can occur for some values. The network topology therefore prevents clusters, but facilitates the emergence of chains of cells which are able to separate the space into distinct regions. This reasoning is confirmed by calculating the cluster coefficients of the networks pictured in figures 1 and 7 which exhibit cluster coefficients of 0.012 and 0.566 respectively.

6   Conclusion

We have shown the role played by the potential network (the network defined by all possible cells and all possible interactions) in defining whether or not it is possible for tolerant and intolerant zones to co-exist in a network. If the cluster coefficient of a network is zero (or close to 0), then it is possible for two distinct zones to co-exist. Although since the origin of networks in immunology (essentially with idiotypic networks) the topology has always raised a lot of interest, this is the first time it has been shown how this topology influences an essential capability of the network: to separate zones of tolerance from immunisation zones. While previous authors have independently decided to make the choice between adopting a binary shape space or a 2D one, this paper intends to show that this choice is far from neutral.

References

1. L.A. Barabasi and Albert.A. Emergence of scaling in random network. *Science*, 286:509–512, 1999.
2. H. Bersini. Self-assertion vs self-recogntion: A tribute to francisco varela. In *Proceedings of ICARIS 2002*, 2002.
3. H. Bersini. Revisiting idiotypic immune networks. In W. Banzhaf and *et al*, editors, *Advances in Artificial Life, 7th European Conference, Proceedings of ECAL 2003*, Lecture Notes in Computer Science, pages 164–174. Springer, 2003.
4. S. Garret. An epitope is not a paratope: Implications for immune network models and clonal selection. In J. Timmis, P. Bentley, and E. Hart, editors, *Proceedings of the 2nd International Conference on Artificial Immune Systems, ICARIS02*, volume 2787 of *Lecture Notes in Computer Science*, pages 217–228. Springer, 2003.
5. E Hart. Not all balls are round: An investigation of alternative recognition-region shapes. In *Artificial Immune Systems, Proceedings of ICARIS 2005*, pages 29–42, 2005.
6. E. Hart and P. Ross. The impact of the shape of antibody recognition regions on the emergence of idiotypic networks. *International Journal of Unconventional Computing*, 2005.
7. N. Jerne. The generative grammar of the immune system. Nobel Lecture, Dec 8th. Chateau de Bellevue, France, 1984.
8. A.S. Perelson. Immune network theory. *Immunological Reviews*, 10:5–36, 1989.
9. R.V. Sole, R. Pastor-Satorras, E. Smith, and T. Kepler. A model of large-scale proteome evolution. *Adv. In Complex Systems*, 5:43–54, 2002.
10. Jon Timmis and Mark Neal. A resource limited artificial immune system for data analyis s. *Knowledge Based Systems*, (3-4):121–130, 2001.
11. F. Varela and A. Coutinho. Second generation immune network. *Immunology Today*, 12(5):159–166, 1991.
12. F. Varela, A. Coutinho, B. Dupire, and N. Vaz. Cognitive networks : Immune, neural and otherwise. *Theoretical Immunology, Series on the Science of Complexity*, 2:359–375, 1988.

On Permutation Masks in Hamming Negative Selection

Thomas Stibor[1], Jonathan Timmis[2], and Claudia Eckert[1]

[1] Department of Computer Science
Darmstadt University of Technology
{stibor, eckert}@sec.informatik.tu-darmstadt.de
[2] Departments of Electronics and Computer Science
University of York, Heslington, York
jtimmis@cs.york.ac.uk

Abstract. Permutation masks were proposed for reducing the number of holes in Hamming negative selection when applying the r-contiguous or r-chunk matching rule. Here, we show that (randomly determined) permutation masks re-arrange the semantic representation of the underlying data and therefore shatter self-regions. As a consequence, detectors do not cover areas around self regions, instead they cover randomly distributed elements across the space. In addition, we observe that the resulting holes occur in regions where actually no self regions should occur.

1 Introduction

Applying negative selection for anomaly detection problems has been undertaken extensively [1,2,3,4]. Anomaly detection problems, also termed one-class classification, can be considered as a type of pattern classification problem, where one tries to describe a single class of objects, and distinguish that from all other possible objects. More formally, one-class classification is a problem of generating decision boundaries that can successfully distinguish between the normal and anomalous class. Hamming negative selection is an immune-inspired technique for one-class classification problems. Recent results, however, have revealed several problems concerning algorithm complexity of generating detectors [5,6,7] and determining the proper matching threshold to allow for the generation of correct generalization regions [8]. In this paper we investigate an extended technique for Hamming negative selection: permutation masks. Permutation masks are immunologically motivated by lymphocyte diversity. Lymphocyte diversity is an important property of the immune system, as it enables a lymphocyte to reacting to many substances, i.e. it induces diversity and generalization. This kind of generalization process inspired Hofmeyr [3,9] to propose a similar counterpart for use in Hamming negative selection. Hofmeyr introduced permutation masks in order to reduce the number of undetectable elements. It was argued that permutation masks could be useful for covering the non-self space efficiently when varying the representation by means of permutation masks (see Fig. 1).

H. Bersini and J. Carneiro (Eds.): ICARIS 2006, LNCS 4163, pp. 122–135, 2006.

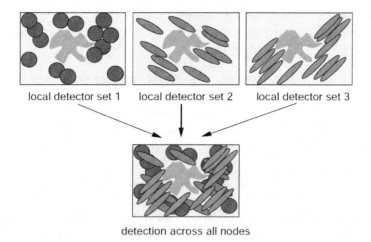

local detector set 1   local detector set 2   local detector set 3

detection across all nodes

Fig. 1. Visualized concept of varying representations by means of permutation masks to reduce the number of undetectable elements. The light gray shaded area in the middle represents the self regions (normal class in terms of anomaly detection). The dark gray shaded shapes represent areas which are covered by detectors with varying representations. The white area represents the non-self space (anomalous class in terms of anomaly detection). This figure is taken from [9].

In the following two sections we briefly introduce the standard negative selection inspired anomaly detection technique.

2   Artificial Immune System

An artificial immune system (AIS) [10] is a paradigm inspired by the immune system and are used for solving computational and information processing problems. An AIS can be described, and developed, using a framework [10] which contains the following basic elements:

- A representation for the artificial immune elements.
- A set of functions, which quantifies the interactions of the artificial immune elements (affinity).
- A set of algorithms which based on observed immune principles and methods.

This 3-step abstraction (representation, affinity, algorithm) for using the AIS framework is discussed in the following sections.

2.1   Hamming Shape-Space

The notion of *shape-space* was introduced by Perelson and Oster [11] and allows a quantitative affinity description between immune components known as antibodies and antigens. More precisely, a shape-space is a metric space with an associated distance (affinity) function.

The Hamming shape-space U_l^Σ is built from all elements of length l over a finite alphabet Σ.

Example 1.

$$\Sigma = \{0,1\} \qquad\qquad \Sigma = \{A,C,G,T\}$$

$$000\ldots000 \qquad\qquad AAA\ldots AAA$$
$$000\ldots001 \qquad\qquad AAA\ldots AAC$$
$$\ldots\ldots\ldots \qquad\qquad \ldots\ldots\ldots$$
$$\ldots\ldots\ldots \qquad\qquad \ldots\ldots\ldots$$
$$\underbrace{111\ldots111}_{l} \qquad\qquad \underbrace{TTT\ldots TTT}_{l}$$

In example 1 two Hamming shape-spaces for different alphabets and alphabet sizes are presented. On the left, a Hamming shape-space defined over the binary alphabet of length l is shown. On the right, a Hamming shape-space defined over the DNA bases alphabet (Adenine, Cytosine, Guanine, Thymine) is presented.

2.2   R-Contiguous and R-Chunk Matching

A formal description of antigen-antibody interactions not only requires a representation (encoding), but also appropriate affinity functions. Percus et. al [12] proposed the *r-contiguous* matching rule for abstracting the affinity of an antibody needed to recognize an antigen.

Definition 1. *An element $e \in U_l^\Sigma$ with $e = e_1 e_2 \ldots e_l$ and detector $d \in U_l^\Sigma$ with $d = d_1 d_2 \ldots d_l$, match with r-contiguous rule, if a position p exists where $e_i = d_i$ for $i = p, \ldots, p+r-1$, $p \leq l-r+1$.*

Informally, two elements, with the *same length*, match if at least r contiguous characters are identical.

An additional rule, which subsumes[1] the r-contiguous rule, is the r-chunk matching rule [13].

Definition 2. *An element $e \in U_l^\Sigma$ with $e = e_1 e_2 \ldots e_l$ and detector $d \in \mathbb{N} \times D_r^\Sigma$ with $d = (p \mid d_1 d_2 \ldots d_r)$, for $r \leq l$, $p \leq l-r+1$ match with r-chunk rule, if a position p exists where $e_i = d_i$ for $i = p, \ldots, p+r-1$.*

Informally, element e and detector d match if a position p exists, where all characters of e and d are identical over a sequence of length r.

We use the term *subsume* as any r-contiguous detector can be represented as a set of r-chunk detectors. This implicates that any set of elements from U_l^Σ that can be recognized with a set of r-contiguous detectors can also be recognized with some set of r-chunk detectors. The converse statement is surprisingly *not* true, i.e. there exists a set of elements from U_l^Σ that can be recognized with a set

---

[1] Include within a larger entity.

of r-chunk detectors, but *not* recognized with any set of r-contiguous detectors. We demonstrate this converse statement on an example, a formal approach is provided in [14].

Example 2. Given a Hamming shape-space $U_5^{\{0,1\}}$, a set $S = \{01011, 01100, 01110, 10010, 10100, 11100\}$ of self elements and a detector length $r = 3$.

All possible generable r-contiguous detectors for the complementary space $U_5^{\{0,1\}} \setminus S$ are $D_{r-contiguous} = \{00000, 00001, 00111, 11000, 11001\}$.

All possible generable r-chunk detectors are
$D_{r-chunk} = \{0|000, 0|001, 0|110, 1|000, 1|011, 1|100, 2|000, 2|001, 2|101, 2|111\}$.

The set $D_{r-contiguous}$ recognizes the elements
$\mathcal{P}_1 = U_5^{\{0,1\}} \setminus (S \cup \{01010, 01101, 10011, 10101, 11101, 11110\})$,
whereas the set $D_{r-chunk}$ recognizes the elements
$\mathcal{P}_2 = U_5^{\{0,1\}} \setminus (S \cup \{10011, 01010, 11110\})$. Hence $|\mathcal{P}_1| \leq |\mathcal{P}_2|$.

Example 2 shows, that the set of r-chunk detectors $D_{r-chunk}$ recognizes more elements of $U_5^{\{0,1\}}$ than the set of r-contiguous detectors $D_{r-contiguous}$ and therefore the r-chunk matching rule subsumes the r-contiguous rule.

3   Hamming Negative Selection

Forrest et al. [1] proposed a (generic[2]) negative selection algorithm for detecting changes in data streams. Given a shape-space $U = S_{seen} \cup S_{unseen} \cup N$ which is partitioned into training data S_{seen} and testing data $(S_{seen} \cup S_{unseen} \cup N)$. The basic idea is to generate a number of detectors for the complementary space $U \setminus S_{seen}$ and then to apply these detectors to classify new (unseen) data as self (no data manipulation) or non-self (data manipulation).

Algorithm 1. Generic Negative Selection Algorithm

---

input : S_{seen} = set of self seen elements
output: D = set of generated detectors
begin
    1. Define self as a set S_{seen} of elements in shape-space U
    2. Generate a set D of detectors, such that each fails to match any element in S_{seen}
    3. Monitor (seen and unseen) data $\delta \subseteq U$ by continually matching the detectors in D against δ.
end

The generic negative selection algorithm can be used with arbitrary shape-spaces and affinity functions. In this paper, we focus on Hamming negative

---

[2] Applicable to arbitrary shape-spaces.

selection, i.e. the negative selection algorithm which operates on Hamming shape-space and employs the r-chunk matching rule and permutation masks.

3.1   Holes as Generalization Regions

The r-contiguous and r-chunk matching rule induce undetectable elements — termed holes (see Fig. 2). In general, all matching rules which match over a certain element length induce holes. This statement is theoretically investigated in [15,14] and empirically explored[3] in [16]. Holes are some[4] elements from $U \setminus S_{seen}$, i.e. elements not seen during the training phase. For these elements, no detectors can be generated and therefore they cannot be recognized and classified as non-self elements. However, the term holes is not an accurate expression, as holes are *necessary* to generalize beyond the training set. A detector set which generalizes well ensures that seen and unseen self elements are *not* recognized by any detector, whereas all other elements are recognized by detectors and classified as non-self. Hence, holes must represent unseen self elements; or in other words, holes must represent *generalization regions* in the shape-space U_l^Σ.

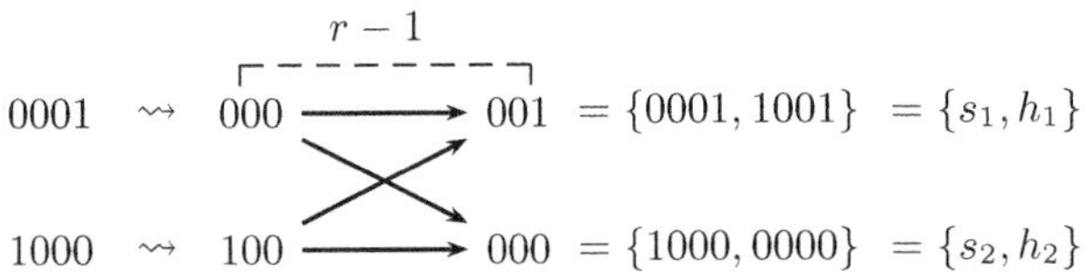

$$
\begin{array}{ccc}
0001 & \rightsquigarrow & 000 \xrightarrow{\quad r-1 \quad} 001 = \{0001, 1001\} = \{s_1, h_1\} \\
1000 & \rightsquigarrow & 100 \xrightarrow{\qquad} 000 = \{1000, 0000\} = \{s_2, h_2\}
\end{array}
$$

Fig. 2. Self elements $s_1 = 0001$ and $s_2 = 1000$ induce holes h_1, h_2, i.e. elements which are not detectable with r-contiguous and r-chunk matching rules for $r = 3$

4   Permutation Masks

Permutation masks were proposed by Hofmeyr [3,9] for reducing the number of holes. A permutation mask is a bijective mapping π that specifies a reordering for all elements $a_i \in U_l^\Sigma$, i.e. $a_1 \to \pi(a_1), a_2 \to \pi(a_2), \ldots, a_{|\Sigma|^l} \to \pi(a_{|\Sigma|^l})$. More formally, a permutation $\pi \in S_n$, where $n \in \mathbb{N}$, can be written as a $2 \times n$ matrix, where the first row are elements $a_1, a_2, \ldots, a_n$ and the second row the new arrangement $\pi(a_1), \pi(a_2), \ldots, \pi(a_n)$, i.e.

$$
\begin{pmatrix}
a_1 & a_2 & \cdots & a_n \\
\pi(a_1) & \pi(a_2) & \cdots & \pi(a_n)
\end{pmatrix}
$$

For the sake of simplicity we will use the equivalent *cycle notation* [17] to specify a permutation. A permutation in cycle notation can be written as $(b_1 \, b_2 \, \ldots \, b_n)$ and means "b_1 becomes b_2, ..., b_{n-1} becomes b_n, b_n becomes b_1. In addition, this notation allows the identity and non-cyclic mappings, for instance $(b_1) \, (b_2 \, b_3) \, (b_4)$ means : $b_1 \to b_1$, $b_2 \to b_3$, $b_3 \to b_2$ and $b_4 \to b_4$.

---

[3] Hamming, r-contiguous, r-chunk and Rogers & Tanimoto matching rule.
[4] The number of holes is controlled by the matching threshold r.

4.1   Permutation Masks for Inducing Other Holes

As explained above, a permutation mask is a bijective mapping and therefore can *increase* or *reduce* the number of holes — there also exists permutation masks which results in self elements which neither increase nor reduce the number of holes. The simplest examples is the identity permutation mask.

For reducing the number of holes, π must be chosen at an appropriate value, and a certain number of detectors must be generable.

Reconsider the self elements $s_1 = 0001$, $s_2 = 1000$ in figure (2). One can see that elements $h_1 = 1001$ and $h_2 = 0000$ are not detectable by the r-contiguous and r-chunk matching rule. However, after applying the permutation mask $\pi_0 = (1\,2\,4\,3)$, i.e.

$$\pi_0(s_1) = 0010, \quad \pi_0(s_2) = 0100$$

one can verify (see Fig. 3) that holes h_1, h_2 are eliminated.

$$\pi_0(0001) \;\rightsquigarrow\; 001 \overset{r-1}{\xrightarrow{\hspace{2cm}}} 010 \;=\{0010\} \;=\{\pi_0(s_1)\}$$

$$\pi_0(1000) \;\rightsquigarrow\; 010 \xrightarrow{\hspace{2cm}} 100 \;=\{0100\} \;=\{\pi_0(s_2)\}$$

Fig. 3. The permutated self elements $\pi_0(s_1)$ and $\pi_0(s_2)$ induce no holes by r-contiguous and r-chunk matching rule

However, it is also clear that $(1\,2\,4\,3)\,(2\,4\,3\,1)$, $(4\,3\,1\,2)$ and $(3\,1\,2\,4)$ represent the same permutation, namely the cycle permutation of $\pi_0 = (1\,2\,4\,3)$. Specifically, all cycle permutations of an arbitrary selected π leads, in terms of the r-chunk and r-contiguous matching, to the same holes.

On the other hand, there do exist permutation masks which do not reduce holes, i.e. $\pi(s_i) = s_j$, for $i \neq j$ and self elements $s_1, s_2, \ldots, s_{|S|}$. An example is the permutation $\pi_1 = (14)(2)(3)$, as $\pi_1(s_1) = s_2$ and $\pi_1(s_2) = s_1$.

Furthermore, as mentioned above, a permutation mask can also increase the number of holes. In our subsequent presented experiments this is illustrated for instance in figures[5] 5(c) and 5(d).

5   Permutation Masks Experiments in Hamming Negative Selection

In [18,8] results were presented which demonstrated the coherence between the matching threshold r and generalization regions when the r-chunk matching rule in Hamming negative selection is applied. Recall, as holes are not detectable by any detector, holes must represent unseen self elements, or in other words holes must represent generalization regions. In the following experiment we will investigate how randomly determined permutation masks will influence the occurrence

---

[5] With and without permutation mask.

of holes (generalization regions). More specifically, we will empirically explore if holes occur in suitable generalization regions when a randomly determined permutation mask is applied. Finally, we explore empirically whether randomly determined permutation masks reduce the number of holes.

Stibor et al. [8] have shown in prior experiments that the matching threshold r is a crucial parameter and is inextricably linked to the input data being analyzed. However, permutation masks were not considered in [8]. In order to study the impact of permutation masks on generalization regions, and to obtain comparable results to previously performed experiments [8], we will utilize the same mapping function and data set. Furthermore, we will explore the impact of permutation masks on an additional data set (see Fig. 4).

5.1 Experiments Settings

The first self data set contains 1000 Gaussian ($\mu = 0.5, \sigma = 0.1$) generated points $p = (x, y) \in [0, 1]^2$. Each point p is mapped to a binary string

$$\underbrace{b_1, b_2, \ldots, b_8,}_{b_x} \underbrace{b_9, b_{10}, \ldots, b_{16},}_{b_y}$$

where the first 8 bits encode the integer x-value $i_x := \lceil 255 \cdot x + 0.5 \rceil$ and the last 8 bits the integer y-value $i_y := \lceil 255 \cdot y + 0.5 \rceil$, i.e.

$$[0, 1]^2 \rightarrow (i_x, i_y) \in [1, \ldots, 256 \times 1, \ldots, 256] \rightarrow (b_x, b_y) \in U_8^{\{0,1\}} \times U_8^{\{0,1\}}$$

This mapping is proposed in [18] and also utilized in [8] — it satisfies a straightforward visualization of real-valued encoded points in Hamming negative selection. The second data set (termed banana data set) is depicted in figure (4) and is a commonly used benchmark for anomaly detection problems [19]. The banana data set is taken from [20] and consists of 5300 points in total. These points are partitioned in two different classes, $\mathcal{C}_+$ which represents points inside the "banana-shape" and class $\mathcal{C}_-$ which contains points outside of the "banana-shape". In this experiment we have taken points from $\mathcal{C}_+$ only for simulating one self-region (similar to figure 1). More specifically, we have normalized with *min-max* method all points from $\mathcal{C}_+$ to the unitary square $[0, 1]^2$. We then sampled 1000 random points from $\mathcal{C}_+$ and mapped those sampled points to bit-strings of length 16.

As the r-chunk matching rule subsumes the r-contiguous rule, i.e. recognize at least as many elements as the r-contiguous matching rule (see section 2.2), we have performed all experiments with the r-chunk matching rule. Furthermore, as proposed in [3,9] we have *randomly* determined permutation masks $\pi \in S_{16}$.

5.2 Experimental Results

In figures (5,6,7,8) experimental results are presented. The black points represent the 1000 sampled self elements, the white points are holes, and the grey points represent areas which are covered by r-chunk detectors. It is not surprising that

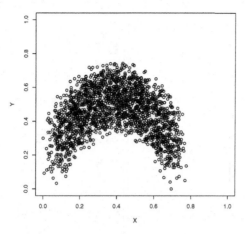

Fig. 4. Banana data set (points from class $\mathcal{C}_+$), *min-max* normalized to $[0, 1]^2$. In an perfect case (error-less detection), the r-chunk detectors should cover regions outside the "banana" shape. The region within the "banana" shape is the generalization region and should consists of undetectable elements, i.e. holes and self elements.

for both data sets, holes occur as they should in generalization regions when $8 \leq r \leq 10$. This phenomena is discussed and explained in [8]. To summarize results from [8], a detector matching length which is not at least as long as the semantical representation of the underlying data — in this case 8 bits for x and y coordinates — results in incorrect generalization regions.

What is more interesting though, is the observation that a (randomly determined) permutation mask shatters the semantical representation of the underlying data (see Fig. 5-8 (b,d,f,h,j,l,n,p,r,t)) and therefore, holes are randomly distributed across the space instead of being concentrated inside or close to self regions. This observation also means that detectors are not covering areas around the self regions, instead they recognize elements which are also randomly distributed across the space. Furthermore one can see that the number of holes — when applying permutation masks (see Fig. 5-8 (b,d,f,h,j,l,n,p,r,t)) — is in some cases significantly higher than without permutation masks (see Fig. 5-8 (a,c,d,e,g,i,k,m,q,s)). This observation could be explained with the previous observation, that permutation masks distort the underlying data and therefore shatter self regions. As a consequence the underlying data is transformed into a collection of random chunks. For randomly determined self elements, Stibor et al. [6] showed that the number of holes increase exponentially for $r := l \to 0$.

Of course this shattering effect is linked very strongly to the mapping function employed. However it is clear that each permutation mask — except the identity permutation — semantically (more or less) distort the data. Furthermore, we believe that finding a permutation mask which does not significantly distort the semantical representation of the data may be computational intractable[6].

---

[6] In the worst-case, one have to check all $n!$ permutations of S_n.

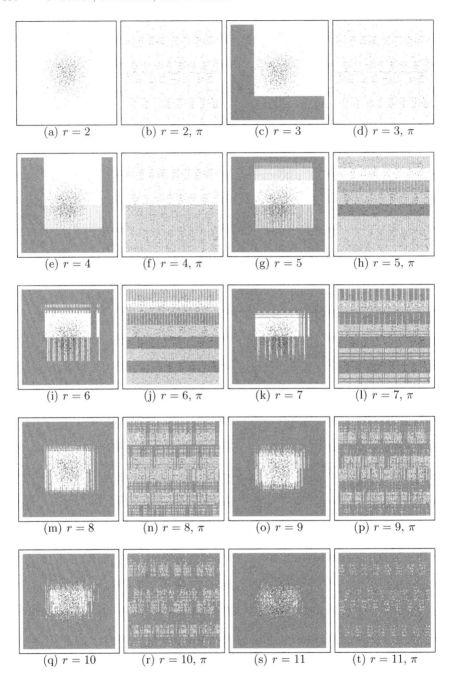

Fig. 5. A visualized simulation run, with 1000 random (self) points generated by a Gaussian distribution with mean $\mu = 0.5$ and variance $\sigma = 0.1$. The grey shaded area is covered by the generated r-chunk detectors, the white areas are holes. The black points are self elements. The captions which include a "π" are simulations results with the randomly determined permutation mask $\pi \in S_{16}$.

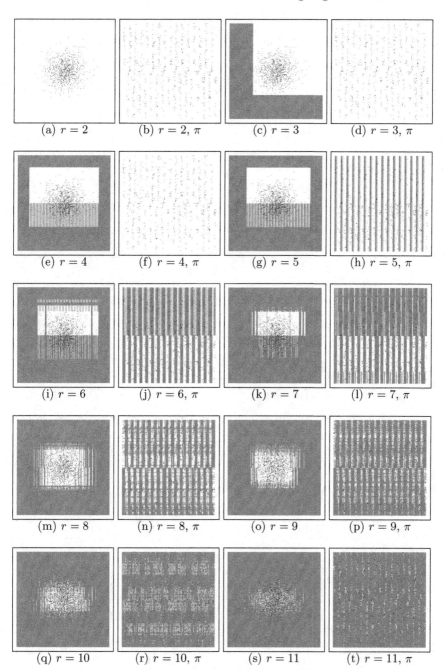

Fig. 6. An additional visualized simulation run, with 1000 random (self) points generated by a Gaussian distribution with mean $\mu = 0.5$ and variance $\sigma = 0.1$. The grey shaded area is covered by the generated r-chunk detectors, the white areas are holes. The black points are self elements. The captions which include a "π" are simulations results with the randomly determined permutation mask $\pi \in S_{16}$.

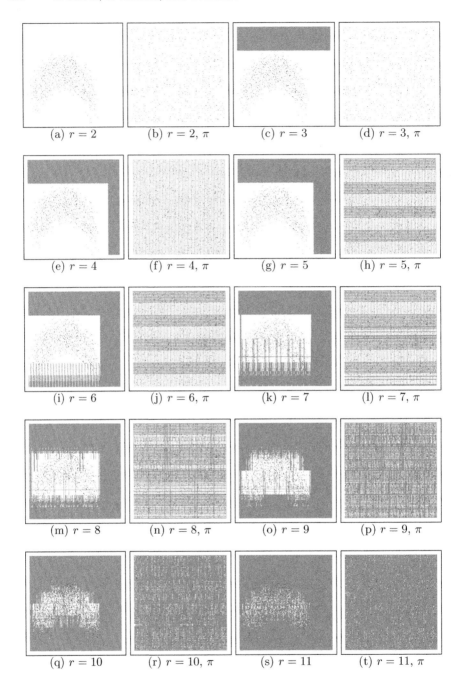

Fig. 7. A visualized simulation run, 1000 randomly sampled (self) points from banana data set. The grey shaded area is covered by the generated r-chunk detectors, the white areas are holes. The black points are self elements. The captions which include a "π" are simulations results with the randomly determined permutation mask $\pi \in S_{16}$.

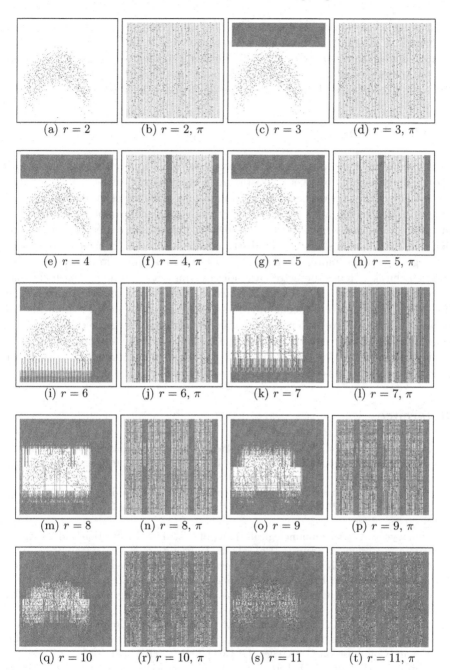

Fig. 8. An additional visualized simulation run, with 1000 randomly sampled (self) points from banana data set. The grey shaded area is covered by the generated r-chunk detectors, the white areas are holes. The black points are self elements. The captions which include a "π" are simulations results with the randomly determined permutation mask $\pi \in S_{16}$.

In order to obtain representative results, we performed 50 simulation runs, each with a randomly determined permutation mask for both data sets. Due to the lack of space to present all 50 simulation runs, we have selected two simulation results at random for each data set (see Fig. 5,6,7,8). The remaining simulation results are closely comparable to results in figures (5,6,7,8).

6   Conclusion

Lymphocyte diversity is an important property of the immune system for recognizing a huge amount of diverse substances. This property has been abstracted in terms of permutation masks in the Hamming negative selection detection technique. In this paper we have shown that (randomly determined) permutation masks in Hamming negative selection, distort the semantic meaning of the underlying data — the shape of the distribution — and as a consequence shatter self regions. Furthermore, the distorted data is transformed into a collection of random chunks. Hence, detectors are not covering areas around the self regions, instead they are randomly distributed across the space. Moreover the resulting holes (the generalization) occur in regions where actually no self regions should occur. Additionally we believe that it is computational infeasible to find permutation masks which correctly capture the semantical representation of the data — if one exists at all. We conclude that the use of permutation masks casts doubt on the appropriateness of abstracting diversity in Hamming negative selection.

References

1. Forrest, S., Perelson, A.S., Allen, L., Cherukuri, R.: Self-nonself discrimination in a computer. In: Proceedings of the 1994 IEEE Symposium on Research in Security and Privacy, IEEE Computer Society Press (1994)
2. Dasgupta, D., Forrest, S.: Novelty detection in time series data using ideas from immunology. In: Proceedings of the 5th International Conference on Intelligent Systems. (1996)
3. Hofmeyr, S.A.: An Immunological Model of Distributed Detection and its Application to Computer Security. PhD thesis, University of New Mexico (1999)
4. Singh, S.: Anomaly detection using negative selection based on the r-contiguous matching rule. In: Proceedings of the 1st International Conference on Artificial Immune Systems (ICARIS), Unversity of Kent at Canterbury Printing Unit (2002) 99–106
5. Kim, J., Bentley, P.J.: An evaluating of negative selection in an artificial immune system for network intrusion detection. In: Proceedings of the Genetic and Evolutionary Computation Conference, GECCO-2001. (2001) 1330–1337
6. Stibor, T., Timmis, J., Eckert, C.: On the appropriateness of negative selection defined over hamming shape-space as a network intrusion detection system. In: Congress On Evolutionary Computation – CEC 2005, IEEE Press (2005) 995–1002
7. Stibor, T., Timmis, J., Eckert, C.: The link between r-contiguous detectors and k-cnf satisfiability. In: Congress On Evolutionary Computation – CEC 2006, IEEE Press (2006 (to appear))

8. Stibor, T., Timmis, J., Eckert, C.: Generalization regions in hamming negative selection. In: Intelligent Information Processing and Web Mining. Advances in Soft Computing, Springer-Verlag (2006) 447–456
9. Hofmeyr, S., Forrest, S.: Architecture for an artificial immune system. Evolutionary Computation **8** (2000) 443–473
10. de Castro, L.N., Timmis, J.: Artificial Immune Systems: A New Computational Intelligence Approach. Springer Verlag (2002)
11. Perelson, A.S., Oster, G.: Theoretical studies of clonal selection: minimal antibody repertoire size and reliability of self-nonself discrimination. In: J. Theor. Biol. Volume 81. (1979) 645–670
12. Percus, J.K., Percus, O.E., Perelson, A.S.: Predicting the size of the T-cell receptor and antibody combining region from consideration of efficient self-nonself discrimination. Proceedings of National Academy of Sciences USA **90** (1993) 1691–1695
13. Balthrop, J., Esponda, F., Forrest, S., Glickman, M.: Coverage and generalization in an artificial immune system. In: GECCO 2002: Proceedings of the Genetic and Evolutionary Computation Conference, New York, Morgan Kaufmann Publishers (2002) 3–10
14. Esponda, F., Forrest, S., Helman, P.: A formal framework for positive and negative detection schemes. IEEE Transactions on Systems, Man and Cybernetics Part B: Cybernetics **34** (2004) 357–373
15. D'haeseleer, P., Forrest, S., Helman, P.: An immunological approach to change detection: algorithms, analysis, and implications. In: Proceedings of the 1996 IEEE Symposium on Research in Security and Privacy, IEEE Computer Society, IEEE Computer Society Press (1996) 110–119
16. González, F., Dasgupta, D., Niño, L.F.: A randomized real-valued negative selection algorithm. In: Proceedings of the 2nd International Conference on Artificial Immune Systems (ICARIS). Volume 2787 of Lecture Notes in Computer Science., Edinburgh, UK, Springer-Verlag (2003) 261–272
17. Knuth, D.E.: The Art of Computer Programming. third edn. Volume 1. Addison-Wesley (2002)
18. González, F., Dasgupta, D., Gómez, J.: The effect of binary matching rules in negative selection. In: Genetic and Evolutionary Computation – GECCO-2003. Volume 2723 of Lecture Notes in Computer Science., Chicago, Springer-Verlag (2003) 195–206
19. Tax, D.M.J.: One-class classification. PhD thesis, Technische Universiteit Delft (2001)
20. Rätsch, G.: Benchmark repository (1998) http://ida.first.fraunhofer.de/projects/bench/benchmarks.htm.

Gene Libraries: Coverage, Efficiency and Diversity

Steve Cayzer[1] and Jim Smith[2]

[1] HP Laboratories, Bristol BS34 8QZ UK
steve.cayzer@hp.com
[2] University of the West of England, Bristol BS16 1QY UK
james.smith@uwe.ac.uk

Abstract. Gene libraries are a biological mechanism for generating combinatorial diversity in the immune system. However, they also bias the antibody creation process, so that they can be viewed as a way of guiding lifetime learning mechanisms. In this paper we examine the implications of this view, by examining coverage, avoidance of self, clustering and diversity. We show how gene libraries may improve both computational expense and performance, and present an analysis which suggests how they might do it. We suggest that gene libraries: provide combinatorial efficiency; improve coverage; reduce the cost of negative selection; and allow targeting of fixed antigen populations.

Keywords: gene libraries, artificial immune systems, antibodies, diversity, Baldwin effect, lifetime learning.

1 Introduction

Immune systems in nature must recognise undesirable antigens while avoiding auto immune reactions. Gene libraries may help both aims; by providing *initialisation bias* away from self space; and by providing a *species memory* to map antigen space. What could this mean for AIS? Could gene libraries be used to intelligently seed our algorithm? In a previous paper [1] we postulated that gene libraries might:

1. improve non-self space coverage – through better placement of detectors (antibodies), over and above random creation;
2. reduce the cost of detector generation by more effectively avoiding self;
3. map the antigen population more accurately; and
4. help deal with co-evolving antigens

In that paper, we showed that option 2 is somewhat easier to achieve than option 1. Here we extend and analyse these results, and tackle option 3. Option 4 is left for future work. The rest of this paper proceeds as follows.

In Section 2 we review the biological background and related AIS research. In Section 3 we provide an initial analysis of the effect of evolving different numbers of libraries in the presence of uniformly distributed populations of self and non-self (antigen) strings. We show that gene libraries can attain superior coverage in this case, and that 2 libraries work as well as, even better than, 1 library. This is significant given the combinatorial advantages of using multiple libraries. All libraries

H. Bersini and J. Carneiro (Eds.): ICARIS 2006, LNCS 4163, pp. 136–149, 2006.

work much better than random creation; we show that libraries give rise to many more antibodies then random creation, due to increased efficiency (chance of producing a valid antibody) – that is, reducing the cost of negative selection.

It is tempting to infer a causal link between efficiency and coverage, but in section 4 we show that concentrating purely on the cost of negative selection actually reduces the number of antibodies produced, by reducing diversity. While these results confirm what might be suspected from a simple combinatorial analysis, in both "real" immune systems, and AIS applications, it is extremely rarely, if ever, the case that either the self or non-self population to be matched is uniformly distributed.

In section 5 we turn our attention to non uniform spaces, and show how different patterns of self and antigen clustering affect both coverage and efficiency. Choosing a number of points in cluster space to analyze, in section 6, we show that gene libraries not only produce more antibodies, but those they do produce are targeted around the antigen clusters. Finally in Section 7 we conclude that gene libraries: provide combinatorial efficiency, improve coverage and reduce the cost of negative selection. Most importantly, they allow the targeting of fixed antigen populations.

2 Background and Related Work

In the biological immune system, both T cell receptors and antibodies are generated by combining fragments from *gene libraries*. The gene library mechanism appears at first to be wasteful: to make a protein of about 200 amino acids we require enough DNA to make almost 12000 amino acids. However this 60-fold redundancy enables 2M combinations; this potential diversity is of course augmented by the well known somatic hypermutation mechanism [2]. The expressed diversity is, of course, likely to be somewhat lower not least become some combinations will be autoreactive (hence screened out by negative selection or other mechanisms [3]). A more detailed account is found in [1] where we speculate that gene libraries, shaped by evolution, are used to guide the B cell creation process to create antibodies with a good chance of success, while preserving the ability to respond to novel threats.

With regard to gene libraries in AIS, a seminal paper by Perelson et al [4] showed that gene libraries can enhance coverage in the absence of a 'self' set. Hightower et al [5] showed that the 'best' coverage was achieved by a high Hamming distance (spread out antibodies) – but not too high. A maximal separation actually allows gaps in coverage (analogous to gaps between disjoint spheres). Oprea & Forrest [6] showed that as the pathogen set size decreases, the structure of the gene library changes, moving from a 'coarse mapping' of antigen space towards a more focused targeting of pathogenic clusters. We present complementary analyses to these papers by studying clustering of both antibodies and antigens.

Other work by Hart and Ross [7,8] and Kim and Bentley [9,10,11] have used gene libraries to improve performance of an AIS application; we argue in [1] that these approaches use the gene library metaphor as an engineering artefact and would benefit from a principled analysis of when and how to use gene libraries. We reiterate our aim that we would like to build a bridge between the established theoretical foundations and current AIS engineering practice.

3 Gene Libraries for Coverage

The most naïve way of looking at antibody creation is a way of covering a multidimensional area (antigen space). This is somewhat complicated by the necessity of avoiding self. Do evolved gene libraries improve such coverage? What about the effect of different numbers of gene libraries? In order to answer these questions, we evolved a number of different library configurations (see table 1) and tested them using 8 bit r contiguous matching on antibodies/antigens of 32 bits.

Table 1. Configuration of gene libraries. We kept the number of antibodies and their size (almost) constant in each case. Each row shows how we created these antibodies using a combination of gene library segments, and how we changed the segment size and number of genes per library in each case. Genome size is calculated as the sum of (#segments * size of segment) for each library.

Number libraries	Segments in each library	Size of each segment	Number antibodies	Genome size
1	1089	32	1089	34848
2	33,33	16,16	1089	1056
3	11,11,9	11,10,11	1089	321
4	6,6,6,5	8,8,8,8	1080	184

For each of these different configurations a generational Genetic Algorithm (GA) was run for 2000 generations. The GA had a population of size 128, used binary tournaments to select parents, one point crossover with probability 0.7 and mutation with a bit-wise probability of 1/genome_len. To assess the effect of random creation in libraries we ran a parallel set of experiments with the bit-wise mutation probability set to 50%. When performed with 1 library this is equivalent to classical random creation without libraries.

Twenty five self sets of 128 proteins were created, each with a corresponding non-self set of 1024 antigens, none of which exactly matched any of the self proteins. These were used as the basis for the 25 runs of each algorithm. Individuals were assessed by creating all of the possible antibodies encoded for (1080 or 1089 as appropriate) and then removing those which were an 8 bit r-contiguous match to any of the self set. The remaining antibodies ("detectors") were used to assess the coverage of the non-self set.

Figure 1 shows the coverage attained by the best-performing individual over 2000 generations (x-axis), averaged over twenty five runs. This illustrates how the use of evolving gene libraries comprehensively outperforms random creation on this basic task. Averaged over the last 500 generations, ANOVA, and by post-hoc testing using Tamhane's T2 test (which does not assume equal variance) revealed that the performance of the 2 libraries was best (98.14%) followed by 1 library (97.80%), followed by 3 libraries (76.20%) and 4 libraries (56.97%). All results are significantly different at the 95% confidence level.

Very similar results can be seen if we compare the average population coverage, although interestingly in this case the use of 1 library gave the best result (97.8%) compared to 97.0% coverage for 2 libraries, again statistically significant.

In order to begin to understand the extremely poor performance of random creation compared to the evolving libraries, we recorded the number of detectors created by each solution; that is the number of antibodies left after negative selection. Figure 2 shows a plot of the mean number of detectors in each generation for the different algorithms, averaged over the 25 runs. This reveals that for all random creation variants the vast majority of the potential antibodies produced are screened out by the negative selection process, so only a very few detectors remain. It is also notable that evolving 1 library produces far fewer detectors than evolving 2, 3 or 4.

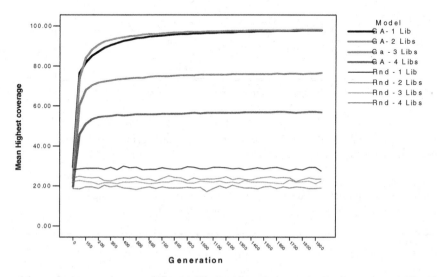

Fig. 1. Coverage of best performing individual over 2000 generations (x axis). Each result shows the % antigens matched (y axis) by antibodies created from a varying number of libraries. The results using random creation are shown for comparison. Values averaged over 25 runs.

Interestingly, when the highest number of detectors per generation is plotted the GA with 4 libraries creates more detectors than the 2, 3 and 1 libraries (in that order) and vastly more than the random methods. Since the mean and best fitness had converged by this time, this indicates that convergence had occurred, but around a very "brittle" region, so that random mutations were producing a few very poor individuals in each generation. This would imply a very "rugged" structure for the library-landscape, (low fitness-distance correlation). Intuitively, as the number of libraries increases, so the combinatorial effects of changing one element of any library become more dramatic: changing one gene in a 1-library system only affects one detector, but if in a 4-library system it makes that fragment rcb-match a self protein it will make 216 detectors auto-reactive. Clearly this merits further investigation.

Table 2 presents the summary data from these experiments; all differences are significant except those between the random variants.

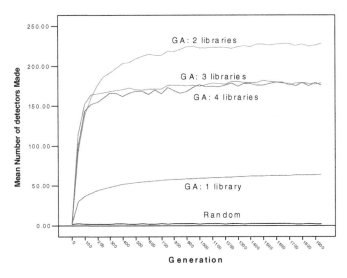

Fig. 2. Mean Number of detectors created (y-axis) against generation (x-axis) for different algorithms. Results are averaged over 25 runs.

Table 2. Mean and standard deviations of observed variables for each algorithm averaged over last 500 generations of 25 runs. Bold type indicates highest performing algorithm.

Model		Mean number of detectors	Highest number of detectors	Mean Coverage	Highest coverage
GA- 1 Lib	Mean	63.2890	64.0814	**97.7844**	97.8075
	Std. Dev.	5.15973	5.40025	1.15710	1.15014
GA- 2 Libs	Mean	**227.1930**	257.1702	97.0047	**98.1453**
	Std. Dev.	21.78812	24.94944	.54271	.51352
Ga – 3 Libs	Mean	178.7102	232.9614	71.3728	76.2019
	Std. Dev.	30.45022	38.96799	1.45540	1.31451
GA – 4 Libs	Mean	178.1495	**277.3882**	50.8206	56.9651
	Std. Dev.	44.95472	67.29847	2.26689	2.24031
Rnd - 1 Lib	Mean	2.2309	6.9018	10.1409	28.6972
	Std. Dev.	.43560	1.24078	1.89157	4.09810
Rnd - 2 Libs	Mean	1.8511	11.2350	6.1164	23.8114
	Std. Dev.	.33315	3.05073	.92953	3.45564
Rnd - 3 Libs	Mean	2.0710	17.7266	4.9721	22.0440
	Std. Dev.	.44342	6.11281	.71997	3.09263
Rnd - 4 Libs	Mean	2.0829	23.0511	3.7466	19.1931
	Std. Dev.	.49558	8.99772	.62348	2.76287

4   Gene Libraries for Avoiding Self

In the above analysis, it would seem that the AIS has optimised for creating a large number of antibodies; clearly it is effective at avoiding self. Could gene libraries provide a bias to assist negative selection; that is, make the creation process cheaper? Certainly, if we change the fitness function to be <u>purely</u> the avoidance of self (ie the success rate of antibody creation) then gene libraries indeed have a profound effect on the cost of negative selection [1].

However, it is possible that this reduction in the cost of negative selection comes at the cost of other desirable features. In order to investigate this hypothesis we used a similar GA setup with simple AIS gene library individuals (3 libraries, 16 bits (5+6+5), 6 bit r-contiguous matching) and measured both the efficiency of producing detectors, and also the diversity of different detectors produced. As can be seen from Figure 3 this 'pure' measure has the effect of reducing genome diversity: in other words, one gets a high proportion of 'safe' (non self reactive) antibodies – but also a large number of duplicates. Clearly there is a trade-off between coverage and cost of creation.

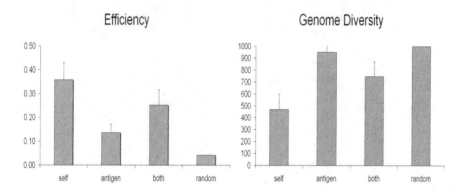

Fig. 3. Effect of using avoidance of self as a fitness function (self), as opposed to coverage (antigen), combined (both) or simply using a random creation strategy. The left figure shows that AIS individuals can evolve gene libraries with a far higher (36%) chance of producing valid antibodies than one whose fitness function measures only coverage (antigens; 13%) and far above random creation (5%). All differences are statistically significant (wilcoxon). In the right figure, the 'self' AIS individuals have roughly half the diversity of the others (unique number of antibodies; 470 cf 950 antigen, 983 random). All differences significant except antigen/random.

5   Mapping Antigen

It is well known that many real proteins fall into "families" with similar configurations, and that in general both the sets of self proteins and possible antigens will come from a non-uniform probability distribution across the space of possible conformations. The same general consideration is true for many real world datasets;

were it not; techniques like k nearest neighbour could not work. In order to investigate what effect this has on the utility, or otherwise, of gene libraries we constructed parameterised data set generators for creating self and non-self sets. Given a number of clusters, (0 being uniform distribution), for each of these a cluster centroid is randomly generated. The rest of the set is evenly divided to become clones of these centroids. For each clone we generate a number of bits to be changed using a zero mean Gaussian distribution with standard deviation 5. That number of positions within the string are chose uniformly at random, and those bits changed to produce the new protein. If this is not a duplicate, it is accepted into the set.

We ran the GA using the same parameters as before for 500 generations for each combination of self and non-self clusters in the range {0,...,5}.

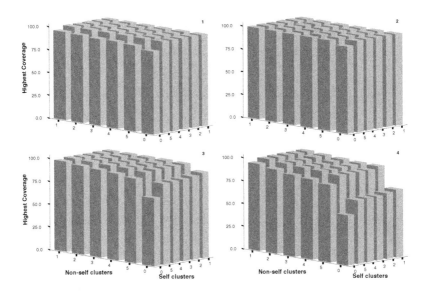

Fig. 4. Best coverage (y-axis) in generation 500 as a function of the number of self (x-axis) and non-self clusters. (z-axis). Graphs show (from top left, clockwise) 1 ,2 ,4 ,3 libraries, and are averaged over 25 runs. Note that 1 cluster is the most tightly clustered; the distribution gets most spread out as number of clusters increases to 5, and then again at 0 clusters (unclustered).

Figure 4 shows the best coverage obtained in the final (500th) generation, as a function of the number of self and non-self clusters. The corresponding plots for the mean coverage are extremely similar. For one library, the GA evolves to give near-perfect coverage except when self is unclustered. As the number of libraries increases, coverage is still very high for multiple clusters, but another effect becomes apparent. Coverage is lower for the unclustered antigens and increases as antigen becomes more clustered, reaching a maximum at 1 antigen cluster. Intuitively, a single antigen cluster is the easiest to cover, but the trend is accentuated for unclustered self which is most likely to induce 'holes' which cover antigen (see section 6).

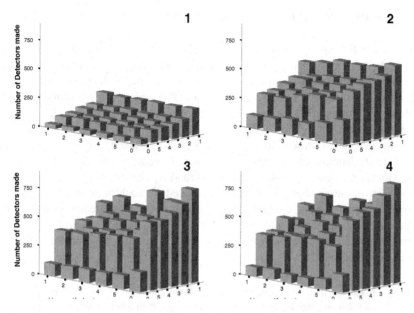

Fig. 5. Mean number of detectors created in final generation (y-axis) as a function of non-self clusters (x-axis) and self-clusters (z-axis). Again, 1 cluster is the most tightly clustered; 0 the least. Note reversed direction of scales. Graphs are average of 25 runs and show (clockwise from top left) 1,2,4,3 libraries.

Figure 5 shows the mean number of antibodies surviving negative selection. In every case this number is highest for 1 self cluster, and decreases through to 5 self-clusters, being lowest for uniformly distributed self; also the point of lowest coverage.

For 1 library, the number of detectors is not strongly affected by the number of non-self clusters, which is what might be expected as the latter has no effect on negative selection. However, as the number of libraries increases the number of detectors created seems to be linked to the number of antigen clusters, rising from 1 to 5 clusters and highest for uniform distribution. This may reflect an increase in the number of duplicate detectors, although a detailed analysis of several sample datasets (section 6) found no duplicates. Alternatively, it may reflect an increasing probability that any randomly placed antibody which does not match self will match an antigen, and so contribute to the fitness of that individual. In other words, as the antigens spread out, so the utility of simply avoiding self increases on average, although the possibility of obtaining complete antigen coverage from the set of detectors also decreases. This would explain the apparent paradox of decreasing coverage (fig 4) for an increasing number of detectors as the antigen becomes less clustered. Put another way, for more clustered antigens the AIS can get higher coverage from a smaller number of tightly focused detectors, a hypothesis which is explored in the next section.

6   Analysis of Coverage

We have seen in the last section that self clustering drives increased coverage and an increase in the number of detectors made. Antigen clustering also increases coverage but decreases the number of receptors made. In this section we take a closer look at these results, to examine the strategies that our AIS employs for covering antigens under different cluster arrangements. For example, is antibody clustered, and how does this clustering change according to environment? In order to answer this question, we analysed representative antibody populations taken from different points in the self cluster/antigen cluster space. In each case we analyzed one representative individual and compared this against (averaged) random performance.

Table 3 shows the number of antibodies produced for each point in cluster space. Interestingly, these figures contain no duplicate detectors. Greater numbers of antibodies are produced by the individuals that use 2 or 3 gene libraries. The number of antibodies created increases with the number of self clusters and decreases with the number of antigen clusters.

Table 3. Number of antibodies produced by gene library individuals for different points in cluster space (data shown graphically in figure 5). The biggest number of antibodies produced for each point in cluster space is shown in bold; for each gene library configuration by underlining. For comparison, random creation (table 2) consistently produces <25 antibodies.

Description	1 lib	2 libs	3 libs
0self - 0antigens	43	**261**	170
0self - 5antigens	38	**157**	94
2self- 2 antigens	<u>124</u>	361	**441**
5self - 0antigens	120	<u>490</u>	**<u>669</u>**
5self - 5antigens	88	343	**579**

We were interested in seeing how coverage compared against the theoretical optimum and a random creation strategy. The latter is easy to test – we just randomly create antibodies (discarding duplicates) until we get the same number that the gene libraries produce. The former is more difficult, but fortunately Wierzchon [12] has shown how this is possible. We used his paper to code an algorithm, the pseudocode of which is shown in Figure 6.

Figure 7 shows that, in general, coverage increases as the antigen clustering increases. Use of one library consistently outperforms random antibodies; two and three libraries require a clustered space to do so. It is important to bear in mind that *random* here refers to the same number of antibodies; as 2 and 3 libraries produce large numbers of antibodies (see table 3), then the same number of (randomly produced) antibodies will of course give high coverage. The cost of creation is not taken into account here, as it is dealt with in Section 3. As reported in section 5, the best coverage is achieved with highly clustered self and antigens.

```
CalculateOptimum(self)

    // get all r-bit templates eg **1100**
    templates = getTemplatesIn(self)

    // see below
    addHoles(templates)

    // count number of proteins induced
    FOR each leaf template eg ****0001
      numInduced = 1

    FOR each non leaf template
      numInduced = SUM numInduced for children
    // Note that undetectable includes self
    undetectable = SUM numInduced for roots
    holes = undetectable - self

    optimum = (nonself - holes)/nonself

addHoles(templates)

    // iterative process
    while (size of templates growing)

      for each template

        // case 1 - children - if *11** and its
        //   ,spouse' *01** are both part of self,
        //   then logically so are the children
        //   *11* and **10*
        IF templates contain spouse THEN
          add children

        // case 2 - parents - if **11* and its
        //   ,sibling' **10* are both part of self
        //   then logically so are the parents
        //   *11** and *01**
        IF templates contain sibling THEN
          add parents
```

Fig. 6. Wierzchon's algorithm [12] for counting number of holes using rContiguous bits. The theoretical optimum is the size of non self space minus the number of holes.

The template algorithm suggested by Wierzchon gives us a useful metric for measuring diversity. Figure 8 shows the number of templates (per antibody or protein) found in the different self sets, antigen sets and corresponding antibodies produced randomly and by the gene libraries. As expected, low numbers of self or antigen clusters give the lowest numbers of templates (i.e. highest degree of clustering). One library gives diverse antibodies, close to, or even higher than, random creation in nature. Two and three libraries give the reverse; much tighter clustering, especially for the 2self-2antigens scenario. Recalling this is a point of high coverage (with less than the maximum numbers of antibodies) this is suggestive of a reason for the libraries' efficacy.

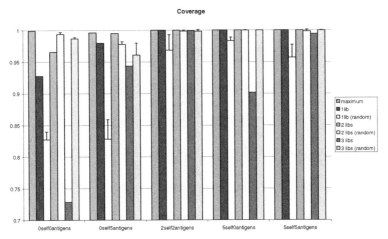

Fig. 7. Coverage values for various cluster configurations and library sizes. In each case, the theoretical maximum antigen coverage (against the given antigen set) is plotted against gene library performance. The random coverage is the coverage achieved using random creation *of the same number of antibodies* (see table 3).

Description	maximum	1lib	random	stdev	2 libs	random	stdev	3 libs	random	stdev
0self0antigens	0.999	0.928	0.827	0.012	0.966	0.994	0.003	0.729	0.987	0.002
0self5antigens	0.996	0.979	0.828	0.031	0.995	0.978	0.004	0.943	0.961	0.019
2self2antigens	1.000	1.000	0.968	0.025	1.000	0.999	0.001	0.999	0.998	0.002
5self0antigens	1.000	1.000	0.983	0.006	1.000	1.000	0.000	0.901	1.000	0.000
5self5antigens	1.000	1.000	0.957	0.020	1.000	0.998	0.003	0.994	1.000	0.000

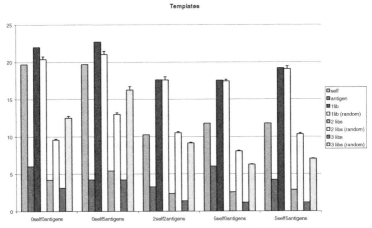

description	self	antigen	1lib	Random	stdev	2lib	random	stdev	3lib	random	stdev
0self0antigens	19.70	6.00	21.98	20.38	0.35	4.20	9.57	0.14	3.11	12.51	0.26
0self5antigens	19.70	4.20	22.71	21.03	0.43	5.41	12.99	0.21	4.20	16.26	0.45
2self2antigens	10.27	3.28	17.60	17.58	0.41	2.37	10.52	0.16	1.38	9.15	0.08
5self0antigens	11.78	6.00	17.53	17.41	0.22	2.57	8.04	0.09	1.18	6.25	0.05
5self5antigens	11.78	4.20	19.20	19.07	0.38	2.89	10.35	0.15	1.16	7.03	0.05

Fig. 8. Number of templates produced in self, antigen, evolved and randomly created libraries

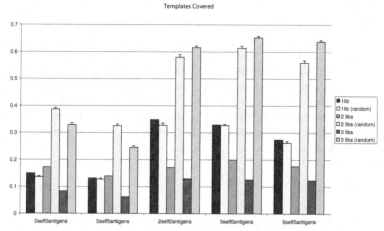

description	1 lib	1 lib (random)	stdev	2 libs	2 libs (random)	stdev	3 libs	3 libs (random)	Stdev
0self0antigens	0.150	0.136	0.003	0.172	0.387	0.006	0.083	0.329	0.007
0self5antigens	0.131	0.127	0.004	0.139	0.326	0.006	0.061	0.245	0.007
2self2antigens	0.348	0.327	0.009	0.171	0.579	0.010	0.129	0.616	0.006
5self0antigens	0.329	0.327	0.004	0.199	0.614	0.007	0.126	0.652	0.005
5self5antigens	0.274	0.262	0.007	0.176	0.558	0.009	0.124	0.637	0.005

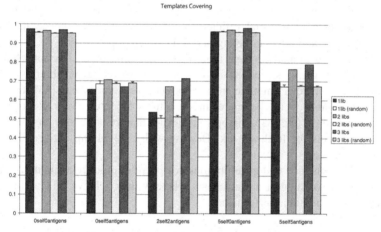

description	1 lib	1 lib (random)	stdev	2 libs	2 libs (random)	stdev	3 libs	3 libs (random)	stdev
0self0antigens	0.974	0.956	0.004	0.965	0.951	0.001	0.970	0.952	0.002
0self5antigens	0.655	0.684	0.016	0.706	0.687	0.006	0.668	0.689	0.006
2self2antigens	0.535	0.504	0.014	0.671	0.512	0.007	0.714	0.512	0.005
5self0antigens	0.962	0.962	0.003	0.971	0.958	0.001	0.981	0.958	0.001
5self5antigens	0.698	0.672	0.011	0.765	0.677	0.004	0.790	0.673	0.005

Fig. 9. Number of antigen templates covered (9a-top) and antibody templates covering (9b – bottom) as a function of number of random or evolved libraries. The former indicates how completely each antigen is covered, the latter how targeted the antibodies are on the antigen population.

Wierzchon's algorithm also allows us to measure degree of targeted coverage. So, for example, the number of antigen templates covered (Figure 9a) show how completely the antigens are matched, while the number of antibody templates covering (Figure 9b) indicate how 'targeted' the antibody set is at that particular antigen population. Again, templates covered (9a) for one library is close to or above 'random' behaviour, while two and three libraries cover far fewer antigen templates, even when delivering superior coverage (for example, 2 libraries with 0self5antigens). The targeting of antibodies (fig 9b) shows a higher than random focusing of templates only in tightly clustered scenarios (eg 2lib2antigens); this is consistent with an antibody population tailored to the fixed antigen set.

7 Conclusions

Gene libraries clearly introduce initialisation bias to antibody creation. We have shown that such bias induces superior coverage, but that this improvement is not purely through reducing the cost of negative selection, nor of combinatorial effects; rather some antigen mapping must be occurring. For unclustered antigens, the antibodies generated retain high diversity; as the antigens become more clustered the antibody population becomes less diverse (fig 8) and more targeted (fig 9). The comparable (even superior) performance of 2 libraries (versus 1 library) is also compelling given the combinatorial advantages. In summary, we suggest that gene libraries: provide combinatorial efficiency; improve coverage; reduce the cost of negative selection; and allow targeting of fixed antigen populations.

We have chosen to analyse gene libraries by assessing their effect on established AIS notions of negative selection and coverage. However, gene libraries will also have an impact on other immune metaphors such as homeostasis [13] and danger [14], and these topics would be interesting directions for future work. Representation other than bit-strings, and mapping operators other than rContiguous bits, would also be suitable subjects for further work. Dealing with co-evolving antigens is another topic for further study.

For now, we conclude that gene libraries do appear to produce a tangible benefit in a defined space, we suggest a mechanism whereby they achieve this, and present a method for analysing their performance.

References

1. Steve Cayzer, Jim Smith, James Marshall & Tim Kovacs (2005) What have gene libraries done for AIS? Proceedings ICARIS-2005, 4th International Conference on Artificial Immune Systems, LNCS 3627, pp 86-99, Springer-Verlag, Banff, Canada.
2. Goldsby, R.A., Kindt, T.J., Osborne, B.A., Kuby, J.: "Immunology" W H Freeman, New York 5th edition (2003)
3. Matzinger, P. The Danger Model: A renewed sense of self. Science 296 (2002) 301-305
4. Perelson, A.S., Hightower, R., Forrest, S. (1996) "Evolution and somatic learning in V-region genes. Research in Immunology 147 pp.202-208

5. Hightower, R., Forrest, S., Perelson, A.S. (1995): The evolution of emergent organization in immune system gene libraries. In: Proceedings of the Sixth International Conference on Genetic Algorithms, Los Altos, CA. Eshelman L.J. (Ed.) Morgan-Kauffman, San Francisco, CA pp.344-350

6. Oprea, M., Forrest, S. (1998): Simulated evolution of antibody libraries under pathogen selection. In: Proceedings of the 1998 IEEE International Conference on Systems, Man and Cybernetics, San Diego, CA

7. Hart, E., Ross, P. (1999a): An Immune System Approach to Scheduling in Changing Environments. In: W.Banzhaf, J.Daida, A.E.Eiben, M.H.Garzon, V.Honavar, M.Jakiela, R.E.Smith (Eds.) Proceedings of Genetic and Evolutionary Computation Conference (GECCO) July 13-17 Morgan Kaufmann pp. 1559-1566

8. Hart, E., Ross, P. (1999b): The Evolution and Analysis of a Potential Antibody Library for Job-Shop Scheduling. In: New Ideas in Optimisation. D. Corne, M.Dorigo & F. Glover (eds), K. McGraw-Hill, London. pp. 185-202

9. Kim, J., Bentley, P. (1999a), The Human Immune System and Network Intrusion Detection. In: 7th European Congress on Intelligent Techniques and Soft Computing (EUFIT '99), Aachen, Germany, September 13- 19.

10. Kim, J., Bentley, P. (1999b): The Artificial Immune Model for Network Intrusion Detection. In: 7th European Congress on Intelligent Techniques and Soft Computing (EUFIT'99), Aachen, Germany, September 13- 19.

11. Kim, J., Bentley, P. J.(2002): A Model of Gene Library Evolution in the Dynamic Clonal Selection Algorithm. In: Proceedings of the First International Conference on Artificial Immune Systems (ICARIS) Canterbury, pp., September 9-11, 2002. pp. 175-182

12. Wierzchon, S (2002) Deriving a concise description of non-self patterns in an artificial immune system. In: New Learning Paradigms in Soft Computing Physica-Verlag (2002) pp.438-458.

13. Hugues Bersini, Why the First Glass of Wine Is Better Than the Seventh, Lecture Notes in Computer Science, Volume 3627, Jan 2005, Pages 100 – 111

14. Aickelin U and Cayzer S (2002): 'The Danger Theory and Its Application to Artificial Immune Systems', Proceedings of the 1st International Conference on Artificial Immune Systems (ICARIS-2002), pp 141-148, Canterbury, UK

Immune System Modeling: The OO Way

Hugues Bersini

CODE/IRIDIA – ULB
CP 194/6
50, av. Franklin Roosevelt
1050 Bruxelles, Belgium
bersini@ulb.ac.be

Abstract. This paper motivates the use of Object Oriented technologies such as OO programming languages, UML and Design Patterns in order to facilitate the development and the communication of immune system software modeling. The introduction justifies the need for immune computer models at different levels of abstraction and for various reasons: pedagogy, testing and study of emergent phenomena and quantitative predictions. Then the benefits allowed by adopting the OO way are further illustrated by simple examples of UML class, state and sequence diagrams and instances of Design Patterns such as the "Bridge" or the "State", helping to question and to clarify the immune objects and relationships. Finally an elementary clonal selection model, restricted to B cells, antibodies and antigens, and fully developed in the OO spirit is presented.

1 Introduction

All scientific disciplines carrying a name that begins with "artificial" (followed by "life", "reality", "intelligence" or "immune system") are similarly suffering from a very ambiguous identity. Their line of research tries to find a way somewhere in the crossroad of engineering (building useful artefacts), natural sciences (biology or psychology – improving the comprehension and prediction of natural phenomena) and theoretical computer sciences (developing and mastering the algorithmic world). Accordingly and depending on which of these perspectives receives more support, they attempt at attracting different kind of scientists and at stimulating different kind of scientific attitudes. While the "Alife" community is recently re-focusing its attention on theoretical biology, engaged in the process of re-attracting genuine biologists in their community, in our more modest AIS community, it is clearly the "engineering" perspective that has been the most represented and still prevails over the years. Since the origin of engineering and technology, nature has offered a reserve of inexhaustible inspirations which have stimulated the development of useful artefacts for man. Artificial life has led to new computer tools, such as genetic algorithms, Boolean and neural networks, robots learning by experience, cellular machines and others which create a new vision of IT for the engineer: parallel, adaptable and autonomous. In this kind of informatics, complex problems are tackled with the aid of simple mechanisms, but infinitely iterated in time and space. In this kind of informatics, the

H. Bersini and J. Carneiro (Eds.): ICARIS 2006, LNCS 4163, pp. 150 – 163, 2006.

engineer must be resigned to partly losing control if he wishes to obtain something useful. The computer finds the solutions by brute force trial and error, while the engineer concentrates on observing and indicating the most promising directions for research. Due to a limited but sharp understanding of the immune system as, first of all, a pattern recognition and classifier system, able to separate and to distinguish the bad from the good stimuli just on the basis of exogenous criteria, the main derived applications have been "classification", "clustering" and "optimisation". In previous ICARIS I already had the opportunity to regret this state of affairs since I can not succeed to see any new useful ideas that "engineers" did not have, even in the absence of the least concern for immunology. As a consequence, I would rather attempt in this paper to make a plea for following the "Alife" re-centring and for a shift from the engineering to the "modelling" perspective, by which the "theoretical immunologist" would turn back to be the more precious partner of the discussion.

But what theoretical immunologists, who obviously did not wait for us in their modelling enterprise ([1, 5, 9, 10, 11, 23, 25, 27]), can expect from us and from this advocated rebalancing. If, so far, we failed to convince the engineers of any possible insight, how else could we convince the immunologist even more knowledgeable of this common topic of interest? What can they expect from these new "merlin hackers", whose ambitions seem, above all, disproportionably naïve? Before answering that key question, I would like to review how computer models of theoretical biology, whoever develops them, can be useful in various ways. These ways will be presented in terms of their increasing importance or by force of impact. First of all, software models can open the door to a new style of training of some major biological principles. This is the case, for example, for Richard Dawkins who, bearing the Darwinian good news, does so with the help of a computer simulation where creatures known as "biomorphs" evolve on a computer screen by means of genetic algorithms. There is nothing here that biologists are not aware of, no new biological fact apart from an unsurpassable illustration of Darwinian principles. However, the fact that ever more surprising and complex biomorphs appear in a deliberately simplified succession of selection, reproduction and mutation, while based on well-known mechanisms, just illustrates how this process works and works well. If a picture is worth a thousand words, this is all the more true of a computer simulation, especially when it is highly coloured and have a "sexy" appearance on the screen. Only informatics can reproduce a near infinity of elementary mechanisms in a confined space and time and reach the surprising although "well-known" outcome in a decent time. I would guess that the cellular automata IMMSIM (immune simulation) model developed these last 15 years by Celada, Seiden and Kleinstein [5, 21] among other roles, fulfils this very important pedagogical one, to explain and illustrate the processes of "immunization" and "memory of previous antigenic exposure". Biologists are not really stunned by what they see, but simply happy to "verify" it and to exploit this software support for pedagogical purposes.

Additionally, computer platforms and simulations can, insofar as they are sufficiently comprehensible, flexible, quantifiable and universal, be used more "experimentally" by the biologist, who will find in them a simplified means of simulating and validating their qualitative understanding of biology. Cellular automata, Boolean networks, genetic algorithms and algorithmic chemistry are excellent examples of software that have been parameterised and used to produce and test different natural phenomena. The predictive power of these software can vary from very qualitative (their results show very general trends similarly present in the real world) to very quantitative (the numbers produced by the computer may be compared to those produced by the real phenomena which we are seeking to model). Even in their most qualitative form and simply due to the fact that they need to be translated into an algorithmic structure, these programs often allow a deep and careful examination of those mechanisms known to be responsible for observed patterns of behaviour. The needed "explicitation" and the writing down in an algorithmic structure of these mechanisms is already the guarantee of an advanced understanding accepted by all. Algorithmic writing is an essential stage in formalising the elements of the model and in rendering them less subjective. John Holland wrote about one definitive virtue of computer models: *"The assumptions underlying the predictions are made explicit, so others can use or modify the assumptions enriching the overall enterprise"* [19]. In a commentary very recently published in "Nature" and entitled *"Can computers help to explain biology"* [4], we can read the following extracts: *"Today, by contrast with descriptions of the physical world, the understanding of biological systems is most often represented by natural-language papers and text books. This level of understanding is adequate for many purposes (including medicine and agriculture) and is being extended by contemporary biologists with great panache. But insofar as biologists wish to attain deeper understanding, they will need to produce biological knowledge and operate on it in ways that natural language does not allow .... Biology narratives of cause and effects are readily systematizable by computers"*

Although algorithmic writing is less demanding than mathematical writing (qualitative agents found in agent-based models or in cellular automata are less precise than the quantitative variables found in differential equations), it requires a great degree of rigour and thus a much sharper clarification of various mechanisms than is found in biological literature in versions still quite ambiguous. The more the model allows to integrate what we know about the reality reproduced, the detailed structures of objects and relationships between them, the more the predictions will move from "tendentious" to quantitative and precise and the easier it will be to validate the model according to Popper's falsificationism, the way in which physicists wish to see biology to evolve. Still more important, new original mechanisms may be discovered, as it is their multiple iterations in time and space, only made possible through the computer, which allows to understand how they underlie the observed emergent behaviour. And this is indeed the territory of "emergent" phenomena and functionalities that only, in addition to nature, software can produce. In the 1950's, when Alan Turing discovered that a simple diffusion phenomenon, propagating itself at different speed, depending on whether it was subject to a negative or positive influence, produces zebra or alternating motifs, he had a considerable effect on a whole section of biology studying the genesis of forms (animal skins, shells of sea creatures). When Kaufmann discovered that the number of attractors in a Boolean network or a neural network has a linear dependency on the number of units in these networks, these results can equally well apply to the number of cells expressed as dynamic attractors in a genetic network or to the quantity of information being stored in a neural network. When some physicists recently observed a non-uniform connectivity in many networks, whether social, technological or biological, showing a small number of nodes with a large number of connexions and a greater number of nodes with far fewer, and when, in addition, they explain the way in which these networks were constituted in time, again biology is clearly affected. When a idiotypic network growing in a real shape space spontaneous separates this space in a "immune" and a "tolerant" zone, although the concentration update mechanism is everywhere the same [3], again this result is far from expected and highlight in new ways the fundamental self/non-self distinction of immunology. And whatever experiment has surprising outcome, scientists will show their face with great expectation. When Perelson et al [26] explain by a simple mathematical model the antagonistic population dynamics of CD4 T cells and HIV virus and qualitatively replicate the long life time of T cell despite the huge presence of virus, again the impact is important. Although still to be construed in a qualitative way, the reproduction of these phenomena by software means help to unveil the underlying mechanisms giving rise to them.

Computer language, although very rigorous, offers more flexibility than any mathematical language. The computer can replay certain scenarios of biological evolution which have taken place over millions of years endlessly, without the programmer having to resort to gnawing at the mouse. This allows the scientist to test several hypotheses, retaining only that one which resembles the current situation most closely. The programmer creates new worlds, worlds which evolve on their own and he can, as necessary, select those which are worth allowing to evolve somewhat. The computer suggests a result and the scientist adapts to it, looking to understand the result and ensuring that it is not a simple artefact linked to the intrinsic limitations of the method of inputting and processing digital information. At last, the "Grail" to reach for any scientific modelling attempt remains the quantitative prediction, a prediction so accurate that a measuring device will be able to validate the modelling by comparing what it measures with the model prediction. Several theoretical immunologists [26, 11, 12] force the way to go beyond qualitative descriptions and to quantify the immune system behaviour through mathematical and computer simulation approaches. As Rob De Boer [11] claims: *"Theoretical immunology is maturing into a discipline where modelling helps to interpret experimental data, to resolve controversies, and – most importantly – to suggest novel experiments allowing for more conclusive and more quantitative interpretations"*. Nevertheless, all other sorts of modelling whatsoever qualitative, on the road to the ideal most predictive one and for reasons mentioned above, like "pedagogy" or the testing of "emergent phenomena", are equally worth the effort.

Since there is no reason why immunologists should be surprised or disagree with these previous arguments, what would they gain in collaborating with researchers in computer science well decided at contributing to this modelling enterprise? I see one strong reason that I will expand below. The immune system is a very complex one, full of chemical actors interacting in complicated ways. These last twenty years computer scientists have been well trained for software simulation of complex systems by learning and practising the "Object Oriented (OO)" tricks, tricks that biologists (natural scientists in general) still seem to be hesitant (mainly because not educated to) to acquire and master. The OO software are simultaneously easy to read and to understand (even for non programmers), simple to build, easy to modularize, to maintain and to adapt. New software tools entirely rely on Object-Orientation (OO), essentially OO programming languages (C++, java, .Net, Python), UML and Design Patterns. From its origins, OO computation has simplified the programming of complex reality by allowing the programming to come closer to the way human perceives this reality (the first OO language was indeed called "SIMULA") instead of being constrained by the processor set of elementary instructions. There is a today trend which makes more and more possible to abstract software engineering from the processor by naturally using high-level human concepts and percepts, simply mapping the actors of the problem on the bricks of the algorithm. Even the way these concepts are cognitively organized (generalization, semantic relations) can be transposed as such in the software. This goes together with the increased use of the standard visual modeling language called UML [16, 24]. UML proposes a set of well defined diagrams (transcending any specific OO programming language) to naturally describe and resolve problems with the high level concepts inherent to the formulation of the problem. It is enough to discover and draw the main actors of the problem and how they do mutually relate and interact in time to build the algorithmic solution of this problem. Departing from these diagrams, more and more automatic code generation tools appear on the market, contributing to make this whole computational frame even more appealing to biologists. On the other hand, Design Patterns (DP) [18, 17, 24] are very convenient and well experimented software recipes to face and resolve programming difficulties often encountered during the development of complex software. The next section of this paper will illustrate how immune knowledge is already intrinsically OO and how accordingly UML and DP should ease the construction of OO models of immune system. In the third section, these OO tricks will be put into practice in a very simplified model of the immune clonal selection and memory, limited to B cells, antigens and antibodies.

2 UML and Design Patterns

Obviously, it is impossible to even briefly give an overview of the hundred modeling symbols composing the 13 UML diagrams. A very simple and didactical introduction to UML is the purpose of Folwer's book [16]. However these symbols are far from being all necessary and a couple of days is enough to acquire those allowing the conception of Class, State and Sequence diagrams, the most useful ones for the simulation of biological systems. For didactics' sake, two excerpts of the Janeway et al's immune system bible [20] will be mapped onto the corresponding UML class diagram. *"The antigen-specific activation of these effector T cells is aided by co-receptors on the T-cell surface that distinguish between the two classes of MHC molecule; cytotoxic cells express the CD8 co-receptor, which binds MHC class I molecules, whereas MHC Class II molecules specific T cells express the CD4 co-receptor, which has specificity for MHC Class II molecules"*. In figure 1, the link between the classes "T cell" and "Receptor" means a "composition" relationship, the receptor being physically and intimately part of the T cell, while the arrow joining the classes "MHC class I" to "MHC Molecule" means a inheritance or specialization relationship, class I and class II being two sub-classes of MHC molecule. The correspondence of figure 1 with the text should be obvious.

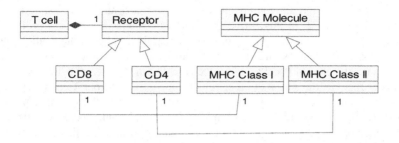

Fig. 1. Extract of page 30 of [20] mapped onto a UML class diagram

Another extract is: *"T cells are activated to produce armed effector T cells when their encounter their specific antigen in the form of a peptide:MHC complex on the surface of an activated antigen-presenting cell (APC) ... The most important APC are the highly specialized dentritic cells ... Macrophages can also be activated to express co-stimulatory and MHC class II molecules ... B cells can also serve as APC in some circumstances... Dentritic cells, macrophages and B cells are often known as profes-sional antigen presenting cells"*

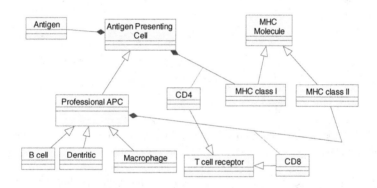

Fig. 2. Extract of page 319 of [20] mapped onto a UML class diagram

In figure 2, looking attentively, the classes CD4 and CD8 are represented as "asso-ciation classes" between APC and MHC, since they interact with APC only when these later express on their surface a MHC molecule. One can see how the second diagram is aimed at completing and refining the previous one by specifying the prop-erties of the T cell receptors and how they do interact with the APC. These two class diagrams still are quite incomplete but need to be taken as simple examples of how UML symbols allow a more formal and computational language, derivable from the qualitative language of immunology, in the way to computer simulations.

In many immune system simulations [1, 6, 7, 21] (included the simple one to be presented in the next section), it is the immune response to pathogens by either T cells or B cells followed by the memorization of this response which is under investigation. Almost all simulations consider a succession of B or T cell states: departing from a naïve state, prior to the antigen encounter, to then reach an "active" state once the antigen is encountered. In this active state, the cell enters in a process proliferation successively producing new clones. Following a certain number of duplication, part of the resulting T or B clones turn into an effector state where they can either produce antibodies (in the case of B cells), kill infected cells (in the case of cytotoxic T cells), suppress or regulate the action of other cells (in the case of helper T cells). This transformation process is at the origin of the immune response to the infecting pathogen. The remaining part of the T or B clones is transformed into memory cells. While immune memory is still a topic of vivid investigation, B and T cells in this new state seem to handle the memory role mainly because their death rate becomes much smaller than their ancestor. Additionally, back to the naïve state and ready in their turn to be activated by an antigen encounter, they appear to be faster to switch to the effector state and even to act more intensively. This whole process can be simply illustrated by the following state-transition UML diagram.

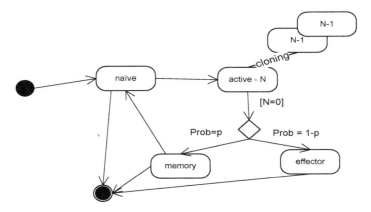

Fig. 3. A basic UML state-transition diagram illustrating the minimal cell transitions at the basis of the immune response and the memorization of this response

The two black disks above and below represent the birth and the death of the considered cell. A state transition diagram theoretically only concerns one unique object and its succession of states while, in this example, as a result of the cloning process, the active, the memory and the effector cells need to be different objects. Still, it is interesting to formally capture in one unique diagram the idea that in order to become memory or effector, a cell has to divide a certain number of times (in this state diagram and in our simulation explained below a clone labeled N disappears to give birth to two clones labeled N-1 and so forth until N=0), only the resulting clones being able to assume this new role. Another principle illustrated by the diagram is the probabilistic transformation of a clone into either a memory or an effector cell. In certain simulations [21], the switch to the memory state takes place before the effector state and as an alternative to it, while in others [6, 7] only a subset of effector cells will be changed into memory cells. There is another problem with this state transition diagram, still resulting from the cloning process. Although represented in the diagram by a transition of the memory cell back to the naïve state and although a memory cell could also become in its turn "active" and "effector", the states through which it transits might be quantitatively different than in the case of the first response. To resolve some of these problems, the third very useful UML type of diagram, the sequence diagram, useful for depicting the interaction between objects in time, can come to the rescue, like illustrated below.

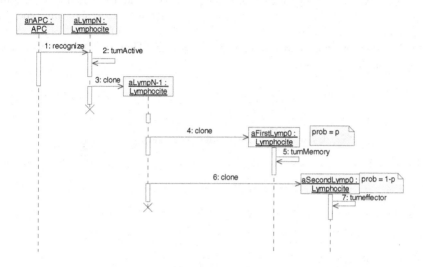

Fig. 4. A UML sequence diagram clarifying some of the ambiguities of the state diagram represented in fig.3. Here three more lymphocyte objects are considered, clones of the first one.

Since the publication of the "Gang of Four" Design Pattern book [18] (classifying, explaining and implementing 23 design patterns), the implementation of these software OO recipes have turned out to be one of the most popular and prolific field of today software technologies. They are not as easy to grasp as the basic principles of OO or the basic symbols of ULM, but they are worth the learning since their implementation testifies of an accurate understanding of the problem to be handled and equally well of the way to map it onto an OO architecture that guarantees readability, flexibility and stability (despite this adaptability). In substance, what DP aim at is to preserve some large space of development variability without affecting the rest of the simulation. Some of them will be presented in the next section while describing the minimal immune system simulation. However, the UML class diagrams discussed before already allow introducing some simple and tricky DP. Among them, the "prototype" DP has to do with the way a new object is created by cloning an existing one (a central aspect of the diagrams above). This DP teaches you for instance not to confuse a shallow copying (a T cell would be cloned without equally cloning the antigen receptor it is composed of) with a deep copying (where the cloning of the container implies the cloning of the content). Once a clone is born and provided many of them are, it is important, for obvious memory reasons, to separate what can be store only once in memory from what has to be distributed distinctively among the clones. This is the role of the "flyweight" DP, looking for common parts in the description of many objects. It forces the programmer and the immunologist to have a clear idea of what is unique to each clone and what is common to all of them (for instance, if the genetic sequence of their receptor is unique, it can be stored only once in the original lymphocyte and make all clones refer to it). The discussion about this DP should also result in a simulation choice between a "type-based simulation", for which an object is a cellular type and a key attribute is its concentration and an "instance-based simulation", for which there are as many objects as cellular instances of any type. The concentration of a type is now derived from the number of explicit objects really present in memory and acting during the simulation. Three other DPs are roughly illustrated in the figure below.

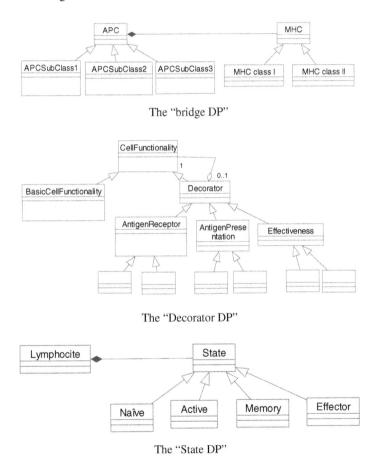

The "bridge DP"

The "Decorator DP"

The "State DP"

Fig. 5. Three among the most useful Design Patterns: The "bridge", the "Decorator" and the "State"

The "bridge" DP aims at keeping clearly separated in the conception and the software two different motivations for the specialization of classes. In the figure, APC can give rise to more specific forms of them and, independently, MHC molecules can be of different sub-classes, indifferently part the APC cell. The difference this DP points out with the previous solution presented in fig.1 should be clarified and resolved by immunologists. The "decorator" DP allows separating a fundamental characteristic of a cell from a set of added functionalities (the decorators) which can vary from a cell to another. It is a much flexible alternative to the use of subclassing. Functionalities can be added or removed simply by adding or deleting wrappers around an object. For instance, one cellular object could present a certain form of antigenic receptor but with no capacity to present antigens. Another cellular object could just be effective in a specific way while a third instance of cell could simultaneously present antigen in a given way and be effective in another. Finally, the "State" pattern is a direct result of the state-transition diagram such as the one presented in figure 3. Each state gives rise to one subclass and all aspects and functions specific to this state (what the cell is doing while in this state, what are the possible transitions from this state) are installed in this subclass. We will turn to that last DP in the next section.

Although I had many times the opportunity to defend the ideas of applying OO principles in biological simulations [2], I had an excellent surprise in discovering a set of recent publications by Irun Cohen (one of our immunologist guests at ICARIS this year), David Harel (the instigator behind the integration of the state-transition diagram in UML) and Sol Efroni (who is developing the software solutions) in which the need of applying OO technologies for immune modeling was advocated with great confidence and impressive software realizations [13, 14]. Extracted from one of this paper [13]: *"Interestingly, most of the experimental data in biology accumulates in an object oriented manner... Concerning the immune system, a significant amount of data exists about its cellular components but very little is known concerning the way these cells collaborate to function as a system... Object orientation fits the way we think, it fits the way the experimental data are collected and it seems suitable for coping with the challenge of understanding how biological objects collaborate to establish a system".* I can't agree more.

3   An Elementary Clonal Selection Model

The simplistic clonal selection and memorization model to be presented in this section is entirely derived from the Seiden, Cellada and Kleinstein IMMSIM software [5, 21]. It is even further simplified to only concentrate on three actors: B cells, antigens and antibodies. As such, it must not to be intended as any relevant attempt in a pure immunological perspective but rather as an illustration of how well UML diagrams and Design Patterns generally apply to this type of simulation. As illustrated in the three plots at the bottom of the next figure (above: showing the evolution of the B cell and antibody populations responding to the pathogenic stimulation and, below: the evolution of the pathogenic population), this simulation is able to reproduce the basic immune response to a pathogenic intrusion (the pathogen is destroyed by the complementary antibodies) and the memorization of this response (the second time the same pathogen is introduced in the system, it is eliminated much faster).

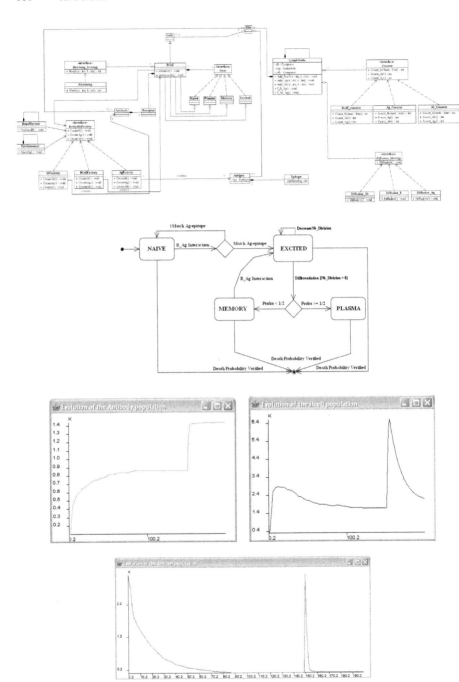

Fig. 6. Above: UML class and state diagrams and below: simulation results of the elementary clonal selection model - evolution in time of the antibody, B cell and antigen concentration

After the first infection, a set of memory B cells is created with longer life time and able to react similarly to the second pathogenic intrusion. Like in IMMSIM, any cell is coded by means of a binary string. Affinity is based on Hamming distance and the simulation is done over a set of sites in a way similar to a cellular automata, except that the presence of neighborhood sites just allow the three immune actors to diffuse through this neighborhood. Instead of describing in more details the immunological aspects which just boil down to a subset of the IMMSIM simulation, it is more advisable here to limit the discussion to the OO aspects. The whole class diagram is hard to read but we will concentrate on some parts of it. Among the most biologically relevant implemented Design Patterns in this simulation, there is for instance the "State" DP, where four subclasses: "Naïve", "Plasma", "Memory", "Excited" inherit from the State class, this latter being connected by a composition link to the class B cell. These subclasses are responsible for 1) implementing the only possible transitions represented in the state-transition diagram below (for instance from "Naïve" to "Excited") 2) coding the specific behaviour of the B cell while being in this specific state (for instance a "Plasma" B cell can produce antibodies and a "Excited" B cell can duplicate). The "Factory" DP is present and responsible for the creation of instances of the three immune actors treated here. For instance, in the case of a binary string coding of the cell, the factory classes care for the generation of this string. Additionally, there is a key connection between the "B cell" factory and the "Ab factory" since B cell of one specific type can only produce antibodies of this same specific type.

When programming in an OO way, programmers aim at encapsulating as much as possible the parts of the simulation which might be subject to a larger variability so as to keep the coding process more stable and linear. The "Template" DP keeps isolate a functionality which is central for the whole simulation to run, but which is susceptible of different implementations. This pattern was used here for implementing the affinity between antigens and antibodies. One possibility for this affinity function, like done in IMMSIM and in many idiotypic networks simulations [3, 7, 26, 27, 15] lies in the use of binary string and the Hamming distance between them. Another possibility is the use of n-dimension shape space [27]. Still other possibilities could be less abstract and take into account more biological details. Nevertheless, whatever affinity version adopted, all the rest of the simulation remains unaffected i.e. the proliferation of B cell and antibodies just depend on the presence of affinity between them and a given antigen. We easily understand how immune simulation could give rise to many instances of this same "template" DP in different places of the code, since many mechanisms composing this simulation are subject to alternatives. This has not been considered here, but this same DP could leave free and well separate from the rest of the code the way any cell grows in concentration, the way it dies, the way it diffuses in space, etc...

4 Conclusions

OO languages, UML and Design Patterns all together allow to tackle the simulation of the immune system in a much more comprehensible, adaptable and effective way. Through the use of UML diagrams, the necessary communication between programmers but also between programmers and biologists is facilitated. Through the use of

Design Patterns, many recipes, well tested and validated by many programmers before, can easily be transposed and adapted to the simulation at hand. Additionally, large space of freedom is provided for effortlessly testing different hypothesis without compromising the rest of the code. As a matter of fact, OO technologies have invaded the software world since programmers are more and more engaged in the development of complex software, their complexity being due to the presence of many actors interacting in subtle ways. Think of "Amazon", "traffic regulation", "meteorology". Without any doubt, the immune system exhibits this kind of complexity.

Although programmers will certainly benefit from OO technologies when conceiving and writing the code of immune system actors and interactions, biologists, even those still in majority, reluctant to software simulation, might also see some interest in the formalism underlying UML diagrams. The use of the diagrams goes not without a deep clarification and disambiguation of the reality to model. To draw a class diagram, a biologist will need to clarify whether a "subclass" link between a type of cell and another type is really a subclass in the OO sense. For that he will need to clearly state what is definitely common between these two types and why does he really perceive the second as a subclass of the first. The "prototype" and "flyweight" patterns will force him to a deeper understanding of the cloning process. The "State" patterns will force him to a better explicitation of what is distinct between cells when they find themselves in distinct states. The "Bridge" patterns will help him to relate or not the many taxonomies which fulfill immunology books and how to relate them. The leaders of the software world (I am referring here to the "Object Management Group") insist more and more in assimilating programming with modeling i.e. in relaxing the coding part to concentrate more on the modeling part. In doing so, they warmly advocate the increased use of UML diagrams and Design Patterns. On account of the extraordinary software developments that the adoption of these new strategies has allowed, I don't see any reason why immunologists interesting in computer simulation should remain immune to this software propaganda and campaign. ICARIS conferences might be ideal opportunities for these immunologist hackers to meet and to confront their diagrams and patterns once a year.

References

1. Antia, R. and M. Lipsitch. 1998 Mathematical models of parasite responses to host immune defenses. Parasitology 115 :pp. 155-167
2. Bersini (1999) Design Patterns for an OO Chemistry - In proceedings of the 1999 European Conference on Artificial Life - MIT Press.
3. Bersini, H. 2002. Self-Assertion vs Self-Recognition: A Tribute to Francisco Varela. Proc. of the first ICARIS Conference – pp. 107-112.
4. Brent, Roger and Jehoshua Bruck,. 2006. Can Computers Help to Explain Biology? Nature (03/23/06) Vol. 440, No. 7083, P. 416
5. Celada, F. and P.E. Seiden. 1992. A computer model of cellular interactions in the immune system. Immunol. Today 13 – pp.56-62
6. Chao, D.L., Davenport, M.P., Forrest, S. and A.S. Perelson. 2003. Stochastic stage-structured modelling of the adaptive immune system. In Proceedings of the IEEE Computer Society Bioinformatics Conference (CSB 2003) – pp. 124-131

7. Chao, D.L., Davenport, M.P., Forrest, S. and A.S. Perelson. 2004. A stochastic model of cytotoxic T cell responses – Journal of Theor. Biol. 228 – pp 227-240.
8. Cohen, IR. 2000: Tending Adam's Garden: Evolving the Cognitive Immune Self, Academic Press, San Diego
9. Cohen, IR. 2002: T-cell vaccination for autoimmune disease: a panorama. In Vaccine 20, pp. 706-710.
10. Cohn, M., Langman, R.E. and J.J. Mata. 2002. A computerized model for the self-non-self discrimination at the level of the Th (Th genesis). I. The origin of "primer" effector Th cells. Int. Immunol. 14:1105.
11. De Boer, R. http://theory.bio.uu.nl/rdb/immune
12. De Boer, R.J. and A.S. Perelson. 1991: Size and Connectivity as Emergent Properties of a Developing Immune Network – Journal of Theor. Biology, Vol. 149, pp. 381-424.
13. Efroni S, Harel D, Cohen IR. 2005 "Reactive animation: Realistic Modeling of Complex Dynamic Systems." 2005 Computer **38**:(1):38-47.
14. Efroni S, Harel D, Cohen IR. 2006. A theory for complex systems: reactive animation. Studies in Multidisciplinarity, Vol.3 Eds (Ray Patton and Laura Mc Namara) – Elsevier – pp. 309-324.
15. Farmer, J.D., N.H. Packard and A.S. Perelson. 1986: The immune system, adaptation and machine learning – Physica D, 22, pp. 187-204.
16. Folwer, M. 2004. UML Distilled – Third Edition – Addison Wesley.
17. Freeman, E., Freeman, E, Sierra, K. and B. Bates. 2004. Head First Design Patterns – O'Reilly Media.
18. Gamma, E., Helm, R. , Johnson, R. and J. Vlissides. 1995. Design Patterns – MA – Addison Wesley
19. Holland, J. 2002 - What is to come and how to predict it – In The Next Fifty Years : Science in the First Half of the Twenty-first Century – Vintage - by John Brockman (Editor)
20. Janeway, C. , Travers, P., Walport, M and M. 2005 Shlomchik: Immunobiology (6th Edition) – Garland Science Publishing.
21. Kleinstein, S.H. and P.E. Seiden, 2000. Computer simulations: simmulating the immune system. Comput. Sci. Eng. 2, pp. 69-77.
22. Kortes Altes, H., Ribeiro, R.M. and R.J. De Boer. 2003. The race between initial T-helper expansion and virus growth upon HIV infection influences polyclonality of the response and viral set-point. Proc. R. Soc. Lond. B 270 - pp. 1349-1358
23. Langman, R.E. and Cohn, M. 2000 A minimal model for the self-non-self distinction: a return to the basics. Semin. Immuno. 13:189
24. Larman C. 2003. Applying UML and Patterns, Second Edition – Prentice-Hall, Inc.
25. Nowak, M.A. and R.M. May 2000. Virus dynamics: mathematical foundations of virology and immunology. Oxford University Press.
26. Perelson, AS, Neumann AU, Markowitz, M., Leonard, JM and D. Ho. 1996. HIV-1 Dynamics in Vivo: Virion Clearance, Infected Cell Life-Span and Viral Generation Time. Science 271 – pp. 1582-1586
27. Perelson A.S. and G. Weisbuch, 1997. Immunology for physicists - Rev. Mod. Phys., 69, pp. 1219-1267.

A Computational Model of Degeneracy in a Lymph Node

Paul S. Andrews[1] and Jon Timmis[1,2]

[1] Department of Computer Science, University of York, UK
[2] Department of Electronics, University of York, UK
{psa, jtimmis}@cs.york.ac.uk

Abstract. This paper highlights degeneracy as being an important property in both the immune system and biology in general. From this, degeneracy is chosen as a candidate to inspire artificial immune systems. As a first step in exploiting the power of degeneracy, we follow the conceptual framework approach and build an abstract computational model in order to understand the properties of degenerate detectors free of any application bias. The model we build is based on the activation of T_H cell in the lymph node, as lymph nodes are the sites in the body where the adaptive immune response to foreign antigen in the lymph are activated. The model contains APC, antigen and T_H cell agents that move and interact in a 2-dimensional cellular space. The T_H cell agent receptors are assumed to be degenerate and their response to different antigen agents is measured. Initial observations and results of our model are presented and highlight some of the possibilities of degenerate detector recognition.

1 Introduction

In a previous work [1] we outlined an approach to exploiting immune ideas not yet used for artificial immune system (AIS) inspiration. We concluded that even though competing and conflicting immune theories are used to inspire AIS, these AIS are still able to perform their tasks well. However, it was observed that many of these AIS were designed with too much of an engineering approach, failing to adequately capture the immunological processes on which they were built. In addition, Hart and Timmis [2] state that current AIS do not offer sufficient advantage over other paradigms available to the engineer. To address this it was suggested that alternative immune ideas should be actively investigated in order to identify useful immune processes that could inspire unique and powerful AIS. As an example of an alternative view of the immune system, we presented the ideas of Cohen [3,4,5] who describes the immune system as a complex adaptive system, the role of which is body maintenance. It was clear from this view that there are many ideas that could inspire the development of new AIS, and the example of receptor degeneracy (the ability of an antigen receptor to respond to different ligands [6]) was highlighted. In order to exploit such an idea we suggested adopting a suitable methodology such as the conceptual framework

H. Bersini and J. Carneiro (Eds.): ICARIS 2006, LNCS 4163, pp. 164–177, 2006.
© Springer-Verlag Berlin Heidelberg 2006

approach [7], which promotes the use of an interdisciplinary set of stages to develop and analyse bio-inspired algorithms in a more principled way.

As a continuation of these ideas we present in this paper the initial stages of our work aimed at exploiting the notion of degenerate immune receptors for use in AIS. By following the conceptual framework approach [7], we have used biological detail drawn from the immunological research literature to build a computational model based on the process of T_H cell activation in the paracortex of a lymph node, in which the T_H cell receptors are assumed to be degenerate. We believe that the model we have developed is a novel tool with a richness of behaviour to enable the investigation of abstract degenerate detectors. Ultimately this investigation aims to generate enough insight to extract algorithmic design principles that will benefit the development of an AIS for pattern classification. It is noted that the degeneracy issues we explore here are not explicitly connected to the ideas of immune networks.

2   Degeneracy

Degeneracy is a property that is not only seen in the immune system, but, according to Edelman and Gally [8], is a ubiquitous biological property present at most levels of biological organisation. They define degeneracy in biology as:

> "the ability of elements that are structurally different to perform the same function or yield the same output"

Examples they give include the genetic code, where different sequences can encode the same polypeptide, and human language, where there many different ways to transmit the same message. They go on to argue that the omnipresence of degeneracy in biology is a result of it being conserved and favoured by natural selection. Additionally, it is noted that degeneracy in biological systems is typically accompanied with complexity, and it is suggested that degeneracy plays a key role in complex systems.

Parnes [9] states that even though degeneracy is a term that has been used in immunology for the last 35 years, it has escaped rigorous definition. For our work, we have adopted the definition given by Cohen [6], which describes antigen receptor degeneracy as the:

> "capacity of any single antigen receptor to bind and respond to (recognize) many different ligands"

Cohen [6] reports that the main consequence of the degeneracy of antigen receptors is *poly-recognition*, whereby a single lymphocyte clone can recognise different antigen epitopes. This causes a problem for the traditional clonal selection theory view of immunology [10] that relies on the strict specificity of lymphocyte clones. In [9], Parnes notes that in immunology there is a notable confusion between the ideas of 'degeneracy', 'cross-reactivity' and 'promiscuity'. The interested reader is referred to the Parnes [9] article for a detailed description of this issue.

As an example of the power of receptor degeneracy, Cohen [6] discusses the example of colour vision in the human eye. The eye possesses millions of colour receptors called cones of which there are only three types (red, green and blue). These receptors are degenerate, each responding to broad range of light wavelengths that overlap between the different cone types. The human brain, however, is able to perceive thousands of specific different colours, thus colour specificity is not encoded by the cones, but achieved via subsequent neuronal firings. Likewise, Cohen [6] envisages a similar recognition scenario in the immune system.

2.1 Exploiting Degeneracy

The description of degeneracy just presented pitches it as an important, advantageous and powerful property at all levels of biological organisation including the immune system. Based on this, we have chosen to investigate the property of degenerate detectors to inspire AIS development. At present there are no instances within the AIS literature where degenerate detectors have been directly addressed, although degeneracy is an issue that is both being discussed [6,9,11] and modelled [12] by immunologists. It is clear that incorporating degenerate detectors into AIS will affect the dynamics of the immune algorithm. Instead of recognition being the responsibility of a single detector, recognition will emerge from the collective response of a set of detectors. The assumed benefit of an AIS with degenerate detectors will be to provide greater scalability and generalisation over existing classifier AIS. Greater scalability can be achieved as the capacity to discriminate patterns collectively by a set of degenerate detectors should be greater than by single detectors. Thus, as the number of patterns to be recognised increases, the number of detectors needed in an AIS with degenerate recognition should be less than that of existing AIS. Better generalisation ability to recognise unseen patterns could be achieved as similar patterns should produce a similar pattern of response from the set of detectors.

To investigate and exploit degeneracy for the benefit of AIS we follow the approach previously outlined by us in [1], which advocates the use of the conceptual framework approach [7] to bio-inspired algorithm design. Following this, and as a first step before building an AIS, we investigate the biology free of any algorithmic application bias via a process of computational modelling. Based on the notion that antigen receptors of lymphocytes are degenerate, the aim of this modelling exercise is to assess the computational impact of lymphocyte antigen receptor degeneracy on epitope/antigen recognition. This includes investigating the recognition properties of sets of degenerate receptors when presented with sets of target antigens. In order to build such a model we first needed to identify a biological process where recognition by degenerate receptors might take place. An investigation of suitable immunological literature identified the lymph nodes as suitable candidate as they are the immune organs where the adaptive immune response to antigen in the lymph are triggered [13]. Biological details of the lymph node and T_H cell activation follow in section 3, which are then used in the design of an abstract computational model of degeneracy in a lymph node presented in section 4.

3   Lymph Nodes

Lymph nodes are examples of the secondary, or peripheral, immune organs, which are the sites where the adaptive immune responses to foreign antigen are initiated. The human body contains many hundred lymph nodes situated at various points in the lymphatic system (lymphatics). They are rich in both lymphocytes and antigen presenting cells (APCs) and so provide an environment where immune responses to antigen in the lymph may be triggered and develop. They thus act as filters of the lymph before it returns to the blood, capturing and responding to foreign antigen that have entered the body via portals of entry such as the skin [14,13].

Lymph nodes are small bean shaped structures connected to the lymphatics via a number of afferent lymph vessels through which lymph enters the node, and a single efferent lymph vessel through which the lymph leaves the node. Each lymph node is also connected to the circulatory system via a lymphatic artery and vein. It is through the lymphatic artery that lymphocytes (mainly naive T and B cells) enter the lymph node. As lymph drains though the node, any antigen present is captured and processed by APCs for presentation to lymphocytes, which consequently initiates the chain of events that results in the adaptive immune response. Antigen may also be transported into the lymph node by APCs, called dendritic cells, that have captured the antigen close to the portal of entry and then migrated to the node via the lymphatics.

The lymph node can be functionally separated into three distinct areas each supporting a different cellular environment: the cortex, the paracortex and the medulla. The cortex supports supports mainly B cells and various APCs (macrophages and dendritic cells), the paracortex supports mainly naive T_H cells and dendritic cells, and the medulla contains mostly lymphocytes including the antibody producing plasma cells. As lymph drains through the lymph node, it slowly percolates though each of these three regions. In the paracortex, the dendritic cells trap and process any foreign antigen and presents it via MHC-II to the naive T_H cells resulting in their activation. These T_H cells then play their part in activating B cells on the edge of the paracortex leading to B cell proliferation. This proliferation takes place in the germinal centres of the cortex, and results in antibody producing plasma cells, some of which migrate to the medulla. This whole process results in the lymph leaving the lymph node being enriched with antibodies and lymphocytes [14].

The segmentation of the lymph node into the three different areas is due to the presence of a particular variety of signalling molecules called chemokines. Both naive T_H cells and dendritic cells activated due to exposure to antigen, express the same cell-surface receptor for a chemokine produced only in the paracortex. This has the effect of attracting both of these cell types into the same area, thus enabling their interaction. Likewise, naive B cells are concentrated in the cortex as they express a receptor for a different chemokine produced only in the cortex. Once T_H and B cells have been activated by antigen/APCs, they lose their chemokine receptors from the cell surface, and therefore migrate towards each other. Thus the structure of the lymph node keeps each of the T and B cells populations in close proximity to the appropriate APCs and also apart from each other until they are in a state in which they are ready to interact with each other [13].

3.1 T_H Activation in a Lymph Node

Naive T_H cells become activated by APCs presenting MHC-II to which antigenic peptides are bound (MHC-P). In order for this activation to take place, a certain level of stimulation is required, an issue determined by two concepts known as affinity and avidity. Affinity is simply the strength of binding between a single binding site (e.g. T cell receptor) and a single ligand (e.g. an MHC-P complex). It can be quantitatively measured using a dissociation constant K_d, which is the concentration of a molecule X required to occupy half of the combining sites of another molecule Y present in a solution. Hence, a smaller K_d represents a stronger or higher affinity [13]. Affinity differs from avidity, which is a measure of the strength of binding between molecules or cells when there is more than one binding site present [15].

T cells become activated when the concentration of MHC-P complexes on an APC reaches a sufficient threshold level [16]. In other words, T cells become activated when an avidity threshold is met, and so T cell activation is affected by both the affinity between the T cell receptor and antigenic peptides presented by the APC, and the concentration of these ligands present. It is possible, therefore, for an APC presenting high concentration of MHC-P complexes with weak affinity to activate a T cell, and conversely an APC presenting a low concentration of MHC-P complexes with high affinity not to activate a T cell. Once a naive T cell has become activated it initiates a process of cellular proliferation and differentiation into effector T cells that can perform their allotted immune functions. In the case of effector T_H cells, they play a crucial role in activating both B and T_C cells which are then in turn able to neutralise pathogens.

4   Degenerate Receptor Lymph Node Model

The previous section described how the activation of naive T_H cells in the paracortex of the lymph node provides the initial recognition event of the adaptive immune response to lymph-borne antigen. The computational model that is described in this section aims to understand how this recognition event is affected by notion that the antigen receptors of T_H cells are degenerate. Specifically, the model is an abstract representation of the activation of T_H cells in the paracortex of the lymph node based on the biological detail presented in section 3, and the assumption that the T_H cell receptors can bind to more than one antigen epitope.

4.1   Overview

The first step in building the model was to extract the relevant details from the biology to enable the identification of a suitable model type. The process of T_H cell activation requires the interaction of three immune agents: dendritic cells (which we shall call APCs from this point forth), foreign antigen and T_H cells. For these agents to interact, they must be spatially close and able to move appropriately. From a computational point of view, these immune agents can be considered as specific agent types within a model, each with its own set of movement and interaction behaviours. Based on these observations a two-layer cellular automaton (CA) type approach in which APC, antigen and T_H cell agents move and interact was chosen as the modelling tool. This was deemed suitable as in a CA each element of the system is modelled individually in a physical space. Having chosen to use this approach, it was possible to reduce some of the complexity present in the real lymph node by reducing it to 2 spatial dimensions. Whilst reducing the spatial complexity of the system, this still enables the elements of the system to move in a non-trivial way.

The approach we have taken to model the immune agents and their movement due to a chemokine, is similar to that of Maree *et al.* [17] who have modelled the movement of *Dictyostelium disciodeum* amoebae due to a chemical gradient. They use a hybrid CA/partial differential equation model, where the CA is used to represent the physical details of the amoebae and the partial differential equation models the chemical gradient. In our model, two separate layers exist: a *chemical space* and an *agent space*. The chemical space models the action of the chemokine produced by the paracortex to attract naive T_H cells and APCs presenting antigen. The agent space provides the environment where the agents of the model can move and interact. Both layers are implemented as 2 dimensional grids of cells, with the agent space placed directly on top of the chemical space. Both grids therefore share the same dimensions and co-ordinate system, so for example grid reference $(2, 3)$ in the agent space would relate directly to the same grid reference in the chemical space. The contents of the cells in the chemical space are integer values representing a level of chemokine, and the contents of the cells in the agent space can either be one of the agent types or empty. See Fig. 1 for pictorial example. Wrap around occurs between the right and left edges of the cellular spaces, but not at the top and bottom. This produces an effect whereby the top of the space represents the afferent lymph vessels where lymph enters the node, and the bottom of the space represents the efferent lymph node through which the lymph leaves the node. Time is represented in the model by discrete steps called iterations, and when the model is simulated it runs for a user defined number of iterations. At each model iteration all the cells in the chemical space update, followed by agent movements in the agent space, and lastly agent interactions.

4.2   Chemical Space

Upon initialisation of the model each cell in the chemical space is set to an integer value representing a chemokine concentration. These values are randomly generated integers between 0 and a user defined maximum value. At each iteration of the model, the chemokine values update according to a diffusion rule, whereby the value at each cell is shared out equally to all the its neighbours.

The neighbourhood used for this comprises nine cells: the original cell and the eight Moore neighbours (the cells to the north, northeast, east, southeast, south, southwest, west and northwest) shown in Fig. 2. When applying the diffusion rule the chemokine value for a cell is integer divided by 9 and the resulting value shared between the neighbours. The remainder, R, from this division is then shared out randomly between the neighbours by generating R random numbers between 0 and 8 inclusive that relate to the positions of the nine neighbours, and incrementing the value of these neighbours by 1. An example of applying this diffusion rule for a cell with a chemokine value of 95 is shown in Fig. 3. Here, each neighbour is first assigned a value of 10 from the integer division step, then five random numbers (e.g. 0, 4, 5, 5 and 7) are generated resulting in the allocation of the remainder, R, to random neighbours. When applying this rule to the entire grid of cells in the chemical space, all cells are initially set to a value of 0 then the diffusion rule is applied to each cell in turn using the old chemokine value of that cell.

The effect of the diffusion rule over a number of iterations is to smooth the chemokine concentration over the entire chemical space, whilst leaving a level of stochasticity at the local level. This stochasticity is important as it provides a small amount of randomness to the agent movements in the model. To simulate the production of chemokine in the paracortex, there is a user defined parameter determining an area in the middle of the chemical space in which chemokine can be added. To provide a stable chemokine gradient, the level of chemokine that is lost at the top and bottom of the chemical space during an update (due to no cell wrap around) is counted and re-injected in the paracortex region. This re-injection takes place once an update of the entire chemical space has taken place, and the paracortex cells to which the chemical is added are determined

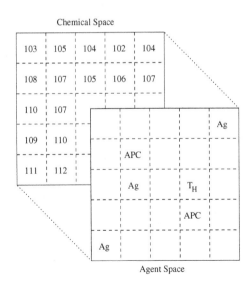

Fig. 1. The two layers of the cellular space with typical values

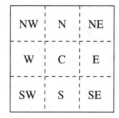

Fig. 2. The Moore neighbourhood where C = central cell, N = north, NE = northeast, E = east, SE = southeast, S = south, SW = southwest, W = west and NW = northwest

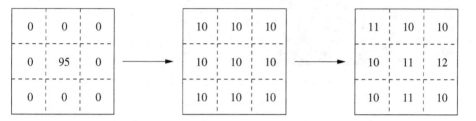

Fig. 3. An example of the stages involved in the diffusion rule in the chemical space

by random numbers. The chemokine gradient produced by these rules can be seen visually in Fig. 4, where the value of chemical is represented by a greyscale value with black being the lowest, and white the highest. Here, a lighter band can be seen in the centre of the space representing the paracortex region.

4.3   Agent Space

Cells in the agent space layer of the model can be either empty or contain one of the following agents types: antigen, APC or T_H cell. Upon initialisation, agents are placed at random positions in the agent space. When updating, all agents within the space move according to rules defined by their agent type. This is followed by all agents interacting with other agents present in their Moore neighbourhood, again according to the rules of their agent type. The functionality of the three agent types, based on the biological details presented in section 3, are described below in turn.

The antigen agents have associated with them a bit string that represents their molecular shape. The movement of the antigen agents mimics the movement of real antigen in the lymph node which drain through the node, entering at the top through afferent lymph vessels and exiting at the bottom via the efferent lymph vessel. The antigen agents, therefore, can only move down or sideways in the agent space, i.e. movements to the east, west, south, southeast and southwest neighbours. At each iteration, a random number determines which of the neighbours the agent moves to. Once an antigen leaves the bottom of the agent space it is automatically reinserted to a cell at the top of the agent space to mimic a

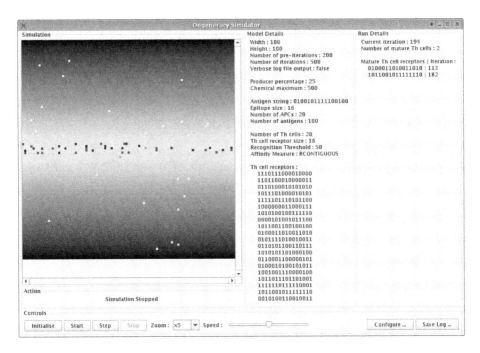

Fig. 4. A snapshot of the simulator user interface with a visual representation of the agent space on top of the chemical space in the left panel

constant flow of antigen through the node. The antigen agents do not themselves initiate any interactions with other agents, although APCs do interact with them which is described below.

The APC agents can be in one of two states that dictate their behaviour: not presenting antigen (naive) or presenting antigen (activated). All APC agents start off in the naive state and move to the activated state upon ingestion of an antigen agent. In the naive state, real dendritic cells (APCs) lack the receptor for the chemokine produced in the paracortex, thus naive APCs in this model move to a Moore neighbour determined by a random number at each iteration. Once activated, real dendritic cells produce the chemokine receptor and move towards the paracortex region. This is mimicked in the model by activated APC agents consulting the chemical space level of the model, and moving to the unoccupied Moore neighbour with the highest level of chemokine, thus following the chemokine gradient. APC agents in both the naive and activated states initiate interactions with antigen agents in their Moore neighbourhood. If the APC is naive it ingests the antigen agent, thus removing it from the agent space. Upon ingesting, the APC becomes activated, and an antigen concentration count for that APC is set to 1. A peptide bit string is generated from the bit string of the antigen that represents the peptide presented by real APCs via MHC for recognition by T_H cells. This peptide bit string is the same length as the T_H cell agent receptors in the model, and is generated as a sub-string of the antigen bit string that was ingested. If the APC agent is activated, it can ingest further antigen agents it interacts with, depending on a model parameter that determines how many antigen agents each APC is allowed to ingest. APC agents also interact with naive T_H cell agents, but this interaction is initiated by the T_H cell agent, and is described below.

All T_H cell agents in the model have associated with them a unique bit string that represents its antigen receptor. Like the APC agents, the T_H cell agents can be in one of two states that affect their behaviour: naive or activated. Again, all T_H cell agents start off in the naive state and move to the activated state upon interaction with a suitable APC agent. Like activated dendritic cells, real naive T_H cells have the receptor for the chemokine produced in the paracortex, thus the movement of naive T_H cell agents in the model is the same as activated APC agents. When real T_H cells become activated, they lose this chemokine receptor and so in the model activated T_H cell agents move to random Moore neighbours. T_H cell agents have associated with them an affinity measure type and activation threshold that is used when they interact with APC agents. Only naive T_H cell agents interact with APC agents, and these APC agents must be in the activated state, and thus, presenting a peptide bit string. When such an APC agent is in the Moore neighbourhood of a naive T_H cell agent, the avidity between the two is calculated. The affinity between the peptide being presented by the APC and the receptor of the T_H cell is calculated. As the antigen and T_H cell receptor are implemented as bit strings, two affinity measures are defined in the model which are the Hamming distance and R-contiguous bits measure. The Hamming distance returns as the affinity the result of applying the XOR operator to the strings, while the R-contiguous bits measure returns the size of the longest run of complementary bits between the strings. This affinity measure is then multiplied by the antigen concentration level of the APC to provide the avidity. This avidity is then compared to the user-defined activation threshold to determine whether the T_H cell becomes activated or not.

4.4   The Simulator

To run useful experiments, a simulator written in the Java programming language is used to execute the model just described. This can be run either interactively via a graphical user interface (see Fig. 4) or on the command line allowing for batch simulation runs. The results of a simulation run, such as the T_T cells that have become activated, can be saved to a log file for future analysis. The simulator has the following user defined parameters which are set via a configuration file:

- Width, w: The width of the cellular space in number of cells. Typically in the range 50 to 200.
- Height, h: The height of the cellular space in number of cells. Typically the same as the width.
- Number of Pre-Iterations, *pre_itns*: The number of simulation iterations before the agents are inserted. During this time only the chemical space settings up date thus allowing it time to settle down from a random initialisation.

- Number of Iterations, *itns:* The number of simulation iterations once the agents have been inserted.
- Chemokine Producer Percentage, *chem_prod:* The percentage of the total chemical space set to be the chemokine producing area.
- Maximum Chemokine Level, *chem_max:* The maximum allowed chemokine value of a chemical space cell upon initialisation of the simulator.
- Maximum Antigen Ingestion, *ag_max:* The maximum number of antigen agents a single APC is allowed to ingest.
- Number of APCs, *apc_num:* The number of APC agents.
- Number of Antigens, *ag_num:* The number of antigen agents.
- Number of T_H Cells, *th_num:* The number of T_H cell agents.
- Recognition Threshold, *recog:* A user defined avidity threshold to determine whether a T_H cell becomes activated upon interaction with an APC.
- Affinity Measure, *aff:* The type of metric used to calculate the affinity between an APC peptipe string and a T_H cell receptor.
- Antigen String, *ag:* The bit string that represents the antigen shape. This is the same for all antigen agents in the simulation.
- T_H Cell Receptors, *ths:* The list of bit strings that represent the unique receptors for each T_H cell in the simulation. The size of the list equals the number of T_H cells parameter.

5   Initial Results and Observations

In this section we first describe the behaviour of the simulator, and then show the type of results it generates. During a typical run of the simulator, a number of emergent behaviours can be seen that result from the rules of the model described above. Firstly, during the pre-iterations stage when only the chemical space updates, a visually stable chemokine gradient emerges that flows from a high concentration in the central paracortex region to a low concentration at the top and bottom of the chemical space. After the pre-iterations have finished, all the agents are inserted into the agent space at random positions and start to move and update as the iterations proceed. As the antigen agents cannot move upwards in the agent space, they cycle as a population from the top to the bottom of the agent space, being ingested as they encounter APC agents. As a results, the number of free antigen agents decreases during a run of the simulator. All the T_H cell agents are inserted in the naive state, so they immediately start to follow the chemokine gradient in the chemical space and soon settle in the centre of the paracortex area where the chemokine gradient is at its greatest. Once in the centre, the naive T_H cell agents continue to move due to the stochasticity in chemokine values at the local level of the chemical space. Like the T_H cell agents, all the APC agents are naive when inserted and thus move randomly until the ingest antigen and become activated. Once activated, they follow the same movement behaviour of the naive T_H cell agents, gravitating to the centre of the paracortex region. Once in the centre, the activated APC agents are close enough to the naive T_H cell agents for them to interact, which results in some of the T_H cell agents becoming activated depending on whether the avidity with the APC agents is above the recognition threshold. Once activated, the T_H cell agents lose their chemokine receptor and start move randomly resulting in them drifting away from the paracortex region. At the end of the simulation iterations, the activated T_H cell agents are noted. Even though the overall behaviour of the agents in the model may be what is expected, it goes some way to justify the model as the individual pieces of biology detail that has been used to build it, combines to produce behaviour (i.e. movement and interactions of immune agents) similar to that seen in real lymph nodes.

Due to the number of parameters that can be changed in the simulator, many different experiments can be run to investigate different issues and effects relating to the behaviour of the model. It is noted that a large numbers of parameters can often hinder the experimentation and results gained from simulations such as ours. However, some initial parameter investigations suggest that the behaviour of the simulator is insensitive to appropriate changes in many of the parameters such as the cellular space sizes and chemical space parameters. These parameters can therefore be kept constant for experimentation into the degenerate receptors. This leaves the simulator with only a small manageable subset of the parameters described above (such as the recognition threshold, antigen receptor and T_H cell receptors) that have a real effect on degenerate recognition in the model. By investigating the effects of these parameters, useful design principles for an AIS algorithm employing similar parameters should become apparent.

As an example, we present the results from an experiment investigating the patterns of 10 unique T_H cell agents with 8-bit receptors that become activated when the simulator is run separately with 20 different 16-bit antigens. For each antigen, the simulator is run 50 times and the percentage of simulations in which each T_H cell agent becomes activated is calculated. The results are shown in Table 1, where a blank entry means that the T_H cell agent did not become activated. The parameters used for this experiment were: $w = 50$, $h = 50$, pre_itns = 100, $itns$ = 500, $chem\_prod$ = 25%, $chem\_max$ = 500, ag_max = 1, apc_num = 10, ag_num 20, th_num = 10, $recog$ = 4 and aff = R-contiguous bits.

The degeneracy of the T_H cells can clearly be seen in the results as each T_H cell is reacting to different antigen ligands (see definition in section 2). We can also see that each of the 20 antigens invokes a unique set (pattern) of T_H cells to become activated. These sets are of different sizes for different antigens, ranging from 2 to 6 T_H cells being activated. It is interesting to note that the 2 T_H cells that become activated by Antigen 9 are also activated by Antigen 8, but the sets differ as Antigen 8 also activated 2 more T_H cells. The percentage values for the T_H cell activations can be seen as a sensitivity that the T_H cell has for the antigen. In general, the results highlight the ability of 10 randomly generated degenerate detectors to collectively distinguish between at least 20 different patterns based on the pattern of response of the detectors. This shows that our model contains degerate detectors capable of reacting in different ways to different patterns, and is therefore a tool we can use for further investigations into the properties degeneracy.

Table 1. Results of a sample experiment showing the percentage of 50 simulations in which the 10 unique T_H cell agents become activated for 20 different 16-bit antigens

	T_H 1	T_H 2	T_H 3	T_H 4	T_H 5	T_H 6	T_H 7	T_H 8	T_H 9	T_H 10
Antigen 1	62	86						64		
Antigen 2		64		62	66		70	56		70
Antigen 3			58			96				
Antigen 4		60	66					62	58	68
Antigen 5							68			62
Antigen 6		84					52	82	60	84
Antigen 7		56					82			
Antigen 8	66	48				64				58
Antigen 9						96				80
Antigen 10							62	62	50	
Antigen 11		60			94			58		
Antigen 12	58		68	60	68		68			
Antigen 13	66							70	60	
Antigen 14	60		90	62			72			
Antigen 15		50						52	74	
Antigen 16	62	84		64				90	56	88
Antigen 17	56	62						74		58
Antigen 18	54		60	58			88	60		
Antigen 19			58	56		64	58		66	66
Antigen 20		82				60		88	90	52

6   Conclusions and Future Work

In this paper we began with a desire to investigate alternative immune ideas for AIS inspiration and identified degeneracy as a possible candidate. By following the suggestions of the conceptual framework approach to bio-inspired algorithm design [7], an abstract computational modelling exercise was chosen to investigate degeneracy as the first step towards AIS design. Lymph nodes were identified as being possible places where degenerate recognition would take place by lymphocytes (in particular T_H cells) as they are the places where the adaptive immune response to foreign antigen in the lymph are initiated. By considering T_H cells to be degenerate, and investigating the biological details of the lymph node and T_H cell activation, an abstract two-layer cellular space model of degeneracy in the lymph node was designed and built, with sample results highlighting the ability of randomly generated detectors to distinguish between patterns based on their collective response. The purpose of the model we have designed is not to explain how the collective T_H response leads to the different ways the immune system responds pathogens. It is, rather, an investigation into the computational recognition capabilities of detectors based on the assumption that these detectors are inherently degenerate.

Further work will concentrate on continuing the conceptual framework [7] path to design and build an AIS that utilises degenerate detectors. Firstly, comprehensive experimentation with the model described in this paper will be used to understand better the recognition abilities of degenerate detectors. This insight will then lead to the identification of design principles for using degenerate detectors. Based on these an AIS with degenerate detectors for the task of pattern classification will be designed and built, that may provide greater scalability and generalisation performance over existing classification AIS.

References

1. Andrews, P.S., Timmis, J.: Inspiration for the next generation of artificial immune systems. In: Proceedings of the 4th International Conference on Artificial Immune Systems (ICARIS 2005), LNCS 3627, Springer (2005) 126–138
2. Hart, E., Timmis, J.: Application areas of AIS: The past, the present and the future. In: Proceedings of the 4th International Conference on Artificial Immune Systems (ICARIS 2005), LNCS 3627, Springer (2005)
3. Cohen, I.R.: Discrimination and dialogue in the immune system. Seminars in Immunology **12** (2000) 215–219
4. Cohen, I.R.: Tending Adam's Garden: Evolving the Cognitive Immune Self. Elsevier Academic Press (2000)
5. Cohen, I.R.: The creation of immune specificity. In Segal, L.A., Cohen, I.R., eds.: Design Principles for Immune Systems and Other Distributed Autonomous Systems. Oxford University Press (2001) 151–159
6. Cohen, I.R., Hershberg, U., Solomon, S.: Antigen-receptor degeneracy and immunological paradigms. Molecular Immunology **40** (2004) 993–996
7. Stepney, S., Smith, R., Timmis, J., Tyrrell, A., Neal, M., Hone, A.: Conceptual frameworks for artificial immune systems. International Journal of Unconventional Computing **1** (2005)
8. Edelman, G.M., Gally, J.A.: Degeneracy and complexity in biological systems. Proceedings of the National Academy of Science (PNAS) **98** (2001) 13763–13768
9. Parnes, O.: From interception to incorporation: Degeneracy and promiscuous recognition as precursors of a paradigm shift in immunology. Molecular Immunology **40** (2004) 985–991
10. Burnet, F.M.: The Clonal Selection Theory of Acquired Immunity. Cambridge University Press (1959)
11. Sercarz, E.E., Maverakis, E.: Recognition and function in a degenerate immune system. Molecular Immunology **40** (2004) 1003–1008
12. Tieri, P., Castellani, G.C., Remondini, D., Valensin, S., Loroni, J., Salvioli, S., Franceschi, C.: Capturing degeneracy of the immune system. In Flower, D., Timmis, J., eds.: To appear: In Silico Immunology. Springer (2007)
13. Abbas, A.K., Lichtman, A.H.: Cellular and Molecular Immunology, 5th edition. Saunders (2003)
14. Goldsby, R.A., Kindt, T.J., Osborne, B.A., Kuby, J.: Immunology 5th edition. W. H. Freeman and Company (2003)
15. Janeway, C.A., Travers, P., Walport, M., Shlomchik, M.: Immunobiology 5th edition. Garland Publishing (2001)
16. Anderton, S.M., Wraith, D.C.: Selection and fine-tuning of the autoimmune t-cell repertoire. Nature Reviews Immunology **2** (2002) 487–498
17. Maree, A.F.M., Panfilov, A.V., Hogeweg, P.: Migration and thermotaxis of Dictyostelium discoideum slugs, a model study. Journal of Theoretical Biology **199** (1999) 297–309

Structural Properties of Shape-Spaces

Werner Dilger

Chemnitz University of Technology
09107 Chemnitz, Germany
dilger@informatik.tu-chemnitz.de

Abstract. General properties of distance functions and of affinity functions are discussed in this paper. Reasons are given why a distance function for $\Re n$ based shape-spaces should be a metric. Several distance functions that are used in shape-spaces are examined and it is shown that not all of them are metrics. It is shown which impact the type of the distance function has on the shape-space, in particular on the form of recognition or affinity regions in the shape-space. Affinity functions should be defined in such a way that they determine an affinity region with positive values inside that region and zero or negative values outside. The form of an affinity function depends on the type of the underlying distance function. This is demonstrated with several examples.

Keywords: Shape-space, distance function, metric, affinity function, affinity region.

1 Introduction

The mostly used definition of shape-spaces is the one introduced by Perelson and Oster in [12]. According to this definition, the interaction between elements of the immune system (cells, antibodies, or molecules) and antigens is determined by properties of shape. Actually, this approach is an abstraction from the real immune system, where the interaction is essentially based on electrical forces due to the charge distribution on the surface of the molecules. The next step of abstraction, then, is the representation of the shape properties by a string of parameters of certain types of values like binary, integer, real, or symbolic.

A basic notion in the Perelson/Oster shape-space is that of complementarity, which means that an immune element and an antigen must have complementary shapes in order to exert affinity on each other. On the basis of the vector representation, in many AIS realizations complementarity has been replaced with similarity (cf. [4]), just by "changing the sign". Different types of affinity have been defined, depending on the type of the shape-space as a vector space, but all of them are based on some distance measure like Euclidean distance or Hamming distance.

In [1], Bersini introduced an alternative definition of a shape-space which on first glance departs considerably from the Perelson/Oster definition. The shape-space is based on $\Re^n$, more precisely on $\Re^2$. However, Bersini uses a special definition of affinity which makes his shape-space particularly interesting. This definition

H. Bersini and J. Carneiro (Eds.): ICARIS 2006, LNCS 4163, pp. 178–192, 2006.
© Springer-Verlag Berlin Heidelberg 2006

incorporates complementarity as mirror image (or complementary) positions in $\mathfrak{R}^2$ together with a fixed affinity region where the immune elements (antibodies) are attracted with graded force. Bersini's approach has been adopted and modified in several ways by Hart and Ross [7] who demonstrate the properties of this kind of shape-space by a number of simulation experiments.

The properties of Bersini's shape-space and some extensions of it were discussed in detail in [6]. The aim of this paper is to give a general framework for the definition of shape-spaces that reveals the similarities and differences between various approaches. Also, I argue that a shape-space defined over $\mathfrak{R}^n$ should be a metric space. This is mainly done in section 2. In section 3, the principles described in section 2 are adopted for finite shape-spaces. Various approaches for defining distance functions on Hamming spaces are examined and it is shown that not all of them are metrics. Based on distance functions, affinity functions can be defined in different ways which are presented in section 4.

2 Structural Aspects of Shape-Spaces

I will make two general presuppositions about shape-spaces. First, a shape-space is a set S of attribute strings of finite length. The values of the attributes can be taken from arbitrary domains. Second, on S a function $d: S \times S \to \mathfrak{R}$ is defined, called "distance function", which satisfies the following conditions: If $\mathbf{x}, \mathbf{y} \in S$ then

(i) $d(\mathbf{x}, \mathbf{y}) \geq 0$

(ii) $d(\mathbf{x}, \mathbf{y}) = 0 \Leftrightarrow \mathbf{x} = \mathbf{y}$

(iii) $d(\mathbf{x}, \mathbf{y}) = d(\mathbf{y}, \mathbf{x})$

There are no additional requirements on d, i.e. one is free to choose an arbitrary two-dimensional function as long as it satisfies the three conditions. Therefore, even such a strange function as the following one can serve as a distance function:

$$d(\mathbf{x}, \mathbf{y}) = \begin{cases} 0, & \text{if } \mathbf{x} = \mathbf{y} \\ 1, & \text{otherwise} \end{cases} \tag{1}$$

Commonly used distance functions on $\mathfrak{R}^n$ are Euclidean and Manhattan distance:

Euclidean $d_E(\mathbf{x}, \mathbf{y}) = \sqrt{\sum_{i=1}^{n} (x_i - y_i)^2}$ (2)

Manhattan $d_M(\mathbf{x}, \mathbf{y}) = \sum_{i=1}^{n} |x_i - y_i|$ (3)

Since the distance function d is a constituent part of a shape-space, I will denote a shape-space in the following as a pair (S, d). Clearly, the function d induces a structure on a shape-space depending on the form of the function, such that two shape-spaces (S, d_1) and (S, d_2) with different distance functions are different even if the underlying set is the same.

An important concept in shape-spaces that is used for the definition of affinity (cf. section 4) is that of complementarity. It can be defined for binary strings in a natural way but can be adopted for arbitrary shape-spaces. The complement of an element $\mathbf{i}$ is denoted as *compl*($\mathbf{i}$). Often the complement is defined with respect to a third element $\mathbf{c}$ and will be denoted by *compl$_c$*($\mathbf{i}$, $\mathbf{c}$) or $\mathbf{i_c}$ for short. If we assume that the distance function is the only structure that is defined on the carrier set of the shape-space (nothing has been said about any other structure) then the complement must be defined by means of the distance function alone. All elements of the space that have the distance $d(\mathbf{i}, \mathbf{c})$ from $\mathbf{c}$ lie on the surface of an n-dimensional ball with center $\mathbf{c}$ and radius $d(\mathbf{i}, \mathbf{c})$. There is a point on this surface that has the distance $2d(\mathbf{i}, \mathbf{c})$ (the diameter of the ball) from $\mathbf{i}$. This point will be taken as the desired element $\mathbf{i_c}$. But is this point uniquely determined? It depends on the distance function d.

For instance for the function we get $d(\mathbf{i}, \mathbf{c}) = d(\mathbf{i_c}, \mathbf{c}) = d(\mathbf{i}, \mathbf{i_c}) = 1$, thus a complementary element cannot be uniquely determined. We want to exclude distance functions of this type and this can be done by an additional condition on distance functions, the so called *triangle inequation* (cf. [10]): For an arbitrary element $\mathbf{z}$

(iv) $d(\mathbf{x}, \mathbf{y}) \leq d(\mathbf{x}, \mathbf{z}) + d(\mathbf{z}, \mathbf{y})$

Notice that with this additional condition the distance function becomes a metric and the shape-space a metric space. Now for the complement $\mathbf{i_c}$ according to the definition above it must hold $d(\mathbf{i}, \mathbf{c}) = d(\mathbf{c}, \mathbf{i_c})$. Together with the triangle inequation we get $d(\mathbf{i}, \mathbf{i_c}) \leq d(\mathbf{i}, \mathbf{c}) + d(\mathbf{c}, \mathbf{i_c}) = 2d(\mathbf{i}, \mathbf{c})$. On the other hand, $\mathbf{i_c}$ shall be the point farthest away from $\mathbf{i}$ but still on the ball, i.e. its distance from $\mathbf{i}$ should be at least the diameter of the ball, in other words, $d(\mathbf{i}, \mathbf{i_c}) \geq 2d(\mathbf{i}, \mathbf{c})$, so altogether $d(\mathbf{i}, \mathbf{i_c}) = 2d(\mathbf{i}, \mathbf{c})$. However, the triangle inequation is only a necessary condition for the existence of such a point, not a sufficient one.

An important concept in metric spaces is the ε-*ball* (cf. [10]). An ε-ball centered at some point $\mathbf{i}$ is the set $b(\varepsilon, \mathbf{i}) = \{\mathbf{x} \in S: d(\mathbf{i}, \mathbf{x}) < \varepsilon\}$. Obviously, the form of the ε-ball depends on the distance function. For the Euclidean distance the ball is defined by $\sqrt{\sum_{i=1}^{n} (x_i - y_i)^2} < \varepsilon$ or $\sum_{i=1}^{n} (x_i - y_i)^2 < \varepsilon^2$ which is a hyperball in $\mathfrak{R}^n$, a ball in $\mathfrak{R}^3$, and a circle in $\mathfrak{R}^2$. For the Manhattan distance, the ε-ball is a hyperrhombus of dimension n with 2^n planes, i.e. in the three-dimensional case it is a regular diamond with eight planes and in the two-dimensional case it is a rhombus, as is shown in [6].

Let us examine these two metrics with respect to complementary elements. Clearly, in the Euclidean metric the complement $\mathbf{i_c}$ of $\mathbf{i}$ is a unique point. All other points on the surface of the ball around $\mathbf{c}$ have a shorter distance from $\mathbf{i}$ than $\mathbf{i_c}$. In the Manhattan metric, things are different. Consider the case illustrated in figure 1 for two dimensions. All points on the thick side of the rhombus have the same distance from $\mathbf{c}$ and therefore also from $\mathbf{i}$, thus there is no unique complementary point $\mathbf{i_c}$. This follows from the Manhattan metric as can be easily proved. Consider the two points $\mathbf{p}$ and $\mathbf{q}$ with the coordinates $(c_1, c_2 - L)$ and $(c_1 + L, c_2)$ for some $L > 0$, L is half the length of the diagonal. An arbitrary point $\mathbf{y}$ on the line between $\mathbf{p}$ and $\mathbf{q}$ has the coordinates $(\lambda c_1 + (1 - \lambda)(c_1 + L), \lambda(c_2 - L) + (1 - \lambda)c_2) = (c_1 + (1 - \lambda)L, c_2 - \lambda L)$ with $0 \leq \lambda \leq 1$. The distance of this point from $\mathbf{c}$ according to Manhattan distance is computed by

$$d_M(\mathbf{c}, \mathbf{y}) = |c_1 - c_1 - (1 - \lambda)L| + |c_2 - c_2 + \lambda L|$$
$$= |(1 - \lambda)L| + |\lambda L| \tag{4}$$
$$= (1 - \lambda)L + \lambda L = L$$

Thus every point on the side has the same distance to the center and this holds for all sides. As a consequence, the length of the side and the length of the diagonal are equal.

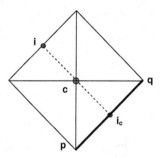

Fig. 1. Complementary element in a Manhattan shape-space

One way to achieve a unique complement is to require that the three points **i**, **c** and **i$_c$** lie on a straight line. This results in an additional condition:

(v) $c_j = \left(i_j + i_{\mathbf{c}_j}\right)/2$ for all $j = 1, \ldots, n$

Notice that this holds only for shape-spaces based on infinite sets, in particular $\mathfrak{R}^n$. Things are different and simpler for finite shape-spaces, in particular Hamming spaces, because here the complement is determined uniquely in a natural way as will be shown in the next section.

3   Finite Shape-Spaces

If V is a finite set of n elements, the power set of V, 2^V, forms a complete lattice with respect to set inclusion. This lattice is isomorphic to the lattice formed by the set H of binary strings of length n with **1** as top and **0** as bottom element and an appropriate partial order on the set. To define such an order we need a function that counts the number of 1's in a string. This is equivalent to computing the sum of the digits of the number; the desired function will be called *ones*, i.e.

$$ones(\mathbf{x}) = \sum_{i=1}^{n} x_i \tag{5}$$

By means of *ones* the partial order $\prec$ on H is defined as follows:

$$\mathbf{x} \prec \mathbf{y} \Leftrightarrow ones(\mathbf{y}) = ones(\mathbf{x}) + 1 \wedge ones(XOR(\mathbf{x}, \mathbf{y})) = 1 \tag{6}$$

Figure 2 shows this lattice for $n = 4$. The set H provided with a distance function is called a (*binary*) *Hamming shape-space*. A usual definition of a distance function on H (cf. e.g. [4]) is the following one:

$$d_{XOR}(\mathbf{x}, \mathbf{y}) = ones(XOR(\mathbf{x}, \mathbf{y})) \tag{7}$$

thus (H, d_{XOR}) is a shape-space. Because of the isomorphism between $(2^V, \subseteq)$ (V a finite set) and $(H, \prec)$ we can restrict the investigation of finite shape-spaces to that of binary Hamming spaces.

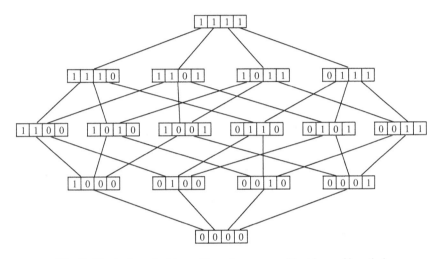

Fig. 2. The lattice of a binary Hamming space with strings of length 4

In section 2 I argued that in $\mathfrak{R}^n$ based shape-spaces distance functions should be metrics in order to define complementary elements. This does not hold for Hamming shape-spaces because here the complement of an element can be defined independently from the chosen distance function. However, one may ask if all distance functions are metrics as some authors believe (e.g. [8]). Therefore some distance functions that are in use for Hamming spaces will be examined in the following.

First, I will show that d_{XOR} is a metric. For this purpose the conditions (i) – (iv) of the definition must be checked. The first three are trivial. The triangle inequation can be proven as follows: Assume $ones(XOR(\mathbf{x}, \mathbf{y})) = k$. Then $\mathbf{x}$ and $\mathbf{y}$ differ in k positions. If $\mathbf{z} = \mathbf{x}$ or $\mathbf{z} = \mathbf{y}$ the triangle inequation is trivially satisfied. If $\mathbf{z} \neq \mathbf{x}$ and $\mathbf{z} \neq \mathbf{y}$ let $ones(XOR(\mathbf{x}, \mathbf{z})) = l$ and $ones(XOR(\mathbf{y}, \mathbf{z})) = m$. This means, $\mathbf{z}$ is identical with $\mathbf{x}$ except in l positions. But then $\mathbf{z}$ must be different from $\mathbf{y}$ in at least $k - l$ positions, otherwise $ones(XOR(\mathbf{x}, \mathbf{y})) < k$, therefore $l + m \geq k$.

Since d_{XOR} is a metric, we can also describe what an ε-ball centered around an element $\mathbf{i}$ would be. It is defined by $b(\varepsilon, \mathbf{i}) = \{\mathbf{x} \in S: ones(XOR(\mathbf{i}, \mathbf{x})) < \varepsilon\}$. The points $\mathbf{x}$ in the ε-ball have the property that they differ from $\mathbf{i}$ in at most $\lfloor \varepsilon \rfloor$ positions, where

$\lfloor \varepsilon \rfloor$ is the greatest integer less than ε. Let $\lfloor \varepsilon \rfloor = k$. Then the surface of the ε-ball is the set of points $\mathbf{x}$ with $ones(XOR(\mathbf{i}, \mathbf{x})) = k$. These points can be reached from $\mathbf{i}$ traversing through the lattice on paths of length k. Take as an example the point 1101 in figure 2. In order to determine the points that can be reached on paths of length 2 from 1101 it is easier to change the lattice of figure 2 such that 1101 becomes the top element, cf. figure 3.

In this lattice we have to go down two steps from the top element and find the elements that are different from $\mathbf{i}$ in exactly two positions. These points form the surface of an ε-ball with $2 \leq \varepsilon < 3$. Notice that for this lattice a variant of the partial order is required. It is defined by

$$\mathbf{x} \prec \mathbf{y} \Leftrightarrow ones(XOR(\mathbf{x}, \mathbf{y})) = 1 \wedge ones(XOR(\mathbf{y}, \mathbf{top})) < ones(XOR(\mathbf{x}, \mathbf{top})) \qquad (8)$$

where $\mathbf{top}$ is the chosen top element, i.e. $\mathbf{i}$. Actually, the lattice of an n-dimensional Hamming space is an n-dimensional diamond that can be turned in arbitrary direction such that every element can become the top element.

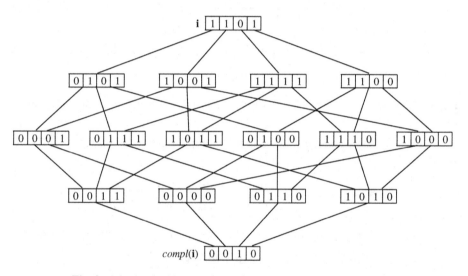

Fig. 3. A lattice for binary strings of length 4 with top element 1101

Usually, the complement of an element $\mathbf{x} \in H$ is defined as the element $\mathbf{y}$ for which $XOR(\mathbf{x}, \mathbf{y}) = \mathbf{1}$ holds, i.e. $compl(\mathbf{x}) = \mathbf{y} \Leftrightarrow XOR(\mathbf{x}, \mathbf{y}) = \mathbf{1}$. Figure 4 illustrates this operation.

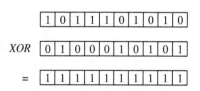

Fig. 4. The operation *compl* in a Hamming space

There are also other distance functions in use for Hamming spaces. One is the r-contiguous bit rule [11]. Its definition is based on the XOR-function like the distance function above. The rule adopts the maximum of a certain set of values that is defined by

$$U(\mathbf{u}) = \{ones(\mathbf{s}) \mid \mathbf{s} \text{ is a substring of } \mathbf{u} \text{ with } ones(\mathbf{s}) = length(\mathbf{s})\} \qquad (9)$$

The condition in U guarantees that the selected substrings only contain 1's. By means of the set U the r-contiguous bit rule can be formulated as

$$r - cont(\mathbf{x}, \mathbf{y}) = max\, U(XOR(\mathbf{x}, \mathbf{y})) \qquad (10)$$

It is easy to see that this definition of the r-contiguous-rule satisfies the first three conditions of a metric. But it does not satisfy the triangle inequation. Figure 5 gives a counterexample. Thus, for any set of binary strings H, $(H, r\text{-}cont)$ is not a metric space.

x | 1 | 0 | 1 | 1 | 1 | 0 | 1 | 0 | 1 | 1 r-cont(**x**, **y**) = 3

y | 1 | 1 | 1 | 0 | 0 | 1 | 1 | 0 | 0 | 1 r-cont(**x**, **z**) = 1

z | 1 | 0 | 1 | 0 | 1 | 1 | 1 | 0 | 0 | 1 r-cont(**y**, **z**) = 1

Fig. 5. An example showing that the r-contiguous-rule does not satisfy the triangle inequation

A variant of the r-contiguous rule is the multiple contiguous bit rule [9]. For its definition the following set V is required:

$$V(\mathbf{x}, \mathbf{y}) = \left\{ ones(\mathbf{s}_i) \middle| \begin{array}{l} \mathbf{s}_i \text{ is the } i^{th} \text{ substring of } \mathbf{u} \text{ with} \\ ones(\mathbf{s}) = length(\mathbf{s}) \geq 2 \text{ and } \mathbf{u} = XOR(\mathbf{x}, \mathbf{y}) \end{array} \right\} \qquad (11)$$

By means of the set V the multiple contiguous bit rule can be defined as follows:

$$mult - cont(\mathbf{x}, \mathbf{y}) = ones(XOR(\mathbf{x}, \mathbf{y})) + \sum_i 2^{weight(s_i)} \qquad (12)$$

Like the r-contiguous bit rule, the multiple contiguous bit rule trivially satisfies the conditions of a distance function. However, it does not satisfy the triangle inequation. This can be shown with the example of figure 5. Figure 6 shows the strings $XOR(\mathbf{x}, \mathbf{y})$, $XOR(\mathbf{x}, \mathbf{z})$, and $XOR(\mathbf{y}, \mathbf{z})$ and the value of $mult$-$cont$ for these strings. So again, $(H, mult\text{-}cont)$ is not a metric space.

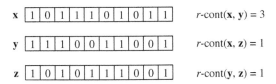

| 0 | 1 | 0 | 1 | 1 | 1 | 0 | 0 | 1 | 0 | $XOR(\mathbf{x}, \mathbf{y})$ $mult$-$cont(\mathbf{x}, \mathbf{y}) = 13$

| 0 | 0 | 0 | 1 | 0 | 1 | 0 | 0 | 1 | 0 | $XOR(\mathbf{x}, \mathbf{z})$ $mult$-$cont(\mathbf{x}, \mathbf{z}) = 3$

| 0 | 1 | 0 | 0 | 1 | 0 | 0 | 0 | 0 | 0 | $XOR(\mathbf{y}, \mathbf{z})$ $mult$-$cont(\mathbf{y}, \mathbf{z}) = 2$

Fig. 6. The strings $XOR(\mathbf{x}, \mathbf{y})$, $XOR(\mathbf{x}, \mathbf{z})$, and $XOR(\mathbf{y}, \mathbf{z})$ with **x**, **y**, and **z** as in figure 6

The similarity measure of Rogers and Tanimoto (abbreviated R/T) has been used as an affinity measure [13]. We will examine the underlying distance function to see if it is a metric. R/T uses the following four auxiliary functions:

$$a(\mathbf{x}, \mathbf{y}) = ones(AND(\mathbf{x}, \mathbf{y}))$$
$$b(\mathbf{x}, \mathbf{y}) = ones(AND(\mathbf{x}, NOT(\mathbf{y}))) \qquad (13)$$
$$c(\mathbf{x}, \mathbf{y}) = ones(AND(NOT(\mathbf{x}), \mathbf{y}))$$
$$d(\mathbf{x}, \mathbf{y}) = ones(AND(NOT(\mathbf{x}), NOT(\mathbf{y})))$$

With these functions the measure is defined as

$$R/T\,(\mathbf{x}, \mathbf{y}) = \frac{a(\mathbf{x}, \mathbf{y}) + d(\mathbf{x}, \mathbf{y})}{a(\mathbf{x}, \mathbf{y}) + d(\mathbf{x}, \mathbf{y}) + 2(b(\mathbf{x}, \mathbf{y}) + c(\mathbf{x}, \mathbf{y}))} \qquad (14)$$

This function has some properties which show that it cannot be interpreted as a distance function.[1] First, since for all $\varphi \in \{a, b, c, d\}$ it holds $\varphi(\mathbf{x}, \mathbf{y}) \geq 0$, it follows that $0 \leq R/T(\mathbf{x}, \mathbf{y}) \leq 1$, i.e. the value domain is normalized, which seems unnatural for a distance function. Second, $R/T(\mathbf{x}, \mathbf{x}) = 1$ because $a(\mathbf{x}, \mathbf{x}) + d(\mathbf{x}, \mathbf{x}) = n$ and $b(\mathbf{x}, \mathbf{x}) = c(\mathbf{x}, \mathbf{x}) = 0$. Thus, R/T does not even satisfy condition (ii) of a distance function. Third, $R/T(\mathbf{x}, \mathbf{y}) = 0$ if and only if $a(\mathbf{x}, \mathbf{y}) = d(\mathbf{x}, \mathbf{y}) = 0$, again because $\varphi(\mathbf{x}, \mathbf{y}) \geq 0$ for all $\varphi \in \{a, b, c, d\}$. (Notice that in this case $b(\mathbf{x}, \mathbf{y}) + c(\mathbf{x}, \mathbf{y}) > 0$.) But $a(\mathbf{x}, \mathbf{y}) = 0$ requires that there is no position where both, $\mathbf{x}$ and $\mathbf{y}$, have a 1, correspondingly for $d(\mathbf{x}, \mathbf{y}) = 0$, i.e. $\mathbf{x}$ and $\mathbf{y}$ are complementary.

These observations lead to the following definition of R/T: In the numerator of the function all positions are counted where $\mathbf{x}$ and $\mathbf{y}$ are equal (either 0 or 1). The same value can be achieved if first XOR is applied, then NOT, and then the number of 1's in the result is counted. In the denominator the same value occurs augmented by the number of positions where $\mathbf{x}$ and $\mathbf{y}$ are different. This gives

$$R/T\,(\mathbf{x}, \mathbf{y}) = \frac{ones(NOT(XOR(\mathbf{x}, \mathbf{y})))}{ones(NOT(XOR(\mathbf{x}, \mathbf{y}))) + 2 \cdot ones(XOR(\mathbf{x}, \mathbf{y}))}$$
$$= \frac{n - ones(XOR(\mathbf{x}, \mathbf{y}))}{n - ones(XOR(\mathbf{x}, \mathbf{y})) + 2 \cdot ones(XOR(\mathbf{x}, \mathbf{y}))} \qquad (15)$$
$$= \frac{n - ones(XOR(\mathbf{x}, \mathbf{y}))}{n + ones(XOR(\mathbf{x}, \mathbf{y}))}$$
$$= \frac{n - d_{XOR}(\mathbf{x}, \mathbf{y})}{n + d_{XOR}(\mathbf{x}, \mathbf{y})}$$

where n is the length of the binary strings. In order to prove the equivalence of the two definitions (14) and (15) we have to show that $a(\mathbf{x}, \mathbf{y}) + d(\mathbf{x}, \mathbf{y}) = n - ones(XOR(\mathbf{x}, \mathbf{y}))$ and $b(\mathbf{x}, \mathbf{y}) + c(\mathbf{x}, \mathbf{y}) = ones(XOR(\mathbf{x}, \mathbf{y}))$. $a(\mathbf{x}, \mathbf{y}) + d(\mathbf{x}, \mathbf{y})$ is the

---

[1] Actually, Rogers and Tanimoto intended to define a similarity measure [15] which is more or less the opposite of a distance function.

number of all positions j where $x_j = y_j$. $XOR(\mathbf{x}, \mathbf{y})$ is the vector with 1's in all positions j where $x_j \neq y_j$ and $ones(XOR(\mathbf{x}, \mathbf{y}))$ is the number of those 1's, thus $n - ones(XOR(\mathbf{x}, \mathbf{y}))$ is the number of those positions where $x_j = y_j$ and therefore both terms have the same value. A similar argument can be given for the second case.

Given some $\mathbf{i} \in H$, the R/T-function has a maximum exactly for the point $\mathbf{y}$ with $\mathbf{i} = \mathbf{y}$, and for all other binary vectors it has some value between 0 and 1. It has a minimum for the point $\mathbf{y}$ which is the complement of $\mathbf{i}$. Thus R/T changes the form of the lattice of figure 2 in such a way that for a special element $\mathbf{i}$ this element becomes the top element and $compl(\mathbf{i})$ the bottom element, cf. figure 3. The function decreases with growing values of $d_{XOR}(\mathbf{x}, \mathbf{y})$ from 1 to 0 in an exponential form. This is shown in figure 7 for $n = 10$.

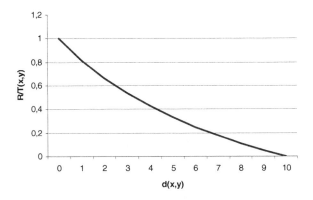

Fig. 7. The form of the Rogers/Tanimoto function for $n = 10$

4   Affinity Functions

Shape-spaces are not defined as abstract structures; rather their main purpose is to describe a special relationship between their elements called *affinity*. The affinity between two immune elements certainly depends on their distance in the shape-space. Several authors, e.g. [2], [3], consider affinity as a constant quantity and are interested in the total amount of influence of other elements on some immune element $\mathbf{x}$. In [1], a more detailed concept of affinity is given. According to it, affinity is a time dependent quantity and in addition depends on the concentration of an element $\mathbf{i}$ that exerts affinity on other elements. I will adopt this approach in the following.

The question is, whether shape is a constant property of immune elements and therefore also the distances between them, in particular antibodies, or not. The shape of an antibody can be modified by mutation. However, according to the usual definitions of mutation, the distances between an element and its mutants are small, so that the mutants of an element $\mathbf{x}$ lie in an ε-ball around $\mathbf{x}$ with small ε. Therefore distance will be considered as a constant quantity in the following, i.e. the distance between $\mathbf{y}$ and $\mathbf{x}$ and that between $\mathbf{y}$ and a mutant of $\mathbf{x}$ are taken as equal.

Affinity, however, will be considered as time dependent. Like in [1], it will be defined as a function that determines the amount of affinity between two elements and at the same time a limited region in the shape-space, the *affinity region*, which has the form of an ε-ball. The affinity function shall have positive but restricted values inside the affinity region and be zero or negative outside.

Let T be the infinite set of time points. The affinity that an element **i** exerts on an element **x** at time t is defined as a function *aff*: $S \times S \times T \rightarrow \Re$ and is denoted by *aff*(**i**, **x**, t). There are two main types of affinity presented in the literature [cf. 5], one called *similarity based* and another called *complementarity based*. In both types, affinity is defined as inversely proportional to distance, i.e. the smaller the distance between **i** and **x** the higher the affinity. The two elements are understood as similar if their distance is small. For the second type of affinity we need the concept of complementarity as defined in section 2. In order to distinguish between the two forms of affinity I will use the notation *aff*$_s$(**i**, **x**, t) for the similarity based affinity and *aff*$_c$(**i**, **x**, t) for the complementarity based affinity. In the second version affinity is defined as inversely proportional to the distance between **x** and **i**$_c$. The points around **i** or **i**$_c$ respectively form an ε-*ball*, which is known as the *recognition region* [5, 14] or the *affinity region* [1].

In the following I will first present a formal treatment of affinity functions and then show, that this is just a generalization of other approaches that explicitly consider concentration of elements in the definition. There are different ways to define the function *aff* such that it has the desired property. The simplest form of *aff* would be a function with a constant (but time dependent) positive value inside the affinity region and zero outside. The affinity region is simply determined by an upper bound to the distance:

$$aff(\mathbf{i}, \mathbf{x}, t) = \begin{cases} a(t) & \text{if } d(\mathbf{i}, \mathbf{x}) \leq b(t) \\ 0 & \text{otherwise} \end{cases} \tag{16}$$

a and b are functions of time, b is used as an upper bound to the distance. The affinity region is an ε-ball around **i** restricted by $b(t)$. The form of the ε-ball depends on the definition of d. However, such a definition seems not adequate because all elements in the affinity region have the same affinity $a(t)$ and there is no difference of affinity between elements close to **i** and those more remote. A more adequate form seems to be a linear function. It has the general form

$$aff(\mathbf{i}, \mathbf{x}, t) = a(t) \cdot d(\mathbf{i}, \mathbf{x}) + b(t) \tag{17}$$

Again, a and b are functions of time. Let us consider some properties of this function, more precisely of *aff*$_s$. *aff*$_s$(**i**, **x**, t) = 0 iff $a(t) \cdot d(\mathbf{i}, \mathbf{x}) + b(t) = 0$ or

$$d(\mathbf{i}, \mathbf{x}) = -\frac{b(t)}{a(t)} \tag{18}$$

We assume that $a(t) \neq 0$. If $a(t) = 0$ then $b(t)$ must also be zero which denotes the extreme case of an affinity region shrunk to a point. The distance between two elements must be a positive value, therefore $b(t)$ and $a(t)$ must have opposite signs. Thus from (18) we get the equation $a(t){\cdot}d(\mathbf{i}, \mathbf{x}) - b(t) = 0$ or $-a(t){\cdot}d(\mathbf{i}, \mathbf{x}) + b(t) = 0$, assuming both, $a(t)$ and $b(t)$, are positive. These equations describe the rim of the affinity region (the surface of an ε-ball). Its form is determined by the distance function d and its size by the functions a and b. The points on the rim are exactly those $\mathbf{x}$ for which $d(\mathbf{i}, \mathbf{x}) = b(t)/a(t)$.

For the points inside or outside the region the inequations that can be derived from the two equations must be treated separately. In the second form of the inequation, $-a(t){\cdot}d(\mathbf{i}, \mathbf{x}) + b(t) < 0$ (i.e. aff is negative) is equivalent to $a(t){\cdot}d(\mathbf{i}, \mathbf{x}) > b(t)$, i.e. for the points outside the affinity region, and $-a(t){\cdot}d(\mathbf{i}, \mathbf{x}) + b(t) > 0$ (aff is positive) is equivalent to $a(t){\cdot}d(\mathbf{i}, \mathbf{x}) < b(t)$, i.e. for the points inside the affinity region. The first form of the inequation would have the (undesired) opposite result. The two cases are illustrated by figure 8. Therefore the only linear version of aff that yields an affinity region with positive values of the affinity function is that of equation (19):

$$aff(\mathbf{i}, \mathbf{x}, t) = -a(t) \cdot d(\mathbf{i}, \mathbf{x}) + b(t) \tag{19}$$

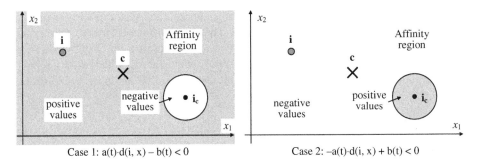

Case 1: a(t)·d(i, x) – b(t) < 0   Case 2: –a(t)·d(i, x) + b(t) < 0

Fig. 8. Regions with positive or negative affinity values depending on the form of the function

Since aff is restricted inside the affinity region by $b(t)$, it adopts a maximum at the point $\mathbf{x} = \mathbf{i}$, its value is clearly $b(t)$. aff can also be defined as a quadratic function:

$$aff(\mathbf{i}, \mathbf{x}, t) = -a(t) \cdot d(\mathbf{i}, \mathbf{x})^2 + b(t) \tag{20}$$

(For simplicity, the linear component of the equation is omitted.) This function is zero if $d(\mathbf{i}, \mathbf{x}) = \sqrt{b(t)/a(t)}$ (the rim of the affinity region), positive if $d(\mathbf{i}, \mathbf{x}) < \sqrt{b(t)/a(t)}$, i.e. inside the region, and negative outside. However, higher order functions would have the unpleasant result that the region of positive values is not coherent, for instance it could look like the shadowed regions in figure 8 for the complementarity based affinity. Therefore such functions will not be considered as adequate representations of affinity.

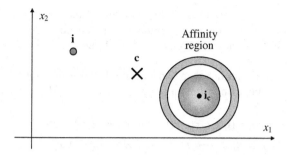

Fig. 9. A non-coherent affinity region

aff can also be defined by a bell-shaped function like the following:

$$aff(\mathbf{i}, \mathbf{x}, t) = a(t) \cdot \frac{e^{-\gamma \cdot d(\mathbf{i}, \mathbf{x})}}{\left(1 + e^{-\gamma \cdot d(\mathbf{i}, \mathbf{x})}\right)^2} \tag{21}$$

This function never adopts the value 0 but its value is very low outside some limited circular region. Thus, by diminishing the function by some small constant we can get the desired version.

To illustrate the definitions in this section, let us consider the complementarity based version of affinity for the two-dimensional shape-space and with linear affinity function. If d is the Euclidean metric, the affinity function is

$$aff_c(i_1, i_2, x_1, x_2, t) = -a(t) \cdot \sqrt{(2c_1 - i_1 - x_1)^2 + (2c_2 - i_2 - x_2)^2} + b(t) \tag{22}$$

The affinity region is defined by the condition $aff_c(i_1, i_2, x_1, x_2, t) = 0$ or $b(t)/a(t) = \sqrt{(2c_1 - i_1 - x_1)^2 + (2c_2 - i_2 - x_2)^2}$ which means that it is a circle with radius $b(t)/a(t)$. The points inside the circle have positive values and the maximum value is at the point $(2c_1 - i_1, 2c_2 - i_2)$, i.e. at the center of the circle. The affinity function has the form of a cone. If d is the Manhattan metric, the affinity function is

$$aff_c(i_1, i_2, x_1, x_2, t) = -a(t) \cdot (|2c_1 - i_1 - x_1| + |2c_2 - i_2 - x_2|) + b(t) \tag{23}$$

The rim of the affinity region is given by $b(t)/a(t) = (|2c_1 - i_1 - x_1| + |2c_2 - i_2 - x_2|)$. Thus it is a rhombus with center $(2c_1 - i_1, 2c_2 - i_2)$ and a pyramid as the form of the affinity function, as was shown in [6]. Let us consider Bersini's version of the function in [1] written in the notation used throughout this paper:

$$aff_c(i_1, i_2, x_1, x_2, t) = C(i_1, i_2, t) \cdot (L - (|2c_1 - i_1 - x_1| + |2c_2 - i_2 - x_2|)) \tag{24}$$

This equation can be slightly transformed such that it is more similar to (23):

$$aff_c(i_1, i_2, x_1, x_2, t) = -C(i_1, i_2, t) \cdot (|2c_1 - i_1 - x_1| + |2c_2 - i_2 - x_2|) + L \cdot C(i_1, i_2, t) \tag{25}$$

With $a(t) = C(i_1, i_2, t)$ and $b(t) = L \cdot C(i_1, i_2, t)$ the two equations become identical. The difference between them is that in Bersini's version b is just the L-fold of a for some constant L. In this respect (23) is more general than (24) although the functions $a(t)$ and $b(t)$ cannot be considered as completely independent from each other. This illustrates that an appropriate interpretation of the function $a(t)$ is as the concentration of $\mathbf{i}$.

For the affinity in Hamming shape-spaces the distance function d_{XOR} is used. With the linear version of the affinity function the two types of affinities have the form

$$aff_s(\mathbf{i},\mathbf{x},t) = -a(t)\cdot ones(XOR(\mathbf{i},\mathbf{x})) + b(t) \qquad (26)$$

$$aff_c(\mathbf{i},\mathbf{x},t) = -a(t)\cdot ones(XOR(compl(\mathbf{i}),\mathbf{x})) + b(t) \qquad (27)$$

Consider the complementarity based affinity. The affinity function adopts its maximum value if $ones(XOR(compl(\mathbf{i}),\mathbf{x})) = 0$ which is equivalent to $XOR(compl(\mathbf{i}), \mathbf{x}) = \mathbf{0}$, and this means $compl(\mathbf{i}) = \mathbf{x}$. Thus, the point of maximum value is just the vector $compl(\mathbf{i})$, and this corresponds to the result in Euclidean and Manhattan shape-spaces where it is the center of the affinity region. The affinity function is zero if $b(t)/a(t) = ones(XOR(compl(\mathbf{i}), \mathbf{x}))$. This holds for all vectors $\mathbf{x}$ that are different from $compl(\mathbf{i})$ in exactly $b(t)/a(t)$ components. For vectors that differ in less than $b(t)/a(t)$ components from $compl(\mathbf{i})$ we have $ones(XOR(compl(\mathbf{i}), \mathbf{x})) < b(t)/a(t)$ and so $aff_c(\mathbf{i}, \mathbf{x}, t) > 0$, and for vectors with more than $b(t)/a(t)$ different components $aff_c(\mathbf{i}, \mathbf{x}, t) < 0$. Thus the vectors with exactly $b(t)/a(t)$ different components form the rim of a region in the Hamming space that can be taken as the affinity region. $aff_c(\mathbf{i}, \mathbf{x}, t)$ has a linear gradient from $compl(\mathbf{i})$ to the rim of the region with respect to the sum of the digits of the vectors. Thus, with respect to the affinity function, the Hamming shape-space can be compared with an iceberg whose top rises up out of the zero surface and the rest is below. This top is the affinity region.

As was shown in section 3, R/T is not a distance function. However, R/T can be used to define an affinity function with d_{XOR} as the underlying distance function. This affinity function is denoted by R/T-aff. R/T-aff is clearly a complementarity based affinity because $R/T(\mathbf{x}, \mathbf{x}) = 1$ (the maximum value) and $R/T(\mathbf{x}, compl(\mathbf{x})) = 0$ as stated above. R/T-aff can be written in the form:

$$R/T - aff(\mathbf{i},\mathbf{x},t) = R/T'(compl(\mathbf{i}),\mathbf{x},t)$$
$$= \frac{b(t)\cdot n - a(t)\cdot ones(XOR(compl(\mathbf{i}),\mathbf{x}))}{b(t)\cdot n + a(t)\cdot ones(XOR(compl(\mathbf{i}),\mathbf{x}))} \qquad (28)$$

With this modification of R/T the affinity function can adopt negative values, which the function R/T itself in a Hamming space could not. It is zero if $ones(XOR(compl(\mathbf{i}), \mathbf{x})) = b(t)\cdot n/a(t)$ and positive if $ones(XOR(compl(\mathbf{i}), \mathbf{x})) < b(t)\cdot n/a(t)$ and this holds for vectors that differ in less than $b(t)\cdot n/a(t)$ components from $compl(\mathbf{i})$. So, figuratively spoken, the iceberg is elevated to a higher level.

To summarize, R/T-aff with the above modification is similar to the affinity function of equation (27), except for the denominator. This is an interesting result because Bersini on one side and Rogers and Tanimoto on the other side clearly had rather different starting points and intended to do different things, but both developed functions that - put down to their principles (and applied to Hamming shape-spaces) -

are very similar. However, there is a difference between both functions because the function of (27) decreases linearly from the center to the border of the affinity region, whereas the function of (28) decreases exponentially as can be seen from figure 7.

5   Conclusion

General aspects of the structure and the dynamics of shape-spaces were presented in this paper. Emphasis was laid on a clear definition of distance functions and it was argued that in $\Re^n$-based shape-spaces only metrics should be used as such functions. It was shown that ε-balls (used as recognition regions) have different shapes depending on the type of the distance function. Several distance functions used in Hamming shape-spaces were examined and it turned out that not all of them are metrics.

With respect to the dynamics, an affinity function was defined as a function by which an element **i** exerts affinity on other elements and its value is determined by the distance between **i** and the other elements. The distance determines the shape of the recognition or affinity region of **i**, and the affinity function its varying size. It was illustrated which impact different distance metrics have on affinity functions. In particular it was shown how the similarity measure of Rogers and Tanimoto, though not being a distance function, can be used to define an affinity function.

The affinity function is the basis for the definition of the dynamics of a shape-space. This has to be worked out in more detail, which means, it must be described how the functions $a(t)$ and $b(t)$ change over time. In [1] they are linked to each other. This has the advantage that the size of the affinity region can be kept fixed and only the function $a(t)$ (or $C(\mathbf{i}, t)$) has to be defined. In [1], it is defined as a function of the total affinity exerted on an immune element **i** by all other immune elements.

In a further developed simulation system the influence of the affinity on the concentration of elements should be defined in a more elaborated way. For instance the influence of other elements like cytokines, which have a different dynamics, should be taken into account. The concentration of antigens should be treated differently from that of the antibodies (as is already done in [1]) and it should be taken into consideration that it cannot only decrease but also increase which means that the immune response fails.

References

[1]   H. Bersini. Self-assertion versus self-recognition: A tribute to Francisco Varela. In *Proceedings of ICARIS 2002*. Canterbury, 2002.

[2]   R.J. De Boer. Information processing in immune systems: Clonal selection versus idiotypic network models. *Cell to Cell Signalling: From Experiments to Theoretical Models*. Academic Press, 1989, 285 – 302.

[3]   R.J. De Boer and A.S. Perelson. Size and connectivity as emergent properties of a developing immune network. *J. of Theoretical Biology*, 149, 1990, 381 – 424.

[4]   L. De Castro and J. Timmis. *Artificial Immune Systems: A new Computational Intelligence Approach*. Springer, 2002.

[5]   V. Detours, H. Bersini, J. Stewart, and F. Varela. Development of an idiotypic network in shape-space. *J. of Theoretical Biology*, 170, 1994.

[6] W. Dilger, S. Strangfeld. Properties of the Bersini experiment on self-assertion. To appear in *Proceedings of GECCO 2006*.

[7] E. Hart and P. Ross. Studies on the implications of shape-space models for idiotypic networks. In *Proceedings of ICARIS 2004*. Springer, 2004, 413 – 426.

[8] E. Hart. Not all balls are round. In *Proceedings of ICARIS 2005*. Springer, 2005,

[9] J.E. Hunt, D.E. Cooke, and H. Holstein. Case memory and retrieval based on the immune system. *Proceedings of the 1st Int. Conference on Case-Based Reasoning Research and Development*, Lecture Notes in Artificial Intelligence, 1010, 1995, 205 – 216

[10] G. McCarty. *Topology. An Introduction with Application to Topological Groups*. McGraw-Hill, New York, 1967.

[11] J.K. Percus, O.E. Percus, and A.S. Perelson. Predicting the size of the T-cell receptor and antibody combining region from consideration of efficient self-nonself discrimination. *Proceedings of the Natl. Acad. Sci. USA*, 90, 1993, 1691 – 1695

[12] A. Perelson and G.F. Oster. Theoretical studies of clonal selection: Minimal antibody repertoire size and reliability of self-nonself discrimination in the immune system. *J. of Theoretical Biology*, 81, 1979, 645 – 670.

[13] D.J. Rogers and T.T. Tanimoto. A computer program for classifying plants. *Science*, 132, 1960, 1115 – 1118.

Integrating Innate and Adaptive Immunity for Intrusion Detection

Gianni Tedesco, Jamie Twycross, and Uwe Aickelin

School of Computer Science & IT (ASAP)
University of Nottingham
NG8 1BB
{gxt, jpt, uxa}@cs.nott.ac.uk

Abstract. Network Intrusion Detection Systems (NIDS) monitor a network with the aim of discerning malicious from benign activity on that network. While a wide range of approaches have met varying levels of success, most IDS's rely on having access to a database of known attack signatures which are written by security experts. Nowadays, in order to solve problems with false positive alerts, correlation algorithms are used to add additional structure to sequences of IDS alerts. However, such techniques are of no help in discovering novel attacks or variations of known attacks, something the human immune system (HIS) is capable of doing in its own specialised domain. This paper presents a novel immune algorithm for application to an intrusion detection problem. The goal is to discover packets containing novel variations of attacks covered by an existing signature base.

Keywords: Intrusion Detection, Innate Immunity, Dendritic Cells.

1 Introduction

Network intrusion detection systems (NIDS) are usually based on a fairly low level model of network traffic. While this is good for performance it tends to produce results which make sense on a similarly low level which means that a fairly sophisticated knowledge of both networking technology and infiltration techniques is required to understand them.

Intrusion alert correlation systems attempt to solve this problem by post-processing the alert stream from one or many intrusion detection sensors (perhaps even heterogeneous ones). The aim is to augment the somewhat one-dimensional alert stream with additional structure. Such structural information clusters alerts in to "scenarios" - sequences of low level alerts corresponding to a single logical threat.

A common model for intrusion alert correlation algorithms is that of the attack graph. Attack graphs are directed acyclic graphs (DAGs) that represent the various types of alerts in terms of their prerequisites and consequences. Typically an attack graph is created by an expert from a priori information about attacks. The attack graph enables a correlation component to link a given

H. Bersini and J. Carneiro (Eds.): ICARIS 2006, LNCS 4163, pp. 193–202, 2006.

alert with a previous alert by tracking back to find alerts whose consequences imply the current alerts prerequisites. Another feature is that if the correlation algorithm is run in reverse, predictions of future attacks can be obtained.

In implementing basic correlation algorithms using attack graphs, it was discovered that the output could be poor when the underlying IDS produced false negative alerts. This could cause scenarios to be split apart as evidence suggestive of a link between two scenarios is missing. This problem has been addressed in various systems [8,6] by adding the ability to hypothesise the existence of the missing alerts in certain cases. [7] go as far as to use out of band data from a raw audit log of network traffic to help confirm or deny such hypotheses.

While the meaning of correlated alerts and predicted alerts is clear, hypothesised results are less easy to interpret. Presence of hypothesised alerts could mean more than just losing an alert, it could mean either of:

1. The IDS missed the alert due to some noise, packet loss, or other low level sensor problem
2. The IDS missed the alert because a novel variation of a known attack was used
3. The IDS missed the alert, because something not covered by the attack graph happened (totally new exploit, or new combination of known exploits)

This work is motivated specifically by the problem of finding novel variations of attacks. The basic approach is to apply AIS techniques to detect packets which contain such variations. A correlation algorithm is taken advantage of to provide additional safe/dangerous context signals to the AIS which would enable it to decide which packets to examine. The work aims to integrate a novel AIS component with existing intrusion detection and alert correlation systems in order to gain additional detection capability.

2   Background

2.1   Intrusion Alert Correlation

Although the exact implementation details of attack graphs algorithms vary, the basic correlation algorithm takes an alert and an output graph, and modifies the graph by addition of vertices and/or edges to produce an updated output graph reflecting the current state of the monitored network system.

For the purposes of discussion, an idealised form of correlation output is defined which hides specific details of the correlation algorithm from the AIS component. This model, while fairly simple, adequately maps to current state of the art correlation algorithms.

Firstly, as in [8], exploits are viewed as a 3-tuple $(vuln, src, dst)$ where vuln is the identity of a know exploit and src and dst refer to two hosts which must be connected for the exploit to be carried out accross the network. An injective function "f" $(ALERT \rightarrow EXPLOIT)$. This is because there may be several variations of a single exploit, each requiring a different signature from the underlying

IDS and consequently producing distinct alerts. Parenthetically, many IDS signatures contain within them meta-data such as the Bugtraq or Mitre Common Vulnerabilities and Exposures (CVE) identification numbers which allows this function to be implemented automatically.

With our assumptions stated we may proceed to define our correlation graph. The output graph, G, is defined as a DAG with exploit vertices (V_e), condition vertices (V_c) and edges (E):

$$G = V_e \cup V_c \cup E$$

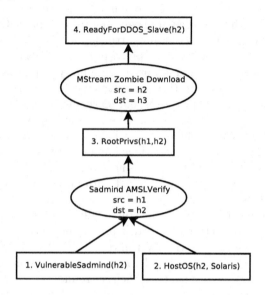

Fig. 1. Example output graph (conditions are boxes and exploits are ellipses)

The two types of vertex are necessary for being able to represent both conjunctive and disjunctive relations between exploits. As we can imagine by looking at Figure 1, any number of exploits may lead to condition 3, namely compromise of root privileges. This would mean that either the "AMSLVerify" exploit *or* some other root exploit may precede "Mstream Zombie Download." In another situation we may want "AMSLVerify" *and* some other exploit to be the precondition. In this case we would simply introduce another pre-requisite condition for that exploit alongside condition 3.

Each disconnected subgraph is considered as a threat scenario. That is to say, a structured set of low level alerts which constitute a single logical attack sequence.

There is a function "vertexstate" $(VERTEX \rightarrow VERTEXSTATE)$ which returns a 3 valued type, $\{HYP, REAL, PRED\}$ for hypothesised, real or predicted respectively. Condition vertices have a function "val" $(VERTEX \rightarrow BOOL)$ which tells us the value of the condition.

In addition to this, exploit vertices contain information about the computer systems involved. Functions for retrieving source and destination addresses and ports are also provided. For the purposes of discussion we will assume that monitored networks are using the familiar TCP/IP protocol suite. Consequently we shall refer to these functions as "src", "dst", "srcport" and "dstport."

2.2 Danger Theory

Over the last decade the focus of research in immunology has shifted from the adaptive to innate immune system, and the cells of innate immunity has moved to the fore in understanding the behaviour of immune system as a whole[2]. Insights gained from this research are beginning to be appreciated and modelled at various levels by researchers building artificial immune systems.

The algorithm described in Section 3 incorporates at a conceptual level mechanisms from both the innate and adaptive immune system although, because of the change in problem domain, these are implemented differently. This section briefly reviews the biological processes and mechanisms which have been drawn upon when designing the algorithm presented in this paper.

The biological immune system as a whole provides effective host defense through the complex interaction of various immune system cells with themselves and their environment, the tissue of the host organism. Dendritic cells (DCs), part of the innate immune system, interact with antigen derived from the host tissue and control the state of adaptive immune system cells.

Antigen is ingested from the extracellular milieu by DCs in their immature state and then processed internally. During processing, antigen is segmented and attached to major histocompatibility complex (MHC) molecules. This MHC-antigen complex is then presented under certain conditions on the surface of the DC. As well as extracting antigen from their surroundings, DCs also have receptors which respond to a range of other signalling molecules in their milieu. Certain molecules, such a lipopolysaccharide, collectively termed pathogen-associated molecular proteins (PAMPs[3]) are common to entire classes of pathogens and bind with toll-like receptors (TLRs) on the surface of DCs.

Other groups of molecules, termed danger signals, such as heat shock proteins (HSPs), are associated with damage to host tissue or unregulated, necrotic cell death and bind with receptors on DCs. Other classes of molecules related to inflammation and regulated, apoptotic cell death also interact with receptor families present on the surface of DCs. The current maturation state of the DC is determined through the combination of these complex signalling networks. DCs themselves secrete cell-to-cell signalling molecules called cytokines which control the state of other cell types. The number and strength of DC cytokine output depends on its current maturation state.

T-cells, members of the adaptive immune system, have receptors which bind to antigen presented in an MHC-antigen complex on the surface of DCs and respond to the strength of the match between receptor and antigen. This response is usually a change in the differentiation state of the T-cell. However, this response is not solely determined by antigen, but also by the levels of cytokines sensed by a range of cytokine receptors present on the surface of T-cells. These receptors are specific for cytokines produced by DCs.

In summary, DCs uptake and present antigen from the environment to T-cells. Also, DCs uptake signals from the environment and produce signals which are received by T-cells. The ultimate response of a T-cell to an antigen is determined by both the antigen presented by the DC and the signals produced by the DC. Section 3 below describes the implementation of this model in the context of a computer intrusion detection problem.

3   The Algorithm

For this purpose the "libtissue" [9,10] AIS framework, a product of a danger theory project [1], will model a number of innate immune system components such as dendritic cells in order to direct an adaptive T-cell based response. Dendritic cells will carry the responsibility of discerning dangerous and safe contexts as well as carrying out their role of presenting antigen and signals to a population of T-cells as in [4].

Tissue and Dendritic Cells. Dendritic cells (henceforth DCs) are of a class of cells in the immune system known as antigen presenting cells. They differ from other cells in this class in that this is their sole discernible function. As well as being able to absorb and present antigenic material DCs are also well adapted to detecting a set of endogenous and exogenous signals which arise in the tissue (IDS correlation graph).

These biological signals are abstracted in our system under the following designations:

1. Safe: Indicates a safe context for developing toleration.
2. Danger: Indicates a change in behaviour that could be considered pathological.
3. Pathogen Associated Molecular Pattern (PAMP)[3]: Known to be dangerous. In our system a distinction is made between activation by endogenous danger signals or through TLR receptors.

All of these environmental circumstances, or inputs, are factors in the life cycle of the DC. In the proposed system, DCs are seen as living among the IDS environment. This is achieved by wiring up their environmental inputs to changes in the IDS output state. A population of DCs are tied to the prediction vertices in the correlation graph, one DC for each predicted attack. Packets matching the prediction criteria of such a vertex are collected as antigen by the corresponding DC. These packets are either stored in memory or logged to disk until the DC matures and is required to present the antigen to a T-cell.

Once a prediction vertex has been added to the correlation graph, the arrival of subsequent alerts can cause that vertex to either be upgraded to an exploit vertex, changed to a hypothesised vertex, or become redundant as sibling vertices are so modified. These possible state changes will result in either a PAMP, danger or safe signal respectively.

These signals initiate maturation and consequent migration of the DC to a virtual lymph node where they are exposed to a population of T-cells.

The signal we are most interested in is the PAMP signal, this occurs when a predicted vertex becomes hypothesised. This provides us with a counterfactual hypothesis to test, ie. "suppose a novel a variation of the attack was carried out." The hypothesis is not unreasonable since:

1. The exploit was predicted already therefore it's prerequisites are met.
2. An exploit which depends on the consequences of the attack was carried out therefore the consequences of the exploit are met.

However this is not enough for a proof, since the standard caveats about the accuracy of the model hold. An attacker may, after all, attempt an attack whose preconditions are not met, the attack will fail, but the IDS cannot know.

Antigen Representation. An important part of the design of an AIS is the representation of the domain data. A number of choices are available [12,13]. For this algorithm we chose to use a natural encoding for the problem domain.

Network packets are blobs of binary data, each one is decoded by the IDS. The decoding process involves extracting, interpreting and validating the relevant features for the purpose of matching the packet against the signature database.

Our proposed algorithm represents each packet as an array of (feature,val) tuples. The array contains a tuple for all possible features and is ordered by feature. Features can be either integers or character strings. Values may be set to wildcards if the corresponding feature is not present in the packet.

This approach imposes a total order on the features. Such an order may be based, for example, on position in the packet which in nearly all cases is invariant and defined in protocol specifications.

Note that this representation shares structural similarities with the actual signatures used in network IDS's. The connection is elaborated in the following sub-section.

T-cells. By the time a DC in our system has received a PAMP signal, matured, migrated to a lymph node and bound to a T-cell it contains a number of candidate packets (our antigen) and an indication of which signal caused migration. The simple T-cell model outlined in this paper only incorporates DC's activated by PAMPs.

The problem here is to select a subset of packets which may contain the novel variation(s) we are looking for. The inverse of the "f" function in our correlation algorithm provides a number of candidate signatures which may be used as a starting point. Thus the additional context is used to significantly reduce the search space in this phase of the algorithm.

In order to find these possible variations, a version of the IDS signature matching algorithm is required which provides meaningful partial matching. Since most signatures entail string searching or regular expression matching this is not a trivial task. For now, it will suffice to simply sum the number of matching criteria in each signature for each packet. If a match is sufficiently close, all the relevant data is output for further analysis. Since most signatures have less than 10 criteria, this may not be effective in all cases, due to the anticipated difficulty in selecting good matching thresholds.

4 Experimental Results

In order to test the algorithm it is important to know how greatly the set of candidate packets for novel attack variations can be reduced. We perform a simple experiment to validate the algorithm in this way. We chose to prototype the algorithm inside Firestorm[14], a signature matching IDS which uses the de-facto standard snort[15] signatures.

A circa 2000 wu-ftpd[11] exploit called "autowux" is to be our novel variation on the snort "FTP EXPLOIT format string" signature (figure 2). These exploits share the same attack methodology, namely exploiting format string overflows in the File Transfer Protocol (FTP) "SITE EXEC" command.

```
alert tcp $EXTERNAL_NET any -> $HOME_NET 21 (msg:''FTP EXPLOIT format
string''; flow:to_server,established; content:  ''SITE EXEC |25 30 32 30
64 7C 25 2E 66 25 2E 66 7C 0A|''; depth: 32; nocase;)
```

Fig. 2. Generic snort signature for FTP format string exploits

The IDS is loaded with a full signature set and is tested to make sure that the autowux exploit packets are not already detected. A contrived attack graph with 3 exploits is also created (see figure 3). An nmap scan is the prerequisite and vulnerability to rootkit installation is the consequence of our "novel" FTP exploit.

The attack scenario is successfully played out across an otherwise quiet test network (run #1). The attack contains on the order of three thousand packets and the problem should be fairly simple because in the absence of background noise a high proportion of the packets are part of the FTP attack (975 of them to be precise). To make things more realistic, a second run of the experiment is carried out in which there is background FTP traffic to our vulnerable host. The background traffic is from the Lincoln Labs FTP data-set[16].

The two data sets were merged based on time deltas between packets, the start packets are synchronised. This provides a realistic and repeatable mix of benign and attack traffic (run #2).

The table below gives initial results for the prototype implementation based on a number of uncontrolled experiments. Total packets is the total number of packets in the merged data set, Ag packets refers to candidate packets in the DC and output packets refers to the final results - ie. those packets in which there is a suspected novel variation of an attack. False positive (FP) and false negative (FN) rates are calculated through manual analysis of the output. In this case, there is one true positive in each data set so all candidate output packets that are not true positives are false positives, so the rate is calculated with $\frac{n-1}{n}$.

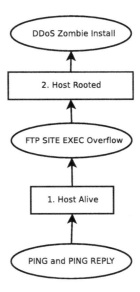

Fig. 3. Contrived attack graph used for experimental purposes

Run #1 is performed on a quiescent network, run #2 is with background traffic as described above.

Table 1. Accuracy of Algorithm with and without Background Traffic

Run	Total Packets	Ag Packets	Output Packets	FP Rate	FN Rate
#1	3,000	975	18	94%	0%
#2	18,000	8,000	30	96%	0%

The table shows that the packets of interest are extracted (eg. 975 / 3000) and that after further processing this is reduced to a mere handful of packets (eg. 18). Overall the detection rate is good, despite the high false positive rates (eg. 94%) which are inherent in the problem.

5 Conclusions and Future Work

In summation, a novel intrusion detection algorithm was presented drawing on theoretical models of innate immunity. The algorithm incorporates within it existing IDS algorithms, but expands on their capability in a limited area, detection of unknown (or 0-day) attacks which are based on other attacks that are previously known to the IDS. The AIS neatly interfaces with the problem domain by treating internal IDS data structures as an artificial tissue environment. Finally the algorithm was evaluated in terms of how accurately the novel variations can be identified.

It should be noted that the results are not directly comparable to other IDS algorithms as the problem being solved is uniquely circumscribed. Rather than designing an anomaly detection algorithm to find previously unknown attacks, a misuse detector and alert correlator are extended to detect a certain kind of anomaly arising from the incomplete models that are invariably used with such algorithms.

Initial results are promising despite the high false positive rate. However since the output is already clustered (all packets which were in a given DC are linked together) it means that as long as there is an upper bound on false positives and the false negative rate is low, there will usually be an accurate detection among each such cluster.

The DCs in the presented model are able to detect specific anomalous patterns of tissue growth and identify where and when novel attacks are taking place. After a DC has made an initial selection of candidate packets, it is then the responsibility of the T-cells to reduce the number of packets still further by detecting structural similarities in the data. DCs are concerned primarily with detecting abnormal behaviour within their environmental context, whereas T-cells are concerned primarily with discerning patterns within the antigen data. The co-ordination of both types of immune cell with each other and the tissue through orthogonal programming interfaces make for neat and efficient solution.

Further investigation in to the T-cell phase of the algorithm should be fruitful. The algorithm presented in this paper is fairly basic and does not incorporate meaningful partial matching which is important for performance and accuracy. A tolerance mechanism might also be useful in integrating the information conveyed by the safe and danger signals to further improve the false positive rate in the difficult cases where malicious traffic differs only slightly from legitimate traffic. Future testing should also incorporate historically problematic attack variations in order to provide a more realistic appraisal of the algorithm.

A mechanism for the automated generation of signatures for the novel variations discovered by the algorithm would be ideal. Work such as [17] shows us that this should, in theory, be possible with acceptable precision.

References

1. U Aickelin, P Bentley, S Cayzer, J Kim and J McLeod. "Danger Theory: The Link between AIS and IDS?" 2nd International Conference on Artificial Immune Systems. 2003.
2. R N Germain. "An innately interesting decade of research in immunology". Nature Medicine. Vol. 10, No. 4, pp. 1307-1320. 2004.
3. CA Janeway Jr. "Approaching the Asymptote? Evolution and Revolution in Immunology." Cold Spring Harb Symp Quant Biol. 54 Pt 1:1-13. 1989.
4. J Greensmith, U Aickelin and S Cayzer. "Introducing Dendritic Cells as a Novel Immune-Inspired Algorithm for Anomaly Detection." 4th International Conference on Articial Immune Systems, pp 153-167. 2005.
5. P Matzinger. "Tolerance, danger and the extended family." Annual Reviews in Immunology, 12:991-1045, 1994.

6. P Ning. D Xu. "Hypothesizing and Reasoning about Attacks Missed by Intrusion Detection Systems." ACM Transactions on Information and System Security Vol. 7, No. 4, pp. 591-627. 2004.
7. P Ning, D Xu. CG Healey and R St. Amant. "Building Attack Scenarios through Integration of Complementary Alert Methods" Proceedings of the 11th Annual Network and Distributed System Security Symposium. 2004.
8. L Wang, A Liu and S Jajoda. "An Efficient Unified Approach to Correlating Hypothesising, and Predicting Intrusion Alerts." Proceedings of European Symposium on Computer Security. 2005.
9. J Twycross and U Aickelin. "Towards a Conceptual Framework for Innate Immunity." Proceedings of the 4th International Conference on Artificial Immune Systems, Banff, Canada, 2005.
10. J Twycross and U Aickelin. "libtissue - implementing innate immunity." Proceedings of the Congress on Evolution Computation. 2006.
11. Washington University FTP Server. http://www.wu-ftpd.org/
12. K. Mathias and D. Whitley. "Transforming the Search Space with Gray Coding." IEEE Conf. on Evolutionary Computation. Volume 1. pp: 513-518, 1994.
13. J Balthrop, F Esponda, S Forrest, M Glickman. "Coverage and Generalization in an Artificial Immune System." Genetic and Evolutionary Computation Conference (GECCO) 2002.
14. G Tedesco. Firestorm Network Intrusion Detection System. http://www.scara-manga.co.uk/firestorm/.
15. M Roesch. Snort Network Intrusion Detection System. http://www.snort.org/
16. Berkeley Labs Internet Traffic Archive Data Set: LBNL-FTP-PKT. http://www-nrg.ee.lbl.gov/LBNL-FTP-PKT.html
17. V Yegneswaran, JT Giffin, P Barford, S Jha. "An Architecture for Generating Semantics-Aware Signatures." Proceedings of USENIX Security Conference, 2005.

A Comparative Study on Self-tolerant Strategies for Hardware Immune Systems

Xin Wang, Wenjian Luo, and Xufa Wang

Department of Computer Science and Technology,
University of Science and Technology of China, Hefei 230027, China
sinbarwx@mail.ustc.edu.cn, {wjluo, xfwang}@ustc.edu.cn

Abstract. Self-Tolerance is a key issue in Hardware Immune Systems. Two novel detector set updating strategies are proposed in this paper as approaches to the self-tolerant problem in Hardware Immune Systems. Compared with previous detector set updating strategies, results of simulation experiments show that the detector sets being updated by the new strategies are less affected by the growing of the self set, and have a better coverage on the non-self space. Moreover, the improvement is notable when the self set is unavailable during the updating of the detector set.

1 Introduction

Hardware Immune System (HIS) is a branch of Artificial Immune Systems. Inspired by the human immune system, a hardware immune system is an approach to hardware fault tolerance, in which the human immune system is mapped to a hardware representation to develop fault detection mechanisms for reliable hardware systems. So far, many works about hardware immune system have already been done. The concept of Immunotronics is proposed by Bradley and Tyrrell, which is claimed as a novel fault-tolerant hardware inspired by immune principles [1, 2]. Canham and Tyrrell proposed a multi-layered hardware artificial immune system based on Embryonic Array [3]. Canham and Tyrrell also developed a novel artificial immune system that has been applied to robotics as an error detection system [4]. Bradley and Tyrrell proposed the architecture for a hardware immune system [5], and they also proposed a novel hardware immune system for error detection on a benchmark state machine [6]. Tarakanov and Dasgupta proposed architecture for immunochips [7].

However, little works are concerned on the self-tolerant problem in HIS under dynamic environments. Inspired by the co-stimulation mechanism which is used to maintain self-tolerance in biological immune systems, algorithms for dealing with the self-tolerance problem in hardware immune system is proposed in [8, 9], and the simulation experiments are carried out on the HIS architecture proposed by Bradley and Tyrrell [1, 5, 6]. The Concurrent Error Detection (CED) [10] is applied to generate co-stimulations (the second signal), and the FSM (Finite State Machine) model is adopted by the experimental system. However, when the growing self set results in some false positives, current strategies for the self-tolerant problem just recruit detectors randomly [8], or even do not recruit any detector [9]. In fact, many works

H. Bersini and J. Carneiro (Eds.): ICARIS 2006, LNCS 4163, pp. 203–214, 2006.

about Negative Selection Algorithm (NSA) [11, 12] have been done [13-16], and some of them can be applied to solve the self-tolerant problem. D'haeseleer proposed a method for counting the number of holes, and presented a greedy algorithm that attempts to reduce the size of the detector set [13]. Zhou and Dasgupata proposed an NSA with variable-coverage detectors in real-valued space [14, 15]. Zhang et al. presented the r-Adjustable NSA in binary string space [16], etc. However, with methods in [13-16], the problem with holes can be only partially avoided by non-autoimmune systems in static environments. Furthermore, in dynamic environments, the self set could change. Therefore, apart from the detector set generation algorithms, the detector set updating strategy is very important for the application of NSA in dynamic environments, and it is a key issue for the self-tolerant problem.

Aiming at the self-tolerant problem in dynamic environments (in which the self set will grow during detection), two detector set updating strategies are proposed in this paper. One of them is inspired by the variable matching length mechanism [14-16], the other just removes the self pattern by stuffing some bits of detector with special symbols. These two novel strategies are compared with the works in [8] and [9]. Results of emulation experiments show that the detector sets being updated by the new strategies are less affected by the growing of the self set, and have a better coverage on the non-self space.

Section 2 briefly introduces the self-tolerant problem and some efforts already made by researchers. Two novel detector set updating strategies are described in detail in section 3. Section 4 is devoted to demonstrating the simulation experimental results. Discussions are given in section 5. Conclusions and future works are given in section 6.

2 Self-tolerance Problem of HIS in Dynamic Environments

Generally the biological immune system is tolerant of the self, i.e. it does not attack the self. But a small quantity of lymphocytes may bind to self and the body will be attacked by the immune system, this response is called autoimmunization. In general, all lymphocytes will suffer the process of negative selection. However, there are still some lymphocytes matching the self released to the blood circulation. The peripheral self-tolerance can be dynamically maintained by a mechanism called co-stimulation. For example, B-cells can be activated only when they receive the first signal from captured pathogens and the second signal from lymphocytes called helper T-cells in the same time. The helper T-cells will provide second signal only if they recognizes the pathogens captured by B-cells as non-self. [17]

In hardware immune systems, if the known self set (the set of known valid state transitions) is incomplete, after the filtration process of the detector set, some detectors may recognize unknown valid state transitions as non-self (invalid state transitions) and give a wrong alarm (a false positive). A co-stimulation mechanism has been developed to maintain the tolerance of self [8, 9].

Self-tolerant problem is an essential issue in both biological immune systems and hardware immune systems under dynamic environments. When the self set grows, the detector set updating strategy is a key component in hardware immune systems. A good detector set updating strategy should have the following characteristics.

(1) It should maintain a low false positive ratio when the new self individual is collected. "False positive" means recognizing a self individual as a non-self.

(2) It should maintain a low false negative ratio after the detector set is updated. "False negative" means recognizing a non-self individual as a self.

(3) The false negative ratio will not clearly increase even if the self set is unavailable.

(4) It has reasonable time and space complexities, and can be easily implemented in hardware immune systems.

In [9], during the detection process, if a detector is activated by a state transition without a co-stimulation signal, it will be deleted from the detector set, and the failure probability of detecting an invalid state transition (the false negative ratio) will be clearly increased. In the ASTA-CED algorithm proposed in [8], if a detector is deleted, a new detector generated randomly will replace the deleted one. But in some cases a new detector can not be generated easily. Moreover, the self set must be kept by the HIS because the newly generated candidate detector should be filtered by the self set to make sure it will not match a known self individual. This is a very time consuming operation, and is not practical for some hardware immune systems.

Two novel detector set updating strategies are introduced in this paper, and compared with the strategies in [8] and [9]. The experimental results show that the detector sets being updated by these two novel strategies are less affected by the growing self set, and have a better coverage on the non-self space.

3 Detector Set Updating Strategies

Before introducing the two novel detector set updating strategies in this section, some symbols used in this paper are defined as following.

r: Matching length threshold. Note that r-continuous-bits matching rule [11] is adopted in this paper.

st: State transition. Here a state transition means a 0/1 string to be monitored [8].

l: The string length of a detector.

m: Maximum continuous matching length between two strings in the corresponding positions.

S: Set of self strings.

R_0: Immature detector set.

R: Mature detector set.

N_{R0}: The number of immature detectors.

N_R: The number of mature detectors.

N_S: The size of the self set.

The overall flowchart of the detector set detecting and updating process is described in Fig. 1. And the process is described as following [8].

(1) Perform partial matching between state transitions and detectors one by one.
(2) If a detector d matches a state transition st, go to (3), or else back to (1).
(3) Report the error. If there is a co-stimulation signal, go to (1).
(4) Update S by inserting st into it.
(5) **Detector set updating strategy:** Update R with the updated S. Using the current R as immature detectors set R_0, every detector in R undergoes a filtration process to avoid matching a known self string. If any detector is deleted, try to generate a new detector.
(6) Go to (1).

The different detector set updating strategies can be adopted at step (5). In the following subsection 3.1 and subsection 3.2, two novel detector set updating strategies are introduced.

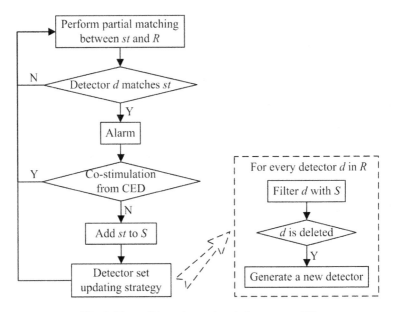

Fig. 1. Flow of detecting and updating process [8]

3.1 Strategy I: Increasing the Partial Matching Length Threshold

The variable matching length mechanism [14-16] is applied in strategy I to perform the detector set updating operation. The following process is the filtration process of a detector in the detector set being updated. If a detector d of the current detector set matches a self string, it will undergo such a filtration process.

(1) Get the maximum matching length m between d and the self string.
(2) If $m=l$, delete d and generate a new detector, or else set the partial matching threshold of d to $m+1$.

The following is the process of trying to generate a new detector when an old detector is deleted in the filtration process listed above.

(1) Generate a new detector d' randomly.
(2) If d' is already included in the current set R, delete it and go back to (1).
(3) Perform partial matching between d' and elements in S one by one, get the maximum matching length m', if $m' = l$, go back to (1).
(4) Set the matching length threshold of d' as $r' = m' +1$, add d' to R.

Since this process could be time consuming, to limit the time cost for generating a new detector, when an old detector is deleted in the updating process, step (1)-(3) in this process will be performed for only a small constant number of cycles.

3.2 Strategy II: Stuffing Some Bits of Detector with a Special Symbol

Firstly, it is assumed that when a detector d (11100111) matches a self string (00100110), the matching bits will be (10011), the maximum continuous matching length $m=5$. If the indices of a detector's bits start from 1, the matching start point $p=3$. The filtration process of a detector is given as follows.

If a detector d matches a self string, some selected matching bits of d will be stuffed with a special symbol. For convenience, the special symbol is indicated by '#' in this paper. Stuffing a matching bit with '#' makes this bit can not match either '0' or '1'. Other matching bits can be kept unchanged. Therefore, the segment that consists of the maximum continuous matching bits and represents some self patterns, is destroyed by the stuffed '#'. And some of useful non-self patterns in this detector are reserved. The key problem is how to choose the minimum number of bits to be stuffed with '#', and these bits could destroy the self patterns and remain the largest number of non-self patterns in this detector.

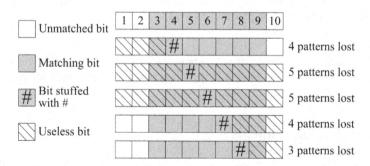

Fig. 2. Choose one bit to be stuffed with '#' when $m<2r$. '#' indicates a symbol other than '0' and '1'. Stuffing a matching bit with '#' makes this bit can not match either '0' or '1'.

Firstly, we consider $m<2r$, then stuffing just one matching bit with '#' will be enough. As shown in Fig. 2, if $l=10$, $r=6$, $p=3$ and $m=7$, replacing the 8th bit with '#' is the best choice, because it has the least number of deleted patterns. When $m < 2r$, the filtration process can be described as following.

(1) Get the matching start point p and the maximum continuous matching length m between the detector d and the matched self string.
(2) If $p \le l - p - m + 2$, stuff the $(p+m-r)$-th bit of d with '#', or else stuff the $(p+r-1)$-th bit of d with '#'.
(3) If the maximum length of contiguous 0/1 bit in d is shorter than r, delete d and try to generate a new detector.

When $m \ge 2r$, set all bits between $(p+r-1, p+m-r)$ as '#'. Obviously, it is very simple when $m \ge 2r$.

Notable, only one segment that the number of the maximum continuous matching bits is no smaller than r, has been considered above. However, when r is small and l is relative large, the number of such segments is possibly more than one. If there are two or more segments of the maximum continuous matching bits not shorter than r, methods for finding the bits to be stuffed by '#' can be designed according to the same idea described above.

Note that if the maximum length of contiguous 0/1 bit in d is shorter than r, the bit replacing operation has made detector d useless because it can not match any self/non-self string in the string space, then d must be deleted and a new detector should be try to be generated.

The following is the process of trying to generate a new detector when a detector is deleted in the process of strategy II. This algorithm is described below.

(1) Generate a new detector d' randomly.
(2) If d' is already included in the current set R, delete it and go back to (1).
(3) Perform partial matching between d' and strings in S one by one, if d' matches any self string, perform the above filtration process of strategy II on d'. If d' is deleted in the filtration process, go to (1).
(4) Add d' to R.

To limit the time cost for generating a new detector, when an old detector is deleted in the updating process, step (1)-(3) in this process will be performed for only a small constant number of cycles.

4 Simulation Experiments

To show the improvements of these two novel detector set updating strategies, they are compared with the strategy used by ASTA-CED algorithm [8] which just delete a detector matching self and try to generate a new one randomly. Binary strings in form of "previous state/current state" are used for representing state transitions and detectors. The framework of the simulation experiment system used in [8, 9] is adopted with some modifications here, as shown in Fig 3.

In Fig. 3, when a detector matches a state transition string from the FSM, the first signal will be sent to the controller, and the parity checking result from CED module will be sent to the controller as the second signal (co-stimulation). According to the first and second signals, the controller will update the detector set R if necessary. In the updating process of R, the state transition string causing false positive will be collected by the self set S as a new self string, and R will be filtered with S. The results record module is used for collecting the performance datum of the system.

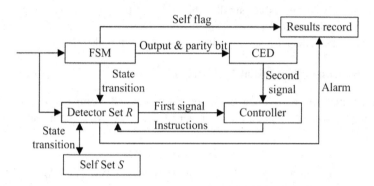

Fig. 3. Simulation experiment system. Different from [8, 9], the self set S is kept by the system, it is used for the filtration process of detector set R in detector set updating steps.

The length of the bit-string is 16, and then the size of string space O is 2^{16}. The "r-continuous-bits" matching rule is adopted here and the initial value of matching length threshold r is fixed to 12.

The detector set updating strategy of ASTA-CED in [8] is temporarily denoted as strategy 0 in these experiments. For convenience, in all tables about experimental results, number 0 denotes strategy 0, I denotes strategy I, and II denotes strategy II.

In an independent run, three strategies have identical initial detector set, which is generated randomly and has $r=12$. The number of self strings N_S is fixed at 3000. The self set of every independent run is generated randomly, and is identical for both the three strategies. The parameter a, which is the proportion of self strings already known in advance among the complete set of self strings, is set to $\{0.9, 0.8, ..., 0.1\}$ for observing the change of the results against it.

Every state transition of the whole string space appears once in an independent run, in which the detector set is updated according to different strategies. The process for generating a new detector will be performed for only 1 cycle when an old detector is deleted from current detector set R in its updating process.

The results take the average values over 10 independent runs for every value of a. There are two parameters taken to make the comparisons: N_R and $\triangle C$. N_R is the number of mature detectors. C is the number of total invalid state transitions covered by the detector set, which represents the non-self coverage degree. And $\triangle C$ is the variation between the initial C at the start of an independent run and the final C at the end of the independent run, it can be defined as $\Delta C = C_{initial} - C_{final}$. The $\triangle C$ also indicates the increasing on the number of false negatives of the strategies.

To prove that the detector sets being updated by the new strategies are less affected by the growing self set, and have a better coverage on the non-self space, comparisons on $\triangle C$ and changes of N_R after detector sets have been updated by the three strategies are given in the following two subsections. In subsection 4.1, the three strategies are compared when initial N_R is fixed, and it can be found out that the $\triangle C$ and the change on N_R of the new strategies are smaller than that of strategy 0. In subsection 4.2, the comparison in subsection 4.1 are repeated when the self set is unavailable during the updating process of detector set, and similar results are found.

4.1   Comparisons When Initial N_R Is Fixed

In this subsection, the experiment is carried out to make the comparisons on $\triangle C$ when three strategies have the same initial number of detectors (N_R). The initial N_R is set to 6000 in this experiment.

Table 1. Comparison on average $\triangle C$ over 10 independent runs when initial N_R is fixed to 6000. Standard deviations are also listed in this table.

a		0.90	0.80	0.70	0.60	0.50	0.40	0.30	0.20	0.10
0	Ave	3696.9	7359.7	10799.0	14481.0	17301.0	20680.0	23152.0	25968.0	28002.0
	Std	315.38	365.71	230.93	359.13	426.68	358.01	819.97	990.19	517.75
I	Ave	2572.2	5059.1	7142.5	9176.5	10788.0	12395.0	13779.0	15120.0	16279.0
	Std	173.71	228.14	133.40	211.05	204.12	225.29	406.82	401.01	338.85
II	Ave	1002.2	1725.5	2133.8	2850.7	3382.9.0	3930.0	4564.2.0	5477.0	6152.0
	Std	101.63	198.10	259.85	314.03	282.94	372.59	247.63	242.43	173.06

Table 1 shows the comparison between the three strategies on average $\triangle C$, the standard deviations are also listed. It can be observed that the values of $\triangle C$ in the results of strategy I and II are lower than that of strategy 0. It means that the increasing on false negative ratio of these two novel strategies is lower than that of strategy 0, i.e. the non-self space coverage of the detector sets being updated by these two new strategies are less affected by the growing of self set. And it can be also seen that strategy II is much better than strategy I from the $\triangle C$'s point of view.

Table 2 lists the average values of final N_R of three strategies after 10 independent runs against values of a, the average numbers of deleted detectors and regenerated (rebirth) detectors are also given, and standard deviations are listed as well. It can be found out that more existent detectors are reserved by strategy I and II during the detector set updating process, i.e. the detector set being updated by the two new strategies are less affected by the growing of self set. And strategy I is a little better than strategy II from the N_R 's point of view.

Table 2. The average values of the final N_R over 10 independent runs against values of a when initial N_R is fixed to 6000. The average numbers of deleted and regenerated (rebirth) detectors are also given in this table. Standard deviations are listed as well.

a		0.90	0.80	0.70	0.60	0.50	0.40	0.30	0.20	0.10
0	Deleted Ave	1254.6	2240.7	3110.2	3769.0	4452.2	5100.9	5809.9	6560.7	7484.0
	Deleted Std	92.292	76.472	69.624	56.115	45.013	99.669	41.439	75.025	41.355
	Rebirth Ave	56.1	156.4	335.2	512.4	796.2	1148.5	1620.2	2217.1	3054.9
	Rebirth Std	7.125	10.146	11.114	20.764	41.787	55.838	46.913	50.516	58.872
	Final Ave	4801.5	3915.7	3225.0	2743.4	2344.0	2047.6	1810.3	1656.4	1570.9
	Final Std	93.131	80.758	71.273	48.040	43.581	57.456	42.802	56.545	53.217
I	Deleted Ave	29.5	57.9	91.7	117.4	137.0	170.9	202.5	223.8	250.1
	Deleted Std	4.720	6.540	8.744	5.190	11.195	13.731	14.183	8.779	17.188
	Rebirth Ave	28.5	55.3	87.4	113.6	132.7	165.2	196.2	217.2	244.2
	Rebirth Std	5.523	6.516	8.566	5.481	11.786	12.621	14.070	8.804	16.396
	Final Ave	5999.0	5997.4	5995.7	5996.2	5995.7	5994.3	5993.7	5993.4	5994.1
	Final Std	1.155	1.430	2.003	2.150	2.057	2.791	1.636	2.989	2.079
II	Deleted Ave	62.8	160.4	303.0	467.3	640.3	876.0	1115.0	1319.8	1591.6
	Deleted Std	13.887	12.572	26.546	23.171	20.575	38.335	31.027	37.821	48.761
	Rebirth Ave	60.1	152.8	290.6	449.4	614.4	847.2	1080.2	1282.2	1544.0
	Rebirth Std	12.940	13.079	23.524	22.599	20.178	35.925	32.152	31.825	48.475
	Final Ave	5997.3	5992.4	5987.6	5982.1	5974.1	5971.2	5965.2	5962.4	5952.4
	Final Std	1.767	1.713	5.103	2.767	4.654	4.517	5.051	7.058	8.181

4.2 Comparisons When the Self Set Is Unavailable

Another experiment is carried out without the self set being kept, i.e. information about known self set is unavailable when the detector set needs to be updated. In this case, the process for generating a new detector in strategy 0 of ASTA-CED [8] can not be performed here. It is noted that the essential difference between the detector set updating strategies in [8] and [9] is whether a new detector is tried to be generated when an old detector is deleted. Therefore, strategy 0 is transformed to the corresponding strategy in [9] now. For convenience, the detector set updating strategy in [9] is also denoted as strategy 0 in this subsection. The initial N_R is still set to 6000.

Table 3. Comparison on average $\triangle C$ between the three strategies when the self set is unavailable during detection. Standard deviations are also listed. Results are got by 10 independent runs. The initial N_R is still set to 6000.

a		0.90	0.80	0.70	0.60	0.50	0.40	0.30	0.20	0.10
0	Ave	3716.6	7524.7	11820.5	16091.9	20500.7	24944.4	29268.6	33805.7	38212.1
	Std	262.52	330.46	396.11	379.30	776.78	481.05	771.70	785.90	785.43
I	Ave	2587.8	5095.4	7468.4	9516.9	11432.6	13035.1	14485.4	15906.2	17111.4
	Std	198.71	189.89	204.72	215.35	355.29	371.95	306.57	314.29	233.93
II	Ave	1730.4	3522.4	5252.0	6827.9	8534.7	9950.0	11286.9	12893.0	14152.8
	Std	147.07	85.57	241.13	186.86	213.49	313.52	180.50	329.17	231.70

Table 3 shows the comparisons between three strategies on average values of $\triangle C$ against a, and standard deviations are also given. It can be observed that $\triangle C$ of strategy I and II is lower than that of strategy 0. It means that the increasing on false negative ratio of these two novel strategies is lower than that of strategy 0, i.e. the non-self space coverage of the detector sets being updated by these two new strategies are less affected by the growing self set. And strategy II performs better than strategy I from the $\triangle C$'s point of view.

Table 4 shows the average values of final N_R of the three strategies after 10 independent runs, and standard deviations are also listed. It is shown that both strategy I and II can remain much more existent detectors than strategy 0, i.e. the detector set being updated by these two new strategies are less affected by the growing of self set. Moreover, strategy I is better than strategy II from the final N_R's point of view.

Table 4. The average values of the final N_R of three strategies after 10 independent runs against values of a when the self set is unavailable during the updating process of detector set. Standard deviations are also listed. The initial N_R is still set to 6000.

a		0.90	0.80	0.70	0.60	0.50	0.40	0.30	0.20	0.10
0	Ave	4768.9	3846.0	3030.1	2391.0	1935.5	1536.4	1229.5	973.4	780.0
	Std	125.629	53.177	84.856	68.772	43.844	33.500	55.588	44.425	44.390
I	Ave	5971.9	5942.3	5916.5	5884.7	5852.9	5832.5	5802.4	5777.8	5755.6
	Std	4.581	6.651	10.320	8.193	11.160	14.547	8.884	11.555	11.568
II	Ave	5945.9	5845.6	5700.5	5527.9	5345.4	5166.9	4948.2	4733.9	4534.2
	Std	11.893	22.102	29.579	28.707	31.146	47.569	27.971	46.912	49.041

5 Discussions

The self-tolerant problem is very important for hardware immune systems under dynamic environment. The ASTA-CED [8] adopted "r-contiguous-bits" matching rule to perform partial matching between detectors and antigens (i.e. invalid state transitions). Compared with the strategy without recruiting detectors in [9], although ASTA-CED has an increased accuracy of detection and a decreased ratio of false positives, it still has an increased failure detection probability (false negative ratio) due to the growing self set.

This paper focuses on the self-tolerant problem in dynamic environments (in which the self set will grow during detection). Two novel detector set updating strategies for HIS are proposed, one of them is endowed with the variable matching length mechanism [14-16], the other just removes the self pattern by stuffing some bits of detector with special symbols.

From the emulation experimental results listed above, it can be observed that, compared with strategies in [8] and [9], the non-self coverage of these two new strategies in this paper are less affected by the growing of the self set, and these two new strategies have a bigger coverage on non-self space. Moreover, the improvements are notable when self set is unavailable during the updating process of detector set. The results also indicate that, the advantages of these two new strategies are more obvious when the parameter a is smaller, i.e., it is more necessary to use these two new strategies in HIS when the self set has a bigger potential of growing. And from the $\triangle C$'s point of view, the progress of strategy II is more notable than that of strategy I.

In addition, strategy I needs an additional space to store every partial matching length of every detector. And strategy II needs two bits for every bit in a detector because '#' is adopted. For example, "00" means '0', "01" means '1', and "11" (or "10") means '#'. Therefore, the space costs of both strategy I and II are larger than that of strategy 0. Furthermore, the implementation complexities of strategy I and strategy II in hardware immune systems are also a little higher than that of strategy 0. However, compared with the advantages of these two new strategies, these disadvantages are not crucial factors in the implementation of many hardware immune systems.

6 Conclusions

Self-Tolerance is a key issue in the research of Hardware Immune Systems. Two novel detector set updating strategies are proposed in this paper. Compared with previous detector set updating strategies in [8] and [9], results of simulation experiments prove that, no matter the self set is available or not, the detector sets being updated by these two new strategies are less affected by the growing of the self set, and the new strategies have a clearly lower increasing on the false negative ratio in a dynamic environment.

There are also some future works that should be studied for improvement, such as embedding these strategies into a real hardware immune system for special applications.

Acknowledgements. This work is supported by National Natural Science Foundation of China (No.60404004) and Nature Science Major Foundation from Anhui Education Bureau (No. 2004kj360zd).

References

1. Bradley, D.W., Tyrrell, A.M.: Immunotronics - Novel Finite-State-Machine Architectures with Built-In Self-Test Using Self-Nonself Differentiation. IEEE Transactions on Evolutionary Computation, Vol. 6(3) (2002) 227-238
2. Tyrrell, A.M.: Computer Know Thy Self!: A Biological Way to Look at Fault Tolerance. Proceedings of 2nd EuroMicro / IEEE Workshop Dependable Computing Systems (1999) 129-135
3. Canham, R., Tyrrell, A.M.: A Learning, Multi-Layered, Hardware Artificial Immune System Implemented upon an Embryonic Array. Proceedings of 5th International Conference on Evolvable Systems, ICES (2003) 174-185
4. Canham, R., Jackson, A.H., Tyrrell, A.M.: Robot Error Detection Using an Artificial Immune System. Proceedings of NASA/DoD Conference on Evolvable Hardware (2003) 199-207
5. Bradley, D.W., Tyrrell, A.M.: The Architecture for a Hardware Immune System. Proceedings of 3rd NASA/ DoD Workshop on Evolvable Hardware. Long Beach, Cailfornia (2001) 193-200

6. Bradley, D.W., Tyrrell, A.M.: A Hardware Immune System for Benchmark State Machine Error Detection. Proceedings of 2002 Congress on Evolutionary Computation. Honolulu, USA (2002)

7. Tarakanov, A., Dasgupta, D.: An Immunochip Architecture and Its Emulation. Proceedings of NASA/DoD Conference on Evolvable Hardware (2002) 261-265

8. Luo, W., Wang, X., Tan, Y., Zhang, Y., Wang, X.: An Adaptive Self-Tolerant Algorithm for Hardware Immune System. Proceedings of 6th International Conference on Evolvable Systems, ICES 2005. Spain (2005) 1-11

9. Wang, X., Luo, W., Wang, X.: Research on an Algorithm with Self-Tolerant Ability in Hardware Immune System (in Chinese). Journal of System Simulation, Vol. 18(5) (2006) 1151-1153

10. Zeng, C., Saxena, N., McCluskey, E.J.: Finite State Machine Synthesis with Concurrent Error Detection. Proceedings of International Test Conference (1999) 672-679

11. Forrest, S., Perelson, A.S., Allen, L., Cherukuri, R.: Self-Nonself Discrimination in a Computer. Proceedings of 1994 IEEE Symposium on Research in Security and Privacy. Los Alamitos, CA (1994) 202-212

12. D'haeseleer, P., Forrest, S., Helman, P.: An Immunological Approach to Change Detection: Algorithms, Analysis and Implications. Proceedings of 1996 IEEE Symposium on Security and Privacy. Los Alamitos, CA (1996) 110-119

13. D'haeseleer, P.: Further Efficient Algorithms for Generating Antibody Strings. Tech. Rep. CS95-3. Dept. Comput. Sci., Univ. New Mexico (1995)

14. Zhou, J., Dasgupata, D.: Augmented Negative Selection Algorithm with Variable-Coverage Detectors. Proceedings of Congress on Evolutionary Computation, CEC, Vol. 1 (2004) 1081-1088

15. Zhou, J., Dasgupata, D.: Real-Valued Negative Selection Algorithm with Variable-Sized Detectors. Proceedings of Genetic and Evolutionary Computation Conference, GECCO-2004. Seattle, Washington USA (2004) 287-298

16. Zhang, H., Wu, L., Zhang, Y., Zeng, Q.: An Algorithm of r-Adjustable Negative Selection Algorithm and Its Simulation Analysis (in Chinese). Chinese Journal of Computers, Vol. 28(10) (2005) 1614-1619

17. Zhou, G.: Principles of Immunology (in Chinese). Scientific and Technical Documents Publishing House, Shanghai (2000)

On the Use of Hyperspheres in Artificial Immune Systems as Antibody Recognition Regions

Thomas Stibor[1], Jonathan Timmis[2], and Claudia Eckert[1]

[1] Department of Computer Science
Darmstadt University of Technology
{stibor, eckert}@sec.informatik.tu-darmstadt.de
[2] Departments of Electronics and Computer Science
University of York, Heslington, York
jtimmis@cs.york.ac.uk

Abstract. Using hyperspheres as antibody recognition regions is an established abstraction which was initially proposed by theoretical immunologists for use in the modeling of antibody-antigen interactions. This abstraction is also employed in the development of many artificial immune system algorithms. Here, we show several undesirable properties of hyperspheres, especially when operating in high dimensions and discuss the problems of hyperspheres as recognition regions and how they have affected overall performance of certain algorithms in the context of real-valued negative selection.

1 Introduction

Work in theoretical immunology has developed various representations for the interactions between antibody and antigen, and affinity metrics for modeling these such interactions. These antibody-antigen binding models were proposed for describing antibody cross-reactivity and multi-specificity [1] or for estimating the antibody repertoire size [2]. This work has provided much of the foundations for the development of artificial immune system (AIS) [3].

AIS is a paradigm inspired by the immune system and is used for solving computational and information processing problems. AIS exploit principles and methods developed by theoretical and experimental immunology, and abstract certain properties which can be implemented in computational systems [3]. In this paper, the abstraction we will consider is the hypersphere. This abstraction of hyperspheres has been used in many artificial immune system algorithms which have been applied to many areas such as anomaly detection, pattern recognition and clustering problems [4,5,6,7,8,9]. In this paper we describe mathematical properties of hyperspheres, which manifest themselves in high-dimensional space, and we provide suggestions on the applicability of hyperspheres as recognition units. Moreover we discuss the applicability of hyperspheres in the context of real-valued negative selection and explain reported poor classification results shown in [6].

H. Bersini and J. Carneiro (Eds.): ICARIS 2006, LNCS 4163, pp. 215–228, 2006.

The paper is organized as follows : In section 2 the real-valued shape-space is outlined and the most commonly used Euclidean distance is presented. Section 3 describes the abstraction of an antibody as a hypersphere. In section 3.1 the known hypersphere volume formula and the construction idea of that formula is shown and properties of that formula are presented in section 4. Next, the maximum volume of hyperspheres with respect to the dimension and the radius is presented in section 4.1, and we highlight unexpected properties of hyperspheres in high dimensions. In section 4.2, based on the mathematical observations, implications on the use of hyperspheres as antibody recognition regions are provided. We then present an algorithm for estimating, as opposed to exactly calculating, the total space of overlapping hyperspheres (section 5). Finally, results in sections 3.1, 4 and 5 are applied to explain in section 6 the poor classification results shown in [6].

2   Real-Valued Shape-Space and Euclidean Distance

The notion of *shape-space* was introduced by Perelson and Oster [1] and allows a quantitative affinity description between antibodies and antigens. More precisely, a shape-space is a metric space with an associated distance (affinity) function. The real-valued shape-space is the n-dimensional Euclidean space $\mathbb{R}^n$, where every element is represented as a n-dimensional point or simply as a vector represented by a list of n real numbers. The Euclidean distance[1] d is the (standard) distance between any two vectors $\mathbf{x}, \mathbf{y} \in \mathbb{R}^n$ and is defined as :

$$d(\mathbf{x}, \mathbf{y}) = \sqrt{(x_1 - y_1)^2 + \ldots + (x_n - y_n)^2} \qquad (1)$$

Moreover, the Euclidean distance d satisfies the metric properties :

non-negativity : $d(\mathbf{x}, \mathbf{y}) \geq 0$

reflexivity : $d(\mathbf{x}, \mathbf{y}) = 0$ iff $\mathbf{x} = \mathbf{y}$

symmetry : $d(\mathbf{x}, \mathbf{y}) = d(\mathbf{y}, \mathbf{x})$

triangle inequality : $d(\mathbf{x}, \mathbf{y}) + d(\mathbf{y}, \mathbf{z}) \geq d(\mathbf{x}, \mathbf{z})$

for all vectors $\mathbf{x}, \mathbf{y}, \mathbf{z} \in \mathbb{R}^n$

and therefore is frequently applied as a distance measurement in AIS algorithms.

3   Hyperspheres as Antibody Recognition Regions

In the original work by Perelson and Oster [1], real-valued shape-space is introduced for estimating the probability that a randomly encountered antigen is recognized by at least one of the antibodies. An antibody is specified by n parameters, e.g. the length, width, charge, etc. and can be described as a n-dimensional

---

[1] Also termed Euclidean norm.

point in the shape-space $\mathbb{R}^n$. Furthermore, an antibody recognizes not only one specific antigen, but several similar antigens which have a certain specificity — this property is called cross-reactivity[2]. In [1] each antibody is represented as a n-dimensional point and its (cross-reactivity) recognition space is modeled as a hypersphere — called an antibody recognition region. Antigens which lie within the hypersphere are recognized by the associated antibody. From an immunological point of view, antibodies recognize antigens which have a complementary binding site instead of similar binding regions (see Fig. 1(a)). This inspired Hart et al. [10] to develop a simulation to investigate empirically complementary binding properties in a immune network, with regard to emerging recognition regions. Hart et al. reported that the resultant immune network depended very much on the affinity metric employed (see [10] for further details).

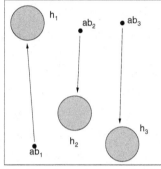 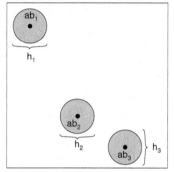

(a) Complementary antibodies recognition regions. Antibodies ab_i recognize all antigens which lie within the complementary hyperspheres h_i

(b) Non-complementary antibodies recognition regions. Antibodies ab_i recognize all antigens which lie within the hyperspheres h_i

Fig. 1. Real-valued Shape-Space with complementer and non-complementer antibody recognition regions (modeling cross-reactivity)

For solving information processing problems, like pattern recognition, anomaly detection and clustering problems, the complementary recognition approach is possibly less appropriate, as it less obvious how one might employ such an idea. For such problems, it is useful to recognize points which are similar instead of complementary and therefore, similarity antibody-antigen recognition approaches are typically applied (see Fig. 1(b)). More precisely, an antibody can be represented as a hypersphere with center $\mathbf{ab} \in \mathbb{R}^n$ and a radius $r \in \mathbb{R}$. An antigen $\mathbf{ag} \in \mathbb{R}^n$ is recognized by an antibody $\mathbf{ab}$, when it lies within the hypersphere, i.e. $d(\mathbf{ab}, \mathbf{ag}) \leq r$.

---

[2] A well described explanation of the difference between cross-reactivity and multi-specificity is provided in [1], page 661.

3.1   Volume of Hyperspheres

The volume of a n-dimensional hypersphere with radius r can be calculated as follows :

$$V(n, r) = r^n \cdot \frac{\pi^{n/2}}{\Gamma\left(\frac{n}{2} + 1\right)}$$

where

$\Gamma(n+1) = n!$ for $n \in \mathbb{N}$ and

$\Gamma(n + \frac{1}{2}) = \dfrac{1 \cdot 3 \cdot 5 \cdot 7 \cdot \ldots \cdot (2n-1)}{2n} \sqrt{\pi}$ for half-integer arguments.

We briefly show the construction idea[3] behind the the volume calculation of hyperspheres. For a in-depth description see [11], where the complete construction and a proof is shown.

The volume $V(n)$ of a n-dimensional *unit sphere* can be constructed inductively

$$V(2) = \pi$$

$$V(3) = \frac{4}{3}\pi$$

$$\vdots$$

$$V(n) = \begin{cases} \dfrac{\pi^{n/2}}{(n/2)!} & , n \text{ even} \\[3mm] \dfrac{2^n \pi^{(n-1)/2}\, ((n-1)/2)!}{n!} & , n \text{ odd} \end{cases}$$

Given a 2-dimensional unit circle

$$C^2 = \{(x_1, x_2) \in \mathbb{R}^2 \mid x_1^2 + x_2^2 \le 1\}$$

The volume $V(C^2)$ can be calculated as a summation of infinitely thin "stripes".

$$V(C^2) = 2 \cdot \int_{-1}^{1} \sqrt{1 - x_2^2}\, dx_2$$

$$= 2 \cdot \int_{0}^{\pi} \sqrt{1 - \cos^2(t)}\, \sin(t)\, dt$$

$$= 2 \cdot \int_{0}^{\pi} \sin^2(t)\, dt$$

$$= \int_{0}^{\pi} dt = \pi$$

---

[3] Taken from [11].

$V(C^2) \to V(C^3)$

$$V(C^3) = \int_{-1}^{1} \pi \left(\sqrt{1 - x_3^2} \right)^2 dx_3$$

$$= \pi \int_{-1}^{1} (1 - x_3^2) \, dx_3$$

$$= \frac{4}{3} \pi$$

$$\vdots$$

$V(C^{n-1}) \to V(C^n)$

$$V(C^n) = V(C^{n-1}) \cdot \int_{-1}^{1} (1 - x_n^2)^{(n-1)/2} \, dx_n$$

$$= \frac{\pi^{n/2}}{\Gamma(\frac{n}{2} + 1)}$$

Proposition 1. *The volume of a n-dimensional hypersphere with radius r is*

$$V(n, r) = r^n \cdot \frac{\pi^{n/2}}{\Gamma\left(\frac{n}{2} + 1\right)} \qquad (2)$$

Proof. see [11]

4 Curse of Dimensionality

The phenomenon "curse of dimensionality" was first mentioned by Bellman [13] during his study of optimizing a function of a few dozen variables in an exhaustive search space. For example, given a function defined on a unitary hypercube of dimension n, in each dimension 10 discrete points are considered for evaluating the function. In dimension $n = 2$, this results in 100 evaluations, whereas in dimension $n = 10$, 10^{10} function evaluations are required. In general, an exponential number of $(1/\epsilon)^n$ function evaluations are required to obtain an optimization error of ϵ and therefore is computationally infeasible, even for a moderate n.

This simple example shows how problems like function optimization, which are computationally feasible in lower dimensions, transform to computationally infeasible problems in higher dimensions. A similar phenomenon (but not from the perspective of computational complexity) can be observed with hyperspheres in high-dimensional spaces, where they loose their familiar properties. In high-dimensions $\mathbb{R}^n$, i.e. $n > 3$, hyperspheres have undesirable properties. These properties (the following corollaries) can be derived directly from proposition (1).

Corollary 1. *The volume of hyperspheres converges to 0 for $n \to \infty$.*

$$\lim_{n \to \infty} V(n, r) = 0$$

Proof.

$$\lim_{n \to \infty} \left(r^n \cdot \frac{\pi^{n/2}}{\underbrace{\Gamma\left(\frac{n}{2}+1\right)}_{\approx \sqrt{2\pi} e^{-n} n^{n+\frac{1}{2}}}} \right)$$

$$= \frac{1}{\sqrt{2\pi}} \lim_{n \to \infty} \left(\frac{\overbrace{(r \, e \, \sqrt{\pi})^n}^{c}}{n^{n+\frac{1}{2}}} \right) = \frac{1}{\sqrt{2\pi}} \lim_{n \to \infty} \left(\frac{c^n}{n^{n+\frac{1}{2}}} \right) = 0$$

□

Corollary 2. *The fraction of the volume which lies at values of the radius between $r - \epsilon$ and r, where $0 < \epsilon < r$ is*

$$V_{fraction}(n, r, \epsilon) = 1 - \left(1 - \frac{\epsilon}{r}\right)^n$$

Proof.

$$1 - \frac{V(n, r - \epsilon)}{V(n, r)} = 1 - \left(\frac{\frac{(r-\epsilon)^n \cdot \pi^{n/2}}{\Gamma\left(\frac{n}{2}+1\right)}}{\frac{r^n \cdot \pi^{n/2}}{\Gamma\left(\frac{n}{2}+1\right)}} \right) = 1 - \left(1 - \frac{\epsilon}{r}\right)^n$$

□

Corollary (1) implies that the higher the dimension the smaller the volume of a hypersphere for a fixed radii. This property is investigated in more detail, in the following section.

Corollary (2) reveals that in high-dimensional spaces, points which are uniformly randomly distributed inside the hypersphere, are predominately concentrated in a thin shell close to the surface or, in other words, at very high dimensions the entire volume of a hypersphere is concentrated immediately below the surface.

Example 1. Given a hypersphere with radius $r = 1$, $\epsilon = 0.1$ and $n = 50$ and k points which are uniformly randomly distributed inside the hypersphere, approximately $1 - \left(1 - \frac{0.1}{1}\right)^{50} \approx 99,5\,\%$ of the k points lie within the thin ϵ-shell close to the surface.

4.1   Volume Extrema

By keeping the radius fixed and differentiating the volume $V(n, r)$ with respect to n, one obtains the dimension[4] where the volume is maximal :

$$\frac{\partial}{\partial n} \left(\frac{r^n \cdot \pi^{n/2}}{\Gamma\left(\frac{n}{2}+1\right)} \right) = \frac{r^n \ln(r) \pi^{n/2}}{\Gamma\left(\frac{n}{2}+1\right)} + \frac{r^n \pi^{n/2} \ln(\pi)}{2\,\Gamma\left(\frac{n}{2}+1\right)} - \frac{r^n \pi^{n/2} \Psi\left(\frac{n}{2}+1\right)}{2\,\Gamma\left(\frac{n}{2}+1\right)} \quad (3)$$

---

[4] The dimension is obviously a nonnegative integer, however we consider term (3) analytically as a real-valued function.

$$\text{where} \quad \Psi(n) = \frac{\partial}{\partial n} \ln \Gamma(n)$$

Vice versa, keeping the dimension fixed and differentiate term (2) with respect to r, it is not solvable in roots, i.e. no extrema exists :

$$\frac{\partial}{\partial r} \left(\frac{r^n \cdot \pi^{n/2}}{\Gamma\left(\frac{n}{2}+1\right)} \right) = \frac{r^n n \pi^{n/2}}{r \Gamma\left(\frac{n}{2}+1\right)} \tag{4}$$

For instance a hypersphere with radius $r = 1$ reaches its maximum volume in dimension 5 and looses volume in lower and higher dimensions. In figure 2 this property is visualized for different radius lengths $r = \{0.9, 1.0, 1.1, 1.2\}$. One can see that for each radius length in dimension from $n = 0$ to $n = 25$, the associated hypersphere reaches a maximal volume in a certain dimension and looses volume asymptotically in higher and lower dimensions.

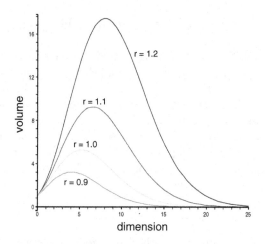

Fig. 2. Hypersphere volume plot for radius lengths $r = \{0.9, 1.0, 1.1, 1.2\}$ and dimension $n = 0, \ldots, 25$. Obviously, n is a nonnegative integer, but the graph is drawn treating n as continuously varying.

Table 1. Dimension where a hypersphere reaches the maximum volume for radius lengths $r = \{0.05, 0.1, 0.2, \ldots, 1.0\}$. Results are obtained by considering term (3) as a real-valued function.

Radius r	0.05	0.1	0.2	0.3	0.4	0.5	0.6	0.7	0.8	0.9	1.0
Dimension $\lfloor n \rfloor$	$-9.17 \cdot 10^7$	-88.94	1.59	1.12	1.0	1.03	1.20	1.53	2.14	3.23	5.27

Table 1 presents the dimension where a hypersphere reaches its maximum volume for different radius lengths. Surprisingly, for radius lengths $r = 0.05$ and $r = 0.1$ the maximum volume lies in negative real-valued numbers. Hence, a volume maximization for such small radius lengths is not feasible, as the dimension is a nonnegative integer.

4.2 Using Hyperspheres as Antibody Recognition Regions in Artificial Immune Systems

The results and observations presented in sections 3.1, 4 and 4.1 indicate that high-dimensional real-valued shape-spaces strongly bias the volume (recognition space) of hyperspheres. A hypersphere, for example with radius $r = 1$ has a high volume in relation to its radius length, up to dimension 15 (see Fig. 2). In higher dimensions ($n > 15$), for $r = 1$ the volume is nearly 0. This means that the recognition space — or in the context of antibody recognition region (covered space) — is nearly 0. In contrast, a radius that is too large ($r > 2$) in high dimensional spaces ($n > 10$) will imply an exponential volume. This exponential volume behavior, in combination with an unprecise volume estimation of overlapping hyperspheres, is the reason for the poor classification results reported in the paper [6] and is discussed in the subsequent sections.

5 Estimating Volume of Overlapping Hyperspheres

In section 3.1 a formula for calculating the exact volume of a hypersphere given by the dimension and the radius was shown. However, many proposed artificial immune system algorithms for solving pattern recognition, anomaly detection and clustering problems using not only *one* but multiple overlapping hyperspheres for classifying points [4,5,6,7,8,9]. Calculating analytically the total volume of overlapping hyperspheres is a very difficult task. Just the simple 2-dimensional case of three overlapping circles with different radii is a mathematical challenge. In the following section we describe a method to estimate the volume of (overlapping) hyperspheres.

5.1 Monte Carlo Integration

The Monte Carlo Integration is a method to integrate a function over a complicated domain, where analytical expressions are very difficult to apply – e.g. the calculation of the volume of overlapping hyperspheres in higher dimensions. Given integrals of the form $I = \int_{\mathcal{X}} h(\mathbf{x}) f(\mathbf{x}) d\mathbf{x}$, where $h(\mathbf{x})$ and $f(\mathbf{x})$ are functions for which $h(\mathbf{x}) f(\mathbf{x})$ is integrable over the space $\mathcal{X}$, and $f(\mathbf{x})$ is a non-negative valued, integrable function satisfying $\int_{\mathcal{X}} f(\mathbf{x}) d\mathbf{x} = 1$. The Monte Carlo integration picks N random points $\mathbf{x}_1, \mathbf{x}_2, \ldots, \mathbf{x}_N$, over $\mathcal{X}$ and approximates the integral as

$$I \approx \frac{1}{N} \sum_{n=1}^{N} h(\mathbf{x}_n) \tag{5}$$

The absolute error of this method is *independent* of the dimension of the space $\mathcal{X}$ and decreases as $1/\sqrt{N}$. By applying this integration method, two fundamental questions arise :

- How many observations should one collect to ensure a specified statistical accuracy ?
- Given N observations from a Monte Carlo Experiment, how accurate is the estimated solution ?

Both question are answered and discussed in [15]. Using the Chebyshev's inequality and specifying a *confidence level* $1 - \delta$, one can determine the smallest sample size N that guarantees an integration error no larger than ϵ. In [15] this specification is called the (ϵ, δ) *absolute error criterion* and leads to the worst-case sample size

$$N := \lceil 1/4\delta\epsilon^2 \rceil \qquad (6)$$

5.2 Monte Carlo Hyperspheres Volume Integration

Using equations (5) and (6) a simple algorithm can be developed which estimates the total space (volume) covered by the hyperspheres inside the unitary hypercube $[0,1]^n$.

Algorithm 1. Monte Carlo Hyperspheres Volume Integration

   input : H = set of hyperspheres, ϵ = absolute error of the estimated volume, δ
            = confidence level
   output: total volume of H
1 **begin**
2 | inside $\longleftarrow$ 0
     | // calculate required worst-case
     | // sample size N
3 | $N \longleftarrow \lceil 1/4\delta\epsilon^2 \rceil$
4 | **for** $i \leftarrow 1$ **to** N **do**
5 | | $\mathbf{x} \longleftarrow$ random point from $[0,1]^n$
6 | | **foreach** $h \in H$ **do**
7 | | | **if** $dist(\mathbf{c}_h, \mathbf{x}) \le r_h$ **then**
                          | // $\mathbf{c}_h$ is center of h, r_h is radius of h
8 | inside $\longleftarrow$ inside + 1
9 | goto 5:
10 | **return** (inside/N)
11 **end**

---

6 Limitation of Real-Valued Negative Selection in Higher Dimensions

In [6] an immune inspired real-valued negative selection algorithm was compared to different statistical anomaly detection techniques[5] for a high-dimensional

---
[5] Parzen-Window, one class SVM.

anomaly detection problem. The investigations observed that the poorest classification results were real-valued negative selection, when compared to the statistical anomaly detection techniques on a 41-dimensional problem set (see [6] for further details). In this section, we attempt to explain this observation.

6.1 Real-Valued Negative Selection

The real-valued negative selection is an immune-inspired algorithm applied for anomaly detection. Roughly speaking, immune negative selection is a process which eliminates self-reactive lymphocytes and ensures that *only* those lymphocytes enter the blood stream that do not recognize self-cells[6]. As a consequence, lymphocytes which survive the negative selection process, are capable of recognizing nearly all foreign substances (like viruses, bacteria, etc.) which do not belong to the body. Abstracting this principle and modeling immune components according to the AIS framework [3] one obtains a technique for anomaly detection :

- Input : S = set of points $\in [0,1]^n$ gathered from normal behavior of a system.
- Output : D = set of hyperspheres, which recognizing a proportion c_0 of the total space $[0,1]^n$, except the normal points.
- Detector generation : While covered proportion c_0 is not reached, generate hyperspheres.
- Classification : If unseen point lies within a hypersphere, it does not belong to the normal behavior of the system and is classified as an anomaly.

A formal algorithmic description of real-valued negative selection is provided in [6].

6.2 Poor Classification Results

In [6] the real-valued negative selection technique (see section 6.1) was benchmarked by means of ROC analysis on a high-dimensional anomaly detection problem. The authors reported a detection rate of approximately $1\% - 2\%$ and a false alarm rate of 0% when applying the real-valued negative selection algorithm. The false alarm rate of 0% can be explained by learning 100% of the training data and benchmarking with the training and testing data — similar false alarm rates results on other benchmarked data sets are reported in [5,16]. Benchmarking with 100% training and testing data should be avoided, as in general it results in a high overfitted learning model and no representative (classification) results on the generalization performance will be obtained.

Moreover, the authors in [6] reported steady space coverage problems: these can be explained also by lack of precision when estimating the volume integration. Using term (6), which gives the worst-case sample size when given ϵ, δ, and applying the inequality

$$N + 1 > \frac{1}{4\delta\epsilon^2} \iff \epsilon > \left(\frac{1}{4\delta(N+1)}\right)^{1/2} \tag{7}$$

---

[6] Cells which belongs to the body.

one can easily see why the authors in [6] reported such steady space coverage problems for the estimated hyperspheres coverage of $c_0 = 80\,\%$. For the parameter c_0 which was originally proposed in [5] one obtains according to [5,6] a sample size of $N = 1/(1 - c_0) = 5$. Evaluating term (7) with a given confidence level of $90\,\%$, one obtains an integration error ϵ of greater than $65\,\%$. Inequality (7) can be used to explain the reported steady space coverage problems, however it does not explain thoroughly the poor classification results described in [6] — this is now explained by means of the results shown in sections 4 and 5.

Investigating the 41-dimensional data set [17], one can statistically verify[7], that the whole normalized non-anomalous class is concentrated at one place inside the unitary hypercube $\mathcal{U} = [0, 1]^{41}$. In [18] this characteristic is called "empty space phenomenon" and arises in any data set that does *not* grow exponentially with the dimension of the space.

In [6] the authors additionally reported, that the real-valued negative selection algorithm terminated when (on average) 1.4 detectors were generated. By generating only one detector (hypersphere) with, for example, a radius $r = 3$ and a detector center which does not necessarily lie inside $\mathcal{U}$, the volume of that hypersphere amounts $5.11 \cdot 10^{10}$. The unitary hypercube $\mathcal{U} = [0, 1]^{41}$ has a total volume of 1, however most of the volume of a hypercube is concentrated in the large corners, which themselves become very long "spikes". This can be verified by comparing the ratio of the distance $\sqrt{n}$ from the center of the hypercube to one of the edges to the perpendicular distance $a/2$ to one of the edges (see Fig. 3).

$$\frac{\left(\sum_{i=1}^{n}(\frac{a}{2})^2\right)^{1/2}}{\frac{a}{2}} = \frac{\left(n\,\frac{a^2}{4}\right)^{1/2}}{\frac{a}{2}} = \sqrt{n} \qquad \text{where } n \text{ is the dimension} \qquad (8)$$

For $n \to \infty$, the term (8) goes to ∞ and therefore the volume is concentrated in very long "spikes" of $\mathcal{U}$.

As a consequence, the hypersphere covers some of those (high-volume) spikes which are lying within the $V_{fraction}$ proportion of the hypersphere. Hence, the real-valued negative selection algorithm terminates with only a very small number of large radii detectors (hyperspheres) which are covering a limited number of spikes. As a result a large proportion of the volume of the hypercube does not lie within the hyperspheres — it lies in the remaining (high-volume) spikes, though the hypersphere volume is far higher than the hypercube volume.

These observations in combination with the unprecise volume integration of overlapping hyperspheres results in the poor classification results reported in [6].

From our point of view, the real-valued negative selection would appear to be a technique that is not well suited for high-dimensional data sets, i.e. data dimensions far higher than 41 — a well established benchmark in the field of pattern classification is for instance the problem of handwritten digit recognition, the dimensionality of this problem domain is 256 [19,20]. We propose this is in part because it makes more sense to formulate a classification model with

---

[7] By means of covariance matrix.

regard to the given training elements, instead of complementary space. The complementary (anomalous) space is exponentially large when compared to the "normal" space in high dimensions. The real-valued negative selection technique attempts to cover this high-dimensional space with hyperspheres, but as we have shown, these have adverse properties in such high-dimensional spaces.

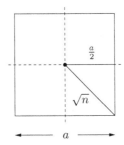

Fig. 3. Distance ratio $\frac{\sqrt{n}}{a/2}$ between a line from center to a corner and a perpendicular line from center to an edge

In [18] Verleysen discusses in detail, this curse of dimensionality problem, with respect to artificial neural networks. He suggests in general to change the distance measure function for high-dimensional problems, for instance by applying a higher-order norm ($h > 2$)

$$d_h(\mathbf{x}, \mathbf{y}) = \sqrt[h]{|x_1 - y_1|^h + \ldots + |x_n - y_n|^h} \qquad (9)$$

instead of the standard Euclidean norm. In the context of *inductive biases*[8], Freitas and Timmis [21] discussed different affinity measures in artificial immune systems. They illustrated the advantages and disadvantages of the 1-norm and 2-norm (see term (9)) and showed how one of these norm when compared to the other norm can lead to an overemphasizing of the distance. As a final summarizing sentence, the authors suggested that when developing an AIS, one should make a careful choice of the norm, as the norm should take into account the characteristics (in our case the dimension) of the data being analyzed. Unfortunately, there seems to be no theoretical results, for correctly choosing the value h with regard to the data dimension [18].

7   Conclusion

The immune system is an impressive recognition system with many appealing properties for the construction of artificial immune system algorithms. Abstracting antibodies as hyperspheres and applying the Euclidean distance metric for quantifying binding strengths, is an established method for modeling and simulating the immune systems.

---

[8] Effectiveness in problem domains.

For developing competitive immune-inspired algorithms the antibody-antigen representation and affinity metric is a crucial parameter. We have found that applying the abstraction of these hyperspheres for immune-inspired algorithms can lead to poor results, especially for high-dimensional classification problems. In this paper, we have shown that these hypersphere have undesirable properties in high dimensions — the volume tends to zero and nearly all uniformly randomly distributed points are close to the hypersphere surface. We have presented these hypersphere properties and have provided an explanation for poor classification results reported in [6]. In addition, we have now explained the limitations of the real-valued negative selection for high-dimensional classification problems, when employing hyperspheres. There is no reason to suggest that the hypersphere properties we have discussed in this paper, are not valid observations for all high-dimensional classification problems where hyperspheres are applied as recognition regions. Therefore, as a result, these adverse hypersphere properties could bias all (artificial immune system) algorithms, which employ hyperspheres as recognition units.

References

1. Perelson, A.S., Oster, G.F.: Theoretical studies of clonal selection: minimal antibody repertoire size and reliability of self-nonself discrimination. In: J. Theor. Biol. Volume 81. (1979) 645–670
2. Percus, J.K., Percus, O.E., Perelson, A.S.: Predicting the size of the t-cell receptor and antibody combining region from consideration of efficient self-nonself discrimination. Proceedings of National Academy of Sciences USA **90** (1993) 1691–1695
3. de Castro, L.N., Timmis, J.: Artificial Immune Systems: A New Computational Intelligence Approach. Springer-Verlag (2002)
4. Gonzalez, F., Dasgupta, D., Nino, L.F.: A randomized real-valued negative selection algorithm. In: Proceedings of the 2nd International Conference on Artificial Immune Systems – ICARIS. Volume 2787 of Lecture Notes in Computer Science., Edinburgh, UK, Springer-Verlag (2003) 261–272
5. Ji, Z., Dasgupta, D.: Real-valued negative selection algorithm with variable-sized detectors. In: Genetic and Evolutionary Computation – GECCO, Part I. Volume 3102 of Lecture Notes in Computer Science., Seattle, WA, USA, Springer-Verlag (2004) 287–298
6. Stibor, T., Timmis, J., Eckert, C.: A comparative study of real-valued negative selection to statistical anomaly detection techniques. In: Proceedings of 4th International Conference on Artificial Immune Systems – ICARIS. Volume 3627 of Lecture Notes in Computer Science., Springer-Verlag (2005) 262–275
7. Watkins, A., Boggess, L.: A new classifier based on resource limited artificial immune systems. In: Proceedings of the 2002 Congress on Evolutionary Computation CEC2002, IEEE Press (2002) 1546–1551
8. Bezerra, G.B., Barra, T.V., de Castro, L.N., Zuben, F.J.V.: Adaptive radius immune algorithm for data clustering. In: Proceedings of 4th International Conference on Artificial Immune Systems – ICARIS. Volume 3627 of Lecture Notes in Computer Science., Springer-Verlag (2005) 290–303

9. Bentley, P.J., Greensmith, J., Ujjin, S.: Two ways to grow tissue for artificial immune systems. In: Proceedings of 4th International Conference on Artificial Immune Systems – ICARIS. Volume 3627 of Lecture Notes in Computer Science., Springer-Verlag (2005) 139–152

10. Hart, E., Ross, P.: Studies on the implications of shape-space models for idiotypic networks. In: Proceedings of 3th International Conference on Artificial Immune Systems – ICARIS. Volume 3239 of Lecture Notes in Computer Science., Springer-Verlag (2004) 413–426

11. Leppmeier, M.: Kugelpackungen von Kepler bis heute. Vieweg Verlag (1997)

12. Bishop, C.M.: Neural Networks for Pattern Recognition. Oxford University Press (1995)

13. Bellman, R.: Adaptive Control Processes: A Guided Tour. Princeton University Press (1961)

14. Mosegaard, K., Sambridge, M.: Monte Carlo analysis of inverse problems. Inverse Problems 18 (2002) 29–54

15. Fishman, G.S.: Monte Carlo Concepts, Algorithms, and Applications. Springer (1995)

16. Stibor, T., Mohr, P.H., Timmis, J., Eckert, C.: Is negative selection appropriate for anomaly detection ? In: Proceedings of Genetic and Evolutionary Computation Conference – GECCO-2005, ACM Press (2005) 321–328

17. Hettich, S. and Bay, S. D.: KDD Cup 1999 Data (1999) http://kdd.ics.uci.edu.

18. Verleysen, M.: Learning high-dimensional data. Limitations and Future Trends in Neural Computation 186 (2003) 141–162

19. Vapnik, V.N.: The Nature of Statistical Learning Theory. Second edn. Springer-Verlag (1999)

20. Schölkopf, B., Platt, J.C., Shawe-Taylor, Shawe-Taylor, Smola, A.J., Williamson, R.C.: Estimating the support of a high-dimensional distribution. Technical Report MSR-TR-99-87, Microsoft Research (MSR) (1999)

21. Freitas, A., Timmis, J.: Revisiting the Foundations of Artificial Immune Systems: A Problem Oriented Perspective. In: Proceedings of the 2nd International Conference on Artificial Immune Systems – ICARIS. Volume 2787 of Lecture Notes in Computer Science., Springer-Verlag (2003) 229–241

A Heuristic Detector Generation Algorithm for Negative Selection Algorithm with Hamming Distance Partial Matching Rule

Wenjian Luo, Zeming Zhang, and Xufa Wang

Department of Computer Science and Technology,
University of Science and Technology of China, Hefei 230027, China
wjluo@ustc.edu.cn, zmzhang@mail.ustc.edu.cn, xfwang@ustc.edu.cn

Abstract. Negative selection algorithm is one of the most important algorithms inspired by biological immune system. In this paper, a heuristic detector generation algorithm for negative selection algorithm is proposed when the partial matching rule is Hamming distance. Experimental results show that this novel detector generation algorithm has a better performance than traditional detector generation algorithm.

1 Introduction

Artificial immune system (AIS) is an emergent bio-inspired research field after artificial neural network and evolutionary computation, which is inspired by biological immune system [1-4]. Negative selection algorithm (NSA) has been proposed for more than ten years, which is one of the most important algorithms and components in artificial immune systems [5]. The detector generation algorithms for negative selection algorithm have been studied for years, too [2, 3, 6, 7]. S. Forrest and her colleagues proposed the linear time detector generation algorithm and the greedy detector generation algorithm for negative selection algorithm with the r-continuous-bits partial matching rule [7]. The negative selection algorithm with r-chunk rule is proposed in [8], and the variable length detector for real-valued shape space is proposed in [9-10]. T. Stibor and his colleagues analyzed the negative selection algorithm theoretically in [11-12]. In addition, evolutionary negative selection algorithms that combine negative selection model and evolutionary operators are also investigated [13]. These are typical works in this field.

However, so far, when the partial matching rule is Hamming distance, there is no efficient detector generation algorithm. As for the previous detector generation algorithm that proposed about ten years ago, it runs in exponential time with respect to the size of the self set [5, 7]. This paper concerns with an efficient detector generation algorithm for negative selection algorithm that adopts Hamming distance as its partial matching rule.

The rest of this paper is organized as follows. Section 2 briefly introduces the traditional detector generation algorithm and its time and space complexities. The new heuristic detector generation algorithm is given in detail in section 3. In section 4,

H. Bersini and J. Carneiro (Eds.): ICARIS 2006, LNCS 4163, pp. 229–243, 2006.

some experiments are done to evaluate the performance of the heuristic detector generation algorithm proposed in this paper. Section 5 includes some discussions. The last section summarizes this paper with a brief conclusion and gives some future works.

2 Exhaustive Detector Generation Algorithm for Negative Selection Algorithm with Hamming Distance Partial Matching Rule

Negative Selection Algorithm (NSA) is a very significant change detection algorithm based on the generation process of T-Cells in biological immune system.

NSA has three steps [5]. (1) Define the self set. Firstly it generates the self set according to the normal data set. (2) Generating detectors. (3) Monitoring the data that we want to protect with the detector set. When the data matches any detector in detector set, anomaly changes occur in the protected data.

The detector generation algorithm is one of the most important components of negative selection algorithm. Fig. 1 shows the typical detector generation algorithm when the partial matching rule is Hamming distance, which runs in exponential time with respect to the size of the self set [5, 7].

---

(1) l : The string length.

(2) r : Hamming distance parameter. If the Hamming distance between two strings is smaller than $l-r$, these two strings match. In other words, if two strings are identical with no less than r bits in the corresponding positions, these two strings match.

(3) S : The self set.

(4) R : The detector set. R is set as an empty set initially.

(5) Generating a string d randomly as a candidate detector.

(6) For any self string s in S, if d matches s, go to (5).

(7) $R \leftarrow R \cup \{d\}$.

(8) If the size of R is large enough, this algorithm terminates. Or go to (5).

Fig. 1. Exhaustive detector generation algorithm

Note that only a binary space for the self and the nonself space is considered in this paper. This algorithm requires generating a number of candidate detectors. And the number of candidate detectors is much larger than the expected number of the detectors. Let N_S denote the size of the self set, N_{R0} represent the number of the candidate detectors, and N_R denote the size of the detector set. The time cost of this algorithm is proportional to N_{R0} and N_S, and the space is determined by N_S [7].

Time complexity: $O(N_{R0} \cdot N_S) = O\left(\dfrac{-\ln P_f}{P_m (1 - P_m)^{N_S}} N_S \right)$,

Space complexity: $O(N_S \cdot l)$.

The failure probability P_f [5] achieved by N_R detectors is

$$P_f = (1 - P_m)^{N_R} . \tag{1}$$

Where P_m is the probability of a match between two random strings.

Since the partial matching rule is Hamming distance, the probability of a match between two random strings is

$$P_m = \sum_{i=r}^{l} \binom{l}{i} \cdot \left(\frac{1}{2}\right)^i \cdot \left(\frac{1}{2}\right)^{l-i} = \frac{1}{2^l} \sum_{i=r}^{l} \binom{l}{i} \tag{2}$$

Normally, P_m is small. Table 1 lists some values of P_m with different l and r.

Table 1. Some values of P_m with different l and r

l	r	P_m	l	r	P_m
8	6	0.1445	32	20	0.1077
8	7	0.0351	32	24	0.0035
16	11	0.1051	32	28	9.6506e-6
16	12	0.0384	32	30	1.2317e-007
16	13	0.0106	64	40	0.0300
16	14	0.0021	64	48	3.8665e-005
16	15	0.0003	64	56	2.7813e-010

Notably, these above formula are under an assumption that all detectors are independent. In this paper, the other formulas are all based on this assumption. Since the candidate detectors are generated randomly, the overlap of the detectors will increase as N_S and P_m increase [7].

3 Heuristic Detector Generation Algorithm for Negative Selection Algorithm with Hamming Distance Partial Matching Rule

3.1 Some Definitions

Firstly, some definitions are given.

Definition 1. Template: A template of order i is a size l string consisting of $l-i$ "blank" symbols (represented by "*" here). For example, "11*1*" is a template of order 3 with two "blanks" [7].

In this paper, a detector is a string that consists of {0, 1, *}, where "*" can match with "0" and "1". Therefore, a template with some "blanks" could be a detector if this template does not match any self individual. Actually, a template is regarded as a candidate detector.

For example, if l=4, r=3 and the self set is {0010, 1001}, template "111*" is a valid detector.

Obviously, this definition of the detector can enlarge the coverage of a detector and decrease the number of detectors needed for a given detection rate.

Definition 2. A candidate detector template of a self string: Given a self string $s = x_1 x_2 x_3 \cdots x_l$, a candidate detector template T_s with order c ($c = l - r + 1$) can be constructed as follows. Select c bits of s randomly and flip these c bits, and let other $r - 1$ bits as "blanks".

For example, T_s can be one of the following templates:

$$\overline{x_1 x_2} \cdots \overline{x_c} \, ** \cdots *,$$

$$\overline{x_1 x_2} \cdots \overline{x_{c-1}} \, * \, \overline{x_{c+1}} \, * \cdots *,$$

$$\overline{x_1 x_2} \cdots \overline{x_{c-2}} \, ** \overline{x_{c+1}} \, * \cdots *,$$

$$\cdots \cdots,$$

$$\text{or } ** \cdots * \overline{x_r} \cdots \overline{x_{l-1} x_l} \, .$$

Template T_s has r-1 "blanks" and c determinate bits. Each bit of c determinate bits is set by flipping the corresponding bit of S . Therefore, the possible number of T_s is

$$\binom{l}{r-1}.$$

Definition 3. A candidate detector template of both a self string and a template: Given a self string $s = y_1 y_2 y_3 \cdots y_l$ and a candidate detector template t with order c, one candidate detector template $T_{t,s}$ with order $c + k$, is constructed by the following method. If $k \leq l - c$, select k-bits of the $l - c$ "blank" bits randomly and set the values of the selected bits by flipping the corresponding bits of S , while other $l - c - k$ bits remain "blank". On the other side, if $k > l - c$, such candidate detector template $T_{t,s}$ does not exist.

For example, if $t = \overline{x_1 x_2} \cdots \overline{x_c} \, ** \cdots *$, then $T_{t,s}$ with order $c + k$ can be one of the following templates:

$$\overline{x_1 x_2} \cdots \overline{x_c} \, \overline{y_{c+1}} \cdots \overline{y_{c+k}} \, * \cdots *,$$

$$\overline{x_1 x_2} \cdots \overline{x_c} \, \overline{y_{c+1}} \cdots \overline{y_{c+k-1}} \, * \, \overline{y_{c+k}} \, * \cdots *,$$

$$\overline{x_1 x_2} \cdots \overline{x_c} \, \overline{y_{c+1}} \cdots \overline{y_{c+k-1}} \, ** \overline{y_{c+k}} \, * \cdots *,$$

$$\cdots \cdots,$$

$$\text{or } \overline{x_1 x_2} \cdots \overline{x_c} \, ** \cdots * \, \overline{y_{l-k+1}} \cdots \overline{y_{l-1} x_l} \, .$$

Obviously, template $T_{t,s}$ has $l - c - k$ "blanks" and $c + k$ determinate bits. The values of the new k determinate bits are set by flipping the corresponding bits of $s = y_1 y_2 y_3 \cdots y_l$. Therefore, the possible number of $T_{t,s}$ is $\begin{pmatrix} l - c \\ k \end{pmatrix}$.

3.2 Heuristic Detector Generation Algorithm

Fig. 2 shows the heuristic detector generation algorithm in detail. The valid detectors generated are stored in R.

---

(1) Denote all elements in the self set as $s_1, s_2, \cdots, s_{N_s}$.

(2) Initialize $R = \Phi$.

(3) Select a self string $s_r (1 \leq r \leq N_s)$ randomly. Randomly generate a candidate detector template with order c ($c = l - r + 1$) of s_r, and the candidate detector template is denoted by d. Therefore, d has $r - 1$ "blanks". Let $m = r - 1$.

(4) Initialize $i = 0$.

(5) Set $i = i + 1$,

    a) If $i = r$, go to (5).

    b) If $i > N_S$, $R \leftarrow R \cup \{d\}$. If the size of R reaches the expected number of the mature detectors or other end conditions are satisfied, the algorithm terminates. Otherwise, go to (3).

    c) If $i \leq N_S$,

        i.   Calculate the number of bits that both d and the self string s_i are identical in the corresponding positions where the bits of d are determinate, and denoted by k. That is to say, no "blank" bit is considered when calculating k.

        ii.   If $k \geq r$, delete d and go to (3).

        iii. If $k = r - 1$, all "blank" bits of d are replaced by the flipped value of the corresponding bits of s_i, and set $m = 0$. Go to (5).

        iv. If $k < r - 1$ and $k + m \leq r - 1$, the candidate detector template d and it's "blank" m bits remain unchanged, go to (5).

        v.   If $k < r - 1$ and $k + m > r - 1$, randomly generate one candidate detector template t with order $l - (r - 1 - k)$ of both d and s_i. And set $d = t$, $m = r - 1 - k$, go to (5).

Fig. 2. The heuristic detector generation algorithm

The detectors generated by the algorithm in Fig. 2 consist of {0, 1, *}. And the "*" can be matched with both "0" and "1". Assume a detector d has b "blanks". Any random string is matched by this detector with a probability of

$$P_{m,b} = \left(\begin{array}{ll} 1 & b > r \\ \displaystyle\sum_{i=r-b}^{l-b} \binom{l-b}{i} \left(\frac{1}{2}\right)^i \left(\frac{1}{2}\right)^{l-i} = \frac{1}{2^{l-b}} \sum_{i=r-b}^{l-b} \binom{l-b}{i} & b \leq r \end{array} \right. \quad (3)$$

In Table 2, some values of $P_{m,b}$ are given.

Table 2. Some values of $P_{m,b}$ with different r and b

l	r	b	$P_{m,b}$	l	r	b	$P_{m,b}$
16	14	0	0.0021	32	28	0	9.6506e-006
16	14	2	0.0065	32	28	2	2.9738e-005
16	14	4	0.0193	32	28	4	8.9996e-005
16	14	6	0.0547	32	28	6	0.0003
16	14	8	0.1445	32	28	8	0.0008
16	14	10	0.3438	32	28	10	0.0022
16	14	12	0.6875	32	28	12	0.0059

Given a detector set $R = \{d_1, d_2, \cdots d_{N_R}\}$, and the numbers of their "blank" bits are $\{b_1, b_2, \cdots, b_{N_R}\}$, the failure probability P_f achieved by these N_R detectors is

$$P_f = \prod_{i=1}^{N_R} (1 - P_{m,b_i}) \quad . \quad (4)$$

As mentioned in section 2, we assume that all detectors are independent here.

4   Experiments

For convenience, the traditional negative selection algorithm is denoted by t-NSA, and the heuristic algorithm given in section 3 is denoted by h-NSA.

In this paper, the following experiments are conducted to evaluate the performance of the heuristic detector generation algorithm proposed in this paper. Every experiments runs 10 times independently.

In section 4.1, experiments are conducted to estimate the average matching number for generating one detector. In both t-NSA and h-NSA, all candidate detectors are generated at random and some of them are removed because of matching one or more self strings. In these two algorithms, the basic operator is the matching operator between the self string and the candidate detector (or the candidate detector template). Therefore, the average matching number for generating one detector can reflect their time costs experimentally.

In section 4.2, comparisons on N_R for fixed P_f are done. At the same time, the actual P_f are given.

In all experiments, the size of the test set is denoted by N_T. Notably, the test set consists of different anomaly strings, and they are generated randomly one by one. That is to say, if an anomaly string is identical to any one of the test set, it can not be added into the test set. In these two algorithms, the self set and test set are generated randomly by *randomize(…)* and *random(…)* functions in visual c++. Suppose the length of string is l. An anomaly string in the test set is generated according to the following steps.

(1) The *random(…)* function is used to generate an integer between 0 and $2^l - 1$ directly, then transform this integer into a binary string.
(2) If this binary string matches any self individual or any one in the test set, go to (1). Or add this binary string into the test set.

In addition, when the length of string is l and the matching length is r, a self string with Hamming distance can cover $\begin{pmatrix} l \\ r \end{pmatrix}$ strings. Therefore, in the following experiments, the size of self set is relatively small. Otherwise, the self set is prone to covering the whole space, and both the detector set and the test set are difficult to be generated.

In the experiments, G_M represents the matching times between all candidate detectors and the self individuals during the generation of detectors. $C_G = \dfrac{G_M}{N_R N_S}$ represents the average cost of generating one matured detector. And this parameter can reflect the algorithms' time cost experimentally. Finally, D_R represents the detection rate. And $D_R = 1 - P_f$.

4.1 Comparisons on G_M and D_R Between h-NSA and t-NSA

Experiment 1. The size of self set N_S is fixed and the size of the detector set N_R varies. Set $l = 16, r = 14$, $N_S = 300$, $N_T = 10000$. And the experimental results are

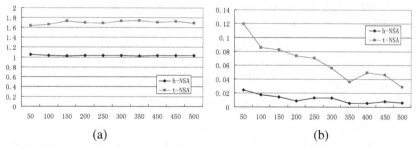

(a)   (b)

Fig. 3. (a) Comparisons on C_G between h-NSA and t-NSA when fixing N_S and varying N_R; (b) Standard deviation of C_G between h-NSA and t-NSA when fixing N_S and varying N_R

Table 3. Comparisons on G_M between h-NSA and t-NSA when fixing N_S and varying N_R

N_R		Max G_M	Min G_M	AVG G_M	STDDEV
50	h-NSA	16120	15167	15675.7	365.22
	t-NSA	28545	22280	24527.7	1792.28
100	h-NSA	31513	30152	30879.1	523.31
	t-NSA	54513	46722	49757.6	2552.35
150	h-NSA	47259	45413	46127.4	646.26
	t-NSA	85156	72262	77705.6	3711.31
200	h-NSA	62433	60703	61734.7	545.77
	t-NSA	109638	94355	101503.9	4410.65
250	h-NSA	79305	76100	77314.0	1008.22
	t-NSA	139078	121987	126130.4	5260.17
300	h-NSA	94836	91775	92897.3	1205.18
	t-NSA	163775	148562	155445.2	5053.12
350	h-NSA	108330	106551	107743.4	600.72
	t-NSA	187053	175327	182479.2	3808.99
400	h-NSA	125041	122900	123915.1	656.90
	t-NSA	215162	197034	204130.6	5960.36
450	h-NSA	141056	138041	139746.7	1108.97
	t-NSA	242589	222226	232088.5	6304.61
500	h-NSA	156130	153357	154610.9	953.22
	t-NSA	260032	246993	252299.7	4340.26

shown in Table 3 and Table 4. For convenience, the experimental results are also shown in Fig. 3 and Fig. 4.

From Table 3 and Fig. 3, it can be observed that when N_S is fixed, the C_G in both h-NSA and t-NSA almost have no notable changes with the increment of N_R. However, when N_S is fixed, it's much more difficult to generate the same number of matured detectors in t-NSA than in h-NSA.

From Table 4 and Fig. 4, it can be observed that the detection ratio D_R of both h-NSA and t-NSA increase with the increment of N_R. But also obviously, the detection ratio D_R of h-NSA is much higher than that of t-NSA for the same number of matured detectors.

From Fig. 3 and Fig. 4, It is also known that the standard deviations of both C_G and D_R in h-NSA are lower than those in t-NSA. So, the h-NSA is more stable than t-NSA.

Table 4. Comparisons on D_R between h-NSA and t-NSA when fixing N_S and varying N_R

N_R		Max D_R	Min D_R	AVG D_R	STDDEV
50	h-NSA	0.3884	0.3082	0.34549	0.027677
	t-NSA	0.1027	0.0918	0.09719	0.004307
100	h-NSA	0.5645	0.4893	0.53586	0.028648
	t-NSA	0.1886	0.1777	0.18409	0.003038
150	h-NSA	0.7112	0.6512	0.67375	0.017377
	t-NSA	0.2621	0.2468	0.25434	0.005868
200	h-NSA	0.7621	0.7025	0.74181	0.017484
	t-NSA	0.3206	0.3072	0.31461	0.003802
250	h-NSA	0.8348	0.8074	0.82325	0.008856
	t-NSA	0.3754	0.358	0.36893	0.004837
300	h-NSA	0.8799	0.8442	0.85341	0.010391
	t-NSA	0.4198	0.4076	0.41702	0.003696
350	h-NSA	0.8932	0.8579	0.87326	0.011136
	t-NSA	0.4625	0.4522	0.45768	0.003748
400	h-NSA	0.922	0.9008	0.91421	0.007709
	t-NSA	0.503	0.4819	0.49338	0.007111
450	h-NSA	0.9422	0.9166	0.9306	0.008074
	t-NSA	0.5326	0.5231	0.52762	0.003233
500	h-NSA	0.9532	0.9285	0.94278	0.007652
	t-NSA	0.5642	0.5487	0.55522	0.00499

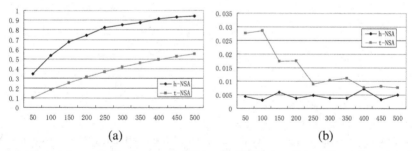

(a)　　　　　　　　　　　　　　(b)

Fig. 4. (a)Comparisons on D_R between h-NSA and t-NSA when fixing N_S and varying N_R ; (b)Standard deviation of D_R between h-NSA and t-NSA when fixing N_S and varying N_R

Experiment 2. The size of matured detectors N_R is fixed, while the size of the self set N_S varies. Set $l = 16, r = 14$, $N_R = 100$, $N_T = 10000$ and the experimental results are shown in Table 5 , Table 6, Fig. 5 and Fig. 6.

Table 5. Comparisons on G_M between h-NSA and t-NSA when fixing N_R and varying N_S

N_S		Max G_M	Min	AVG G_M	STDDEV
50	h-NSA	5000	5000	5000.0	0
	t-NSA	5686	5252	5426.8	151.14
100	h-NSA	10000	10000	10000.0	0
	t-NSA	12434	11360	11716.2	344.96
200	h-NSA	20383	20000	20107.3	148.86
	t-NSA	30275	26272	28499.5	1365.31
300	h-NSA	32055	30527	31052.8	448.16
	t-NSA	56718	44809	49433.9	3574.93
400	h-NSA	44248	40796	42513.5	979.37
	t-NSA	95220	73279	81900.0	6532.52
500	h-NSA	58264	53215	55599.7	1324.18
	t-NSA	145005	120985	129361.7	7175.92
600	h-NSA	71615	65516	68209.4	1916.98
	t-NSA	212944	168734	187648.0	13928.35
700	h-NSA	88921	78691	82592.2	3309.34
	t-NSA	332533	225637	275329.4	33571.90
900	h-NSA	119346	111265	115244.9	3135.51
	t-NSA	688482	471133	562326.6	75176.57
1100	h-NSA	165563	135428	151418.2	9687.97
	t-NSA	1199136	969823	1124476.0	69780.24

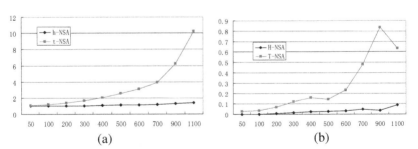

(a)   (b)

Fig. 5. (a)Comparisons on C_G between h-NSA and t-NSA when fixing N_R and varying N_S; (b) Standard deviation of C_G between h-NSA and t-NSA when fixing N_R and varying N_S

From Table 5 and Fig. 5, when the N_R is fixed, the C_G of both h-NSA and t-NSA increase with the increment of N_S. However, the average matching numbers for generating one matured detector in h-NSA is much less than in t-NSA, especially when N_S is large. And the increasing speed of C_G in t-NSA is much higher than in h-NSA.

Table 6. Comparisons on D_R between h-NSA and t-NSA when fixing N_R and varying N_S

N_S		Max D_R	Min D_R	AVG D_R	STDDEV
50	h-NSA	0.9543	0.9303	0.94203	0.008844
	t-NSA	0.1876	0.1814	0.1849	0.002486
100	h-NSA	0.8474	0.7381	0.79412	0.028445
	t-NSA	0.1894	0.1751	0.18214	0.004446
200	h-NSA	0.6863	0.5956	0.63463	0.032304
	t-NSA	0.1911	0.1751	0.18222	0.005227
300	h-NSA	0.5652	0.5154	0.53954	0.019914
	t-NSA	0.1882	0.1763	0.18168	0.003982
400	h-NSA	0.5125	0.4433	0.48044	0.025536
	t-NSA	0.1868	0.1709	0.17724	0.005197
500	h-NSA	0.4869	0.3991	0.44081	0.027283
	t-NSA	0.1789	0.1674	0.17409	0.003515
600	h-NSA	0.4684	0.3966	0.43301	0.025968
	t-NSA	0.1803	0.164	0.17158	0.005298
700	h-NSA	0.4454	0.3975	0.41809	0.015273
	t-NSA	0.1782	0.1645	0.17116	0.00441
900	h-NSA	0.4425	0.3809	0.40513	0.020728
	t-NSA	0.1772	0.1663	0.17173	0.003877
1100	h-NSA	0.4121	0.3635	0.38717	0.016699
	t-NSA	0.1771	0.1567	0.16774	0.00544

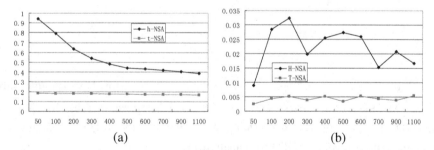

(a)   (b)

Fig. 6. (a)Comparisons on D_R between h-NSA and t-NSA when fixing N_R and varying N_S; (b) Standard deviation of D_R between h-NSA and t-NSA when fixing N_R and varying N_S

From Table 6 and Fig. 6, when the N_R is fixed, the detection ratio D_R of h-NSA decrease with the increment of N_S. However, the D_R of h-NSA is always higher than it of t-NSA. From Table 6, the D_R of t-NSA decreases slowly. It is noted that as

N_S increases, the D_R of t-NSA will also decrease much more and smaller than the expected P_f because of the overlap of the detectors [7]. Related experiments will be given in subsection 4.2.

From Fig. 5 and Fig. 6, it is also known that the standard deviation of C_G in h-NSA is much less than it in t-NSA, while the standard deviation of D_R in h-NSA is little higher than it in t-NSA. However, the standard deviation of D_R in h-NSA is always little than 0.055, and this is acceptable since its detection rate is much higher than that of t-NSA.

4.2 Comparisons on N_R for Fixed P_f

In this subsection, the experiments are conducted to show the efficiency of h-NSA for fixed P_f.

In this experiment, the expected detectors number N_R is calculated by the formula of $N_R = \dfrac{-\ln P_f}{P_m}$ in t-NSA [5, 7]. In h-NSA, the N_R is gotten after the following steps.

(1) Initialize $N_R = 0$ and $CP_f = 1$.

(2) According to the h-NSA described in section 3.2, one detector is generated.

(2.1) Calculate $P_{m,b}$ as formula (3) for this detector.

(2.2) $CP_f = CP_f * (1 - P_{m,b})$.

(2.3) $N_R = N_R + 1$.

(3) If $CP_f > P_f$, go to (2).

(4) End.

In Table 7, 'P_f (actual)' means the real values of P_f are gained by experimentally testing. And the size of the test set, namely N_T, are also given in Table 3. N_T is set as 10000 except one the case of $l=16$, $r=12$ and $N_S = 60$ (because it is difficult, and often impossible to generate 10000 anomaly strings).

From Table 7, it is shown that the needed matured detectors N_R of h-NSA is much less than that of t-NSA for the same P_f. And the real value of P_f of h-NSA is much nearer to the expected P_f too. In fact, as N_S and P_m increase, the real P_f of t-NSA is much larger than the expected P_f, namely 0.1.

Table 7. Comparisons on N_R between h-NSA and t-NSA when $P_f = 0.1$

| | | | | h-NSA | | t-NSA | |
l	r	N_S	N_T	N_R	P_f (actual)	N_R	P_f (actual)
16	12	40	10000	41	0.07807	60	0.09135
16	12	60	1000	44	0.0883	60	0.0817
16	14	400	10000	412	0.11729	1102	0.23623
16	14	600	10000	550	0.10292	1102	0.25111
16	14	800	10000	634	0.07293	1102	0.28565
18	16	600	10000	345	0.13309	3510	0.51912
18	16	800	10000	402	0.12499	3510	0.57223
20	18	800	10000	267	0.13108	11443	0.71051
20	18	1000	10000	286	0.13679	11443	0.75233

Furthermore, as shown in subsection 4.1, the average matching numbers for generating one matured detector in h-NSA is much less than in t-NSA. Therefore, to generate detectors enough for the same expected P_f, the time cost of h-NSA is much less than that of t-NSA.

5 Discussions

In this section, the time complexities of these two algorithms are discussed and compared. In both t-NSA and h-NSA, the basic operator is the matching operator between the self strings and the candidate detectors. The match times G_M can reflect the time cost to some extent. From the experimental results in section 4, it is shown that the G_M of h-NSA is much less than it of t-NSA under the same parameters. Therefore, the experimental results have demonstrated that the time cost of h-NSA is less than it of t-NSA.

Actually, the time complexity of these two algorithms can be denoted by

$$O(N_{R0} \cdot N_S) = O(\frac{N_R}{P_S} \cdot N_S), \qquad (5)$$

where P_S means the survivable probability of an initial random detector.

From equation (2) and equation (3), it is true that $P_{m,b} \geq P_m$, and the equal is satisfied only when $b = 0$. According to equation (1), equation (4) and $P_{m,b} \geq P_m$, for the same expected P_f, the needed detectors number N_R of h-NSA is less than that of t-NSA.

As for h-NSA, there are $r - 1$ "blank" bits in the initial candidate detectors. And the number of "blank" bits tends to decrease in the course of matching other self strings. When the number of "blank" bits is zero, the corresponding candidate detector in h-NSA has the same probability to survive as that in t-NSA. The survivable probability can be represented by $P_S = (1 - P_m)^{N_S^L}$, where N_S^L is the number of the left self strings to be matched when the number of "blank" bits is zero. Obviously, $N_S^L < N_S$, so the survivable probability P_S of a random detector in h-NSA is higher than in t-NSA. Especially, as for h-NSA, an initial candidate detector has $r - 1$ "blanks". Therefore, it represents 2^{r-1} initial random candidate detectors in t-NSA. And in h-NSA the survivable probability P_S of an initial random detector is 2^{r-1} times higher than it in t-NSA.

Therefore, according to equation (5), the time cost of h-NSA is less than that of t-NSA.

In addition, the space complexity of h-NSA is equal to that of t-NSA, as shown in section 2. It is noted that to store "blank" bits, every bit of a detector in h-NSA needs two bits. For example, "00" means" "0", "01" means "1", and "10" (or "11") can be used to denote "*".

6   Conclusions and Future Works

A heuristic detector generation algorithm for negative selection algorithm with Hamming distance partial matching rule is proposed in this paper. This is a good supplement for negative selection algorithm since previous efficient detector generation algorithms are most for the r-continuous-bits partial matching rule. There are also some future works to be done, such as a heuristic detector generation algorithm on higher alphabets while not a binary space. Another, this heuristic detector generation algorithm will also be applied to practical applications. Generally, the practical data set has somewhat special distributions, while not the random distribution that is tested in this paper. Since the candidate detector in the heuristic detector generation algorithm is generated according to the self individuals, the performance of h-NSA is expected to be more competitive in practical applications.

Acknowledgements. This work is partly supported by the National Natural Science Foundation of China (NO. 60404004) and Nature Science Major Foundation from Anhui Education Bureau (NO. 2004kj360zd).

References

1. Emma Hart, Jonathan Timmis. Application Areas of AIS: the Past, the Present and the Future. Proc. the 4th International Conference on Artificial Immune Systems (ICARIS), Lecture Notes in Computer Science, Vol. 3627, Springer-Verlag (2005) 483-497
2. D. Dasgupta, Z. Ji, et al. Artificial Immune System(AIS) Research in the Last Five Years. Proc. the IEEE Congress on Evolutionary Computation (CEC), Canberra, Australia (2003) 123-130
3. L. N. de Castro, J. Timmis. Artificial Immune Systems: a New Computational Intelligence Approach. Springer-Verlag, London (2002)

4. A. O. Taraknaov, V. A. Skormin and S. P. Sokolova. Immunocomputing: Principles and Applications. Springer-Verlag (2003)
5. S. Forrest, A. S. Perelson, L. Allen, and R. Cherukuri. Self-nonself Discrimination in a Computer. Proc. the 1994 IEEE Symposium on Research in Security and Privacy, Los Alamitos, CA (1994) 202-212
6. M. Ayara, J. Timmis, L. N. de Lemos, R. de Castro, R. Duncan. Negative Selection: How to Generate Detectors. Proc. the First International Conference on Artificial Immune Systems, J. Timmis and P. J. Bentley, Editors (2002) 89-98
7. P. D'haeseleer, S. Forrest, P. Helman. An Immunological Approach to Change Detection: Algorithms, Analysis and Implications. Proc. the 1996 IEEE Symposium on Security and Privacy, Los Alamitos, CA (1996) 110-119
8. J. Balthrop, F. Esponda, S. Forrest, M. Glickman. Coverage and Generatization in an Artificial Immune System. Proc. the 2002 Genetic and Evolutionary Computation Conference, (2002) 3-10
9. Z. Ji and D. Dasgupata. Augmented Negative Selection Algorithm with Variable-Coverage Detectors. Proc. Congress on Evolutionary Computation, CEC, Vol. 1, 2004 (1081-1088)
10. Z. Ji and D. Dasgupata. Real-Valued Negative Selection Algorithm with Variable-Sized Detectors. Proc. the 2004 Genetic and Evolutionary Computation Conference, Seattle, Washington USA (2004) 287-298
11. T. Stibor, K. Bayarou, C. Eckert. An Investigation of R-chunk Detector Generation on Higher Alphabets. Proc. the 2004 Genetic and Evolutionary Computation Conference, Lecture Notes in Computer Science, Vol. 3102, Springer-Verlag (2004) 229-307
12. T. Stibor, P. Mohr, J. Timmis and C. Eckert. Is Negative Selection Appropriate for Anomaly Detection? Proc. the 2005 Genetic and Evolutionary Computation Conference (GECCO), Washington DC, USA, ACM Press (2005) 321-328
13. Wenjian Luo, Xufa Wang, et al. Evolutionary Negative Selection Algorithms for Anomaly Detection. Proc. the 8th Joint Conference on Information Sciences (JCIS'2005), the 7th International Conference on Computational Intelligence and Natural Computing (CINC'2005), held in conjunction with the 8th Joint Conference on Information Sciences (JCIS'2005), Salt Lake City, Utah (2005) 440-445

A Novel Approach to Resource Allocation Mechanism in Artificial Immune Recognition System: Fuzzy Resource Allocation Mechanism and Application to Diagnosis of Atherosclerosis Disease

Kemal Polat[1], Sadık Kara[2], Fatma Latifoğlu[2], and Salih Güneş[1]

[1] elcuk University, Dept. of Electrical & Electronics Engineering,
42075, Konya, Turkey
kpolat@selcuk.edu.tr, sgunes@selcuk.edu.tr
[2] Erciyes University, Dept. of Electronics Eng., 38039,
Kayseri, Turkey
fdirgenali@tse.org.tr, kara@erciyes.edu.tr

Abstract. Artificial Immune Recognition System (AIRS) has showed an effective performance on several problems such as machine learning benchmark problems and medical classification problems like breast cancer, diabets, liver disorders classification. In this study, the resource allocation mechanism of AIRS was changed with a new one determined by Fuzzy-Logic. This system, named as Fuzzy-AIRS was used as a classifier in the diagnosis of atherosclerosis, which are of great importance in medicine. The proposed system consists of the following parts: first, we obtained features that are used as inputs for Fuzzy-AIRS from Carotid Artery Doppler Signals using Fast Fourier Transform (FFT), then these obtained inputs used as inputs in Fuzzy-AIRS. While AIRS algorithm obtained 75% maximum classification accuracy for 150 resources using 10-fold cross validation, Fuzzy-AIRS obtained 100% maximum classification accuracy in the same conditions. These results show that Fuzzy-AIRS proved that it could be used as an effective classifier for the medical problems.

Keywords: Artificial Immune Recognition System (AIRS), Fuzzy resource allocation mechanism, Atherosclerosis disease, Carotid artery, Fast Fourier Transformation.

1 Introduction

Atherosclerosis is the buildup of fatty deposits called plague on the inside walls of arteries. Plaques can grow large enough to significantly reduce the blood's flow through an artery. As an artery becomes more and more narrowed, less blood can flow through. The artery may also become less elastic (called "hardening of the arteries"). Atherosclerosis is the main cause of a group of cardiovascular diseases [1].

H. Bersini and J. Carneiro (Eds.): ICARIS 2006, LNCS 4163, pp. 244–255, 2006.

Atherosclerosis is usually diagnosed after symptoms or complications have arisen. There are a number of tests in diagnosing vascular diseases, including blood tests, electrocardiogram, stress testing, angiography, ultrasound, and computed tomography. Angiography is used to look inside arteries to see if there is any blockage and how much [2, 3]. This is the most accurate way to assess the presence and severity of vascular disease. On the other hand this technique involves injecting dye directly into the arteries. Therefore this is a much more invasive.

Having so many factors to analyze to diagnose the Atherosclerosis disease of a patient makes the physician's job difficult. A physician usually makes decisions by evaluating the current test results of a patient and by referring to the previous decisions she or he made on other patience with the same condition. The former method depends strongly on the physician's knowledge. On the other hand, the latter depends on the physician's experience to compare her patient with her earlier patients. This job is not easy considering the number of factors she has to evaluate. In this crucial step, she may need an accurate tool that lists her previous decisions on the patient having same (or close to same) factors.

In this study, resource allocation of AIRS was changed with its equivalence formed with Fuzzy-Logic to increase its classification performance by means of resource number. The effects of this change were analyzed in the applications using Carotid Artery Doppler Signals. Fuzzy-AIRS, which proved it self to be used as an effective classifier in medical field by reaching its goal, has also provided a considerable decrease in the number of resources. In all applications conducted, Fuzzy-AIRS obtained high classification accuracies for diagnosis of Atherosclerosis disease.

The remaining of the paper is organized as follows. We present the used procedure in the next section. In Section 3, we give the used algorithm called Artificial Immune Recognition System and Fuzzy resource allocation mechanism. In Section 4, we give the experimental data to show the effectiveness of our method. Finally, we conclude this paper in Section 5 with future directions.

2   The Procedure

Fig.1 shows the procedure used in the proposed system. It consists of four parts: (a) Measurement of Carotid Artery Doppler Signal, (b) Spectral Analysis (AIRS inputs were selected), (c) Artificial Immune Recognition System with fuzzy resource allocation mechanism and (d) Classification results (Atherosclerosis and healthy).

2.1   Hardware and Demographic Acknowledgments

Carotid arterial Doppler ultrasound signals were acquired from 60 patients and 54 healthy volunteers. The patient group included thirty-three males and twenty-seven females with an established diagnosis of atherosclerosis through coronary or aorto-femoropopliteal (lower extremity) angiography (mean age: 45 years; range: 25-69 years). Healthy volunteers including thirty-five males and nineteen females (mean age: 26 years; range: 20-39 years) were young non-smokers who appeared not to bear any risk of atherosclerosis. The two study groups represent the upper and lower

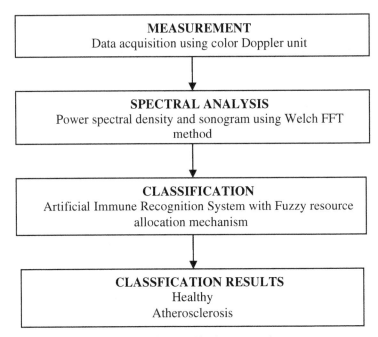

Fig. 1. The Procedure used in the proposed system.

extremes of the arterial compliance. We have utilized Toshiba PowerVision 6000 Doppler Ultrasound Unit in the Radiology Department for data acquisition.

A linear ultrasound probe of 10 MHz was used to transmit pulsed ultrasound signals to the proximal left common carotid artery. In all tests performed on the patients and healthy subjects, the insonation angle and the presettings of the ultrasound were kept constant.

2.2 Spectral Analysis of Carotid Artery Doppler Signals

Welch method of power spectrum estimation was applied on the Doppler data. Blood flow can only be considered statistically stationary for typically 10 to 20 ms. Therefore acquired Doppler data was grouped in frames of 512 data points and the method was applied on these frames. Welch's method is one among the classical methods of spectrum estimation based on FFT.

2.2.1 Welch Method of Spectral Analysis

FFT based Welch method is defined as classical (Nonparametric) method. It is made the second modification of periodogram spectral estimator, which is to window data segments prior to computing the periodogram [4-9]. If avaliable information on the signal consists of the samples $\{x(n)\}_{n=1}^{N}$, the periodogram spectral estimator is given by;

$$\hat{P}_{PER}(f) = \frac{1}{N}\left|\sum_{n=1}^{N} x(n)\exp(-j2\pi f n)\right|^2 \tag{1}$$

Where $\hat{P}_{PER}(f)$ is the estimation of periodogram. In the Welch method, signals are divided into overlapping segments, each data segment is windowed, periodograms are calculated and then average of periodograms is found. $\{x_l(n)\}$, l=1,...,S are data segments and each segment's length equals M. Note that, the overlap is often chosen to be 50%. The Welch spectrum estimate is given by:

$$\hat{P}_w(f) = \frac{1}{S}\sum_{l=1}^{s} \hat{P}_l(f) \tag{2}$$

$$\hat{P}_l(f) = \frac{1}{M}\frac{1}{P}\left|\sum_{n=1}^{M} v(n)x_l(n)\exp(-j2\pi f n)\right|^2 \tag{3}$$

where $\hat{P}_l(f)$ is the periodogram estimate of l^{TH} segment, $v(n)$ is the data-window, P is total average of $v(n)$ and given as $P = 1/M\sum_{n=1}^{M}|v(n)|^2$, $\hat{P}_w(f)$ is the Welch PSD estimate, M is the length of each signal segment and S is the number of segments.

Then, Evaluation of $\hat{P}_w(f)$ at the frequency samples basically requires the computation of the following discrete Fourier transform (DFT):

$$X(k) = \sum_{n=1}^{N} x(n)\exp(-j\frac{2\pi}{N})^{nk} , \quad k=0,..., N\text{-}1 \tag{4}$$

Where $X(k)$ is expressed as the discrete Fourier coefficient, N is the length of available data and $x(n)$ is the input signal on the time domain. The procedure that computes Eq. (4) is called as FFT algorithm. The Welch PSD can be efficiently computed by the FFT algorithm. Variance of an estimator is one of the measures often used to characterize its performance. For 50% overlap and triangular window, variance for the Welch method is given by;

$$\text{var}(\hat{P}_w(f)) = \frac{9}{8S}\text{var}(\hat{P}_l(f)) \tag{5}$$

Where $\hat{P}_w(f)$ the Welch PSD is estimate and $\hat{P}_l(f)$ is the periodogram estimate of each signal interval [4-10].

A sonogram is plotted with the frequency components and power spectral density values sequenced on the timeline. Time is on the x-axis, while frequency is on the y-axis and gray value of the display represents the corresponding power spectral density.

3 AIRS Classifier Algorithm

AIRS is a resource limited supervised learning algorithm inspired from immune metaphors. In this algorithm, the used immune mechanisms are resource competition, clonal selection, affinity maturation and memory cell formation. The feature vectors presented for training and test are named as Antigens while the system units are called as B cells. Similar B cells are represented with Artificial Recognition Balls (ARBs) and these ARBs compete with each other for a fixed resource number. This provides ARBs, which have higher affinities to the training Antigen to improve. The memory cells formed after the whole training Antigens were presented are used to classify test Antigens. The algorithm is composed of four main stages, which are initialization, memory cell identification and ARB generation, competition for resources and development of a candidate memory cell, and memory cell introduction. Table 1 summarizes the mapping between the immune system and AIRS.

Table 1. Mapping between the Immune System and AIRS

Immune System	AIRS
Antibody	Feature Vector
Recognition Ball	Combination of feature vector and vector class
Shape-Space	Type and possible values of the data vector
Clonal Expansion	Reproduction of ARBs that are well matched antigens
Antigens	Training data
Affinity Maturation	Random mutation of ARB and removal of the least stimulated ARBs
Immune Memory	Memory set of mutated ARBs
Metadynamics	Continual removal and creation of ARBs and memory cells

We give the details of our algorithm below.

1. Initialization: Create a set of cells called the memory pool (M) and the ARB pool (P) from randomly selected training data.

2. Antigenic Presentation: for each antigenic pattern do:

(a) Clonal Expansion: For each element of M, determine its affinity to the antigenic pattern, which resides in the same class. Select the highest affinity memory cell (mc) and clone mc in proportion to its antigenic affinity to add to the set of ARBs (P).

(b) Affinity Maturation: Mutate each ARB descendant of the highest affinity mc. Place each mutated ARB into P.

(c) Metadynamics of ARBs: Process each ARB using the resource allocation mechanism. This process will result in some ARB death, and ultimately controls the population. Calculate the average stimulation for each ARB, and check for termination condition.

(d) Clonal Expansion and Affinity Maturation: Clone and mutate the randomly selected subset of the ARBs left in P based on their stimulation level.

(e) Cycle: While the average stimulation value of each ARB class group is less than a given stimulation threshold go to step 2.c.

(f) Metadynamics of Memory Cells: Select the highest affinity ARB of the same class as the antigen from the last antigenic interaction. If the affinity of this ARB with the antigenic pattern is better than that of the previously identified best memory cell mc then add the candidate (mc-candidate) to memory set M. If the affinity of mc and mc-candidate are below the affinity threshold, remove mc from M.

3. Classify: Classify data items using the memory set M. Classification is performed in a k-Nearest Neighbor fashion with a vote being made among the k closest memory cells to the given data item being classified.

We can characterize AIRS as follows:

- Memory: The memory of the AIRS algorithm is in the pool of memory cells developed through exposure to the training data (experiences);

- Adaptation: The adaptation occurs primarily in the ARB pool. With each new experience, AIRS evolves a candidate memory cell in reaction to this experience. If this memory cell is of sufficient quality, then the memory structure is adapted to include in it.

- Decision-making: The initial decision is which memory cell is the most similar to the incoming training antigen. This cell is used as a progenitor for a pool of evolving cells. During classification, the primary classification decision is made based on the k most similar memory cells to the data item being classified.

These steps are repeated for each training antigen. After training, test data are presented only to memory cells. k-NN algorithm is used to determine the classes in test phase. For more detailed information about AIRS, the reader is referred to [11, 12].

3.1 Fuzzy resource allocation mechanism

The competition of resources in AIRS allows high-affinity ARBs to improve. According to this resource allocation mechanism, half of resources are allocated to the ARBs in the class of Antigen while the remaining half is distributed to the other classes. The distribution of resources is done according to a number that is found by multiplying stimulation rate with clonal rate. In the study of Baurav Marwah and Lois Boggess, a different resource allocation mechanism was tried [13]. In their mechanism, the Ag classes occurring more frequently get more resources. Both in classical AIRS and the study of Marwah and Boggess, resource allocation is done linearly with affinities. This linearity requires excess resource usage in the system, which results long classification time and high number of memory cells.

In this study, to get rid of this problem, resource allocation mechanism was done with fuzzy-logic. So there existed a non-linearity because of fuzzy-rules. The difference in resource number between high-affinity ARBs and low-affinity ARBs is bigger in this method than in classical approach.

The input variable of Fuzzy resource allocation mechanism is stimulation level of ARB hence the output variable is the number of resources, which will be allocated to that ARB. As for the other fuzzy-systems, input membership functions as well as output membership functions were formed. The input membership functions are shown in Fig. 2.a.

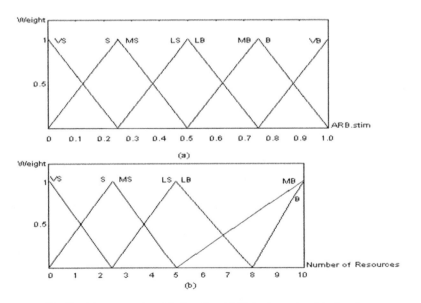

Fig. 2. a) Input membership function, b) Output membership function

The input variable, ARB.stim, varies between 0 and 1. A membership value is calculated according to this value using input membership functions. In this calculation, two points are get which are the cutting points of membership triangles by the input value, ARB.stim. Also these points are named as membership values of input variable for related membership function. The minimum of these points is taken as the membership value of input variable x, ARB.stim (Eq. (6)).

$$\mu_{A \cap B}(x) = MIN(\ \mu_A(x),\ \mu_B(x)),\ x \in x \tag{6}$$

Here in Eq. (6), $\mu_A(x)$ is the membership value of x in A and $\mu_B(x)$ is the membership value of x in B, where A and B are the fuzzy sets in universe X. The calculated input membership value is used to get the output value through output membership functions, which are shown in Fig. 2.b

In the x-axis of Fig. 2.b, allocated resource number that will be calculated using the membership functions for the ARB is shown which changes between 0-10. The weight in the y-axis, which is the input membership value get as explained above, intersects the membership triangles at several points. The rule base for Fuzzy Resource Allocation is seen in Fig. 3.

if ARB.stim= VS and S
   then Output= (VS' + S') / 2

if ARB.stim= S and MS
   then Output= (S' + MS') / 2

if ARB.stim= MS and LS
   then Output= (MS' + LS') / 2

if ARB.stim= LS and LB
   then Output= (LS' + LB') / 2

if ARB.stim= LB and MB
   then Output= (LB' + MB') / 2

if ARB.stim= MB and B
   then Output= (MB' + B') / 2

if ARB.stim= B and VB
   then Output= (B' + VB') / 2

Fig. 3. Rule base for fuzzy resource allocation

Here VS, S, MS...etc are the labels of input membership triangles and VS',S', MS'...etc are the labels of output membership values. The rules in Fig. 3 define which points will be taken to average. For example if the input value cuts the triangles VS and S among the input membership functions, then the points to be averaged will be only the ones of VS' and S' triangles in the output membership functions.

Whereas determining membership value and getting output value using fuzzy-rules are of crucial importance, another important point is determination of linguistic values used in the input and output membership functions, which are shown in Table 2.

Table 2. Linguistic values for input and output membership functions

Input	Output
VS- Very Small	**VS'**- Very Small
S- Small	**S'**- Small
MS- Middle Small	**MS'**- Middle Small
LS- Little Small	**LS'**- Little Small
LB- Little Big	**LB'**- Little Big
MB- Middle Big	**MB'**- Middle Big
B- Big	**B'**- Big
VB- Very Big	

These linguistic values were determined in such a manner that the allocated resource number for ARBs which have stimulation values between 0 and 0.50 will be less while for ARBs which have stimulation values between 0.50 and 1 will be more.

4   The Experimental Results

In this section, we present the performance evaluation methods used to evaluate the proposed method. Finally, we give the experimental results and discuss our observations from the obtained results.

4.1   Performance Evaluation

4.1.1   Classification Accuracy
In this study, the classification accuracies for the datasets are measured using Eq.(7) [11]:

$$accuracy(T) = \frac{\sum_{i=1}^{|T|} assess(t_i)}{|T|}, t_i \in T$$

$$assess(t) = \begin{cases} 1, & if \ classify(t) = t.c \\ 0, & otherwise \end{cases} \tag{7}$$

where T is the set of data items to be classified (the test set), $t \varepsilon T$, $t.c$ is the class of item t, and classify(t) returns the classification of t by AIRS [11].

4.1.2   Sensitivity and Specificity Analysis
For sensitivity and specificity analysis, we use the following expressions.

$$sensitivity = \frac{TP}{TP + FN}(\%) \tag{8}$$

$$specificity = \frac{TN}{FP + TN}(\%) \tag{9}$$

where TP, TN, FP and FN denote true positives, true negatives, false positives, and false negatives, respectively.

True positive (TP): An input is detected as a patient with atherosclerosis diagnosed by the expert clinicians.

True negative (TN): An input is detected as normal that is labeled as a healthy person by the expert clinicians.

False positive (FP): An input is detected as a patient that is labeled as a healthy by the expert clinicians.

False Negative (FN): An input is detected as normal with atherosclerosis diagnosed by the expert clinicians.

4.1.3 k-Fold Cross-Validation

K-fold cross validation is one way to improve the holdout method. The data set is divided into *k* subsets, and the holdout method is repeated *k* times. Each time, one of the *k* subsets is used as the test set and the other *k-1* subsets are put together to form a training set. Then the average error across all *k* trials is computed. The advantage of this method is that it is not important how the data is divided. Every data point appears in a test set exactly once, and appears in a training set *k-1* times. The variance of the resulting estimate is reduced as *k* is increased. The disadvantage of this method is that the training algorithm must be rerun from scratch *k* times, which means it takes *k* times as much computation to make an evaluation. A variant of this method is to randomly divide the data into a test and training set *k* different times. The advantage of this method is that we can independently choose the size of the each test and the number of trials [14].

4.2 Results and Discussion

Fuzzy-resource allocation mechanism provided Fuzzy-AIRS to classify Atherosclerosis disease with 100% classification accuracy using 10-fold cross validation.

The relation between resource number and classification accuracy in Fuzzy-AIRS and AIRS for the diagnosis of Atherosclerosis disease is shown in Table 3 and 4. Also they present the obtained classification accuracy and sensitivity and specifity values of AIRS and Fuzzy-AIRS classifier algorithms. As can be seen in Table 3 and Table 4, AIRS with fuzzy resource allocation mechanism is very effective classifier more than original AIRS. This improvement in performance is also very important especially in medical field and in applications that use large datasets.

Table 3. The obtained classification accuracies, sensitivity and specifity values for AIRS classifier algorithm using 10-fold cross validation

Number of Resources	Classification Accuracy (%)	Sensitivity	Specificity
50	75	100	66.67
100	58.33	100	54.54
150	50	0	50
200	75	100	66.67
250	58.33	100	54.54
300	58.33	66.67	55.55
350	58.33	100	54.54
400	66.67	100	60
450	75	100	66.67
500	66.67	100	66.67

Table 4. The obtained classification accuracies, sensitivity and specifity values for Fuzzy-AIRS classifier algorithm using 10-fold cross validation

Number of Resources	Classification Accuracy (%)	Sensitivity	Specificity
50	75	100	66.67
100	91.66	85.71	100
150	100	100	100
200	100	100	100
250	91.66	100	85.71
300	100	100	100
350	100	100	100
400	100	100	100
450	100	100	100
500	100	100	100

5 Conclusions and Future Work

With the improvements in expert systems and ML tools, the effects of these innovations are entering to more application domains day-by-day and medical field is one of them. Decision-making in medical field can sometimes be a trouble. Classification systems that are used in medical decision-making provide medical data to be examined in shorter time and more detailed.

In this study, the resource allocation mechanism of AIRS that is among the most important classification systems of Artificial Immune Systems was changed with a new one that was formed using fuzzy-logic rules.

In the application phase of this study, Carotid Artery Doppler Signals were used. In the classifications of Atherosclerosis disease, the analyses were conducted to see the effects of the new resource allocation mechanism.

According to the application results, Fuzzy-AIRS showed a considerably high performance with regard to the classification accuracy especially for diagnosis of Atherosclerosis disease. The reached classification accuracy of Fuzzy-AIRS for Atherosclerosis disease is 100%.

AIRS is going one step ahead among the other classifiers with the aid of improvements done in the algorithm. The proposed change in this study has produced very satisfactory results to use the classifier in other medical datasets. Other application areas are also open for Fuzzy-AIRS to experiment with. One of the further studies can be using the fuzzy mechanisms in other Artificial Immune Systems similar to AIRS.

Acknowledgments. This study has been supported by Scientific Research Project of Selcuk University (Project No: 05401069).

References

1. T. Hirai, S. Sasayama, T. Kawasaki and S. Yagi,: Stiffness of systemic arteries in patients with myocardial infarction. A noninvasive method to predict severity of coronary atherosclerosis, Circulation, (1989) 78 –86.
2. C. Stefanadis, C. Stratos, H. Boudoulas, C. Kourouklis and P. Toutouzas,: Distensibility of the ascending aorta, comparison of invasive and non-invasive techniques in healthy men and in men with coronary artery disease. Eur. Heart J., (1990) 990–996.
3. A.M. Dart, F. Lacombe, J.K. Yeoh, J.D. Cameron, G.L. Jennings, E. Laufer and D.S. Esmore,: Aortic distensibility in patients with isolated hyper-cholesterolaemia, coronary artery disease, or cardiac transplant. Lancet, (1991) 270–273.
4. D. Evans,: Doppler Signal Analysis. Ultrasound in Med. & Biol., 26 (2000)13–15.
5. V. D. Saini, N. C. Nanda & D. Maulik,: Basic principles of ultrasound and Doppler effect. Doppler echocardiography, 1993.
6. B. Sigel,: A brief history of Doppler ultrasound in the diagnosis of peripheral vascular disease. Ultrasound Med. Biol., 24 (1998)169–176.
7. M. M,uller, P. Ciccotti, W. Reiche, T. Hagen,: Comparison of color flow Doppler scanning, power Doppler scanning, and frequency shift for assessment of carotid artery stenosis. J. Vasc. Surg., 34(2001) 1090–1095.
8. D.H. Evans, W.N. McDicken, R. Skidmore, J.P. Woodcock, : Doppler Ultrasound: Physics. Instrumentation and Clinical Applications, 1989.
9. P.J. Vaitkus, R.S.C. Cobbold, K.W. Johnston,: A comparative study and assessment of Doppler ultrasound spectral estimation techniques part II: methods and results. Ultrasound Med. Biol., 14(1988) 673–688.
10. Van Asten WN, Beijneveld WJ, Pieters BR et al.,: Assessment of aortoiliac obstructive disease by Doppler spectrum analysis of blood flow velocities in the common femoral artery at rest and during reactive hyperemia. Surgery, 109(1991) 633–639.
11. Watkins, A.: AIRS: A Resource Limited Artificial Immune Classifier, A Thesis Submitted to the Faculty of Mississippi State University (2001).
12. Watkins, A., and Timmis, J.: Artificial Immune Recognition System (AIRS): Revisions and Refinements, Proc. Int. Conf. on Artificial Immune Systems (ICARIS), (2002) 99-106.
13. Goodman DE, Boggess L, Watkins A.: An Investigation into the source of power for AIRS, an artificial immune classification system. In Proceedings of the International Joint Conference on Neural Networks (IJCNN'03), Portland, Oregon July (2003) 1678-1683.
14. Kohavi, R, and Provost, F.,: Glossary of Terms. Editorial for the Special Issue on Applications of Machine Learning and the Knowledge Discovery Process, 30 (1998) 2/3.

Recognition of Handwritten Indic Script Using Clonal Selection Algorithm

Utpal Garain[1], Mangal P. Chakraborty[1], and Dipankar Dasgupta[2]

[1] Indian Statistical Institute, 203, B.T. Road, Kolkata 700108, India
[2] The University of Memphis, Memphis, TN 38152
utpal@isical.ac.in, dasgupta@memphis.edu

Abstract. The work explores the potentiality of a clonal selection algorithm in pattern recognition (PR). In particular, a retraining scheme for the clonal selection algorithm is formulated for better recognition of handwritten numerals (a 10-class classification problem). Empirical study with two datasets (each of which contains about 12,000 handwritten samples for 10 numerals) shows that the proposed approach exhibits very good generalization ability. Experimental results reported the average recognition accuracy of about 96%. The effect of control parameters on the performance of the algorithm is analyzed and the scope for further improvement in recognition accuracy is discussed.

Keywords: Clonal selection algorithm, character recognition, Indic scripts, handwritten digits.

1 Introduction

Several immunological metaphors are now being used (in a piecemeal) for designing Artificial Immune Systems (AIS) [1]. These approaches can broadly classified into three groups namely, immune network models [2], negative selection algorithms [3], and clonal selection algorithms [4]. This paper investigates a new training approach for clonal selection algorithm (CSA) and its application to character recognition. Earlier CSA was used for a 2-class problem to discriminate pair of similar character patterns [5], the present study extends it for a m-class classification problem.

Training in CSA so far is modeled as one pass method where each antigen undergoes single training phase. Once the training on all antigens is over, an immune memory is produced and used for solving classification problem (as used in [5] and [6]). Our work presents a new training algorithm where a refinement phase is used to fine-tune the initial immune memory that is build from the single pass training. In the refinement stage, training of an antigen depends on its recognition score. Incorrect recognition of an antigen triggers further training. This process continues until the immune system suffers from negative learning or it is over-learned.

Recognition of handwritten Indic numerals has been considered to study the performance of the modified CSA. Because of its numerous applications for postal automation, bank check reading, etc., the document image analysis researchers have been studying the problem for last several years and a number of methods have been proposed.

H. Bersini and J. Carneiro (Eds.): ICARIS 2006, LNCS 4163, pp. 256 – 266, 2006.

While some of these are biologically inspired approaches such as neural networks [7], genetic algorithms [8], AIS approaches remained unexplored for this application; though AIS techniques have been applied to several pattern recognition problems [9-14].

The rest of the paper is organized as follows. Section-2 describes the CSA with the proposed retraining scheme. Section-3 provides the experimental details and report results highlighting the performance of the CSA in classifying handwritten numerals. This section also exhibits the performance of the new retraining scheme over the previously used single-pass approach. In addition, section-3 discusses the effect of CSA control parameters on its performance, and section-4 provides some concluding remarks.

2 Classification Using Clonal Selection Algorithm

Let AG represent a set of training data (antigens) and ag_i represents an individual member of this set: $AG = \{ag_1, ag_2, ..., ag_k\}$. Each ag_i has two attributes: *class*: $ag.c \in C = \{c_1, c_2, ...c_n\}$ ($n = 10$ for digit classification) and *feature vector*: $ag.f$. Let the immune memory, $IM = \{m_1, m_2, ..., m_m\}$ where m_i is a memory cell having two attributes similar to those of an individual antigen. For any m_i, $m_i.c \in C = \{c_1, c_2, ...c_n\}$ is the class information and $m_i.f$ is the feature vector.

Binary images of handwritten numerals are first size-normalized in a 48x48 matrix whose each element is binary. This matrix is used as a feature map for the experiments. Similarity between two such feature matrices $S(F_1, F_2)$ a measure of auto-correlation coefficient between F_1 and F_2 as defined below:

$$S(F_1, F_2) = \frac{1}{2} - \frac{s_{10}s_{01} - s_{00}s_{11}}{2\sqrt{(s_{11} + s_{10})(s_{01} + s_{00})(s_{11} + s_{01})(s_{10} + s_{00})}} \tag{1}$$

where s_{00}, s_{11}, s_{01}, and s_{10} denote the number of zero matches, one matches, zero mismatches, and one mismatches, respectively. It is to be noted that S gives values in the range [0, 1], where 1 indicates the highest and 0 signifies the lowest similarity between two samples. We used this metric to measure similarity/affinity during antibody-antibody or antigen-antibody interactions.

Training has two phases: Phase-I is the same as was used in [6], while Phase-II incorporates a refinement process. Phase-I involves three stages namely, initialization of immune memory, clone generation, and selection of clones to update the immune memory. These stages are briefly discussed below.

Initialization: This stage deals with choosing some antigens as initial memory cells to initialize the immune memory. In the present study, only one antigen from each class is randomly chosen to initialize the immune memory (IM). It is to be noted that the number of initial cells has certain effect on system's performance as illustrated in [6].

Clone generation: For a given antigen ag_i, its closest match (say, m_i) is, at first, chosen from the existing IM as follows:

$$stim(ag_i, m_i) \geq stim(ag_i, m_j), \text{ for all } j \neq i \text{ and } m_j.c = ag_i.c \tag{2}$$

The function $stim()$ is used to measure the response of a b-cell to an antigen or to another b-cell and is directly proportional to the similarity between the feature matrices as defined in equation (1). After a memory cell m_i (renamed as m_{match}) is selected for a training antigen ag_i, m_{match} goes through a proliferation process (Proliferation-I), known as *somatic hyper-mutation* that generates a number of clones of m_{match}. The exact number of clones is determined by three parameters, namely, (i) hyper-mutation rate, (ii) clonal rate and (iii) $stim(ag_i, m_{match})$. Note that the first two parameters are user-defined.

Each clone is produced through mutation (controlled by MUTATION_RATE, a user defined parameter) at selected sites of m_{match}'s feature matrix. No clone is an exact copy of m_{match}. The algorithms for Proliferation-I and the generation of mutated clones are outlined in Algorithm-I and II, respectively. These algorithms are similar to the ones described in [6]. On completion of hyper-mutations, a stimulation value is computed for each element $b_j \in B$ as $stim(b_j, ag_i)$. Here b_j denotes an individual b-cell clone and B represents the entire cloned population.

In order to minimize the computational cost in generating clones, a modified version of the resource limitation policy [15] is incorporated. The modified version considers only the recent clones generated for the current antigen undergoing the (maturation) training process. The method does not consider clones generated for previous antigens i.e. present implementation considered the entire resource for the current antigen's class only.

Stopping criterion defined in equation (3) is used to terminate the training on an antigen ag_i. If this criterion is not met then further proliferation of existing (i.e. survived after resource limitation) b-cells is invoked. In this stage (i.e. Proliferation-II), each survived b-cell, i.e. b_j is proliferated to produce a number of clones determined by the resources allocated to it. Proliferation-II process is similar to one for proliferation-I outlined in Algorithm-I except the calculation of the number clones to be generated from each surviving b-cell (b_j). This number is determined only by the CLONAL_RATE and $stim(ag_i, b_j)$.

$$\frac{\sum_{j=1}^{|B|} b_j.stim}{|B|} > STIMULATION\_THRESHOLD \tag{3}$$

Algorithm I. Hyper-mutation/Proliferation-I

Let B is the set of b-cell clones to be created due to somatic hyper-mutation started with m_{match}.

Initially $B=\{m_{match}\}$.

Let N_c denote the number of clones and calculated as,

$\quad N_c \leftarrow$ HYPER_MUTATION_RATE * CLONAL_RATE * $stim(ag_i, m_i)$

While ($|B| \leq N_c$)

Do

$\quad$ *mut* $\leftarrow$ false   //*mut* is a Boolean variable

$\quad$ Call *mutate*(m_i, *mut*)

$\quad$ Let b_j denote a mutated clone of m_i

$\quad$ If (*mut*) Then $B \leftarrow B \cup b_j$

Done

Algorithm II. Production of Mutated Clones

mutate(x, flag){

For each binary feature element (i, j) in *x.f* // *note that x.f is basically a matrix*

Do

    Generate a random number, *r* in [0, 1]

    If (*r* < MUTATION_RATE) Then

        $x.f_{i,j} \leftarrow$ toggle(*x.f*$_{i,j}$)

        flag $\leftarrow$ true

    Endif

Done

}

Clone selection and update of immune memory: Once the training criterion in equation (3) is met for an antigen, the most stimulated (*w.r.t.* the current antigen undergoing training) *b*-cell among the survived ones is selected as a candidate (let $b_{candidate}$ denote this cell) to be inserted into immune memory. This process is outlined in Algorithm III that is similar to one in [6]. This algorithm makes use of two parameters *AS* (average stimulation) and α (a scalar value). The parameter α is a user-defined one, whereas *AS* is measured from the input training antigen set as the average stimulation between all pairs of the mean values of the antigen classes.

Algorithm III: Update of immune memory

CandStim $\leftarrow$ *stim*(*ag*$_i$, $b_{candidate}$)

MatchStim $\leftarrow$ *stim* (*ag*$_i$, m_{match})

CellAff $\leftarrow$ *stim*(m_{match}, $b_{candidate}$)

If (*CandStim* > *MatchStim*)

      IM $\leftarrow$ *IM* $\cup$ $b_{candidate}$ // insertion into the immune memory

      If (*CellAff* > $\alpha \times AS$)

            IM $\leftarrow$ *IM* $-$ m_{match} // memory replacement

Phase-II of the training algorithm: Note that the training in Phase-I is a one-pass method i.e. the system is trained only once on a training antigen. At the end of the training phase, the immune memory i.e. $IM_0=\{m_1, m_2, ..., m_m\}$ is produced. In the present implementation, training involves a second phase namely Phase-II that employs a refinement process. In this method recognition and training go hand in hand to obtain a better immune memory from its initial version i.e. IM_0.

In this phase, recognition of the all the training antigens is done first using the immune memory (*IM*$_i$, *i*=0, 1, ...) obtained in the previous stage (say, *i*-th stage). Classification strategy outlined next is used for recognition of antigens and the recognition accuracy is noted. Next, antigens for which incorrect classification is recorded act as a bootstrap samples that undergo further training involving clone generation, selection and updating immune memory as outlined above in Phase-I of the training. This results in an updated immune memory (*IM*$_{i+1}$), which is then used for classification of all the training antigens. This newer version is retained if better (than what was obtained using IM_i) recognition accuracy is obtained. Otherwise, IM_i is reloaded and the Phase-II terminates.

It is observed that for a few iterations of Phase-II newer versions of the immune memory continue to produce better recognition accuracy and then there is degradation in accuracy, signaling a negative (or over) learning in the system. In fact, instead of using the training antigen set, a separate validation set can be used in this refinement phase. This modification would be considered in the future extension of the present study.

Classification strategy: Classification is implemented by a k-nearest neighbor (k-NN) approach. For a target antigen (ag), k (an odd number) closest (w.r.t. ag) memory cells are selected from the immune memory IM. Closeness is measured by the *stim* function i.e. *stim*(ag, m_i) for all i, $m_i \in IM$. Next, k m_i's are grouped based on their class labels. Class of the largest sized (a majority-voting strategy) group identifies ag.

3 Experimental Details

Two different datasets (DS1 and DS2) [16] have been used to test the proposed classification approach based on clonal selection algorithm (CSA). These datasets DS1 and DS2 contain samples for handwritten numerals in two major Indic scripts namely, Devanagari (Hindi) and Bengali, respectively. Unlike English, Chinese, Japanese, etc., studies in Indic script handwriting recognition are rare and this provides additional motivation to this present work to deal with datasets of handwriting in Indian languages. Moreover, datasets consisting of a large number of samples for handwritten digits in Indic scripts are recently available [16] in public domain and this facilitates training and testing of an approach and comparing it with other competing methods.

Both the datasets contain real samples collected from different kinds of handwritten documents such as postal mails, job application forms and railway ticket reservation forms, passport application forms, etc. For our experiment, each dataset consists of 12,000 samples (equal number of samples for each class). DS1 samples are randomly selected from a collection of 22,556 Devanagari numerals written by 1049 persons and DS2 samples are taken from a set of 12,938 Bengali numerals written by 556 persons. Some samples for each digit class are shown in fig 1. The datasets are divided are into six equal sized partitions. Training is conducted on samples from five partitions and classification is tested on the sixth partition. This realizes a six-fold experiment that results in six test runs. The results reported next are averaged over these six runs.

Experiments are carried out under two different training policies, L1: training is single pass and L2: proposed method that employs refinement process. Recognition accuracies under these two environments are reported in Table 1 and it is observed that L2 outperforms L1 by a significant margin. However, L2 generates a slightly larger sized immune memory than the one produced by L1. Significant difference is observed in the time units required for training. On a Pentium-IV (733 MHz, 128 RAM) PC, L1 takes quite less CPU time than L2 that involves additional refinement phase. However, there is hardly any difference in the time needed for classification by the two approaches. The system can classify about 50 characters per second. Abso lute time units taken during training and testing are outlined in Table 2 below.

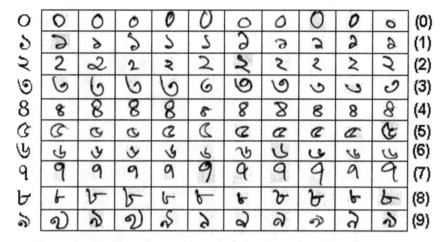

Fig. 1. Hundred random samples from the dataset of Bengali handwritten numerals

Performance of the proposed refinement stage is studied to check how rapidly the system attains the maximum classification rate on the training set. In fact, it's the first local maximum where the training terminates and at present, the system does not attempt to find the global one. The response of the additional training module is shown in fig. 2 for the dataset DS1. A similar behaviour is obtained for the other dataset too.

In fig. 2 it is to be noted that the recognition accuracy gradually increases till the 8th iteration after which the accuracy degrades and training terminates. Number of antigens undergo training in each pass is also plotted by a line curve in fig. 2. Please note that iteration 0 represents the initial Phase-I training where all 10,000 antigens were trained.

Table 1. Recognition accuracies and size of immune memory with two different training algorithms

	Recognition accuracy		Size of immune memory	
Dataset	L1	L2	L1	L2
DS1	93.31%	96.23%	912	1283
DS2	92.57%	95.68%	1103	1472

Table 2. CPU Time for training and classification using two different training algorithms

	Time to train		Classification speed (#characters per second)	
Dataset	L1	L2	L1	L2
DS1	5 H 14 Min	7 H 05 Min	52	49
DS2	5 H 19 Min	7 H 22 Min	51	47

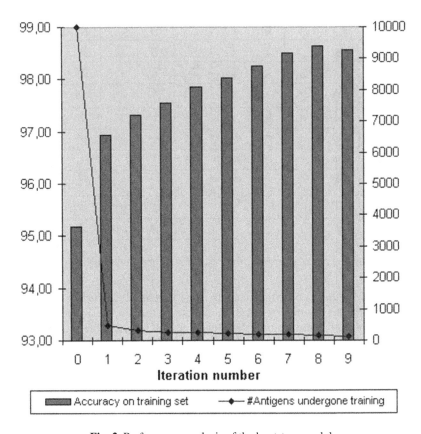

Fig. 2. Performance analysis of the bootstrap module

Next, the effects of parameters are studied for two different measures: (i) recognition accuracy and (ii) size of the immune memory. Results are reported here for the new training algorithm. Almost similar effects have been observed on both the datasets and results on DS1 are shown in Fig 3. Finally, the effect of k in k-nearest neighbour classification is examined and it is observed that k = 5 gives the best performance. Recognition accuracies for different values of k are shown in Fig. 4. The overall results reported in Table 1 are obtained with k = 5, stimulation threshold = 0.89, number of resources = 400, mutation rate = 0.008, affinity threshold scalar, α = 0.4, hyper-mutation rate = 2 and clonal rate = 10 (the last two parameters are used in Algorithm-I of section 2).

Classification results are further grouped into three classes, *correct*: a sample is properly classified; *incorrect*: a sample is wrongly classified, and *reject*: the system cannot classify a sample. A rejection is reported when no single class gets majority among the k choices returned by the classifier. Table 3 presents the average classification results taking these three aspects into consideration.

Table 3. Classification results

Dataset	% correct	% incorrect	% reject
DS1	96.23	2.14	1.63
DS2	95.68	2.44	1.88

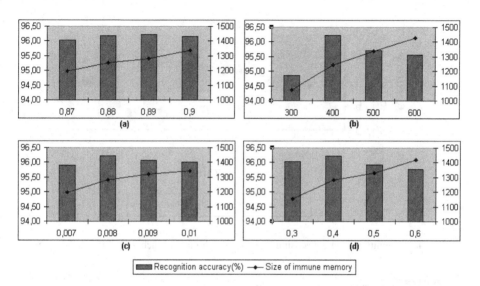

Fig. 3. Effect of different parameters on recognition accuracy and size of immune memory: (a) stimulation threshold (refer equation (3)), (b) number of resources used for resource limitation, (c) Mutation rate (refer Algorithm-II), and (d) Affinity threshold scalar, α as used in Algorithm-III

Fig. 5 presents the class-wise classification rates. Recognition of the digit '0' attains highest recognition score in both scripts. On the other hand, samples of ২ (digit '2') in Hindi and ৯ (digit '9') in Bengali result in the lowest classification rates as 89.32% and 90.52%, respectively. Study of the confusion matrix identifies several similar-shaped character pairs. For example, many samples from १ (digit '1') and २ (digit '2') in Hindi dataset and from ১ (digit '1') and ৯ (digit '9') in Bengali dataset resulted in confusion during classification. Some post-processing can be employed to discriminate such confusion pairs. In this context, a previous study [5] reported promising ability of an AIS-based approach for discrimination of similar-shaped character pairs. The same approach can also be employed here to further improve the classification accuracy. Such multi-level recognition scheme is considered as a future extension of the present study.

Comparison with other existing studies: As mentioned earlier that there are many studies on recognition of handwritten digits in English and Oriental scripts. However, there are only a few reports on Indic script. A recent study [17] makes use of fuzzy model based recognition scheme and reports recognition accuracy of about 95% on a dataset containing about 3500 handwritten samples for Devanagari digits. Study in [18] used neural net as classifier and achieved an accuracy of 93.26% on the same dataset used here for recognition of handwritten Bengali digits.

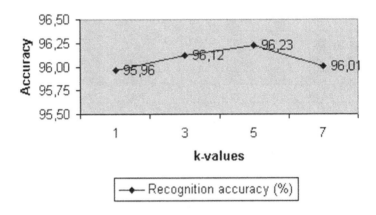

Fig. 4. Recognition accuracies using k nearest neighbor approach with different k values

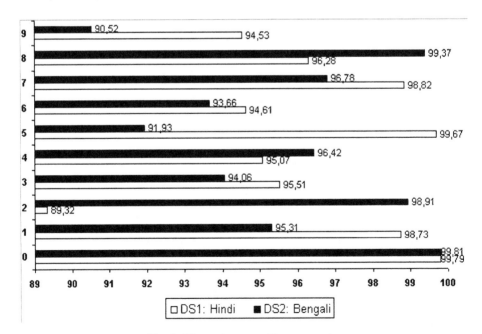

Fig. 5. Class-wise recognition accuracies

Compared to these approaches and achievements, the proposed AIS-based method can be viewed as a potential alternative. However, it is to be noted that no study employs the same feature set. Authors in [17] use some grid-based features, [18] considers wavelet coefficients as features whereas, a size normalized binary image array has been used as feature in the present study. Use of distance measure also differs from one study to another. Therefore, a direct comparison needs replication of these experiments using a uniform feature set and the same distance measure. Our future study will consider this aspect to bring out a judicious comparison between an AIS-based framework and other approaches using different learning paradigm.

4 Conclusions

This paper presents an application of a clonal selection algorithm for recognition of handwritten Indic numerals. In particular, a 2-phase clonal selection algorithm implementing a retraining scheme is proposed, and experiments using different datasets are performed. Reported results show that this new method outperforms the previously used single pass method. Overall classification performance shows that this method compares well with the existing approach. In particular, the proposed scheme achieves recognition accuracy of about 96% that is comparable to the previous approaches.

This study uses a feature vector and a simple distance measure to explore the feasibility of an AIS-based approach as an alternative classification tool. Since encouraging results have been obtained in this experiment, future extension of this study would include examination of different feature sets and distance measures to further improve the recognition accuracy.

Reference

1. D. Dasgupta, Z. Ji, and F. Gonzalez, F, "Artificial immune system (AIS) research in the last five years," in Congress on Evolutionary Computation (CEC'03), 2003, Volume: 1, pp. 123- 130.
2. Zheng Tang, Koichi Tashima, and Qi P. Cao, "Pattern recognition system using a clonal selection-based immune network," Systems and Computers in Japan, Volume 34, Issue 12, pp. 56 - 63, 2003.
3. Z. Ji and D. Dasgupta, "Real-valued negative selection algorithm with variable-sized detectors," in LNCS 3102, Proceedings of GECCO, pages 287–298, 2004.
4. L. N. d. Castro and F. J. V. Zuben, "Learning and Optimization Using the Clonal Selection Principle," *IEEE Transactions on Evolutionary Computation, Special Issue on Artificial Immune Systems*, vol. 6, pp. 239-251, 2002.
5. U. Garain, M. P. Chakraborty, D. Dutta Majumder, "Improvement of OCR Accuracy by Similar Character Pair Discrimination: an Approach based on Artificial Immune System," to be presented in the 18th Int. Conf. on Pattern Recognition (ICPR), August 2006, Hongkong.
6. A.B. Watkins, "AIRS: a resource limited artificial immune classifier," *Master's dissertation*, Dept. of Computer Science, Mississippi State University, 2001.

7. Keith Price Bibliography on use of Neural Networks for recognition of Numbers and Digits at http://iris.usc.edu/Vision-Notes/bibliography/char1019.html
8. C. de Stefano, A. Della Cioppa, and A. Marcelli, "Handwritten Numeral Recognition by Means of Evolutionary Algorithms," in Proc. of the 5th Int. Conf. on Document Analysis and Recognition (ICDAR), Bangalore, India, page: 804-808, 1999.
9. J. H. Carter, "The Immune System as a model for Pattern Recognition and classification," Journal of the American Medical Informatics Association. Vol. 7, no. 3, pp.28-41, 2000
10. L. N. de Castro and J Timmis, "Artificial Immune Systems: A Novel Approach to Pattern Recognition," in Artificial Neural Networks in Pattern Recognition (Eds. L Alonso J Corchado and C Fyfe), pp. 67-84. University of Paisley, January 2002.
11. S. Forrest, B. Javornik, R. E. Smith and A. S. Perelson, "Using genetic algorithms to explore pattern recognition in the immune system," in Evolutionary Computation 1:3, pp. 191-211, 1993.
12. Jennifer A. White and Simon M. Garrett, "Improved Pattern Recognition with Artificial Clonal Selection," in the Proc. of 2nd Int. Conf. on Artificial Immune Systems (ICARIS), September 1-3, 2003, Napier University, Edinburgh, UK.
13. Y. Cao and D. Dasgupta, "An Immunogenetic Approach in Chemical Spectrum Recognition," Advances in Evolutionary Computing (Eds. Ghosh & Tsutsui), Chapter 36, Springer-Verlag, January 2003.
14. Tarakanov and V. Skormin, "Pattern Recognition by Immunocomputing," in the proceedings of the special sessions on artificial immune systems in Congress on Evolutionary Computation, 2002 IEEE World Congress on Computational Intelligence, Honolulu, Hawaii, May 2002.
15. J. Timmis, "Artificial Immune Systems: a novel data analysis techniques inspired by the immune network theory," PhD Thesis, University of Wales, Aberystwyth, 2001.
16. U. Bhattacharya and B. B. Chaudhuri, "Databases for research on recognition of handwritten characters of Indian scripts," in Proc. of the 8th Int. Conf. on Document Analysis and Recognition (ICDAR), Seoul, Korea, vol. II, page: 789-793, 2005.
17. M. Hanmandlu and O.V. Ramana Murthy, "Fuzzy Model Based Recognition of Handwritten Hindi Numerals," Proc. Int. Conf. on Cognition and Recognition, Dec. 2005, pp. 490-496. http://www.studentprogress.com/appln/colleges/cogrec/
18. U. Bhattacharya, T. K. Das, A. Dutta, S. K. Parui, and B. B. Chaudhuri, "A Hybrid scheme for handwritten numeral recognition based on Self Organizing Network and MLP," in Int. J. on Pattern Recognition and Artificial Intelligence (IJPRAI), Volume 16, pp. 845-864, 2002.

Diophantine Benchmarks for the B-Cell Algorithm

P. Bull[1], A. Knowles[2], G. Tedesco[3], and A. Hone[4]

[1] Department of Computer Science, University of Aberystwyth,
Aberystwyth SY23 3DB, U.K.
plb3@aber.ac.uk
[2] Department of Electronics, University of York, York YO10 5DD, U.K.
ack500@york.ac.uk
[3] School of Computer Science, University of Nottingham,
Nottingham NG8 1BB, U.K.
gxt@cs.nott.ac.uk
[4] Institute of Mathematics, Statistics & Actuarial Science, University of Kent,
Canterbury CT2 7NF, U.K.
anwh@kent.ac.uk

Abstract. The B-cell algorithm (BCA) due to Kelsey and Timmis is a function optimization algorithm inspired by the process of somatic mutation of B cell clones in the natural immune system. So far, the BCA has been shown to be perform well in comparison with genetic algorithms when applied to various benchmark optimisation problems (finding the optima of *smooth* real functions). More recently, the convergence of the BCA has been shown by Clark, Hone and Timmis, using the theory of Markov chains. However, at present the theory does not predict the average number of iterations that are needed for the algorithm to converge. In this paper we present some empirical convergence results for the BCA, using a very different *non-smooth* set of benchmark problems. We propose that certain Diophantine equations, which can be reformulated as an optimization problem in integer programming, constitute a much harder set of benchmarks for evolutionary algorithms. In the light of our empirical results, we also suggest some modifications that can be made to the BCA in order to improve its performance.

1 Introduction

Artificial immune systems (AIS) constitute a fairly new approach to biologically inspired computing, that seek to exploit the mechanisms inherent in the natural immune system for computational purposes. So far, the application of the AIS approach to problems such as fault detection and network security has been quite successful (see [de Castro and Timmis 2002b] for a variety of applications). However, it is still not clear for which classes of problems it is appropriate to use AIS techniques. Moreover, even in situations where AIS methods are known to be successful, there is a dearth of theory to explain why they work.

Some of the first steps in the precise theoretical analysis of AIS were taken by Villalobos-Arias et al. [Villalobos et al. 2004], who have shown the convergence

H. Bersini and J. Carneiro (Eds.): ICARIS 2006, LNCS 4163, pp. 267–279, 2006.

of a multiobjective optimization algorithm, and subsequent work of Clark et al. [Clark et al. 2005] proved analogous results for the B-cell algorithm of Kelsey and Timmis [Kelsey and Timmis 2003]. In each of these works, the respective algorithms were described exactly in terms of Markov chains, and the theory of the latter implied convergence to the optima with probability one, in the limit when the number of iterations goes to infinity. There is a large amount of literature concerning the use of genetic algoritms (GAs) as function optimizers (see e.g. [Dasgupta and McGregor 1992, De Jong 1992]), and in this setting there is already a precedent for applying Markov chain methods [Vose 1995].

Although the convergence of optimization algorithms like the BCA is a nice theoretical property, it is not immediately useful from a practical point of view: one cannot wait for infinitely many iterations! The Markov chain theory applied to the BCA (see [Clark et al. 2005]) describes the algorithm in terms of a matrix of probabilities, known as the transition matrix. The transition matrix has 1 as its eigenvalue of largest modulus. In order to get a precise estimate of the average rate of convergence of the algorithm, in terms of the so called mixing time [Dyer et al. 2006, Hunter 2003], one would need to estimate the eigenvalue of the transition matrix which is second largest in size. For some problems, such as certain sampling algorithms considered by Jerrum [Jerrum 2005], the mixing time can be estimated, but for the BCA the transition matrix (and hence its second largest eigenvalue) is highly problem-dependent, and so it is not clear that a good universal estimate can be obtained.

The aim of this paper is to get some empirical results on the performance of the BCA applied to some specific problems, in order to see (on average) what proportion of trials converge to a solution to these problems. In the original paper by Kelsey and Timmis [Kelsey and Timmis 2003], the BCA was shown to perform very well compared with GAs and hybrid GAs when these algorithms were applied to a standard set of benchmark function optimization problems, including the problem of finding a global minimum of the "Camelback" function

$$f(x, y) = (4 - 21x^2/10 + x^4/3)x^2 + xy + (-4 + 4y^2)y^2. \tag{1}$$

Kelsey and Timmis found that the BCA outperformed a certain hybrid GA in the sense that it performed fewer function evaluations to get the same optimum solutions. All the standard problems considered in [Kelsey and Timmis 2003] were smooth, real-valued functions of this type (in one or several variables). For smooth function landscapes like these, various hill-climbing algorithms (even deterministic ones) and GAs are known to be quite successful at obtaining solutions. An important difference between the BCA and GAs is that the BCA does not use crossover. Here we propose a more challenging set of benchmark problems, namely the solution of Diophantine equations, which are likely to provide a fertile testing ground for new algorithms.

In the next section we briefly describe the B-cell algorithm (BCA), before explaining how to use it to solve Diophantine problems in the following section. After presenting our experimental results, we conclude with various suggestions for ways to modify and improve the BCA.

2   The B-Cell Algorithm

An important aspect of the adaptive immune response is the huge diversity in lymphocyte populations, which allows essentially any possible antigen to be recognized. For B cells, this diversity is generated in two quite different ways. (See section D of [Lydyard et al. 2004] for an overview.) Firstly, at the germline level (in the absence of antigen), diversity arises due to random selection and recombination of the genes that code for immunoglobulins. Secondly, further diversity is generated by somatic mutation, when (in the presence of antigen) B cells undergo costimulation with T-helper cells and a population of B cell clones is produced. The somatic mutation means that the clones potentially have a higher affinity for the antigen than their parent cells.

The B-cell algorithm (BCA) is loosely based on this process of somatic mutation in B cell clones. There is some evidence in the immunological literature [Lamlum 1999] that mutation occurs in *clusters* of regions within cells. The novel feature of the BCA is the use of an analogous notion applied to bit strings: mutation is applied to contiguous regions along the string. This mutation mechanism is referred to as the *contiguous somatic hypermutation* operator (described in more detail below).

The BCA takes bit strings (vectors) of length L, which represent a point in the search space; this could correspond to bit-encoded double-precision numbers, integers, or any other way of encoding the coordinates in search space. These vectors are considered to be the B cells within the system (although the analogy with biology is very loose: the B cells are identified with their genetic code, and with the associated immunoglobulins). Each B cells is associated with a vector $\underline{v} \in P$, where P is the population, and the objective function g can be evaluated at $\underline{v}$ to give $g(\underline{v})$, which corresponds to the fitness of the cell. An efficient population size for many functions can be small in contrast with genetic algorithms; a population size of five would be typical. In fact, as noted in [Clark et al. 2005], in the original specification of the algorithm the separate members of the population evolve independently, so there is no difference between running the algorithm N times with a population of size one, or once (i.e. in parallel) with population size N. Unlike standard GAs, the BCA does not use crossover. However, in practice Kelsey has used a heuristic for culling the weakest member of the population in each generation [Kelsey 2006], which effectively introduces an interaction between the different members. (Whether this is the right heuristic to use will be discussed later.)

Within every iteration (or generation) of the algorithm, each B-cell $\underline{v}$ is cloned to produce a *clonal pool*, $C(\underline{v})$. For *each* B cell within the population, all the adaptation takes place within $C(\underline{v})$. The size of C is typically the same size as the population P (but this does not have to be the case). Each B-cell $\underline{v}' \in C(\underline{v})$ is subjected to the contiguous somatic hypermutation operator. The BCA is outlined in figure 1.

An unusual feature of the BCA is the form of the mutation operator. This operates by subjecting *contiguous* regions of the vector to mutation. In essence a more focused search is undertaken: in [Clark et al. 2005] this is understood

1. *Initialisation*: create an initial random population of
   individuals P;
2. *Main loop*: $\forall \underline{v} \in P$:
   (a) *Affinity Evaluation*: evaluate $g(\underline{v})$;
   (b) *Clonal Selection and Expansion*:
       i. *Clone each B-cell*: for each $\underline{v} \in P$, produce a pool of clones $C(\underline{v})$;
       ii. *Contiguous mutation*: For each $\underline{v} \in P$, apply the contiguous somatic hy-
           permutation operator to every $\underline{c} \in C$;
       iii. *Affinity Evaluation*: evaluate each clone by applying
           g; if a clone is fitter than its parent B-cell $\underline{v}$, then replace $\underline{v}$ by $\underline{c}$;
3. *Cycle*: repeat from step 2 until some stopping criterion
   is met.

Fig. 1. Outline of the B-Cell Algorithm

in terms of the bias inherent in the mutation operator, which overall tends to mutate the least significant bits with higher probability than the most significant ones. Rather than selecting multiple random sites for mutation, a random site (or *hotspot*) is chosen within the vector, along with a random length; the vector is then subjected to mutation from the hotspot until the length of the contiguous region has been reached.

3 Diophantine Equations as Optimization Problems

A Diophantine equation is an algebraic equation

$$f(x, y, z, \ldots) = 0$$

which must be solved over the integers $\mathbb{Z}$. Diophantine problems have a long and distinguished pedigree in number theory [Mordell 1969]. As the recent proof by Wiles and Taylor of Fermat's last theorem shows, they also constitute some of the hardest problems in modern mathematics. While it is well known that there are infinitely many Pythagorean triples of integers (x, y, z) satisfying

$$x^2 + y^2 = z^2,$$

Fermat's assertion that

$$x^N + y^N = z^N, \qquad N \geq 3$$

has no integer solutions turned out to be an incredibly difficult thing to prove. Hilbert's tenth problem is the general problem of deciding when a Diophantine equation has integer solutions, and Matiyasevich proved the undecidability of this problem. Moreover, Matiyasevich showed that any statement in a formal system can be encoded as an equivalent Diophantine problem (see chapter 3 in [Manin and Panchishkin 2005] for instance).

We propose that Diophantine problems make good (and difficult) benchmarks for testing AIS and other evolutionary algorithms. There are two main reasons why we have decided to consider Diophantine equations: firstly, because when they arose in some work on discrete dynamics [Hone 2006], the fourth author wanted a simple algorithm that could find solutions without performing an exhaustive search; and secondly, some Diophantine problems are close to an associated smooth optimization problem, and so can be considered as being intermediate between smooth fitness landscapes and the hardest deceptive problems [Dasgupta 1994].

Using a simple idea mentioned in [Hone and Kelsey 2004], it is easy to convert any Diophantine equation into an optimization problem, namely that of minimizing the function

$$g(x, y, z, \ldots) = |f(x, y, z, \ldots)|$$

over $\mathbb{Z}$ (or equivalently one can minimize $f(x, y, z, \ldots)^2$). Thus one wants to obtain integers $x, y, z, \ldots$ which give the global minimum value zero for this function. Why are these problems hard? Well, in general one has no idea whether a given problem has any solutions at all. Furthermore, although these algebraic functions are smooth when considered as functions of real variables, the function landscape over the integers can be very spiky (since there can be many real minima which are very close to integer-valued local minima).

In this paper, we consider four different test problems. The prototype example will be Markoff's equation

$$x^2 + y^2 + z^2 = 3xyz \tag{2}$$

which has important applications in number theory, where it arises in the theory of quadratic forms and Diophantine approximation (see [Burger 2000] for an overview). We have chosen this example because it is known how to generate all the solutions in a cube of a given size, and furthermore Zagier has shown [Zagier 1982] that the number of positive triples (x, y, z) with

$$0 < x \leq y \leq z \leq T$$

that satisfy (2) grows like

$$C \log^2(3T)$$

for a constant $C \approx 0.1807$. When applying the BCA to finding solutions of (2), the latter asymptotic result should be helpful in measuring how the algorithm scales with the problem size, but we will not address this issue here.

Our first test problem is to solve a special case of (2), setting $z = 433$, which reduces it to the 2D problem of finding positive integers that satisfy

$$f(x, y) = x^2 + y^2 + 433^2 - 1299xy = 0. \tag{3}$$

Part of the function landscape for the above problem is plotted (logarithmically) in figure 2. We use the full 3D Markoff equation (2) as our second test problem, and a variant considered by Mordell [Mordell 1969], namely

$$x^2 + y^2 + z^2 + 2xyz - 5 = 0, \tag{4}$$

as the third test problem.

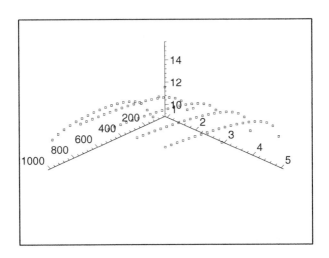

Fig. 2. Contour plot of the function $\ln|f(x, y)|$, with f as in equation (3), for positive integer values of $x \leq 1000$ along the sections $y = 1, 2, 3, 4, 5$

Our fourth, and hardest, problem is a Diophantine equation related to sequences of points on an elliptic curve (and associated with some integer sequences suggested by Michael Somos [Gale 1991]), which is given by

$$z^2 + (9x^2 - 37y)xz + 9y^2(y + 2x^2) = 0. \tag{5}$$

For this last problem, we do not explicitly know how to generate all the solutions, although an obvious one is $(x, y, z) = (1, 1, 1)$. We explain how we applied the BCA to these four problems in the next section, and how the difficulty of the problems led us to suggest various ways of making modifications to the algorithm.

4   Experimental Setup

For the first and second problems we applied the BCA to search between 0 and 1023 for each variable, in 2D and 3D respectively. For the more difficult three-dimensional problems for which solutions exist with negative integer values, a full 16 bit integer was used for each variable, giving a search space of size $65536^3 \approx 3 \times 10^{14}$. On the simplest 2D problem the algorithm performed reasonably well, finding a solution within 100 iterations more than 95% of the time. However in the other cases, the algorithm would often get stuck at a local optimum with a small value of the objective function g, and would make very slow progress until much of the search space had been searched. For example, for the first problem for equation (3) in 2D, the points $(x, y) = (1, 165)$ and $(165, 1)$ are two local minima

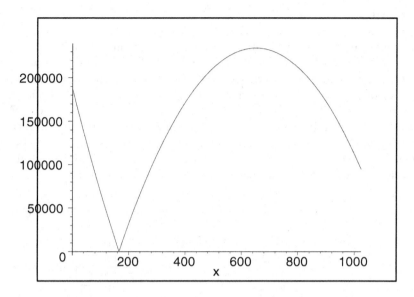

Fig. 3. Plot of the function $|f(x, 1)|$, with f as in equation (3)

over the integers, since they are very close to a *real*-valued minimum of $|f(x, y)|$ - see figure 3, and note that $f(x, 1) = 0$ when $x = (1299 - \sqrt{937441})/2 \approx 165.39$.

Our initial data seemed to indicate that this "sticking" would happen to a given population member within a very small number of iterations (of the order of 100). In addition to this, Kelsey's heuristic procedure for culling weakest members seemed to make little difference to the algorithm's performance. These problems led us to experiment with several modifications to the BCA, designed to improve its efficiency:

1. Megamutation (i): If the fitness of an individual in the population has not changed after 75 iterations, a fully randomising mutation operator is applied to that individual's clones: in other words, they are reset to random strings.
2. Megamutation (ii): Extend megamutation by allowing clones with a lower fitness to replace their parents regardless of their relative fitness.
3. Anti-elitism: At each iteration the fittest member of the population is killed and replaced with a randomly initialized individual.
4. Megamutation (ii) + Anti-elitism: All modifications combined.

Of course the anti-elitism strategy is only suitable for problems where the value of the optimum solution is known *a priori*, such as these Diophantine problems where we know that the value zero is an absolute minimum of $g(x, y, z) = |f(x, y, z)|$. For problems where this is not the case, memory cells added into the algorithm may be appropriate (in order to store the best solution so far).

5 Results

All four versions of the algorithms were tested on the three Diophantine equations in 3D. A version of the algorithm which combined anti-elitism with the second variant of the megamutation was also tested on the fourth equation. All the algorithms used a population size and clone size of 10. The mutation rate (probability of flipping each bit in the hotspot) was held fixed at 0.5. Each experiment was run 100 times with various numbers of maximum iterations, depending on the equation. The maximum number of iterations was set by observing the rate of convergence of the algorithms on each equation, and noting that convergence almost never occurred beyond a certain point.

Table 1. Number of iterations out of 100 in which algorithm converged on the optimum

Problem	Iterations	BCA	Algorithm #1	#2	#3	#4
#2	4,000	53	78	100	100	n/a
#3	100,000	36	90	84	100	n/a
#4	1,000,000	4	5	69	77	77

Table 1 shows the number of runs which converged before the maximum number of iterations was reached. The algorithms with megamutation found greater numbers of optimal solutions than the original algorithm for all three equations in 3D. However, the anti-elitist algorithm equalled or outperformed all the other algorithms, converging for all the runs for equations 2 and 3, and converging 77% of the time for equation 4. No improvement was found by combining the megamutation with the anti-elitism.

Table 2. Number of fitness evaluations (mean and standard deviation) for problem #2

Algorithm:	BCA	#1	#2	#3
Mean Fitness Evaluations $\times 10^4$	6.3	4.7	2.6	4.4
Standard Deviation $\times 10^4$	10.0	9.3	2.8	4.9

Table 2 shows the average and standard deviations of the number of evaluations which were required to achieve convergence, thus giving an idea of the amount of computational effort involved. This includes only the runs when the algorithm did converge to an optimal solution (since it only makes sense to measure the average evaluations to the convergence when an optimal solution was actually found). The megamutations reduced the average number of evaluations required for equations 2 and 3, when compared with the original BCA. However, the number of evaluations increased with megamutation on equation 4. The anti-elitism reduced the number of evaluations on all equations. Both the megamutations and the anti-elitism also reduced the standard deviation of all three equations. Observe that the standard deviations in table 2 are huge: in most cases, larger than the means. We have also calculated the analogous statistics for problems #3 and #4 (see tables 3 and 4), but because of the large spread of these distributions they are probably not the most meaningful statistics to quote. To provide more detailed information, in figures 4,5 and 6 we have plotted bar charts displaying the number of times (runs) out of 100 that the BCA or a variant converged in a given number of steps (function evaluations).

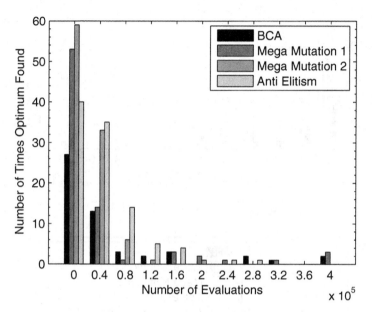

Fig. 4. Bar chart for problem #2

Table 3. Number of fitness evaluations (mean and standard deviation) for problem #3

Algorithm:	BCA	#1	#2	#3
Mean Fitness Evaluations $\times 10^6$	2.4	2.1	2.1	0.57
Standard Deviation $\times 10^6$	3.1	2.5	2.6	0.67

Table 4. Number of fitness evaluations (mean and standard deviation) for problem #4

Algorithm:	BCA	#1	#2	#3
Mean Fitness Evaluations $\times 10^7$	4.0	6.3	5.3	3.9
Standard Deviation $\times 10^7$	4.9	2.6	3.0	3.2

Since the megamutations provide a method of dealing with local optima, which the original BCA does not have, the algorithms with megamutation are less likely to remain stuck for long periods of time and thus can reduce the number of evaluations needed. The higher number of evaluations needed by the megamutation algorithms for equation 4 can be explained as follows: when the original BCA

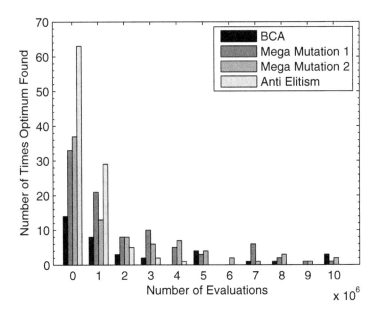

Fig. 5. Bar chart for problem #3

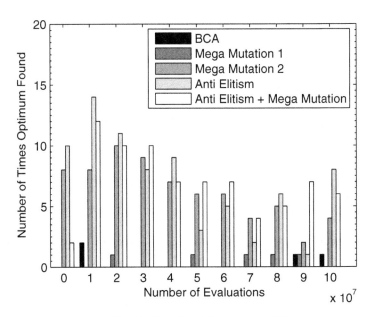

Fig. 6. Bar chart for problem #4

finds an optimal solution, it does so within a small number of iterations, thus the amount of work done by a successful BCA run is quite small, as most runs tend to get stuck in local optima. Unfortunately, as we can see from table 1, very few BCA runs are successful on equation 4. The megamutation algorithms (particularly the second version) find solutions with greater frequency, however they spend more time moving in and out of the local optima from which the BCA never escapes.

Culling the fittest member of the population (as with anti-elitism) may at first seem counter-intuitive. However, if its fitness does not change for a certain given period of time, the fittest member of the population is highly likely to be stuck in one of the most difficult local optima. If it has a better fitness than it would have in other nearby local optima, then its chances of escape are the slimmest of the whole population. Thus it does make sense to cull the fittest individual, since that individual has the lowest chance of improvement. This makes anti-elitism a more intelligent (or targeted) culling, as opposed to the "cull everything that doesn't move for a while" approach of the megamutation.

6   Conclusions

This work has benchmarked the B-Cell algorithm on four Diophantine equations. We have implemented three modified versions of this algorithm, all of which outperformed the original in terms of the probability of finding a global optimum within a given number of iterations and demonstrated a reduction of the average number of function evaluations needed for a global optimum to be found. The most successful modification is anti-elitism, which culls the fittest member of the population when its fitness has not changed within a certain specified number of steps.

Further work remains to be done, including:

1. Attempt to solve the same Diophantine equations using genetic algorithms and/or swarm optimization for comparison with these results.
2. Apply the anti-elitism modified version of the BCA to other optimization problems to gain a more general determination of its advantages.
3. Design and test a variant of the anti-elitism algorithm utilizing memory cells, for problems where the optimal fitness value is not known.

There is a substantial literature on so-called deceptive problems for GAs, and on finding modifications that result in better performance of GAs upon application to these sorts of problems (see [Dasgupta 1994], for instance). Thus it would also be good to use deceptive problems as another set of benchmarks for AIS algorithms. In fact, for a Diophantine equation, there can be points with very small but non-zero values of $g = |f|$ (i.e. local optima) that are far from the actual solutions in search space, so in this sense Diophantine equations correspond to a particular class of deceptive problems.

It is also worth mentioning here that, quite recently [Andrews 2006], Paul Andrews showed us his implementation of the AIS algorithm opt-aiNet, another optimization algorithm introduced in [de Castro and Timmis 2002a]. When opt-aiNet was applied to the simplest of our benchmarks (problem #1), it appeared to perform very badly. In every trial that we saw, most of the fittest members of the population remained near one of the local optima $(1, 165)$ or $(165, 1)$;

other popular local minima were at $(2, 74)$, $(9, 16)$ and their images under the reflection $x \leftrightarrow y$. However, this version of opt-aiNet was using (approximations to) real numbers respresented in floating-point, which were then rounded to the nearest integer; thus the comparison is not a fair one. It would be worth making a proper comparison between these two algorithms in future, also comparing with the results of [Timmis and Edmonds 2004].

In its most basic form (once the search space has been defined) the BCA requires only one parameter to be specified, namely the mutation rate (i.e. the probability that each bit in the hotpsot on a string will flip). Including the megamutation strategy requires at least one additional parameter to be set, namely the number of steps to wait before megamutation is applied. So far, we have not explored the effect of scaling on the performance of the algorithm; the benchmark problem #2 should be good for large-scale numerical tests, because the asymptotic growth of the number of solutions is known in advance. Finally, it would be good to develop other practical and theoretical methods for the analysis of convergence of the BCA and similar algorithms.

Acknowledgements. This work was carried out at the Easter School on Artificial Immune Systems at the University of Aberystwyth in April 2006. We are grateful to the ARTIST network for organization and financial support. Andy Hone also thanks the EPSRC for funding the project *Nonlinear dynamics of artificial immune systems* with a Springboard Fellowship.

References

[Andrews 2006] Andrews, P. Private communication (2006); opt-aiNet code available at http://www.elec.york.ac.uk/ARTIST/code.php

[Burger 2000] Burger, E. Exploring the Number Jungle: a Journey into Diophantine Analysis. Providence, RI, American Mathematical Society (2000).

[de Castro and Timmis 2002a] de Castro, L and Timmis, J. An Artificial Immune Network for Multimodal Function Optimisation, in *Proceedings of IEEE World Congress on Evolutionary Computation* (2002) 669–674.

[de Castro and Timmis 2002b] de Castro, L and Timmis, J. Artificial Immune Systems: A New Computational Intelligence Approach. Springer-Verlag (2002).

[Clark et al. 2005] Clark, E., Hone, A., and Timmis, J. A Markov Chain Model of the B-Cell Algorithm, in *Proceedings of ICARIS 2005*, C. Jacob et al. (Eds.). Springer LNCS **3627** Springer-Verlag (2005) 318–330.

[Dasgupta and McGregor 1992] Dasgupta, D. and McGregor, D.R. Nonstationary Function Optimization using the Structured Genetic Algorithm, Parallel Problem Solving from Nature 2 (Proc. 2nd Int. Conf. on Parallel Problem Solving from Nature, Brussels 1992), pages 145–154, 1992, Amsterdam, Elsevier

[Dasgupta 1994] Dasgupta, D. Handling Deceptive Problems Using a different Genetic Search, in *Proceedings of the First IEEE Conference on Evolutionary Computation 1994, IEEE World Congress on Computational Intelligence* (1994) 807–811.

[De Jong 1992] DeJong, K. Are genetic algorithms function optimizers? Parallel Problem Solving from Nature **2**, *Proceedings of the Second Conference on Parallel Problem Solving from Nature*, Brussels: North-Holland (1992) pages 3–13.

[Dyer et al. 2006] Dyer, M., Goldberg, L.A., Jerrum, M. and Martin, R. Markov chain comparison. *Probability Surveys* **3** (2006) 89–111.

[Gale 1991] Gale, D. The strange and surprising saga of the Somos sequences. *Mathematical Intelligencer* **13 (1)** (1991), 40–42.

[Hone and Kelsey 2004] Hone, A. and Kelsey, J. Optima, extrema and artificial immune systems. In Proceedings of ICARIS 2004, G. Nicosia et al. (Eds.), Springer LNCS **3239** (2004) 80–90.

[Hone 2006] Hone, A.N.W. Diophantine non-integrability of a third order recurrence with the Laurent property, *J. Phys. A: Math. Gen.* **39** (2006) L171–L177.

[Hunter 2003] Hunter, J.J. Mixing Times with Applications to Perturbed Markov Chains. Preprint, Institute of Information and Mathematical Sciences, Massey University (2003).

[Jerrum 2005] Jerrum, M. Algorithmically feasible sampling: what are the limits? Talk at London Mathematical Society meeting, University College London, 7th October 2005.

[Kelsey and Timmis 2003] Kelsey, J and Timmis, J. Immune Inspired Somatic Contiguous Hypermutation for Function Optimisation. Lecture Notes in Computer Science **2723** Cantu-Paz et al. (Eds.) Proc. of Genetic and Evolutionary Computation Conference (GECCO) 2003, 207–218.

[Kelsey et al. 2003] Kelsey, J., Timmis, J. and Hone, A. Chasing Chaos. In R. Sarker et al. (Eds.), *Proceedings of the Congress on Evolutionary Computation*, Canberra, Australia, December 2003. IEEE, pages 413–419.

[Kelsey 2006] Kelsey, J. Private communication (2006).

[Krishnakumar 1989] Krishnalumar, K. Micro-genetic algorithms for stationary and non-stationary function optimization. In SPIE Proceedings: *Intelligent Control and Adaptive Systems*, pages 289-296.

[Lamlum 1999] Lamlum, H, et. al. The type of somatic mutation at APC in familial adenomatous polyposis is determined by the site of the germline mutation: a new facet to Knudson's 'two-hit' hypothesis. *Nature Medicine*, 1999, **5**: pages 1071-1075.

[Lydyard et al. 2004] Lydyard, P., Whelan, A. and Fanger, M. *Immunology*. 2nd edition; New York, Abingdon: Taylor & Francis (2004).

[Manin and Panchishkin 2005] Manin, Y.I. and Panchishkin, A.A. *Introduction to Modern Number Theory*. 2nd edition; Berlin, Heidelberg, New York: Springer (2005).

[Mordell 1969] Mordell, L.J. *Diophantine Equations*. London: Academic Press (1969).

[Timmis and Edmonds 2004] Timmis, J. and Edmonds, C. A Comment on opt-AiNET: An Immune Network Algorithm for Optimisation, in *Genetic and Evolutionary Computation*, D. Kalyanmoy et al. (Eds.). Springer LNCS **3102** Springer-Verlag (2004) 308–317.

[Villalobos et al. 2004] Villalobos-Arias, M. Coello Coello, C.A. & Hernandez-Lerma, O. Convergence analysis of a multiobjective artificial immune systems algorithm, in *Proceedings of ICARIS 2004*, G. Nicosia et al. (Eds.). Springer LNCS **3239** Springer-Verlag (2004) 226–235.

[Vose 1995] Vose, M.D. Modeling simple genetic algorithms. *Evolutionary Computation* **3**, number 4 (1996) 453–472.

[Zagier 1982] Zagier, D. On the Number of Markoff Numbers Below a Given Bound. *Mathematics of Computation* **39**, number 160 (1982) 709–723.

A Population Adaptive Based Immune Algorithm for Solving Multi-objective Optimization Problems

Jun Chen and Mahdi Mahfouf

Dept. of Automatic Control and Systems Engineering, The University of Sheffield
Mappin Street, S1 3JD, Sheffield, United Kingdom
Phone: +44 (0) 114 222 5607; Fax: +44 (0) 114 222 5624
{jun.chen, m.mahfouf}@sheffield.ac.uk

Abstract. The primary objective of this paper is to put forward a general framework under which clear definitions of immune operators and their roles are provided. To this aim, a novel Population Adaptive Based Immune Algorithm (PAIA) inspired by Clonal Selection and Immune Network theories for solving multi-objective optimization problems (MOP) is proposed. The algorithm is shown to be insensitive to the initial population size; the population and clone size are adaptive with respect to the search process and the problem at hand. It is argued that the algorithm can largely reduce the number of evaluation times and is more consistent with the vertebrate immune system than the previously proposed algorithms. Preliminary results suggest that the algorithm is a valuable alternative to already established evolutionary based optimization algorithms, such as NSGA II, SPEA and VIS.

1 Introduction

Bio-Inspired Computing lies within the realm of Natural Computing, a field of research that is concerned with both the use of biology as inspiration for solving computational problems and the use of the natural world experiences to solve real world problems. The increasing interest in this field lies in the fact that nowadays we are having to deal with more and more complex, large, distributed and ill-structured systems, while on the other hand, one cannot help noticing that the apparently simple structures and organizations in nature are capable of dealing with the most complex systems and tasks with ease. Artificial Immune Systems (AIS) is one such recognized computing paradigm, which has been receiving more attention recently.

Most previous research efforts in the AIS area were mainly concerned with fault diagnosis [1], computer security [2], and data analysis [3, 4] and only very recently have a few attempts seen AIS extended to the optimization field, and most of them being dedicated to solving single objective optimization problems (SOP) [5, 6]. The reason behind this is that it is relatively easy to create a direct link between real immune system and the aforementioned three application areas, e.g. in applications of data analysis, clusters to be recognized are easily related to antigens (Ag), and the set of solutions to distinguish between these clusters is linked to antibodies (Ab) [3]. However, such direct links are vague in the optimization field, especially in the MOP field. The main difficulty in exploiting immune metaphors for optimization problems

H. Bersini and J. Carneiro (Eds.): ICARIS 2006, LNCS 4163, pp. 280–293, 2006.
© Springer-Verlag Berlin Heidelberg 2006

is to find a way to define Ag and the *affinity* since there is no explicit Ag population to be recognized. For SOP, since there is only one objective to be achieved the objective itself can be viewed as Ag. Therefore, the *affinity* can be defined as the evaluation of the objective function for a given Ab [5]. Such an implicit definition of Ag is reckoned to be more difficult to be used in a MOP context for the objectives are now multiple.

In [7], the authors argued that AIS has, in its elementary structure, the main features required to solve MOP. There have been several attempts to address this in the literature [8~12] but none of these presented a formal systematic framework due to the aforementioned reasons. Some of them are coupled with other evolutionary mechanisms [8, 12], and others sacrifice some biological metaphors in exchange for a better performance [9, 10]. If one wishes to make AIS a new alternative computing paradigm to solve MOP, clear definitions of each part of the immune metaphors and their corresponding roles added to a general accepted framework are more pressing at the moment than any specific algorithms. Furthermore, identifying the difference between AIS and the traditional evolutionary algorithms for solving MOP and what it is the extra strength that AIS can offer is more meaningful than just providing relatively better comparative results.

Based on such understanding, this paper presents a systematical AIS framework to solve MOP with clear definitions and roles of the immune metaphors to be employed. The new algorithm is mostly inspired by Clonal Selection [13] and Immune Network [14, 15] theories, and is mainly based on the previous research in [3~5]. After comparing this algorithm to other state-of-the-art MOP algorithms using the ZDT1~ZDT4 benchmark functions, emphasis is placed on the following: 1) the difference between AIS and traditional evolutionary algorithms, 2) the extra advantages that are exclusively inherent in AIS and alike. Finally, it will be argued that if one considers each objectives' combination as a unique antigen intruding on the immune system, MOP is also an ideal test bed for the immune mechanism simulation.

2   Background

2.1   Multi-objective Optimization

Many real-world problems are inherently of a multi-objective nature with often conflicting issues. Generally, MOP consists of mini/maximizing the vector function:

$$f(x) = [f_1(x), f_2(x), \dots, f_m(x)]^T \cdot \tag{1}$$

subject to J inequality and K equality constraints as follows:

$$g_j(x) \geq 0 \quad j = 1, \dots J; \quad h_k(x) = 0 \quad k = 1, \dots K \cdot \tag{2}$$

where $x = [x_1, x_2, \dots, x_n]^T \in \Omega$ is the vector of decision variables and Ω is the feasible region. There are two main methods that allow to deal with MOP, namely the ideal multi-objective optimization procedure and the preference-based multi-objective optimization procedure [16]. The fundamental difference between these two is that the latter relies heavily on the experiences of the particular user and the obtainable higher-level problem information. The higher-level information is used to choose a preference vector so that multiple objectives can be aggregated into a single objective. In doing so, MOP is actually transformed into SOP. However, because of its high dependence on preference information this approach is sometimes subjective and impractical. Facing the possibility of lacking the problem information, the ideal multi-objective optimization procedure has been given more attention. Through this method, a set of trade-off solutions is found. By finding the set of solutions humans can understand the problem in greater depth, and finally a single optimal solution to a specific scenario is finally decided.

The prevalence of the ideal method calls for a new philosophy to deal with the problem since one wants to find a set of uniform-distributed optimal solutions simultaneously through a single run, rather than several runs. For this reason, population-based *Genetic algorithm* (GA) steps in sight. GA was originally developed to solve SOP. In this case, all solutions in the population will finally converge to a single optimum. To make traditional GA suitable to maintain a solution set, the sharing method is used [17]. In this way and alike, different species can format and co-exist in the final population. Despite its great ability in maintaining trade-off solutions and dealing with non-convex problems, population-based GA suffers from two main problems:

1. It is sensitive to the setting of the sharing parameters.
2. It depends highly on the population size to preserve its search capability.

Solving the above problems is our initial intention to develop a population adaptive based immune algorithm (PAIA), which is further discussed in Section 3.

2.2   The Immune System

The vertebrate immune system is highly complex and possesses multi layers. Here, what one is interested in is the third layer, namely, the adaptive immune system, which can learn and adapt to most previously unseen antigens, and can respond to such patterns quickly in the next sample. Among many immunological models, the Clonal Selection and the Immune Network theories are the two branches which were emulated in this work. Another immune metaphor which was exploited is the way that the immune system controls its Abs' concentration.

Clonal Selection Principle. The Clonal Selection Principle describes the basic features of an immune response to an antigenic stimulus, and establishes the idea that only those cells that recognize the antigen are selected to proliferate. The key procedures are: 1) *Selection*: the B-cell with a higher affinity than a threshold is selected to clone itself; 2) *Proliferation*: the selected B-cells produce many offspring with the same structure as themselves; the clone size is proportional to the individual's affinity; 3) *Affinity Maturation*: this procedure consists of *Hypermutation* and *Receptor Editing* [18]; in the former case, clones are subjected to a high-rate mutation in order to differentiate them from their parents; the higher the affinity, the lower the mutation rate; in the latter case, cells with a low affinity, or self-reactive cells, can delete their self-reactive receptors or develop entirely new receptors; 4) *Reselection*: after *affinity* *maturation*, the mutated clones and edited cells are reselected to ensure that only those cells with a higher affinity than a certain threshold survive. The whole process is performed iteratively until a certain stable state is achieved. In PAIA, the principle is used to provide a selection pressure to effectively drive the population towards the Pareto front over many iteration steps.

Immune Network Theory. According to this theory, Abs not only have paratopes but also epitopes. This results in the fact that Abs can be stimulated by recognizing other Abs, and for the same reason can be suppressed by being recognized. Consequently, the immunological memory can be acquired by this self-regulation and mutual reinforcement learning of B-cells. In [19], Farmer *et al.* created an immune network model defined by a differential equation which demonstrates that Abs' concentration is determined by two activations-Abs' activation and Ags' activation, one suppression-Abs' suppression, and *Apoptosis*. The suppression function is a mechanism that allows to regulate the over-stimulated B-cells to maintain a stable memory. This metaphor is used in PAIA to regulate the dynamics of the population.

Abs' Concentration. Initially, only a small number of B-cells cruise in the body. If they encounter foreign Ags, some of them are activated and then they proliferate. The immune system should maintain a specific Abs concentration. This process is adaptive, i.e. the number of clones that are proliferated during the activation process and how many of them are maintained at each iteration step and at the end in order to neutralize Ags is adaptive. This makes sense since if a large number of initial B-cells is available then undoubtedly it can kill any Ags at the cost of spending more energy to activate B-cells and secrete Abs. However, only an optimal number of B-cells during each step is necessary (less means more time is needed to reach the required concentration; more means redundant B-cells are introduced). This is the main inspiration for us to design PAIA's structure so that the population is adaptive at each iteration step.

3   The Algorithm

The synthesis of the above three immune metaphors generates the new algorithm-Population Adaptive Based Immune Algorithm (PAIA), which aims to:

1. provide a generic AIS framework for MOP solving;
2. make the population size adaptive to the problem;
3. reduce the evaluation times so that only the necessary evaluations are carried out;

Here, we mainly discuss the last two aims, and leave the first one until after presenting the whole algorithm. The last two aims are related to the last problem raised in Section 2.1 which needs detailing. To preserve the search capability, all population-based GAs require a sufficiently large population, and such a population is fixed during the search mechanism. This makes the initial population size crucial to the success of such algorithms. Deb pointed out in [16] that NSGA II failed to converge to the true Pareto front for ZDT4 using a population of 100. He suggested (but not proved) that 500 may be needed for a successful outcome. Hence, the population size is obviously problem-contingent. This leads to following legitimate question: how can one know that the population size is sufficient for a more complicated problem? And on the other hand, how can one be sure that the population size is not redundant for a simpler problem? If one failed in the first scenario the true Pareto front can never be approached; or if they failed in the second case one could end up with many redundant evaluation times, which is more severe than it looks since in real life it is expensive and time consuming to evaluate objective functions [20]. However, due to its mating scheme and selection mechanism population-based GA has to have its population size fixed.

Can AIS, as a new computing paradigm, offer a solution? This paper gives the answer by addressing the following two questions:

1. Does one still need to fix the size of the population?
2. Can the population size adapt to the problem so that the initial population size is no longer crucial to the success of the algorithm?

If the answers to both questions are 'yes', then another problem to be addressed is how one can control the population size during the search. The problem is tackled by emulating the third immune metaphor discussed in Section 2.2. The accomplishment of aim 2 makes aim 3 automatically achieved since only the necessary Abs are preserved during each step.

3.1 The PAIA Algorithm

The basic definitions are first given so that one can describe the algorithm with clarity:

- **Antigen (Ag):** Ag is the problem to be optimized.
- **Antibody (Ab):** Ab is the candidate solutions of the problem to be optimized.
- **Ag-Ab affinity:** for SOP, it is defined as the objective (fitness) value; for MOP, it is determined by using the non-dominance concept, i.e. solutions in the first non-dominated front have the highest affinity, then the second front, and so on.
- **Ab-Ab affinity (Abs' affinity):** it is defined as the distance (refer to Eqs. (3)) in the decision variable space between one randomly chosen Ab in the first non-dominated front and the one in the remaining population.
- **Ab-Ab suppression (Abs' suppression/Network suppression):** when two Abs are very close to each other, they can recognize each other. The result is that one of them is suppressed and deleted. Unlike Abs' affinity, this term is defined as the *Euclidian* distance in the objective space.

The PAIA algorithm can be described via the following steps:

1. **Initialization:** a random Ab population is first created.
2. **Identify_Ab:** one random Ab in the first non-dominated front is identified.
3. **Activation:** the identified Ab is used to activate the remaining dominated Abs. Dominated Abs' affinity value (NB: affinity is the inverse of the affinity value) is calculated according to Eqs. (3), where n is the dimension of the decision variables.

$$aff \_ val_d = \sum_{i=1}^{n} \left| x_{identified}(i) - x_d(i) \right| / n \cdot \tag{3}$$

The non-dominated Abs' affinity value is calculated as follows: **I.** if the size of dominated Abs is not zero, the affinity value equals the minimum affinity value of the dominated Ab divided by two; **II.** otherwise, the affinity value is calculated according to Eqs. (4), where N is the size of non-dominated Abs.

$$aff \_ val_{nd} = \sum_{j=1}^{N} (\sum_{i=1}^{n} \left| x_{identified}(i) - x_j(i) \right| / n) / N \cdot \tag{4}$$

In this way, Ag-Ab affinity is indirectly embedded in Abs' affinity since non-dominated Abs always have the smallest affinity value (the highest affinity).

4. **Clonal Selection:** Clonal selection consists of three steps: **I.** Abs with the smallest affinity value are selected, i.e. non-dominated Abs are always selected; **II.** Abs in the remaining population with affinity value smaller than a threshold (δ) are selected; **III.** unselected Abs are kept in a different set.

5. **Clone: I.** for selected Abs, a maximum clone size (N_{cmax}) is pre-defined; then a fraction of N_{cmax} is allocated to each selected Ab according to its affinity percentage, i.e. the higher the percentage the larger the fraction is assigned; **II.** Unselected Abs are cloned once regardless of their affinity.

6. **Affinity Maturation: I.** selected Abs are submitted to *hypermutation*, i.e. one dimension of the Ab is randomly chosen to mutate; the mutation rate is proportional to the affinity value (inversely proportional to affinity); the whole process is calculated using Eqs. (5). **II.** unselected Abs are submitted to *receptor editing* which means that more than one dimension (two, in PAIA) are randomly chosen to mutate; the mutation rate is calculated using Eqs. (5).

$$x_{new}(i) = x_{old}(i) + \alpha \cdot N(0,1) \quad i = 1,\ldots,n; \quad \alpha = \exp(aff \_ val) / \exp(1) \cdot \tag{5}$$

where $N(0, 1)$ is a Gaussian random variable with zero mean and standard deviation 1. i represents the dimension that has been chosen to mutate.

7. **Reselection:** the mutated/edited clones and their corresponding parents are combined together and reselected: **I.** all non-dominated Abs are selected; **II.** if the number of current non-dominated Abs (NCR) is less than the initial population size (IN), Abs from the next non-dominated front are selected according to their recalculated Abs' affinity value (the ones with smaller affinity values are favoured) to fill the difference between these two; this process continues until the difference is filled; **III.** only when NCR is greater than IN and greater than the number of the non-dominated Abs in the last iteration (NPR) can *Network Suppression* be invoked to suppress any too-close Abs.

8. **Network Suppression:** the *Euclidian* distance in objective space between any two Abs is calculated; if it is less than a predefined network threshold (σ) the one with the larger affinity value is suppressed and deleted; this operator is invoked in step 7 when certain conditions are satisfied.

9. **Iteration:** the process is repeated from step 2 until certain conditions are met.

In the following, some differences between PAIA and previous research are highlighted. Further discussion can also be found in Section 5.

- In PAIA, the initial population size can be any number (even 1). However, only an optimal initial size can lead to the most efficient way of dealing with the problem.
- Most previous research did not emulate Clonal Selection. In PAIA, it is emulated to fully exploit the selected Abs so that they have more opportunities to be cloned and mutated in the early iteration steps, which can speed up the convergence.
- Most previous works used a fixed clone size for every Ab. In PAIA the clone size is adaptively decided by the number of selected Abs and their affinities.
- A new method (Eqs. (5)) is proposed to calculate the mutation rate, which ensures that the mutation rate is at least 0.37^1. The exploration ability is thus preserved even when all Abs converge to a single (sub) optimum.
- In PAIA, the population size is not fixed, but is finally controlled by σ. The population is regulated by network suppression so that any too-close Abs are suppressed. The way to invoke network suppression is adaptive to the search process.

3.2 The Generic AIS Framework

Although PAIA is a specific MOP algorithm, the main structure of the algorithm can be extracted as a generic AIS framework for MOP solving, as shown in Fig. 1.

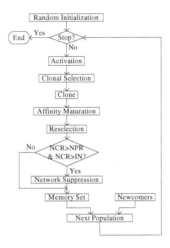

Fig. 1. Generic AIS framework for MOP solving (NCR: the number of current non-dominated Abs; NPR: the number of non-dominated Abs in the last iteration; IN: the initial Abs size)

Two kinds of activation are emulated, namely Ag-Ab activation and Ab-Ab activation, so that one obtains information from both the objective space (Ag-Ab affinity) and the decision variables space (Abs' affinity) to select Abs. The Clonal Selection and Clone prefer good Abs by giving them more chances to be cloned so that they always dominate the whole population. Affinity Maturation increases the diversity of the population so that more objective landscape can be explored. Reselection ensures that good mutants are inserted into the memory set and bad Abs *apoptosis*. Network

---

[1] If Abs are normalized, then *aff_val* is within 0~1; so α is within 0.37~1 according to Eqs. (5).

Suppression regulates the population so that it is adaptive to the search process. Newcomers are used to further increase the diversity of Abs (it is not used in PAIA and is included here for completion). It is argued here that each part of the framework can be implemented in various means; while the basic structure remains unchanged.

4 Experiments

The proposed approach is compared to two well-known algorithms-NSGA II [16] and SPEA [21], and another immune algorithm-VIS proposed by Freschi *et al.* [7]. By comparing with NSGA II and SPEA, it is shown that PAIA is a valuable alternative to standard algorithms; by comparing with VIS, the difference between these two immune algorithms is identified. ZDT1~ZDT4 test suite [16] is used for such a comparison. These test functions have two objectives and represent the same type of problems with a large decision variable space, a concave and discrete Pareto front, and many local optima. Results of NSGA II and SPEA are taken from [16] with a population size of 100 and a maximum of 250 generations. This gives a total number of 25000 evaluation times. To make the comparison fair, VIS is also run using the same setting (26000 for ZDT4). For PAIA, although the population is adaptive the final population can be controlled by σ. Hence, one can set an adequate value for σ so that the final population size and evaluation times are around 100 and 25000 respectively. NSGA II failed to converge for ZDT4 even with a larger number of evaluation times, while on the other hand, although some algorithms may not fully converge within 25000 evaluations they have no difficulty to converge using larger evaluations. For this reason, one can also compare PAIA and VIS when both have fully converged (otherwise, it is only the best results to be used). Two performance metrics, namely the Generational Distance (GD) and the Spread Δ [16], are used and are defined as follows [11]:

- **Generational Distance:** GD measures the closeness of the obtained Pareto solution set Q from a known set of Pareto-optimal set P^*.

$$GD = \frac{(\sum_{i=1}^{|Q|} d_i^m)^{1/m}}{|Q|} .$$
(6)

For a two-objective problem (m=2), d_i is the *Euclidean* distance between the solution $i \in Q$ and the nearest member of P^*.

- **Spread:** Δ measures the diversity of the solutions along the Pareto front in the final population.

$$\Delta = \frac{\sum_{m=1}^{M} d_m^e + \sum_{i=1}^{|Q|} |d_i - \bar{d}|}{\sum_{m=1}^{M} d_m^e + |Q| \bar{d}} .$$
(7)

where d_i is the distance between the neighbouring solutions in the Pareto solution set Q. $\bar{d}$ is the mean value of all d_i. d_m^e is the distance between the extreme solutions of P^* and Q along the mth objective.

4.1 Experiment 1 (25000 Evaluations)

In this experiment, the number of iterations was set to 280, IN = 7, δ = 0.4, and N_{cmax} = 95 for all four test problems; σ = 0.0074 for ZDT1~ZDT3 and 0.0078 for ZDT4 so that the final population size and evaluations are around 100 and 25000 respectively. The results are obtained as the average values of 10 independent runs and are shown in Fig. 2.

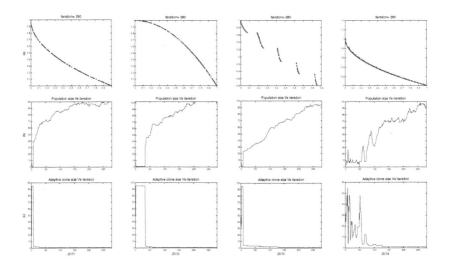

Fig. 2. (a) Pareto solutions obtained by PAIA on ZDT1~ZDT4; (b) Adaptive population size Vs iteration; (c) Adaptive clone size (the assigned maximum clone size among all Abs) Vs iteration

Table 1. Mean and variance values relating to the convergence measure GD

Algorithm	ZDT1		ZDT2		ZDT3		ZDT4	
	GD	σ^2	GD	σ^2	GD	σ^2	GD	σ^2
NSGA II	8.94e-4	0	8.24e-4	0	4.34e-2	4.20e-5	3.228	7.3076
SPEA	1.25e-3	0	3.04e-3	2.00e-5	4.42e-2	1.90e-5	9.514	11.321
VIS	1.81e-3	1.97e-7	1.21e-3	1.04e-6	1.58e-3	2.26e-7	0.1323	4.20e-2
PAIA	1.43e-4	1.56e-9	1.04e-4	2.2e-11	1.58e-4	4.6e-10	1.20e-3	1.88e-7

The results shown in Tables 1, 2 and 3 indicate that PAIA reached a better performance than any of other three algorithms using similar evaluation times. From Fig. 2 (b), one can see that the population adaptively increases/decreases during each iteration step and can be finally controlled by σ, which means that only necessary Abs are maintained during the search and at the end. From Fig. 2 (c), one can see that the clone size is adaptively decided by the number of selected Abs and their corresponding affinities. If the number of selected Abs is small, each selected Ab can be assigned a large clone size so that the population is large enough to explore the objective space.

Although the results of PAIA for ZDT4 are much better than for other algorithms', it has not fully converged to the true Pareto front. This result can be further improved by using more iteration steps and such results can be found in experiment 2.

Table 2. Mean and variance values relating to the diversity measure Δ

Algorithm	ZDT1		ZDT2		ZDT3		ZDT4	
	Δ	σ^2	Δ	σ^2	Δ	σ^2	Δ	σ^2
NSGA II	0.4633	4.16e-2	0.4351	2.46e-2	0.5756	5.08e-3	0.4795	9.84e-3
SPEA	0.7302	9.07e-3	0.6781	4.48e-3	0.6657	6.66e-4	0.7321	1.13e-2
VIS	0.5420	8.25e-3	0.6625	2.58e-2	0.6274	1.60e-2	0.1011	1.37e-3
PAIA	0.3368	1.10e-3	0.3023	7.07e-4	0.4381	1.50e-3	0.3316	1.20e-3

Table 3. Final population size and evaluation times of PAIA

Test suite	Final Population		Evaluation Times	
	Mean	Max/min	Mean	Max/min
ZDT1	96	101/87	25372	26467/24494
ZDT2	101	106/96	25950	26649/25371
ZDT3	94	102/89	25365	26155/24587
ZDT4	96	103/85	25910	26654/25203

4.2 Experiment 2 (Full Convergence)

In this experiment, the number of iterations was set to 180 for ZDT1 and ZDT2, to 280 for ZDT3 and to 500 for ZDT4. Other parameters remained unchanged.

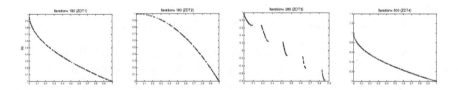

Fig. 3. Pareto solutions obtained by PAIA on ZDT1~ZDT4

Through this experiment, it was found that PAIA possesses very fast convergence properties. For ZDT1 and ZDT2, 180 iterations were enough for convergence, and for ZDT4 500 iterations were sufficient. For all the four test problems, both algorithms obtained good performances (except ZDT4 in VIS) in terms of both metrics. From Table 5, one can see that PAIA generally uses fewer evaluations to achieve good results. Although it used 46899 evaluations to fully converge, it only used 25910 (see Table 3) evaluations to obtain similar results as those produced by VIS (see Table 4). This is due to two reasons: 1) PAIA only preserves necessary Abs during each iteration step so that only the necessary evaluations are carried out; 2) PAIA uses adaptive clone size so that only the necessary clone size is assigned to each selected Ab. One can see from Fig. 2 (c) that in most cases the clone size is 1. While on the other hand, VIS and most previous works use a fixed clone size (4 in VIS). This generally leads to two main problems: 1) in the early stage, a fixed clone size may not be large enough to speed up the convergence; 2) in the later stage, a fixed clone size may be too large so that at each iteration step many unnecessary clones are produced.

Table 4. Mean and variance values of GD and Δ for PAIA and VIS

Algorithm	ZDT1		ZDT2		ZDT3		ZDT4	
	GD	σ^2	GD	σ^2	GD	σ^2	GD	σ^2
VIS	1.32e-4	1.12e-9	1.10e-4	2.2e-12	1.23e-4	1.9e-11	1.23e-3	1.12e-6
PAIA	1.58e-4	2.31e-9	1.06e-4	5.7e-11	1.58e-4	4.6e-10	4.96e-4	1.53e-8
Algorithm	Δ	σ^2	Δ	σ^2	Δ	σ^2	Δ	σ^2
VIS	0.3142	6.31e-4	0.2123	3.12e-3	0.3451	1.22e-3	0.0834	1.12e-4
PAIA	0.3522	1.10e-3	0.3443	1.50e-3	0.4381	1.50e-3	0.3058	1.00e-3

Table 5. Final population size and evaluation times of PAIA and VIS

Test suite	Final Population		Evaluation Times	
	PAIA(mean)	VIS	PAIA(mean)	VIS
ZDT1	93	100	15844	28523
ZDT2	95	100	15856	29312
ZDT3	94	100	25365	32436
ZDT4	97	100	46899	38956

5 Discussions

5.1 The Differences Between AIS and Population-Based GA

It is clear that the proposed algorithm-PAIA offers significant advantages. However, as already stated in Section 1, presenting comparative good results is not the main objective of this study. It was felt that only when the differences between AIS and traditional population-based GAs are clarified, can one fully exploit the extra advantages that are exclusively included in AIS. The fundamental differences can be summarized as follows:

1. **Reproduction mechanism:** AIS represents a type of asexual reproduction; while on the other hand, population-based GA represents the counterpart. Through the latter, the offspring is produced by crossing the chromosomes of both parents. Through the former, each Ab copies itself to produce many clones.
2. **Selection scheme:** For population-based GA, good solutions are selected into the mating pool with high probability. For AIS, good solutions are always selected.
3. **Evolution strategy:** For population-based GA, the whole population evolves by using crossover. The hypothesis is that if both parents are the good ones their crossed offspring would have a high probability of becoming even better solutions; mutation is only used to jump out of the local optima (diversity is very important), otherwise, GA is likely to lead to premature convergence; for AIS, since clones are

duplicates of their predecessors the evolution of the population depends on muta-tion of the clones.

4. **Elitism:** For population-based GA, during each generation, the whole population is replaced with the offspring after mating; so 'elitism' has to be introduced to pre-serve good solutions found so far, otherwise they would be lost during generations; for AIS, the mutated clones and their predecessors are mixed together to compete for survival, so the 'elitism' is inherently embedded in AIS

5. **Population control:** For the population-based GA, since one has to specify the size of the mating pool in the first place the population size is thus fixed during each generation; if one only selects good solutions into the mating pool and makes the pool size flexible to the number of selected solutions GA could end up reaching premature convergence due to its evolutionary strategy; a reasonable pool size is necessary so that in the early stages sub-optimal solutions can also be included in the pool to increase population diversity; for AIS, a mating pool does not exist hence the population can be flexible and finally controlled by the mutual influences of Abs.

5.2   Extra Strength of AIS

If one recognizes all these differences AIS should offer extra strengths, which have been implemented in PAIA and are summarized as follows:

1. **Adaptive population.** Network suppression was first proposed in [3] to perform data analysis. In PAIA, it is used to regulate the population. The main point is that: it allows any selected Ab to get into to the population as long as it is far enough from any other Ab. This flexible rather than fixed population plus adaptive clone size make the population adaptive in the problem.

2. **Initial population size is not crucial to the success of PAIA.** Due to the nature of the adaptive population, whatever initial size is used the population can be adap-tively adjusted to a reasonable size according to the need of the problem. Although the results are not shown in this paper, in other experiments it was found that one can use any number as the initial population size (even 1) and the results in terms of performance metrics are equivalently good as the ones presented in this paper. The only difference is if an optimal initial size is chosen the evaluations can be largely reduced.

3. **Fast convergence.** In PAIA, even a small initial size (e.g. 7) can give a very fast convergence because one only selects good Abs and let them reproduce with an adaptive clone size. In the early iterations this cannot only provide sufficient Abs to support the search but also accelerates the convergence.

4. **Only necessary evaluations are exercised.** Since only a necessary population size and clones are maintained and produced in each iteration step, only necessary evaluations are carried out. One can see from Table 5 that PAIA used 46899 evaluations to converge for ZDT4. If one uses the same setting for NSGA II (a population of 100 and 500 generations) 50000 evaluations would be needed.

5. **Parameter less.** The only parameter crucial to the success of PAIA is the way to calculate the mutation rate. However, an adequate combination of parameters can efficiently tackle this problem (using a fewer evaluations).

5.3 MOP-Ideal Test Bed for Immune Mechanism Simulation

Figure 2 (b) is a reflection of the immune response from Ab when stimulated by Ag. It can be seen that the population (Ab concentration) keeps increasing with the presence of antigenic stimulus until a stable concentration level is achieved. If without local extrema, then a problem (i.e. ZDT1~ZDT3) can be regarded as an unvaccinated immune system (whose Ab concentration bears characteristics illustrated in the first three graphs in Figure 2 (b), and such a characteristic is seen as primary immune response). On the other hand, when a problem has many local extrema and these extrema share some resemblances (ZDT4), it corresponds to an immune system with continuous vaccinations. As in the last graph of Figure 2 (b), the Ab concentration initially reacts as a primary response, however, in the following vaccinations the peak values match each set of extrema and this is recognized here as secondary response. Therefore, if a test problem is adequately designed according to the above principle, MOP will be an ideal test bed for the immune mechanism simulations.

6 Conclusions and Further Research

Our conclusion is that, as a solution to a MOP, AIS offers advantages over traditional population-based GA schemes. Such superiority is based on the fact that AIS is inspired by a different regime of natural mechanisms. As a result, one could identify two directions for future research; one is to improve PAIA such as its mutation operator and termination condition. The other is to further compare and understand the differences between AIS and GA so that one can be confident in deciding which one is more suitable to handle a specific problem.

Acknowledgements

The authors would like to thank Dr. Fabio Freschi for his kind help in providing the results of applying VIS to the ZDT1~ZDT4 test suite.

References

1. Ishida, Y.: Fully Distributed Diagnosis by PDP Learning Algorithm: Towards Immune Network PDP Model. Proc. of the IEEE International Joint Conference on Neural Networks. San Diego, USA (1990) 777-782
2. Forrest, S., Perelson, A. S., Allen, L., Cherukuri, R.: Self-Nonself Discrimination in a Computer. Proc. Of IEEE Symposium on Research in Security and Privacy. Oakland, USA (1994) 202-212
3. de Castro, L. N., Von Zuben, F. J.: aiNet: An Artificial Immune Network for Data Analysis In: Abbass, H. A., Sarker, R. A., Newton, C. S. (eds.): Data Mining: A Heuristic Approach. Idea Group Publishing, USA (2001) 231-259
4. Timmis, J.: Artificial Immune Systems: A Novel Data Analysis Technique Inspired by the Immune Network Theory. PhD Dissertation, Department of Computer Science, University of Wales (2000)

5. de Castro, L. N., Timmis, J.: An Artificial Immune Network for Multimodal Function Op timization. Proc. Of the IEEE Congress on Evolutionary Computation (CEC' 2002), Vol. 1. Honolulu, Hawaii (2002) 699-704

6. Kelsey, J., Timmis, J.: Immune Inspired Somatic Contiguous Hypermutation for Function Optimization. In: Cantu-Paz, E. et al. (eds.): Proc. of Genetic and Evolutionary Computation Conference (GECCO). Lecture Notes in Computer Science, Vol. 2723. Springer Berlin/Heidelberg (2003) 207-218

7. Freschi, F.: Multi-Objective Artificial Immune System for Optimization in Electrical Engineering. PhD Thesis, Politecnico di Torino, Department of Electrical Engineering, Torino, Italy (2006)

8. Yoo, J., Hajela, P.: Immune Network Simulations in Multicriterion Design. Structural Optimization, Vol. 18 (1999) 85-94

9. Cruz Cortes, N., Coello Coello, C. A.: Multiobjective Optimization Using Ideas from the Clonal Selection Principle. In: Cantu-Paz, E. et al. (eds.): Genetic and Evolutionary Computation (GECCO'2003). Lecture Notes in Computer Science, Vol. 2723. Springer Berlin/Heidelberg (2003) 158-170

10. Coello Coello, C. A., Cruz Cortes, N.: Solving Multiobjective Optimization Problems Using an Artificial Immune System. Genetic Programming and Evolvable Machines, Vol. 6, No. 2. Springer Netherlands (2005) 163-190

11. Wang, X. L., Mahfouf, M.: ACSAMO: An Adaptive Multiobjective Optimization Algorithm using the Clonal Selection Principle. The First European Symposium on Nature-inspired Smart Information Systems. Albufeira, Portugal (2005)

12. Jiao, L. C., Gong, M. G., Shang, R. H.: Clonal Selection with Immune Dominance and Anergy Based Multiobjective Optimization. In: Coello Coello, C. A. et al. (eds.): Proc. of the Third International Conference on Evolutionary Multi-Criterion Optimization (EMO'2005). Lecture Notes in Computer Science, Vol. 3410. Springer Berlin/Heidelberg (2005) 474-489

13. Burnet, F. M.: The Clonal Selection Theory of Acquired Immunity. Cambridge at the University Press, UK (1959)

14. Jerne, N. K.: Towards a Network Theory of the Immune System. Ann. Immunology (Inst. Pasteur), Vol. 125C (1974) 373-389

15. Perelson, A. S.: Immune Network Theory. Immunological Review, Vol. 110 (1989) 5-36

16. Deb, K.: Multi-Objective Optimization using Evolutionary Algorithms. Chichester, U.K.: Wiley (2001)

17. Goldberg, D. E.: Genetic Algorithms for Search, Optimization, and Machine Learning. Reading, MA: Addison-Wesley (1989)

18. de Castro, L. N., Von Zuben, F. J.: artificial Immune Systems: Part I-Basic Theory and Applications. Technical Report, TR-DCA 02/00. School of Computing and Electrical Engineering, State University of Campinas, Brazil (1999)

19. Farmer, J. D., Packard, N. H.: The Immune System, Adaptation, and Machine Learning. Physica, Vol. 22D. North-Holland, Amsterdam (1986) 187-204

20. Smith, R. E., Dike, B. A., Stegmann, S. A.: Fitness Inheritance in Genetic Algorithms. Proc. of ACM Symposiums on Applied Computing (ACM'95) (1995) 345-350

21. Zitzer, E., Thiele, L.: An Evolutionary Algorithm for Multi-objective Optimization: The Strength Pareto Approach. TIK-Report, No. 43. Computer Engineering and Communication Networks Lab (TIK), Swiss Federal Institute of Technology, Switzerland (1998)

omni-aiNet: An Immune-Inspired Approach for Omni Optimization

Guilherme P. Coelho and Fernando J. Von Zuben

Laboratory of Bioinformatics and Bioinspired Computing - LBiC
Department of Computer Engineering and Industrial Automation - DCA
School of Electrical and Computer Engineering - FEEC
University of Campinas - UNICAMP
PO Box 6101, 13083-970 Campinas, SP, Brazil
{gcoelho, vonzuben}@dca.fee.unicamp.br

Abstract. This work presents omni-aiNet, an immune-inspired algorithm developed to solve single and multi-objective optimization problems, either with single and multi-global solutions. The search engine
is capable of automatically adapting the exploration of the search space
according to the intrinsic demand of the optimization problem. This proposal unites the concepts of omni-optimization, already proposed in the
literature, with distinctive procedures associated with immune-inspired
concepts. Due to the immune inspiration, the omni-aiNet presents a population capable of adjusting its size during the execution of the algorithm,
according to a predefined suppression threshold, and a new grid mechanism to control the spread of solutions in the objective space. The omni-
aiNet was applied to several optimization problems and the obtained
results are presented and analyzed.

1 Introduction

During the last decades, the optimization field has been benefited from the continued sprouting of efficient optimization algorithms. These algorithms have been
applied to an expressive number of different real-world problems, leading to very
encouraging results. However, optimization problems appear in different types
and forms: some may have a single objective (known as single-objective optimization problems); some may have multiple conflicting objectives (known as
multi-objective optimization problems); some problems may have only one global
optimum, requiring the task of finding this optimum; and other problems may
contain more than one global optimum in the search space, thereby requiring the
task of simultaneously finding multiple global optimal solutions. This variability
in features and objectives guided to the proposition of algorithms specialized in
each kind of problem, what forced users to know different algorithms in order to
solve different kinds of optimization problems.

A straight attempt to revert this tendency was made by Deb and Tiwari
[8]. In their work, they propose and evaluate a single evolutionary optimization
algorithm for solving different kinds of function optimization problems: single or

H. Bersini and J. Carneiro (Eds.): ICARIS 2006, LNCS 4163, pp. 294–308, 2006.

multi-objective problems and uni or multi-global problems. The proposed *omni-optimizer* algorithm, hereafter denoted DT omni-optimizer, is mainly based on a *ranking* procedure that uses a modified *constrained dominance* principle and adapts itself to solve different kinds of problems. Further explanation of this ranking procedure will be given in Section 4.

In the field of evolutionary computation, a relatively novel computational paradigm, namely Artificial Immune System (AIS), was originated from attempts to model and apply immunological principles to problem solving in a wide range of areas such as optimization, data mining, computer security and robotics [4]. Three advantages of advanced AISs over other population-based strategies are: (*i*) they are inherently able to maintain population diversity (modules with some resemblance with niching and fitness sharing are intrinsic parts of the algorithm); (*ii*) the size of the population at each generation is automatically defined according to the demands of the application; and (*iii*) local optimal solutions are simultaneously preserved once located.

Based on the successful application of AISs to several kinds of function optimization problems ([3], [5] and [7]), this work presents a novel proposal called *omni-aiNet*, which unites the flexibility given by the principles of the DT omni-optimizer [8] with the intrinsic advantages of AISs over other population-based strategies. The results obtained with this basic version of omni-aiNet indicated that the algorithm is very effective to deal with demanding scenarios, although some improvements are still required.

This paper is organized as follows. Section 2 presents a brief introduction to the concepts of AISs and the main immunological theories that inspired the proposed algorithm. Section 3 introduces some formalism of function optimization and depicts the notation that will be used throughout the paper. Section 4 presents and details the proposed algorithm, and Section 5 outlines a brief conceptual comparison between omni-aiNet and the DT omni-optimizer [8]. The description of the experiments and the presentation of the obtained results are fulfilled in Section 6. Finally, Section 7 draws some concluding remarks.

2   Artificial Immune Systems

The natural immune system can be considered one of the most important components of superior living organisms. The permanent cycle of recognition and combat against pathogens (infectious foreign elements) has the goal of keeping the organism healthy. The molecular patterns expressed in those invading pathogens or *antigens* are responsible for triggering the immune response when properly recognized by the immune cells.

Some of the cells with major roles in the immune response are the *lymphocytes*, which can be divided into two types: B lymphocytes (B cells) and T lymphocytes (T cells). The present description will focus only on the B cells. When an antigen is detected, the B cells that best recognize the antigen (best *affinity*) will proliferate by cloning. Some of the clones will differentiate into *plasma cells* (the main *antibody secretors*) while the others will differentiate into *memory cells*. These *memory cells* guarantee a faster response to similar antigens that may invade the organism in the future. After the cloning phase, the new generated cells suffer a process of *hypermutation* with variation rates inversely proportional to each cell affinity to the antigen (the highest affinity cells suffer the lowest variation and vice-versa). The resulting cells with best affinity are subsequently selected to remain in the B cell population, while the cells with lower affinity and cells that have become harmful to the organism after the hypermutation are eliminated.

This cloning and hypermutation processes are essential parts of the *Clonal Selection Principle* [2]. This principle is one of the main inspirations of the proposed algorithm.

Another important immune concept is the *Immune Network Theory* proposed by Jerne [11]. This theory states that antibodies are not only capable of recognizing antigens, but they are also capable of recognizing each other. When an antibody is recognized by another one, it is suppressed. This mechanism allows the immune system to remain in a dynamic equilibrium and to respond accordingly to each external stimuli (antigen invasion).

Founded on the *Immune Network Theory* and on the *Clonal Selection Principle*, the self-maintenance of diversity in the population and the simultaneous search for multiple high-quality solutions are distinctive aspects of immune-inspired algorithms devoted to the solution of optimization problems.

The omni-aiNet algorithm is proposed here as a new member of the aiNet family of algorithms, which consists of four immune inspired algorithms. The first algorithm, aiNet (Artificial Immune Network) was proposed by de Castro and Von Zuben in [6] to perform data analysis and clustering tasks. In a subsequent work, de Castro and Timmis developed a version of aiNet for multimodal optimization problems, called opt-aiNet (Artificial Immune Network for Optimization) [5]. The third algorithm, copt-aiNet was further proposed by Gomes *et al.* in [9] as an extension of opt-aiNet for combinatorial optimization tasks. The fourth algorithm, dopt-aiNet (Artificial Immune Network for Dynamic Optimization) [7], is an improved and extended version of opt-aiNet for time-varying fitness functions. In all works, the authors demonstrated empirically the suitability of the cited algorithms for each kind of optimization problem, with competitive results when compared to the literature. The essence of the proposal presented in this work, omni-aiNet (Artificial Immune Network for Omni-optimization), is mainly based on opt-aiNet, but incorporates some mechanisms introduced by dopt-aiNet.

3   Basic Optimization Concepts

The main goal of this section is to formalize the kind of problems that will be treated in this work and to give definitions of some concepts commonly adopted in optimization (specially multi-objective optimization) that will be used in the remaining parts of the paper.

In this work, all problems that will be treated by omni-aiNet will be considered as a constrained M-objective ($M \geq 1$) minimization problem as follows:

$$\text{Minimize } (f_1(x), f_2(x), \ldots f_M(x)),$$

$$\begin{aligned}
\text{Subject to} \quad & g_j(x) \geq 0, & j = 1, 2, \ldots, J, \\
& h_k(x) = 0, & k = 1, 2, \ldots, K, \\
& x_i^L \leq x_i \leq x_i^U, & i = 1, 2, \ldots, n,
\end{aligned} \tag{1}$$

where n is the number of variables (dimension of the problem), J is the number of inequality constraints, K is the number of equality constraints, x_i^L is the lower bound of variable i and x_i^U is the upper bound of variable i. The only mandatory constraints for the algorithm are the bounds of the search space (x_i^L and x_i^U).

For the problem given in Formulation 1, n-variable solution vectors that satisfy all constraints are called *feasible* solutions. These solutions will be optimal if they individually satisfy a number of Karush-Kuhn-Tucker optimality conditions, which involves finding the gradients of objective and constraint functions [1].

When we have a single objective f, the optimal solutions correspond to the points that have the smallest values of f, considering the whole search space (in a minimization problem). However, for several objective functions, the notion of "optimal" solution changes, because the aim now is to find good trade-offs among the objective functions. In this case, the most commonly adopted notion of optimality is the one associated with the *Pareto front*. A solution x^* belongs to the Pareto front if there is no other feasible solution x capable of minimizing an objective without simultaneously increasing at least one of the others.

Other important concepts that will be frequently used in this work are *Pareto dominance* and *Pareto optimal set*. For the *Pareto dominance*, a vector $u = (u_1, \ldots, u_k)$ is said to dominate a vector $v = (v_1, \ldots, v_k)$ (denoted by $u \preceq v$) if and only if $\forall i \in \{1, \ldots, k\}, u_i \leq v_i$ and $\exists i \in \{1, \ldots, k\} : u_i < v_i$.

The *Pareto optimal set* for a multi-objective optimization problem $f(x)$ is given by $\wp^* := \{x \in \Omega \mid \neg \exists\, x' \in \Omega\ f(x') \preceq f(x)\}$, where Ω is the domain of x.

Therefore, the *Pareto front* ($\wp_F$) for a given $f(x)$ and $\wp^*$ is defined as $\wp_F := \{u = f = (f_1(x), \ldots, f_M(x)) \mid x \in \wp^*\}$.

4 The omni-aiNet Algorithm

The omni-aiNet algorithm works with a real-coded population of antibodies that correspond to the candidate solutions for the optimization problem. The concept of a population of antigens is not explicitly used, once only the affinity measures (value of the objective functions being optimized) are available. The omni-aiNet basically follows the same main steps of the opt-aiNet algorithm [5], as can be seen in Figure 1. However, the essential aspects of each step are different. Additionally, to increase the convergence capability of the algorithm, it was added a variation mechanism known as *Gene Duplication*, which will be described in Section 4.3.

The algorithm starts by randomly generating an initial population of size N_i (N_i is defined by the user). Each individual generated is within the range of the variables. After the creation of the initial population, the algorithm enters a

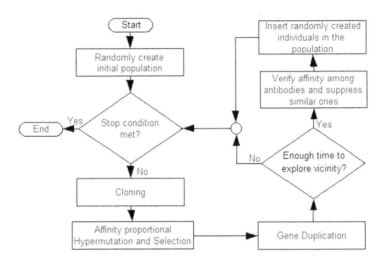

Fig. 1. Main steps of omni-aiNet

loop where the stop criterion is the number of generations (also defined by the user). Within this loop, the main steps of the algorithm are executed: Cloning, Hypermutation, Selection and Gene Duplication. The suppression of individuals and insertion of new randomly generated ones are made from N_{gs} to N_{gs} generations (N_{gs} is defined by the user). The value of N_{gs} should be greater than one to give enough time for the algorithm to explore the vicinity of each solution before the suppression of similar individuals.

The following Subsections will present a detailed description of the main steps presented in Figure 1.

4.1   Cloning and Hypermutation

The first step of each generation of the algorithm is the *cloning* phase. In this phase, for all individuals in the antibody population, N_c identical copies (clones) are generated. The parameter N_c must be defined by the user. Then, this population of clones suffer a process of genetic variability known as *hypermutation*.

The hypermutation mechanism applies to each generated clone, a random variation with rates inversely proportional to its affinity to the antigen (also known as its *fitness*). In this algorithm, it was adopted the *polynomial mutation* mechanism, where a new individual is given by $c' = c + \gamma \times \Delta_{max}$, with c the parent individual, c' the new clone, and Δ_{max} the maximum shift that the individual can suffer in direction γ without violating the domain of the variables. The value of γ is given by:

$$\gamma = \begin{cases} (2u)^{\frac{1}{\eta+1}} - 1, & \text{if } u < 0.5 \\ 1 - [2(1-u)]^{\frac{1}{\eta+1}}, & \text{if } u \geq 0.5 \end{cases} \tag{2}$$

where u is a random number with uniform distribution in $[0, 1]$.

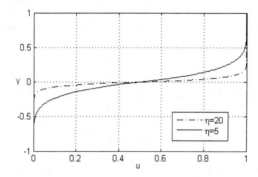

Fig. 2. The influence of η over γ, as a function of u

The parameter η is responsible for the amplitude of the mutation and is defined according to each individual (parent antibody) fitness. Several tests were made and it was empirically defined that $\eta \in [5, 20]$, which makes γ vary with u (u is a random number) in the region between the two boundaries (dashed and full curves) in Figure 2.

Since it is desired a mutation rate inversely proportional to the fitness, before the cloning process the population of antibodies is ranked and divided into ordered classes (as will be explained in Subsection 4.2). The individuals of the first class receive the value $\eta = 20$ (smaller variation), the individuals of the last class receive $\eta = 5$ (greater variation) and the individuals of the remaining classes receive η values equispaced in $[5, 20]$, always giving higher values of η to individuals in the best classes (better individuals).

4.2 Selection, Ranking and Grid Processes

After the cloning and hypermutation phases, the algorithm has now a population of size $N' = N + N \times N_c$ (where N is the size of the original population and N_c is the number of clones per individual). From this population, the N best individuals should be selected to constitute the new antibody population. This selection phase is described in Algorithm 1.

Algorithm 1. Pseudo-code for the selection phase.

$[F_1, F_2, \ldots] \leftarrow \text{ranking}(P_t);$ ▷ Best class in F_1 and so on.
$P_{t+1} \leftarrow \emptyset;$ ▷ Initializing the new population
$j \leftarrow 1;$
while $|P_{t+1} \bigcup F_j| \leq N$ **do**
     $P_{t+1} \leftarrow P_{t+1} \bigcup F_j;$ ▷ Inserts the j-th class in the population
     $j \leftarrow j + 1;$
end while
$L \leftarrow j;$ ▷ Last class to be included (partially)
$rem \leftarrow N - |P_{t+1}|;$ ▷ Num. of individuals that still can be inserted in the pop.
$P_g \leftarrow \text{grid}(F_L, rem);$ ▷ Selection of the remaining individuals
$P_{t+1} \leftarrow P_{t+1} \bigcup P_g;$

In the above pseudo-code, the first step is to rank the population of clones and parents into ordered classes, according to the "quality" of each individual. This measure of "quality" of each individual can be given by the concept of *constrained ϵ-dominance*, originally proposed by [8].

The term ϵ-dominance is a modification of the concept of Pareto Dominance presented in Section 3. A vector $\boldsymbol{u} = (u_1, \ldots, u_k)$ is said to ϵ-dominate a vector $\boldsymbol{v} = (v_1, \ldots, v_k)$ if and only if $\forall i \in \{1, \ldots, k\}, u_i \leq v_i$ and $\exists i \in \{1, \ldots, k\} :$ $u_i < v_i - \epsilon_i$. The parameter ϵ is calculated from a user-defined parameter δ as in $\epsilon_i = \delta \times (maxValue_i - minValue_i)$, where $maxValue_i$ is the maximum value for coordinate i and $minValue_i$ is the minimum value for coordinate i. In this context, it is said that a solution $\mathbf{i}$ *constrained ϵ-dominates* a solution $\mathbf{j}$ if any of the following conditions are true: (*i*) solution $\mathbf{i}$ is feasible and solution $\mathbf{j}$ is not feasible; (*ii*) both solutions $\mathbf{i}$ and $\mathbf{j}$ are NOT feasible but solution $\mathbf{i}$ has a smaller *constraint violation* than solution $\mathbf{j}$; and (*iii*) both solutions $\mathbf{i}$ and $\mathbf{j}$ are feasible and solution $\mathbf{i}$ ϵ-dominates solution $\mathbf{j}$.

The *constraint violation* for a solution a is given by $CV(a) = \sum_{j=1}^{J} \gamma(g_j(a)) + \sum_{k=1}^{K} |h_k(a)|$, where $h_k(a)$ is the value of the k-th equality constraint for solution a, $g_j(a)$ is the value of the j-th inequality constraint for solution a, $\gamma(g_j(a)) = 0$ if $g_j(a) > 0$ and $\gamma(g_j(a)) = |g_j(a)|$ if $g_j(a) \leq 0$.

In this context, the *ranking* procedure divides the population allocating to Class one the solutions in the population that are not constrained ϵ-dominated by any other solution, to Class two the solutions constrained ϵ-dominated only by the solutions in Class one, and so on. Given that the ranking is made over the parents and mutated clones, and the best classes are defined first, the algorithm is then capable of implementing an elitism within a single population, without the need of an auxiliary population as many multi-objective optimization algorithms do.

Frequently in the selection process, the number of individuals in the class to be inserted into the population is greater than the remaining "vacancies" (the number of individuals that are still allowed to enter the population). Under these circumstances, the algorithm must find another way to select individuals expressing the same performance according to the ranking mechanism. In omni-aiNet, a *grid* procedure is proposed. This procedure selects N_r solutions from a given class F_L. To do so, it detects the kind of problem being optimized (single or multi-objective) and works on each axis (dimension) of the variable space (for single-objective problems) or of the objective space (for multi-objective problems), selecting the $N_a = N_r/N_{axis}$ (where N_{axis} is the dimension of the variable or objective space) more spaced solutions. For each axis, the procedure finds the maximum and minimum solutions and divides the interval between these extreme values into N_a *cells* and selects the N_a solutions closest to the center of each cell. This procedure tries to keep the solutions spread in the variable or objective space, therefore contributing to the diversity of solutions in the population.

4.3 Gene Duplication

Besides the polynomial hypermutation, the omni-aiNet algorithm also incorporates a second technique of genetic variation, known as *Gene Duplication*. This mutation consists of the duplication of parts of the elements in the DNA chain during the chromosome reading. According to Ohno [12] and Holland et al. [10], this mutation has an important role in the evolution of species.

This mechanism has already been proposed by de França et al. [7] as a relevant operator in dopt-aiNet. Basically, it randomly selects a coordinate i of the antibody and replaces every element in the remaining coordinates by x_i whenever this replacement improves the performance of the antibody.

4.4 Suppression, Binary Tournament and Random Insertion

The main goal of the *Suppression* phase of the algorithm is to eliminate redundancy among individuals in the population and to maintain diversity when associated with the insertion of new randomly generated individuals in the population (*Random Insertion*).

In the Suppression phase, the Euclidean distance in the variable space among every individual in the population is calculated and normalized with respect to the maximum distance found so far. In this context, the individuals close enough to each other according to a suppression threshold (defined by the user) are subject to a *Binary Tournament* procedure and the worst one is eliminated from the population.

This Binary Tournament follows basically the same criteria used in the ranking procedure, which means that a given solution **i** is preferred to a solution **j** if (i) **i** is feasible and **j** is not feasible; (ii) **i** has a smaller Constraint Violation than **j** and both are not feasible; and (iii) both solutions are feasible and **i** ϵ-dominates **j**. If both solutions are feasible and there is no ϵ-dominance among then, the winner solution is randomly selected.

The Random Insertion is a mechanism that contributes to the diversity of the population by inserting N_{rand} new individuals randomly generated into the population (N_{rand} must also be defined by the user).

The Suppression and Random Insertion steps of the algorithm, together with cloning and hypermutation phases, are also responsible for other important characteristic of omni-aiNet: the dynamic variation of the population size. The algorithm is then allowed to define a proper number of antibodies in the population at each iteration, according to the specified suppression threshold.

5 Comparative Analysis

This section presents a brief conceptual and comparative analysis between omni-aiNet and Deb and Tiwari's omni-optimizer (DT omni-optimizer) [8]. Besides the distinct bio-inspiration, the omni-aiNet and the DT omni-optimizer algorithms present several conceptual differences that may lead each algorithm to perform differently according to the characteristics of the problems being treated.

The most evident difference between omni-aiNet and DT omni-optimizer is that the latter works with a population of fixed size, while omni-aiNet can adjust the number of individuals according to each problem and to the suppression threshold defined by the user. This characteristic gives more flexibility to the search engine, once the algorithm automatically adjusts the number of individuals, providing a better allocation of computational resources.

Although both algorithms use the polynomial mutation as one of the mechanisms of genetic variability, the probability of activation of this mechanism is much smaller in the DT omni-optimizer than in omni-aiNet, once the latter presents a polynomial hypermutation as its main mechanism of genetic variability. Also, omni-aiNet automatically determines the parameter η according to the ranking of each individual, while in the DT algorithm this parameter is defined by the user. The other mechanisms of genetic variability are also different in both algorithms: DT presents crossover between the individuals in the population, while omni-aiNet presents gene duplication.

The last main difference between both algorithms is associated with the way each omni-optimizer treats the diversity and spacing of solution in both variable and objective spaces. While omni-aiNet presents the mechanisms of Suppression, Random Insertion and Grid, described in Sections 4.2 to 4.4, the DT algorithm uses a metric of *Crowding Distance* to select the individuals with greater distances from their neighbours in variable and objective space (further information about this metric and procedure can be found in [8]).

Both algorithms present the same number of parameters to be adjusted by the user: omni-aiNet demands the proper tuning of the size of initial population, number of generations, number of generations between suppressions, number of clones per individual, number of randomly generated individuals, suppression threshold and δ; while the DT omni-optimizer requires the definition of the size of initial population, number of generations, distribution index for crossover, probability of crossover, distribution index for mutation, probability of mutation and δ. More information about these parameters can be found in [8].

6   Experimental Results

This section presents the results of the preliminary experiments with the omni-aiNet algorithm. Special attention will be devoted to multi-objective problems, so that single objective instances (uni and multi-global) are incorporated only to indicate the ability to perform omni-optimization.

For the multi-objective problems, the omni-aiNet algorithm was compared to the original version of the omni-optimizer algorithm, proposed by Deb and Tiwari [8] (DT omni-optimizer) and kindly provided by the authors, and the comparative results are presented in Subsections 6.3 and 6.4. Once Deb and Tiwari's software package does not provide the number of fitness evaluations per iteration, the comparison will be founded on the capability to reproduce the Pareto front, and whenever an equivalence exists between parameters, they will receive the same settings. For the non-equivalent parameters, the DT omni-optimizer was run with simulated binary crossover (with $\eta_c = 20$), polynomial mutation (with $\eta_m = 20$), crossover probability of 0.8 and mutation probability of $1/n$ (where n is the number of variables) for all problems. The population size and number of iterations depends on the problem and will be given in what follows. In all simulations in Subsections 6.3 and 6.4, omni-aiNet has always been run with the number of generations and individuals in the initial population smaller than or equal to the ones adopted for the DT omni-optimizer.

6.1 Single-Objective Uni-global Problem

The omni-aiNet algorithm was applied to the following single objective uni-global constrained test problem:

$$\text{Minimize} \quad f(x) = \exp(x),$$
$$\text{Subject to } g(x) = \exp(x) - 5 \geq 0, \tag{3}$$
$$0 \leq x \leq 3,$$

This problem has a single optima located at $x = 1.609$. The omni-aiNet could successfully find this global solution. The simulation was made with the following parameters: initial population of 20 individuals, 20 generations, 10 generations between suppressions, 5 individuals in Random Insertion, a suppression threshold of 0.01, 5 clones per individual and $\delta = 0$.

The main aspect to be emphasized here is that the population converges to a single individual (global solution), indicating that the algorithm is capable of automatically adjusting the amount of computational resources to the kind of problem being treated.

6.2 Single-Objective Multi-global Problems

In this section, two single-objective multi-global problems were considered. The first problem is a single variable problem having 21 different global optimal solutions and given by:

$$\text{Minimize } f(x) = \sin^2(\pi x), \ x \in [0, 20]. \tag{4}$$

For this problem, eight simulations were made with an initial population of 60 individuals, for 50 generations (being 10 the number of generations between suppressions), with 20 individuals in Random Insertion, a suppression threshold of 0.01, 10 clones per individual and $\delta = 0.05$. The final ϵ-nondominated solutions for one of these simulations (24 solutions in the final population) are presented in Figure 3-a. The omni-aiNet algorithm found an average of 19.75 ± 0.71 of the 21 global optimal solutions of this problem, and kept in the final population an average of 22.63 ± 1.93 individuals. The average number of individuals in the final populations were higher than the average number of global solutions found because some non-optimal individuals presented distances from the other elements in the population greater than the defined suppression threshold, which prevented their suppression.

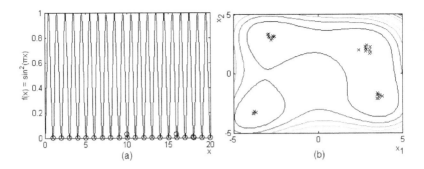

Fig. 3. The final ϵ-nondominated solutions for (a) $f(x) = \sin^2(\pi x)$ and (b) Himmelblau's function

The second problem is known as Himmelblau's function and is given by:

$$\text{Minimize } f(x_1, x_2) = (x_1^2 + x_2 - 11)^2 + (x_1 + x_2^2 - 7)^2, \quad -5 \leq x_1, x_2 \leq 5. \quad (5)$$

For this problem, there are four minima, each having a functional value equal to zero. As can be seen in Figure 3-b, the regions of these minima concentrated the final solutions found by the algorithm (31 solutions). The parameters used were 60 generations, 50 individuals in the initial population, 20 individuals in Random Insertion, a suppression threshold of 0.005, 5 clones per individual and $\delta = 0.05$. During the execution of omni-aiNet, the population size decreased with the convergence of the algorithm, finishing with 31 individuals (including the four solutions) whose distance among each other is within the predefined suppression threshold.

Again, the results presented in Figure 3 seems very promising, once for both problems the algorithm was capable of identifying the global solutions with a fine tuning of the population size according to the demand.

6.3 Multi-objective Uni-global Problems

Two problems were selected as test functions for the multi-objective uni-global problem category: the 30-variable ZDT1 test function, that has a convex Pareto Front and the 30-variable ZDT2 test function, that is the nonconvex counterpart to ZDT1. The details of each problem can be found in [13]. Figures 4 and 5 present the true Pareto front (solid lines) and the Pareto front found by (a) the omni-aiNet; and (b) DT omni-optimizer algorithm for problems ZDT1 and ZDT2, respectively. The parameters used for omni-aiNet were 50 generations, 100 individuals in the initial population, 10 generations between suppressions, 5 individuals in Random Insertion, a suppression threshold of 0.001, 3 clones per individual and $\delta = 0.01$. For the DT omni-optimizer, it was used $\delta = 0.01$, 100 generations and a population of 100 individuals.

As can be seen in Figures 4 and 5, for both problems the omni-aiNet produced a final population of solutions much closer to the real Pareto front and with a better coverage of this front than the DT omni-optimizer.

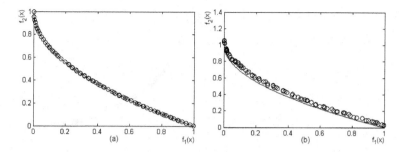

Fig. 4. The final ε-nondominated solutions for ZDT1 problem, obtained by (a) omni-aiNet (79 solutions) and (b) DT omni-optimizer.

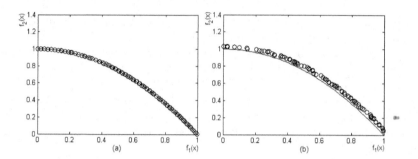

Fig. 5. The final ε-nondominated solutions for ZDT2 problem, obtained by (a) omni-aiNet (92 solutions) and (b) DT omni-optimizer

6.4 Multi-objective Multi-global Problem

The multi-objective multi-global problem used in this work was designed by Deb and Tiwari in [8] and is given by:

$$\text{Minimize } f_1(x) = \sum_{i=1}^{5} \sin(\pi x_i),$$
$$f_2(x) = \sum_{i=1}^{5} \cos(\pi x_i), \qquad (6)$$
$$\text{subject to} \quad 0 \leq x_i \leq 6$$

Both objectives of this problem are periodic functions with period 2, such that Pareto optimal solutions correspond to $x_i \in [2m + 1, \ 2m + 3/2]$, where m is an integer. Figure 6 presents the ε-nondominated solutions obtained by (a) omni-aiNet and (b) DT omni-optimizer. The omni-aiNet parameters were 100 generations, 400 individuals in the initial population, 3 generations between suppressions, 200 individuals in Random Insertion, a suppression threshold of 0.006, 2 clones per individual and $\delta = 0.001$. For this problem, the obtained results for DT omni-optimizer were achieved with $\delta = 0.001$, 100 generations and a population of 400 individuals.

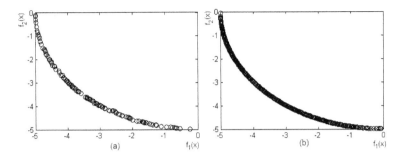

Fig. 6. The final ε-nondominated solutions for the multi-objective multi-global problem, obtained by (a) omni-aiNet (212 solutions) and (b) DT omni-optimizer

As can be seen in Figure 6, the omni-aiNet had problems in covering the whole Pareto front, specially in the region close to $f_1(x) = 0$. Moreover, it can be said that the DT omni-optimizer also presented a smoother coverage of the Pareto front than the one presented by omni-aiNet, what can be assigned to its larger final population.

Figure 7 presents the solutions obtained by the optimizers in the variable space. This figure illustrates the multimodality of this problem, once distinct points in the variable space can be mapped to the same point in the Pareto front.

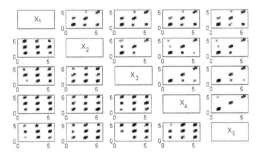

Fig. 7. Pareto optimal solutions with DT omni-optimizer (lower-left) and omni-aiNet (upper-right). The axes in an (i, j)-plot correspond to variables x_i and x_j.

As can be seen, the DT omni-optimizer clearly overcomes the omni-aiNet performance in finding the multiple global solutions of the problem. However, it could be noticed during the execution of omni-aiNet, that the algorithm was capable of finding all the multiple global solutions of the problem but was unable to keep them in the population until the end of its execution. These solutions were discarded from the population specially due to intrinsic characteristics of the Selection and Grid mechanisms. In the Selection phase, if a solution i in a region close to a global optima is slightly better than a solution j in the region close to another global optima of the problem, the mutated clones of solution i tend to be better than the mutated clones of solution j and sometimes even better than solution j at all. Therefore, the solution i and probably the most of its mutated clones are selected to continue in the population while solution j, that corresponds to a different optima of the problem, may be discarded. Other important aspect that lead to the above results is the fact that the Grid procedure analyzes only the objective space in multi-objective problems to select the most spread solutions, without considering any information of the spread of these solutions in the variable space. The obtained results for the ZDT1 and ZDT2 problems showed that this mechanism seems to be efficient in multi-objective uni-global problems, but needs improvements to treat multi-objective multi-global optimization problems.

7   Concluding Remarks

This work presented a new immune-inspired algorithm for omni-optimization, called omni-aiNet, capable of solving single and multi-objective problems, with a single or multiple global optimal solutions. The proposed algorithm unites the concepts of omni-optimization proposed by Deb and Tiwari [8] to principles of Artificial Immune Systems, giving to the algorithm the capabilities of dynamically adjusting its population size and avoiding high levels of redundancy within the population.

The omni-aiNet was applied to several optimization problems with distinct characteristics and compared to the performance of the DT omni-optimizer algorithm [8]. The obtained results showed that the proposed approach seems very promising, once it was even capable of outperforming the DT omni-optimizer for two of the problems treated in this work. However, further improvements are still necessary to the omni-aiNet algorithm, specially to its diversity maintenance mechanism when both the spaces of objectives and variables are considered.

For future work, besides the necessary improvements to the algorithm, a more rigorous series of tests should also be made, covering a wider range of problems and comparing the results not only to the Deb and Tiwari's omni-optimizer, but also to other well known state-of-the-art algorithms. Sensitivity analysis should also be made to detect the impact of each input parameter on the overall performance of the algorithm.

Acknowledgment

This work has been supported by grants from Fapesp, Capes and CNPq. The authors would like to specially thank Prof. Kalyanmoy Deb and Santosh Tiwari for providing their omni-optimizer software package and for all the support given.

References

1. Bazaraa, M. S., Sherali, H. D., Shetty, C. M.: *"Nonlinear Programming: Theory and Algorithms"*, John-Wiley & Sons, 2nd. ed., 1993.
2. Burnet, F. M.: *"Clonal Selection and After"*, In Bell, G. I., Perelson, A. S., Pimgley Jr, G. H. (Eds.): Theoretical Immunology, Marcel Dekker Inc., pp. 63–85, 1978.
3. Coello Coello, C. A., Cortés, N. C.: *"Solving Multiobjective Optimization Problems Using an Artificial Immune System."* In: Genetic Programming and Evolvable Machines, vol. 6, pp. 163–190, 2005.
4. de Castro, L. N., Timmis, J.: *"An Introduction to Artificial Immune Systems: A New Computational Intelligence Paradigm"*, Springer-Verlag, 2002.
5. de Castro, L. N., Timmis, J.: *"An Artificial Immune Network for Multimodal Funcion Optimization"*, In: Proc. IEEE CEC, USA, pp. 669–674, 2002.
6. de Castro, L. N., Von Zuben, F. J.: *"aiNet: An Artificial Immune Network for Data Analysis"*, In Abbass, H. A., Sarker, R. A., Newton, C. S. (Eds.): Data Mining: A Heuristic Approach, Idea Group Publishing, USA, Chapter XII, pp. 231-259, 2001.
7. de França, F. O., Von Zuben, F. J., de Castro, L. N.: *"An Artificial Immune Network for Multimodal Funcion Optimization on Dynamic Environments."* In: Proc. GECCO, Washington, DC, USA, pp. 289–296, 2005.
8. Deb, K., Tiwari, S.: *"Omni-optimizer: A Procedure for Single and Multi-objective Optimization."* In Coello Coello, C. A., Aguirre, A. H., Zitzler, E. (Eds.): Proc. 3rd. EMO, Mexico. LNCS, vol. 3410, pp. 47–61, 2005.
9. Gomes, L. C. T., de Sousa, J. S., Bezerra, G. B., de Castro, L. N., Von Zuben, F. J.: *"Copt-aiNet and the Gene Ordering Problem"*, In: Information Technology Magazine, Catholic University of Brasília, vol.3, no.2, pp. 27-33, 2003.
10. Holland, P. W. H., Garcia-Fernandez, J., Williams, N. A., Sidow, A.: *"Gene Duplications and Origins of the Vertebrate Development"*, In: Dev. Supp., pp. 125-133, 1994.
11. Jerne, N. K.: *"Towards a Network Theory of the Immune System"*, Ann. Immunol., Inst. Pasteur, vol. 125C, pp. 373–389, 1974.
12. Ohno, S: *"Evolution by Gene Duplication"*, Allen and Unwin, London, UK, 1970.
13. Zitzler, E., Thiele, L., Deb, K.: *"Comparison of Multiobjective Evolutionary Algorithms: Empirical Results"*, In: Evol. Computation, vol. 8, no. 2, pp. 173-195, 2000.

Immune Procedure for Optimal Scheduling of Complex Energy Systems

Enrico Carpaneto, Claudio Cavallero, Fabio Freschi, and Maurizio Repetto

Dept. of Electrical Engineering,
Politecnico di Torino, Torino, Italy
{enrico.carpaneto, claudio.cavallero,
fabio.freschi, maurizio.repetto}@polito.it
http://www.polito.it/cadema

Abstract. The management of complex energy systems where different power sources are active in a time varying scenario of costs and prices needs efficient optimization approaches. Usually the scheduling problem is is formulated as a Mixed Integer Linear Programming (MILP) to guarantee the convergence to the global optimum. The goal of this work is to propose and compare a hybrid technique based on Artificial Immune System (AIS) and linear programming versus the traditional MILP approach. Different energy scheduling problem cases are analyzed and results of the two procedures are compared both in terms of accuracy of results and convergence speed. The work shows that, on some technical cases, AIS can efficiently tackle the energy scheduling problem in a time varying scenario and that its performances can overcome those of MILP. The obtained results are very promising and make the use of immune based procedures available for real-time management of energy systems.

1 Introduction

Distributed energy generation systems are becoming more and more widespread in the power grid. This increase is driven by the growing demand of energy for industrial and civil purposes and by energy market deregulation. In this way, the classic passive electric grid with few power plants is overcome by an active network where dispersed nodes can generate power on their own and, possibly, they offer power to the grid. This solution has many advantages, some drawbacks and certainly it requires an accurate energy management. Design and optimization of the energy local network is, in fact, quite different from the one of the classical energy grid.

In particular, starting from the fact that loads very often requires both electric and thermal power, the local system can be of Combined Heat and Power (CHP) type. The combined production of electric and thermal energy leads to the use, in a positive way, of the thermal energy usually wasted in the thermodynamic cycle. This energy can be efficiently employed to satisfy the requirements of thermal loads both domestic and or industrials. Since heat cannot be efficiently transferred to far sites, its source must be located close to the load and thus

H. Bersini and J. Carneiro (Eds.): ICARIS 2006, LNCS 4163, pp. 309–320, 2006.

also this characteristic requires that energy is produced in a distributed way all over the network. The energy management of this system needs to take into account local loads and generators, with different nominal powers, reliability and pollution levels and the possible presence of energy storage units. In addition, all these characteristics and requirements change with time: for instance load profiles, price of energy bought from or sold to the electrical network etc.. An accurate scheduling of the system must ensure the use of the most economical power sources, fulfilling operational constraints and load demand.

The management of the energy system requires the definition of the on/off status of the machines and the identification of their optimal production profile of them. When the start-up/shut-down profile is set, the problem can be approached by means of Linear Programming (LP). The definition of the on/off status of the sources is referred to as *scheduling* and it requires the introduction of logical variables, which define in each time interval (e.g. one hour, one quarter of an hour etc.) the power source availability. As a consequence, the complete problem must deal with both continuous (power levels) and integer (on/off status) variables. This problem can be stated as a Mixed Integer Linear Programming problem (MILP) [1]. Even if this approach guarantees to find out the global minimum of the cost function, the use of MILP needs a branch and bound, or similar approaches, whose computational cost is shown to exponentially increase with the number of branches. Instead of a full LP approach, an heuristic optimization algorithm can be used to define the on/off status of the power sources, leaving to an inner LP module the optimization of a particular configuration. An Artificial Immune System (AIS) algorithm can be efficiently employed in this phase and its use is shown to be quite efficient if all operational constraints are embedded inside the scheduling interval definition [2].

In this paper, a comparison of the two techniques, MILP and AIS-LP is presented, both approaches are described and comparisons are carried out in terms of results accuracy and convergence speed to the optimum.

2   Definition of Energy Management Problem

The outline of the system under study is represented in Fig. 1, where:

- P_e is the electrical power produced by the CHP;
- P_t is the thermal power produced by the CHP;
- B_t is the heat produced by a boiler which fulfills the thermal load when production of electric power is neither needed nor economically convenient;
- D_t is the heat produced in the thermodynamic cycle which is not used by the thermal load and it is thus released into the atmosphere;
- P_p and P_s are the electrical power purchased from or sold to the external network respectively;
- S_t is the stored thermal energy;
- U_e and U_t are the electrical and thermal power required by the load;

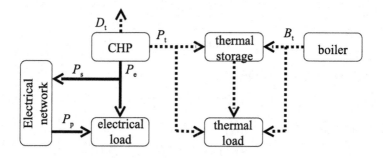

Fig. 1. Structure of a CHP. Straight lines: electrical power fluxes, dotted lines: thermal power fluxes.

In each time interval (i), thermal and electrical power of a CHP are linked by a linear relation

$$P_t(i) = k_t P_e(i) \tag{1}$$

The energy management problem of the CHP system regards the definition of the best arrangement of production levels of the power unit to minimize the management costs and fulfilling all loads requirements. The problem is defined over a scheduling period (e.g. one day, one week etc.) where loads, costs, fares etc. can change. The scheduling period is subdivided in $N_{\text{intervals}}$ time intervals of length Δt. During each interval all CHP characteristics and load data are assumed to be constant.

Besides plant data, some operational constraints have to be imposed on the power source like:

– *Minimum On Time* (MOT): minimum time interval during which CHP must be on when it is switched on;
– *Minimum Shut-down time* (MST): minimum time interval which CHP must be off since it was turned off;
– *Maximum ramp rate*: maximum power rate of the source

The unit production costs of the node, expressed in €/kWh, are:

– c_e: cost coefficient of electric energy produced by the CHP;
– c_t: cost coefficient of thermal energy produced by the boiler;
– $c_p(i)$, $c_s(i)$: prices of purchased and sold energy at i-th time interval.

By using the previous definitions it is possible to write a global cost function (in €) over the scheduling period

$$f_{\text{CHP}} = \sum_{i=1}^{N_{\text{intervals}}} \left[c_e P_e(i) + c_p(i) P_p(i) - c_s(i) P_s(i) + c_t B_t(i) \right] \Delta t \tag{2}$$

The optimization problem can be stated as

$$\text{minimize } f_{CHP} \tag{3}$$

subject to operational constraints

1. electrical balance: $P_e(i) + P_p(i) - P_s(i) = U_e(i)$;
2. thermal balance: $P_t(i) + B_t(i) - D_t(i) + \dfrac{S_t(i-1) - S_t(i)}{\Delta t} = U_t(i)$;
3. dissipation of thermal power produced by CHP: $D_t(i) - P_t(i) \leq 0$;
4. thermal and electrical CHP characteristic (1): $k_t P_e(i) - P_t(i) = 0$;
5. MOT, MST and ramp limit satisfaction.

Variables are bounded by their upper and lower bounds

$$
\begin{aligned}
P_e^{\min} &\leq P_e(i) \leq P_e^{\max} \\
0 &\leq B_t(i) \leq B_t^{\max} \\
0 &\leq P_s(i) \\
0 &\leq P_p(i) \\
0 &\leq D_t(i) \\
0 &\leq S_t(i) \leq S_t^{\max}
\end{aligned}
\tag{4}
$$

The first bounds do not hold during the starting-up and shutting-down phases.

3   Mixed Integer Scheduling Approach

The scheduling problem can be directly formulated as a MILP [1,3]. This means that the problem is still linear, but it has both continuous and integer variables. This class of problems can be solved by exact methods like Branch and Bound technique [4]. The MILP approach requires to define the on/off status of the CHP as a logical variable $\delta(i)$ defined for all i-th time interval. Moreover, two additional sets of logical variables must be considered to take into account MOT/MST constraints and up/down ramps [5] (see Fig. 2)

$$
y(i) = \begin{cases} 1 \text{ if CHP turns on at } i - \text{th time interval} \\ 0 \text{ otherwise} \end{cases}
\tag{5}
$$

$$
z(i) = \begin{cases} 1 \text{ if CHP turns off at } i - \text{th time interval} \\ 0 \text{ otherwise} \end{cases}
\tag{6}
$$

The complexity of the problem hardly depends on time discretization, because the finer the discretization the higher the number of integer variables. Besides, the model of ramp limits, MOT and MST limits introduce several additional constraints which must be explicitly added to the model. In [5] it is shown that it is possible to model start-up and shut-down power trajectories with eleven

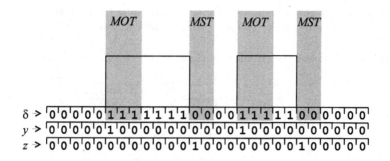

Fig. 2. Binary variables of MILP approach

constraints. Finally, it is common to define an upper limit to the number of turns on and off during the scheduling period $N_{\text{on}} = N_{\text{off}} = N_{\text{change}}$.

$$\sum_{i=0}^{N_I} y(i) \leq N_{\text{change}}$$

$$\sum_{i=0}^{N_I} z(i) \leq N_{\text{change}} \qquad (7)$$

For instance, for a one-day scheduling period with the CHP in one day, and $N_{\text{on}} = N_{\text{off}} = 1$, this means that CHP can be turned on and off just once.

4   Immune Scheduling Approach

The second approach is based on the opt-aiNet version [6] of the clonal selection algorithm. The optimization procedure (AIS-LP) is divided into two nested stages: the inner one is the LP problem derived in Section 2 which defines the optimal production levels at each time interval once the on/off profiles are defined. The outer stage is responsible defining the on/off status of the generation units.

It is useful to use as degrees of freedom of the optimization the time amplitudes of the on and off intervals τ_j of the CHP (Fig. 3). These values are treated as integer variables representing the number of on and off intervals of each control period. The variables are then decoded in terms of 0-1 strings representing, for each utility, its on/off status. This assumption drastically simplify the optimization search. The number of available solutions is in fact equal to M^N, where N is the number of degrees of freedom and M the number of possible values assumed by each variable. A fine discretization does not affect the number of variables but only their range of values M, thus the overall complexity of the problem is polynomial. With a MILP approach, M is always equal to 2, because the problem is modeled by binary variables. The time discretization affects the value of N, giving rise to an exponential complexity of the problem. Moreover, in AIS-LP approach, the value of M is restricted when including MOT/MST constraints. Thus the modeling of technical constraints reduces the search space allowing a faster convergence to the optimal solution. Table 1 The definition of

Table 1. Number of available configurations for two time discretizations

	$\Delta t = 1$ hour		$\Delta t = 0.25$ hour	
	MILP	AIS-LP	MILP	AIS-LP
M	2	24	2	96
N	24	2	96	2
M^N	16.8×10^6	576	79.2×10^{27}	9216

on/off intervals τ as optimization variables requires an algorithm without complex operators. This consideration is due to the fact that it is not easy to keep the feasibility of solutions. Thus algorithms with crossover and recombination operators, like Genetic Algorithm and Evolution Strategy must be excluded *a priori*. The AIS has the advantage of using the mutation operator only, and its memory capability will be exploited in a future work to handle the time varying scenarios in real time optimization. The AIS-LP performances can be enhanced

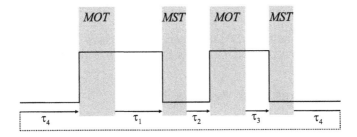

Fig. 3. Representation of the variables for the AIS-LP approach: intervals τ_j

by using problem-specific information:

- creation of feasible initial population which satisfies the equality constraints

$$\sum_i \tau_i = N_{\text{intervals}} - N_{\text{on}}\text{MOT} - N_{\text{off}}\text{MST} = N_{\text{free}} \tag{8}$$

- modified mutation operator to generate of feasible-only clones.

For these reasons some immune operators must be customized to solve the specific problem. In particular the mutation operator is not related to the actual fitness of the parent cell. Algorithms 1 and 2 report the pseudocodes of the generator of new cells and mutation operator, respectively.

The use of problem-specific information drastically decreases the dimension of the search space [2], making the AIS-LP approach more suited for high dimensional or fine discretized problems [7].

Algorithm 1. New cells generation

1: **for all** newcells **do**
2:     $sum \leftarrow 0$
3:     **for** $i \leftarrow 1, N_{\text{intervals}}$ **do**   ▷ Random initialization
4:         $cell(i) \leftarrow \text{random}()$
5:         $sum = sum + cell(i)$
6:     **end for**
7:     **for** $i \leftarrow 1, N_{\text{intervals}}$ **do**   ▷ Normalization and interization
8:         $cell(i) \leftarrow \text{INT}(N_{\text{free}} \times cell(i)/sum)$
9:     **end for**
10: **end for**

Algorithm 2. Mutation

1: **for all** clones **do**
2:     **for** $i \leftarrow 1, N_{\text{intervals}}$ **do**
3:         $mutaz(i) \leftarrow \text{random}()$
4:         **if** $0 \leq mutaz(i) \leq 1/3$ **then** $mutaz(i) \leftarrow -1$
5:         **if** $1/3 \leq mutaz(i) \leq 2/3$ **then** $mutaz(i) \leftarrow 1$
6:         **if** $2/3 \leq mutaz(i) \leq 1$ **then** $mutaz(i) \leftarrow 0$
7:     **end for**
8:     **for** $i \leftarrow 1, N_{\text{intervals}}$ **do**
9:         $clone(i) = parent(i) + mutaz(i) - mutaz(i-1)$ ▷ Feasible mutation
10:        **if** $clone(i) \leq xlow(i)$ **then**   ▷ Fix mutation to the lower bound
11:            $clone(i) \leftarrow xlow(i)$
12:            $mutaz(i) \leftarrow 0$
13:        **end if**
14:       **if** $clone(i) \geq xup(i)$ **then**   ▷ Fix mutation to the upper bound
15:           $clone(i) \leftarrow xup(i)$
16:           $mutaz(i) \leftarrow 0$
17:        **end if**
18:     **end for**
19: **end for**

5   Proof of Principle Test Case

MILP and AIS-LP are tested on a simple but effective energy management problem. The structure of the CHP node is the one of Fig. 1; the operational data of the devices are reported in Table 2. The thermal storage unit is considered to have a maximum capacity of 300 kWh. Energy price profiles are shown in Fig. 4. Several scheduling instances are solved with a quarter of hour time sampling ($\Delta t = 0.25$ hours), thus a one day scheduling period has $N_{\text{intervals}} = 96$, two days scheduling $N_{\text{intervals}} = 192$ etc. Results are compared in terms of convergence time and number of objective function calls. It must be remarked that a comparison in terms of the mere number of objective function calls can be misleading because the linear problem solved by MILP and AIS-LP are different.

Table 2. Main operational data used in the test case

	$P_e^{\min}$ kW	$P_e^{\max}$ kW	MOT hour	MST hour	Ramp limit $\frac{kW}{h}$
CHP	200	600	5	4	170
Boiler	0	800	none	none	none

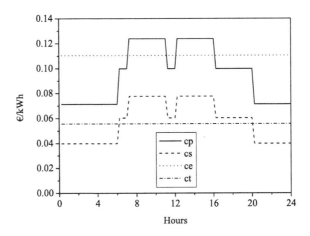

Fig. 4. Profile of costs purchased (c_p) and sold (c_s) electrical power

These differences can be explained by noting that the number of variables, number of constraints and number of non zero elements in coefficients matrix are not the same for two formulations. The main differences in the LP formulation between AIS-LP and MILP are summarized in Table 3. The larger MILP

Table 3. Comparison of dimensions of different LP problems (N_{MOT}: number of minimum on time intervals, N_{MST}: number of minimum shutdown time intervals, N_{up}: number of time intervals needed to reach, $P_e^{\min}$ during start-up phases, N_{dw}: number of time intervals needed to reach zero power during shut-down phases)

	AIS-LP	MILP
nr. of constraints	$6N_{\mathrm{intervals}}$	$21N_{\mathrm{intervals}} + 2$
nr. of variables	$7N_{\mathrm{intervals}}$	$10N_{\mathrm{intervals}}$
matrix elements	$35N_{\mathrm{intervals}}^2$	$210N_{\mathrm{intervals}}^2$
non zeros	$14N_{\mathrm{intervals}}$	$(48 + N_{\mathrm{MOT}} + N_{\mathrm{MST}} + 8N_{\mathrm{dw}} + 8N_{\mathrm{up}})N_{\mathrm{intervals}}$

model is due to the fact that operational constraints (ramp limits and MOT and MST constraints) have to be taken into account directly in the linear model whereas AIS-LP approach manage these limits in the external loop, as described in Section 4.

The parameter setting of AIS-LP is:

- population cardinality: 10;
- number of clones: 5;
- number of inner iterations: 5;
- convergence criterion: the search ends if the objective function value does not improve for more than ten external generations.

Results are averaged on 10 independent runs to take into account the statistical variation of performances due to the stochastic nature of the algorithm.

6   Discussion

In Fig. 5 MILP and AIS-LP are compared with respect to the computational time (in seconds) to converge to the optimal value on a Pentium IV 2.8 GHz. These data are displayed versus dimension of problem, represented by the value of $N_{intervals}$.

Fig. 5 shows two important properties. Firstly, there is a crossover between the two curves of MILP and AIS-LP. This fact leads to the consideration that the computational time of MILP approach becomes impracticable for large instances, i.e. for fine discretization and/or long period managements.

Secondly, by analyzing each curve, it is possible to find that MILP has an exponential dependence of the computational time on the cardinality of the problem, while AIS-LP has a quadratic rule. The previous considerations are confirmed by the analysis of Fig. 6 which shows the number of LP problems solved by the two techniques. In this case the number of LP problem is linearly dependent on the cardinality of the problem. It is also worth noting that the solutions found by AIS-LP and MILP models share the same objective function

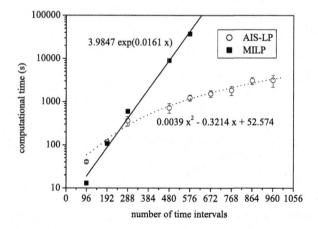

Fig. 5. Computational time of the two procedures vs number of time intervals. AIS-LP computational time has a quadratic dependence on the cardinality of the problem.

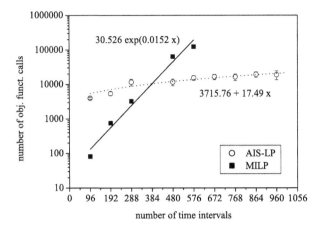

Fig. 6. Number of objective function calls of the two procedures vs number of time intervals. The number of LP problems solved by AIS-LP is linearly dependent on time discretization.

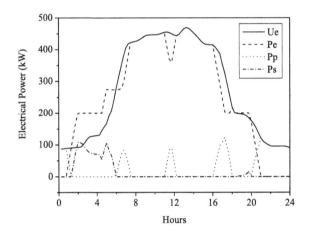

Fig. 7. One day electrical power profiles

values, or are slightly different. This fact shows that AIS-LP procedure converges to the exact solution.

Figs. 7, 8 and 9 show the electrical and thermal power and energy storage profiles of a one day scheduling.

The following remarks can be made:

a) the CHP starts early in the morning in order to store heat energy and satisfy the first thermal load peak of the day. Excess electrical power is sold to the external network;

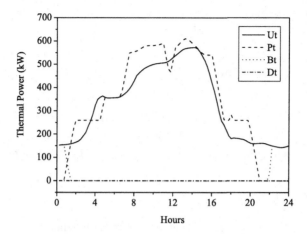

Fig. 8. One day thermal power profiles

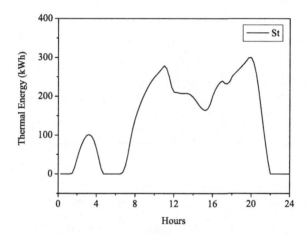

Fig. 9. One day thermal storage energy profile

b) the electrical load is always supplied by the CHP except for few time intervals; by looking at Fig. 8 it is possible to note that CHP production never follows thermal load. This fact is explained by the role of thermal storage;

c) the boiler is requested to produce thermal power only during night hours, when the CHP electrical production is neither needed nor economical;

d) during night hours, thermal storage reaches its upper limit for some time intervals. This fact means that the possibility of storing more thermal energy would be useful to reduce costs.

The effectiveness of the optimal scheduling is evidenced by referring the optimal objective function to the cost of a non cogenerative system, where the electrical load is supplied by the external network and the thermal power is produced by the boiler only. In this case

$$f_{\text{noncogenerative}} = \sum_{i=1}^{N_{\text{intervals}}} [c_p(i)U_e(i) + c_t U_t(i)] \, \Delta t \qquad (9)$$

$$f_\% = \frac{f_{\text{CHP}}}{f_{\text{noncogenerative}}} 100. \qquad (10)$$

The one day scheduling allows to save money of about 34% ($f_\% = 66\%$).

Acknowledgments

This work is supported by the European project High Efficiency polyGEneration appLication "HEGEL" No. 20153, 6th Framework Programme - Priority 6.1 - Sustainable Energy Systems.

References

1. Arroyo, J.M., Conejo, A.J.: Optimal response of a thermal unit to an electricity spot market. IEEE Transaction on Power Systems **15** (2000) 1098–1104
2. Carpaneto, E., Freschi, F., Repetto, M.: Two-stage optimization of a single chp node. In: Cigre 2005 Athens Symposium. (2005) 303–310
3. Gomez-Villalva, E., Ramos, A.: Optimal energy management of an industrial consumer in liberalized markets. IEEE Transactions on Power Systems **18** (2003) 716 723
4. Wolsey, L.A., Nemhauser, G.L.: Integer and Combinatorial Optimization. 1st edition edn. Wiley-Interscience (1999)
5. Arroyo, J.M., Conejo, A.J.: Modeling of start-up and shout-down power trajectories of themal units. IEEE Transaction on power systems **19** (2004) 1562–1568
6. de Castro, L.N., Timmis, J.: An Artificial Immune Network for Multimodal Function Optimization. In: Proceedings of the 2002 Congress on Evolutionary Computation, CEC 2002. Volume 1. (2002) 699–704
7. Deb, K., Reddy, A.R., Singh, G.: Optimal scheduling of casting sequences using genetic algorithms. Journal of Materials and Manufacturing Processes **18** (2003) 409–432

Aligning Multiple Protein Sequences by Hybrid Clonal Selection Algorithm with Insert-Remove-Gaps and BlockShuffling Operators

V. Cutello[1], D. Lee[2], G. Nicosia[1], M. Pavone[2], and I. Prizzi[3]

[1] Department of Mathematics and Computer Science
University of Catania
Viale A. Doria 6, 95125 Catania, Italy
{vctl, nicosia, mpavone}@dmi.unict.it
[2] IBM-KAIST Bio-Computing Research Center
Department of BioSystems, KAIST
373-1, Guseong-dong, Yuseong-gu, Daejeon, Republic of Korea
dhlee@biosoft.kaist.ac.kr, mario@biosoft.kaist.ac.kr
[3] Diogenes Research Center, Catania, Italy
prizzi@crsdiogenes.it

Abstract. Multiple sequence alignment (MSA) is one of the most important tasks in biological sequence analysis. This paper will primarily focus on on protein alignments, but most of the discussion and methodology also applies to DNA alignments. A novel hybrid clonal selection algorihm, called an aligner, is presented. It searches for a set of alignments amongst the population of candidate alignments by optimizing the classical *weighted sum of pairs* objective function. Benchmarks from BaliBASE library (v.1.0 and v.2.0) are used to validate the algorithm. Experimental results of BaliBASE v.1.0 benchmarks show that the proposed algorithm is superior to PRRP, ClustalX, SAGA, DIALIGN, PIMA, MULTIALIGN, and PILEUP8. On BaliBASE v.2.0 benchmarks the algorithm shows interesting results in terms of SP score with respect to established and leading methods, i.e. ClustalW, T-Coffee, MUSCLE, PRALINE, Prob-Cons, and Spem.

Keywords: bioinformatics, multiple sequence alignment, protein sequences, immune algorithms, clonal selection algorithms, hypermutation operator.

1 Introduction

Proteomics Multiple Sequence Alignment (MSA) plays a central role in molecular biology, as it can reveal the constraints imposed by structure and function on the evolution of whole protein families [1]. MSA has been used for building phylogenetic trees, identification of conserved motifs, and predicting secondary and tertiary structures for RNA and proteins [2].

H. Bersini and J. Carneiro (Eds.): ICARIS 2006, LNCS 4163, pp. 321–334, 2006.

In order to be able to align a set of bio-sequences a reliable objective function able to measure an alignment in terms of its biological plausibility through an analytical or computational function is needed. Alignment quality is often the limiting factor in the analysis of biological sequences — defining an appropriate and efficient objective function can remove this limitation. It is an active research field [3]. A simple objective function to optimize is the *weighted sums-of-pairs* (SP) with affine gap penalties [4], where each sequence receives a weight proportional to the amount of independent information it contains [5] and the cost of the multiple alignment is equal to the sum of the cost of all the weighted pairwise substitutions.

This research paper proposes a Hybrid Clonal Selection Algorithm (CSA) which incorporates specific perturbation operators for MSA of amino-acids sequences. The obtained results show that the proposed Immune Algorithm is comparable to state-of-art algorithms.

2   The Multiple Sequence Alignment Problem

To determine if two biological sequences have common sub-sequences is the most popular sequence analysis problem. As described in [2] there are four fundamental topics: (1.) what *kinds of alignment* should be considered; (2.) the *scoring function* adopted to evaluate alignments; (3.) the *alignment algorithm* designed to find optimal (or suboptimal) scoring alignments; (4.) the statistical methods used to assess the *significance of an alignment score*. This paper focuses on the key issues of design and efficient implementation of alignment algorithms of finding optimal and suboptimal alignments of protein structures — but the technique is also applicable to DNA alignments.

Definition 1 *[Sequence Alignment]. Let $S = \{S_1, S_2, \ldots, S_n\}$ be a set of n sequences (strings) over a finite alphabet Σ, each sequence S_i consisting of ℓ_i ordered characters $s_{i,j}$:*

$$S_i = s_{i,1}s_{i,2} \ldots s_{i,\ell_i}, \quad \forall i = 1, 2, \ldots, n$$

Let $\hat{\Sigma}$ a new alphabet: $\hat{\Sigma} = \Sigma \cup \{-\}$ by adding the symbol dash '-' to represent gaps.

Then a set $\hat{S} = \{\hat{S}_1, \hat{S}_2, \ldots, \hat{S}_n\}$ of sequences over the alphabet $\hat{\Sigma}$ is called a **sequence alignment** *of the set of sequence S, if the following properties are fulfilled:*

1. All strings in $\hat{S}$ have the same length $\hat{\ell}$ with

$$\max_{i=1\ldots n}(\ell_i) \leq \hat{\ell} \leq \sum_{i=1}^{n} \ell_i.$$

$\hat{S}$ can be interpreted as $n \times \hat{\ell}$ matrix where the $i-th$ row contains string $\hat{S}_i$.
2. Ignoring gaps, sequence $\hat{S}_i$ is identical with sequence S_i, $\forall i = 1, 2, \ldots, n$.
3. $\hat{S}$ has no columns that contains gaps only.

When $n = 2$ a *pairwise sequence alignment* is found, with $n \geq 3$ *multiple sequence alignment*. Solving the sequence alignment problem requires a *scoring function* to evaluate alignments. A simple scoring function is a distance function (another scoring function is the similarity approach). Having a distance function $d(\hat{S}_i, \hat{S}_j)$ for any aligned sequences $\hat{S}_i$ and $\hat{S}_j$, the pairwise alignment problem can be stated as follows:

Definition 2 *[Pairwise alignment problem].* *Let* $S = \{S_1, S_2\}$ *be a set of 2 sequences over the alphabet* Σ. *Compute the alignment* $\hat{S} = \{\hat{S}_1, \hat{S}_2\}$ *of* S *over the alphabet* $\hat{\Sigma}$ *that minimises the distance* $d(\hat{S}_1, \hat{S}_2)$.

Hence, the multiple sequence alignment problem can be stated as follows:

Definition 3 *[Sum-of-pairs multiple alignment problem]*
Let $S = \{S_1, S_2, \ldots S_n\}$ *be a set of n sequences over the alphabet* Σ. *Compute the alignment* $\hat{S} = \{\hat{S}_1, \hat{S}_2, \ldots, \hat{S}_n\}$ *of* S *over the alphabet* $\hat{\Sigma}$ *that minimises the sum of the distance over all pairs* $\hat{S}_i$, *and* $\hat{S}_j$:

$$\min_{\hat{S}} = \left(\sum_{i=1}^{n-1} \sum_{j=i+1}^{n} d(\hat{S}_i, \hat{S}_j) \right)$$

The scoring functions previously defined are too simple to be used when aligning real biological sequences. A scoring function needs to be based on the similarity of the characters occurring in the sequences, e.g. amino-acids. For instance, for two amino-acids, aa_i and aa_j, we need a measure of the probability that they have a common ancestor, or that one aa is the result of one or several mutations of the other. This measure can be formulated as follows:

Definition 4 *[Scoring matrix].* *Let* M *be a* $\ell \times \ell$ *scoring matrix, where* ℓ *is the cardinality of the alphabet* Σ, *which for any two characters* a *and* b *of the alphabet* Σ *has the following properties:*

1. $M(a, b) = M(b, a)$, $\forall a, b \in \Sigma$,
2. $M(a, -) = GEP$, *where GEP is a fixed gap penalty,*
3. $M(-, -) = 0$.

In general a gap of lenght h has a penalty score of $h \times GEP$, where $GEP < 0$ is the fixed gap (extension) penalty. This is called the *linear gap penalty function*. From a biological point of view a more appropriate penalty score is the *affine gap penalty function*, (AGPS): given an aligned sequence $\hat{S}_i$, the first gap receives a *gap opening penalty*, $GOP < GEP < 0$, which is stronger than penalty for gap extending spaces. Hence, a gap of lenght h has a cost of $GOP + (h-1)GEP$. The most common scoring matrices are the PAM and BLOSUM series. These scoring matrices have been developed based on observed mutations in the nature. In order to minimise redundant information, based on the relatedness of the given sequences, each sequence usually receives a weight proportional to the amount of independent information it contains. This kind of information can be derived from a phylogenetic tree for the sequences.

Definition 5 [Weighted symbol score]. *Let W be such a weight matrix for every pair of aligned sequences. Then the weighted symbol score for the aligned sequences $\hat{S}_i$ $\hat{S}_j$ is defined as:*

$$WSS(\hat{S}_i, \hat{S}_j) = W_{ij} \sum_{k=1}^{\hat{\ell}} M(\hat{s}_{i,k}, \hat{s}_{j,k})$$

Sequence weights can be determined by constructing a guide tree from known sequences — this is the approach used in this paper. These definitions lead to the most common faced sum-of-pairs multiple alignment problem: optimizing a weighted sum-of-pairs function with affine gap penalties.

Definition 6 [Sum-of-pairs multiple alignment problem]
Let $S = \{S_1, S_2, \ldots, S_n\}$ be a set of n sequences over the alphabet Σ. Compute the alignment $\hat{S} = \{\hat{S}_1, \hat{S}_2, \ldots, \hat{S}_n\}$ of S over the alphabet $\hat{\Sigma}$ that maximises the weighted symbol score and the affine gap penalty score for all aligned sequences $\hat{S}_i$:

$$\max_{\hat{S}} \left(\sum_{i=1}^{n-1} \sum_{j=i+1}^{n} WSS(\hat{S}_i, \hat{S}_j) + \sum_{i=1}^{n} AGPS(\hat{S}_i) \right) \tag{1}$$

For multiple protein sequence alignment, the weighted sum-of-pairs with affine gap penalties is a popular objective function included in many MSA packages. The problem of finding the multiple alignment was investigated in [6] and [7], and proved to be a NP-hard problem. However, the results presented in [7] was proved using a *not metric scoring matrix* (zero distance between two identical residues), which is different from the actual scoring matrices used in multiple alignments. Therefore, in [6], the authors improved the previous investigation using a fixed metric score matrix through a reduction from the *Minimum Vertex Cover*, a classical NP complete problem [8]. Multiple sequence alignment (MSA) decision problems can be formulated as: given a set $S = \{S_1, \ldots, S_n\}$ of sequences, a sum-of-pairs objective function, and an integer C. MSA checks for alignments of S, which have value C or less.

3   Hybrid Clonal Selection Algorithm

This work presents a Clonal Selection Algorithm (CSA) [30] with new hypermutation operators for solving the multiple sequence alignment problem. CSAs are a special class of Immune algorithms (IAs) inspired by the human Clonal Selection Principle [31]. They are effective methods for search and optimization in real-world applications. The algorithm is population based where each individual of the population is a *candidate solution* belonging to the fitness landscape of a given computational problem. It uses two different methodologies to create the initial population, as well as new hypermutation operators which insert or remove gaps in the sequences.

Gap columns which have been matched are moved to the end of the sequence. Next the remaining elements (amino acids in this work) and existing gaps are

shifted into the freed space. The designed CSA considers only two immunological entities: antigens (Ags) and B cells. The Ag is the problem to solve, i.e. a
given MSA instance, and B cells are the candidate solutions, i.e. a set of alignments, that have solved (or approximated) the initial problem [32,33]. Tackling
the multiple sequence alignment problem Ags and B cells are represented by a
sequences matrix.

Let $\Sigma = \{A, R, N, D, C, E, Q, G, H, I, L, K, M, F, P, S, T, W, Y, V\}$ be the alphabet, where each symbol represents twenty amino acids and let $S = \{S_1, S_2,$
$\ldots, S_n\}$ be the set of $n \geq 2$ sequences with length $\{\ell_1, \ell_2, \ldots, \ell_n\}$, such that $S_i \in$
Σ^*. Therefore, an Ag is represented by a matrix of n rows and $max\{\ell_1, \ldots, \ell_n\}$
columns, whereas for the B cells a $(n \times \ell)$ matrix was used, with $\ell = (\frac{3}{2} \cdot$
$max\{\ell_1, \ldots, \ell_n\})$. These values where taken from experimental the proposed algorithm was able to develop more *compact alignments*. In particular, for the B
cells a binary matrix was used, where $s'_{i,j} = 0$ refers to a gap in the alignment
and $s'_{i,j} = 1$ to a residue with $1 \leq i \leq n$ and $1 \leq j \leq \ell$.

A   Initialize the Population

Two different strategies were used to create the initial population $(t = 0)$ of
candidate alignments. The first strategy, *random_initialization*, is based on the
use of random *"offsets"* to shift the initial sequences in the following way: an
offset is randomly chosen in the range $[0, (\ell - \ell_i)]$ by a uniform distribution and
then the sequence S_i is shifted from an offset positions towards the right side of
the row i, of the current B cell.

A second way to initialize the population was analyized, seeding the initial
population with CLUSTALW and *CLUSTALW-seeding*. However, a percentage
of the population was initialized using the offsets strategy described above to
avoid the algorithm getting trapped in a local optima. Hence, the second strategy
creates a percentage of initial alignments using CLUSTALW and the remaining
alignments are determined by a random offsets creation.

Preliminary experimental results show that the proposed algorithm achieves
better performance using the second strategy. Therefore, all results shown in
this paper were obtained using a combination of the two previously introduced
strategies (80% of B cell population by CLUSTALW seeding and 20% of B cell
population by random_initialization using the random offsets).

The presented hybrid IA incorporates the classical *static cloning operator*,
which clones each B cell *dup* times producing an intermediate population $P_{N_c}^{(clo)}$
of $N_c = d \times dup$ B cells, where d is the population size).

The basic mutation processes which are considered in pairwise alignment and
multiple sequence alignments are: *substitutions* which change sequences of amino
acids, as well as *insertions* and *deletions* which add or remove amino acids and/or
gaps. In a first version of the algorithm the classical hypermutation and hypermacromutation operators where used: first operator flips a bit, using a number of
mutations inversely proportional to the fitness function value [34], whereas the
hypermacromutation simply swaps two randomly choosen subsequences. However, the first experiments produced non optimal alignments obtained, leading

Table 1. Pseudo-code of the proposed hybrid immune algorithm for the MSA

Hybrid Immune Algorithm$(d, dup, \tau_B, T_{max})$
1. $t \leftarrow 0$;
2. $FFE \leftarrow 0$;
3. $N_c \leftarrow d \times dup$;
4. $P_d^{(t)} \leftarrow$ Initialize_Population(d);
5. Strip_Gaps$(P_d^{(t)})$;
6. Evaluate$(P_d^{(t)})$;
7. $FFE \leftarrow FFE + d$;
8. **while** $(FFE < T_{max})$**do**
9. $\quad P_{N_c}^{(clo)} \leftarrow$ Cloning $(P_d^{(t)}, dup)$;
10. $\quad P_{N_c}^{(gap)} \leftarrow$ Gap_operators $(P_d^{(clo)})$;
11. $\quad$ Strip_Gaps$(P_{N_c}^{(gap)})$;
12. $\quad$ Evaluate$(P_{N_c}^{(gap)})$;
13. $\quad FFE \leftarrow FFE + N_c$;
14. $\quad P_{N_c}^{(block)} \leftarrow$ BlockShuffling_operators $(P_d^{(clo)})$;
15. $\quad$ Compute_Weights$()$;
16. $\quad$ Normalize_Weights$()$;
17. $\quad$ Strip_Gaps$(P_{N_c}^{(block)})$;
18. $\quad$ Evaluate$(P_{N_c}^{(block)})$;
19. $\quad FFE \leftarrow FFE + N_c$;
20. $\quad ({}^aP_d^{(t)}, {}^aP_{N_c}^{(gap)}, {}^aP_{N_c}^{(block)}) =$ Elitist-Aging$(P_d^{(t)}, P_{N_c}^{(gap)}, P_{N_c}^{(block)}, \tau_B)$;
21. $\quad P_d^{(t+1)} \leftarrow (\mu + \lambda)$-Selection$({}^aP_d^{(t)}, {}^a P_{N_c}^{(gap)}, {}^a P_{N_c}^{(block)})$;
22. $\quad t \leftarrow t + 1$;
23. **end_while**

---

to frequent premature convergence to the local optimal during the convergence process. Therefore, we have developed new hypermutation operators, specific to the multiple sequence alignments, which insert or remove gaps in the sequences — called *GAP operator* or *BlockShuffling operator*.

B   GAP Operator

This operator acts on the cloned B cells generating a new population $P_{N_c}^{(gap)}$. It is based on two procedures, one inserts (INSGAP), and the other removes (REMGAP) adjacent sequences of gaps. Initially, the GAP operator chooses what procedure to apply using a random uniform distribution, i.e. if a number of adjacent gaps needs to be inserted into the sequences or removed. Then a number k, in the range $[1, \theta]$, of (adjacent) gaps is randomly choosen, where θ represents a percentage of the alignments length. After several experiments setting $\theta = 2\%$ was obtained.

The INSGAP PROCEDURE can be summarize in the following steps: split the n sequences in z groups. During the experimental tests, $z = 2$ has been the best setting for the performances of the proposed algorithm. Hence, we can rephrase this step as follows: randomly choose a value $m \in [1, n[$, and split the n sequences into two groups: $1st$ group from 1 to m sequences, and $2nd$ group from $(m + 1)$ to n; randomly choose two integer values x and y, in such way that k adjacent gaps are insterted beginning from column x for the first group, and from column y for the second group; randomly choose a subsequence shift direction D, either left or right; finally, to insert the k adjacent gaps in the relative positions for each sequence, and shift the subsequence to the D direction. During the shifting phase, it is possible to miss $n \geq 0$ bits with value 1; in this case, InsGap will select n bits with value 0, different from the k gaps inserted, and they will be flipped to 1, rebuilding the correct sequence. Figure 1, plot (a), shows an example of how the InsGap procedure works, with $k = 3$, $m = 2$ and right shift direction.

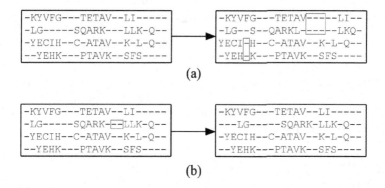

(a)

(b)

Fig. 1. GAP operator has the purpose to insert, by *InsGap* procedure (a), or remove, by *RemGap* procedure (b), adjacent gaps into the proposed alignment

RemGap procedure, simply, remove k adjacent gaps, and move the subsequences towards a randomly chosen direction, either left or right. Plot (b) of figure 1 shows an example of such an operator.

C BlockShuffling Operator

The second perturbation operator is the BlockShuffling operator, which is based on the block definition. This operator moves aligned blocks left or right: a block is selected in each alignment starting from a random point in a sequence.Three different approaches where developed: BlockMove moves whole blocks either to the left or to the right; BlockSplitHor divides the blocks in two levels, upper and lower, and shifting only one level, randomly chosen; and BlockSplitVer, which randomly choose a column in the block which divides it into two sides (left and right), and shifting only one side, randomly chosen as well. Figure 2 summarizes the three operators.

Finally, the function Strip_Gaps($P^{(*)}$) moves matched gap columns to the right end side of the matrix. This function is always applied before the fitness function is evaluated.

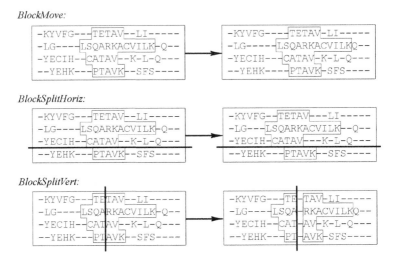

Fig. 2. *BlockShuffling operator* has the purpose to shifting blocks of amino acids or gaps. Upper plot shows the *BlockMove* operator; middle plot drawing how *BlockSplitHor* works, choosing the *4th* row to divide the block in two level; lower plot shows *BlockSplitVer* operator performing a right shift.

Evaluate(P) computes the sum-of-pairs objective function of each B cell in the population P, i.e. the proposed alignment quality, using the equation 1.

The aging operator, used by the algorithm eliminates old B cells in the populations $P_d^{(t)}$, $P_{N_c}^{(gap)}$ and $P_{N_c}^{(block)}$, whilst maintaining high diversity in order to avoid premature convergence. The maximum number of generations a B cell can remain in the population is determined by the parameter τ_B :. When a B cell reaches $\tau_B + 1$ it is erased from the current population, even if it is a good candidate solution. The only exception is made for the best B cell present in the current population: (*Elitist-Aging*).

A new generation $P_d^{(t+1)}$ of d B cells is obtained by selecting the "survivors" after the aging operator was applied to the populations — the resulting populations are: $^a P_d^{(t)}$, $^a P_{N_c}^{(gap)}$ and $^a P_{N_c}^{(block)}$. The $(\mu + \lambda)$-selection operator (with $\mu = d$ and $\lambda = 2N_c$) reduces an offspring B cell population of size $\lambda \geq \mu$ to a new parent population of size μ. Such a selection operator guarantees monotonicity in the evolution dynamics.

Finally, T_{max} is the maximum number of fitness function evaluations and the termination criterion.

Table 1 shows the pseudo-code of the described hybrid immune algorithm. The functions COMPUTE_WEIGHTS() and NORMALIZE_WEIGHTS() compute and normalize the weights of the sequences using a rooted tree, which is used for the evaluation of the objective function.

4 The State-of-Art Methods for MSA

The most popular method to solve MSA is based on *Dynamic Programming* (DP) [9], which guarantees a mathematically optimal alignment. However, the method is limited to a small number of short sequences, since the size of the problem space increases with the number of sequences and their length. To overcome this problem several heuristic approaches, based on different strategies, have been developed to effectively deal with the computational complexity of the problem.

All current methodologies of multiple alignment are heuristics and can be classify in three main categories: *progressive alignments, exact algorithms* and *iterative alignments*.

Progressive Alignments. In progressive alignment methods multiple alignments are performed, first aligning the closest sequences and then the more distant ones are added. Although this approach has the advantage of being simplistic and very fast, it does not guarantee any level of optimization.

Therefore, the main drawback of this approach is that once a sequence has been aligned it cannot be modified, causing possible conflicts with successively added sequences. Alignment programs based on this approach are MULTALIGN [10], PILEUP [11], CLUSTALX [12], CLUSTALW [13], T-COFFEE [14]. Their strategy is to align sequences in a progressive manner using a consistency-based objective function in order to minimize possible errors. SPEM (sequence and Secondary-structure Profiles Enhanced Multiple alignment) [15] combines a sequence-based method with a consistency-based refinement for pairwise alignment, a progressive algorithm for multiple alignment and PROBCONS [16] a practical tool for progressive protein multiple sequence alignment based on *probabilistic consistency* which is a novel scoring function for measuring alignment quality.

Exact algorithms. In contrast to the previous approach, PIMA [17] uses local dynamic programming to align only the most conserved motifs. In the default setting it makes use of two alignment methods, maximum linkage and sequential branching, to decide the order of alignments ML_PIMA and SB_PIMA respectively. Exact algorithms were developed to align multiple sequences simultaneously [18]. High memory requirement, high computational effort and limitation on the number of sequences limit their usage. A new divide and conquer algorithm [19] extending their capabilities was developed.

Iterative alignments. Iterative alignment methods depend on algorithms able to produce an alignment and to refine it through a series of iterations until no further improvements can be made. They are based on the idea that the solution to a given problem can be computed by modifying an already existing *sub-optimal solution.* Aligners which are based on this approach are:

- DIALIGN [20,21], a consistency-based algorithm which attempts to use local information in order to guide a global alignment, i.e. to construct multiple alignments based on segment-to-segment comparisons — such segments are incorporated into a multiple alignment using an iterative procedure.

- PRRP [22] optimizes a progressive global alignment by iteratively dividing the sequences into two groups which are realigned using a global group-to-group alignment algorithm.
- HMMT [23] is based on Hidden Markov Model (HMM), using simulated annealing (SA) to maximize the probability that a HMM represents the sequences to be aligned.
- MUSCLE (multiple sequence comparison by log-expectation) [24] is based on similar strategies used by PRRP.
- SAGA (Sequence Alignment by Genetic Algorithm) [25] is a genetic algorithm based on COFFEE (Consistency Objective Function For alignmEnt Evaluation) objective function [26]. The model described in SAGA has received considerable interest in the evolutionary computation community.
- Another iterative alignment method is Praline [27]; it begins with a preprocessing of the sequence to align.

In general, Evolutionary Algorithms tend to be suitable tools for the MSA [28] and can be used to effectively search in large solution spaces. But they spend a lot of time gradually improving potential solutions before reaching a solution comparable to deterministic methodologies [29]. This is due to a random initialization of the candidate alignments.

5   Results

The immune algorithm presented has been tested on the classical benchmark BaliBASE version 1.0 and version 2.0. BAliBASE (Benchmark Alignment data-BASE) [36] is a database developed to evaluate and compare all multiple alignments programs containing high quality (manually refined) multiple sequence alignments.

BAliBASE is divided into two versions: the first version contains 141 reference alignments and is divided into five hierarchical reference sets containing twelve representative alignments. Moreover, for each alignment the *core blocks* are defined. They are the regions which can be reliably aligned and they represent 58% of residues in the alignments. The remaining 42% are in ambiguous regions which cannot be reliably aligned.

Reference 1 contains alignments of equi-distant sequences with similar length, reference 2 contains alignments of a family (closely related sequences with > 25% identity) and 3 "orphan" sequences with < 20% identity, reference 3 consists of up to four families with < 25% identity between any two sequences from different families and references 4 and 5 contain sequences with large N/C-terminal extensions or internal insertions. For an extensive explanation of all references please refer to [3].

In the second version, BAliBASE v.2.0 [37], all alignments present in the first version have been manually verified and it includes three new reference sets: repeats, circular permutations and transmembrane proteins. It consists of 167

Table 2. SP values given by several methods on the BAliBase v.1.0 benchmark (http://bips.u-strasbg.fr/fr/Products/Databases/BAliBASE/) for multiple sequence alignment

Aligner	Ref 1(82)	Ref 2(23)	Ref 3(12)	Ref 4(12)	Ref 5(12)	Overall(141)
Hybrid CSA	80.7	**88.6**	**77.4**	70.2	82.0	**79.7**
DIALIGN [20]	77.7	38.4	28.8	**85.2**	83.6	62.7
CLUSTALX [12]	85.3	58.3	40.8	36.0	70.6	58.2
PILEUP8 [11]	82.2	42.8	33.3	59.1	63.8	56.2
ML_PIMA [17]	80.1	37.1	34.0	70.4	57.2	55.7
PRRP [22]	**86.6**	54.0	48.7	13.4	70.0	54.5
SAGA [25]	70.3	58.6	46.2	28.8	64.1	53.6
SB_PIMA [17]	81.1	37.9	24.4	72.6	50.7	53.3
MULTALIGN [10]	82.3	51.6	27.6	29.2	62.7	50.6

Table 3. Alignment accuracies given by several methods on the the BAliBASE v.2.0 benchmark (http://bips.u-strasbg.fr/fr/Products/Databases/BAliBASE2/) for multiple sequence alignment [15]

Aligner	Ref 1(82)		Ref 2(23)		Ref 3(12)		Ref 4(12)		Ref 5(12)		Overall(141)	
	SP	CS	SP	CS	SP	CS	SP	CS	SP	CS	SP	CS
SPEM [15]	**90.8**	83.9	93.4	57.3	81.4	56.9	**97.4**	**90.8**	97.4	**92.3**	**91.5**	78.6
MUSCLE [24]	90.3	**84.7**	64.4	60.9	82.2	61.9	91.8	74.8	**98.1**	92.1	91.0	**78.7**
PROBCONS [16]	90.0	83.9	**94.0**	**62.6**	**82.3**	**63.1**	90.9	73.6	**98.1**	91.7	90.8	78.4
T-COFFEE [14]	86.8	80.0	93.9	58.5	76.7	54.8	92.1	76.8	94.6	86.1	88.2	74.6
PRALINE [27]	90.4	83.9	**94.0**	61.0	76.4	55.8	79.9	53.9	81.8	68.6	88.2	73.9
CLUSTALW [13]	85.8	78.3	93.3	59.3	72.3	48.1	83.4	62.3	85.8	63.4	85.7	70.0
Hybrid CSA	82.7	65.3	91.9	41.3	78.6	36.2	70.5	31.9	83.6	56.9	81.4	46.3

reference alignments with more than 2100 sequences. The three new references contain 26 protein families with 12 distinct repeat types, 8 transmembrane families and 5 families with inverted domains.

Table 2 shows the average SP score obtained by the described alignment tools on every instance set of BAliBASE v.1.0. The values refer to the Sum of Pairs score, calculated by the "*baliscore.c*" program. As it can be seen in the table, Hybrid CSA performs well on the Ref 2 and Ref 3 sets. The values obtained aid to raise the overall score, which is higher compared to the results published by the Bioinformatic platform of Strasbourg[1].

Table 3 shows the average SP and Column Score (CS) values obtained by the compared tools on every group of instances belonging to the BAliBASE v.2.0 database. The Column Score is defined as the number of correctly aligned columns present in the generated alignments, divided by the total number of aligned columns in the core blocks of the reference alignment.

---

[1] http://bips.u-strasbg.fr/fr/Products/Databases/BAliBASE/

The values used in table3 are drawn from data reported in [15]. Hybrid CSA obtains comparable values of SP score on Ref 1, Ref2 and Ref 5 — despite the fact that the value obtained on Reference 3 is the fourth best value. This table also shows that future effort should focus on improving the CS metric.

6   Conclusions and Future Works

Experimental results of benchmark BaliBASE v.1.0 show that the proposed algorithm is superior to PRRP, ClustalX, SAGA, DIALIGN, PIMA, MULTIALIGN and PILEUP8. Whilst on BaliBASE v.2.0 the algorithm shows interesting results in terms of SP score with respect to established and leading methods, e.g. ClustalW, T-Coffee, MUSCLE, PRALINE, ProbCons and Spem.

A strong point of the IA is the ability of generating more than a single alignment for every MSA instance. This behaviour is due to the stochastic nature of the algorithm and the populations evolved during the convergence process. Another advantage of the aligner is that the alignment process is not affected by the presence of distant sequences in the starting protein set. As shown by the experimental results, the scoring function used by the IA produces high SP values and low CS scores, therefore future work will first focus on the improvement of the CS score values using the T-Coffee scoring function. The second step will be the more accurate tuning of the parameters and the operators in order to improve the convergence speed.

Acknowledgments

This work was supported by the National Research Laboratory Grant (2005-01450) from the Ministry of Science and Technology. D.L. and M.P. would like to thank CHUNG Moon Soul Center for BioInformation and BioElectronics for providing research and computing facilities.

References

1. Eidhammer I., Jonassen I., Taylor W. R.; *"Protein Bioinformatics,"* Chichester, West Sussex, UK, Wiley, (2004)
2. Durbin R., Eddy S., Krogh A., Mitchison G.; *"Biological sequence analysis"*, Cambridge, UK, Cambridge University Press (2004)
3. Thompson J. D., Plewniak F., Ripp R., Thierry J.C., Poch O.; "Towards a Reliable Objective Function for Multiple Sequence Alignments", in J. Mol. Biol., vol. 301, pp. 937-951 (2001)
4. Altschul S. F., Lipman D. J.; *"Trees stars and multiple biological sequence alignment,"* in SIAM Journal on Applied Mathematics, vol. 49, pp. 197–209, (1989).
5. Altschul S. F., Carroll R. J., Lipman D. J.; *"Weights for data related by a tree,"* in Journal on Molecular Biology, vol. 207, pp. 647–653, (1989).
6. Bonizzoni P., Della Vedova G.; *"The Complexity of Multiple Sequence Alignment with SP-score that is a Metric,"* in Theoretical Computer Science, vol. 259 (1), pp. 63–79 (2001).

7. Wang L., Jiang T.; "*On the complexity of multiple sequence alignment,*" in Journal of Computational Biology, vol. 1, pp. 337–348, (1994)
8. Garey M. R., Johnson D. S.; "*Computers and Intractability: A Guide to the Theory of NP-Completeness,*" Freeman, New York (1979).
9. Gupta S. K., Kececioglu, J. D., Schaffer A.; "*Improving the practical space and time efficiency of the shortest-paths approach to sum-of-pairs multiple sequence alignment,*" in Journal of Computational Biology, vol. 2, pp. 459–472, (1995)
10. Corpet F.; "*Multiple sequence alignment with hierarchical clustering,*" in Nucleic Acids Research, vol. 16, pp. 10881–10890, (1988)
11. Wisconsin Package v.8; Genetics Computer Group, Madison, WI. www.gcg.com
12. Thompson J. D., Gibson T. J., Plewniak F., Jeanmougin F., Higgins D. G.; "*The ClustalX windows interface: flexible strategies for multiple sequence alignment aided by quality analysis tools,*" in Nucleic Acids Research, vol. 24, pp. 4876–4882, (1997)
13. Thompson J. D., Higgins D. G., Gibson T. J.; "*CLUSTAL W: improving the sensitivity of progressive multiple sequence alignment through sequence weighting, position-specific gap penalties and weight matrix choice,*" in Nucleic Acids Research, vol. 22, pp. 4673–4680, (1994)
14. Notredame C., Higgins D. G., Heringa J.; "*T-Coffee: a novel method for fast and accurate Multiple Sequence Alignment,*" in Journal Molecular Biology, vol. 302, pp. 205–217, (2000)
15. Zhou H., Zhou Y.; "*SPEM: Improving multiple sequence alignment with sequence profiles and predicted secondary structures,*" in Bioinformatics, vol. 21, pp. 3615–3621, (2005)
16. Do C. B., Mahabhashyam M. S. P., Brudno M., Batzoglou S.; "*ProbCons: Probabilistic consistency-based multiple sequence alignment,*" in Genome Research, vol. 15, pp. 330–340, (2005)
17. Smith R. F., Smith T. F.; "*Pattern-induced multi-sequence alignment (PIMA) algorithm employing secondary structure-dependent gap penalties for use in comparative protein modelling,*" in Protein Engineering, vol. 5, pp. 35–41,(1992).
18. Carrillo H., Lipman D. J.; "*The Multiple Sequence Alignment Problem in Biology,*" in SIAM Journal on Applied Mathematics, vol. 48, pp. 1073–1082, (1988)
19. Stoye J., Moulton V., Dress A. W.; "*DCA: an efficient implementation of the divide-and conquer approach to simultaneous multiple sequence alignment,*" in Bioinformatics, vol. 13 (6), pp. 625–626, (1997)
20. Morgenstern B., Frech K., Dress A., Werner T.; "*DIALIGN: Finding local similarities by multiple sequence alignment,*" in Bioinformatics, vol. 14, pp. 290–294,(1998)
21. Morgenstern B., Frech K., Dress A., Werner T.; "*DIALIGN 2: improvement of the segment-to-segment approach to multiple sequence alignment,*" in Bioinformatics, vol. 15, pp. 211–218, (1999)
22. Gotoh O; "*Further improvement in methods of group-to-group sequence alignment with generalized profile operations,*" in Bioinformatics, vol. 10 (4), pp. 379–387, (1994)
23. Eddy S. R.; "*Multiple alignment using hidden Markov models,*" in 3rd International Conference on Intelligent Systems for Molecular Biology, vol. 3, pp. 114–120, (1995)
24. Edgar R. C.; "*MUSCLE: multiple sequence alignment with high accuracy and high throughput,*" in Nucleic Acids Research, vol. 32, pp. 1792–1797, (2004)
25. Notredame C., Higgins D.G.; "*SAGA: sequence alignment by genetic algorithm,*" in Nucleic Acids Research, vol. 24, pp. 1515–1539, (1996)
26. Notredame C.; "*COFFEE: an objective function for multiple sequence alignments,*" in Bioinformatics, vol. 14, pp. 407–422, (1998)

27. Simossis V. A., Heringa J.; *"PRALINE: a multiple sequence alignment toolbox that integrates homology-extended and secondary structure information,"* in Nucleic Acids Research, vol. 33, pp. 289–294, (2005)

28. Shyu C., Sheneman L., Foster J. A.; *"Multiple Sequence Alignment with Evolutionary Computation,"* in Genetic Programming and Evolvable Machines, vol. 5, pp. 121-144, (2004)

29. Nguyen H. D., Yoshihara I., Yamamori K., Yasunaga M.; *"Aligning Multiple Protein Sequences by Parallel Hybrid Geneti Algorithm,"* in Genome Informatics, vol. 13, pp. 123–132, (2002)

30. Cutello V., Nicosia G.; *"An Immunological Approach to Combinatorial Optimization Problems"*, Advances in Artificial Intelligence - IBERAMIA 2002, 8th Ibero-American Conference on AI, Seville, Spain, November 12-15, 2002. Springer, Lecture Notes in Computer Science, vol. 2527, pp. 361-370, (2002)

31. Nicosia G.; *"Immune Algorithms for Optimization and Protein Structure Prediction,"* Ph.D. Dissertation, Department of Mathematics and Computer Science, University of Catania, Italy (2004)

32. Cutello V., Narzisi G., Nicosia G., Pavone M.; *"Clonal selection algorithms: A comparative case study using effective mutation potentials,"* in 4th International Conference on Artificial Immune Systems (ICARIS), pp. 13–28 (2005)

33. Cutello V., Nicosia G., Pavone M., Timmis J.; *"An Immune Algorithm for Protein Structure Prediction on Lattice Models,"* to appear in IEEE Transaction on Evolutionary Computation.

34. Cutello V., Nicosia G., Pavone M.; *"Exploring the capability of immune algorithms: A characterization of hypermutation operators,"* in 3rd International Conference on Artificial Immune Systems (ICARIS), pp. 263–276 (2004)

35. Taylor W. R.; *"A flexible method to align a large number of sequences,"* in J. Mol. Evol., vol. 28, pp. 161-169, (1988)

36. Thompson J. D., Plewniak F., Poch O.; *"BAliBASE: a benchmark alignment database for the evaluation of multiple alignment programs,"* in Bioinformatics, vol. 15, pp. 87–88 (1999).

37. Bahr A., Thompson J. D., Thierry J. C., Poch O.; *"BAliBASE (Benchmark Alignment dataBASE): Enhancements for Repeats, Transmembrane Sequences and Circular Permuations,"* in Nucleic Acids Research, vol. 29 (1), pp. 232–326 (2001).

Controlling the Heating System of an Intelligent Home with an Artificial Immune System

Martin Lehmann and Werner Dilger

Chemnitz University of Technology
09107 Chemnitz, Germany
martin.lehmann@s2000.tu-chemnitz.de,
dilger@informatik.tu-chemnitz.de

Abstract. Intelligent Home is nowadays an established technology. Actually, most existing realizations of the Intelligent Home cannot really adapt to the needs of the inhabitants of the home so that they can learn typical user behavior. In this paper we present an AIS that can perform the usual control functions but in addition is also able to adapt to varying requirements and to learn. The AIS is network based. The antigens represent the requests to the home and the antibodies the responses to these requests. Both incorporate the relevant parameters in their structure. Antibodies are produced according to the bone marrow model and a sort of reinforcement learning mechanism is implemented. The operation of the AIS is described by a scenario.

Keywords: Intelligent home, AIS-network, B-cell, antibody, antigen, adaptation.

1 Introduction

The intelligent home (iHome) is a technology that is in use since about the nineties as a by-product of building automation. It comprises several functions of which usually not all are installed in a realization. The mostly used functions are those for the security of the home. Other useful functions are control of temperature (heating and cooling) and of light. Existing realizations of the iHome operate with standard routines controlling certain parameters that are preset by the user. They cannot adapt themselves to varying requests of the users and they cannot learn typical user behavior and predict the needs of the users, in other words, they are not intelligent in the meaning of the word as it is used in AI or CI.

A first step to the control of an iHome by means of an AIS was made in [2]. However, only some terminology from AIS was adopted in that paper, it lacked a deep understanding of AIS principles. Mozer has done a lot of interesting work in building an iHome (his own one) (cf. [8]). His approach is based on neural networks, probably because he is a psychologist working in the Cognitive Neuroscience community at Boulder.

The iHome can be viewed as a kind of robot, though not a mobile but a stationary one. It is equipped with sensors and effectors of different types according to the needs of its functions. However, there are some important differences between the iHome and normal robot. The robot can be viewed more or less as a point-like entity,

H. Bersini and J. Carneiro (Eds.): ICARIS 2006, LNCS 4163, pp. 335 – 348, 2006.

whereas for the iHome spatial extension is an essential property. A robot exists in a certain environment and behaves according to its tasks and the conditions of the environment. The iHome also has an environment but it consists not only of the world outside the building but also of the world inside. In this part of the environment the iHome has to serve the varying requests of the inhabitants.

From the different parts of the iHome we have chosen the heating system because with respect to temperature the requests of the inhabitants are not constantly changing, rather there exist typical scenarios that are to be followed and that can be learned by the iHome. These scenarios are specified to single rooms in the house, certain daytimes, and the weekdays. The iHome must be flexible enough to react to deviations from the scenarios triggered by the inhabitants and to adapt to changes of the scenarios in time. In any case the iHome has to take into account the weather conditions outside.

Section 2 of this paper gives an overview of the heating system of a home. Section 3 describes how the requirements of the heating system must be formalized to build an AIS for controlling such a system. Based on the definitions in section 3 the AIS is modeled in section 4 with the structure of the antigens and antibodies, the network, and the bone marrow model. The results of a few simulated tests that are designed according to various needs of the inhabitants are presented in section 5. Finally, section 6 concludes the paper.

2   Some Properties of the Heating System of a Home

Figure 1 shows a heating system. Components like radiators and outlets of heated water are represented only once for simplicity. As can be seen from the figure, in a modern heating system one tries to reduce the costs of heating making use of different energy sources not only fossil fuels, e.g. solar energy. Also, the control of the temperature by the system tries to minimize the costs by reducing temperature by some degrees when a room is not used.

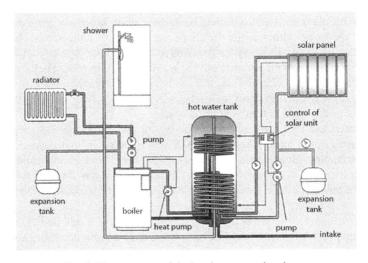

Fig. 1. The structure of the heating system in a home

The most important factors that should be regarded for the control of the heating system are the outdoor temperature, indoor temperature, type of the room, frequency of use, daytime, weekday, and ventilation. For the outdoor temperature an air temperature sensor must be installed outside the home. The indoor temperature is measured by air temperature sensors in each room. The temperature should be on a level that is pleasant to the inhabitants. Here, feedback can be given by the inhabitants by adjusting the temperature. The type of the room and the frequency of use are closely related. The frequency can be measured by motion detectors in the rooms. It clearly varies according to the type of the room but also to the daytime and even to the weekday. Daytime and weekday are in general important for the temperature, e.g. during the night, the temperature can be reduced. Ventilation also plays a role because a well controlled ventilation produces a good indoor climate and saves energy.

3   The Structure and Functioning of the AIS

The architecture of the AIS for the heating system is shown in figure 2. It consists of three components: the central unit, the AIS-network and the bone marrow. The central unit serves as an interface to the outside world, i.e. to the hardware of the heating system. It receives signals and produces antigens from these signals, and in the opposite direction it transforms the output of the network into commands to the heating system. The bone marrow produces new B-cells and adapts them to the needs of the AIS-network if necessary. The AIS-network performs reactions to the stimulations by antigens and antibodies by the operations selection and mutation, both based on the affinity between the elements.

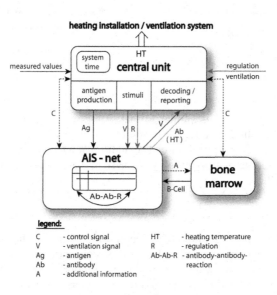

Fig. 2. The architecture of the AIS

3.1 Antibodies

The antibodies have a structure similar to those of Farmer and colleagues [3]. They consist of three components: a paratope, an encoding of the temperature, and an idiotope, cf. figure 3. Both, paratope and idiotope, have four attributes encoding the type of the room, the weekday, the daytime, and the frequency of use (of the room). The encoding of the temperature contains the current heating temperature and the optimal temperature. The last one is used to adapt the heating temperature to changes of the current temperature caused by regulations or ventilations By its paratope an antibody can recognize epitopes as parts of antigens but also idiotopes of other antibodies. The encoding of the temperature is evaluated in the central unit and is used to control the heating system.

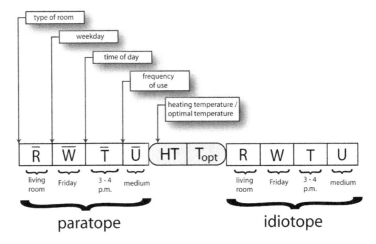

Fig. 3. The structure of the antibodies

3.2 Antigens

The structure of the antigens is similar to that of the paratopes of the antibodies. It consists of the same four attributes, but in addition it has two other attributes encoding the indoor and the outdoor temperature. The additional attributes are required for the adaptation of the optimal temperature by the system and so indirectly of the heating temperature as well.

3.3 B-cells

B-cells are used as carriers of antibody molecules. In addition to the antibody a B-cell has three attributes that encode parameters for the concentration, the ageing, and the selection of the cell. The value of the concentration parameter describes the concentration of the antibody in the network; the other two parameters are used to control the selection and elimination of the cell.

3.4 The Bone Marrow

The bone marrow (figure 4) produces the B-cells and hands them over to the AIS-network. For this purpose, first antibodies are composed of arbitrarily chosen parts. They are considered as immature and have to mature which means that the room temperature must be adapted to the values required for the different rooms. The value of the temperature parameter is computed from the encoding of the room and the frequency of use and of a predefined value for each room. In addition, it is adapted by signals from the network that record modifications of relevant antibodies in the system. The mature antibodies are completed to B-cells by values for the three parameters for concentration, ageing, and selection.

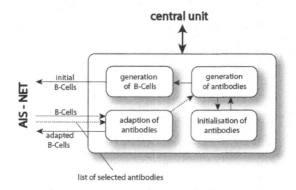

Fig. 4. The structure of the bone marrow

3.5 The Central Unit

The central unit is the interface between the AIS and the heating system as well as the ventilation system, cf. figure 5. With respect to the heating and ventilation system, it stores measured values from the hardware and commands from the inhabitants concerning regulation and ventilation, and on the other side, sends commands to the heating and the ventilation system. With respect to the AIS, it decodes the information delivered by antibody molecules, it produces stimuli that act as a kind of interrupt signals and are considered in this context as co-stimulative signals, and produces antigens from the measured values and the commands. In addition, it controls the other two components of the AIS, the network and the bone marrow.

The AIS-network is controlled by means of a number of parameters that can be regulated by the central unit. Among them are the initial size of the population, the size of the whole network, the number of elements that are best suited for the affinity computation as well as those that are worst suited, the number of elements that are best suited for mutation as well as those that are worst suited, the number of new elements, the number of elements to be eliminated, and the mutation rate. The bone marrow is controlled by regulation of the production of initial antibodies, the adaptation of initial elements, the initial values of the B-cells, and other parameters.

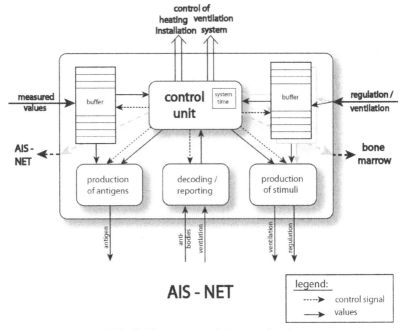

Fig. 5. The structure of the central unit

3.6 The AIS-Network

The network is the heart of the AIS. In cooperation with the central unit and the bone marrow it realizes three main functions: It determines the antibody that fits best to an antigenic stimulus (the so called *key element*), it processes the co-stimulative signals

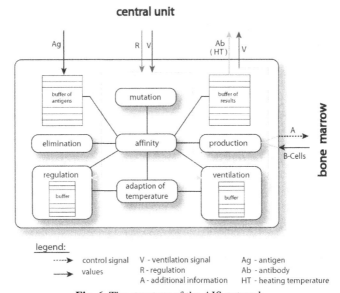

Fig. 6. The structure of the AIS-network

concerning the adaptation to the desires of the inhabitants, and it processes the co-stimulative signals that control the ventilation. The network is shown in figure 6.

In principle, the network consists of a number of functions that are closely connected with each other such that there is a strong interdependence between them. These functions control the buffer for the antigens and for the results, they compute the affinities between antigens and antibodies and among antibodies, they determine the mutation of antibodies and the production of new ones, they adapt the temperature parameter according to the desires of the users, they eliminate useless elements, they determine the key elements by a number of interrelated sub-functions, and finally select the best suited antibody.

4 The Realization of the AIS

A prerequisite for the AIS is the encoding of the attribute values. Some of them are real values, others are symbolic. For a uniform representation we decided to encode them as binary strings. In order to do this the real type parameters are divided into a finite number of intervals and their values are replaced with these intervals so that we end up with only a finite domain for each parameter. The implementation has been done in Java. For each main function and main component a class together with a number of subclasses is defined. Each class has a function for the input of values and an output function. The encoding is shown by the example of the codes for the rooms and some important classes of the implementation are described in more detail in the following subsections.

4.1 The Code of the Rooms as an Example for the Encoding

Each room in the house is encoded by a binary string according to the following criteria:

* Duration of use,
* frequency of use,
* preferred time of use,
* preferred temperature.

For instance for the bathroom and the living room we fixed values according to table 1:

Table 1. Parameter values for the encoding of rooms

	Duration of use	Frequency of use	Preferred time of use	Preferred Temperature
Bathroom	low	often	morning/evening	22 – 24 °C
Living Room	high	only once	evening	20 – 22 °C

All rooms are encoded according to this scheme. The values of the criteria mentioned above are encoded in such a way that the codes of similar values are close to each other. Table 2 gives an example for the frequency of use. This encoding has the effect that an antigen with high affinity to one of the three values low, medium, and high has also a certain affinity to the other values.

Table 2. Encoding of values

Frequency of use	Code
none	00000
low	11100
medium	11101
high	11111

4.2 The Class Definitions for Antibodies and Antigens

The two classes have similar structure and are responsible for the access to the parameter values. They can be created by the user, but normally antigens are produced by the central unit while antibodies are produced by the AIS-network. The method for the input of values in the definition of an instance of the class Antigen for instance is Antigen(), the method for displaying the relevant values of an instance is AgPrint(). The creation of an antigen is illustrated in figure 7, the output of the method AgPrint() is shown in figure 8.

```
Antigen Ag = new  Antigen(„110111111",
                          „11111101",
                          „01110111",
                          „11111",
                          11,
                          -5);
```

Fig. 7. Creation of an antigen

```
Ag:    110111111    11111101    01110111    11111   11  -5
Des:   living room  &  Tuesday  &  0 – 1 a.m. & no use
```

Fig. 8. Displaying an antigen

The output shows the codes for the room, day, time, and use, further the outdoor temperature (11), and the outdoor temperature (-5). In the antibody class the first four parameters correspond to the paratope part of the antibody and have the same meaning as in the antigen class, while the last two parameters represent the heating temperature and the optimal temperature. In addition, the antibody class contains four parameters for the idiotope part and their values are initialized complementary to those of the paratope part. An antibody with high affinity to the antigen of figure 8 would have the first six components shown in figure 9.

```
Ag:    001000000    00000010    00000000    00000   I !!11!! I 11 I
Des:   living room  &  Tuesday  &  2 – 3 a.m. & no use
```

Fig. 9. An antibody with high affinity to the antigen

The total affinity between antigen und antibody is determined as the sum of the affinities of the corresponding parts of both plus certain weights for these parts, e.g. for the room 0.00, for the day 0.10, for the time 0.25, and for the use 0.75. These weights reflect the priority between the parts. The total affinity is computed by

$$D = \sum_{i=1}^{L} \delta_i \quad \text{with } \delta_i = \begin{cases} 1 & \text{if } Ab \neq Ag \\ 0 & \text{otherwise} \end{cases}$$

L is the number of parts in the definition of the antigens, i.e. $L = 6$ in the example above. Codes for neighbored day times get an additional weight such that an antibody for time t_{j+1} has a greater affinity to the actual antigen (representing time t_j) than an antibody for a previous time.

4.3   The Class Definition for the AIS-Network

This class, called AIS, has the method AIS() by which a new network is created, i.e. an initial population of antibodies. There are methods for the ventilation and the regulation of the heating system. The most important method is upgradeAIS() which performs the network algorithm. The algorithm follows that of de Castro and von Zuben but is extended by some elements from clonal selection theory, in particular the co-stimulative signals that are used to represent regulation and ventilation signals given by the users. It proceeds in the following steps:

Determine the current antigen
Check co-stimulative signals
Create a list with a fixed number of new B-cells (from the bone marrow)
For each B-cell in the network do
    Select the antibody molecule form the B-cell
    Compute its affinity to the antigen
    If the affinity is higher than those of the elements in the list, add the B-cell to
        the list
    If the affinity is lower than a certain threshold value, mark the cell as useless
    Determine the concentration and the age of the B-cell
    If the affinity of the B-cell's antibody is higher than that of the elements in the
        list of B-cells, add the cell to the list and possibly remove another one
Fix the key element for the current room according to the best one of the B-cells
Generate a list of mutated antibodies from the list of best B-cells
    Determine the mutation rate
    Generate a mutated antibody according to the mutation rate
    Store the antibodies in a special list
Eliminate antibodies whose affinity is lower than that of the last element in the list
    of best B-cells
Eliminate a predefined number of elements from the list of useless elements

5   A Test Scenario

We have tested the system with a number of scenarios that show the different functionalities of the system, i.e. how the system adapts itself to various needs of the inhabitants and to regulation and ventilation signals. The test data were produced by means of the class `createAntigens`. We will demonstrate the processing of the system with a scenario that shows how the system adapts to co-stimulative signals for ventilation and regulation while the behavior of the users stays unchanged.

The scenario starts with a list of 10×24 antigens which represents the input of 24 antigens (one for each hour of the day) ten times. Together with the antigens at certain times co-stimulative signals for the regulation are sent to the system. At the beginning of a week new signals for ventilation are prefixed and stored in the AIS which are processed at the defined times. The settings are repeated for each week with minor modifications to simulate the behavior of the system during several weeks. Figure 10 shows how the values of the temperature change during one day of the second week. The first to weeks represent the initialization phase of the system.

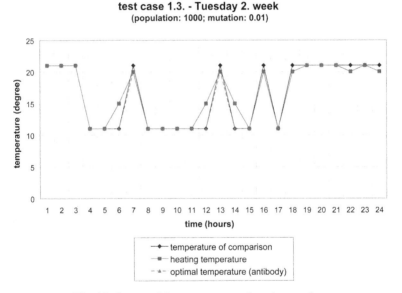

Fig. 10. Course of the temperature values for one day

Figure 11 shows how the system reacts on two regulation signals in the 2nd (up by 3° C) and in the 7th hour (down by 2° C) and on a (prefixed) ventilation signal in the 13th hour. The ventilation signal causes the heating temperature to go down. The system keeps the modifications by the regulation and ventilation signals and adapts the heating and the optimal temperature in the following weeks. This is achieved by new or mutated antibodies that are introduced into the network.

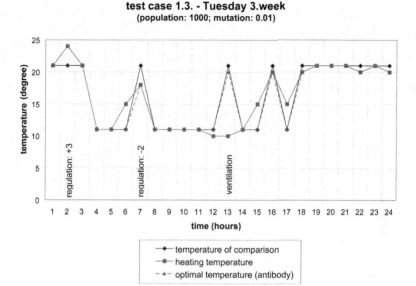

Fig. 11. Regulation and ventilation signals

In figure 12 the down regulated signal in the 7th hour is again regulated up by 3° C and an additional ventilation signal in the 17th hour is given. The system immediately adapts to the regulation signal since appropriate antibodies are still available, and it adapts to the ventilation signal in the same manner as to the first one in figure 10.

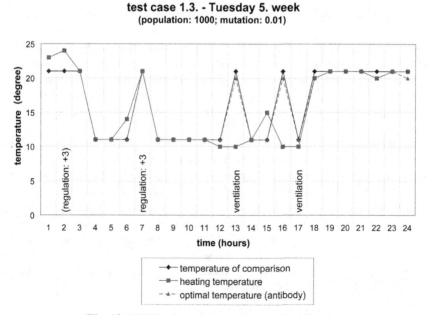

Fig. 12. Additional regulation and ventilation signals

Figure 13 shows the situation after an additional regulation signal. The temperature in the 2nd hour is regulated down by 5° C. This influences the antibodies that are associated with the 2nd hour in this room and at this day. The regulation in the 7th hour is kept unchanged since the antibodies associated with this hour are not influenced. The ventilation signals shown in figure 12 are removed from the system because they had only a temporally suppressing effect and the system can adapt to the normal behavior very quickly.

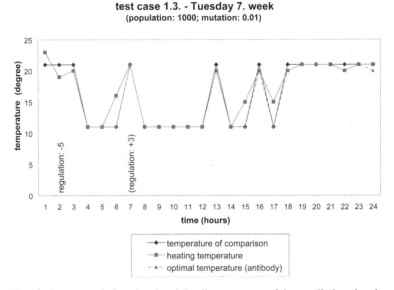

Fig. 13. A new regulation signal and the disappearance of the ventilation signals

Finally, figure 14 shows the unchanged effect of the previously done regulations and how the system has optimally adapted to the desires of the users. This can be seen by comparing figures 13 and 14. The heating temperature is regulated down in the 1st hour and up in the 12th hour because the system has learned that the users expect a lower temperature at the 2nd hour and at the 13th hour and so it starts in time with regulating up or down.

The purpose of this scenario was to demonstrate how the system can adapt to regulation and ventilation signals which are treated as co-stimulative signals. As we have seen in our experiments, it is rather easy for the system to learn the "normal" behavior of the users, i.e. the usual course without interrupt signals. But the aim that we had with this system was to make it able to adapt quickly to special demands from the users (by interrupt signals) without forgetting the normal course of events and being able to get back to it as soon as possible. Interrupt signals have only local effects around the hour where they are sent. In particular the ventilation signals influence the system only temporally so that it quickly returns to the normal course when the signals are no longer delivered.

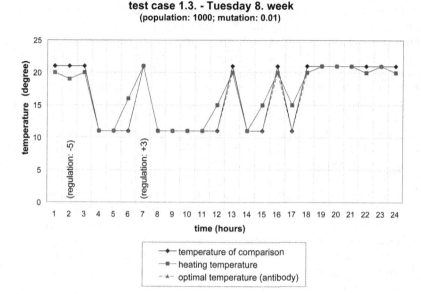

Fig. 14. The final adaptation of the system to the desires of the inhabitants

The reason for this behavior of the system lies in the use of the antibodies that are specialized to rooms, weekdays, and hours. When an adaptation is required at some hour, the antibodies responsible for the normal behavior in this hour are not completely eliminated; rather some of them survive for some time and can be easily reactivated if necessary. This makes the system able to quickly re-adapt when the deviating behavior is no longer required, and this is important for a flexible use of the system in the context of the intelligent home.

6   Conclusion

We have described an Artificial Immune System that has been developed for the control of an intelligent home. Such a system should be able to learn the normal behavior of the inhabitants which is assumed to be constant for most of the time. This assumption is certainly correct for most people. The system must be able to differentiate between days, times, and rooms in the house. In addition, the use in the home requires the ability to quickly adapt to spontaneously sent signals from the users and to re-adapt to the normal behavior later.

We have presented in this paper an implementation of an AIS that satisfies the needs of the intelligent home and we have demonstrated how it operates by a certain test scenario that in particular deals with the problem of adaptation to commands deviating from the normal behavior. We have tested the system in a number of other scenarios not included in this paper. In these scenarios the regular use, the regular use with a break of two weeks of no use, the regular use with a change of use after a number of weeks, irregular use with frequent changes, and the control of several rooms. In all these cases, the system adapted pretty well to the various requirements. In addition, we did some tests to determine optimal values for the relevant parameters in the system like mutation rate and adaptation of concentration.

Further developments on an AIS for the intelligent home should include other components of the home, e.g. the lighting system. We have already developed an AIS for such a system, but this is based on the clonal selection theory, and it turned out that the results are not as convincing as those based on a network approach. The appropriate choice of the parameter values is always a problem in an AIS. It depends on the deployment of the AIS therefore it would be a good idea to have some kind of meta-learning system that is able to adapt the parameters to the current application.

Finally, the question remains about the actual deployment in a house that has all the required technology at its disposal. The heating control system we have presented has a clearly defined interface to the outside world, in this case to the world of the hardware of the heating system via the central unit. It is responsible for the translation of incoming signals into antigens and it produces commands to the heating system from the antibodies. For the test of the system it does not matter if the signals are real or simulated. However in general, reality is different from simulation to some degree. Therefore we hope that we can connect it one day to the iPhon-software of ESF Software Company. iPhon is a control system for building automation ([6]) but has also been deployed for the control of iHomes. If the AIS will be successfully tested in combination with iPhon, it may be possible to implement it in one of the homes where iPhon is in use.

References

1. L.N. de Castro and F.J. von Zuben. aiNET: An artificial immune network for data analysis. In *Data Mining: A heuristic approach,* H.A. Abbass, R.A. Sarker, and C.S. Newton (eds.), Idea Group Publishing, USA, 2001, 231 - 259
2. W. Dilger. Decentralized autonomous organization of the intelligent home according to the principle of the immune system. In Proceedings of IEEE System, Man, and Cybernetics Conference, Orlando 1997, 351 – 356.
3. J.D. Farmer, S.A. Kauffman, N.H. Packard, and A.S. Perelson. Adaptive dynamic networks as models for the immune system and autocatalytic sets. *Ann. of the New York Academy of Sciences,* 504, 1987, 118 – 131
4. E. Hart, P. Ross, A. Webb, and A. Lawson. A role for immunology in "Next generation" robot controllers. In *Proceedings of ICARIS 2004,* Edinburgh, Springer LNCS 2787, 2003, 46 – 56
5. A. Ishiguro, Y. Watanabe, T. Kondo, Y. Shirai, and Y. Uchikawa. Immunoid. A robot with a decentralized behavior arbitration mechanisms based on the immune system. In *Proceedings of ICMAS Workshop on Immunity-Based Systems.* Nagao, 1996, 82 – 92
6. ESF Software GmbH. http://www.esf-software.com/de/home/index.php
7. M. Krautmacher, W. Dilger. AIS based robot navigation in a rescue scenario. In *Proceedings of ICARIS 2005,* Catania, 2005, Springer LNCS 3239, 106 – 118
8. M.C. Mozer. Lessons from an adaptive house. In D. Cook and R. Das (eds.), *Smart environments: Technologies, protocols, and applications.* Hoboken, NJ, J. Wiley & Sons, 2005, 273 - 294

Don't Touch Me, I'm Fine: Robot Autonomy Using an Artificial Innate Immune System

Mark Neal[1], Jan Feyereisl[2], Rosario Rascunà[3], and Xiaolei Wang[4]

[1] Computer Science, University of Wales, Aberystwyth, UK
[2] School of Computer Science, University of Nottingham, UK
[3] CCNR, University of Sussex, UK
[4] Electrical and Communications Engineering, Helsinki University
of Technology, Espoo, Finland

ARTIST Network: Student Spring School, Aberystwyth, UK
April 2006

Abstract. A model for integration of low-level responses to damage, potential damage and component failure in robots is presented. This model draws on the notion of inflammation and introduces an extensible, sub-symbolic mechanism for modulating high-level behaviour using the notion of artificial inflammation. Preliminary results obtained via simulation are presented and demonstrate the potential benefits of such a scheme. Additionally the system maps the robot's physiological state-space, which is defined in terms of the levels and sources of inflammatory response. This is achieved using Kohonen's Self-Organizing Map algorithm to arrange the states experienced during the lifetime of the robot. The future use of this map for diagnosis and localization of faults and for the generation of specific high-level remediation behaviour is also discussed.

Keywords: Artificial Immune Systems, Human Immune Systems, Innate Immunity, TLR, PAMPs, Inflammation, SOM, Robot.

1 Introduction

With a few rare exceptions such as [10,4], the innate immune system has been neglected in artificial immune systems [3], especially in the field of robotics which appears to have much to be gained from such an approach. The functions making up this part of the immune system, offer a number of useful analogies that can be exploited in a robotic system. In the quest for autonomy an artificial innate immune system can be applied in order to create systems which are aware of their own state. This could allow them to maintain a "healthy", homeostatic balance and achieve self sufficiency. In order to achieve this a robot must contain a number of proprioceptive[1] sensors, monitoring various state measures across

---

[1] proprioceptive: sensing internal body state.

H. Bersini and J. Carneiro (Eds.): ICARIS 2006, LNCS 4163, pp. 349–361, 2006.

the physical domain of the robotic system [2]. An analogy emerges here with Toll-Like Receptors (TLRs) as sensors of potentially problematic signals within the body. Such signals are known as Pathogen Associated Molecular Patterns (PAMPs) [9]. In robotic systems simple sensors capable of detecting problematic circumstances (eg. "motor3 overheating") can often be used locally to help remediate the problem without recourse to high-level software and control systems. This is directly analogous to the types of action taken by innate immune system components (such as macrophages) endowed with TLRs. Difficulties arise in engineering complex robotic systems (or other electro-mechanical systems) which attempt to integrate the input from large numbers of such local sensing and remediation devices into high-level control systems. It rapidly becomes impossible to predict all possible combinations of problem and remediation action, and computationally expensive to process all this information in the high-level controller. A number of approaches to robot control have addressed this problem with varying degrees of success, the best known being [1]. The notion of artificial inflammation allows the integration of information about low-level response patterns into a small number of global signals which represent the "state of health" of the system throughout time. These simple inflammatory signals can then be used via schemes such as neuro-endocrine control [7,8] to modulate high-level control systems appropriately.

The representation of the states of the robotic system using Kohonen's Self-Organizing Maps (SOM) [6] allows the sources of the inflammation to be localized within individual nodes in order to both diagnose problems at intermediate levels (eg. "motor compartment 2 overheating") and to allow higher-level remediation to be appropriately targeted on the components that directly affect the inflamed parts of the robot.

A description of the physiology of a robot follows, including the analogy drawn from the innate immune system. Next, a step-by-step description of the model is used to show exactly how it works both in this specific case and how the scheme works in general. A proof of concept experiment is described, supported by the results obtained and a commentary on what the results show. This is followed by some conclusions, including advantages and disadvantages of the proposed model.

2   Robot Physiology

In general a robot is a complex system made up of numerous interacting components that can fail or malfunction alone as well as in combination. Typical components also include automatic damage protection functions and circuits such as locally switched cooling fans and automatic overheat cut-outs. Analogies between such components and the innate immune system are presented here. Firstly the function of TLRs in the innate immune system is the detection of PAMPs. In a robot the proprioceptive sensors which monitor the state of the robot can be considered to be analogous to TLRs. For example a temperature sensor, measuring the temperature of a motor within a robot might have a TLR associated with it containing a function (see Figure 1) which determines if the TLR gets triggered and by what amount. PAMPs, in terms of robotics are signals received by the robot's proprioceptive sensors (TLRs). These can trigger the TLRs starting the immune response in order to prevent possible damage in the long run. For example a temperature which exceeds various predefined thresholds might trigger responses designed to limit or prevent damage. In the natural innate immune system the action of TLRs leads to the generation of an inflammatory response via a number of pathways and mechanisms. This response is initially characterized by the generation, accumulation and diffusion of cytokines through the local tissues and into the bloodstream. In the longer term, continued inflammation results in a sustained "stress response" which has wide-ranging and diverse effects at a number of levels. This can affect physiological responses, behaviour and psychological state. These responses might vary from protection of an inflamed area, to the reduction of use of a limb due to localized pain through to increased sleep periods in severe cases. These varied responses can be incorporated into an innate artificial immune system with the help of the SOM. This can be achieved by activating the SOM using the current state vector of the robot (represented by the states of activation of all TLRs in the robot) and responding appropriately to affect the high-level controller, by releasing hormone into a neuro-endocrine controller for example. Whilst not implemented here assignment of remediation activities to particular nodes of the SOM (such as specification of which hormone to release) could be achieved automatically by examining which components of the robot are the source of the inflammation and selectively suppressing control system components which access those components. In the first instance this is a reasonable assumption, but in those cases where this response is insufficient to prevent further inflammation the SOM can be used to "spread" the inflammatory response to neighbouring nodes in order to suppress activity of components in closely related states. The gradual spreading of inflammation through the SOM ensures that the dependence on "engineered-in" relationships between component failures and remediation activities is only used in the first instance. When such relationships are incompletely or incorrectly assigned, the spreading to other closely related remediation activities improves the likelihood of an appropriate response being elicited in a computationally inexpensive and extensible manner.

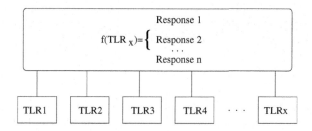

Fig. 1. Schematic of the TLRs' functions

For example, this could enable the system to locally engage in an activity in an inflamed area in order to prevent damage. In the case of an overheating motor this localisation feature ensures that a nearby fan gets switched on, rather than a fan in a distant part of the robot.

The inflammatory response is simply accumulated over time from the individual TLR response levels. The sum of TLR activity is calculated at each time step and added to the current inflammation level. Also at each time step the inflammation level is geometrically decayed. Thus the formula for updating the inflammation at each time step is as follows:

$$inf_{t+1} = decay \times (inf_t + \sum_{x=1}^{n} f(TLR_x)) \tag{1}$$

where inf_t is the inflammation level at time t, $decay$ is a scalar in the range $0 < decay < 1$ and $f(TLR_x)$ is the activation level of the x'th individual TLR from a set of n in the complete system.

3   Innate Autonomy

A detailed description of the functionality of the model follows, presenting a framework for robot autonomy based on the innate immune system.

Assuming a simplistic robot comprising of four motors, two fans and four sensors each measuring the temperature of one motor, a description of each step of the model is given. The robot is initially in a stable, homeostatic state from which it will deviate over the duration of the description of the model. The homeostatic state is defined to be when the four motors are operating continuously with the fans switched off. All four motors can be switched on and off at any point in time, according to the activity of TLRs (based on the motor temperatures). Both fans can also be triggered (also by the TLRs) to cool the motors.

3.1   PAMPs

At regular intervals sensors within the robot collect data about the robot's state and convert this data into signals. These signals are analogous to PAMPs in the human body. These signals are collected by the corresponding TLRs in order to monitor and respond locally to the state of the system. In our example robot these are simply the temperatures of each individual motor.

3.2   TLRs

If one motor is overheating while the others are functioning correctly, the associated sensor generates a PAMP which is passed to the related TLR. A PAMP is defined to be a sensor reading that deviates from normal according to a predefined function, which operates as part of the TLR. Each TLR has a predefined set of responses as shown in Figure 1. Once the TLR receives the signal (ie. the temperature reading), it evaluates it according to predefined condition and response pairs shown in Table 1. The TLR also returns the inflammation level associated with the particular response:

$$y = f(TLR_x) \tag{2}$$

where x denotes the TLR in question and y denotes the inflammation level associated with the action that should be performed when the robot is in that state. Such functions can be implemented in terms of simple mathematical functions, lookup tables, fuzzy logic operators or any other appropriate technique. An example input could be the value 50, which represents the temperature of one of the motors and a response is generated according to the following lookup table (for example):

Table 1. Function table

Condition	Response
$T_x < 40°C$	$\emptyset$
$40°C < T_x < 80°C$	Fan On
$T_x > 80°C$	Fan On, Motor Off

This means, that the outcome of the function f will be the action *Fan On*. This is a local immediate response to the trigger of a single TLR. If the temperature is within the acceptable range, no action will be taken.

	Response$_1$	Response$_2$	...	Response$_n$
TLR$_1$	1.0	1.0	...	$f(TLR_1)$
TLR$_2$	0.0	0.0	...	$f(TLR_2)$
...	...	...	...	...
TLR$_x$	...	...	...	$f(TLR_x)$
$\sum_{m=1}^{x} f(TLR_m)$	...	...	...	...

Fig. 2. Input Feature Vector

In this model implementation, the stable state inflammation level is represented with the real value 0.0, while the TLR triggered state is 1.0. This is the contribution to the inflammation level described above. Once the model collects the outputs of the TLR functions of each individual TLR, a vector is created from the responses as shown in Figure 2. This vector is used as input to the SOM and the sum of its components is used to update the inflammation level according to equation 1.

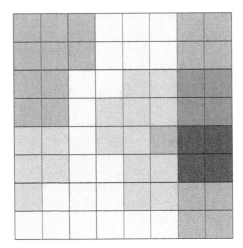

Fig. 3. Self-Organizing Map trained using data acquired from the simulated robot control system. The upper left corner represents normal operation states, and the dark patch in the lower right quadrant represents states where many or all of the TLRs are responding. Other regions of the map represent states where fewer TLRs are responding.

3.3   Self-organizing Maps

The higher level state representation of the robot is encoded using a SOM [5].

The strength of a SOM algorithm in the context of this work is the way it deals with multidimensional input vectors. The algorithm is able to cope with large amounts of n-dimensional data and find correlations between them. This means that a system incorporating a SOM is highly scalable, as large numbers of input sensors can be dealt with. Upon finding a correlation between input vectors, the algorithm locates an appropriate neuron within the SOM, which consequently gets activated. This process is performed in an unsupervised manner, thus avoiding tedious and possibly inaccurate supervised methods, which would only allow a limited set of states to be represented within the map. A SOM is a low dimensional representation of the input data which preserves the topological properties of the input and explicitly represents multiple relationships between similar states. This feature enables the proposed system to evolve the map in a way which can be exploited for the purpose of inflammation. Neurons within the SOM which are topologically in close proximity represent states with certain similarities and thus result in only slightly different responses when activated. This is in contrast to most traditional statistical analysis methods such as cluster analysis or minimal spanning trees which do not unambiguously and explicitly represent such rich relationships between data items. The SOM also allows the possibility of learning on-the-fly without requiring discontinuous reorganisations of the state map which can result using statistical analyses such as cluster analysis.

The SOM contains all possible states of the robot, distributed across the map in a topologically ordered fashion and clustered according to similarity of the states. Initially the SOM is trained on a set of known problematic as well as stable states. This gives the map an informed starting point, from which it can evolve and adapt over the lifetime of the robot. A major feature of a SOM is the clustering effect which means that general robotic states can be identified in the maps produced when trained in this way. An example of this is the stable/homeostatic state; this state will be represented within the SOM by a cluster of similar nodes in which most of the TLR responses are zero. This can be seen in figure 3 in the top left corner of the map. In contrast the dark region in the lower right quadrant of the map has clustered all the states in which two motors are overheating and can be considered to be a stressed state of the robot, and if the robot remains in this state for long periods then inflammation will result and spread the activation throughout the map.

The input into the SOM is the TLR vector, which contains all TLR responses. This vector is presented to the SOM and the algorithm finds the node within the map which is closest to the input feature vector. In our case this is measured using the Euclidean distance.

3.4   Neuro-endocrine Control

The system then passes on the responses, which correspond to the winning node within the SOM, in order to influence the higher level control mechanism's behaviour. This response could be achieved in a number of ways, but perhaps a good candidate would be using a neuro-endocrine control system [7,8] where the artificial hormone is simply the inflammation level. These neuro-endocrine controllers rely on standard multi-layer perceptron neural networks with the simple addition of sensitivity to hormone concentrations built into their synapses. Thus the neural networks in the control system could be selectively (selection being performed by the SOM) suppressed by the application of the inflammation level as an artificial hormone at their synapses in the (now standard) neuro-endocrine way:

$$u = \sum_{i=0}^{nx} w_i \cdot x_i \cdot inf_t \tag{3}$$

where n is the number of synapses at the artificial neuron, w_i is the weight associated with the i'th synapse, x_i is the input to that synapse and inf_t is the inflammation level at the time t. This new activation level is then used with the standard output function:

$$o = \frac{1}{1 + e^{-u}} \tag{4}$$

where o is the output from the neuron in question. This provides a simple but effective way of affecting the higher level control systems of the robot.

3.5 Spreading Inflammation

The clustering effect of the SOM offers a way of dealing with local as well as more widespread problems in a way which is analogous to inflammation. The robot is in a stable/homeostatic state if all its actuators are working correctly. Once problems start to occur, the nodes which become activated within the SOM fall outside the cluster of the stable behaviour. Once in such an unstable state the artificial innate immune system first deals with the problem locally at the level of TLRs. In case this local prevention does not return the robot to a stable state within a short period of time, inflammation starts to spread to neighbouring nodes of the current state node. This way the system deals with the problem by performing similar, yet slightly different responses, until the problem is rectified and the robot is returned to a stable state (a node within the SOM is activated which belongs to the cluster of stable/homeostatic behaviour).

4 Proof of Principle

A proof of principle implementation has been developed to demonstrate the key features of the operation of the model as described above. The model contains a small number of TLRs and uses inflammation responses generated by them to modify behaviour of a very simple high level control system. The inflammation response is integrated across the system and is decayed in the manner indicated above. Simple physical models of heating and cooling of motors are included in the simulation. The SOM component is not currently integrated into the system, but the vectors representing the system state were collected during the execution of the model and were used to train an SOM to prove the principle. This implementation has been performed as a simulation containing the important parts of the robot's functionality. The following results were obtained, supporting the proposed principle and its viability in a future physical system implementation.

4.1 Description of the Model

The simulated robot has two motor compartments: one for the front two wheels and one for the rear two wheels. Each wheel has a separate motor as is common in all-terrain robots. Each compartment also has a single cooling fan which is responsible for cooling the pair of motors in that compartment. Each motor has a TLR associated with it which monitors the motor's temperature. Each TLR has three possible states. The "normal" state is that the motor is enabled and the fan is switched off. When the motor reaches a predefined threshold temperature the TLR will activate and switch on the fan in that compartment. If the motor reaches a second, higher threshold temperature which endangers the motor then the TLR will activate a thermal cut-out which cuts all current to the motor in question in order to allow it to cool. This disables the motor and thus deprives the high-level control system and the robot as a whole of the use of that motor. The simulation ensures that the temperature of the motors increases proportionally to the current passing through it. The motor model also includes a simplistic but sufficiently realistic cooling curve, the effects of which can be discerned in figure 5. The current applied to the motor is controlled by a high-level control system, which in the simulation is a simple fixed sequence of instructions. The purpose of the simulation is to demonstrate the action of the innate immune system components, and thus the implementation of a neuro-endocrine controller was not deemed necessary.

It is important to note that decisions are taken by the TLRs without the intervention of the high level control system, and they have to be considered as the first response of the immune system. The high level control system might then be influenced to change its behaviour depending on the inflammation present in the system through a scheme such as the neuro-endocrine controller outlined above (see section 3.4). In this model a more simplistic high-level control mechanism is used, but importantly it *is* affected by the inflammation level and modifies the requested current taking this inflammation level into account. This is a very simplistic remediation mechanism.

5   Results

Figure 4 shows how increasing current causes an increase in inflammation. The oscillations in the inflammation are due to the action of the TLRs switching the cooling fans and the motors themselves on and off. The effect of the inflammation is also to reduce the currents requested by the high level control system using a simple inversely proportional relationship (see Figure 6). The high-level control system is at the same time always attempting to return the motor currents to the requested levels.

Figure 5 shows the temperature of one motor over a period of time varying with the current. For a current of 0.1, after reaching the limit temperature of 40 (this value was fixed arbitrarily) a response is performed by the TLR which causes the fan to switch on. This operation causes the temperature of the motor to decrease. However the high level control system is trying to return current to the requested level. Considering a current of 0.1 the fan is always able to control the temperature. This pattern can also be seen when the current is 0.2. A different case occurs when the current is 0.5, this means that the high level control system is driving the motor at a high rate in order to fulfill its aim. This causes the TLR to activate the fan and frequently switch off the motor to prevent damage.

Figure 6 shows the effects of varying current over time in different motors and the resultant inflammation level. In this experiment motor1 simulates the occurrence of a fault, resulting in excessive current at time step 500. This causes the inflammation level to rise in steps as the requested current increases at time steps 1000 and 1500. The dramatic increase in inflammation at time step 2000 is due to the failure of the fan to cool motor1 and subsequent coincidental failure of motor2 and motor3. This inflammation comes from the activity of TLRs 2 and 3 as they activate the other fan and switch off the motors when required. At time step 2500 the faults are removed from the motors and the system returns to normal operation. This type of over-current condition can result from sticky

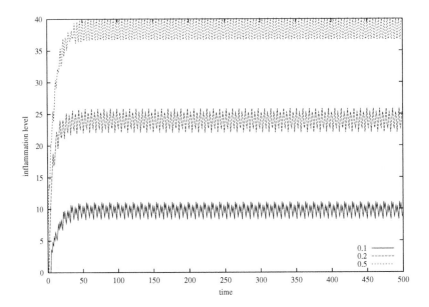

Fig. 4. Increasing current causes increasing inflammation level

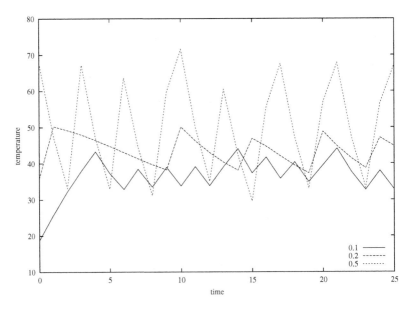

Fig. 5. Impact of varying motor current over the time

motor bearings or fouling of axles by long grass and is relatively common in drive motors of all-terrain robots. The figure illustrates the way in which the inflammation level varies and responds to the state of the robot and how it can rapidly return to "normal" when faults are dealt with.

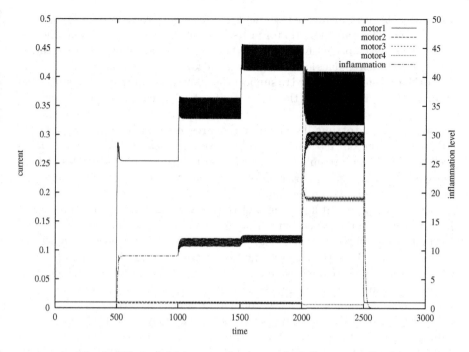

Fig. 6. Effect of the current change on the inflammation level

Figure 3 shows the SOM as generated using the state input feature vectors taken from the above experiments. A clear cluster, representing the homeostatic state, can be seen in the upper left region of the table. This cluster comprises of states which contain value 0 for all TLR responses. This value represents no triggering activity of the TLRs. By contrast, the dark region in the lower right quadrant represents triggering of TLRs both to switch on a fan and to switch two motors off to prevent damage. The region in the centre of the bottom row represents triggering of a single fan, and is bordered by regions to the left and right which represent switching on the fan in the other motor compartment (left) and switching off a motor in the overheating compartment (right). These adjacent regions can be used to highlight what might happen if inflammation caused by the single fan in the first motor compartment persists and is required to spread through the SOM. Activation of the adjacent regions mentioned will trigger preventative high-level actions appropriate for these closely related states. For example reducing current in the affected motors is likely to be one of the actions taken in order to pre-empt the triggering of the TLRs in the other components.

6   Conclusion

A scheme for incorporating low-level damage prevention and maintenance activities into a coherent biologically inspired control paradigm has been proposed, based on an innate immune system. Three important aspects of the innate immune system have been applied with clear analogies between a robotic and a human immune system. These are the notion of TLRs, inflammation and localisation. The system has been developed with the help of a SOM as an adaptive state representation of the robot, which enables local as well as global failure prevention and ratification. A model has been implemented to support the above given principles. Results from performed experiments show that the activity of TLRs causes an incremental inflammatory response over time, in case the robot is not returned to a stable state in a reasonable period of time. This inflammatory response can be used along with the SOM to locate the affected area of the robot in order to deal with it on a more global level. The presented preliminary results support the described principles and encourage future development of a real robot implementation incorporating immune, neural and endocrine control components.

Some of the potential advantages of this scheme are highlighted throughout the earlier parts of the paper, but perhaps one of the most significant is that it offers a relatively simple mechanism for integrating existing engineering knowledge of how to deal with particular problems locally with the higher level and less well defined parts of the control system. Some potential disadvantages include: that the engineer must still manually assign fault conditions and remediation activities for local conditions which leaves room for oversight and error; the overhead of maintaining a system-wide map of the robot's state may cause problems (whilst maintaining the SOM is unlikely to be computationally expensive, the gathering of its input data from all over the robot could be problematic); and last but by no means least, it is not yet clear how such an innate system might fit into a full multi-layer artificial immune system for a robot. Apart from the obvious next step (implementing the system as described on a real robot), a pressing piece of future work will be identification of how this might be achieved.

It is also interesting to consider the effect of the system on the combination of task achieving behaviour and survival behaviour. Whilst the mechanism here does not explicitly address this (potential) conflict, it does provide an interesting possibility when combined with the neuro-endocrine control systems described above and elsewhere. The "soft" switching, suppression and promotion of behaviours is precisely what this conflict requires in order to achieve the sorts of complex trade-offs that are observed in nature. The addition of an inflammation based driver for such behaviour mediation provides an additional homogeneous driver *specifically for maintenance of homeostasis*. This is an important step forward as it provides a truly integrated mechanism for promotion of survival behaviours within task achieving robot systems.

Acknowledgements

This paper arose as a direct result of the ARTIST Network[2] funded Student Spring School held at Aberystwyth on April 8-13th 2006. Whilst the direct contributors are listed as authors we would like to thank all of those who attended

---

[2] ARTIST is an EPSRC (UK) funded network to support artificial immune systems research.

for help, discussions and ideas. In particular we would like to thank Julie Greensmith for coaching us on the functioning of the innate immune system and the inflammatory response.

References

1. R Brooks. A robust layered control system for a mobile robot. *IEEE Journal of Robotics and Automation*, 2(1):14–23, 1986.
2. W. Clancey. *Situated Cognition: On Human Knowledge and Computer Representations*. Cambridge University Press, 1997.
3. L N de Castro and J Timmis. *Artificial Immune Systems: A New Computational Intelligence Approach*. Springer-Verlag, 2002.
4. J. Greensmith, U. Aickelin, and S. Cayzer. Introducing Dendritic Cells as a Novel Immune-Inspired Algorithm for Anomaly Detection. In *Proceedings of the 4th International Conference on Artificial Immune Systems*, volume 3627, 2005.
5. T Kohonen. Self-organised formation of topologically correct feature maps. *Biological Cybernetics*, 43:59–69.
6. Teuvo Kohonen. *Self-organising Maps*. Springer, 1995.
7. M. Neal and J. Timmis. Timidity: A Useful Mechanism for Robot Control? *Informatica*, 27(4):197–204, 2003.
8. M Neal and J Timmis. *Recent Advances in Biologically Inspired Computing*, chapter : Once more unto the breach... towards artificial homeostasis? IGP, 2004.
9. L Sompayrac. *How the immune system works*. Blackwell, 2002.
10. Bruce C. Trapnell Jr. A peer-to-peer blacklisting strategy inspired by leukocyte-endothelium interaction. In *Proceedings of the 4th International Conference on Artificial Immune Systems*, volume 3627, 2005.

Price Trackers Inspired by Immune Memory

William O. Wilson, Phil Birkin, and Uwe Aickelin

School of Computer Science, University of Nottingham,UK
{wow, pab, uxa}@cs.nott.ac.uk

Abstract. In this paper we outline initial concepts for an immune inspired algorithm to evaluate price time series data. The proposed solution evolves a short term pool of trackers dynamically through a process of proliferation and mutation, with each member attempting to map to trends in price movements. Successful trackers feed into a long term memory pool that can generalise across repeating trend patterns. Tests are performed to examine the algorithm's ability to successfully identify trends in a small data set. The influence of the long term memory pool is then examined. We find the algorithm is able to identify price trends presented successfully and efficiently.

1 Introduction

The investigation of time series data for analysis and prediction of future information is a popular and well studied area of research. Historically statistical techniques have been applied to this problem domain, however in recent years the use of evolutionary techniques has seen significant growth in this area. Neural networks [6] [13], genetic programming [7], and genetic algorithms [3] are all examples of methods that have been recently applied to time series evaluation and prediction.

However the use of immune inspired (IS) techniques in this field has remained fairly limited [9]. IS algorithms have been used with success in other fields such as pattern recognition [2], optimisation [5], and data mining [8]. In this paper we propose an IS approach, using *trackers* to identify trends in time series data, and take advantage of the associative learning properties exhibited by the natural immune system.

The time series proposed for investigation in this paper is that of price movements (Section 2) and the approach used to identify trends in price data is inspired by the immune memory theory of Dr Eric Bell [1]. His theory indicates the existence of two separately identifiable memory populations which are ideally suited to recognise long and short term trends prevalent in time series data. In Section 3 we discuss this immune memory theory and introduce other immune mechanisms which form part of our algorithm. The algorithm itself is then presented in Section 4. The methodology for testing the algorithm, the results and discussions of the results are documented in Sections 5, 6 and 7 respectively, before concluding in Section 8.

H. Bersini and J. Carneiro (Eds.): ICARIS 2006, LNCS 4163, pp. 362–375, 2006.
© Springer-Verlag Berlin Heidelberg 2006

2   Analysis and Representation of Price Trends

In our approach price data is converted to price movements over time and presented to the system as an antigen. The change in price at time t_i is calculated as the closing price at time t_i less that of t_{i-1}. Price movements are then banded to simplify classification. For example a price rise between \$0 and \$1 is categorised as a \$1 price rise and stored as the antigen Ag = [1]. The classification boundary (in this case 1) can be altered as required depending on the level of detail needed in the evaluation. Price movements are then stored in chronological order within a vector representing the antigen. The antigen provides a historical record of price changes over a particular period. The objective of our algorithm is to identify the trends prevalent within that antigen.

A **trend** 'T' is defined as a sequence of continuous price changes, whose length exceeds one, that are seen to repeat at least once within the antigen. This paper provides a proof of concept that such a trend detection mechanism is possible.

3   Development of Long and Short Term Memory

The flexible learning approach offered by the immune system is attractive as an inspiration but without an adequate memory mechanism knowledge gained from the learning process would be lost. Memory therefore represents a key factor in the success of the immune system. A difficulty arises in implementing an immune memory mechanism however, because very little is still known about the biological mechanisms underpinning memory development [11]. Theories such as antigen persistence and long lived memory cells [10], idiotypic networks [4], and homeostatic turnover of memory cells [12] have all attempted to explain the development and maintenance of immune memory but all have been contested. The attraction of the immune memory theory proposed by Dr Eric Bell is that it provides a simple, clear and logical explanation of memory cell development. This theory highlights the evolution of two separate memory pools, 'memory primed' and 'memory revertant' [1], see Figure 1.

Antigen presented by dendritic cells in the lymph node causes naive cells to undergo blast transformation and become activated, increasing proliferative capacity, and responsiveness but becoming short lived in the process due to their instability. This rapidly expanding population forms the short lived memory primed pool. The purpose of this growing pool is to drive the affinity maturation process to cope with the huge diversity in the potential antigen repertoire. These cells migrate to the periphery in an attempt to interact with further antigens. If antigen contact is achieved the memory primed cells terminally differentiate into effector cells to counter the antigen, after which point they die.

The high rate of apoptosis of memory primed cells means most will die during circulation of the periphery, however a small minority that fail to achieve secondary antigen exposure do survive and return to the lymph node to reach a memory revertant state. These cells down-regulate cytokine production and

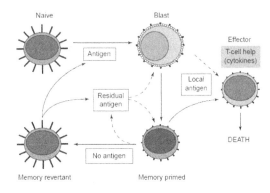

Fig. 1. Immune memory development [1]

apoptotic pathways and revert back to a naive like state. The key difference to naive cells however is that these revertant cells are able to homeostatically turnover, producing clones to sustain knowledge of an antigen experience over the long term. These two distinct memory pools, and the transfer mechanism between them, represent a key difference to other memory theories, and prove the inspiration for memory development in our algorithm.

In our solution the equivalent of the short term memory pool is generated using a derivative of the popular clonal selection algorithm [5] which proliferates all successfully bound candidates. The short term memory pool evolves through a special form of mutation, and is regulated through apoptosis. Successful candidates from the short term memory pool then transfer to the long term memory pool for permanent storage. This pool can then be utilised during future antigen presentations to aid in identification. These mechanisms are discussed in detail in Section 4.

4   An Immune Inspired Trend Evaluation and Prediction Solution

The pseudo code for the proposed Trend Evaluation Algorithm (TEA) is detailed in Program 1. Each of the significant operations in the TEA is then described in the subsequent sections. All parameters noted in these sections have been chosen using educated guesses based on previous experience, no formal sensitivity analysis has been performed to date but will form part of our future work.

4.1   Tracker Pool Construction and Initialisation

The TEA comprises a population of individual 'trackers' whose purpose is to identify the price trends located within an antigen. Each tracker is a vector consisting of multiple price change estimates, much like the antigen. The price estimates are generated using a Gaussian distribution and converted to price

Program 1 . TEA Pseudo Code

```
Convert oil price data to form antigen 'Ag'
Generate naive tracker pool 'TP'
For generations 1 to N
{
    Present Ag to each tracker 'Ti'
    Calculate affinity 'AF' between Ag and Ti
    Identify optimal match sequence 'MS'in Ti
    Calculate stimulation factor 'SF' of MS
    Calculate match length 'ML' of MS
    If (AF < bind threshold) && (SF or ML > previous SF, ML values)
    {
        Clone Tracker in proportion to ML
        Determine mutation mechanism & mutate clone
        Add clones to TP
    }
    Identify long term (LT) memory candidates from TP
    Transfer successful candidates to LT memory pool
    Apoptose TP
}
```

categories. The initial tracker pool is set at 20 trackers and the length of each tracker is randomly generated on initialisation to contain between one and four price estimates.

4.2 Antigen Presentation and Tracker Binding

The algorithm runs for 50 generations. During each generation the latest price change value is calculated and provided to the TEA and added to the current antigen. In generation 'n' the TEA will obtain the nth price change value and present it, along with all previous price values, as an antigen to the current tracker population.

The affinity between the antigen and each tracker is calculating as the numerical difference between the price values in the antigen and the tracker. A bind threshold of zero produces a continuous set, or sub-set, of the tracker that identically matches a part of, or the whole of, the antigen. All possible continuous permutations of the tracker are assessed against the antigen to find the longest matching sequence 'MS' between the two entities. For example, given antigen A1 [0.5, 1, 2] and tracker T1 [1, 2, 1], the MS would be [1,2] after all permutations of T1 and A1 were investigated.

During the binding process the stimulation factor 'SF' for the current MS is determined. This corresponds to the number of times MS is seen to repeat within the antigen. The match length 'ML' of the tracker is calculated as the length of MS. If SF and ML both exceed 1 then the MS represents a recurring trend within the antigen and that tracker is flagged as a candidate for proliferation. To avoid excessive population growth, proliferation candidates only undergo proliferation if their SF or ML values exceed those attained in the previous generation. The tracker is seen to have improved its fitness to an antigen trend (in terms of length of match, or frequency of occurrence) and as such is cloned.

4.3   Proliferation and Mutation

All trackers that meet the proliferation criteria are cloned, forming the short term memory pool theorised in Section 3. The number of clones generated during a match is proportional to the ML for that match. This was decided because a proliferation mechanism, using ML as a driver, in conjunction with the mutation mechanism, encourages successful trackers to evolve and lengthen to match ever longer trends.

Clones undergo mutation within the TEA in one of two unique forms, selected randomly with a probability of 0.5.

- **Mutation by Extension:** Here a new price estimate is generated randomly using a Gaussian distribution and added to the end of the clone.
- **Mutation by Shortening:** Here a randomly selected price estimate within the tracker is eliminated.

Extension mutation allows the clone, whose parent was a successful match to a trend, to anticipate the next price movement in that trend. The tracker clone evolves to increase the length of it's MS as it tries to detect longer and more complex price trends. During the binding process some trackers will contain redundant price information. Redundant price information is defined as any price values within the tracker that are not included in the MS of that tracker. The shortening mutation permits the trackers a random chance to rid themselves of redundant information and improve the accuracy of the resulting memory pool.

4.4   Long Term Memory Transfer

During each generation all trackers undergoing proliferation become candidates for entry into the long term memory pool. Trackers that have a MS not recorded in the memory pool will automatically be transferred into the pool for preservation. Candidates with a MS identical to that of one of the memory trackers will only replace that memory if they contain less redundant information than that memory tracker. The memory pool thus reflects the most efficient matching trackers in the population up to that point in time.

4.5   Apoptosis

To ensure the tracker population returns to a stable equilibrium 10% of the current tracker population is selected at random and eliminated. Both high and low affinity trackers have the same probability of death. If the population falls below its minimal limit of 20 the remaining population will automatically clone to repopulate the pool, reflecting homeostatic turnover observed in nature.

To reflect the instability and high death rate prevalent in the short term memory pool clones are eliminated five generations after their creation if they do not improve on their affinity to an antigen trend. This ensures excessive population growth is carefully regulated and a return to a stable population level soon after antigen presentation ceases.

Reviewing the mechanisms within the TEA one can see a close similarity exists to algorithms such as CLONALG [5], however a number of notable differences exist. Compared to CLONALG apoptosis occurs across all population members in the TEA, not just the lowest affinity members. In addition, due to it's specialised nature, mutation in the TEA is not directly related to affinity fit. TEA also proliferates all bound trackers to form the short term memory pool, encouraging diversity in the search space. The process in CLONALG is more elitist, as only the 'n' fittest population members are proliferated and mutated, and from these only the best fitting clone becomes a memory candidate. All remaining clones are eliminated. In essence CLONALG skips the short term memory pool stage as it looks to find the best fitting candidate using the minimum of resources. In comparison the TEA maintains the population of clones in order to match and anticipate patterns arising in the data fed live to the system.

5   Testing Methodology

5.1   Methodology

In order to test the ability of the TEA to identify trends in a data series, a simple antigen 'A' was constructed. 'A' contains 20 fictitious price movements, and 8 trends, T1 to T8. These represent the complete set of trends in A in accordance with the definition described in Section 2. The antigen and trends T1 to T8 are listed in Table 1.

To assess the ability of the TEA to associate new novel antigen with those experienced during past presentations we split antigen A at the mid point into

Table 1. Antigen data sets with observed trends

Antigen	Price Movements
A	[1, 2, 1, -0.5, 1, 2, 1, 0.5, -0.5, 0.5, 2, 1, 2, -0.5, 2, 1, 2, -0.5, 1, 1.5]
A1	[1, 2, 1, -0.5, 1, 2, 1, 0.5, -0.5, 0.5]
A2	[2, 1, 2, -0.5, 2, 1, 2, -0.5, 1, 1.5]
Trends	
T1	[1, 2] - seen in A, A1 and A2
T2	[1, 2, 1] - seen in A and A1
T3	[2, 1] - seen in A, A1 and A2
T4	[1, 2, -0.5] - seen in A and A2
T5	[2, -0.5] - seen in A and A2
T6	[2, 1, 2] - seen in A and A2
T7	[2, 1, 2, -0.5] - seen in A and A2
T8	[-0.5, 1] - seen in A

two subsets A1 and A2, both of length 10. A1 represents the training data set from which the TEA will develop a long term memory of trends associated with A1. A2 represents the testing data set which the TEA will have to examine in the light of information preserved from the experience of A1.

A1 contains three simple trends, T1, T2 and T3. They are closely related, in terms of the price movements they contain, so presenting A1 to the TEA represents a simple challenge to ensure the TEA operates correctly.

A2's purpose is to test the ability of the TEA to handle a more complex antigen with more diverse trends. A2 comprises 6 trends, T1 and T3 as were noted in A1, in addition to four new trends T4 to T7. Compared to A1 we have increased the number of trends from three to six and increased their length and diversity, making it more difficult for the TEA to find all the trends in A2.

It is hypothesized that although trends T4, T5, T6 and T7 are more complex to identify from knowledge of A2 alone, after experiencing trends T1, T2, and T3 from A1's presentation, which are related to T4 to T7, the TEA should develop some form of association between the trends leading to an easier recognition of these new patterns. To test this hypothesis we define the following 4 experiments.

In experiment 1 the training set A1 will be presented to the TEA from generations 1 to 10. The testing set A2 is then presented to the TEA from generations 30 to 40. The TEA is run for 50 generations and the experiment repeated and results averaged across 10 runs. The frequency of detection of trends T1 to T7 is recorded across all runs. To give a base line comparison where there is no memory in the system experiment 1 assumes no knowledge of A1 is carried forward in the TEA during A2's presentation. At the point of A2's presentation the tracker population is replaced by the random tracker population created in generation 0. The TEA therefore has to learn to recognise trends in A2 from scratch.

Experiment 2 investigates the impact of incorporating feedback from the long term memory pool into the TEA. We repeat the previous experiment, but the tracker population at generation 30 is repopulated using clones from the long term memory pool. We identify whether any association properties become apparent in the TEA by examining the frequency with which the trackers in the long term memory pool have detected the trends in A2 as compared to experiment 1.

Experiment 3 investigates the issue of scalability in the TEA. Experiments 1 and 2 present antigen sub sets of only 10 data items at a time. We now scale up the information presented to evaluate the impact on the TEA's performance. Experiment 3 presents the complete antigen A to the TEA from generation 1 to 20, doubling the size of the information presented. Results in terms of population sizes, trend detection rates and memory pool efficiency are then to be compared with experiments 1 and 2.

Experiment 4 compares the performance of the TEA against a random search. Each tracker generated during execution represents a potential search solution; given the high population levels anticipated in the TEA one could argue that a large randomly generated tracker population would also succeed in identifying the trends prevalent in an antigen. Experiment 4 generates a random population of trackers, whose size is approximately equivalent to the population levels generated during experiments 2 and 3 to examine whether the TEA performs better than a random search in terms of trend detection rates and memory efficiency.

5.2   Performance Evaluation

The results of the TEA are evaluated as an average across 10 runs. The performance of the algorithm is assessed using two measures i) the number of trends identified against the maximum available for detection and ii) the efficiency of the trackers in the long term memory pool to map to the trends. Efficiency can be measured as the number of price change values included in the memory tracker that are not contained within the match sequence 'MS'. For example if the trend to be found was [2.0, 2.5] and the best fitting tracker was [2.0, 2.5, 3.0] the price value 3.0 within the tracker is redundant given the MS of [2.0, 2.5]. The degree of efficiency, or to be more precise inefficiency, would therefore be calculated as 1 over 3, or 33%. The TEA was written in C++ and run on a windows machine with a Pentium M 1.7 Ghz processor with 1.0 Gb of RAM.

6   Results

The results of experiments 1 to 3 are discussed in the following sections and are listed in Table 2 whilst those of experiment 4 are found in Table 3. TEA execution times varied from approximately 40 to 50 seconds for experiments 1 and 2, and 7 to 8 minutes for experiment 3.

Table 2. Detection rate and memory efficiency results

Experiment	Trend Detection Frequency								Total	Detection Rate
	T1	T2	T3	T4	T5	T6	T7	T8		
1	10	10	10	6	2	1	0	n/a	39	55.7%
2	9	9	10	9	9	7	3	n/a	56	80.0%
3	10	10	10	10	9	10	8	10	77	96.3%

Experiment	Redundant memory values								Total	Inefficiency Rate
	T1	T2	T3	T4	T5	T6	T7	T8		
1	0	2	0	0	0	1	0	n/a	3	3.2%
2	0	0	0	0	0	2	1	n/a	3	2.1%
3	0	0	0	0	0	0	1	3	4	2.0%

6.1   Experiment 1. No Long Term Memory Pool Interaction

In accordance with Section 5 A1 was presented to the TEA from generations 1 to 10. The tracker population at generation 30 was replaced by the randomly generated tracker population from generation 1. A2 was then presented from generations 30 to 40. Figure 2 illustrates the total tracker population in response to these presentations, whilst Figure 3 shows the population of trackers that specifically match trends T1 to T7.

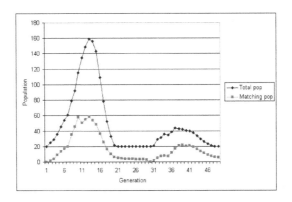

Fig. 2. Total Tracker and total matching tracker populations with no memory feedback

Regarding the presentation of A1, Table 2 shows the TEA is able to identify and develop memory trackers that map with 100% success to trends T1, T2 and T3 for each of the 10 runs. There are no redundant price values in the memory pool resulting in 100% memory efficiency. However the TEA is less successful in indentifying trends T4 to T7 from the subsequent presentation of A2.

The secondary response in Figure 2 is minimal because no memory of the trends from A1 are carried forward in the system, resulting in the TEA having to relearn the trends presented. This led to a poor mapping to A2's trends due to their increased number and complexity.

Trends T1 and T2 were again recognised within A2 and the new trend T4 was identified with 60% success across the 10 runs, however the remaining trends (T5, T6 and T7) were only rarely detected. In total 39 (55.7%) of the 70 possible trends were found across the 10 runs, with 3.2% memory inefficiency.

6.2   Experiment 2. Long Term Memory Pool Interaction

In this experiment the tracker population is replaced with clones from the memory pool in generation 30. This provides the potential to learn from the trends memorised in response to A1, to create associations with the novel trends in A2. Table 2 shows feedback from the memory pool has a significant impact on the performance of the TEA compared to experiment 1. The total number of trends now mapped by memory trackers increases by 43.6% to 56 trends, giving a detection rate of 80% compared to the previous coverage of 55.7%. The TEA is now able to consistently detect trends T4, T5, and T6 and even manages to identify the elusive T7 with a 30% success rate. Memory inefficiency fell to 2.1% with 3 redundant price values included in the memory population.

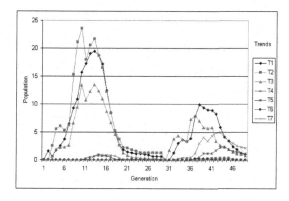

Fig. 3. Trackers matching trends T1 to T7 with no memory feedback

It should be noted however that due to apoptosis during run 4 of the experiment a number of important trackers were eliminated before they had a chance to bind. This resulted in the TEA failing to detect 6 of the 7 available trends in this run. Omitting this unusual occurrence from our analysis would have boosted the current 80% detection rate to 87%.

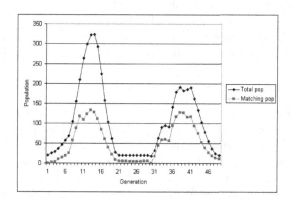

Fig. 4. Total Tracker and total matching tracker populations with memory feedback

Figures 4 and 5 show the total tracker population levels and tracker populations that match the specific trends T1 to T7. Figure 4 shows a more pronounced secondary response to A2 compared to that in Figure 2, with the maximum population rising to 191 trackers compared to that of 44 in experiment 1. Looking at the population of trackers that map to specific trends (Figure 5) we see evidence of stronger responses to the trends in A2, as seen in Figure 3. Thus knowledge of the trends seen from A1's presentation have improved the TEA's recognition of new, novel trends that have some association with those previously seen. This leads to the 43.6% improvement in trend detection.

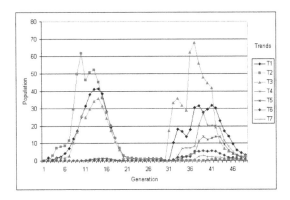

Fig. 5. Trackers matching trends T1 to T7 with memory feedback

This experiment was repeated to examine the impact of removing the shortening mutation function from the TEA. Considering presentation of A1 the tracker population levels reached a slightly higher peak of 218 compared to 191 with no shortening, however the impact on the quality of the memory pool was significant. Whilst the TEA's detection rate for trends T1 and T2 varied insignificantly, without shortening the detection rate for T3 fell from 100% to 10%, T3 was undetected in 9 of the 10 execution runs. Of more concern was the fact that the resulting memory pool contained 33 redundant price values compared to the 100% memory efficiency found through using mutation by shortening. It is clear that the shortening mutation is vital for the proper performance of the TEA.

6.3   Experiment 3. Antigen Scalability

To assess scalability antigen A was presented to the TEA from generations 1 to 20. Scanning A we see a new trend T8 becomes apparent when we combine subsets A1 and A2. Detection of this trend would not be possible in any of the previous experiments because its occurrence in A1 and A2 does not satisfy the definition of a trend in those individual sub sets. This highlights an issue with the approach as the point of split in the antigen has an impact on the potential number of trends to be detected in the sub parts of that antigen, this issue is addressed later.

The tracker population reaches a maximum of 2,244 trackers compared to the maximum population in experiment 2 of 323. The memory pool created is able to successfully map to 77 of the 80 possible trends across the 10 runs (96.3% coverage). The TEA failed to find T7 twice and T5 once. Memory inefficiency dropped to 2% as 4 excess price values were noted in the memory pool.

6.4   Experiment 4. Comparison with Random Search

From experiments 2 and 3 approximately 1,000 and 4,000 trackers respectively were generated by the TEA in order to generate the memory pool of solutions.

To compare the results of experiments 2 and 3 with a random search, a random population was generated consisting of 1,000, 4,000, 10,000 and 20,000 trackers. Given the longest trend (T7) has four price values, and can be found by the TEA with no data redundancy, each random tracker had a randomly determined length between one and four. The randomly generated population would then be mapped to antigen A, and the memory trackers compared to those of experiments 2 and 3 to see whether the TEA can outperform a purely random search. Results are shown in Table 3, ticks indicate the trend was found, crosses indicate the trend was not detected.

Table 3. Trends detected using a random search

Pop Size	Analysis of Trends Detected								Total
	T1	T2	T3	T4	T5	T6	T7	T8	
1,000	✓	X	✓	X	✓	X	X	n/a	3
4,000	✓	✓	✓	✓	✓	X	X	✓	6
10,000	✓	✓	✓	✓	✓	✓	X	✓	7
20,000	✓	✓	✓	✓	✓	✓	X	✓	7

With a randomly generated population of size 1,000 only 3 of the 7 trends T1 to T7 were detected. The random search failed to find trends T2, T4, T6 and T7. In comparison, during experiment 2 the TEA found 6 trends consistently, missing only T7 70% of the time. The detection rate of the TEA is twice that of the random search with just 1,000 trackers.

With 4,000 random trackers 6 of the 8 trends are found, trends T6 and T7 were undetected by the random search. Increasing the random population size to 10,000 trackers, 7 of the 8 trends are detected as T6 is now found. The random search fails to find T7, even if we increase the tracker population to 20,000. This contrasts to experiment 3 where the TEA, with only 4,000 trackers, can generate a memory pool that detects T1, T2, T3, T4, T6 and T8 every time across all 10 runs, and T5 and T7 9 and 8 times out of 10 respectively. The TEA therefore outperforms a random search.

7 Discussion

From experiment 1 it is seen that the TEA can evolve a population of trackers that generate a memory pool able to successfully map to trends in a simple data set (such as A1) with 100% accuracy and efficiency. Increasing the number and complexity of the trends to be found, as was achieved through the presentation of A2, causes the algorithm to struggle to identify these potential trends.

Without knowledge of the trends from A1 being carried forward in the system, detection rates of the TEA to the more complex trends falls significantly. This can be corrected in the TEA by increasing the degree of proliferation to raise the detection rate in the system. But what is of interest to us in this paper is whether the TEA can learn, through feedback from its long term memory pool, to associate what it has memorised from previous experiences to aid in the investigation of new novel antigen. Comparing the results of experiments 1 and 2 we see incorporation of the memory pool has a beneficial effect on the ability of the TEA to map to and memorise trends in a more complex antigen. Compared to its naive counterpart the inclusion of the long term memory pool boosts trend recognition from 55.7% to a potential 87.%, whilst inefficiency in the memory pool is kept consistently low at 2.1%.

The reason for this improvement can be seen if we view the trends within the antigen subsets A1 and A2, as shown in Table 1. Trends T1, T2 and T3, located within A1, have price change combinations involving rises of $1 or $2. Recognition and development of memory trackers associated with these trends would assist the TEA in identifying trends T4, T6 and T7 in A2 as they too have price combinations that involve price rises of $1 and $2. If memory trackers can be successfully evolved to map to these trends during presentation of A1, as was shown in experiment 2, then the TEA can utilise that knowledge and associate new novel trends with those already seen, instigating a more successful response. Without the ability to associate new experiences with past knowledge the performance of the TEA declines significantly, as expected.

Although the antigen investigated here is very small and simplistic, it is important for the TEA to scale to handle larger antigens. Experiment 3 gives us an indication of the scalability of the system as antigen sizes increase. Comparing test experiments 2 and 3 we see increasing the antigen size by 100% from 10 to 20 causes the maximum tracker population to increase from 323 trackers to 2,244, leading to an exponetial growth problem. Splitting antigen A into it's two component parts, as done in experiment 3, results in significantly lower population sizes whilst still maintaining a high detection rate. This is only possible if we carry forward the long term memory pool and feed it back into the tracker population to assist in future antigen recognitions. In this way we can avoid the scalability issue whilst maintaining a high degree of accuracy in the TEA.

However, from test 3 it was evident that separating antigen A at the mid point results in trend T8 now not being recognised as a trend within the component parts A1 and A2. T8 exists within A1 and A2 but is not repeatedly stimulated so has a SF of 1, therefore it does not conform to the definition of a trend in either A1 or A2. To avoid this issue the algorithm could be re-run with alternative split points to generate an overall memory pool; this will be investigated in future work. From analysis in experiment 4 we can also conclude that the TEA performs significantly better than a random search in identifying trends prevailing in a small data set.

8   Conclusion

This paper presents an immune inspired algorithm that is successful in identifying trends in a small simple data set. The authors theorise that these techniques can be expanded and applied to larger time series data sets to identify trends over time. Potential scalability issues can be addressed by breaking the data into more manageable subsets, so long as memory generated from previous presentations is fed back into the TEA prior to new data presentation. Using this approach the algorithm can learn through association from past experiences to maintain a high success rate in detecting and recording prevalent trends.

References

1. E. B. Bell, S. M. Sparshott, and C. Bunce. CD4+ T-cell memory, CD45R subsets and the persistence of antigen - a unifying concept. *Immunology Today*, 19:60–64, February, 1998.
2. J. H. Carter. The immune system as a model for pattern recognition and classification. *Journal of American Medical Informatics Association*, pages 28–41, January 2000.
3. S. H. Chen. *Genetic Algorithms and Genetic Programming in Computational Finance*. Kluwer Academic Publishers: Dordrecht, 2002.
4. D. Chowdhury. Immune networks: An example of complex adaptive systems. *In Artificial Immune Systems and their Applications, D. Dasgupta (ed)*, pages 89–104, 1999.
5. L. N. de Castro and F. J. Von Zuben. Learning and optimization using the clonal selection principle. *IEEE Transactions on Evolutionary Computation*, 6(3): 239–251, 2002.
6. M. Ghiassi, H. Saidane, and D. K. Zimbra. A dynamic artificial neural network model for forecasting time series events. *International Journal of Forecasting*, 21:341–362, 2005.
7. C. Grosan, A. Abraham, S. Y. Han, and V. Ramos. Stock market prediction using multi expression programming, 2005.
8. T. Knight and J. Timmis. AINE: An immunological approach to data mining. In N. Cercone, T. Lin, and X. Wu, editors, *IEEE International Conference on Data Mining*, pages 297–304, San Jose, CA. USA, 2001.
9. I. Nunn and T. White. The application of antigenic search techniques to time series forecasting. *GECCO*, pages 353–360, June 2005.
10. A. S. Perelson and G. Weisbuch. Immunology for physicists. *Rev. Modern Phys.*, 69:1219–1267, 1997.
11. W. Wilson and S. Garrett. Modelling immune memory for prediction and computation. In *3rd International Conference in Artificial Immune Systems (ICARIS-2004)*, pages 386–399, Catania, Sicily, Italy, September 2004.
12. A. Yates and R. Callard. Cell death and the maintenance of immunological memory. *Discrete and Continuous Dynamical Systems*, 1:43–59, 2001.
13. G. Zhang, D. E. Patuwo, and M. Y. Hu. Forecasting with artificial neural networks: The state of the art. *International Journal of Forecasting*, 14:35–62, 1998.

Theoretical Basis of Novelty Detection in Time Series Using Negative Selection Algorithms

Rafał Pasek

Wrocław University of Technology, 27 Wybrzeże Wyspiańskiego 50-370 Wrocław, Poland
rafal.pasek@pwr.wroc.pl

Abstract. Theoretical basis of Novelty Detection in Time Series and its relationships with State Space Reconstruction are discussed. It is shown that the
methods for estimation of optimal state-space reconstruction parameters may be
used for the estimation of immunological novelty detection system's parameters. This is illustrated with a V-detector system detecting novelties in
Mackey-Glass time series.

1 Introduction

Novelty Detection in Time Series (NDinTS) problem is a time-sensitive version of a
general Novelty Detection (ND) problem known also as Anomaly Detection. Many
different formulations of this problem exist in the literature, including both the time-
sensitive [10, 11] and time-insensitive version [6, 14]. They all have three common
elements: (1) problem space, with the finite or infinite number of elements; (2) input
data, which is a set of elements that belongs to the normal class; (3) result, which is a
mapping that classifies all elements as normal or novel. Therefore, Anomaly
Detection can be seen as a two-class classification problem, in which only the
examples from one class are available for the training [6]. The typical solution relies
on the model of known normal data, a distance measure and a threshold value to
decide whether the element is normal or novel. A wide review of existing approaches
can be found in [1].

The problem of Novelty Detection in Time Series was also approached using the
Artificial Immune Systems based on the Negative Selection Algorithm (NSA). This
approach, as many others, utilizes the sliding window procedure [10, 11, 12, 14, 15,
16, 19] to reduce the problem to a time-insensitive variant. Theoretical analysis of this
procedure shows, that it is an equivalent to the Method of Delays (MOD) – a well
known procedure in the domain of system's dynamics reconstruction. It is then
possible to find sliding window's parameters using existing methods for estimation of
optimal reconstruction parameters.

The rest of this paper is organized as follows. In section 2 the formal definitions of
Novelty Detection and its time-sensitive variant are introduced and also the NSA based
approach and sliding window procedure are defined. Section 3 is a short introduction
to the analysis of dynamical systems and state space reconstruction. Basing on this it is

H. Bersini and J. Carneiro (Eds.): ICARIS 2006, LNCS 4163, pp. 376 – 389, 2006.
© Springer-Verlag Berlin Heidelberg 2006

shown that the sliding window procedure and MOD are equivalent, and also the well known methods of state space reconstruction parameters estimation are discussed. In section 4 the results of V-detector novelty detection system on Mackey-Glass time series are presented and discussed. The summary is presented in section 5.

2 Problem Definition

To be able to define the NDinTS, the general ND problem must be defined first.

Def. 1. The problem space P is a space containing all elements subject to classification by novelty detection system.

Def. 2. A problem's element is any element e that belongs to the problem space P.

Def 3. The classification mapping is a mapping $classify:P \rightarrow \{normal, novel\}$, that assigns each element of the problem space to with one of two classes: *normal, novel.* [1]

Def. 4. The normal subspace P_- is a set of elements classified as *normal*
$P_- =_{df} \{e \in P |\ classify(e) = normal\}$.

Def. 5. The novel subspace P_+ is set of elements classified as *novel*
$P_+ =_{df} \{e \in P |\ classify(p) = novel\}$.

The problem can be formulated as follows: given a subset S of a normal subspace P_-, estimate the classification mapping. As it was stated in Section 1, the common approach is based on a model of normal data. It can be informally defined as follows:

Def. 6. A model M_X is a finite mathematical representation of systems behavior given by a set of problem's elements X. $M_X \in M$.

Def. 7. A misfit function $F(M,e)$ is a function $F:M \times P \rightarrow R$ that determines how much the element e does not fit into the model M.

Def. 8. A novelty detection system NDS is an ordered triple (F, M_S, p), such that: F is a misfit function, M_S is a model of input data set S, p is a misfit threshold value.

Def. 9. An estimated classification mapping $classify\_est(NDS, e)$ is a mapping defined as follows[2]:

$$classify\_est(NDS,e) =_{df} \begin{cases} normal & iff \quad F(M_S,e) < p \\ novel & iff \quad F(M_S,e) \geq p \end{cases}$$

---

[1] In the Artificial Immune Systems nomenclature, the classes and the following subspaces P_- and P_+ sets are usually named *Self* and *Non-Self.*

[2] There are also other definitions of classification mapping that allows more then one level on novelty or even a non-crisp discrimination.

2.1   Novelty Detection in Time Series

Considering the problem of NDinTS it is common to perceive the source of data as a dynamical system with unknown dynamics. The input data are available in the form of series of values gathered in consecutive time moments.

Def. 10. A (univariate) discrete time series X is a series of values generated by some dynamical system in consecutive time moments labeled with natural numbers. $X: x_0, x_1, \dots, x_N$.

Sliding Window Procedure. To reduce the problem to a time-insensitive variant a so called sliding window procedure is used. This procedure has three integer parameters: window length m; observation delay τ and offset Δ and as a result it produces a set of observations.

Def. 11. An observation $x_{t,m,\tau}$ is a vector of m consecutive values of a series of every τ-th value taken from X starting from moment t: $x_{t,m,\tau} =_{df} (x_t, x_{t+\tau} \dots, x_{t+(m-1)\tau})$

The offset parameter does not influence the observation itself, but defines how far the "window" is moved to generate another observation. If $x_{t,m,\tau}$ is the current observation, then the next observation is $x_{t+\Delta,m,\tau}$.

Novelty. A novelty can be informally defined as every observation in the tested time series B that is surprising given to the fact that B has been generated by the same system as some exemplary series A. The concept of "surprise" is being formulated in different ways in literature, depending on the considered problem and approach. The most commonly used approach relies on the reduction of problem to the time-insensitive version.

Def 12. A set of available observations $Obs_{X,m,\tau}$ is a set of every m-sized observations with a delay of τ in time series X:

$$Obs_{X,m,\tau} =_{df} \bigcup_{0 \le t \le N-m+1} \{x_{t,m,\tau}\}$$

We can then define the NDinTS as a ND problem in which the problem space is a space of all m-sized observations and input data $S = Obs_{A,m,\tau}$

2.2   Evaluation of Results

The estimated classification mapping introduces a separation of the problem space P onto two distinct subspaces P_{NDS+}, P_{NDS-}, where $P_{NDS+} =_{df} \{e \in P | classify\_est(NDS, e) = novel\}$ and $P_{NDS-} =_{df} \{e \in P | classify\_est(NDS, e) = normal\}$. The optimal result is the one in which this separation is equal the one introduced by *classify*, so the following must be met:

Cond. 1. $P_{NDS-} = P_-$ (which is equivalent to $P_{NDS+} = P_+$)

Def. 13. A perfect novelty detection system NDS^* is a novelty detection system for which the condition 1 is true.

From the Condition 1 we have $P_{NDS*.} = P.$, but $S \subseteq P.$, so the following is an essential condition for a perfect novelty detection system:

Cond. 2. $P_{NDS*.} \supseteq S$

It is then clear that the perfect novelty detection system requires $P_{NDS*.}$ to be a superset[3], of the given set of normal elements S. In general the separation of P resulting form *classify* and *classify_est* mappings are not identical. Two types of classification errors can be identified: type 1 – false positives and type 2 – false negatives. They are expressed by two factors, *error_rate* (*also known as false_alarm_rate*) and *reject_rate* defined as follows: error_rate = FN/TP+FN; reject_rate = FP/TN+FP, where:

FP is the number of elements e for which: *classify(e)=normal* $\wedge$ *classify_est(e)=novel*
FN is the number of elements e for which: *classify(e)=novel* $\wedge$ *classify_est(e)=normal*
TP is the number of elements e for which: *classify(e) = classify_est(e)= normal*
TN is the number of elements e for which: *classify(e) = classify_est(e)= novel*

To compare any two detection systems ROC curves are commonly used. They present the effect *error_rate* on *reject_rate* or the effect of false alarm rate on *detection_rate=1-reject_rate*.

2.3 Immunological Approach to ND

Artificial Immune Systems (AIS) follows the paradigm of natural immune system (NIS) [13] which works as a natural self – non-self discrimination system. Therefore Novelty Detection is one of the major areas of AIS application [17]. There were also few attempts to apply them to a NDinTS problem [10, 11, 12, 14, 15, 16, 19]. Of a special interest are the systems based on a Negative Selection Algorithm (NSA), proposed in the first, so called naïve version by Forrest et al. in [9].

The NSA based immunological novelty detection systems use the negative characterization scheme, which means that the model M is focused on representing not the input data S itself, but its complement. Due to the imperfect nature of model the two approaches are not equivalent [4]. A comprehensive analytical comparison of positive and negative characterization schemes may be found in [4, 5], for experimental comparisons see [15, 47]. There is a dispute whether the negative characterization is a proper approach to AD/ND [17]. It is being criticized in [2, 47, 48]. The major drawbacks mentioned are high dependability on parameters values and high computational cost. In [3] a response to these charges is given with the suggestion that choosing proper values of parameters reduce the computational complexity to linear.

Leaving this dispute apart in the rest of this work the negative characterization based immunological system is discussed. The complement of input data set S is modeled with a set of so called detectors.

Def. 14. An immunological model M^{IMM} is a set D of detectors:
$M^{IMM} =_{df} D$, *where* $D =_{df} \{d_1, d_2, ..., d_k\}$

---

[3] This superset can be regarded as a generalization of S.

Def. 15. A <u>detection area</u> *DetArea(d)* of a detector *d* is a set of problem elements that are detected by *d*.

We say that a detector *d* detects a problem element *e* (denoted by *d*<u>m</u>*e*) iff. *e* belongs to a detection area of *d*. A set of detectors *D* detects a problem element *e* (denoted *D*<u>m</u>*e*) iff. *e* is detected by a detector *d* that belongs to *D*. This can be stated using mathematical notation as: $d\underline{m}e \Leftrightarrow e \in DetArea(d)$, $D\underline{m}e \Leftrightarrow \exists d \in D \cdot d\underline{m}e$.

Def. 16. An <u>immunological model's misfit function</u> F^{IMM} is a function defined as follows:

$$F^{IMM}\left(M^{IMM}, e\right) =_{df} \begin{cases} 1 & \text{iff. } D\underline{m}e \\ 0 & \text{iff. } \neg D\underline{m}e \end{cases}$$

Def. 17. An <u>immunological novelty detection system</u> NDS^{IMM} is an ordered triple $(F^{IMM}, M^{IMM}, 1)$.

By setting novelty threshold to *1* it is granted that the elements detected by *D* are classified as novelties.

Sliding Window Procedure Parameters. For an NDinTS problem the source of data is a system with an unknown dynamics. In the most known immunological approaches the following systems were used: a cutting machine [10, 12, 16], a refrigeration system [11] an aircraft system [19] and a computer network [14, 15]. In the above mentioned works the parameters of sliding window procedure were established in an arbitrary manner and in some of them the values were not reported. In [10, 12] only *5* and *7* were used for window length. In [11] *m=5,7,8,10*, but no information about the delay and offset is given. In [19] there is no information on the window length and in [14, 15] the window length *m=1* and *3*. It seems then that these parameters do not attract the attention of the authors as much as other parameters of immunological novelty detection system.

The rest of this work is a discussion on the impact of these parameters and some expectations following the Takens embedding theorem. This needs some introduction into dynamical systems area.

3 Introduction to Dynamical Systems Analysis

Some basic concepts must be defined first.

Def. 18. A system's <u>state space</u> or a <u>phase space</u> is a *k*-dimensional space of orthogonal coordinates, which represents every variables necessary to define the momentary state of a system.

Def. 19. A <u>dynamical system</u> *DS* is an ordered pair *(X, f)*, where *X* is a subset of state space and *f:X→X* is a mapping in this space. Usually *X=R^k*.

Def. 20. A <u>state vector</u> or simply a <u>state</u> is a vector $x=(x_1, x_2, ..., x_k) \in X$.

The mapping f defines the evolution of the dynamical system, by determining the next state $x_{n+1}=f(x_n)$.[4] Te above definitions concerns the systems with discrete time (cascades). For continuous time systems (flows) the evolution is given by a set of k differential equations $\dot{x} = F(x)$.

Def. 21. A <u>trajectory</u> or an <u>orbit</u> is a series of consecutive states of a system.

For a class of systems, known as dissipative systems (see [26]), the trajectory usually settles on a subset of state space known as attractor.

Def. 22. An <u>attractor</u> A of a dynamical system $DS=(X,f)$ is a bounded closed subset of system space $A \subset X$ that is invariant $f(A)=A$ and has such a neighborhood that every trajectory from it settles on A.

From the invariant property of an attractor it follows that if the state of a system converges to an attractor, then every consecutive states belongs to the attractor as well.

In some special occasions a dissipative dynamical system can be sensitive to a initial state. In these case even the smallest difference in the initial conditions gets strengthen in time and two close trajectories disperse quickly. Such systems are called chaotic [46]. The attractor of a chaotic dynamical system is usually a fractal set and has an non-integer fractal dimension, and is being called a strange attractor.

An exemplary chaotic system is represented by the Mackey-Glass (MG) equation, introduced in [45] as a model of blood cells production. Its dynamics is defined with a following equation:

$$\dot{x} = \frac{0.2x(t - \tau_{MG})}{1 + x(t - \tau_{MG})^{10}} - 0.1x \tag{1}$$

MG system belongs to the class of delayed feedback systems [32] that are common for biological systems. Systems from this class have a infinite-dimensional state space, because to establish its initial condition a generic function over a set $[-\tau, 0]$ is needed. For delayed feedback systems the attractor's dimension can by arbitrary high, but if the delay is small system's dynamics is usually low-dimensional, e.g. for MG with $\tau=17$ the dimension of attractor is about 2 [29].

3.1 State Space Reconstruction

One of the most widely used methods for dynamic systems analysis is the state space reconstruction, proposed in [23] and justified on theoretical basis in [30] and [31]. It allows for the reconstruction of system's underlying dynamics basing on the univariate time series. There are three basic approaches to state space reconstruction [24]: (1) the Method of Delays (MOD); (2) the derivatives method; and (3) the principal components method. The simplest and most popular (although not chronologically first) is MOD [20, 21, 22, 28, 32, 33, 34, 35]. In the method of delays a reconstructed system space is represented by a delay vector, defined as follows:

---

[4] Assuming an autonomous system, in which f does not depend on n.

Def. 23. A delay vector *x(t)* of an univariate time series *X* is a vector: $x(t) = (x(t-(d-1)\tau), ..., x(t-\tau), x(t))$, where: d, τ - dimension and delay of reconstruction respectively - are the reconstruction's parameters.

In the d-dimensional reconstructed state space delay vectors form a reconstructed attractor. In [30] Takens formulated a theorem that if the dimension of reconstruction is big enough, namely bigger than twice the dimension of underlying attractor, then the delay vectors form an embedding of the original system space[5]. This means that the mapping from the original attractor to the reconstructed one is one-to-one and reversible, so every element of the original attractor is mapped onto one element of the reconstructed attractor and vice-versa.

This theorem, known as Takens embedding theorem, applies also to the attractor's neighborhood. Therefore it can be said that at least in the vicinity of the attractor, the states that do not belong to the attractor in the original state space are mapped onto states that do not belong to the attractor in the reconstructed space. This is a very important property of an embedding as it is very closely related to the NDinTS problem. The connection is due to the fact that the sliding window procedure is no more than a state space reconstruction using MOD. To see this we must introduce the definition of a delay vector for a discrete time series:

Def. 24. A delay vector $x_{t,m,\tau}$ for a discrete univariate time series is a vector: $x_{t,m,\tau} =_{df} (x_t, x_{t+\tau} ..., x_{t+(m-1)\tau})$

It is an equivalent to the definition 11, which defined on observation. It may be then said that:

Theorem 1. If the source of a time series A is a dynamical system, which state already converged to an attractor, then the observations set $Obs_{A,m,\tau}$ form a reconstruction of the underlying attractor in m-dimensional reconstructed state space.

From theorem 1 it follows that for the observation set $Obs_{A,m,\tau}$ applies all the implications of Takens theorem and its generalizations. Therefore:

Theorem 2. If the window length m is big enough, so that observations set $Obs_{A,m,\tau}$ forms an embedding of the original attractor, then:
(a) the states that belongs to the original attractor are mapped onto $Obs_{A,m,\tau}$
(b) the states from the original attractor's vicinity that do not belong to this attractor are mapped onto the supplement of $Obs_{A,m,\tau}$

The immunological novelty detection system detects only the elements that does not belong to the input data set. From Theorem 2 it follows that the supplement of input

---

[5] Precisely: if the dynamical system and the observed quantity are generic, then the delay-coordinate map from a d-dimensional compact manifold M to R^{2d+1} is a diffeomorphism on M. Generalized in [25] for a compact-invariant subset of R^k, and furthermore in [22] for a finite-dimensional subset of infinite-dimensional state space.

data set $Obs_{A,m,\tau}$ consist of a states that do not belong to the original attractor. Therefore a type (1) novelties detected by a novelty detection system can be defined as follows:

Def. 25. A type (1) novelty is a state that does not belong to the original attractor.

The type (1) novelties are then caused by the change in the underlying system's dynamics that causes the trajectory to diverge from the attractor. [6]

3.2 Reconstruction Parameters

The parameters of reconstruction may be mapped directly to the sliding window procedure parameters. While the proper reconstruction ensures the detection of type (1) novelties, the Takens theorem itself, which underlies theorem 2, does not give any guidance on how those parameters should be fixed. Only the minimal sufficient value of m is given. What's more, the assumptions for Takens theorem, which is an infinite series of noise free data, are unrealistic [20]. In the real problems only a finite series is given. This may lead to another type of novelties.

Def. 26. A type (2) novelty is a state that does belong to the original attractor but is not observed in the exemplary time series A.

While type (1) novelties are caused by change in the dynamics of the system, type (2) novelties are the results of not having the full information. In general to represent a whole attractor an infinite time series $A*$ is needed, from which only a subseries A is known. From the condition 1 it follows that the perfect novelty detection in time series system a following must be true:

Cond. 3. $P_{NDS-} = Obs_{A*}$

The generalization of input data should then reconstruct a whole attractor basing on an observed finite series A, so that only the type (1) novelties are detected.

Having only a finite set of imperfect data makes estimation of reconstruction dimension more difficult, and also makes the reconstruction quality dependant on the value of delay [20, 32]. Nevertheless many methods of estimating the proper reconstruction parameters have been proposed. A small survey of them is presented in the next few paragraphs. This methods may be used to estimate the values for sliding window procedure parameters.

Reconstruction delay. Commonly two limits are given for the value of τ [20]: the lower – so that the reconstructed attractor is expanded from the diagonal; and the upper – so that the attractor does not fold on itself. The most popular methods are based on a decorrelation (linear or general) of successive element of series [33], the geometrical expansion from the diagonal [28] or a mean time between peeks [20]. For references to works presenting other approaches like higher-order correlations, fill-factor, wavering products, small-window solution, see [28]. Many authors [20, 21, 27, 28] suggest that the independent parameter that should be estimated is not the lag

---

[6] Assuming that the observed system already converged to the attractor.

between two consecutive elements of delay vector τ, but rather the lag between the first and the last element $\tau_w=(m-1)\tau$. In particular in [28] it is shown that the correlation integral does depend on τ_w, but not on τ and m separately.

Reconstruction dimension. The reconstruction dimension as the most important parameter of reconstruction attracted major attention [34, 35, 36, 37, 38, 39, 40, 41]. In [41] a comparison of the most popular algorithms is presented. The methods can be divided into three categories [35, 34]: (1) estimating the attractor's invariant; (2) singular value decomposition; and (3) checking the smoothness of reconstruction.

Methods from the first class are based on the fact that several values are attractor's invariants (e.g. the correlation integral [42]) and therefore their value should be the same for all faithful reconstructions. Increasing the dimension of reconstruction one can find a minimal dimension after which the selected invariant's value does not change, meaning that the reconstruction is proper. The main drawbacks of these methods is their sensitivity to data and the computational complexity [34].

In singular value decomposition the orthogonal directions in the reconstructed space are identified and sorted according to the variance of the trajectory's projection onto them [27]. Apart from its strong theoretical basis, its major advantage is higher tolerance of noise.

Methods from the third class are based on the fact, that in the not faithfully reconstructed attractor (due to the too small reconstruction dimension) the states that are away in the original space can be mapped into neighbors in the reconstructed space. The most commonly used method is the False Nearest Neighbors (FNN) proposed in [37] and its variants [34, 38]. In FNN the so called false nearest neighbors are counted, which are the states that are neighbor in k-dimensional reconstruction but are not longer neighbor in $k+1$-dimensional reconstruction. The optimal reconstruction dimension is then the one for which the number of false nearest neighbors falls to 0.[7] For a justification of this approach see [39, 40].

The main drawback of the FFN method is the necessity to fix two subjective parameters, therefore it is worth noticing that in the work [34] a modification of FFN that does not need any parameters is given.

Window Offset. Although this parameter does not have a typical equivalent in the method of delays, some suggestions may be made basing on the MOD literature. Setting Δ to a value other than 1 means that some of the data will not be used for the reconstruction. Therefore the value 1 is recommended, as most of the methods mentioned above are sensitive to the amount of data [34].

4   Experiments and Results

In this section some results of an advanced immunological novelty detection system on a benchmark chaotic series are presented and confronted with the expectations arising from Theorem 2.

Observed system. Mackey-Glass time series generated with the 4th order Runge-Kutta method is used. It is assumed that $\tau_{MG}=17$ models the normal data series A.

---

[7] Or a minimal value for a noised data [43,44].

Series B^+ generated with $\tau_{MG}=20$ is used to check the *detection_rate*. A third series B^- with $\tau_{MG}=17$ but for another initial condition is used to check the *false_alarm_rate*.
Reconstruction parameters. The reconstruction delay parameter was set to $\tau=50$, which is suggested in [20] as a mean time between peaks. The reconstruction dimension was estimated using the method proposed in [34] to $d=5$, which is consistent with the minimal sufficient reconstruction dimension $d=2d_a+1$ where d_a is the attractor's dimension equal to 2 for $\tau_{MG}=17$.
Tested detection system. A modified version of V-detector algorithm is used to generate detectors. This algorithm was firstly introduced in [7] for the Anomaly Detection problem, and the enhanced in [8] and [18]. Its special feature is the stop condition, which is based on testing the hypothesis about achieving a requested minimal coverage of P subspace. The only modification introduced is that the generated detectors are added to the resulting detector set at once. Still only n last tries are taken into account when testing the hypothesis as in the original algorithm.

4.1 Experiments

A series of experiments using the above mentioned input and test data were conducted, for different values of parameters r_S and m. The measured values are *detection_rate* (DR), *false_alarm_rate* (FAR), size of resulting detectors set (DC), and an average detection rate (DR/DC). For all tests the parameters of V-detector: the required coverage p confidence level α were set to p=0,9, α=0,95. The results presented in figures 1-3 were averaged over 100 runs.

4.2 Results

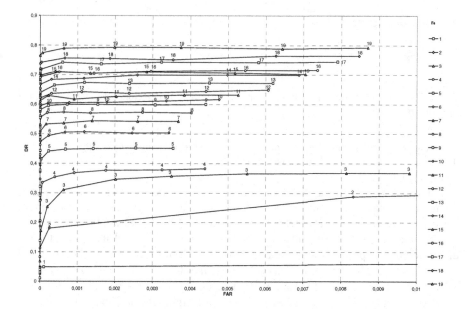

Fig. 1. The ROC curves

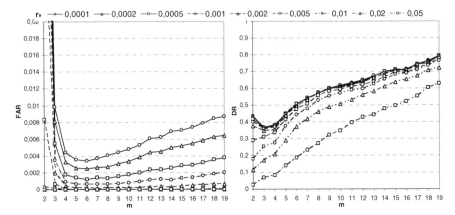

Fig. 2. The effect of window length *m* on the *false_alarm_rate* (left) and *detection_rate* (right)

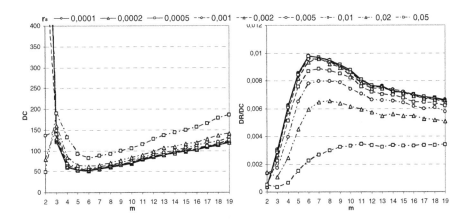

Fig. 3. The effect of window length *m* on the size of resuzlting detectors set (left) and average detection rate (right)

As it can be seen on the **Fig. 1**, increasing the window length *m* results in a better detection. A more accurate analysis requires checking the effect of *m* on DR and FAR separately on **Fig. 3**.

For a *false_alarm_rate* a well-defined minimum over the *m=5* and *6* can be seen. It seems then that to minimize the type 1 detection errors the window length corresponding to the estimated minimal reconstruction dimension can be used.

The *detection_rate* clearly increases with *m*. The strange local maximum for the dimension of 2 is probably due to the fact that the selected reconstruction delay $\tau=50$ is valid only for this dimension. This is because only for *m=2* the window lag $\tau_w=(m-1)\tau$ is equal to the suggested value *50*. It can be also seen that the big values of r_S have negative effect o DR. It is caused by the effect of merging the neighbor trajectories in the reconstructed state space, and is less visible in higher-dimensional spaces because the distance between trajectories increases with the dimension of reconstruction.

The bottom two graphs on the **Fig. 3** depicts the effect of m on the size of resulting detectors set (DC) and average detection rate (DC/TC). For both of them there is a clear optima for $m=5,6,7$. For these values of m the resulting set of detectors is smallest, and the generated detectors have the biggest average detection rate, defined as a ratio of DC to TC. It seems that the average detection rate is optimal for $m=6$ rather than for $m=5$. This may be due to the fact, that the series used for calculating DR was generated with $\tau_{MG}=20$. For this value the dimensionality of the underlying attractor is greater than 2 and the estimated optimal reconstruction dimension is 6.

5 Summary

The formal basis for Novelty Detection in Time Series problem and the sliding window procedure in particular indicates the close connection with a state space reconstruction method, known as Method of Delays. This encourages taking advance of the wide spectrum of solutions presented in the dynamical systems analysis literature. Especially the methods for estimation of optimal reconstruction parameters can be used to fix the parameters of the sliding window procedure.

The experiments conducted for an chaotic time series showed that the estimated optimal reconstruction dimension coincides with the optima of several detection system's characteristics. More experiments are needed to check also the effect of reconstruction lag.

References

1. M.Markou, S.Singh. Novelty Detection: A Review. Signal Processing, vol. 83, issue 12: 2481--2497; 2003
2. J.Kim, P.Bentley. An Evaluation of Negative Selection in an Artificial Immune System for Network Intrusion Detection. In GECCO-2001: 1330--1337; 2001
3. J.Balthrop, S.Forrest, M.R.Glickman. Revisiting LISYS: Parameters and Normal Behavior. In CEC-2002: 1045--1050; 2002
4. F.Esponda, S.Forrest, P.Helman. A Formal Framework for Positive and Negative Detection Schemes. IEEE Trans. Syst., Man Cybernet., 34: 357--373; 2004
5. F.Esponda, S.Forrest, P.Helman. The Crossover Closure and Partial Match Detection. L.N. in Computer Science, vol. 2787: 249--260; 2003
6. F.González. A Study of Artificial Immune Systems Applied to Anomaly Detection. PhD thesis, USA The University of Memphis; 2003
7. Z.Ji, D.Dasgupta. Real-Valued Negative Selection Algorithm with Variable-Sized Detectors. In GECCO-2004: 287--298; 2004
8. Z.Ji, D.Dasgupta. Augmented Negative Selection Algorithm with Variable-Coverage Detectors. In CEC-2004: 1081--1088; 2004
9. S.Forrest, A.Perelson, L. Allen, R.Cherukuri. Self-Nonself Discrimination in a Computer. In IEEE Symposium on Research in Security and Privacy; 1994
10. D.Dasgupta, S.Forrest. Novelty Detection in Time Series Data using Ideas from Immunology. In 5th International Conference on Intelligent Systems; 1996

11. D.Taylor, D.W.Corne. An Investigation of the Negative Selection Algorithm for Fault Detection in Refrigeration Systems. L.N. in Computer Science, vol. 278; 2003

12. D.Dasgupta, S.Forrest. Tool Breakage Detection in Milling Operations using a Negative-Selection Algorithm. Tech.rep.CS95-5, Computer Science, University of New Mexico; 1995

13. S.A.Hofmeyr. An Interpretative Introduction to the Immune System. tech. rep. University of New Mexico; 1999

14. D.Dasgupta, F.Gonzalez. An Immunity-Based Technique to Characterize Intrusions in Computer Networks. IEEE Trans. Evol. Comput. 6: 1081--1088; 2002

15. F.González, D.Dasgupta. An Immunogenetic Technique to Detect Anomalies in Network Traffic. In GECCO-2002; 2002

16. D.Dasgupta, S.Forrest. Artificial Immune Systems in Industrial Applications. In IPMM'99

17. E.Hart, J.Timmis. Application Areas of AIS: The Past, The Present and The Future. L.N. in Computer Science, vol. 3627; 2005

18. Z.Ji, D.Dasgupta. Estimating the Detector Coverage in a Negative Selection. In GECCO-2005; 2005

19. D.Dasgupta K. KrishnaKumar, D.Wong, M.Berry. Negative Selection Algorithm for Aircraft Fault Detection. L.N. in Computer Science, vol. 3239; 2004

20. D.Kugiumtzis. State Space Reconstruction Parameters in the Analysis of Chaotic Time Series - the Role of the Time Window Length, Physica D, 95: 13--28; 1996

21. M.Small, C.K.Tse. Optimal embedding parameters: A modeling paradigm. Physica D, 194: 283--296; 2004

22. J.C.Robinson. A topological delay embedding theorem for infinite-dimensional dynamical systems. Nonlinearity, vol. 18, issue 5: 2135--2143; 2005

23. N.H.Packard, J.P.Crutchfield, J.D.Farmer, R.S.Shaw. Geometry from a time series. Phys. Rev. Let. 45: 712--716; 1980

24. J.F.Gibson, J.D.Farmer, M.Casdagli, S.Eubank. An analytic approach to practical state space reconstruction. Physica D, 57; 1992

25. T.Sauer, J.A.Yorke, M.Casdagli. Embedology. Journal of Stat. Phys., 65: 579--616; 1991

26. D.Ruelle, F.Takens. On the nature of turbulence. Comm. Math. Phys. 20: 167--192; 1971

27. D.S.Broomhead, G.P.King. Extracting qualitative dynamics from experimental data. Physica D, 20: 217--236, 1986

28. M.T.Rosenstein, J.J.Collins, C.J. De Luca. Reconstruction expansion as a geometry-based framework for choosing proper delay times. Physica D, 73: 82--98; 1993

29. A.A.Tsonis. Chaos: From Theory to Applications. Plenum Press, New York; 1992

30. F.Takens. Detecting strange attractors in turbulence, Dynamical Systems and Turbulence. L.N. in Mathematics, vol. 898: 366--381; 1981

31. R. Mane. On the dimension of the compact invariant sets of certain nonlinear maps. Dynamical systems and turbulence, Warwick; 1981

32. M.J.Bünner, M.Ciofini, A.Giaquinta, R.Hegger, H.Kantz, R.Meucci, A.Politi. Reconstruction of systems with delayed feedback: I. Theory. EPJ D, vol 10, issue 2; 2000

33. S.S.Sharif, J.H.Taylor. Chaos in Nonlinear Dynamical Systems, Interim Report on Vibration Mechanisms of the EH101 Helicopter; 2001

34. L. Cao. Practical method for determining the minimum embedding dimension of a scalar time series. Phys. Rev. A 45: 3403--3411; 1992

35. M.Ataei, B.Lohmann, A.Khaki-Sedigh, C.Lucas. Model based method for estimating an attractor dimension from uni/multivariate chaotic time series with application to Bremen climatic dynamics. Chaos, Solutons and Fractals 19: 1131--1139; 2004

36. H.Froehling, J.P.Crutchfield, D.Farmer, N.H.Packard, R.Show. On determining the dimension of chaotic flows. Physica D, vol. 3, issue 3: 605--617; 1981
37. M.B.Kennel, R.Brown, H.D.I.Abarbanel. Determining embedding dimension for phase-space reconstruction using a geometrical construction. Phys.Rev. A 45: 3403--3411; 1992
38. M.B.Kennel, H.D.I.Abarbanel. False neighbors and false strands: A reliable minimum embedding dimension algorithm. Tech.rep., Institute for Nonlinear Science and Department of Physics, University of California, San Diego, Mail Code 0402, La Jolla, CA 92093-0402
39. W.Liebert, K.Pawelzik, H.G.Schuster. Optimal embeddings of chaotic attractors from topological considerations. Europhys. Lett. 14, 521; 1991
40. Z.Aleksic. Estimating the embedding dimension. Physica D, 52; 1991
41. Th.Buzug, G.Pfister. Comparison of algorithms calculating optimal embedding parameters for delay time coordinates. Physica D, 58:127--137; 1992
42. P.Grassberger, I.Procaccia. Measuring the strangeness of strange attractors. Phys. D; 1983
43. D.Kugiumtzis, N.Christophersen. State Space Reconstruction: Method of Delays vs Singular Spectrum Approach. Report No 236, Dept of Informatics, Univ. of Oslo; 1997
44. M.Casdagli, S.Eubank, J.D.Farmer, J.Gibson. State space reconstruction in the presence of noise. Physica D, 51: 52-98; 1991
45. M.C.Mackey, L.Glass. Science, vol. 197, pp. 287--289, 1977. Oscillations and chaos in physiological control systems. Science, vol. 197: 287--289; 1977
46. E.N.Lorenz. Deterministic non-periodic flow. J.of Atmospheric Science, vol. 357; 1963
47. T.Stibor, J.Timmis, C.Eckert. A Comparative Study of Real-Valued Negative Selection to Statistical Anomaly Detection Techniques. L.N. in Computer Science, vol. 3627; 2005
48. M.Ebner, H.G.Breunig, J.Albert. On the Use of Negative Selection in an Artificial Immune System. In GECCO-2002; 2002

Danger Is Ubiquitous: Detecting Malicious Activities in Sensor Networks Using the Dendritic Cell Algorithm

Jungwon Kim, Peter Bentley, Christian Wallenta,
Mohamed Ahmed, and Stephen Hailes

Department of Computer Science, University College London,
Malet Place, London, U.K., WC1E 6BT
{J.Kim, P.Bentley, C.Wallenta, M.Ahmed, S.Hailes}@cs.ucl.ac.uk

Abstract. There is a list of unique immune features that are currently absent from the existing artificial immune systems and other intelligent paradigms. We argue that some of AIS features can be inherent in an application itself, and thus this type of application would be a more appropriate substrate in which to develop and integrate the benefits brought by AIS. We claim here that sensor networks are such an application area, in which the ideas from AIS can be readily applied. The objective of this paper is to illustrate how closely a Danger Theory based AIS - in particular the Dendritic Cell Algorithm matches the structure and functional requirements of sensor networks. This paper also introduces a new sensor network attack called an *Interest Cache Poisoning Attack* and discusses how the DCA can be applied to detect this attack.

Keywords: Danger Theory, Artificial Immune Systems, Sensor Networks, Interest Cache Poisoning Attack.

1 Introduction

Danger threatens living organisms every day of their lives. Intuitively, one might therefore suppose that a successful strategy in our immune systems would be to detect danger instead of relying solely on the detection of antigens that identify specific pathogens. A hotly debated hypothesis in immunology known as the Danger Theory [13] proposes just this. This theory suggests that the human immune system can detect danger in addition to antigens in order to trigger appropriate immune responses. The Danger Theory states that appropriate immune responses produced by the immune system emerge from the balance between the concentration of danger and safe signals within the tissue of a body, not by discrimination of self from non-self.

Danger also threatens modern computer networks every day. Aickelin *et al.* [1] presented the first in-depth discussion on the application of Danger Theory to intrusion detection and the possibility of combining research from wet and computer laboratory results. Their work aimed to build a computational model of Danger Theory in order to define, explore, and find danger signals. Greensmith *et al* [5] employed Dendritic Cells (DCs) within a Danger Theory based artificial immune system (AIS). DCs are a class of antigen presenting cells that ingest antigens or

H. Bersini and J. Carneiro (Eds.): ICARIS 2006, LNCS 4163, pp. 390–403, 2006.
© Springer-Verlag Berlin Heidelberg 2006

protein fragments in the tissue. DCs are also receptive to danger signals in the environment that may be associated with antigens. Greensmith *et al* abstracted several properties of DCs that would be useful for anomaly detection and proposed the DC algorithm (DCA) to accommodate these properties. Recent work by the same authors [6] has also shown some initial results of using the DCA to detect port scanning. The outcome demonstrated the capability of the DCA as an anomaly detector.

As Hart and Timmis stated in [8], after a decade of research in the area of AIS, the researchers in the AIS community pose a question on whether there is a distinctive niche application area that AIS can provide unique benefits that is not presented by other existing approaches. They also highlighted a list of unique immune features that are currently absent from the existing AIS and other intelligent paradigms. We argue that some of these features can be inherent in an application itself, and thus this type of application would be a more appropriate substrate in which to develop and integrate the benefits brought by AIS. We claim here that sensor networks are such an application area, in which the ideas from AIS can be readily applied. The objective of this paper is to illustrate how closely Danger theory based AIS, in particular the DCA matches the structure and functional requirements of sensor networks.

The paper first reviews literature related to the Danger Theory based AIS. Section 3 illustrates how properties and functional requirements of sensor networks conform to an artificial tissue. Section 4 introduces a new sensor network attack called the *'Interest cache poisoning attack'* and section 5 discusses how the DCA can be applied to detect this attack. Finally, section 6 concludes this work with future work.

2 Danger Theory Based AIS

2.1 Previous Work

Since the first in-depth discussion of Danger Theory on the possibility of computing research [1], Bentley *et al* [3] introduced the concept of artificial tissue in order to adapt danger and safe signals (apoptosis and necrosis) thereby triggering artificial immune responses within an AIS. The authors stressed that the tissue is an integral part of immune function, with danger signals being released when tissue cells die under stressful conditions. Related work by Greensmith *et al* [5] employed DCs within AIS that coordinated T-cell immune responses. Kim *et al* [11] continued Greensmith *et al*'s work by discussing T-cell immunity and tolerance for computer worm detection. This work presented how three different processes within the function of T-cells, namely T-cell maturation, differentiation and proliferation could be embedded within the Danger Theory-based AIS. Twycross and Aickelin [15] provided a review of biological principles and properties of innate immunity, and showed how these could be incorporated into artificial models. In this work, authors addressed six properties of the innate immune system that would influence the capability of AIS. The same authors implemented the libtissue software that provides an innate immunity framework [16]. Finally, Le Boudec and Sarafijanovic [14] were also influenced by the idea of the Danger Theory, and chose to regard a packet loss in the network as a danger signal. Danger signals were used as co-stimulation signals confirming successful detection.

2.2 Dendritic Cell Algorithm

This paper focuses specifically on the Dendritic Cell Algorithm [5,6,7] of Greensmith *et al*, which abstracted a number of properties of DCs that are possibly advantageous to design AIS for anomaly detection.

In the human immune system, during the antigen ingestion process, immature DCs experience different types of signals that indicate the context (either safe or dangerous) of an environment where the digested antigens exist. The different types of signals lead DCs to differentiate into two types: mature and semi-mature. Chemical messages known as cytokines produced by mature and semi-mature DCs are different and influence the differentiation of naïve T-cells into several distinctive paths such as helper T-cells or killer T-cells. In order to employ these properties of DCs, Greensmith *et al.* categorised DC input signals into four groups – *PAMPs* (signals known to be pathogenic), *Safe Signals* (signals known to be normal), *Danger Signals* (signals that may indicate changes in behaviour) and *Inflammatory Cytokines* (signals that amplify the effects of other signals). When each artificial DC experiences the combination of these four different signal groups released by the artificial tissue, it interprets the context of ingested antigens by using a signal processing function, which weights each type of input signal differently. The output of a signal processing function determines the differentiation status of DCs (either semi-mature or mature).

3 Artificial Immune Systems Applied to Sensor Networks

The parallels between intrusion detection and immunity have long been the source of inspiration for AIS researchers, but conventional computer networks do not closely resemble the dynamic, distributed and fluid nature of organisms and their immune systems well. There is, however, a type of network that does share many of these features: sensor networks. In the following sections, we introduce this type of network and outline one popular routing protocol, known as *Directed Diffusion* [9].

3.1 Sensor Network Overview

Sensor networks are an emerging technology and research area in the rapidly growing field of ubiquitous computing [4], aimed at providing distributed and massively parallel monitoring in heterogeneous physical environments. Sensors are typically low-cost, limited capacity, mass production units, consisting of no more than (i) a sensing unit, (ii) a processing unit, (iii) memory, (iv) a transceiver and (v) a power unit [2]. Their aim is two fold: (i) to faithfully execute their intended task, and (ii) to efficiently manage their limited resources, such as energy, so as to maximise their lifetime. The following features of sensor networks distinguish them from traditional computing environments [2, 4]:

P1: Constrained resources – limited in physical capacity, bandwidth, cost, etc.

P2: High-density – number and density of sensor nodes can be several orders of magnitude higher than the mobile nodes in an ad hoc mobile network.

P3: Fidelity though redundancy – due to their physical constraints, individual nodes are prone to failure through deliberate attack or normal malfunction. The redundancy of nodes is used to compensate for this.

P4: Flexibility – aimed at operating under diverse conditions with minimal structured support, for example deployment in remote areas.

P5: Dynamic network topology - the topology may change often.

P6: Frequently data centric - IP addresses are not used, all nodes perform data-centric routing.

P7: Self-organising – network connectivity is often ad-hoc and dynamically maintained.

P8: Distributed computation – each node carries out simple data processing locally and sends out the partially processed data to other nodes. The chain of partial processing by individual nodes provides an aggregated solution.

Together, these properties have provided the catalyst for a wide range of new applications, including environmental monitoring, disaster relief operations, military control/surveillance and health monitoring [2].

3.2 Directed Diffusion

In addition to the distributed and dynamic nature of sensor network hardware, one popular routing method is equally suggestive of natural immune metaphors: the *Directed Diffusion* protocol. This is a routing algorithm used to gather data sensed by a large number of sensor nodes and disseminate to a node that requests such data [9]. Directed Diffusion works in two phases, an initial exploratory phase that is followed by a reinforcement phase. Together these phases make up the three different stages discussed in Fig. 1.

The requesting node, referred to as the 'sink node' may request data from one or multiple other sensor nodes. As shown in Fig. 1(a), the sink periodically broadcasts its 'interest' packets (containing a description of the sensing task e.g. the regular reading of a patient's blood pressures) to its neighbours. Interest packets are then propagated throughout the whole network, resulting in creation of gradient fields representing the possible data flow paths from the source, back to the sink as shown in Fig. 1(b). Once the sink receives its requested data, it is then in a position to choose between its various neighbours by reinforcing the paths deemed most advantageous, for example based on the quality of service on the path that led to the neighbour, as shown in Fig. 1(c). As a result, though during the exploratory data packets are forwarded toward the sink node along multiple paths, the gradient refinement process chooses the most preferred path.

Reinforcements in Directed Diffusion come in two forms: positive and negative. Positive reinforcement encourages data flow along a given path, and the result is that data flows at a higher rate through the given path. In contrast, negative reinforcement discourages data flow along given paths, thereby reducing the rate at which data is sent through the path. The result is that the algorithms is dynamically able to tune its performance (with respect to the data flow path) based on arbitrary criteria.

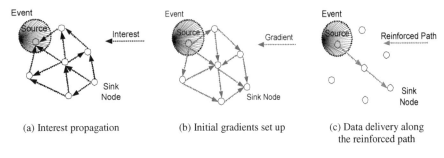

(a) Interest propagation   (b) Initial gradients set up   (c) Data delivery along
                                                                              the reinforced path

Fig. 1. Directed Diffusion [9]

3.3   Wireless Sensor Tissue

Readers familiar with the field of AIS should find the properties of the sensor network using Directed Diffusion very familiar, because they mirror many of the properties of AIS algorithms. In this work we regard sensor networks as a suitable metaphor for the tissue of an organism - with diffusing packets acting as signals between cells. Using the work of Bentley [3] and Tycross [15] to aid this analogy:

- Tissue cells have limited processing, storage, and communication capacity; while a cell has its own capability of processing and storage, it takes a limited amount of input proteins such as cytokines or binds to a restricted number of neighbour cells. As described in *(P1)* sensor networks share these features.
- Biological tissue comprises a large number of cells. A tissue cell is the basic structural and functional unit, capable of functioning independently. A sensor network is similarly structured, see *(P2)*.
- Each cell is prone to failure: cells in biological tissue are continuously exposed to pathogenic attacks, just as individual nodes of a sensor network are at risk, see *(P3)*. Later sections explain how an immune algorithm can integrate with a sensor network to help detect and overcome such attacks.
- The cells in living tissue move and reorganise themselves, just as nodes of a sensor network may move or be deployed in different places and have variable topologies, see *(P4)* and *(P5)*.
- Communication between biological cells is through the diffusion of signalling proteins and the matching of antigenic patterns; communication between sensor network nodes (using the Directed Diffusion protocol) is through diffusion and the matching of packets, see *(P6)*.
- Tissue cells are self-organising, growing without predetermined global control; the spatial and temporal information is passed by signals while receptors help the entire structure of the tissue develop. Likewise a sensor network automatically and dynamically forms its connectivity, see *(P7)*.
- Biological tissue cells are distributed, they work in parallel, signalling to each other to perform the desired functions. A sensor network is a truly distributed system with nodes that are processing in parallel and communicating with each other, see *(P8)*.

As discussed, the sensor network itself plays the role of artificial tissue and therefore the development of a separate artificial tissue as suggested in [3] and [15] is unnecessary.

4   Poisoning Sensor Networks

The analogy between sensor networks and tissue can also incorporate ideas of harm and damage. There are various types of vulnerabilities identified in sensor network environments that are often not found in conventional wired networks. This work focuses on vulnerabilities in sensor network routing protocols that rely on presence of limited capacity caches to keep a track of state of the network, for example the next hop for a packet. Directed Diffusion is one such protocol. Such protocols are typically optimised for nodes with limited resources and for specific applications, with little consideration for security.

In their seminal work Karlof and Wagner [10] analysed diverse attacks against sensor network routing protocols and introduced some countermeasures. Notable attacks discussed include: Selective forwarding, Sinkhole attacks, Sybil attacks, Wormhole attacks, HELLO flood attacks and Acknowledge spoofing. In this paper, we introduce a new attack called the 'Interest Cache Poisoning Attack', which can easily disrupt multiple data paths in a network. The attacks discussed in [10] exploit the vulnerabilities of sensor networks that are also found from mobile ad-hoc networks. In contrast, the interest cache poisoning attack reflects the vulnerability of data-centric approaches which are often adopted for routing in sensor networks.

Under the Directed Diffusion protocol, each node maintains an interest cache that records the history of received interest packets. Each entry contains an interest and gradient(s) towards neighbouring node(s) that have sent the interest packets, such that when a data packet arrives, a node looks up its interest cache in order to find the next hop for the data. If there is a matching interest, the node forwards the data packet to the neighbour node(s) indicated by the gradient(s). Otherwise the data packet is dropped. The basic idea of the interest cache poisoning attack is to inject fabricated interest packets to replace benign entries in the interest caches of other nodes. The attack is ideally aimed at nodes on established data paths that shall be referred to as the targets of the attack.

For example, in our study of Tiny Diffusion - an implementation of the Directed Diffusion protocol for real sensor nodes running the TinyOS[1], we found that: (i) An interest cache always has a fixed size and (ii) whenever a new interest packet arrives and the cache is full, the oldest entry is replaced. Therefore to realise a successful attack, the attacker can take advantage of the normal behaviour of the target by forcing it to drop the content of its cache. The attack works in two phases: First by flooding the target with bogus interests, thereby forcing it to drop those interests in its cache already. This leads to the second phase of the attack, when the requested data that was intended for distribution arrives, since the target no longer has gradients to those interested in it and will be forced to drop it.

---

[1] TinyOS is an open-source operating system designed for wireless embedded sensor networks. (http://www.tinyos.net/)

This process will result in the disruption of data packet delivery to the sink node. Ideally, a given cache entry needs to be wiped out before the first data packet from the source node arrives at the target node. Otherwise the attack may succeed but may not be able to completely suppress the data flow. Though mechanistically different, the effect of this attack is analogous to that of '*DNS cache-poisoning*' (http://en.wikipedia.org/wiki/DNS_cache_poisoning). However, we cannot use the same methods of protection against *DNS cache-poisoning* (i.e., randomised ports, restricted relaying, etc.) since these are aimed at the control plane and the *Interest Cache Poisoning Attack* is performed on the data plane.

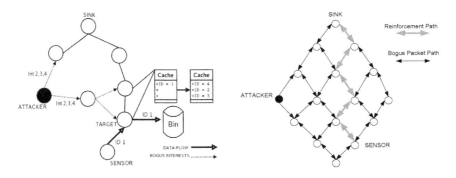

(a) Interest Cache Poisoning Attack Overview   (b) Bogus interest packet propagation

Fig. 2. Interest Cache Poisoning Attack

Fig. 2 (a) shows the impact of the attack. The attacker sends out the bogus packets and fills up the cache of the nodes on the data path. The bogus interests will replace the original interest with ID 1. When the requested data with ID 1 arrives later, the target node will just drop it. This is because there is no matching entry in the cache. As shown in Fig. 2 (b), the attack will even be successful if the attacker is not next to the target node. The attack exploits the flooding behaviour of Directed Diffusion. Whenever a node receives a new interest packet it will rebroadcast it to all its neighbours. Hence, the bogus interest packets are spread and affect the caches of many nodes, eventually the cache of a target node. As a result, the impact of bogus packets can propagate over an entire network and disrupt multiple paths of data packet delivery.

5 Using the DC Algorithm to Detect Interest Cache Poisoning

Sensor networks using Directed Diffusion share a surprising number of similarities with biological tissue, including susceptibility to poison. Here we propose a security solution for sensor networks utilising Directed Diffusion with the aim of detecting cache poisoning attacks. The mechanism incorporates an immune algorithm inspired by the responsiveness of DCs in the human immune system to danger signals.

5.1 System Overview

Figure 3 shows the overall architecture of the Danger Theory based AIS, which employs the DC algorithm (DCA). Our Danger Theory based AIS comprises of two stages: (i) Detecting misbehaving nodes and (ii) detecting antigens and responding to the detected antigens. The DCA performs the first stage of the job, detecting misbehaving nodes. The second stage of the job involves sending immune cells and signals between the nodes of the sensor network. This may be performed by a different immune inspired algorithm such as the one introduced in [11]. This paper focuses on the first stage.

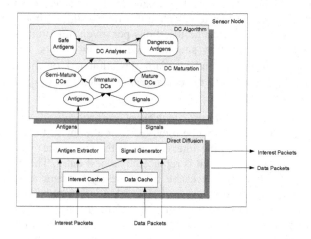

Fig. 3. DC algorithm and Directed Diffusion execute on a sensor node

A sensor node employing Directed Diffusion maintains two tables; the interest cache and the data cache and handles two types of packets; interest packets and data packets. While there are four possible sources of antigens and signals for input to the DCA, namely: (i) The interest cache, (ii) the data cache, (iii) interest packets and (iv) data packets. The signal generator and an antigen extractor are implemented as a sub-module of Directed Diffusion, thereby integrating the AIS into the protocol. When a packet arrives at a node, Directed Diffusion updates the interest and/or a data cache according to its local cache update rules [9], and extracts the signals and antigens from the packet(s) and/or cache(s). These are then passed to the DCA.

The immature DCs of the DCA sample the antigens and store them in their internal storage. They also combine various input signals using the signal weighting function shown in equation (1). The evaluation of the input signals results in output cytokines that differentiate between the immature DCs, to either become semi-mature or mature DCs. Antigens contained in semi-mature DCs are regarded as being collected under a normal condition, in contrast to the antigens stored by mature DCs that are collected under attack conditions. The DC analyser of the DCA reviews all the antigens stored in semi-mature and mature DCs and determines the state of each antigen as either "benign" or "malicious".

5.2 Signals

The DCA uses the four different types of input signals discussed in Section 5.1. In the following, we introduce various input signals that can be collected from a sensor network environment in order to detect an interest cache poisoning attack. Signals are categorised into the four groups: (i) Danger Signals (*DS*), (ii) Safe Signals (*SS*), (iii) PAMP signals (*PS*) and (iv) Inflammatory Cytokines (*IC*). A detailed explanation on how these four categories are defined is presented in [5].

- *DS1 - Generated from the interest cache insertion rate*

This is the first Danger Signal collected from abnormal interest cache insertion rates. *DS1* signals are aimed at indicating that bogus interest packets have corrupted the interest cache of a node. In order to calculate this rate, a sliding time window is used to track the number of interest cache insertions per given time unit (such as 10 sec) and a total count is calculated by summing the window counts. After a minimum training period, the mean (μ) and standard deviation (σ) of the total count are calculated. *DS1* is generated with the concentration given by $(X_i - \mu) / \sigma$, where X_i is the count of in window i.

- *DS2 - Generated from the interest cache entry expiration*

There are two ways for an entry to be removed from the interest cache: (i) When its expiration time (a predefined time interval set by the sink node) has passed, or (ii) when the cache is already full and it is replaced by a new entry. Though a sink is able to overwrite its own entries in a cache by carelessly sending a large number of different interests during a short time interval, within in a well-behaved network, we do not expect this behaviour to be the norm. Therefore, the overwriting of entries long before their expiration time can indicate the presence of an attack. In order to identify such an event, the expiration field is checked whenever an entry is inserted. The concentration of a *DS2* signal is the time difference between the expiration time and the entry overwriting time. Overwriting a very recent entry will lead to a much stronger signal than overwriting a nearly expired entry.

- *SS - Generated from the arrival of data packets*

This measurement shows that the data requested by the sink node has been forwarded to a given node. The nature of the Safe Signal is to indicate normal data flow. The absence of a Safe Signal does not necessarily indicate the existence of an attack, but a Safe Signal can be used to suppress a false detection alert. The entry of a data cache, which records the data packet forwarded, would serve this purpose. Whenever a data packet that matches an interest in the interest cache arrives, it will be forwarded and recorded in the data cache. Therefore, whenever a new entry is inserted into the data cache, an *SS* is generated and the concentration of the *SS* is 1.0.

- *PS - Generated from the data delivery failure at the sink node*

A PAMP signal is a strong indicator of a pathogenic presence. For an interest cache poisoning attack, the failure of data delivery to the sink node strongly indicates the possibility of an attack. Though delivery failures may result from many factors such as node failures on the established path or the absence of sensor nodes generating the requested data - the PAMP signal definitively establishes that what was expected did not happen and can be used to launch further investigation. This relative difference of confidence in abnormal behaviour makes the PAMP signal stronger than a Danger

Signal. For this purpose, the failure of requested data delivery would cause the sink node to generate a *PS* signal. Unlike other signals, that are just generated locally and not forwarded to other nodes, the *PS* is forwarded to other nodes. In order to transport the *PS* signal, a re-sent interest packet is used, with concentration of 1.0.

- *IC1 - Generated from the changes in gradient directions*
This process aims to detect the onset of an attack through analysing the change in the gradient directions. Relative change in the number of gradients per neighbour indicates the addition or removal of paths to a data source by that neighbour and consequently the number of paths that go through the given neighbour. The normal behaviour of Directed Diffusion is such that if the majority of the maintained gradients point to a given neighbour, a node would expect that neighbour to be closer to the sink node than the other entities in the cache. This is because the only process that should result in an increase in the frequency of gradients to a given neighbour is the consequence of reinforcements applied to paths through that neighbour. In our analogy, inflammatory cytokine (IC) amplifies the effects of the other three types of signals but it alone is not sufficient to cause the maturation of a DC. *IC1* signals are generated by identifying bursts in the frequency of gradients to given neighbours. The concentration of *IC1* signals represents the magnitude of the changes. Though *IC1* alone is not strong enough to indicate an attack, i.e. it could be the result of a normal topology change; it still indicates a disturbance that should be noted. It therefore represents an *IC* and not a *DS*.

- *IC2 - Generated from data without matching interest cache entry*
The reception of a data packet that cannot be matched to an interest in the cache can be used as an indicator of a problem. Though this does not necessarily indicate the presence of an attack, for example as the result of different interest expiration times, it still identifies anomalous situations. The concentration of *IC2* is 1.0.

5.3 Antigens

From the view point of Danger Theory, antigens together with signals trigger immune responses. Antigens can originate from pathogens, the self or foreign cells. Immune cells attempt to bind antigens presented by semi-mature or mature DCs. When the receptors of immune cells bind to antigens passed by mature DCs, the immune cells become activated and later respond to new antigens binding to their receptors, i.e. killing antigens. In contrast, when the receptors of immune cells bind to antigens presented by semi-mature DCs, the immune cells become suppressed and later do not respond to new antigens binding to the receptors[2].

Likewise, the receptors of immune cells are used to find targets (antigens) of their immune responses. The AIS proposed in this work is required to have two types of responses. The first response is to identify an attacker node where a fabricated interest packet is created and sent out, and then to exclude this node from a sensor network. The second response is to identify bogus interest packets and then to stop forwarding them. For an interest cache poisoning attack, a node that is receiving bogus packets

---

[2] Or the receptors of immune cells binding antigens presented by semi-mature DCs will bind to the receptors of other immune cells and suppress the responses released by these other immune cells. Regulatory T cells are such immune cells.

(and thus its cache is being poisoned), might poison its neighbour nodes by forwarding the bogus packets. If the AIS excludes this kind of node from a sensor network, it runs the risk of disabling the entire network. In this case, a more desirable response could be to continue the delivery of genuine packets while stopping the forwarding of bogus interest packets. This work focuses on making the second response and hence regards interest packets as antigens. In future work we aim to add further antigens to trigger the first type of response – identifying an attacker node.

5.4   The Ubiquitous Dendritic Cell Algorithm

Detailed description of the original DCA is presented in [7] and a simplified pseudo-code of the ubiquitous DCA (UDCA) is shown in fig 4. UDCA is a variation of DCA that is designed to detect 'Interest Cache Poisoning Attacks' on sensor networks. UDCA has several properties that distinguish it from existing AIS. In the following section, we address the key elements of UDCA that could be particularly beneficial in detecting malicious activities in sensor networks, and their implementation in UDCA.

- UDCA attempts to collect signals from *multiple* data sources: Although multiple signals provide richer information to make a detection decision, they require temporal calibration. Line 8-14 of fig. 4 shows that a DC continuously calculates a new output cytokine with new signals and antigens collected at each DC maturing cycle (DC_Mat_Cycle). New output cytokines are then added to previously estimated ones until the CSM cytokine reaches a migration threshold. This allows a DC to collect signals indicating a possibly identical status of context despite being generated asynchronously. Hence, UDCA fine-tunes delays between multiple signals using a CSM value update with migration threshold.
- UDCA maps the context information delivered by signals with antigens in a *temporal* manner: antigens (interests) are gathered when signals are generated (see Signal_Generator and Antigen_Extractor at fig. 4). Depending on the type of signals, one or multiple antigens can be paired with a signal. For instance, in the UDCA (for SIG_new in Antigen_Extractor at fig.4), DS2, SS and PS will be paired with one interest packet triggering the signal generation. However, for DS1, IC1 and IC2, all the interests that exist at an interest cache when these signals are generated will be selected as antigens. In this case, the antigen extractor collects antigens that are temporally close to signals since the signals are generated from the changes at multiple entries of interest caches or an absence of matching benign interest.
- UDCA combines multiple signals to judge an antigen context status: the diverse nature of signals contribute differently when judging an antigen context status. Empirical data obtained from immunologists' experimental results[3] suggest the weight values given in table 1. Equation (1) is a weighting function that determines the output cytokine by combining four types of input signals. This weighting function is used to handle a possible inconsistency existing between various signals. A given antigen can be judged by different signals in a

---

[3] These results were obtained by the research team led by Dr. Julie McLeod, Dr. Rachel Harry and Charlotte Williams at University of West England.

contradictory manner – "semi-mature" and "mature". In this case, the equation (1) determines a final decision by assigning a different weight to each signal. The line 10 – 19 of fig.4 shows this stage of UDCA processing.

```
PROCEDURE DC_Maturation(Ag_pop)
1   Let DC_Mat_Cycle = 1;
2   Creates a DC population, DC_pop;
3   A migration threshold value is randomly generated from a given range
4   Set a generated migration threshold value to each DC in DC_pop
5   Do
6   {
7      For each DC from DC_pop
8         Sample antigens, AGs, from Ag_pop, with replacement
9         Store sampled antigens to DC's internal antigen storage
10        Copy the signals paired with AGs to DC's internal signal storage
11        Calculate the concent. for CSM, MAT, SEMI-MAT cytokine of DC using (1)
12
13        Add CSM, MAT, SEMI-MAT cytok. to
14           total CSM, MAT, SEMI-MAT cytokine concent. respectively
15        If a total CSM cytokine concent. > an assigned migration threshold
16           If SEMI-MAT cytokine concent. > MAT cytokine concent.
17              DC is moved to semi-mature DC population, SEMI_MAT_DC_pop
18           else
19              DC is moved to mature DC population, MAT_DC_pop
20           endif
21           call DC_Analyser(SEMI_MAT_DC_pop, MAT_DC_pop)
22        endIf
23     endFor
24     Empty Ag_pop;
25     DC_Mat_Cycle++;
26  } while ( DC_Mat_Cycle < Max_DC_Cycle )

PROCEDURE DC_Analyser(SEMI_MAT_DC_pop, MAT_DC_pop)
1   For each antigen Ag from SEMI_MAT_DC_pop and MAT_DC_pop
2      Counts the number of times presented by SEMI_MAT_DC or MAT_DC
3      If SEMI_MAT_COUNT > MAT_COUNT
4         Ag is malicious
5      else
6         Ag is benign
7      endIF
8   endFor
9   For each DC from SEMI_MAT_DC_pop and MAT_DC_pop
10  Reset a migration threshold value of DC
11  Set CSM, MAT, SEMI_MAT cytokine concent. of DC to be 0
12  Set total CSM, MAT, SEMI_MAT cytokine concent. of DC to be 0
13  Empty antigen and signal storages of DC
14  Move the DC to DC_pop from  SEMI_MAT_DC_pop or MAT_DC_pop
15  EndFor

PROCEDURE Signal_Generator(Interest Cache, Data Cache, Packets)
1   Generates a new signal, SIG_new  // as described in section 5.2
2   If  SIG_new is generated
3      Call Antigen_Extractor(Interest Cache, SIG_new)
4   endIf

PROCEDURE Antigen_Extractor(Interest Cache, SIG_new)
1   Check through an Interest Cache
2   Select interests matching to SIG_new
3   Each selected interest becomes an antigen
4   Add pairs of an antigen with SIG_new to Ag_pop
```

Fig. 4. Pseudo code of the UDC algorithm to detect malicious activites

Table 1. Suggested weights used for Equation (1), which is a signal weighting function [6]. W_P, W_D, W_S, C_P, C_D, C_S are weights and concentrations of PS, DS, SS respectively.

Weight	csm	semi	mat
W_P	2	0	2
W_D	1	0	1
W_S	2	3	-3

$$C_{[csm,semi,mat]} = \frac{(W_p{*}C_p)+(W_s{*}C_s)+(W_D{*}C_D)}{|W_p|+|W_s|+|W_D|} * \frac{1+IC}{2} \quad (1)$$

- UDCA employs a population of DCs to determine the final antigen context status: as shown DC_Analyser procedure of UDCA in fig. 4, the context status of each antigen is determined by the collective decisions of multiple DCs'. Each DC samples antigens and its migration threshold values are set differently (see line 2-3 of fig.4). These allow each DC to judge the context of one antigen differently and the final decision on a given antigen is therefore made from the aggregations from multiple DCs.
- UDCA does not employ a pattern matching based detection: UDCA concentrates on identifying bogus interest packets and filtering them out. This is another different trait from other existing AISs, which usually employ pattern matching to detect an on-going attack. UDCA detects an attack by examining how much a given node is misbehaving via generated signals. It then collects data (=antigens) for the next AIS algorithm to perform a pattern matching detection, which is required to produce responses. In responding, an AIS needs to react to a malicious antigen before it damages a monitored system and causes generations of signals. It is necessary for an artificial immune responder to have a pattern matching based detection. Therefore, UDCA plays the role of the innate immune system that presents the context information with matching antigens to the adaptive immune system [3], [15].

6   Conclusion

This work introduces the concept of sensor networks as a new application area for AIS research and argues that some AIS features are inherent in sensor networks. We illustrate how closely a Danger Theory based AIS, in particular the dendritic cell algorithm (DCA), matches the structure and functional requirements of sensor networks. This work also introduces a new sensor network attack called an interest cache poisoning attack and discusses how the DCA can be applied to detect an interest cache poisoning attack.

Currently we have implemented a number of different versions of an interest cache poisoning attacks by varying the bogus packet sending rates, the number of sink node interest subscriptions and the location of an attacker. In addition, various types of signals introduced in this paper have been being generated. The attacks and the signal generator have been being implemented under a network simulator, J-Sim (www.j-sim.org) and TOSSIM (www.cs.berkeley.edu/~pal/research/tossim.html). As discussed in this paper, UDCA appears to be an attractive solution to filter out bogus packets but the more detailed features of UDCA need to be further investigated. In future work, we aim to thoroughly study the appropriateness of a weight function used, the sensitivity analysis of various parameters, and the efficiency required to be used in a limited environment like a sensor node.

Acknowledgments

This project is supported by the EPSRC (GR/S47809/01).

References

1. Aickelin, U. Bentley, P., Cayzer, S., Kim, J., and McLeod, J.: Danger Theory: the Link between AIS and IDS. In Proc. of the 2nd Int. Conf. on AIS (ICARIS-03), (2003) 147-155.
2. Akyildiz, I. F. et al.: A Survey on Sensor Networks, IEEE Communication Magazine, Aug., (2002) 102-114.
3. Bentley, P., Greensmith, J., and Ujjin, S. : Two ways to grow tissue for AIS, In Proc. of the 3rd Int. Conf. on AIS (ICARIS-05), Springer-Verlag (2005) 139-152
4. Estrin, D., Cullar, D., Pister, K., and Sukhatme, G. : Connecting the Physical World with Pervasive Networks, Pervasive Computing, (2002) 59-69
5. Greensmith, J., Aickelin, U. and Cayzer, S. : Introducing Dendritic Cells as a Novel Immune-Inspired Algorithm for Intrusion Detection, In Proc. of ICARIS-05, Springer-Verlag (2005) 153-167
6. Greensmith, J., Twycross, J., and Aickelin, U.: Dendritic Cells for Anomaly Detection, In Proc. of IEEE Cong. on Evolutionary Computation (CEC-06), Vancouver, Canada (2006).
7. Greensmith, J. et al.: Articulation and Clarification of the Dendritic Cell Algorithm, submitted to ICARIS-2006
8. Hart, E., and Timmis, J. : Application Areas of AIS : The Past, The Present and The Future, In Proc. of the 3rd Int. Conf. on AIS (ICARIS-05), (2005) 483-497
9. Intanagonwiwat, C. et al : Directed Diffusion for Wireless Sensor Networking, IEEE/ACM Trans. on Networking, Vol.11, No.1, Feb (2003) 2-16.
10. Karlof, C., and Wagner, D. : Secure routing in wireless sensor networks: attacks and countermeasures, Ad Hoc Networks, (2004) 293-315
11. Kim, J., Wilson, W., Aickelin, U. and McLeod, J. : Cooperative Automated Worm Response and Detection ImmuNe Algorithm (CARDINAL) inspired by T-cell Immunity and Tolerance, In Proc. of the 3rd Int. Conf. on AIS (ICARIS-05), (2005) 168-181
12. Kim, J. et al, Immune System Approaches to Intrusion Detection – a Review, under review.
13. Matzinger, P.: Tolerance, danger and the extended family. Annual Reviews in Immunology, 12 (1994) 991-1045
14. Sarafijanovic, S. and Le Boudec, J. : An AIS for misbehaviour detection in mobile ad-hoc networks with virtual thymus, clustering, danger signals and memory detectors, In Proc. of the 2rd Int. Conf. on AIS (ICARIS-04), Springer-Verlag (2005) 342-356
15. Twycross, J. and Aickelin, U. : Towards a conceptual framework for innate immunity, In Proc. of the 3rd Int. Conf. on AIS (ICARIS-05), Springer-Verlag (2005) 153-167
16. Twycross, J. and Aickelin, U.: libtissue – implementing innate immunity, In Proc. of the CEC-06, Vancouver, Canada (2006) to appear.

Articulation and Clarification of the Dendritic Cell Algorithm

Julie Greensmith, Uwe Aickelin, and Jamie Twycross

CS&IT, University of Nottingham, UK, NG8 1BB
{jqg, uxa, jpt}@cs.nott.ac.uk

Abstract. The Dendritic Cell algorithm (DCA) is inspired by recent work in innate immunity. In this paper a formal description of the DCA is given. The DCA is described in detail, and its use as an anomaly detector is illustrated within the context of computer security. A port scan detection task is performed to substantiate the influence of signal selection on the behaviour of the algorithm. Experimental results provide a comparison of differing input signal mappings.

Keywords: dendritic cells, artificial immune systems, anomaly detection.

1 Introduction

Artificial immune systems (AIS) are a collection of algorithms developed from models or abstractions of the function of the cells of the human immune system. The first, and arguably the most obvious, application for AIS is in the protection of computers and networks, through virus and intrusion detection[2]. In this paper we present an AIS approach to intrusion detection based on the Danger Theory, through the development of an algorithm based on the behaviour of *Dendritic Cells* (DCs). DCs have the power to suppress or activate the immune system through the correlation of signals from an environment, combined with location markers in the form of antigen. A DCs function is to instruct the immune system to act when the body is under attack, policing the tissue for potential sources of damage. DCs are natural anomaly detectors, the sentinel cells of the immune system, and therefore the development of a DC based algorithm was only a matter of time. The Dendritic Cell Algorithm (DCA) was introduced in 2005 and has demonstrated potential as a classifier for a static machine learning data set[4] and anomaly detector for real-time port scan detection[5]. The DCA differs from other AIS algorithm for the following reasons:

- multiple signals are combined and are a representation of environment or context information
- signals are combined with antigen in a temporal and distributed manner
- pattern matching is not used to perform detection, unlike negative selection[6]
- cells of the innate immune system are used as inspiration, not the adaptive immune cells and unlike clonal selection, no dynamic learning is attempted

H. Bersini and J. Carneiro (Eds.): ICARIS 2006, LNCS 4163, pp. 404–417, 2006.

The aim of this paper is to demonstrate the anomaly detection capabilities of the DCA and to clarify which features of the algorithm facilitate detection.

2   Dendritic Cells *in vivo*

The DCA is based on the function of dendritic cells whose primary role is as an antigen presenting cell. DCs behave very differently to the cells of the adaptive immune system. Before describing the function of the algorithm we give a general overview of DC biology, introducing different cells, organs and their behaviour. More information on natural DCs can be found in [9].

In vivo, DCs can perform a number of different functions, determined by their state of maturation. Modulation between these states is facilitated by the detection of signals within the tissue - namely danger signals, PAMPs (pathogenic associated molecular patterns), apoptotic signals (safe signals) and inflammatory cytokines which are described below. The maturation state of a DC is determined by the relative concentrations of these four types of signal. The state of maturity of a DC influences the response by T-cells, to either an immunogenic or tolerogenic state, for a specific antigen. Immature DCs reside in the tissue where they collect antigenic material and are exposed to signals. Based on the combinations of signals received, maturation of the DCs occurs generating two terminal differentiation states, mature or semi-mature. Mature DCs have an activating effect while semi-mature DCs have a suppressive effect. The different output signals (termed output cytokines) generated by the two terminal states of DCs differ sufficiently to provide two different contexts for antigen presentation, shown abstractly in Figure 1.

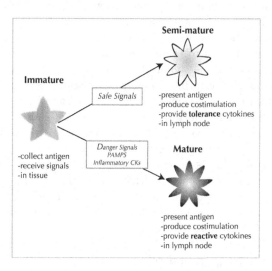

Fig. 1. An abstract view of DC maturation and signals required for differentiation. CKs denote cytokines

The characteristics of the relevant signals are summarised below:

- PAMPS are pre-defined bacterial signatures, causing the maturation of immature DCs to mature DCs through expression of 'mature cytokines'.
- Danger signals are released as a result of damage to tissue cells, also increasing mature DC cytokines, and have a lower potency than PAMPs.
- Safe signals are released as a result of regulated cell death and cause an increase in semi-mature DC cytokines, and reduce the output of mature DC cytokines
- Inflammatory cytokines are derived from general tissue distress and amplify the effects of the other three signals but are not sufficient to cause any effect on immature DCs when used in isolation.

3   Dendritic Cells *in silico*

The Dendritic Cell Algorithm (DCA) was developed as part of the Danger Project[1], which aims to find the missing link between AIS and Intrusion Detection through the application of the danger theory[8]. The danger theory proposes that the immune system responds when damage to the host is detected, rather than discriminating between self and non-self proteins. The project encompasses artificial tissue[3] and T-cells[7], and the libtissue framework[11]. The DCs are the detection component developed within this project.

3.1   Libtissue

Libtissue is a software system which allows the implementation and testing of AIS algorithms on real-world problems based on principles of innate immunology [10], [11]. It allows researchers to implement AIS algorithms as a collection of cells, antigen and signals interacting within a tissue compartment. The implementation has a client/server architecture, separating data collection from data processing. Input data to the tissue compartment is generated by sensors monitoring environmental, behavioural or context data through the libtissue client, transforming this data into antigen and signals. AIS algorithms can be implemented within the libtissue server, as libtissue provides a convenient programming environment. Both client and server APIs allow new antigen and signal sources to be added to libtissue servers, and the testing of the same algorithm with a number of different data sources. Input data from the tissue client is represented in a tissue compartment contained on the tissue server. A tissue compartment is a space in which cells, signals and antigen interact. Each tissue compartment has a fixed-size antigen store where antigen provided by libtissue clients is placed. The tissue compartment also stores levels of signals, set either by tissue clients or cells.

3.2   Abstract View of the DCA

The DCA is implemented as a *libtissue* tissue server. Input signals are combined with a second source of data, such as a data item ID, or program ID number. This is achieved through using a population of artificial DCs to perform aggregate sampling and data processing. Using multiple DCs means that *multiple* data items in the form of antigen are sampled *multiple times*. If a single DC presents incorrect information, it becomes inconsequential provided that the majority of DCs derive the correct context. The sampling of data is combined with context information received during the antigen collection process. Different combinations of input signals result in two different antigen contexts. Semi-mature antigen context implies antigen data was collected under normal conditions, whereas a mature antigen context signifies a potentially anomalous data item. The nature of the response is determined by measuring the number of DCs that are fully mature, represented by a value, **MCAV** - the *mature context antigen value*. If the DCA functions as intended, the closer this value is to 1, the greater the probability that the antigen is anomalous. The MCAV value is used to assess the degree of anomaly of a given antigen. By applying thresholds at various levels, analysis can be performed to assess the anomaly detection capabilities of the algorithm.

The DCA has three stages: *initialisation, update and aggregation*. Initialisation involves setting various parameters and is followed by the update stage. The update stage can be decomposed into *tissue update* and *cell cycle*. Both the tissue update and cell cycle form the `libtissue` tissue server. Signal data is fed from the data-source to the tissue server through the tissue client.

The tissue update is a continuous process, whereby the values of the tissue data structures are refreshed. This occurs on an event-driven basis, with values for signals and antigen updated each time new data appears in the system. Antigen data enters tissue update in the same, event driven manner. The updated signals provide the input signals for the population of DCs.

The cell cycle is a discrete process occurring at a user defined rate. In this paper, 1 cell cycle is performed per second. Signal and antigen from the tissue data structures are accessed by the DCs during the cell cycle. This includes an update of every DC in the system with new signal values and antigen. The cell cycle and update of tissue continues until a stopping criteria is reached, usually until all antigen data is processed. Finally, the aggregation stage is initiated, where all collected antigen are subsequently analysed and the MCAV per antigen derived.

3.3   Parameters and Structures

The algorithm is described using the following terms.

- Indices:
  $i = 0, ..., I$ input signal index;
  $j = 0, ..., J$ input signal category index;
  $k = 0, ..., K$ tissue antigen index;
  $l = 0, ..., L$ DC cycle index;
  $m = 0, ..., M$ DC index;
  $n = 0, ..., N$ DC antigen index;
  $p = 0, ..., P$ DC output signal index.

– Parameters:
I = maximum number of input signals per category;
J = maximum number of categories of input signal;
K = maximum number of antigen in tissue antigen vector;
L = maximum number of DC cycles;
M = maximum number of DCs in population;
N = maximum number of antigen contained per DC ;
P = maximum number of output signals per DC;
Q = number of antigens sampled per DC for one cycle.

– Data Structures:
$DC_m = \{s^{DC}(m), a^{DC}(m), \bar{o}(m), t(m)\}$- a DC within the population;
$T = \{S, A\}$ - the tissue;
S = tissue signal matrix;
s_{ij} = a signal type i, category j in the signal matrix S;
A = tissue antigen vector;
a_k = antigen index k in the tissue antigen vector;
s^{DC} =DC signal matrix;
a^{DC} = DC antigen vector;
o = temporary output signal vector for DC_m;
$o(m)$ = output signal p in the output signal vector of DC_m;
$\bar{o}_p$ = cumulative output signal vector for DC_m;
t_m = migration threshold for DC_m;
w_{ijp} = transforming weight from $s_{ij}\ o_p$.

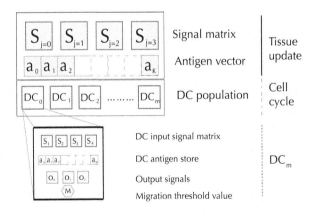

Fig. 2. Tissue and Cell Update components, where $S_{i,j}$ is reduced to S_j

The data structures are represented graphically in Figure 2. Each DC_m transforms each value of $s^{DC}(m)$ to $o_p(m)$ using the following equation with suggested values for weightings given in Table 1. Both the equation and weights are derived from observing experiments performed on natural DCs (personal communication from Dr J. McLeod and colleagues, UWE, UK), and information presented in Section 2 (more details found in [4]).

$$o_p(m) = \frac{\sum_i \sum_{j \neq 3} W_{ijp} s_{ij}^{DC}}{\sum_i \sum_{j \neq 3} |W_{ijp}|} * \frac{\sum_i W_{i3p}(s_{i3}^{DC}+1)}{\sum_i |W_{i3p}|} \qquad \forall p$$

Table 1. Examples of weights used for signal processing

w_{ijp}	$j = 1$	$j = 2$	$j = 3$	j= 4
$p = 1$	2	1	2	1
$p = 2$	0	0	3	1
$p = 3$	2	1	-3	1

The tissue has containers for signal and antigen values, namely S and A. In the current implementation of the DCA, there are 4 categories of signal ($j = 3$) and 1 signal per category ($i = 0$). The categories are derived from the 4 signal model of DC behaviour described in Section 2 where: $s_{0,0}$ = PAMP signals, $s_{0,1}$ = danger signals, $s_{0,2}$ = safe signals and $s_{0,3}$ = the inflammatory signal. An antigen store is constructed for use within the tissue cycle where all DCs in the population collect antigen, which is also introduced to the tissue in an event driven manner.

The cell cycle maintains all DC data structures. This includes the maintenance of a population of DCs, DC_m, which form a sampling set of size M. Each DC has an input signal matrix, antigen vector, output signals, and migration threshold. The internal values of DC_m are updated, based on current data in the tissue signal matrix and antigen vector. The DC input signals, s_{ij}^{DC}, use the identical mapping for signal categories as tissue s_{ij} and are updated every cell cycle iteration. Each s_{ij}^{DC} for DC_m is updated via an overwrite every cell cycle. These values are used to calculate output signal values, o_p, for DC_m, which are added cumulatively over a number of cell cycles to form $\bar{o}_p(m)$, where $p = 0$ is costimulatory value, $p = 1$ is the mature DC output signal, and $p = 2$ is the semi-mature DC output signal.

3.4   The DCA

The following pseudocode shows the initialisation stage, cycle stage, tissue update and cell cycle.

```
initialise parameters {I, J, K, L, M, N, O, P, Q}
while (l < L)
    update A and S
    for m = 0 to M
        for 0 to Q
            DCm samples Q antigen from A
            for all i = 0 to I and all j = 0 to J
```

$$s_{ij}^{DC} = s_{ij}$$
for $n = 0$ to N
    DC_m processes a_{nm}^{DC}
    for p to P
      compute o_p
      $\bar{o}_p(m) = \bar{o}_p(m) + o_p$
    if $o_0(m) > t_m$
      DC_m removed from population
      DC_m migrate to Lymph node
  l++

analyse antigen and calculate MCAV

3.5 Lymph Node and Antigen Aggregation

Once DC_m has been removed from the population, the contents of a_n^{DC} and values $\bar{o}_{pm}$ are logged to a file for the aggregation stage. Once completed, s_{ij}^{DC}, a_n^{DC} and $\bar{o}_{pm}$ are all reset, and DC_m is returned to the sampling population. The re-cycling of DCs continues until the stopping condition is met $(l = L)$. Once all data has been processed by the DCs, the output log of antigen-plus-context is analysed. The same antigen is presented multiple time with different context values. This information is recorded in a log file. The total fraction of mature DCs presenting said antigen (where $\bar{o}_1 > \bar{o}_2$) is divided by the total amount of times the antigen was presented namely $\bar{o}_1/(\bar{o}_1 + \bar{o}_2)$. This is used to calculate the *mean mature context antigen value* or MCAV.

3.6 Signals and Antigen

An integral part of DC function is the ability to combine multiple signals to influence the behaviour of the cells. The different input signals have different effects on cell behaviour as described in Section 2. The semantics of the different category of signal are derived from the study of the influence of the different signals on DCs *in vitro*. Definitions of the characteristics of each signal category are given below, with an example of an actual signal per category. This categorisation forms the signal selection schema.

- PAMP - s_{i0} *e.g. the number of error messages generated per second by a failed network connection*
  1. a signature of abnormal behaviour e.g. an error message
  2. a high degree of confidence of abnormality associated with an increase in this signal strength
- Danger signal - s_{i1} *e.g. the number of transmitted network packets per second*
  1. measure of an attribute which significantly increases in response to abnormal behaviour
  2. a moderate degree of confidence of abnormality with increased level of this signal, though at a low signal strength can represent normal behaviour.

- Safe signal - s_{i2} *E.g. the inverse rate of change of number of network packets per second. A high rate of change equals a low safe signal level and vice versa.*
  1. a confident indicator of normal behaviour in a predictable manner or a measure of steady- behaviour
  2. measure of an attribute which increases signal concentration due to the lack of change in strength
- Inflammatory signal -s_{i3} *e.g. high system activity when no user present at a machine*
  1. a signal which cannot cause maturation of a DC without the other signals present
  2. a general signal of system distress

Signals, though interesting, are inconsequential without antigen. To a DC, antigen is an element which is carried and presented to a T-cell, without regard for the structure of the antigen. Antigen *is* the data to be classified, and works well in the form of an identifier, be it an anomalous process ID[5] or the ID of a data item [4]. At this stage, minimal antigen processing is performed and the antigen presented is an identical copy of the antigen collected. Detection is performed through the correlation of antigen with signals.

4   Return of the Nmap - the Port Scan Experiment Revisited

The purpose of these experiments is as follows:

1. To validate the theoretical model which underpins the DCA
2. To investigate sensitivity to changes in the treatment of signals
3. To apply the DCA to anomaly detection for computer security

4.1   Port Scanning and Data

In this paper, port scanning is used as a model intrusion. While a port scan is not an intrusion *per se*, it is a 'hacker tool' used frequently during the information gathering stage of an intrusion. This can reveal the topology of a network, open ports and machine operating systems. The behaviour of *outgoing* port scans provide a small scale model of an automated attack. While examination of outgoing traffic will not reveal an intruder at the point of entry, it can be used to detect if a machine is subverted to send anomalous or virally infected packets. This is particularly relevant for the detection of scanning worms and botnets. The DCA is applied to the detection of an outgoing port scan to a single port across a range of IP addresses, based on the ICMP 'ping' protocol.

Data is compiled into 30 sessions, namely 10 attack, 10 normal and 10 control sessions. Each session includes a remote log-in to the monitored machine via SSH, and contains an event. The attack session includes a port scan performed by popular port scanning tool `nmap`, using the $-sP$ option for an ICMP 'ping' scan, across a range of 1020 IP addresses. The normal session includes a transfer of a file of 2.5MB from the monitored machine to a remote server. The control session has no event and allows us to observe any signal deviations caused through monitoring the SSH session.

4.2 Signals and Antigen

Data from the monitored system are collected for the duration of a session. These values are transformed into signal values and written to a log file. Each signal value is a normalised real-number, based on a pre-defined maximum value. For this experiment the signals used are PAMPs, danger and safe signals. Inflammatory cytokines (S_{i4}) do not feature as they are not relevant for this particular problem. PAMPs are represented as the number of "destination unreachable" errors-per-second recorded on the ethernet card. When the port scan process scans multiple IP addresses indiscriminately, the number of these errors increases, and therefore is a positive sign of suspicious activity. Danger signals are represented as the number of outbound network packets per second. An increase in network traffic could imply anomalous behaviour. This alone would not be useful as legitimate behaviour can cause an increase in network packets. The safe signals in this experiment are the inverse rate of change of network packets per second. This is based on the assumption that if the rate of sending network packets is highly variable, the machine is behaving suspiciously. None of these signals are enough on their own to indicate an anomaly. In these experiments the signals are used to *detect* the port scan, and to *not detect* the normal file transfer.

During the session each process spawned from the monitored ssh session is logged through capturing all system calls made by the monitored processes using strace. Antigen is created with each system call made by a process, with antigen represented as the process ID value of a system call. Each antigen is processed subsequently by the DCA, and those presented with context are assigned a MCAV for assessment.

4.3 The Experiments

Experiments are performed to examine the influence of using different signal mappings. In these experiments a signal designed to be a PAMP is used as a danger signal and vice versa. The same is performed with PAMP and safe signals. We hypothesise based on previous experience using the DCA that it will be robust to incorrect signal mapping between danger and PAMP signals, but will lose detection accuracy if a safe signal is switched with a PAMP.

We also examine the effect of multiple antigen sampling on the performance of the algorithm. The DCA is designed so each DC can present multiple antigen on migration from the sampling population. Each DC presents a small subset of the total antigen within the tissue for its lifetime in the cell cycle. If multiple copies of the same antigen are used, robust coverage of input antigen can be achieved. To investigate the influence of multiple antigen presentation, an experiment is performed through limiting the antigen storage capacity (N) of each DC to 1. If less antigen is presented, the accuracy of the DCA could be impeded. An additional version of the DCA, known as 'DCLite', is implemented as the most basic form of the algorithm. DCLite uses one context signal, with $N = 1$, as in experiment M4. Based on our working knowledge of the data and of the DCA, we predict that it not possible to perform anomaly detection with the PAMP signal ($S_{0,1}$) alone. The performance of the algorithm under the various conditions is assessed through analysing the MCAV values. Five experiments are performed:

M1 using the suggested 'hand selected' input signals
M2 danger and PAMP signal swapped
M3 PAMP and safe signal swapped
M4 using a DC antigen vector size of 1, with signal mapping M1
M5 DC antigen vector of size 1 and using the PAMP signal only (DCLite)

Experiments M1 - M5 are performed for all individual attack and normal datasets as separate runs. Each data session is analysed by the DCA 3 times for each experiment (a total of 240 runs). Parameters for the experiments are as follows: $I = 1; J = 4; K = 500; L = 120; M = 100; N = 50; P = 3; Q = 1$. All experiments are performed on a AMD Athlon 1GHz Debian Linux machine (kernel 2.4.10) with all code implemented in C (gcc 4.0.2).

4.4   Results

The mean MCAV for each process type and each session type, both attack and normal, are recorded and presented in Table 2. Any process generating a non-zero MCAV is considered for analysis and termed a *process of interest*. The MCAV values for the 4 processes of interest for the attack sessions are represented in

Table 2. MCAV values for each experiment across each dataset

Expt.	Attack							
	nmap		pts		bash		sshd	
	mean	stdev	mean	stdev	mean	stdev	mean	stdev
M1	0.82	0.04	0.67	0.11	0.18	0.22	0.02	0.24
M2	0.86	0.27	0.78	0.12	0.28	0.27	0.19	0.35
M3	0.90	0.04	0.62	0.13	0.99	0.33	0.96	0.02
M4	0.82	0.21	0.55	0.14	0.16	0.26	0.13	0.27
M5	1.00	0.00	1.00	0.00	1.00	0.00	1.00	0.00

Expt.	Normal							
	scp		pts		bash		sshd	
	mean	stdev	mean	stdev	mean	stdev	mean	stdev
M1	0.14	0.29	0.12	0.25	0.01	0.02	0.01	0.01
M2	0.24	0.33	0.18	0.29	0.04	0.03	0.05	0.09
M3	1	0	1	0	1	0	1	0
M4	0.19	0.25	0.1	0.17	0.01	0.03	0.05	0.08

Figure 3. This shows experiment M1-M4 for the two normal processes of the bash shell (bash) and ssh demon (sshd) and the two anomalous processes namely the nmap and the pseudo-terminal slave (pts) which displays the nmap output. The MCAV values for the anomalous processes is significantly higher than that of the normal processes for experiments M1, M2 and M4. Experiment M3 does not show the same trend, though interestingly the nmap MCAV is not significantly different to the values for experiments M1, M2 and M4. All MCAV values for experiment M5 equal 1 because antigen is never presented in a semi-mature context due to lack of other signals. The normal session is represented in a similar manner, also shown in Figure 3. Significantly lower values for MCAV for all processes are reported, with the exception of experiment M3. The processes of interest include the bash shell, ssh demon, the file transfer (scp) and a forwarding client (x-forward). In the control experiment the mean MCAV values for all presented antigen were zero - no processes of interest could be highlighted. From this we can assume that the process of remote log-in is not enough to change the behaviour of the machine. All antigens were presented in a safe context implying steady-state system behaviour reflected through the MCAV output of the algorithm.

4.5   Analysis

In experiment M1 distinct differences are shown in the behaviour of the algorithm for the attack and normal datasets. The MCAV for the the anomalous process is significantly larger than the MCAV of the normal processes. This is encouraging as it shows that the DCA can differentiate between two different types of process based on environmentally derived signals. In experiment M2 the PAMP and danger signals were switched. In comparison with the results presented for experiment M1, the MCAV for the anomalous process is not significantly different (paired t-test $p < 0.01$). However, in experiment M2, the standard deviations of the mean MCAVs are generally larger and is especially notable for the nmap process. Potentially, the two signals could be switched (through accidental means or incorrect signal selection) without altering the performance of the algorithm significantly. Experiment M3 involved reversing the mapping of safe and PAMP signals. The safe signal is generated continuously when the system is inactive and when mapped as a PAMP constantly generated full maturation in the artificial DCs, shown by the high MCAV value for all processes indiscriminately. Interestingly, in M3 the MCAV value for the anomalous processes in the attack datasets is lower than the normal process' value. For the normal dataset, all processes are classified as anomalous, all resulting in a MCAV of 1, a 100% false positive rate. These three experiments show that adding some expert knowledge is beneficial to the performance of the algorithm. It also supports the use of the proposed signal selection schema for use within the algorithm and has highlighted one key point - danger and PAMP signals should increase in response to a change in the system, whereas a PAMP must be the opposite, namely an indicator of little change within the system.

By comparing the results from experiment M1 and M4, the influence of multiple antigen sampled per DC can be observed. In M4, the anomalous processes'

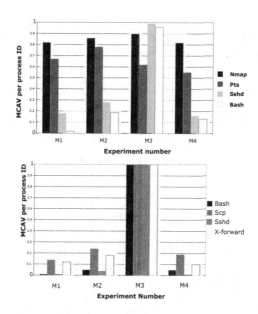

Fig. 3. The rate of detection for attack (upper graph) and normal (lower graph) for the 4 processes of interest (MCAV value) for experiments M1-M4 is shown

MCAV are significantly greater than that of the normal processes. In comparison with M1, the detection of the anomalous processes was not significantly different for nmap, and was slightly lower for the pts process. Conversely, the MCAV for all normal processes from both the attack and normal datasets was greater than in experiment M1. Examination of the number of antigen presented revealed that fewer antigens per process were presented than in experiment M1. This implies that the MCAV values were generated from a smaller set size and could be responsible for the differences in detection. Multiple antigen sampling can improve the detection of anomalous processes while reducing the amount of normal processes presented as anomalous. More experiments must be performed using a range of antigen vector sizes to confirm this result. Experiment M5 yielded interesting results, showing it is not possible to discriminate between normal and anomalous (nmap) processes based on the PAMP signal alone. In M5, 3 out of the 10 datasets yielded no results, with insufficient PAMP signal generated to cause antigen presentation. For the remaining 7 datasets, all processes of interest produced a MCAV of 1. No discrimination was made between the normal and anomalous processes. In the absence of being able to discriminate based on the MCAVs, it may still be possible to determine the anomalous process for M5 based on the ratio of presented antigen to antigen input. The ratio for nmap antigen over the 7 successful runs is 0.054, and 0.02 for the ssh demon. A paired T-test shows that the sshd antigen ratio was significantly larger than the nmap ratio, further confirming the poor performance of DC Lite. One possible explanation for the poor performance of the DCA is that the safe signal is vital to provide some 'tolerance' for the processes which run constantly such as the ssh demon. Further investigations will be performed with the use of safe signals and the role of active suppression in the performance of the DCA.

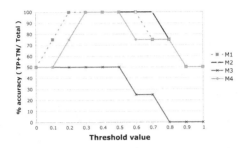

Fig. 4. Analysis of attack data for experiment M1-M4 in terms of accuracy at different thresholds

The accuracy for experiments M1-M4 is calculated by applying increasing threshold values to the MCAV values for the attack datasets, within a range of 0-1 at 0.1 intervals. If the MCAV value of a process exceeds this threshold then the process is classed as anomalous. The number of true positives and true negatives are calculated. The accuracy is calculated for each experiment (accuracy = true positives+true negatives / total number of processes) and the results of this analysis are presented in Figure 4. This figure shows that for experiment M1, if the threshold is between 0.2 and 0.7 the anomaly detection accuracy is 100%. For experiment M2 100% accuracy is also achieved, but is in the range of 0.3-0.8. M4 is of interest, as the range at which 100% accuracy is achieved is reduced in comparison to M1 and M2. As expected M3 performs significantly poorer than all others, also shown in Figure 4. For the normal dataset a similar analysis showed lower rates of false positives for increasing thresholds, with the exception of M3.

5   Conclusions

In this paper the DCA has been described in detail and interesting facets of the algorithm have been presented. The importance of careful signal selection has been highlighted through experiments. The DCA is somewhat robust to misrepresentation of the activating danger and PAMP signals, but care must be taken to select a suitable safe signal as an indicator of normality. In addition, the influence of multiple antigen presentation by each DC was investigated. Reduced antigen throughput, a decrease in detection of true positives and an increase in the rate of false positives are observed. The process by which these signals are combined has been described, and how changes in the semantic mappings of the signals influence the algorithm. Data processing was performed by a population of DCs, and multiplicity in sampling produced improved results. The baseline experiment highlighted that it is not possible to perform detection using a predefined 'signature-based' signal, regardless of how the results are analysed. Not only have we demonstrated the use of the DCA as an anomaly detector, but have also uncovered elements of behaviour previously unseen from the application of this algorithm.

Many aspects of this algorithm remain unexplored such as the sensitivity of the parameters and scalability in terms of number of cells and number of input signals. Our future work with this algorithm includes a sensitivity analysis and the generation of a solid baseline for comparison, in addition to performing similar signal experiments with a larger, more realistic, real-time problem.

Acknowledgements

This project is supported by the EPSRC (GR/S47809/01).

References

1. U Aickelin, P Bentley, S Cayzer, J Kim, and J McLeod. Danger theory: The link between ais and ids. In *ICARIS-03, LNCS 2787*, pages 147–155, 2003.
2. U Aickelin, J Greensmith, and J Twycross. Immune system approaches to intrusion detection - a review. In *ICARIS-04, LNCS 3239*, pages 316–329, 2004.
3. P Bentley, J Greensmith, and S Ujjin. Two ways to grow tissue for artificial immune systems. In *ICARIS-05, LNCS 3627*, pages 139–152, 2005.
4. J Greensmith, U Aickelin, and S Cayzer. Introducing dendritic cells as a novel immune-inspired algorithm for anomaly detection. In *ICARIS-05, LNCS 3627*, pages 153–167, 2005.
5. J. Greensmith, J. Twycross, and U. Aickelin. Artificial dcs for anomaly detection. In *Congress on Evolutionary Computation*, page TBA, 2006.
6. S Hofmeyr. *An immunological model of distributed detection and its application to computer security*. PhD thesis, University Of New Mexico, 1999.
7. J. Kim, W. Wilson, U. Aickelin, and J. McLeod. Cooperative automated worm response and detection immune algorithm (cardinal) inspired by t-cell immunity and tolerance. In *ICARIS-04, LNCS 3239*, 2005.
8. P Matzinger. Tolerance, danger and the extended family. *Annual Reviews in Immunology*, 12:991–1045, 1994.
9. T R Mosmann and AM Livingstone. Dendritic cells: the immune information management experts. *Nature Immunology*, 5(6):564–566, 2004.
10. J. Twycross and U. Aickelin. Towards a conceptual framework for innate immunity. In *ICARIS-05, LNCS 3627*, 2005.
11. J. Twycross and U. Aickelin. libtissue - implementing innate immunity. In *Congress on Evolutionary Computation (CEC-2006)*, page TBA, 2006.

Immune-Inspired
Adaptive Information Filtering

Nikolaos Nanas[1], Anne de Roeck[1], and Victoria Uren[2]

[1] Computing Department, The Open University, Milton Keynes, MK7 6AA, U.K.
{N.Nanas, A.deRoeck}@open.ac.uk
[2] Knowledge Media Institute, The Open University, Milton Keynes, MK7 6AA, U.K.
{V.S.Uren}@open.ac.uk

Abstract. Adaptive information filtering is a challenging research problem. It requires the adaptation of a representation of a user's multiple interests to various changes in them. We investigate the application of an immune-inspired approach to this problem. Nootropia, is a user profiling model that has many properties in common with computational models of the immune system that have been based on Franscisco Varela's work. In this paper we concentrate on Nootropia's evaluation. We define an evaluation methodology that uses virtual user's to simulate various interest changes. The results show that Nootropia exhibits the desirable adaptive behaviour.

1 Introduction

Information Filtering (IF) systems seek to provide a user with relevant information based on a tailored representation of the user's interests, a *user profile*. The user interests are considered to be long-term. Consequently, a user may be interested in more than one topic in parallel. Also, changes in user interests are inevitable and can vary from modest to radical. In addition to short-term variations in the level of interest in certain topics, new topics of interest may gradually emerge and interest in existing topics may wane. Adaptive IF deals with the problem of adapting the user profile to such interest changes.

Profile adaptation to changes in a user's multiple interests is a fascinating and challenging problem that has already attracted biologically-inspired approaches. Evolutionary IF systems maintain a population of profiles (chromosomes) to represent a user's interests and apply Genetic Algorithms–inspired by natural evolution–to evolve the population and thus adapt the profiles to changes in them. These approaches treat profile adaptation as a continuous optimisation problem and tackle it by performing combined global and local search in a stochastic, but directed fashion.

Profile adaptation however is not a traditional optimisation problem. As Fillipo Menczer puts it [1], it is a "multimodal" and time-dependent one, where convergence to a single optimum should be avoided. A user's multiple and changing interests translate into an information space where there are multiple optima that change over time. It has been argued and supported experimentally [2,3],

H. Bersini and J. Carneiro (Eds.): ICARIS 2006, LNCS 4163, pp. 418–431, 2006.
© Springer-Verlag Berlin Heidelberg 2006

that in time dependent optimisation problems, like profile adaptation, where the optimum, or optima, change over time, GAs suffer due to their elitist character. GAs converge and there is a progressive loss in diversity as the optimum prolifer-ates and spreads over the population. This can cause evolutionary IF systems to specialise to one area (topic) of interest and reach a state which inhibits further adaptation.

The immune system's ability to discriminate between the host organism's own molecules (self) and foreign, possibly harmful, molecules (non-self), serves well as a metaphor to the problem of IF. Typically, Immune-inspired IF systems employ a dynamic repertoire of profile representations (antibodies) that learn to discriminate between relevant information (self) and non-relevant information (non-self). The composition of this repertoire changes in a way that, in contrast to GAs, not only maintains, but also boosts diversity. As we further discuss in the next section, this characteristic may prove advantageous when dealing with adaptive IF. Despite this potential however, the application of immune-inspired approaches to the problem of adapting the user profile to changes in the user's multiple interests has not been fully explored yet. Existing immune-inspired IF systems concentrate on traditional routing applications where profiles are trained in a batch mode and then used for filtering. Profile adaptation is either ignored, or treated simply by periodically repeating the training process.

To explore the application of immune-inspired ideas to the problem of profile adaptation we evaluate in this paper Nootropia[1], a user profiling model that has been introduced in [4,5]. The immune network is used as a metaphor to build a network of terms that represents a user's multiple interests (section 3.1) and that adapts to changes in them through a process of self-organisation (section 3.2). The evaluation methodology (section 4) uses virtual users to simulate a variety of interest changes. The results show that through self-organisation a user profile that represents more than one topic of interest can adapt to both modest and radical interest changes. They exhibit the profile's ability both to "learn" and to "forget" and signify the importance of the network structure during this process. The evaluation methodology itself is of interest because it reflects more accurately than existing standards the multimodal and time-dependent nature of adaptive IF. The current work is part of ongoing research on biologically inspired IF that seeks to compare AIS and GAs on this challenging problem.

2   Evolutionary and Immune-Inspired IF

The insight behind GAs is that the fundamental components of biological evo-lution can be used to evolve solutions to problems within computers. They are stochastic search techniques that have been traditionally applied to optimisation problems. Typically in evolutionary IF a population of profiles, which collec-tively represent the user interests, is maintained [6,7,8,9]. The population evolves according to user feedback. Individual profiles that better represent the user

---

[1] Greek word for: "an individual's or a group's particular way of thinking, someone's characteristics of intellect and perception".

interests become fitter, reproduce and proliferate, while those that do not receive positive feedback are eventually removed from the population. The elitist character of GAs is reflected in the way selection for reproduction is performed. In evolutionary IF systems chromosomes are commonly selected for reproduction according to their relative fitness. This can be accomplished simply by selecting a fixed percentage of the most fit chromosomes [6], but to control the pace of evolution, this percentage may be varied according to the overall filtering performance [8]. To more accurately mimic natural evolution, one may assign to each chromosome reproduction probability proportional to its fitness using *roulette wheel* selection [7]. In any case, the most fit individuals are more likely to mate and produce offspring that inherit their features (keywords). Diversity is progressively lost as the optimum profile proliferates and takes over the population. This can cause evolutionary IF systems to overspecialise to one of the topics of interest and reach a state which inhibits further adaptation.

Fillipo Menczer proposes a remedy to this loss of diversity. Arachnid [1] and InfoSpiders [9] are two similar systems that use a population of agents that autonomously crawl the web and filter information on behalf of the user. To avoid a bias towards the most successful individuals a local selection schema is adopted. Individuals are not selected for reproduction by comparing their fitness (e.g. by ranking them according to decreasing weight), but rather, to reinforce diversity, each individual reproduces once its fitness is over a certain threshold.

This solution points towards the direction of Artificial Immune Sustems (AIS). AIS are not meant to be accurate models of the biological immune system, but use relevant processes and concepts. Simply put[2], the main actors of the immune system are *antibody* molecules that are responsible for recognising a class of foreign, *antigen* molecules. In the case of IF, antibodies typically correspond to user profiles and antigens to information items. How well an antibody recognises an antigen, in other words their *affinity* to the antigen depends on their structure. In IF terms, affinity usually corresponds to the relevance score that a profile assigns to an information item. When the affinity between an antibody and an antigen is over a threshold the immune system's *primary* response is triggered. The antibody clones rapidly and thus the concentration of successful antibodies increases. The cloning process is not accurate, but is subjected to *somatic hypermutation* that results in slightly different antibodies, possibly a better match to the invading antigen. Further diversity of antibody repertoire is maintained through replacement of a percentage of antibodies with new types of antibodies that the bone marrow produces. With these processes the immune system achieves adaptive pattern matching in the presence of different types of antigens.

At the same time the immune system should avoid recognising and destroying the host organism's own molecules. This ability for self–non-self discrimination is what makes the immune system a particularly appealing metaphor . According to one view, it is achieved through *negative selection*, that causes immature

---

[2] For more details in AIS see [10,11,12].

antibodies that match the organism's molecules to die. Alternatively, Jerne's *idiotypic network theory* suggests that in addition to antigens, antibodies can recognise other antibodies. The antibody-to-antibody recognition can operate on multiple levels, forming chains of suppression and reinforcement, creating complex reaction networks, which regulate the concentration of self-matching antibodies [13].

AIS are particularly good at maintaining and boosting diversity. This is achieved in two ways. *Heterostasis*, the preservation of diversity, is implicitly accomplished using local selection mechanisms. In accordance with Menczer's own solution for reinforcing diversity in GAs, an antibody is typically selected to clone based on its affinity to an antigen and not its relative importance (fitness) with respect to the rest of the cells. Furthermore, algorithms based on idiotypic network theory achieve diversity explicitly using suppression of similar antibodies. *Heterogenesis*, on the other hand, refers to the introduction of diversity and is accomplished either through somatic hypermutation, or the recruitment of new cells.

By combining heterostasis with heterogenesis, immune-inspired IF systems appear well suited to the problem of profile adaptation. With heterostasis sufficient coverage of the information space is achieved for the representation of a user's multiple interests, while it is also ensured that new, previously unmet information items (antigens) can be recognised. Heterogenesis, further facilitates the exploration of new areas in the information space. By maintaining and boosting diversity, these systems may prove effective in adapting a user profile to both short-term variations and long-term changes in the user's interests. They may prove advantageous, comparing to evolutionary approaches, in maintaining their viability during adaptation.

This potential in applying AIS to the problem of profile adaptation in content-based filtering has not been explored yet. Existing immune-inspired approaches to IF concentrate instead on learning, in a batch mode, to discriminate between relevant (self) and non-relevant (non-self) information items. In [14] for example, AIS have been used for filtering computer generated graphics. Antibodies and antigens are both modelled as 9 digit, real valued vectors and their affinity is measured as the maximum arithmetic distance between two matching digits. [15] applied AIS to the problem of binary document classification. Antibodies and antigens are binary keyword vectors of fixed length, where some of the bits are masked with the special "don't care" symbol #. The affinity between cells is measured as the percentage of matching bits, ignoring any #. Finally, AIS have also been applied to the task of email filtering [16]. Here antibodies and antigens (emails) are both modelled as unweighted keyword vectors of varied length and their affinity measured as the proportion of common keywords. A similar application is described in [17] where antibodies correspond to regular expressions composed by randomly recombining information from a set of libraries. These immune-inspired approaches to IF either don't deal with profile adaptation, or treat it implicitly with periodic retraining of the profiles.

3 Nootropia

Nootropia is the first attempt to apply ideas drawn from the immune system to the problem of profile adaptation to changes in a user's multiple interests. The model is described in detail in [5], where it is argued that Nootropia has common characteristics with computational models of the immune system that have been developed within the the context of Maturana and Varela's *autopoietic theory* [18]. According to Varela the immune system is not antigen driven, but instead, an *organisationally closed* network that reacts autonomously in order to define and preserve the organism's identity, in what is called *self-assertion* [19]. This is achieved through two types of change: variation in the concentration of antibodies called the *dynamics* of the system, and, on the other hand, a slower recruitment of new cells (produced by the bone marrow) and removal of existing cells, called the *metadynamics*. While dynamics play the role of reinforcement learning, the metadynamics function as a distributed control mechanism which aims at maintaining the viability of the network through an on-going shift in the immune repertoire [20]. One significant aspect of the immune network's metadynamics is that the system itself is responsible for selecting new cells for recruitment in what is called *endogenous selection*. In this paper, we only briefly describe Nootropia's profile representation and adaptation and concentrate instead on the model's evaluation.

3.1 Profile Representation

Inspired by Varela's view of the immune network, in Nootropia, a term network is used to represent a user's multiple interests. This profile representation is described in detail in [4], along with a process for initialising the network based on a set of documents that are relevant to the user. It is depicted in figure 1(left). Terms in the network correspond to antibodies and links denote antibody-to-antibody recognition. A term's weight corresponds to the antibody's concentration and measures how important the term is regarding the user's interests. A link's weight on the other hand, corresponds to the affinity between antibodies and measures the statistical dependencies that exist between semantically and syntactically correlated terms. Terms in the network are ordered according to decreasing weight. This gives rise to separate term hierarchies, one for each general topic that is discussed in the relevant documents (e.g. two overlapping topics in fig. 1(left)). This is a significant transformation that is the basis for the non-linear evaluation of documents according to the represented topics.

More specifically, when confronted with a new document D, profile terms that appear in D are activated (fig 1(right)). Subsequently, each activated term disseminates part of its activation to activated terms higher in the hierarchy that it is linked to. The amount of activation that is disseminated between two activated terms is proportional to the weight of the corresponding link.

It is then possible to calculate the document's relevance score based on the final activation of activated terms. In the simplest case, this is done using equation 1, where A is the set of activated profile terms, NT the number of terms in

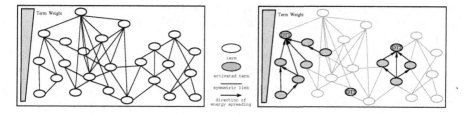

Fig. 1. Hierarchical Term Network: (left) deactivated, (right) activated

the document, and w_i the weight of an activated term t_i. Alternatively, additional evidence derived from the pattern of activation can also be taken into account. In equation 2, $S1(D)$ is complemented with the additional factor $log(1 + (b+d)/b)$. We call b the "breadth" of the document, that can be estimated as the number of activated terms that did not disseminate any energy (fig. 1(right): terms DT1, DT2 and DT3). d stands for the "depth" of the document and is estimated as the number of activated terms that disseminated energy. Hence, $S2(D)$ which has been adopted for our experiments, awards documents which activate connected subnetworks and not isolated terms.

$$S1(D) = \frac{\sum_{i \in A} w_i \cdot E_i^f}{log(NT)} \tag{1}$$

$$S2(D) = S1_D \cdot log(1 + \frac{b+d}{b}) \tag{2}$$

This directed spreading activation process takes into account the term dependencies that the network represents to establish non-linear document evaluation. How much a term contributes to a document's relevance score depends not only on its weight, but also on the term's place within the hierarchy and its links to other terms. It depends on the current network structure. This is a property of the model that distinguishes it from traditional approaches to IF, like the vector space model, which ignore term dependencies. It has been argued and supported experimentally that it is this property which allows the effective representation of multiple topics with a single user profile [4].

3.2 Profile Adaptation

Once the user profile is initialised its life cycle begins and can be used to evaluate documents. Based on the assigned relevance scores and an appropriate threshold a distinction can be made between relevant (self) and non-relevant (non-self) documents. Nevertheless, documents are typically presented to the user in decreasing relevance order and is left to the user to decide which documents to read. The user expresses satisfaction, or dissatisfaction, of the filtering results through relevance feedback. Here we only consider binary feedback[3] where the

---

[3] Scaled feedback is also possible.

user marks viewed documents as either relevant, or not. Changes in the user interests are reflected by changes in the content of documents that received user feedback. Nootropia's adaptation in response to user feedback is achieved through a process that is described in detail in [5]. In accordance with Varela's view, the process is not antigen driven. Relevant documents and their terms correspond to the production of antibodies by the bone marrow, to which the immune network reacts structurally.

In summary, the process comprises five deterministic steps. Given a document that received positive feedback, terms in the document are weighed and those with weight over a certain threshold are extracted. Some of the extracted terms already appear in the profile (immune repertoire) and some are new. In the second step, we employ a local selection scheme. Each of the profile terms that is also contained in the document, is selected and its weight (concentration) is increased by its weight in the document. Terms are not selected based on their relative importance. The overall additional weight is subsequently subtracted evenly from all profile terms. Therefore, during this step, the overall profile weight remains constant, but a redistribution of weight towards terms that appear in the relevant document takes place. These variations in the weight (concentration) of terms (antibodies) correspond to the networks dynamics. They cause changes in the ordering of terms. Eventually, some terms loose their weight. These terms are removed from the profile and the sum of their initial weight, i.e. the weight of each new profile term, is evenly subtracted from the remaining terms. The fourth step of the process involves the new extracted terms. These are added to the profile with initial weight equal to their weight in the relevant document. The recruitment and removal of terms (antibodies) implements the network's metadynamics. Finally, links between existing and new terms are generated and the weight of existing links is updated. It is important to note that due to the way document evaluation is performed the survival of a newly recruited term depends not only on its initial weight, but also $\hat{1}_\lambda\hat{1}\frac{1}{2}$ the current network structure and $\hat{1}_\lambda\hat{1}\frac{1}{2}$ the term's place in it. In other words endogenous selection takes place since it is the network itself which selects those terms that will survive.

In the case of a document that received negative feedback, only the first three of the above five steps take place. The process differs in that during the second step, the weight of profile terms that have been extracted from the document gets decremented, rather than incremented, by their weight in the document. The overall subtracted weight is then equally divided among all profile terms.

According to [5] the above process allows the profile to adapt through self-organisation of the network's structure. Hierarchies that correspond to topics that received positive feedback grow, while those that did not receive positive feedback decline. Such variations in the size of hierarchies can allow the profile to quickly adapt to short-term variations in user interests. In a similar way, more substantial long term changes can also be accounted for. A new hierarchy may develop when a new topic of interest emerges. On the other hand, a hierarchy that corresponds to a topic that is no longer interesting progressively disintegrates and is eventually forgotten. Negative feedback is not essential for forgetting a topic, but, as we will see, facilitates the process. The way different hierarchical subnetworks are formulated to account for the topics of interest is reminiscent of the work in [21], where the author describes a deterministic algorithm for generating meta-stable network structures based on multivariate data. An extensions of this work has been applied in the context of ubiquitous computing [22].

Overall, with Nootropia, a single multi-topic profile can be theoretically adapted to both short-term variations and occasional more radical interest changes. In contrast to evolutionary algorithms, a single structure and not a population of profiles, is adapted through a deterministic process, rather than through probabilistic genetic operations. It remains to be shown experimentally that this is indeed an effective approach to profile adaptation.

4   Experimental Evaluation

The main goal of this paper is to demonstrate Nootropia's ability to adapt to a variety of interest changes in a user's multiple interests. For this purpose we needed an evaluation methodology that reflects the multimodal and time dependent nature of this problem. Unfortunately no existing evaluation standard fulfilled our requirement. Even the adaptive filtering track of the well established Text Retrieval Conference, concentrates on evaluating the ability of a profile, that represents a single topic category, to adapt to modest changes in the content of documents about that topic. It does not simulate radical changes in a user's multiple interests. For the evaluation of Nootropia and other biologically inspired solutions to IF a more challenging setting is required. After all, the removal of the filtering track from the last TREC conferences leaves a gap in the evaluation of adaptive IF systems.

4.1   Evaluation Methodology

The evaluation methodology uses virtual users and a variation of the routing subtask of the 10th TREC's (TREC-2001) filtering task[4]. TREC-2001 adopts the Reuters Corpus Volume 1 (RCV1), an archive of 806,791 English language news stories[5], which have been manually categorised according to topic, region, and industry sector. The TREC-2001 filtering track is based on 84 out of the 103 RCV1 topic categories. Furthermore, it divides RCV1 into 23,864 training stories and a test set comprising the rest of the stories.

Since changes in a user's interests are reflected by variations in the distribution of feedback documents about different topics, then we may simulate a virtual user's interests in the following way. Given RCV1's classification, a virtual user's current interests may be defined as a set of topics (e.g. $R1/R2/R3$) [23]. A radical, long-term change of interest may then be simulated by removing, or adding, a topic to this set. For example, if the user is no longer interested in

---

[4] For more details see: http://trec.nist.gov/data/t10_filtering/T10filter_guide.htm
[5] http://about.reuters.com/researchandstandards/corpus/index.asp

Table 1. Simulated interest changes

Learn two topics in parallel		Learn a new topic	
l.1	$R6/R21$	*n*.1	$R6/R21 \rightarrow R6/R21/R20$
l.2	$R10/R32$	*n*.2	$R10/R32 \rightarrow R10/R32/R50$
l.3	$R41/R79$	*n*.3	$R41/R79 \rightarrow R41/R79/R58$
l.4	$R26/R68$	*n*.4	$R26/R68 \rightarrow R26/R68/R1$
l.5	$R23/R37$	*n*.5	$R23/R37 \rightarrow R23/R37/R41$
l.6	$R44/R53$	*n*.6	$R44/R53 \rightarrow R44/R53/R79$
Forget a topic		**Penalise a topic**	
f.1	$R6/R21/R20 \rightarrow R6/R21$	*p*.1	$R6/R21/R20 \rightarrow R6/R21/\neg R20$
f.2	$R10/R32/R50 \rightarrow R10/R32$	*p*.2	$R10/R32/R50 \rightarrow R10/R32/\neg R50$
f.3	$R41/R79/R58 \rightarrow R41/R79$	*p*.3	$R41/R79/R58 \rightarrow R41/R79/\neg R58$
f.4	$R26/R68/R1 \rightarrow R26/R68$	*p*.4	$R26/R68/R1 \rightarrow R26/R68/\neg R1$
f.5	$R23/R37/R41 \rightarrow R23/R37$	*p*.5	$R23/R37/R41 \rightarrow R23/R37/\neg R41$
f.6	$R44/R53/R79 \rightarrow R44/R53$	*p*.6	$R44/R53/R79 \rightarrow R44/R53/\neg R79$

topic $R3$, then we may denote such a change as $R1/R2/R3 \rightarrow R1/R2$. Similarly, we present here results for four kinds of simulated interests (or tasks) and six sets of topics (table 1). In an attempt to overcome known problems with the large number of test documents per topic in RCV1 [24], we have chosen instead topics with a small number of relevant documents.

The first task involves virtual users with parallel interest in two topics. It does not simulate a radical change of interest, but tests the ability of the system to learn two topics simultaneously and adapt to short-term variations in the user's level of interest in these topics. In the second task, the initial interest in two topics is followed by the emergence of a third topic of interest. As already described in the example, in the third task the virtual user is no longer interested in one of the initial three topics. The fourth kind of interest change is similar to the third, with the difference that the virtual user explicitly indicates the change of interest through negative feedback (denoted with "$\neg$").

For each of the above tasks we start with an empty profile that is subsequently adapted to the initial set of interesting topics. For that purpose we use a set of documents comprising the first 30 documents per topic in RCV1's training set. The documents are ordered according to publication date and therefore their distribution is not homogeneous, but rather reflects the temporal variations in the publication date of documents about each topic. It simulates fast, short-term variations in the virtual user's interests. For tasks that include radical changes in the virtual user's interests (tasks n, f and p), the same process is subsequently executed using the first 30 training documents per topic in the set following the change of interest. Training documents that correspond to negated topics have been used as negative feedback.

During the first adaptation phase for task l and the second for tasks n, f and p, the profile is used every five training documents to filter the complete

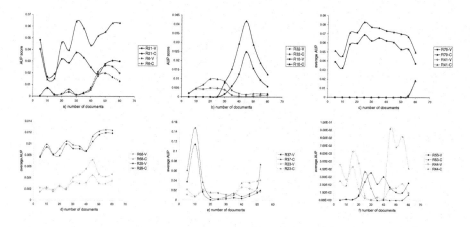

Fig. 2. Learning two topics in parallel: a) $l.1$ b) $l.2$ c) $l.3$ d) $l.4$ e) $l.5$ f) $l.6$

test set. It is then evaluated on the basis of an ordered list of the best 3000[6] scoring documents, using the *Average Uninterpolated Precision* (AUP) measure. The AUP is defined as the sum of the precision value–i.e. percentage of filtered documents that are relevant–at each point in the list where a relevant document appears, divided by the total number of relevant documents. AUPs absolute value depends on the number of relevant documents and consequently, no direct comparison between the AUP scores of different topics can be made. Instead, we concentrate on how each topic's score changes during the adaptation phase. Note also that the above evaluation methodology is deterministic and will produce the same results for a specific evaluation task and profile configuration.

4.2 Results

The proposed evaluation methodology is an attempt to take into account the multi-modal and time-dependent nature of the profile adaptation problem. It tests, in a controlled and reproducible fashion, the ability of a profile to learn multiple topics in parallel and adapt to a variety of interest changes. Here it is used to evaluate a profile based on Nootropia (denoted C) and a baseline version (denoted V) where links between terms are ignored. With their comparison we wish to highlight the importance of adopting a network structure.

Figures 2 to 5 present the experimental results. Each graph depicts for each topic the fluctuation of AUP score (Y-axis) as the number of feedback documents that have been processed increases (X-axis). Whenever required a second Y-axis has been used to account for large differences in the AUP score of topics. For tasks n, f and p, the figures present for visualisation reasons the average AUP score for the two persistent topics of interest in each case (depicted with dashed line).

---

[6] This number has been increased from 1000 according to TREC's guidelines to 3000 as an additional remedy to problems deriving from the large number of relevant documents per topic in RCV1.

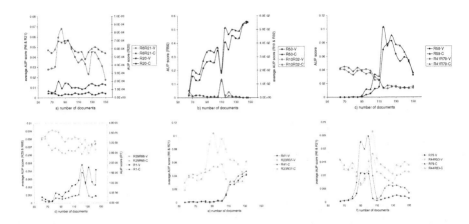

Fig. 3. Learning a third topic of interest: a) $n.1$ b) $n.2$ c) $n.3$ d) $n.4$ e) $n.5$ f) $n.6$

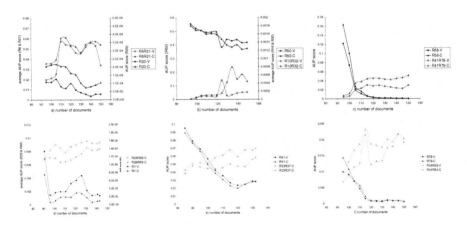

Fig. 4. Forgetting the third topic of interest: a) $f.1$ b) $f.2$ c) $f.3$ d) $f.4$ d) $f.5$ f) $f.6$

This facilitates the comparison between C and V, but obscures fluctuations in the individual scores of the persistent topics.

The results indicate that through self-organisation Nootropia can adapt successfully to a variety of changes in the user interests. Figure 2 indicates that two topics of interest can be learned in parallel. In most cases, despite fluctuations the final AUP of the involved topics is larger than zero. We can also observe that the fluctuations in score between topics in the same task are usually symmetric. Although they are exaggerated due to the fixed number of evaluation documents[7], they are nevertheless indicative of the profile's ability to quickly adapt to short-term variations in the user's interests.

---

[7] Documents relevant to each topic compete for a place in the list of 3000 evaluation documents.

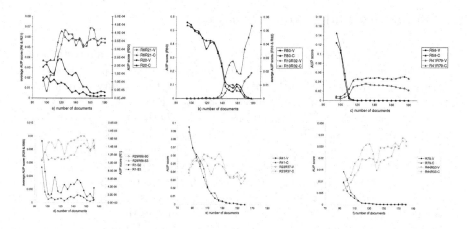

Fig. 5. Negating the third topic of interest: a) *p*.1 b) *p*.2 c) *p*.3 d) *p*.4 e) *p*.5 f) *p*.6

According to figure 3, learning a new, emerging topic of interest can also be handled. In all cases the score of the new topic (bold line) shows an overall increase. In addition to symmetric short-scale fluctuations between the scores of the new and existing topics, we observe in many cases an overall drop in the average score of the existing topics. Like before, this is partially due to the fixed number of evaluation documents. Nevertheless, with the exception of task *n*.2, the profile represents all three topics at the end of the adaptation phase.

The results for the third task are equally promising (fig. 4). Nootropia seems able to forget a no longer interesting topic. In all cases, there is an overall drop in the AUP score of the topic that no longer receives positive feedback (bold line). It is usually followed by an increase in the score of the remaining two topics for reasons already explained. However, only in tasks *f*.3 and *f*.6 is the waning topic completely forgotten. In the rest of the cases a longer adaptation period might be necessary. When, on the other hand, the no longer interesting topics explicitly receive negative feedback, we observe a larger overall decrease in their score (fig. 5). This is clear in all cases. Now only in tasks *p*.1 and *p*.4 isn't the no longer interesting topic completely forgotten.

Finally, the comparison between the full version (C) and its baseline version (V), where links between terms are ignored, produced interesting results. For most tasks C outperforms V. This finding demonstrates the importance of links not only for representing multiple topics[8], but also when adapting to changes in them. It highlights the significance of the network structure and of the additional information that it encodes, in defining and preserving the user's interests. There are however, inconsistencies in the performance of C over V. For example, the fourth combination of topics (R1/R29/R68) did not produce positive results in any of the tasks (graph *d* in figures 2, 3, 4 and 5). This inconsistency in performance prompts us for further improvements in the model, like maintaining only links with large weights and calibrating term and link weights.

---

[8] As it is also argued in [4].

5   Summary and Future Research

In adaptive IF, user profile adaptation to changes in the user's interests poses a challenging and fascinating research problem that invites the application of biologically inspired solutions. In this paper we evaluated the ability of an immune-inspired user profiling model, called Nootropia, to adapt to various changes in a user's multiple interests. The evaluation methodology that we employed is based on the routing subtask of TREC 2001, but extends it in various ways. It modifies it to reflect the multi-modal and time dependent nature of adaptive IF. The results demonstrate that Nootropia exhibits the wanted adaptive behaviour. It can learn two topics in parallel and reflect their short-term variations, learn an emerging topic of interest, and forget a no longer interesting topic. In this later case negative feedback is not necessary, but it facilitates the process. They also demonstrate the importance of links and of the network structure that terms and links compose.

We may argue that this first attempt to apply immune-inspired ideas to the problem of adaptive IF has been promising and is worth further investigation. Nootropia, a self-organising network of terms that exhibits dynamics, metadynamics, endogenous selection and other properties in common with Varela's view of the immune network, performed satisfactory in the task of adapting to simulated changes in a user's multiple interests. The evaluation methodology itself poses a challenging setting for the evaluation of biological inspired algorithms in general. We wish to improve and standardise this methodology to conduct comparative experiments between Nootropia and an evolutionary approach. We seek to provide further evidence that the ability of AIS to boost and maintain diversity, in contrast to the elitist character of GAs, proves advantageous given the challenge of adaptive IF. In general, we hope to promote further constructive interaction between biologically inspired computing and IF.

References

1. Menczer, F.: ARACHNID: Adaptive retrieval agents choosing heuristic neighborhoods for information discovery. In: 14th International Machine Learning Conference. (1997) 227–235
2. Gaspar, A., Collard, P.: From GAs to artificial immune systems: Improving adaptation in time dependent optimization. In: Proceedings of the Congress on Evolutionary Computation. Volume 3., IEEE Press (1999) 1859–1866
3. Simoens, A., Costa, E.: An immune system-based genetic algorithm to deal with dynamic environments: Diversity and memory. In: Sixth International Conference on Neural Networks and Genetic Algorithms, Springer (2003) 168–174
4. Nanas, N., Uren, V., de Roeck, A., Domingue, J.: Multi-topic information filtering with a single user profile. In: 3rd Hellenic Conference on Artificial Intelligence, (2004) 400–409
5. Nanas, N., Uren, V., de Roeck, A.: Nootropia: a user profiling model based on a self-organising term network. In: 3rd International Conference on Artificial Immune Systems, (2004) 146–160

6. Sheth, B.D.: A Learning Approach to Personalized Information Filtering. Master of Science, Massachusetts Institute of Technology (1994)
7. Winiwarter, W.: PEA - a personal email assistant with evolutionary adaptation. International Journal of Information Technology **5**(1) (1999)
8. Moukas, A., Maes, P.: Amalthaea: An evolving multi-agent information filtering and discovery system for the www. Autonomous Agents and Multi-Agent Systems, (1998) 59–88
9. Menczer, F., Monge, A.E.: Scalable web search by adaptive online agents: An infospiders case study. In Klusch, M., ed.: Intelligent Information Agents: Agent-Based Information Discovery and Management on the Internet. Springer-Verlag (1999) 323–347
10. Dasgupta, D., ed.: Artificial Immune Systems and Their Applications. Springer-Verlag Berlin and Heidelberg GmbH & Co. K (1998)
11. Castro, L.N., Timmis, J.: Artificial Immune Systems: A New Computational Intelligence Approach. Springer-Verlag UK (2002)
12. Tarakanov, A.O., Skormin, V.A., Sokolova, S.P.: Immunocomputing: Principles and Applications. Springer Verlag (2003)
13. Farmer, J.D., Packard, N.H., Perelson, A.S.: The immune system, adaptation, and machine learning. Physica 22D (1986) 187–204
14. Chao, D.L., Forrest, S.: Information immune systems. Genetic Programming and Evolvable Machines **4** (2003) 311–331
15. Twycross, J., Cayzer, S.: An immune-based approach to document classification. Technical Report HPL-2002-292, HP Research Bristol (2002)
16. Secker, A., Freitas, A.A., Timmis, J.: Aisec: an artificial immune system for e-mail classification. In: Congress on Evolutionary Computation, IEEE (2003) 131–139
17. Oda, T., White, T.: Immunity from spam: An analysis of an artificial immune system for junk email detection. In: 4th International Conference on Artificial Immune Systems, (2005) 276–289
18. Maturana, H.R., Varela, F.J.: Autopoiesis and Cognition. Dordrecht, Holland (1980)
19. Varela, F.J., Coutinho, A.: Second generation immune network. Immunology Today **12** (1991) 159–166
20. Bersini, H., Varela, F.: The immune learning mechanisms: Reinforcement, recruitment and their applications. In: Computing with Biological Metaphors. Chapman Hall (1994) 166–192
21. Neal, M.: Meta-stable memory in an artificial immune network. In: 2nd International Conference on Artificial Immune Systems, (2003) 168–180
22. Mohr, P.H., Ryan, N., Timmis, J.: Exploiting immunological properties for ubiquitous computing systems. In: 3rd International Conference on Artificial Immune Systems, (2004) 277–289
23. Widyantoro, D.H., Loerger, T.R., Yen, J.: Learning user interests dynamics with a three-descriptor representation. JASIS **52**(3) (2000) 212-225
24. Robertson, S., Soboroff, I.: The TREC 2001 filtering track report. In: TREC-10. (2001)

An Immune Network for Contextual Text Data Clustering

Krzysztof Ciesielski, Sławomir T. Wierzchoń, and Mieczysław A. Kłopotek

Institute of Computer Science, Polish Academy of Sciences,
ul. Ordona 21, 01-237 Warszawa,Poland
{kciesiel, stw, klopotek}@ipipan.waw.pl

Abstract. We present a novel approach to incremental document maps creation, which relies upon partition of a given collection of documents into a hierarchy of homogeneous groups of documents represented by different sets of terms. Further each group (defining in fact separate context) is explored by a modified version of the aiNet immune algorithm to extract its inner structure. The immune cells produced by the algorithm become reference vectors used in preparation of the final document map. Such an approach proves to be robust in terms of time and space requirements as well as the quality of the resulting clustering model.

1 Introduction

Analyzing the number of terms per query in one billion accesses to the Altavista site, [10], it was observed that in 20.6% queries no term was entered; one quarter used just one term in a search, and the average was not much higher than two terms! This justifies our interest in looking for a more "user-friendly" interfaces to web-browsers.

According to so-called Cluster Hypothesis, [16], relevant documents tend to be highly similar to each other, and therefore tend to appear in the same clusters. Thus, it is possible to reduce the number of documents that need to be compared to a given query, as it suffices to match the query against cluster representatives first. However such an approach offers only technical improvement in searching relevant documents. A more radical improvement can be gained by using so-called document maps, [2], where a graphical representation allows additionally to convey information about the relationships of individual documents or group of documents. Document maps are primarily oriented towards visualization of a certain similarity of a collection of documents, although other usage of such the maps is possible – consult Chapter 5 in [2] for details.

The most prominent representative of this direction is the WEBSOM project. Here the Self-Organizing Map (SOM [14]), algorithm is used to organize miscellaneous text documents onto a 2-dimensional grid so that related documents appear close to each other. Each grid unit contains a set of closely related documents. The color intensity reflects dissimilarity among neighboring units: the lighter shade the more similar neighboring units are. Unfortunately this approach

H. Bersini and J. Carneiro (Eds.): ICARIS 2006, LNCS 4163, pp. 432–445, 2006.
© Springer-Verlag Berlin Heidelberg 2006

is time and space consuming, and rises questions of scaling and updating of document maps (although some improvements are reported in [15]). To overcome some of these problems the DocMINER system was proposed in [2].

In our research project BEATCA, [13], oriented towards exploration and navigation in large collections of documents a fully-fledged search engine capable of representing on-line replies to queries in graphical form on a document map has been designed and constructed [12]. A number of machine-learning techniques, like fast algorithm for Bayesian networks construction [13], SVD analysis, Growing Neural Gas (GNG) [9], SOM algorithm, etc., have been employed to realize the project. BEATCA extends the main goals of WEBSOM by a multilingual approach, new forms of geometrical representation (besides rectangular maps, projections onto sphere and torus surface are possible); further we experimented with various modifications of the entire clustering process by using the SOM, GNG and immune algorithms.

In this paper we focus on some problems concerning application of an immune algorithm to extract clustering structure. In section 2 we present our hierarchical, topic-sensitive approach, which appears to be a robust solution to the problem of scalability of map generation process (both in terms of time complexity and space requirements). It relies upon extraction of a hierarchy of concepts, i.e. almost homogenous groups of documents described by unique sets of terms. To represent the content of each context a modified version the aiNet [7] algorithm was employed – see section 3. This algorithm was chosen because of its ability of representing internal patterns existing in a training set. To evaluate the effectiveness of the novel text clustering procedure, it has been compared to the aiNet and SOM algorithms in section 4. In the experimental sections 4.5-4.7 we have also investigated issues such as evaluation of immune network structure and the influence of the chosen antibody/antigen representation on the resulting immune memory model. Final conclusions are given in section 5.

2   Contextual Local Networks

In our approach – like in many traditional IR systems – documents are mapped into m-dimensional term vector space. The points (documents) in this space are of the form $(w_{1,d}, ..., w_{m,d})$ where m stands for the number of terms, and each $w_{t,d}$ is a weight for term t in document d, so-called term frequency/inverse document frequency ($tfidf$) weight:

$$w_{t,d} = w(t, d) = f_{td} \cdot log\left(\frac{N}{f_t}\right) \tag{1}$$

where f_{td} is the number of occurrences of term t in document d, f_t is the number of documents containing term t and N is the total number of documents.

The vector space model has been criticized for some disadvantages, polysemy and synonymy, among others, [3]. To overcome these disadvantages a contextual approach has been proposed relying upon dividing the set of documents into a number of homogenous and disjoint subgroups each of which is described by unique subset of terms. In the sequel we will distinguish between *hierarchical* and *contextual* model. In the former the set of terms, with $tfidf$ weights (eq. (1)), is identical for each subgroup of documents, while in the later each subgroup is represented by different subset of terms weighted in accordance with the equation (3). Finally, when we do not split the entire set of documents and we construct a single, "flat", representation for whole collection – we will refer to *global* model.

The contextual approach consists of two main stages. At first stage a hierarchical model is built, i.e. a collection D of documents is recurrently divided – by using Fuzzy ISODATA algorithm [4] – into homogenous groups consisting of approximately identical number of elements. Such a procedure results in a hierarchy represented by a tree of clusters. The process of partitioning halts when the number of documents inside each group meets predefined criteria[1]. To compute the distance $dist(d, c)$ of a document d from a centroid c, the next function was used: $dist(d, c) = 1 - < d/||d||, c/||c|| >$, where the symbol $< \cdot, \cdot >$ stands for the dot-product of two vectors. Given m_{dG} the degree of membership of a document d to a group G this document is assigned to the group with highest value of m_{dG}.

The second phase of contextual document processing is division of terms space (dictionary) into – possibly overlapping – subspaces of terms specific to each context (i.e. the group extracted in previous stage). The fuzzy membership level, m_{tG}, representing importance of a particular term t in a given context G is computed as:

$$m_{tG} = \frac{\sum_{d \in G} (f_{td} \cdot m_{dG})}{f_G \cdot \sum_{d \in G} m_{dG}} \qquad (2)$$

where f_G is the number of documents in the cluster G, m_{dG} is the degree of membership of document d to group G, f_{td} is the number of occurrences of term t in document d. We assume that a term t is relevant for a given context G if $m_{tG} > \epsilon$, where ϵ is a parameter.

Removing non-relevant terms leads to the topic-sensitive reduction of the dimension of the terms space. This reduction results in new vector representation of documents; each component of the vector is computed according to the equation:

$$w_{tdG} = f_{td} \cdot m_{tG} \cdot log \left(\frac{f_G}{f_t \cdot m_{tG}} \right) \qquad (3)$$

where f_t is the number of documents in the group G containing term t.

To depict similarity relation between contexts (represented by a set of contextual models), additional "global" map is required. Such a model becomes the root of contextual maps hierarchy. Main map is created in a manner similar to previously created maps with one distinction: an example in training data is a weighted centroid of referential vectors of the corresponding contextual model: $x_i = \sum_{c \in M_i} (d_c \cdot v_c)$, where M_i is the set of cells in i-th contextual model, d_c is the density of the cell and v_c is its referential vector.

---

[1] Currently a single criterion saying that the cardinality c_i of i-th cluster cannot exceed a given boundaries $[c_{min}, c_{max}]$. This way the maps created for each group at the same level of a given hierarchy will contain similar number of documents.

The whole process of learning contextual model is to some extent similar to hierarchical learning [11]. However, in our approach each constituent model, and the corresponding contextual map, can be processed independently (particularly, in parallel). Also a partial incremental update of such model appears to be much easier to perform, both in terms of model quality, stability and time complexity. The possibility of incremental learning stems from the fact that the very nature of the learning process is iterative. So if new documents come, we can consider the learning process as having been stopped at some stage and it is resumed now with all the documents. We claim that it is not necessary to start the learning process from scratch neither in the case that the new documents "fit" the distribution of the previous ones nor when their term distribution is significantly different. This claim is supported by experimental results presented e.g in [13].

3   Immune Approach to Text Data Clustering

One of main goals of the BEATCA project was to create multidimensional document maps in which geometrical vicinity would reflect conceptual closeness of documents in a given document set.

In SOM algorithm, [14] each unit of an $m \times m$ grid contains so-called reference vector v_i, whose dimension agrees with the dimension of training examples. The training examples are repeatedly presented to the network until a termination criterion is satisfied. When an example $x(t)$ is presented at time t to the network, its reference vectors are updated according to the rule

$$v_i(t + 1) = v_i(t) + \alpha_i(t) \cdot (x(t) - v_i(t)), i = 1, ..., |m| \times |m| \tag{4}$$

where $\alpha_i(t)$ is so-called learning rate varying according to the recipe: $\alpha_i(t) = \epsilon(t) \cdot exp\left(-\frac{d(i,w)}{\sigma^2(t)}\right)$. Here $\epsilon(t)$ and $\sigma(t)$ are two user defined monotone decreasing functions of time called, respectively, step size (or cooling schedule) and neighborhood radius. The symbol $d(i, w)$ stands for the distance (usually Manhattan distance) between i-th unit and so-called winner unit (i.e. the unit which reference vector is most similar to the example $x(t)$).

The main deficiencies of SOM are (cf. [1]): (a) it is order dependent, i.e. the components of final weight vectors are affected by the order in which training examples are presented, (b) the components of these vectors may be severely affected by noise and outliers, (c) the size of the grid, the step size and the size of the neighborhood must be tuned individually for each data-set to achieve useful results, (d) high computational complexity.

GNG [9] uses the same equation (4) to update reference vectors but with fixed learning rate α. Further its output is rather graph and not a grid. The main idea is such that starting from very few nodes (typically, two), one new node is inserted ever λ iterations near the node featuring the local local error measurement. There is also a possibility to remove nodes: every λ iterations the node with lowest utility for error reduction is removed. The main disadvantages of GNG are (cf. [1]): (a) in comparison with SOM it requires larger number of control parameters which should be tuned, (b) because of fixed learning rate it lacks stability, (c) rather elaborated technique for visualizing resulting graph must be invented.

An immune algorithm is able to generate the reference vectors (called antibodies) each of which summarizes basic properties of a small group of documents treated here as antigens[2]. This way the clusters in the immune network spanned over the set of antibodies will serve as internal images, responsible for mapping existing clusters in the document collection into network clusters. In essence, this approach can be viewed as a successful instance of exemplar-based learning giving an answer to the question "what examples to store for use during generalization, in order to avoid excessive storage and time complexity, and possibly to improve generalization accuracy by avoiding noise and overfitting", [17].

3.1   aiNet Algorithm for Data Clustering

The artificial immune system aiNet [7] mimics the processes of clonal selection, maturation and apoptosis [8] observed in the natural immune system. Its aim is to produce a set of antibodies binding a given set of antigens (i.e. documents). The efficient antibodies form a kind of immune memory capable to bind new antigens sufficiently similar to these from the training set.

Like in SOM, the antigens are repeatedly presented to the memory cells (being matured antibodies) until a termination criterion is satisfied. More precisely, a memory structure M consisting of matured antibodies is initiated randomly with few cells. When an antigen ag_i is presented to the system, its affinity $aff(ag_i, ab_j)$ to all the memory cells is computed. The value of $aff(ag_i, ab_j)$ expresses how strongly the antibody ab_j binds the antigen ag_i. From a practical point of view $aff(ag_i, ab_j)$ can be treated as a degree of similarity between these two cells[3]. The greater affinity $aff(ag_i, ab_j)$, the more stimulated ab_j is.

The idea of clonal selection and maturation translates into next steps (here σ_d, and σ_s are parameters). The cells which are most stimulated by the antigen are subjected to clonal selection (i.e. each cell produces a number of copies proportionally to the degree of its stimulation), and each clone is subjected to mutation (the intensity of mutation is inversely proportional to the degree of stimulation of the mother cell). Only clones cl which can cope successfully with the antigen (i.e. $aff(ag_i, cl) > \sigma_d$) survive. They are added to a tentative memory, M_t, and the process of clonal suppression starts: an antibody ab_j too similar to another antibody ab_k (i.e. $aff(ab_j, ab_k) > \sigma_s$) is removed from M_t. Remaining cells are added to the global memory M.

These steps are repeated until all antigens are presented to the system. Next the degree of affinity between all pairs $ab_j, ab_k \in M$ is computed and again too

---

[2] Intuitively by antigens we understand any substance threatening proper functioning of the host organism while antibodies are protein molecules produced to bind antigens. A detailed description of these concepts can be found in [8].

[3] In practical applications this measure can be derived from any metric dissimilarity measure $dist$ as $aff(ag_i, ab_j) = \frac{d_{max} - dist(ag_i, ab_j)}{d_{max}}$, where d_{max} stands for the maximal dissimilarity between two cells.

similar (in fact: redundant) cells are removed from the memory. This step represents network suppression of the immune cells. Lastly $r\%$ (one more parameter) worst individuals in M are replaced by freshly generated cells. This ends one epoch, and next epoch begins until a termination condition is met.

Among all the parameters mentioned above the crucial one seems to be the σ_s as it critically influences the size of the global memory. Each memory cell can be viewed as an exemplar which summarizes important features of "bundles" of stimulating it antigens.

3.2   Robust Construction of Mutated Antibodies

In case of high-dimensional data, such as text data represented in vector space, calculation of stimulation level is quite costly (proportional to the number of different terms in dictionary). Thus, the complexity of an immune algorithm can be significantly reduced if we could restrict the number of required expensive recalculations of stimulation level. The direct, high-dimensional calculations can be replaced by operations on scalar values on the basis of the simple geometrical observation that a stimulation of a mutated antibody clone can be expressed in terms of original antibody stimulation.

Such optimization is based on the generalized Pythagoras theorem: if v_1, v_2, v_3 are the sides of a triangle ($v_1 + v_2 + v_3 = 0$) then $|v_3|^2 = |v_1|^2 + |v_2|^2 - 2|v_1||v_2|cos(v_1, v_2)$. We can define mutated clone m as: $m = kd + (1 - k)c$, where c is cloned antibody, d is antigen (document) and k is the mutation level (random).

Taking advantage of equation (4) and Pythagoras theorem (where $v_1 := d' = k \cdot d$, $v_2 := c' = (1 - k) \cdot c$, $v_3 := -m$) and having calculated original antibody stimulation $aff(c, d)$, we can calculate mutated clone stimulation level $aff(m, d)$.

Dually, we can find mutation threshold k so that mutated antibody clone stimulation $aff(m, d) < \sigma_d$. Precisely, we are looking for k_0 such that $aff(m, d) = \sigma_d$, which in turn can be used to create mutated antibody for random mutation level $k \in (0, k_0)$. The advantage of such an approach is the reduction of the number of inefficient (too specific) antibodies, which would be created and immediately removed from the clonal memory. Analogically to the previous inference, if we define $p := aff(c, d)$, $x := -p|d| + p^2|c| + \sigma_d^2(p|d| - c)$, $y := |d|^2 - 2p|c||d| + p^2|c|^2 - \sigma_d^2(|d|^2 - |c|^2 + 2p|c||d|)$ and $z := \sigma_d \cdot |d| \sqrt{(p^2 - 1) \cdot (\sigma_d^2 - 1)}$, then $k_0 = \frac{|c| \cdot (x+z)}{y}$.

3.3   Stabilization Via Time-Dependent Parameters

Typical problem with immune based algorithms is the stabilization of the size of the memory cells set. This explains why we decided to use time dependent parameters. For each parameter p, we defined its initial value p_0 and the final value p_1 as well as the time-dependent function $f(t)$, such that $p(t) = f(t)$ and $p(0) = p_0$, $p(T) = p_1$ where T is the number of learning iterations.

In particular, both $\sigma_s(t)$ and $\sigma_d(t)$ are reciprocally increased, while $m_b(t)$ – the number of clones produced by a cell – is linearly decreased with time:

$\sigma(t) = \sigma_0 + (\sigma_1 - \sigma_0) \cdot \frac{t \cdot (T+1)}{T \cdot (t+1)}$ and $m_b(t) = m_0 + \frac{m_1 - m_0}{T} \cdot t$, where $\sigma_0 = 0.05$, $\sigma_1 = 0.25$ for $\sigma_s(t)$; $\sigma_0 = 0.1$, $\sigma_1 = 0.4$ for $\sigma_d(t)$; $m_0 = 3$, $m_1 = 1$ for $m_b(t)$.

4   Experimental Results

In the following sections, the overall experimental design as well as quality measures are described. Since immune network can be treated both as a clustering and a meta-clustering (clusters of clusters) model, beside commonly used clustering quality measures (unsupervised and supervised), we have also investigated immune network structure. The discussion of results is given in Sect. 4.3-4.7.

4.1   Quality Measures of the Clustering

Various measures of quality have been developed in the literature, covering diverse aspects of the clustering process. The clustering process is frequently referred as "learning without a teacher", or "unsupervised learning", and is driven by some kind of similarity measure. The optimized criterion is intended to reflect some esthetic preferences, like: uniform split into groups (topological continuity) or appropriate split of documents with known a priori categorization. As the criterion is somehow hidden, we need tests if the clustering process really fits the expectations. In particular, we have accommodated for our purposes and investigated the following well known quality measures of clustering [19,5]:

Average Document Quantization: average cosine distance (dissimilarity) for the learning set between a document and the cell it was classified into.

This measure has values in the $[0,1]$ interval, the lower values correspond respectively to more "smooth" inter-cluster transitions and more "compact" clusters. The two subsequent measures evaluate the agreement between the clustering and the a priori categorization of documents (i.e. particular newsgroup in case of newsgroups messages).

Average Weighted Cluster Purity: average "category purity" of a cell (cell weight is equal to its density, i.e. the number of assigned documents): $AvgPurity = \frac{1}{|D|} \sum_{n \in N} max_c (|D_c(n)|)$, where D is the set of all documents in the corpus and $D_c(n)$ is the set of documents from category c assigned to the cell n. Similarly, *Average Weighted Cluster Entropy* measure can be calculated, where the $D_c(n)$ term is replaced with the entropy of the categories frequency distribution.

Normalized Mutual Information: the quotient of the entropy with respect to the categories and clusters frequency to the square root of the product of category and cluster entropies for individual clusters [5].

Again, both measures have values in the $[0,1]$ interval. The higher the value is, the better agreement between clusters and *a priori* given categories.

4.2   Quality of the Immune Network

Beside the clustering structure represented by cells, idiotypic network should be also treated as a meta-clustering model. Similarity between individual clusters is expressed by graph edges, linking referential vectors in antibodies. Thus, there is a need to evaluate quality of the structure of the edges.

There is a number of ways to evaluate idiotypic model structure. In this paper we present the one which we have found to be the most clear for interpretation. This approach is based on the analysis of the edge lengths of the minimal spanning tree (MST) constructed over the set of antibodies, in each iteration of the learning process.

4.3   Experimental Settings

The architecture of BEATCA system supports comparative studies of clustering methods at the various stages of the process (i.e. initial document grouping, initial topic identification, incremental clustering, graph model projection to 2D map and visualization, identification of topical areas on the map and its labeling) – consult [13] for details. In this paper we focus only on the evaluation and comparison of the immune models.

This study required manually labelled documents, so the experiments were executed on a widely-used 20 Newsgroups document collection[4] of approximately 20 thousands newsgroup messages, partitioned into 20 different newsgroups (about 1000 messages each). As a data preprocessing step in BEATCA system, entropy-based dimensionality reduction techniques are applied [12], so the training data dimensionality (the number of distinct terms used) was 4419.

Each immune model have been trained for 100 iterations, using previously described algorithms and methods.

4.4   Impact of the Time-Dependent Parameters

In the first two series of experiment, we compared models built with time-dependent parameters $\sigma_s(t)$ and $\sigma_d(t)$ with the constant, a priori defined values of σ_s and σ_d. As a reference case we took a model where $\sigma_s(t)$ was changed from the initial value 0.05 up to 0.25 and $\sigma_d(t)$ from 0.1 up to 0.4 (cf. section 3.3).

First, we compare the reference model and the four models with constant σ_d. Parameter σ_s has been changed identically as in reference model. The values of σ_d varied from the starting value in the reference model (0.1) up to the final value (0.4) by 0.1 step. The results[5] are presented in Figure 1.

Fig. 1(a) presents variance of the edge length in the minimal spanning tree built over the set of antibodies in the immune memory in i^{th} iteration of the learning process. At first glance one can notice instability of this measure for high values of σ_d. Comparing stable values, we notice that the variance for the reference network has the highest value. It means that the idiotypic network contains both short edges, connecting clusters of more similar antibodies and longer edges, linking more distant antibodies, probably stimulated by different subsets of documents (antigens). Such meta-clustering structure is desirable and preferred over networks with equidistant antibodies (and, thus, low edge length variance).

---

[4] http://people.csail.mit.edu/jrennie/20Newsgroups/
[5] All figures present average values of the respective measures in 20 contextual nets.

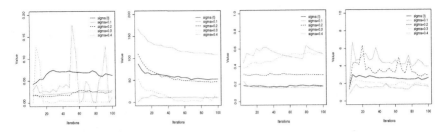

Fig. 1. Time-dependent σ_d: (a) edge length variance (b) network size (c) quantization error (d) learning time

Comparing network sizes, Fig. 1(b), and quantization error, Fig. 1(c), we observe that for the highest values of σ_d, the set of antibodies reduces to just a few entities; on the other hand - for the lowest values almost all antibodies (universal and over-specialized) are retained in the system's memory. It is not surprising that the quantization error for a huge network (e.g. $\sigma_d = 0.1$) is much lower than for smaller nets. Still, the time-dependent $\sigma_d(t)$ gives similarly low quantization error for moderate network size. Also, both measures stabilize quickly during learning process. Learning time, Figure 1(d), is – to some extent – a function of network size. Thus, for the reference model, it is not only low but very stable over all iterations.

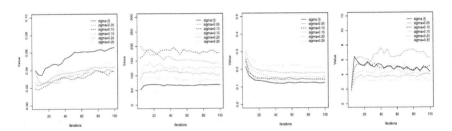

Fig. 2. Time-dependent σ_s: (a) edge length variance (b) network size (c) quantization error (d) learning time

In the next experiment – dually – we compare reference model and another five models with constant σ_s (and varying σ_d). Analogically to the first case, the values of σ_s varied from the initial value 0.05 up to the final value in the reference model 0.25 by 0.05 step. The results are presented in Fig. 2. Due to the space limitations, we restrict the discussion of the results to the conclusion that also in this case time-dependent parameter $\sigma_s(t)$ had a strong, positive influence on the resulting immune model.

A weakness of the approach seems to be the difficulty in selecting appropriate values of the parameters for a given dataset. We investigated independently changes to the values of both parameters, but it turns out that they should be changed "consistently"; that is the antibodies should not be removed too quickly, nor aggregated too quickly. However, once found, there is a justified hope that for an incrementally growing collection of documents the parameters do not need to be sought anew, but rather gradually adopted.

4.5 Scalability and Comparison with Global Models

Comparing hierarchical and contextual models described in section 2, with a "flat", global model the most noticeable difference is the learning time[6]. The total time for 20 contextual networks accounted for about 10 minutes, against over 50 minutes for hierarchical network and almost 20 hours (*sic!*) for a global network. Another disadvantage of the global model is high variance of the learning time at single iteration as well as the size of the network. The learning time varied from 150 seconds to 1500 seconds (10 times more!) and the final network consisted of 1927 antibodies (two times more than for contextual model). It should also be noted that in our experimental setting, each model (local and global) has been trained for 100 iterations, but it can be seen (e.g. Figure 4) that the local model stabilizes much faster. Recalling that each local network in the hierarchy can be processed independently and in parallel, it makes contextual approach robust and scalable[7] alternative to the global immune model.

One of the reasons for such differences of the learning time is the representation of antibodies in the immune model. The referential vector in an antibody is represented as a balanced red-black tree of term weights. If a single cell tries to occupy "too big" portion of a document-term vector space (i.e. it covers documents belonging to different topics), many terms which rarely co-occur in a single document have to be represented by a single red-black tree. Thus, it becomes less sparse and - simply - bigger. On the other hand, better separation of terms which are likely to appear in various topics and increasing "crispness" of topical areas during model training leads to faster convergence and better models, in terms of previously defined quality measures. While the quantization error is similar for global and contextual model (0.149 versus 0.145, respectively), then both supervised measures - showing correspondence between documents labels (categories) and clustering structure - are in favor to contextual model. The final value of the Normalized Mutual Information was 0.605 for the global model and 0.855 for the contextual model and Average Weighted Cluster Purity: 0.71 versus 0.882 respectively.

We have also executed experiments comparing presented immune approach with SOM models: flat (i.e. standard, global Kohonen's map) and our own variant of contextual approach - the hierarchy of contextual maps (C-SOM). To compare immune network structure, with the static grid of SOM model, we have built minimal spanning tree on the SOM grid. Summary of the results can be seen in Figure 3. Again, global model turned out to be of lower quality than

---

[6] By learning time we understand the time needed to create an immune memory consisting of the set of antibodies representing the set of antigens (documents).

[7] Especially with respect to growing dimensionality of data, what - empirically - seem to be the most difficult problem for immune-based approach.

both contextual SOM and contextual AIS model. Similarly to the global immune model, also in this case the learning time (over 2 hours) was significantly higher than for the contextual models. Surprisingly, the average edge in contextual SOM model was much longer than in case of contextual immune network and standard SOM, what may be the result of the limitations of the rigid model topology (2D grid). The discussion of the edge length distribution (Figure 3(b)) we defer to the section 4.7.

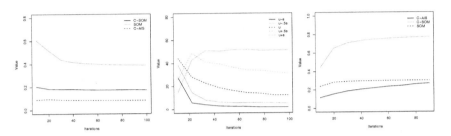

Fig. 3. Immune model vs. SOM: (a) quantization error (b) SOM (MST on SOM grid) edge length distribution (c) average edge length

4.6   Contextual Versus Hierarchical Model

The next series of experiments compared contextual model with hierarchical model. Figures 4(a) and 4(b) presents network sizes and convergence (wrt Average Document Quantization measure) of the contextual model (represented by black line) and hierarchical model (grey line).

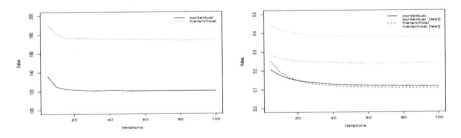

Fig. 4. Contextual vs. hierarchical model: (a) network size (b) quantization error

Although convergence to the stable state is fast in both cases and the quantization error is similar, it should be noted that this error is acquired for noticeably smaller network in contextual case (and in shorter time, as mentioned in previous section).

However, the most significant difference is the generalization capability of both models. For this experiment, we have partitioned each context (group of documents) into training and test subsets (in proportion 10:1). Training documents were used during learning process only, while the quantization error was computed for both subsets. The results are shown in Figure 4(b) – respective learning data sets are depicted with black lines while test data sets with grey lines. Nevertheless quantization error for learning document sets are similar, the difference lies in test sets and the hierarchical network is clearly *overfitted*. Again, there's no room to go into detailed study here, but it can be shown that this undesirable behavior is the result of the noised information brought by additional terms, which finally appears to be not meaningful in the particular context (and thus are disregarded in contextual weights w_{dtG}).

4.7 Immune Network Structure Investigation

To compare robustness of different variants of immune-based models, in each learning iteration, for each of the immune networks: contextual [Fig. 5(b)], hierarchical [Fig. 5(c)], global [Fig. 5(d)] and MST built on SOM grid [Fig. 3(c)], the distributions of the edge lengths have been computed. Next, the average length u and the standard deviation s of the length have been calculated and edges have been classified into five categories, depending on their length, l: shortest edges with $l \leq u-s$, short with $l \in (u-s, u-0.5s]$, medium with $l \in (u-0.5s, u+0.5s]$, long with $l \in (u+0.5s, u+s]$ and very long edges with $l > u+s$.

Additionally, in Figure 5(a), we can see average length of the edges for hierarchical and contextual immune networks (dashed and solid black lines, respectively) and complete graphs on both models' antibodies (cliques - depicted with grey lines). Actually, in both cases clustering structure has emerged and the average length of the edge in the immune network is much lower than in the complete graph. However, the average length for the contextual network is lower, whereas variance of this length is higher. It signifies more explicit clustering structure.

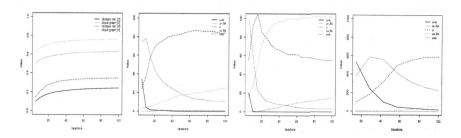

Fig. 5. Edge length distrib.: (a) complete (b) contextual (c) hierarchical (d) global net

There are quite a few differences in edge length distribution. One can notice than in all models, the number of shortest edges diminishes with time. It is coherent with the intention of gradual elimination of the redundant antibodies from the model. However, such elimination is much slower in case of the global model, what is another reason of slow convergence and high learning time. Also in case of SOM model, which has a static topology and no removal of inefficient cells is possible, we can see that the model slowly reduces the number of redundancies, represented by too similar referential vectors.

On the extreme side, the dynamics of the longest edges' distribution is similar in case of the contextual and the global model, but distinct in case of the hierarchical model. This last contains much more very long edges. Recalling that the variance of the edge lengths has been low for this model and the average length has been high, we can conclude that hierarchical model is generally more discontinuous. The same is true for the SOM model, which is another indication of the imperfection of the static grid topology.

5   Concluding Remarks

The contextual model described in this paper admits a number of interesting and valuable features in comparison with global and hierarchical models used traditionally to represent a given collection of documents. Further, when applying immune algorithm to clustering the collection of documents, a number of improvements was proposed. These improvements obey:

- Identification of redundant antibodies by means of the fast agglomerative clustering algorithm [13].
- Fast generation of mutated clones without computation of their stimulation by currently presented antigen. These mutants can be characterized by presumed ability of generalization (cf. section 3.2).
- Time-dependent parameters σ_d and σ_s. In general we have no a recipe allowing to tune both the parameters to a given dataset. In original approach [7] a trial-and-error method was suggested. We observed that in highly dimensional space the value of σ_d is almost as critical as the value of σ_s. Hence we propose a "consistent" tuning of these parameters – cf. section 3.3. The general recipe is: carefully (i.e. not to fast) remove weakly stimulated and too specific antibodies and carefully splice redundant (too similar) antibodies.
- Application of the CF-trees [18] for fast identification of winners (most stimulated memory cells) [6].

With these improvements we proposed a new approach to mining high dimensional datasets. The contextual approach described in section 2 appears to be fast, of good quality (in term of indices introduced in sections 4.1 and 4.2) and scalable (with the data size and dimension).

Clustering high dimensional data is both of practical importance and at the same time a big challenge, in particular for large collections of text documents. The paper presents a novel approach, based on artificial immune systems, within the broad stream of map type clustering methods. Such approach leads to many interesting research issues, such as context-dependent dictionary reduction and keywords identification, topic-sensitive document summarization, subjective model visualization based on particular user's information requirements, dynamic adaptation of the document representation and local similarity measure computation. We plan to tackle these problems in our future work. It has to be stressed that not only textual, but also any other high dimensional data may be clustered using the presented method.

References

1. A. Baraldi and P. Blonda, A survey of fuzzy clustering algorithms for pattern recognition, IEEE Trans. on Systems, Man and Cybernetics, 29B(1999), 786–801
2. A. Becks, Visual Knowledge Management with Adaptable Document Maps, GMD research series, 2001, 15, ISBN 3-88457-398-5
3. M.W. Berry, Z. Drmač, E.R. Jessup, Matrices, vector spaces and information retrieval, SIAM Review, Vol. 41, No. 2, pp. 335-362
4. J.C. Bezdek, S.K. Pal, Fuzzy Models for Pattern Recognition: Methods that Search for Structures in Data, IEEE, New York, 1992
5. C. Boulis, M. Ostendorf, Combining multiple clustering systems, Proc. of 8th European Conference on Principles and Practice of Knowledge Discovery in Databases (PKDD-2004), LNAI 3202, Springer-Verlag, 2004
6. K. Ciesielski, et al. Adaptive document maps, in: Proceedings of the Intelligent Information Processing and Web Mining (IIS:IIPWM'06), Ustron, 2006
7. L.N. de Castro, F.J. von Zuben, An evolutionary immune network for data clustering, SBRN'2000, IEEE Computer Society Press, 2000
8. L.N. de Castro, J. Timmis, Artificial Immune Systems: A New Computational Intelligence Approach. Springer 2002
9. B. Fritzke, Some competitive learning methods, draft available from http://www.neuroinformatik.ruhr-uni-bochum.de/ini/VDM/research/gsn/JavaPaper
10. M. Gilchrist, Taxonomies for business: Description of a research project, 11 Nordic Conference on Information and Documentation, Reykjavik, Iceland May 30 - June 1, 2001, URL: http://www.bokis.is/iod2001/papers/Gilchrist_paper.doc
11. C. Hung, S. Wermter, A constructive and hierarchical self-organising model in a non-stationary environment, Int. Joint Conference in Neural Networks, 2005
12. M. Kłopotek, M. Dramiński, K. Ciesielski, M. Kujawiak, S.T. Wierzchoń, Mining document maps, in Proceedings of Statistical Approaches to Web Mining Workshop (SAWM) at PKDD'04, M. Gori, M. Celi, M. Nanni eds., Pisa, 2004, pp.87-98
13. M. Kłopotek, S. Wierzchoń, K. Ciesielski, M. Dramiński, D. Czerski, Conceptual Maps and Intelligent Navigation in Document Space (in Polish), to appear in: Akademicka Oficyna Wydawnicza EXIT Publishing, Warszawa, 2006
14. T. Kohonen, Self-Organizing Maps, Springer Series in Information Sciences, vol. 30, Springer, Berlin, Heidelberg, New York, 2001
15. K. Lagus, S. Kaski, T. Kohonen, Mining massive document collections by the WEBSOM method Information Sciences, Vol 163/1-3, pp. 135-156, 2004
16. C.J. van Rijsbergen, Information Retrieval, London: Butterworths, 1979, URL: http://www.dcs.gla.ac.uk/Keith/Preface.html
17. D.R. Wilson, T.R. Martinez, Reduction techniques for instance-based learning algorithms, Machine Learning, 38(2000), 257-286
18. T. Zhang, R. Ramakrishan, M. Livny, BIRCH: Efficient data clustering method for large databases, in: Proc. ACM SIGMOD Int. Conf. on Data Management, 1997
19. Y. Zhao, G. Karypis, Criterion functions for document clustering: Experiments and analysis, url: http://www-users.cs.umn.edu/~karypis/publications/ir.html

An Immunological Filter for Spam

George B. Bezerra[1], Tiago V. Barra[1], Hamilton M. Ferreira[1],
Helder Knidel[1], Leandro Nunes de Castro[2], and Fernando J. Von Zuben[1]

[1] Laboratory of Bioinformatics and Bio-Inspired Computing (LBIC)
Department of Computer Engineering and Industrial Automation
University of Campinas, Unicamp, CP: 6101, 13083-970, Campinas/SP, Brazil
[2] Catholic University of Santos, UniSantos, 11070-906, Santos/SP, Brazil

Abstract. Spam messages are continually filling email boxes of practically every Web user. To deal with this growing problem, the development of high-performance filters to block those unsolicited messages is strongly required. An Antibody Network, more precisely SRABNET (Supervised Real-Valued Antibody Network), is proposed as an alternative filter to detect spam. The model of the antibody network is generated automatically from the training dataset and evaluated on unseen messages. We validate this approach using a public corpus, called PU1, which has a large collection of encrypted personal e-mail messages containing legitimate messages and spam. Finally, we compared the performance with the well known naïve Bayes filter using some performances indexes that will be presented.

1 Introduction

A pathogen is a specific causative agent (as a bacterium or virus) of disease. In the same way a junk email, also commonly called spam and defined typically as unsolicited and undesired electronic messages, can be seen as some sort of disease to a personal computer. It tends to require a high percentage of memory and network packages to store and transmit spam.

Resource allocation apart, spam forces undesired content into our mailboxes, impairs our ability to communicate freely, and costs Internet users billions of dollars annually. According to SpamCon foundation, the U.S. businesses lost about US$4 billion[1] in productivity in 2004 because of spam, and those losses can be even higher without an intervening technology or policy to curb unwanted messages. Some solutions have been applied to avoid spam like legislation prohibiting the sending of spam and blacklists (lists containing addresses of known spam senders). Nevertheless, these methods are usually not very effective, once the spam senders have, in the majority of the cases, "shell addresses"(i.e. addresses used once and then discarded), they can change their addresses regularly to avoid being blacklisted [1].

The problem of detecting spam messages is popular and can be interpreted as a binary classification task. However, what turns this classification task a hard

---

[1] In SpamCon foundation, http://spamcon.org/ . Accessed in 05/01/2006.

H. Bersini and J. Carneiro (Eds.): ICARIS 2006, LNCS 4163, pp. 446–458, 2006.

one is the large overlapping between these classes and the inherent conceptual drift of the spam set [2,3]. The most used technique to detect spams is the Bayesian analysis [4,5,6], but other machine learning techniques have been used to detect or categorize spams, as Support Vector Machines [7], decision trees [8,9] and case-based reasoning [3].

If we interpret the spams as pathogens, the use of the natural immune system as inspiration to develop new methods, to detect or to categorize spam, is well supported, as can be seen in [10,11,12,13]. Here, we propose the use of a supervised version of a Real-Valued Antibody Network [14]. The antibody network will work as a classifier of new messages.

The paper is organized as follows: in Section 2 the antibody network is presented together with some previous works; in Section 3 the corpus are described and its pre-processing methods are described in Section 4; some performance measures are introduced in Section 5 and the results are presented in Section 6. Analytical and concluding remarks are outlined in Section 7.

2   Applying the SRABNET to Capture Spam

De Castro et al. [15] proposed a growing artificial binary antibody repertoire to recognize antigens, which was called AntiBody NETwork (ABNET). Boolean weights were adopted for antigens and antibodies. Knidel et al. [16] extended that previous work and proposed real-valued vectors to represent the weights of the network (RABNET), for data clustering tasks.

In classification problems with labelled samples, it is important to use that information to improve the performance of the model. Based on this idea, citeKnidel2006 proposed a supervised version of the RABNET called SRABNET (Supervised Real-Valued Antibody Network), which is well suited for such classification tasks, once it uses the label of the samples during the evolution of the system.

Inspired by ideas from neural networks and artificial immune systems, the SRABNET assumes a population of antigens (Ag) to be recognized by an antibody repertoire (Ab) modeled as a one-dimensional competitive supervised network with real-valued weights. Being a supervised approach, the first difference from RABNET [16] is that at the beginning of the network adaptation, while RABNET starts with only one antibody, the SRABNET will present one antibody assigned to each class. The weights of these initial antibodies are defined by the arithmetic mean taken in the space of attributes from all the data belonging to the class to which the antibody is assigned.

In summary, the following features are associated with SRABNET:

- Competitive network with supervised learning;
- Constructive network structure, with growing and pruning phases governed by an implementation of the clonal selection principle; and
- Real-valued connection weights in an Euclidean shape-space [17].

Although there are similar stages in the learning algorithms of RABNET and SRABNET, the way they are implemented will depend upon the learning paradigm: supervised or unsupervised. As SRABNET is founded on supervised learning, new ideas have been proposed for the stages that follow.

2.1   Weight Updating

The weight updating procedure for SRABNET is similar to the one used in Learning Vector Quantization (LVQ) [18], [19]. Equation (2) shows the weight updating rule used here, where α is the learning rate and Ab_K is the antibody that wins the competition for representing antigen Ag. In other words, the most similar antibody is the one that presents the highest affinity (minimum Euclidean distance) to the given antigen as in equation 1.

$$K = arg\,min_k \|Ag - Ab_k\|, \forall k \qquad (1)$$

$$Ab_K(t+1) = \begin{cases} Ab_K(t) + \alpha * (Ag - Ab_K(t)), \text{ If } Class(Ab_k) = Class(Ag) \\ Ab_K(t) - \alpha * (Ag - Ab_K(t)), \text{ Otherwise.} \end{cases} \qquad (2)$$

According to equation 2, if the antibody has the same label, or class, of the antigen which it is recognizing, its weights are updated towards the weight pattern of the antigen. Otherwise, the antibody is moved away from the antigen in the shape space.

2.2   Network Growing

The network growing is performed at each epoch. The antibody chosen to be duplicated is the one that represents an antigen with the lowest affinity (highest Euclidean distance). The location of the new antibody in the shape space, associated with a weight vector, is defined as the midpoint of the straight line connecting the antibody to be duplicated and that antigen with the lowest affinity.

In Fig. 1(a-b) the duplication process is depicted; the sample with a circle is the antigen with the lowest affinity and the cloned antibody is marked with a square. The new antibody will belong to the class with the maximum number of elements (antigens) among the elements that will now be represented by this new antibody. A tie will lead to a random choice of the class. Depending on the distribution of antigens in the shape space, the class to be attributed to the newly-generated antibody may differ from the class of its immediate ancestor as illustrated in Fig. 1(b-c). The dynamic of the whole process to obtain the final network structure can be seen in Fig. 1(a-h).

2.3   Network Pruning

The pruning on the network occurs when an antibody does not win or when it does not represent at least one antigen. In supervised learning, each class should have at least one antibody representing its samples. Based on this requisite, the pruning process is not performed if the antibody to be pruned is the unique representative of that class. In a more immunological view, the antibodies that were not stimulated by any antigen suffer apoptosis.

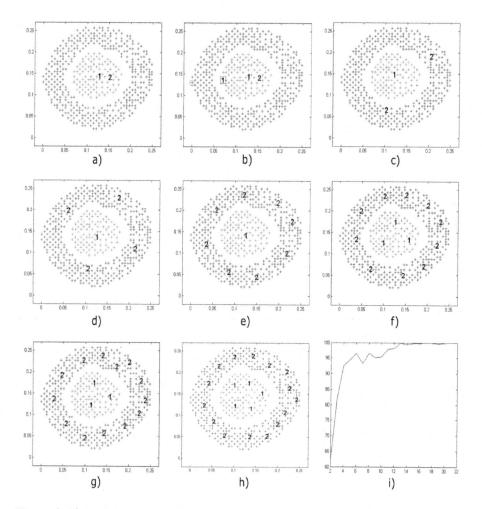

Fig. 1. (a-h) Dynamic of the training stage presenting the growing and the re-labeling process. (i) Performance of the different networks.

2.4 Convergence Criterion

The learning procedure involves a constructive network, and it is a challenging task to automatically decide when the network should stop growing. To perform this task, an approach was developed based on two concepts. The first one is the *reference network*, that represents the network with the best performance so far. The other concept is called *convergence window* and is related to the number of networks that will have its performances compared to the *reference network*. These concepts are illustrated in Fig. 2 and in Fig. 3. The size of the convergence window defines the number of networks to be compared to the *reference network*, and it is the unique user-defined parameter of the algorithm. The performance evaluation, at this point, is achieved by using only the training dataset.

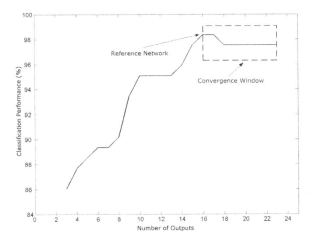

Fig. 2. The use of a convergence window to evaluate the stopping criterion

Once defined the size (s) of the convergence window, the approach proposed here evaluates the performance of networks with increasing numbers of antibodies but restricted to the convergence window. If any of the topologies within this window presents better performance than a given *reference network*, the reference network will then be replaced by the better performance network, as can be seen in Fig. 3. If none of the topologies within the convergence window presents better performance than the reference network, the convergence criterion is satisfied and the learning procedure halts, finishing the topology adaptation. In this case the resultant topology will be the reference network.

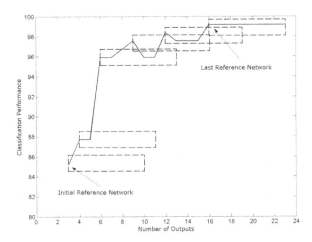

Fig. 3. Dynamics of the convergence window and reference network updating

For example, in Fig. 3 it is assumed a window of size 7. The last reference network will be the network with 16 antibodies. The networks with 17, 18, 19, 20, 21, 22 and 23 antibodies are evaluated for comparison. Since the classification performance of these networks are not superior to that produced by the reference network, the convergence criterion was reached and the resultant topology will be the network with 16 antibodies. The maximum number of antibodies to be inserted into the network is given by the quarter part of the dataset size. This limit of the number of antibodies in the network is a empirical value and was chosen based on previous tests. In this implementation, the performance criterion used is the TCR (Total Cost Ratio), that will be better explained in Section 5.

2.5   SRABNET PseudoCode

The steps described in the previous subsections are presented here in a pseudocode█ format.

Algorithm 1. Pseudo-code of the SRABNET algorithm

1: **Begin**
2: Initialization;
3: Initialize the network with one antibody per class, using the training dataset. The weight vector of each antibody corresponds to the mean of the samples belonging to the class to which the antibody was assigned;
4: **while** the convergence criterion is not met **do**
5:    **for** each input pattern (antigen) **do**
6:       Present a randomly chosen antigen to the network;
7:       Calculate the Euclidean distance between the antigen presented and the antibodies in the network;
8:       Find the winner antibody according to Eq. (1);
9:       Increase the concentration level of the winner;
10:      Update the weights of the winner antibody according to Eq. (2);
11:   **end for**
12:   Choose the antibody to be cloned. The antibody to be cloned will be the one that recognizes the antigen with the lowest affinity (highest Euclidean distance);
13:   The weight vector of the new antibody is the midpoint between the parent antibody and the antigen with the lowest affinity;
14:   The new antibody will belong to the class with the maximum number of elements among the ones recognized by the new antibody;
15:   **if** the concentration level of a given antibody is zero and it is not the unique of its class **then**
16:      prune it from the network
17:   **end if**
18: **end while**
19: **End**

Supported by the dynamic behavior illustrated in Fig. 1, the pseudo-code describes the whole algorithm including the growing and pruning processes.

3   The Corpus Used

The corpus that will be used to validate the proposal is the PU1 [4]² corpus and consists of 1099 messages, with spam rate of 43.77%, divided as follows:

- 481 spam messages. These are all the spam messages over a period of 22 months, excluding non-English messages and duplicates of spam messages sent on the same day.
- 618 legitimate messages, all in English, over a period of 36 months.

All the messages have header fields and HTML tags removed, leaving only subject line and mail body text, resulting in 24,748 words in total vocabulary. Each token was mapped to a unique integer to ensure the privacy of the content. There are four versions of this dataset: with or without stemming and with or without stop-word removal. Stop-word removal is a procedure to remove most frequent used words as 'and, for, a' and the stemming is the process of reducing a word to its root form (e.g. 'learner' becomes 'learn'). These methods are used mainly to reduce the dimensionality of feature space aiming at improving the classifier's prediction. However, Androutsopoulos et al. [4] demonstrated that stop-word removal and stemming may not promote a statistically significant improvement. That is why we have adopted in the experiments to be presented, the version without stemming and stop-word removal, although we have considered a simple procedure to dimensionality reduction aiming at alleviating the data sparseness problem.

4   Pre-processing Stage

The pre-processing is an important step in all pattern recognition and information retrieval task. In this stage, the dataset and the samples inside it are turned into some interpretable pattern for the system that will learn from them. Here, we have conceived this step as the development of a representation for the samples (Section 4.1) and the reduction of the number of attributes (Section 4.2).

4.1   Messages Representation

The first stage of the design of representation is to define how the messages will be encoded. Each individual message can be represented as a binary vector denoting which features were present or absent in the message. This is frequently referred to as the bag of words approach. A feature in this context is a word, w_i, and each message, x_d, is represented as depicted in Eq. 3, where i is the number of words of the entire corpus and d is the number of documents or messages of the dataset.

$$x_m = w_{m1}, w_{m2}, \ldots, w_{mi} \quad m = 1, 2, \ldots, d \tag{3}$$

---

² The PU corpora may be downloaded from http://www.iit.demokritos.gr/skel/i-config/.

4.2   Dimensionality Reduction

When we are dealing with textual information, the feature space tends to be large, usually on the order of several thousands of attributes (words). Hence, a method to reduce this number of attributes is required. According to [20] the attributes that appear in most of the files are not relevant in order to separate these documents because all the classes have instances that contain those attributes. In addition, as we are working with only two different classes (spam and legitimate), words that appear rarely in the files have a low weight in the identification of the class. So, the attributes that appear less than 5% and more than 95% in all documents of the corpus were removed. At the final, the dimension of the feature vectors is 751. The benefit of dimension reduction also includes, in some cases, an improvement in prediction accuracy [21].

5   Performance Measures

Once generated a classifier, it is necessary to obtain some indexes that can measure its performance and facilitate the comparison with other classifiers. In pattern recognition and information retrieval, when there are multiple categories, performance measures such as recall and precision are used. Although spam detection is a binary classification task, these measures will be used here to estimate the accuracy of the methods.

We will adopt the same notation used in [4,22], using L and S to represent legitimate and spam message respectively; and $n_{L \to S}$ (legitimate to spam or false positive) and $n_{S \to L}$ (spam to legitimate or false negative) to denote the two error types, respectively. Then, the spam recall and the spam precision are defined here as follows in equations 4 and 5.

$$SR = \frac{n_{S \to S}}{n_{S \to S} + n_{S \to L}} \tag{4}$$

$$SP = \frac{n_{S \to S}}{n_{S \to S} + n_{L \to S}} \tag{5}$$

In anti-spam filtering, misclassifying a legitimate mail as spam is worse than letting a spam message pass the filter. If a spam goes through the filter, the only inconvenience that it may cause is the time wasted to remove that message from the inbox. However, if an important legitimate mail message was misclassified, a real disaster can happen. When the error types (false positive and false negative) have distinct relevance the usual precision and recall measures can not express well the performance and it is necessary to adopt some cost sensitive evaluation measures.

Androutsoupoulos et al. [4] introduced a weighted accuracy measure (WAcc) that assign to false positive a higher cost than false negative and has been used in some spam filtering benchmarks [4,8,22]. WAcc is defined as:

$$WAcc = \frac{\lambda.n_{L \to L} + n_{S \to S}}{\lambda.N_L + N_S}, \quad WErr = \frac{\lambda.n_{L \to S} + n_{S \to L}}{\lambda.N_L + N_S} \tag{6}$$

where N_L is the total number of legitimate messages, and N_S the total number of spams.

With this, WAcc treats false positive λ times more costly than false negatives. In other words, when a false positive occurs it is counted as λ errors; and when it is classified correctly, it counts λ successes [22]. Nevertheless, as suggested by the same author, to avoid some problems with high values of WAcc, we will adopt the baseline versions of weighted accuracy and weighted error rate as depicted in Eq. 7 and the total cost ratio (TCR) as another measurement of the spam filtering effects, shown in Eq. 8. Note that the baseline here is the case where no filter is present: legitimate messages are never blocked and spams can always pass the filter.

$$WAcc^b = \frac{\lambda.N_L}{\lambda.N_L + N_S}, \quad WErr^b = \frac{N_S}{\lambda.N_L + N_S} \tag{7}$$

$$TCR = \frac{WErr^b}{WErr} \tag{8}$$

TCR seems to be a suitable performance indicator and it was used, as said before, to control the convergence criterion of the antibody network. Large TCR values indicate better performance. In cases where TCR ≤ 1 , taking on the baseline (not using any filter) is better.

Androutsopoulos et al. [4] proposes three different values for λ: $\lambda = 1$, 9, and 999. When λ is set to 1, spam and legitimate mails are weighted equally; when λ is set to 9, a false positive is penalized nine times more than a false negative; for the setting of $\lambda = 999$, more penalties are put on false positive. Such a high value of λ is suitable for scenarios where messages marked as spam are deleted directly. In this work, the values adopted to λ are 9 and 999, since the main difference between spam filtering and general text categorization task is the weight given to the two types of error.

If the cost is proportional to wasted time, an intuitive meaning for TCR is the following: it measures how much time is wasted to delete manually all spam messages when no filter is used (NS), compared to the time wasted to delete manually any spam messages that passed the filter plus the time needed to recover from mistakenly blocked legitimate messages [4].

6   Experiments

6.1   Experimental Results

To obtain the values of SP, SR, WAcc and TCR, 30 runs were performed using a ten-fold cross-validation method, which makes our results less prone to random variation. In each run, the entire data set was split in ten subsets: nine for training and one for testing. It is important to note that in ten-fold cross validation experiments, as suggested in [4], TCR is computed as average of $WErr^b$ divided by the average $WErr$ and not as the average of the TCR's of the individual folds, as this effectively ignores folds with TCR $\ll 1$.

The well-known naïve Bayes was chosen to be the filter for comparison due to its wide application in the context of spam filtering [1,4,6].

In Tables 1 and 2, the performance indexes for naïve Bayes and SRABNET are presented. The values are the average of the 30 runs and the symbol ($\pm$) means the standard deviation. As the entire dataset is mixed at the beginning of the algorithm to promote ten-fold cross validation, there is nothing to hinder that at least one fold have only legitimate or only spam in it. In this case, we did not use these values to compute the average. It is important to stress that this 'peculiarity' just occurs with the naïve Bayes filter. This occurs mainly because the naïve Bayes filter uses only the samples from training set to calculate the probability of a sample be a spam or not. With this, if the training set have just legitimate messages the value attributed to the probability of a message be spam is strongly affected. In this scenario all the messages will be classified as legitimate.

Table 1. Performance Measures with $\lambda = 9$

Filter	Spam Recall (%)	Spam Precision (%)	WAcc (%)	TCR
naïve Bayes	14.17	73.05	34.45 ± 1.71	1.08 ± 0.4
SRABNET	**85.90**	**97.37**	$\mathbf{97.18 \pm 0.14}$	$\mathbf{2.85 \pm 0.02}$

Table 2. Performance Measures with $\lambda = 999$

Filter	Spam Recall (%)	Spam Precision (%)	WAcc (%)	TCR
naïve Bayes	14.38	72.16	35.61 ± 1.77	0.05 ± 0.06
SRABNET	**60.21**	**97.73**	$\mathbf{98.38 \pm 0.09}$	0.07 ± 0.001

For $\lambda = 999$, both filters score TCR < 1, this is probably due to the very high weight given to false positives ($L \to S$). As a result, none of the filters manages to eliminate these errors completely. That is, higher values of λ benefits the baseline filter (without one), once that no false positives occurs. Despite theses results, SRABNET still remains as the best filter keeping into consideration WAcc and even TCR.

For $\lambda = 9$, both filters reach a TCR > 1, with the antibody network clearly overcoming the naïve Bayes filter. This is mainly due the fact that the immune algorithm does not make any assumption on the independence of the attributes, allowing a better positioning of the prototypes (antibodies) on the feature space.

The poor performance of the naïve Bayes in all values of λ can be attributed to the method applied here to reduce dimensionality. The concise information that remains in the feature vector, may probably deceive the Bayesian classifier.

6.2   Future Work

Further important analysis includes corpora where the data (messages) have a temporal sequence. Some experiments, with artificial datasets have already been

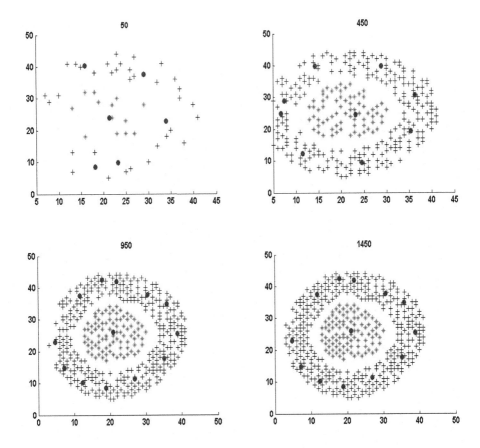

Fig. 4. Temporal behavior of SRABNET when applied to a dynamic environment, with more and more samples arriving along time

done as shown in Fig. 4. This dataset was used by Knidel et al. in [14] to illustrate the robustness of the algorithm on classes with non-convex distributions, but in this case we are trying to illustrate the temporal behavior of the messages. In this pictorial example, the messages are being described solely by two numerical attributes. To reproduce the behavior of SRABNET in Fig. 4, in what we call a dynamic environment, we determined a sequence of steps. In each iteration the algorithm takes samples to from all the previous steps to training and test on the next step samples of the dataset. Each time a new test is performed, the training set grows with the addition of the previous step samples and the algorithm is retrained. Intuitively , we can realize that the larger the dataset, the lower the value of the error rate on the test data. However, the generalization capability of the model to unseen samples reduces if it becomes too specialized (overtrained).

In the context where the data changes over time, a good model is the one that can track the changes of distribution, or in this case the change of concept, of the data that arrives. As a consequence, the model built on old data, in some cases inconsistent, becomes inappropriate to the new data. This problem is known as conceptual drift and must be the main concern when synthesizing a model from dynamic data [2]. Secker et al. [13] had already proposed the use of an artificial immune system for this task, somehow comparable with the perfomance produced by the naïve Bayes approach.

7 Conclusions

In this paper we have proposed the application of a supervised antibody network called SRABNET for spam filtering. Based on the use of a weighted index, total cost ratio (TCR), to control the convergence window we obtained a better performance with a robust network. Then, the use of SRABNET as a spam filter instead of naïve Bayes has shown to be an interesting choice for the user.

Even with the high accuracy of the antibody network, its performance can be improved by adding some distinctive and domain specific features in the representation as performed by Sahami et al. [5]. In [1] a comparison of methods for feature selection is presented, including information gain (IG), Mutual Information (MI) or Chi squared (χ^2). We believe that the use of advanced feature selection techniques will accentuate the discriminant capability of filters for spam.

Acknowledgment

The authors would like to thank CNPq and UOL (Universo On Line) for their financial support.

References

1. O'Brien, C., Vogel, C.: Spam filters: Bayes vs. chi-squared; letters vs. words. In: ISICT '03: Proceedings of the 1st international symposium on Information and communication technologies, Trinity College Dublin (2003) 291–296
2. Tsymbal, A.: A case-based approach to spam filtering that can track concept drift. Technical Report TCD-CS-2004-15, Trinity College Dublin (2004)
3. Cunningham, P., Nowlan, N., Delany, S.J., Haah, M.: A case-based approach to spam filtering that can track concept drift. Technical Report TCD-CS-2003-16, Trinity College Dublin (2003)
4. Androutsopoulos, I., Koutsias, J., Chandrinos, K.V., Spyropoulos, C.D.: An experimental comparison of naïve Bayesian and keyword-based anti-spam filtering with personal e-mail messages. Proceedings of the 23rd Annual International ACM SIGIR Conference on Research and Development in Information Retrieval (2000) 160–167
5. Sahami, M., Dumais, S., Heckerman, D., Horvitz, E.: A Bayesian approach to filtering junk e-mail. In: AAAI-98 Workshop on Learning for Text Categorization. (1998) 55–62

6. Graham, P.: A plan for spam. Available on: http://paulgraham.com/spam.html (2003)
7. Drucker, H., Vapnik, V., Wu, D.: Support vector machines for spam categorization. IEEE Transactions on Neural Networks **10** (1999) 1048–1054
8. Carreras, X., Màrquez, L.: Boosting trees for anti-spam email filtering. In: Proceedings of the 4th International Conference on Recent Advances in Natural Language Processing, Tzigov Chark, BG (2001)
9. Androutsopoulos, I., Paliouras, G., Karkaletsis, V., Sakkis, G., Spyropoulos, C.D., Stamatopoulos, P.: Learning to filter spam e-mail: A comparison of a naïve Bayesian and a memory-based approach. In: Proceedings of the Workshop on Machine Learning and Textual Information Access, 4th European Conference on Principles and Practice of Knowledge Discovery in Databases. (2000) 1–13
10. Oda, T., White, T.: Immunity from spam: An analysis of an artificial immune system for junk email detection. In: Proceedings of the 4th International Conference on Artificial Immune Systems (ICARIS). (2005) 276–289
11. Oda, T., White, T.: Developing an immunity to spam. In: Genetic and Evolutionary Computation - GECCO 2003. Genetic and Evolutionary Computation Conference, Chicago, IL, USA. Lecture Notes in Computer Science, Vol. 2723, Springer. (2003) 231–242
12. Oda, T., White, T.: Increasing the accuracy of a spam-detecting artificial immune system. In: Proceedings of the Congress on Evolutionary Computation (CEC 2003), Canberra, Australia. (2003) 390–396
13. Secker, A., Freitas, A.A., Timmis, J.: AISEC: An artificial immune system for e-mail classification. In: Proceedings of the Congress on Evolutionary Computation. (2003) 131–139
14. Knidel, H., de Castro, L.N., Von Zuben, F.J.: A supervised constructive neuro-immune network for pattern classification. In: IJCNN'06: Proceedings of the 2006 Conference on International Joint Conference on Neural Networks. (2006)
15. de Castro, L.N., Von Zuben, F.J., de Deus Jr, G.A.: The construction of a Boolean competitive neural network using ideas from immunology. Neurocomputing **50** (2003) 51–85
16. Knidel, H., de Castro, L.N., Von Zuben, F.J.: RABNET: a real-valued antibody network for data clustering. In: GECCO '05: Proceedings of the 2005 conference on Genetic and evolutionary computation, New York, NY, USA, ACM Press (2005) 371–372
17. Segel, L.A., Perelson, A.S.: Computations in shape space: a new approach to immune network theory. In Perelson, A., ed.: Theoretical Immunology. Volume 2 of SFI Series on Complexity. Addison Wesley (1988) 321–343
18. Kohonen, T.: Self-organization and associative memory: 3rd edition. Springer-Verlag New York, Inc., New York, NY, USA (1989)
19. Kohonen, T.: Self-organizing maps. Springer-Verlag, Berlin (2000)
20. Zuchini, M.H.: Aplicações de mapas auto-organizáveis em mineração de dados e recuperação de informação. Master's thesis, UNICAMP (2003)
21. Yang, Y., Pedersen, J.O.: A comparative study on feature selection in text categorization. In Fisher, D.H., ed.: Proceedings of ICML-97, 14th International Conference on Machine Learning, Nashville, US, Morgan Kaufmann Publishers, San Francisco, US (1997) 412–420
22. Zhang, L., Zhu, J., Yao, T.: An evaluation of statistical spam filtering techniques. ACM Transactions on Asian Language Information Processing (TALIP) **3** (2004) 243–269

Author Index

Lecture Notes in Computer Science

For information about Vols. 1–4034

please contact your bookseller or Springer

Vol. 4088: Z.-Z. Shi, R. Sadananda (Eds.), Agent Computing and Multi-Agent Systems. XVII, 827 pages. 2006. (Sublibrary LNAI).

Vol. 4085: J. Misra, T. Nipkow, E. Sekerinski (Eds.), FM 2006: Formal Methods. XV, 620 pages. 2006.

Vol. 4079: S. Etalle, M. Truszczyński (Eds.), Logic Programming. XIV, 474 pages. 2006.

Vol. 4077: M.-S. Kim, K. Shimada (Eds.), Geometric Modeling and Processing - GMP 2006. XVI, 696 pages. 2006.

Vol. 4076: F. Hess, S. Pauli, M. Pohst (Eds.), Algorithmic Number Theory. X, 599 pages. 2006.

Vol. 4075: U. Leser, F. Naumann, B. Eckman (Eds.), Data Integration in the Life Sciences. XI, 298 pages. 2006. (Sublibrary LNBI).

Vol. 4074: M. Burmester, A. Yasinsac (Eds.), Secure Mobile Ad-hoc Networks and Sensors. X, 193 pages. 2006.

Vol. 4073: A. Butz, B. Fisher, A. Krüger, P. Olivier (Eds.), Smart Graphics. XI, 263 pages. 2006.

Vol. 4072: M. Harders, G. Székely (Eds.), Biomedical Simulation. XI, 216 pages. 2006.

Vol. 4071: H. Sundaram, M. Naphade, J.R. Smith, Y. Rui (Eds.), Image and Video Retrieval. XII, 547 pages. 2006.

Vol. 4070: C. Priami, X. Hu, Y. Pan, T.Y. Lin (Eds.), Transactions on Computational Systems Biology V. IX, 129 pages. 2006. (Sublibrary LNBI).

Vol. 4069: F.J. Perales, R.B. Fisher (Eds.), Articulated Motion and Deformable Objects. XV, 526 pages. 2006.

Vol. 4068: H. Schärfe, P. Hitzler, P. Øhrstrøm (Eds.), Conceptual Structures: Inspiration and Application. XI, 455 pages. 2006. (Sublibrary LNAI).

Vol. 4067: D. Thomas (Ed.), ECOOP 2006 – Object-Oriented Programming. XIV, 527 pages. 2006.

Vol. 4066: A. Rensink, J. Warmer (Eds.), Model Driven Architecture – Foundations and Applications. XII, 392 pages. 2006.

Vol. 4065: P. Perner (Ed.), Advances in Data Mining. XI, 592 pages. 2006. (Sublibrary LNAI).

Vol. 4064: R. Büschkes, P. Laskov (Eds.), Detection of Intrusions and Malware & Vulnerability Assessment. X, 195 pages. 2006.

Vol. 4063: I. Gorton, G.T. Heineman, I. Crnkovic, H.W. Schmidt, J.A. Stafford, C.A. Szyperski, K. Wallnau (Eds.), Component-Based Software Engineering. XI, 394 pages. 2006.

Vol. 4062: G. Wang, J.F. Peters, A. Skowron, Y. Yao (Eds.), Rough Sets and Knowledge Technology. XX, 810 pages. 2006. (Sublibrary LNAI).

Vol. 4061: K. Miesenberger, J. Klaus, W. Zagler, A. Karshmer (Eds.), Computers Helping People with Special Needs. XXIX, 1356 pages. 2006.

Vol. 4060: K. Futatsugi, J.-P. Jouannaud, J. Meseguer (Eds.), Algebra, Meaning, and Computation. XXXVIII, 643 pages. 2006.

Vol. 4059: L. Arge, R. Freivalds (Eds.), Algorithm Theory – SWAT 2006. XII, 436 pages. 2006.

Vol. 4058: L.M. Batten, R. Safavi-Naini (Eds.), Information Security and Privacy. XII, 446 pages. 2006.

Vol. 4057: J.P.W. Pluim, B. Likar, F.A. Gerritsen (Eds.), Biomedical Image Registration. XII, 324 pages. 2006.

Vol. 4056: P. Flocchini, L. Gąsieniec (Eds.), Structural Information and Communication Complexity. X, 357 pages. 2006.

Vol. 4055: J. Lee, J. Shim, S.-g. Lee, C. Bussler, S. Shim (Eds.), Data Engineering Issues in E-Commerce and Services. IX, 290 pages. 2006.

Vol. 4054: A. Horváth, M. Telek (Eds.), Formal Methods and Stochastic Models for Performance Evaluation. VIII, 239 pages. 2006.

Vol. 4053: M. Ikeda, K.D. Ashley, T.-W. Chan (Eds.), Intelligent Tutoring Systems. XXVI, 821 pages. 2006.

Vol. 4052: M. Bugliesi, B. Preneel, V. Sassone, I. Wegener (Eds.), Automata, Languages and Programming, Part II. XXIV, 603 pages. 2006.

Vol. 4051: M. Bugliesi, B. Preneel, V. Sassone, I. Wegener (Eds.), Automata, Languages and Programming, Part I. XXIII, 729 pages. 2006.

Vol. 4049: S. Parsons, N. Maudet, P. Moraitis, I. Rahwan (Eds.), Argumentation in Multi-Agent Systems. XIV, 313 pages. 2006. (Sublibrary LNAI).

Vol. 4048: L. Goble, J.-J.C.. Meyer (Eds.), Deontic Logic and Artificial Normative Systems. X, 273 pages. 2006. (Sublibrary LNAI).

Vol. 4047: M. Robshaw (Ed.), Fast Software Encryption. XI, 434 pages. 2006.

Vol. 4046: S.M. Astley, M. Brady, C. Rose, R. Zwiggelaar (Eds.), Digital Mammography. XVI, 654 pages. 2006.

Vol. 4045: D. Barker-Plummer, R. Cox, N. Swoboda (Eds.), Diagrammatic Representation and Inference. XII, 301 pages. 2006. (Sublibrary LNAI).

Vol. 4044: P. Abrahamsson, M. Marchesi, G. Succi (Eds.), Extreme Programming and Agile Processes in Software Engineering. XII, 230 pages. 2006.

Vol. 4043: A.S. Atzeni, A. Lioy (Eds.), Public Key Infrastructure. XI, 261 pages. 2006.

Vol. 4042: D. Bell, J. Hong (Eds.), Flexible and Efficient Information Handling. XVI, 296 pages. 2006.

Vol. 4041: S.-W. Cheng, C.K. Poon (Eds.), Algorithmic Aspects in Information and Management. XI, 395 pages. 2006.

Vol. 4040: R. Reulke, U. Eckardt, B. Flach, U. Knauer, K. Polthier (Eds.), Combinatorial Image Analysis. XII, 482 pages. 2006.

Vol. 4039: M. Morisio (Ed.), Reuse of Off-the-Shelf Components. XIII, 444 pages. 2006.

Vol. 4038: P. Ciancarini, H. Wiklicky (Eds.), Coordination Models and Languages. VIII, 299 pages. 2006.

Vol. 4037: R. Gorrieri, H. Wehrheim (Eds.), Formal Methods for Open Object-Based Distributed Systems. XVII, 474 pages. 2006.

Vol. 4036: O. H. Ibarra, Z. Dang (Eds.), Developments in Language Theory. XII, 456 pages. 2006.

Vol. 4035: T. Nishita, Q. Peng, H.-P. Seidel (Eds.), Advances in Computer Graphics. XX, 771 pages. 2006.